New IPv6 Transition Technology

Xing Li · Congxiao Bao

New IPv6 Transition Technology

IPv6-Only, IPv6-Mostly and IPv4 as a Service

Science Press
Beijing

Springer

Xing Li
Tsinghua University
Beijing, China

Congxiao Bao
Tsinghua University
Beijing, China

ISBN 978-981-95-8426-0 ISBN 978-981-95-8427-7 (eBook)
https://doi.org/10.1007/978-981-95-8427-7

Jointly published with China Science Publishing & Media Ltd.
The print edition is not for sale in China mainland. Customers from China mainland please order the print book from: China Science Publishing & Media Ltd.

The original submitted manuscript has been translated into English. The translation was done using artificial intelligence. A subsequent revision was performed by the author(s) to further refine the work and to ensure that the translation is appropriate concerning content and scientific correctness. It may, however, read stylistically different from a conventional translation.

Translation from the Chinese Simplified language edition: "新一代IPv6过渡技术: IPv6单栈和IPv4即服务" by Xing Li and Congxiao Bao, © China Science Publishing & Media Ltd. 2024. Published by China Science Publishing & Media Ltd. All Rights Reserved.

This Springer imprint is published by the registered company Springer Nature Singapore Pte Ltd.
The registered company address is: 152 Beach Road, #21-01/04 Gateway East, Singapore 189721, Singapore

Foreword

We are at a critical moment in history. Faced with various new challenges in social development, the Internet has played an important and irreplaceable role. The Internet unites us and makes humanity stronger than ever before.

Now, we still need to solve the problem of Internet address exhaustion, so that the Internet can continue to operate and expand. The new Internet must have the ability to provide reliable services to global users. This is the fundamental reason why we call on everyone to fully embrace IPv6 in the second decade of the twenty-first century. Many Internet pioneers have provided convincing examples for the deployment of IPv6, especially IPv6-only. That is to say, the Internet still has efficient operating capabilities without relying on the old IPv4.

Therefore, we believe that: IPv6 can provide almost unlimited IP address space and a wide range of end-to-end innovation space and is the globally recognized solution to the problem of IPv4 address shortage.

Promoting the widespread deployment of IPv6-only is not only the basis for making the Internet more flat, efficient, and secure, but also the inevitable choice for promoting the comprehensive upgrade of Internet technology and industrial ecology. IPv6 will empower network information technology, industrial development, and innovative applications.

IPv6 technology will make immeasurable contributions to the current and future digital economy.

IPv6-only Internet has laid a solid foundation for the expansion and innovative application of information infrastructure worldwide. IPv6-only is the first and possibly the last major upgrade of the Internet in the next few decades, let us make the right choice for the benefit of all mankind with practical actions.

I am pleased to write the Forword for this book, looking forward to the global Internet transition to IPv6-only.

Vint Cerf, Reston, Virginia, USA — Vinton Cerf

Preface

The Internet, as the cornerstone of modern information infrastructure, is rapidly reshaping the global digital ecosystem. From universal access and the widespread adoption of mobile Internet to the explosive growth of cloud computing, Internet of Things (IoT), and AI agents, evolving network demands have outpaced the capabilities of traditional IPv4. However, the transition to IPv6 is not merely a simple protocol replacement but a systemic shift spanning network architecture, device compatibility, application layer adjustments, and operational models.

The authors of this book are key members of the technical team responsible for the design, construction, and operation of CERNET (China Education and Research Network) in 1994 and IPv6-only CERNET2 in 2004. In 1997, they established China's first IPv6 testbed. In 2006, they developed stateless IPv4/IPv6 translation technology (IVI), enabling seamless interoperability between IPv6-only CERNET2 and the IPv4 CERNET as well as the IPv4 Internet. The authors began participating in IETF standardization efforts for transition technologies in 2007, contributing to working groups such as Behave, Softwire, and V6ops. They are co-authors of several key IPv6 transition RFCs, including RFC4925, RFC6052, RFC6144, RFC6145, RFC6219, RFC6791, RFC7597, RFC7598, RFC7599, and RFC7915. From 2008 to the present, they have been developing a series of translation techniques and deploying them in production networks. Since 2017, the authors have been guiding the design and deployment of the multi-slicing IPv6-only CERNET3 network.

This book offers cutting-edge IPv6 transition technologies, grounded in the author's firsthand experience, and provides comprehensive insights into architecture, granular design, and operational aspects. It explores innovative approaches to IPv6 transition, for IPv4-reachable IPv6-only and IPv6-mostly, as well as IPv4 as a Service (IPv4aaS).

Through the IPv6 transition process, the authors of this book argue that practical, bit-and-byte design should be guided by principles of Internet architecture. Indeed, studying the protocol translation and address mapping mechanisms between IPv4 and IPv6 provides an insightful method for understanding both IPv4 and IPv6 protocols. Ultimately, the authors' experience highlights that the rapidly evolving technological landscape often leads to incompatibilities between innovative technologies and widely adopted legacy systems. Therefore, designing a technical architecture that facilitates a seamless transition is critical. The case of achieving interoperability between IPv4 and IPv6 Internet protocols through translation mechanisms serves as a relevant example of this challenge.

This book is ideal for researchers and engineers designing and implementing Internet protocols—particularly with a focus on IPv6 transition technologies. It is also highly relevant for network operators managing diverse network environments, including LANs, WANs, ISPs, data centers, IXs, and more. Additionally, it serves as a key resource for researchers and engineers working on the design of future Internet architectures. Finally, it is an essential reference for educators and students specializing in telecommunications and networking at colleges and universities.

The structure of this book is as follows.

Chapter 1, "Introduction," is a historical review, including the birth of ARPANET, especially the introduction of the historical experience of the first Internet transition from "NCP to TCP/IP."

Chapter 2, "Internet Design Principles," systematically introduces the design principles of IPv4 and IPv6, and the guiding significance of these design principles for the second Internet transition from "IPv4 to IPv6."

Chapter 3, "Evolution of IPv6 Transition Technology," comprehensively introduces traditional IPv6 transition technology and discusses the dilemma of traditional IPv6 transition technology and the research process of the new generation of IPv6 transition technology.

Chapter 4, "New-Generation IPv6 Transition Scenarios," comprehensively and systematically analyzes the application scenarios, technical framework, and components of the new-generation IPv6 transition technology.

Chapter 5, "Protocol Processing Techniques," systematically discusses the principles of network layer protocols, including the header structures of IPv4 and IPv6, ICMP, ICMPv6, TCP, and UDP. Based on this, it provides methods for translating and encapsulating between IPv4 and IPv6.

Chapter 6, "Address Mapping Techniques," systematically discusses the principles of Internet addressing, including the structure and usage of IPv4 and IPv6 addresses. Based on this, it provides mapping algorithms between IPv4 and IPv6 addresses.

Chapter 7, "Domain Name Support Techniques," introduces the domain name system in IPv6 transition technology, specifically including DNS64 that enables IPv6 computers to access IPv4 computers, and DNS46 that enables IPv4 computers to access IPv6 computers.

Chapter 8, "Parameter Discovery and Configuration Techniques," introduces supporting protocols involved in IPv6 transition technology, including discovery of the IPv6 prefix through DNS and configuration of the IPv6 prefix via DHCPv6 or through RA. The chapter also covers DHCPv4 Option 108 (IPv6-mostly) and discussion of the BGP extension.

Chapter 9, "Single Translation," introduces Stateless Translation Technology (IVI), Stateless Translation Address Sharing Extension Technology (1: *N* IVI), and Stateful Single Translation Technology (NAT64).

Chapter 10, "Stateless Double Translation and Encapsulation," introduces Stateless IPv4/IPv6 Double Translation Technology (dIVI and MAP-T) and Stateless Encapsulation Technology (MAP-E).

Chapter 11, "Stateful Double Translation and Encapsulation," introduces Stateful Double Translation Technology (464XLAT), Stateful Tunneling Technology (DS-Lite), and User State Tunneling Technology (LW-4o6).

Chapter 12, "Stateless IPv6 Prefix Translation," introduces Stateless IPv6/IPv6 Prefix Translation Technology (NPTv6) and Stateless Double IPv6 Prefix Translation Technology (dNPTv6).

Chapter 13, "IPv6-Only Network Transition Roadmap," presents the trend, summarizes the new-generation transition technologies discussed in this book, and provides an IPv6-only network transition roadmap.

Chapter 14, "Unit Systems of IPv6-Only Network," introduces IPv6-only servers that can communicate with IPv4, IPv6-only local area networks, IPv6-only home broadband, and IPv4 public network services and virtual private network services based on IPv6 networks (IPv4 as a Service: IPv4aaS).

Chapter 15, "Integrated Systems of IPv6-Only Network," introduces IPv6-only campus networks, IPv6-only metropolitan area networks, IPv6-only backbone networks, IPv6 virtual private networks, IPv6-only data centers, IPv6 exchange centers, etc.

Chapter 16, "Transition of Future Network Protocols," reviews the evolution of Internet transition technologies and makes suggestions for the design of future network transition technologies.

The appendix includes the protocol parameters involved in IPv4/IPv6 transition technology.

Beijing, China — Xing Li
October 2025 — Congxiao Bao

Acknowledgments The authors express their gratitude to all the teachers and students of the IVI research group at Tsinghua University. We are deeply indebted to the experts from CNGI and CERNET for their invaluable contributions. Special thanks go to the continuous support provided by national projects for the advancement of IVI technology research. We also acknowledge the co-authors and partners of the IETF Behave, Softwire, and V6ops working groups.

Our sincere appreciation goes to the ISPs and vendors, such as CERNET.com, Huawei, ZTE, Cisco, Juniper, Bitway, Centec, Google, Apple, Sohu, China Telecom, China Unicom, and China Mobile, for their interest, support, and implementation of the IPv4/IPv6 translation technologies. We are grateful to indirectionnet.com for its high-quality series of stateless and stateful IPv4/IPv6 translators.

We thank the editors at Springer for their dedicated efforts in publishing this book and the editors at Science Press for their work on the Chinese version. Finally, we express our heartfelt thanks to the families of the authors for their unwavering understanding and support throughout the research process.

Competing Interests The authors have no competing interests to declare that are relevant to the content of this manuscript.

Contents

Acronyms

ACK	Acknowledgement
ACL	Access Control List
ACM	Association for Computing Machinery
AF	Address Family
AH	Authentication Header
AHHP	ARPANET Host-to-Host Protocol
ALG	Application Layer Gateway
AMT	Automatic Multicast Tunneling
API	Application Programming Interface
ARPA	Advanced Research Projects Agency
ARP	Address Resolution Protocol
AS	Autonomous System
ASM	Any Source Multicast
ATM	Asynchronous Transfer Mode
BBN	Bolt, Beranek, and Newman company
Behave	Behavior Engineering for Hindrance Avoidance
BGP	Border Gateway Protocol
BIB	Binding Information Bases
BRAS	Broadband Remote Access Server
CGN	Carrier-Grade NAT
CIDR	Classless Inter-Domain Routing
CLNP	Connectionless Network Protocol
CPE	Customer Premises Equipment
CPU	Central Processing Unit
CRC	Cyclic Redundancy Check
DAD	Duplicate Address Detection
DARPA	Defense Advanced Research Projects Agency
DCCP	Datagram Congestion Control Protocol
DCE	Data Communication Equipment
DECNET	Digital Equipment Corporation Network
DF	Don't Fragment

DHCP	Dynamic Host Configuration Protocol
DLA	Defense Logistics Agency
DNS	Domain Name System
DNSSEC	DNS Security Extensions
DNSSL	DNS host Search List
DoD	Department of Defense
DoH	DNS over HTTPS
DoS	Denial of Service
DoT	DNS over TLS
E2E	End to End
EGP	Exterior Gateway Protocol
ESP	Encapsulating Security Payload
EUI	Extended Unique Identifier
EUROCOMP	European Computer Conference
FIND	Future Internet Network Design
FQDN	Fully Qualified Domain Name
FTP	File Transfer Protocol
GGP	Gateway-to-Gateway Protocol
GRE	Generic Routing Encapsulation
HIP	Host Identity Protocol
HMAC	Hash-based Message Authentication Code
HPN	High Performance Network
HTML	Hypertext Markup Language
HTTP	Hypertext Transfer Protocol
HTTPS	Hypertext Transfer Protocol Secure
IAB	Internet Architecture Board
IANA	Internet Assigned Numbers Authority
ICCC	International Computer Communications Conference
ICE	Interactive Connectivity Establishment
ICMP	Internet Control Message Protocol
ICP	Initial Connection Protocol
ICP	Internet Code Point
ICP	Internet Content Provider
ID	Identifier
IEEE	Institute of Electrical and Electronics Engineers
IEN	Interim Engineering Note
IESG	Internet Engineering Steering Group
IETF	Internet Engineering Task Force
IGMP	Internet Group Management Protocol
IGP	Interior Gateway Protocol
IGRP	Interior Gateway Routing Protocol
IID	Interface Identifier
IMAP	Internet Message Access Protocol
IMP	Interface Message Processors
IoT	Internet of Things

IP	Internet Protocol
IPng	Internet Protocol next generation
ISATAP	Intra-Site Automatic Tunnel Addressing Protocol
ISDN	Integrated Services Digital Network
ISIS	Intermediate System to Intermediate System routing protocol
ISN	Initial Sequence Number
ISOC	Internet Society
ISO	International Organization for Standardization
ISP	Internet Service Provider
IX	Internet Exchange
L2TP	Layer 2 Tunneling Protocol
LAN	Local Area Network
LIR	Local Internet Registry
LISP	Locator/ID Separation Protocol
MAC	Media Access Control
MAN	Metropolitan Area Network
MIB	Management Information Base
MILNET	Military Network
MIT	Massachusetts Institute of Technology
MITM	Man-in-the-Middle attack
MLD	Multicast Listener Discovery
MPLS	Multi-Protocol Label Switching
MSDP	Multicast Source Discovery Protocol
MSS	Maximum Segment Size
MTU	Maximum Transmission Unit
NAPT	Network Address and Protocol Translation
NAT	Network Address Translation
NCC	Network Coordination Centre
NCP	Network Control Program
NDP	Neighbor Discovery Protocol
NetSE	Network Science and Engineering
NMAP	Network Mapper
NSAP	Network Service Access Point
NSFNET	National Science Foundation Network
NSP	Network Specific Prefix
NTP	Network Time Protocol
OSI	Open Systems Interconnection
OS	Operation System
OSPF	Open Shortest Path First
PCP	Port Control Protocol
PIM	Protocol Independent Multicast
PIP	Paul's Internet Protocol
PLC	Prefix Length Code
PLPMTUD	Packetization Layer Path MTU Discovery
PMTUD	Path MTU Discovery

POP	Point Of Presence
POP	Post Office Protocol
PPP	Point-to-Point Protocol
RA	Router Advertisement
RDNSS	Recursive DNS Server
RFC	Request for Comments
RIID	Rendezvous Point Interface ID
RIP	Routing Information Protocol
RIR	Regional Internet Registry
ROAD	Routing and Addressing Group
RPC	Remote Procedure Call
RPF	Reverse Path Forwarding
RP	Rendezvous Point
RSVP	Reservation Protocol
RTCP	Real-time Transport Control Protocol
RTP	Real-time Transport Protocol
SCTP	Stream Control Transmission Protocol
SIGCOMM	Special Interest Group on Data Communication
SIPP	Simple Internet Protocol Plus
SIP	Session Initiation Protocol
SIP	Simple Internet Protocol
SLAAC	Stateless Address Autoconfiguration
SLO	Service Level Objective
SMTP	Simple Mail Transfer
SNMP	Simple Network Management Protocol
SOCKS	Protocol for Sessions Traversal Across Firewall Securely
SPX	Sequenced Packet Exchange Protocol
SSH	Secure Shell protocol
SSID	Service Set Identifier
SSL	Secure Sockets Layer
SSM	Source Specific Multicast
STUN	Session Traversal Utilities for NAT
TCP	Transmission Control Protocol
TLA	Top-Level Aggregator
TLS	Transport Layer Security
TLV	Type-Length-Value
TUBA	TCP and UDP with Bigger Addresses
TURN	Traversal Using Relay NAT
UDP	User Datagram Protocol
UE	User Equipment
ULA	Unique Local IPv6 Unicast Addresses
URL	Uniform Resource Locator
uRPF	Unicast Reverse Path Forwarding
UUCP	Unix-to-Unix Copy Protocol
VPN	Virtual Private Network

VRRP	Virtual Router Redundancy Protocol
VXLAN	Virtual Extensible LAN
WAN	Wide Area Network
WG	Working Group
XML	Extensible Markup Language

Part I
Foundations

Chapter 1
Introduction

Over the past few decades, the development of the Internet has led to the widespread adoption of the Internet Protocol version 4 (IPv4). However, the rapid expansion of network scale has exposed critical limitations, including the exhaustion of IPv4 address space and the limited scalability of routing infrastructure. In February 2011, the Internet Assigned Numbers Authority (IANA) allocated its final five available/eight address blocks to the Regional Internet Registries (RIRs). As a result, all global IPv4 addresses have been exhausted, with regional Internet registries also depleting their IPv4 address pools at an accelerated rate [1].

All global IPv4 addresses have been allocated. There are still over 3 billion people worldwide who have not yet accessed the Internet. Emerging cloud computing, Internet of Things (IoT), and even Artificial Intelligence (AI) applications and agents are also booming. As a resource that is becoming increasingly scarce, IPv4 addresses are becoming more and more expensive.

As the core protocol of the next-generation Internet network layer, the version 6 of the Internet Protocol (IPv6) was announced by the Internet Engineering Task Force (IETF) in December 1995 (RFC1883 [2]). Compared with IPv4, IPv6 supports 2^{128} addresses. This vast space meets the address demands of IoT devices and enables each Internet-connected host to have a unique address—both now and in the future. This means that each host can transparently communicate with any other host and can be traced back to its source, ensuring the security of the network. In addition, IPv6 optimizes hierarchical address structure and routing mechanisms, and has better quality of service (QoS) and security. Therefore, in order to continue to maintain the rapid growth of the Internet, transitioning to IPv6 is necessary and urgent [3].

In fact, the current transition from IPv4 to IPv6 is the second transition in the history of the Internet. The first transition of the Internet took place on January 1, 1983. It was a "flag day" style hard switch, that is, the original Network Control Program (NCP) was stopped on a specific date, and the new Transmission Control Protocol/Internet Protocol (TCP/IP) was started [4]. The first transition of the Internet

X. Li and C. Bao, *New IPv6 Transition Technology*,
https://doi.org/10.1007/978-981-95-8427-7_1

was very smooth, and eventually made the IPv4 Internet the most important infrastructure in today's information society. To understand why the first transition of the Internet was smooth and steady, but the second transition from IPv4 to IPv6 has not been completed for many years, it is necessary to review the history of the Internet [4–6].

1.1 First-Generation Internet

1.1.1 ARPANET

In 1961, Leonard Kleinrock at MIT published the first paper on packet switching theory. In 1964, Paul Baran of RAND published "On Distributed Communications Networks," proposing packet switching networks designed to withstand node outages, particularly those caused by nuclear first strikes. His article described three types of network topologies, as illustrated in Fig. 1.1. The conclusion drawn is that only distributed networks exhibit the maximum resilience against destruction [7].

In 1967, Lawrence G. Roberts joined the Defense Advanced Research Projects Agency (DARPA) of the United States Department of Defense and published the Advanced Research Projects Agency Network (ARPANET) proposal [8]. The ARPANET team designed the NCP. In 1969, the four nodes of ARPANET (University of California, Los Angeles, Stanford Research Institute, University of California, Santa Barbara, and University of Utah) were successfully connected based on NCP, marking the official beginning of the world's first packet-switched network [4], as shown in Fig. 1.2.

In 1972, Robert E. Kahn organized a very successful ARPANET demonstration at the International Computer Communications Conference (ICCC), publicly showcasing this new network technology for the first time. After that, ARPANET developed rapidly.

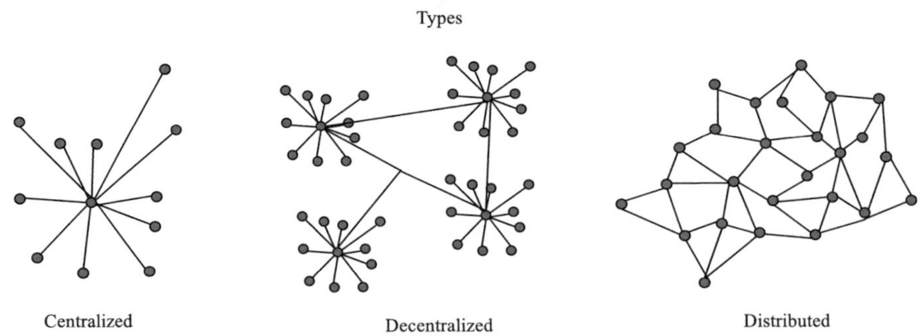

Fig. 1.1 Three types of network topologies

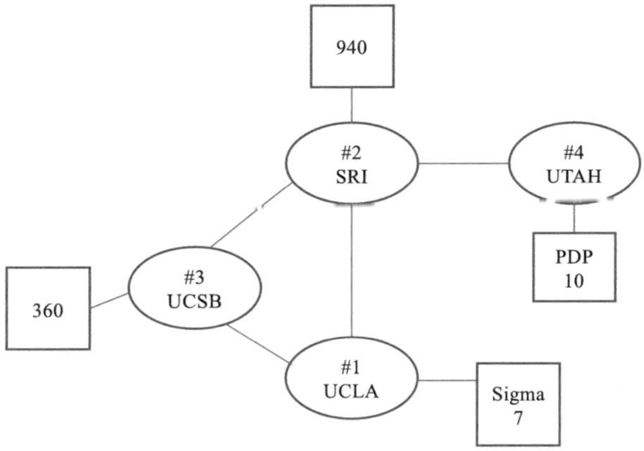

Fig. 1.2 ARPANET topology in 1969

In summarizing the experience of ARPANET, Craig Partridge of BBN proposed six principles in network architecture design [6].

(1) Stick to your vision.
(2) Think about work and data flow, not applications.
(3) Accept you can't answer some questions.
(4) Don't hoard your problems.
(5) Don't worry about backward compatibility.
(6) Don't get caught up in implementation issues.

In 1988, David Clark of MIT summarized the design philosophy of ARPANET [9] into the following points:

Goal 0: An "effective" technique for multiplexed utilization of existing interconnected networks.

Goal 1: Internet communication must continue despite loss of networks or gateways.

Goal 2: The Internet must support multiple types of communication service.

Goal 3: The Internet architecture must accommodate a variety of networks [underneath].

Goal 4: The Internet architecture must permit distributed management of its resources.

Goal 5: The Internet architecture must be cost effective.

Goal 6: The Internet architecture must permit host attachment with a low level of effort.

Goal 7: The resources used in the Internet architecture must be accountable.

Clark emphasized that the order of these design philosophies is also very important. When these priorities are reversed, a completely different network architecture may be designed.

Interestingly, Craig Partridge explicitly stated, "Don't worry about backward compatibility." Similarly, Clark's design principles made no reference to compatibility with legacy networks such as the telephone system. In fact, ARPANET was the world's first large-scale packet-switched network, which was revolutionary compared to the circuit-switched telephone network. Had compatibility with the telephone network been prioritized during ARPANET's design, it might have limited the development of a truly revolutionary packet-switched architecture. However, we believe that in the global transition from IPv4 to IPv6, the absence of a method to achieve "backward compatibility" has been the primary obstacle to the widespread adoption of IPv6.

1.1.2 NCP

The initial ARPANET used NCP [10]. NCP is a transit protocol run for ARPANET hosts. NCP is a simplex protocol that establishes connections based on user addresses. NCP reserves an odd port and an even port for the user's application program. NCP provides connection and traffic control between different host processes. NCP is shown in Fig. 1.3.

The communication protocol between interface message processors (IMP) includes physical layer, data link layer, and network layer protocols, implemented between IMPs. The communication protocol between IMP and host has different physical layers, data link layers, and network layer specifications. Therefore, NCP essentially provides a transport layer composed of an ARPANET host-to-host protocol (AHHP) and an initial connection protocol (ICP). The functions of these protocols are as follows:

(1) AHHP defines a program for transmitting unidirectional data streams with traffic control between two hosts.
(2) ICP defines the process of establishing a pair of communication data streams between two host processes.

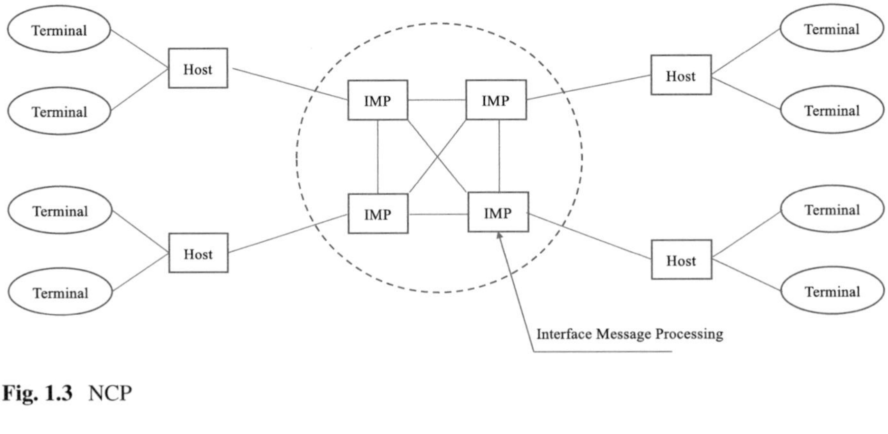

Fig. 1.3 NCP

(3) Application protocols (such as remote login (Telnet), file transfer protocol (FTP), and simple mail transfer protocol (SMTP)) access network services through the interface to the top of NCP.

The Network Control Protocol's (NCP's) addressing and forwarding mechanism follows a straightforward evolutionary path through three generations, based on the destination address format [10,11].

(1) First generation: The IMP number is encoded with 8 bits, and the host number is encoded with 2 bits.
(2) Second generation: The IMP number is expanded to 16 bits, and the host number is expanded to 8 bits.
(3) Last generation: Added logical addressing, that is, 16-bit flat addressing with 2 flag bits (RFC878 [12]).
(4) Therefore, it can address 2^{14} hosts without the source node needing to know the location of the receiving host. When a host connects to ARPANET, it notifies the IMP of the logical names it will use. The IMP then propagates this information across the network by forwarding it in the flat address space.

1.1.3 TCP/IP

When NCP is used for other networks (satellite packet networks and terrestrial wireless packet networks) and interconnected with ARPANET, NCP cannot address the downstream networks and hosts connected by IMP. Since ARPANET is very reliable, NCP does not have a mechanism for handling end-to-end host errors. Therefore, the initial motivation for developing a new protocol (which eventually became TCP/IP) was to implement global addressing across networks and to add error handling for heterogeneous networks [4,11].

The new protocol in design should have four basic principles:

(1) Each distinct network would have to stand on its own and no internal changes could be required to any such network to connect it to the Internet.
(2) Communications would be on a best effort basis. If a packet didn't make it to the final destination, it would shortly be retransmitted from the source.
(3) Black boxes would be used to connect the networks; these later are named gateways and routers. There would be no information retained by the gateways about the individual flows of packets passing through them, thereby keeping them simple and avoiding complicated adaptation and recovery from various failure modes.
(4) There would be no global control at the operations level.

In 1973, Vinton Cerf joined Robert Kahn's project, and they jointly created the next-generation transmission control protocol (TCP) [13]. In the early versions of this technology, there was only one core protocol, TCP. This protocol proposed an 8-bit network field and a 16-bit host field (referred to as TCP fields). They believed at the time that:

(1) The 8-bit network field allows for the selection of up to 256 different networks, which seemed sufficient for the foreseeable future.
(2) The host field allows for up to 65,536 different hosts to be addressed, which seemed more than enough for any given network.

In 1977, the Advanced Research Projects Agency of the U.S. Department of Defense signed contracts with BBN, Stanford University, and University College London to develop verification versions of the protocol on different hardware platforms: TCPv1 and TCPv2. During the development process, TCP/IP had to support voice and other sensitive applications that are delay-sensitive but not packet loss-sensitive. Vinton Cerf, Danny Cohen, and Jon Postel then divided the functions of TCP into two protocols: TCP and IP, becoming TCPv3 and IPv3, which then evolved into the stable TCP/IPv4, ultimately forming the famous TCP/IP hourglass model, as shown in Fig. 1.4 [11].

As can be seen from Fig. 1.4: IP is the core of the Internet. The data to be transmitted is broken down into datagrams of a certain size by the source node, each datagram carries a complete destination address and source address, and the network delivers the datagram from the source node to the destination node based on the destination address of the datagram. Each datagram is transmitted independently, there is no need to set up a central control point in the network, and network devices (routers) deliver the datagram to the next router based on a distributed routing algorithm, hoping to eventually deliver it to the destination node.

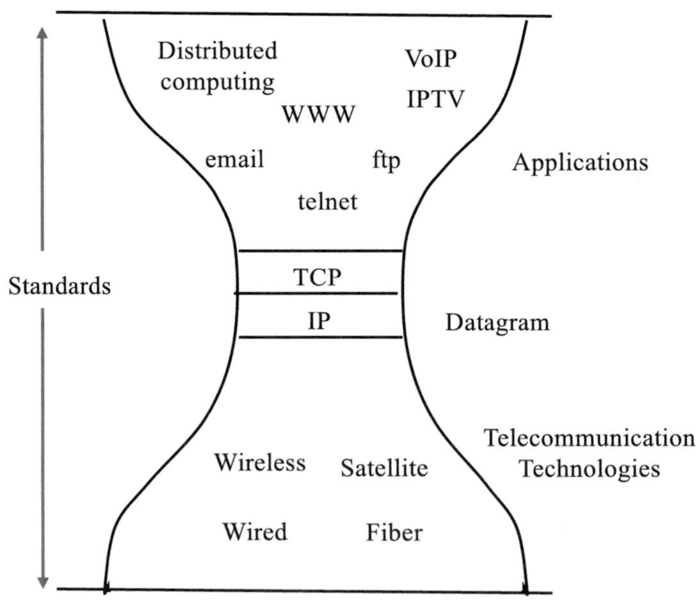

Fig. 1.4 TCP/IP hourglass model

The most important function of IP is addressing. It should be pointed out that: for scalability, the possibility of variable-length addresses was indeed considered at the time. However, the team implementing the network devices stated that the overhead of handling variable-length datagram headers was unacceptable, and ultimately chose a 32-bit fixed-length address [11]. The original structure of the 32-bit address was 8 bits for network identification and 24 bits for host address (RFC760 [14]). In 1981, RFC791 [15] defined a more flexible class structure, where Class A addresses have an 8-bit network identifier and a 24-bit host address. Class B addresses have a 16-bit network identifier and a 16-bit host address. Class C addresses have a 24-bit network identifier and an 8-bit host address.

Looking back at history, the original TCP/IP design team was very forward-thinking, designing "variable-length address" and "source routing" schemes [11]. Due to the limitations of people's understanding of the scale of the global information network at the time, and the capabilities of hardware devices and software algorithms, the "variable-length address" scheme was not chosen. Because the "source routing" was implemented using the option field in the IPv4 datagram header, which could not achieve high performance, "source routing" has never been widely used in practice.

IP does not guarantee the quality of transmission, all it can do is "best effort." The Internet uses end-to-end TCP to ensure the correctness of data transmission (retransmission mechanism) and the fairness of bandwidth usage (flow control algorithm). For applications like audio or video that are insensitive to data loss but sensitive to delay, the Internet uses the User Datagram Protocol (UDP).

IP has very low requirements for the underlying communication lines, so it can run on any communication line. The transport layer protocols TCP or UDP provide generic support to the upper layer, so any application can be developed.

From 1978 to 1983, multiple research centers developed and implemented the TCP/IP prototype system. In March 1982, the U.S. Department of Defense announced that TCP/IP would become the standard for military computer networks.

1.1.4 The First Transition: From NCP to TCP/IP

The RFC801 released in November 1981 [16] provided a transition plan from NCP to TCP, the content of which is as follows.

1. *Necessity of Transition*

ARPANET, launched in 1969 and began normal operation in 1971, had been in service for over 10 years by 1980. Although ARPANET provided reliable services and supported various research activities, changes occurred during this period, necessitating continuous improvements to ARPANET.

In the past few years, ARPA sponsored more computer networks. These networks used different lower-layer network communication technologies (wireless broadcast digital packet networks, satellite networks, etc.). Obviously, the NCP used by ARPANET at that time was insufficient for use in these networks. Therefore, in 1973,

ARPA began to support the research of new technologies, resulting in IP and TCP. The U.S. Department of Defense decided to use IP and TCP as the standard protocols for all packet networks within its management scope. Therefore, the ARPANET management committee decided to apply these protocols to the ARPANET as soon as possible.

2. *Feasibility of Transition*

At that time, ARPANET had already implemented TCP/IP on several hosts, and some of its services could be used normally. Therefore, any new host connected to ARPANET should only implement TCP/IP services.

Since it was impossible to convert all hosts to TCP at the same time, it was necessary to provide temporary dual-stack hosts (relay hosts) for bridging NCP-only and TCP-only. These relay hosts (running both NCP and TCP/IP) would support Telnet, FTP, and mail services on both NCP and TCP. These relay hosts began to provide services in November 1981 and began to operate stably in January 1982.

It was expected that during the early transition process, there would be many NCP-only hosts and a few TCP-only hosts, so the load on the relay hosts would be relatively light. As the transition progressed, more TCP-supporting hosts and fewer NCP single-stack hosts would appear. Therefore, most hosts on ARPANET at that time would become "dual-stack" hosts (supporting both NCP and TCP/IP), so the load on the relay hosts would not increase too much.

3. *Overall Transition Plan*

On January 1, 1982, every organization connected to ARPANET began to deploy TCP/IP on their hosts. The complete transition from NCP to TCP/IP was completed on January 1, 1983.

It was not enough to only implement IP (RFC791 [15]), Internet Control Message Protocol (ICMP) (RFC792 [17]), TCP (RFC793 [18]), and address allocation (RFC790 [19]). The main services also had to be available on this TCP/IP basis. These services mainly included: remote login (Telnet) (RFC764 [20]); FTP (RFC765 [21]); and SMTP (RFC788 [22], RFC780 [23], and RFC772 [24]).

4. *Milestones*

Table 1.1 presents the milestones of the first transition from NCP to TCP/IP.

5. *Issues in Implementation*

The following issues need special attention during implementation:

(1) Technical details of the Name Tables (hosts.txt).
(2) Technical details of the Mail Programs.
(3) Implementation issues of TCP/IP. Do not take "shortcuts," i.e., implement non-standard protocols. These non-standard protocol implementations include but are not limited to: ① the IP layer (i) does not perform checksum verification, (ii) does not handle fragmentation, (iii) does not handle redirection, (iv) does not handle options, (v) does not perform error handling, etc.; ② the TCP layer (i)

Table 1.1 Milestone events of the transition from NCP to TCP/IP

Historical event	Status and time
First TCP/IP service	Completed before 1982
First TCP single-stack service	Completed before 1982
Remote login protocol and file transfer protocol	Completed before 1982
Ad Hoc mail transfer protocol (RFC780 [23])	Completed before 1982
Start of switch day	January 1982
SMTP (RFC788) [22]	January 1982
General TCP/IP service	July 1982
Majority of hosts support TCP and use TCP services	November 1982
Last NCP single-stack host switched, all TCP/IP service, end of relay service	January 1983

does not perform checksum verification, (ii) does not perform reordering, (iii) does not handle options, (iv) does not perform error handling; and ③ the host does not maintain a complete mapping table.

6. *Relay Service*

Relay service means deploying "forwarding hosts," with the following modes.

(1) **Remote Login**

TCP-only host using NCP-only service as shown in Fig. 1.5.
NCP-only host using TCP-only service as shown in Fig. 1.6.

(2) **File Transfer Protocol**

TCP-only host copies files from NCP-only server.

(1) Remotely log into the forwarding host and use the forwarding host for file transfer, as shown in Fig. 1.7.

(2) Perform file transfer between the local host and the forwarding host, as shown in Fig. 1.8.

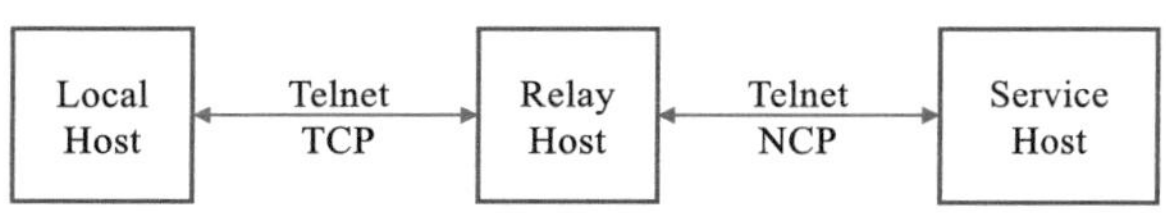

Fig. 1.5 TCP-only host using NCP-only service

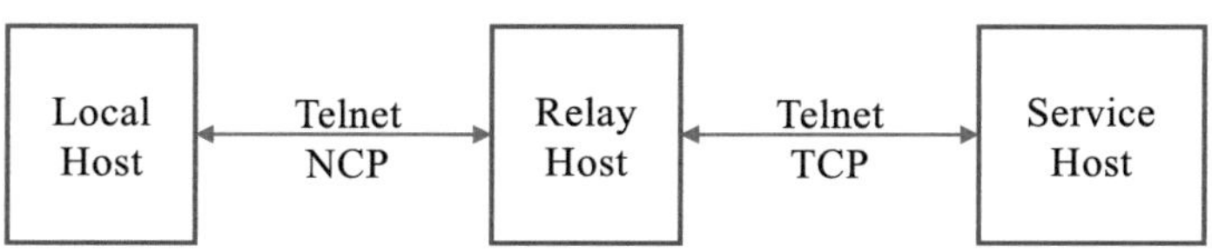

Fig. 1.6 NCP-only host using TCP-only service

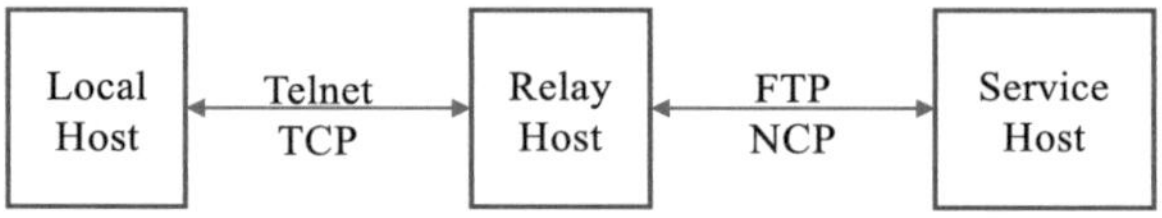

Fig. 1.7 Step one

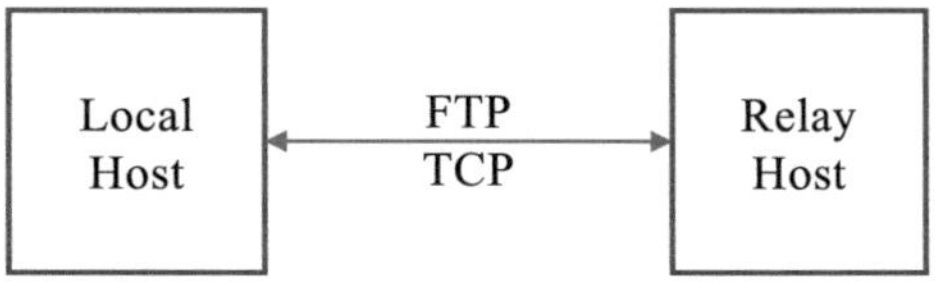

Fig. 1.8 Step two

(3) SMTP

TCP-only sends a message to the NCP-only host, as shown in Fig. 1.9.

TCP-only host sends a message to the NCP-only host, but at that time the NCP-only host does not support SMTP, so use FTP to send the contains of the mail message, as shown in Fig. 1.10.

NCP-only host sends a message to the TCP-only host, but the NCP-only host does not support SMTP, so file transfer is used, as shown in Fig. 1.11.

7. *Transition Timeline*

The timeline for the transition from NCP to TCP/IP is shown in Table 1.2.

On January 1, 1983, ARPANET completed the transition from NCP to TCP/IP. This was a "flag day" transition, requiring all hosts to switch simultaneously. Due to the comprehensive planning mentioned above, the transition process went very smoothly [4].

The first transition of the Internet (from NCP to TCP/IP) achieved great success within a year. The experience can be summarized as follows:

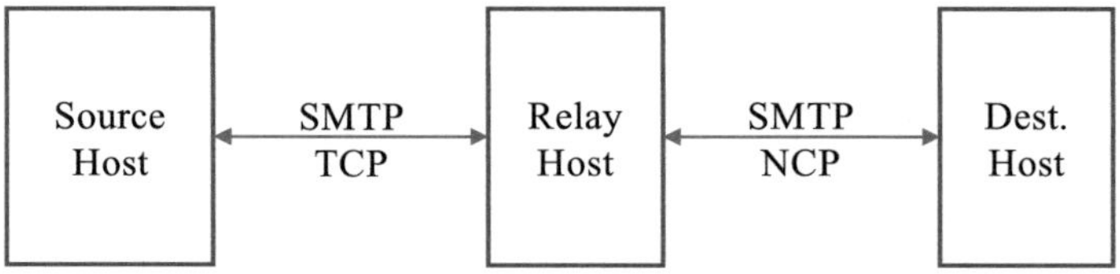

Fig. 1.9 TCP-only host sends a message to NCP-only host (first scenario)

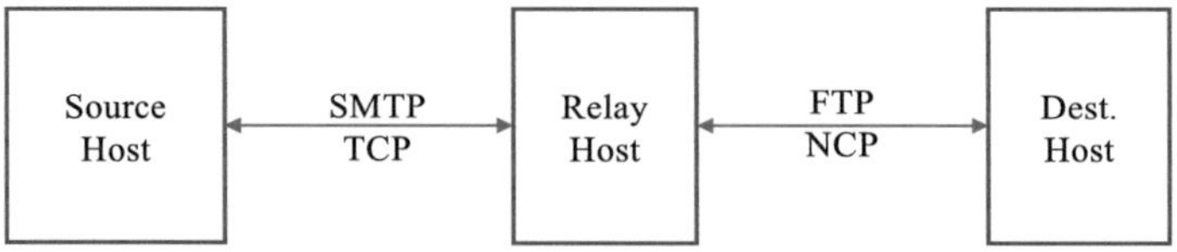

Fig. 1.10 TCP-only host sends a message to NCP-only host (second scenario)

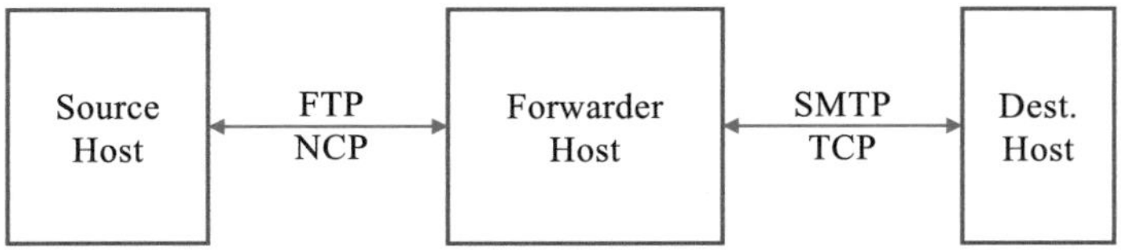

Fig. 1.11 NCP-only host sends a message to TCP-only host

Table 1.2 Transition timeline from NCP to TCP/IP

Total number of hosts	Number of dual-stack hosts	Number of NCP hosts	Number of TCP hosts	Load	Date
200	20	178	2	356	January 1982
210	40	158	12	1896	March 1982
220	60	135	25	3375	May 1982
225	95	90	40	3600	July 1982
230	100	85	45	3825	September 1982
240	125	55	60	3300	November 1982
245	155	20	70	1400	December 1982
250	170	0	80	0	December 31, 1982
250	0	0	250	0	January 1, 1983

(1) Although TCP/IP is not compatible with NCP, TCP/IP has unique function that NCP does not have, and NCP does not have a workaround for this function.
(2) The transition from NCP to TCP/IP was implemented in a single management domain (ARPANET), which could be enforced. The scale of the network involved was not large, and the applications that needed support (Telnet, FTP, SMTP, etc.) were not many.
(3) A transition period of 1 year was clearly set. During the transition period, translation services were provided for all applications (i.e., NCP-only hosts and TCP/IP-only hosts could communicate through relays). At the same time, existing NCP-only hosts had to be upgraded to dual-stack hosts that support both NCP and TCP/IP, and new hosts had to be TCP/IP-only.
(4) A "flag day" was clearly set, and support for NCP was stopped after the "flag day."

In 1983, the National Science Foundation Network (NSFNET) decided to use TCP/IP. In the same year, ARPANET was reorganized into two parts: the civilian

ARPANET and the military network (MILNET). In 1984, the International Organization for Standardization (ISO) officially recognized TCP/IP. In accordance with the Open Systems Interconnection (OSI) principle, TCP/IP has become the de facto international standard. In 1985, TCP/IP became part of the UNIX operating system. Subsequently, almost all operating systems gradually supported TCP/IP. With the expansion of networks such as NSFNET, ARPANET ceased operation in 1990. In 1995, the research-oriented NSFNET gradually retired, and the Internet entered a booming commercial development stage.

1.2 Next-Generation Internet

1.2.1 IPv6

TCP/IP was initially designed to interconnect ARPANET with a few other limited networks of the U.S. military. The designed IPv4 addressing range was 2^{32}, theoretically about 4 billion addresses.

In January 1991, the Internet Architecture Board (IAB) held a meeting, the results are logged in RFC1287 [25], which includes the following statements:

(1) Addressing and routing are the most pressing architectural issues, as they directly relate to the continued expansion of the Internet.
(2) The Internet architecture needs to be able to scale to 10^9 networks.
(3) There should not be plans for a series of “small” changes to the architecture, but instead, plans should be made to address the exhaustion of the address space. As a long-term action plan, the 32-bit address space should be replaced.
(4) Multiple paths from the source host to the destination host need to be supported to meet the needs of different types of service (TOS). Therefore, the source node or intermediate node must be able to control route selection.

Subsequently, the IETF established the Routing and Addressing Group (ROAD), the main conclusions of which are seen in RFC1380 [26].

ROAD identified the following challenges facing the Internet at the time:

(1) Class B address exhaustion.
(2) Routing table explosion.
(3) IP address space exhaustion.

To address these challenges, ROAD provided short-term, medium-term, and long-term solutions.

(1) The short-term solution is to solve the problem of Class B address exhaustion (the short-term solution does not allow modification of the terminal system). This goal led to the invention of Classless Inter-Domain Routing (CIDR [27]) technology, which also solved the problem of routing table explosion. Around

1993, the IETF issued a series of RFC standards related to CIDR, which has become the core addressing mechanism of the Internet.

(2) The medium-term solution is to solve the problem of IP address exhaustion (the medium-term solution allows upgrading of the terminal system). This goal resulted in two sub-solutions. ① Local address solution: Large enterprises with multiple internal hosts use a private address space to address these hosts, rather than using a global address. The domain name of the host is globally unique, but its IP address is unique only within the local routing domain. This led to the birth of Network Address Translation (NAT) devices, which greatly changed the end-to-end nature of the original design of the Internet. For private address space, see RFC1597 [28]. ② Next-generation internet protocol (Internet Protocol Next Generation, IPng) solution: This is actually the long-term solution.

(3) In addition to solving the address problem, the long-term solution should also solve issues such as quality-of-service (QoS) control, bandwidth reservation, and mobility. This is the next-generation Internet architecture solution.

In order to formulate a long-term plan (IPng), the IAB drafted a proposal at the Kobe meeting in Japan in June 1992. The draft suggests using the connectionless network protocol (CLNP) in the seven-layer model of the International Standardization Organization OSI as the addressing scheme for IPng. The IAB considers this a reasonable path because OSI designed the CLNP with a variable-length addressing space, which can solve the problem of address exhaustion. The IAB revised the plan eight times in less than 2 weeks. However, when the IETF community saw the draft, they were extremely angry, believing that the IAB was selling the Internet to OSI, an enemy and defeated opponent that the IETF had been fighting for many years. The IETF community believes that the IAB has no right to make such a decision. In addition, the IETF, which was mainly composed of academic and government researchers at the time, was dissatisfied with the complex and expensive OSI system. At the IETF 24 meeting held in Cambridge, Massachusetts in July 1992, IETF participants protested against the IAB's unilateral decision. About 700 IETF participants asked the Internet Society to intervene and ensure that the IETF continues to control the process of specifying Internet standards. Under these circumstances, the IAB compromised and reopened the IETF's selection process for IPng of different experiments (IP versions) [29], which eventually led to IPv6 becoming the standard for IPng.

Table 1.3 provides a list of IP version numbers.

IPv4 is the widely used Internet network layer protocol, version 5 is a stream protocol, which is rarely used.

From 1992 to 1994, the IETF community conducted a series of analyses on the needs of IPng, see RFC1498 [37], RFC1686 [38], RFC1679 [39], RFC1681 [40], RFC1667 [41], RFC1636 [42], and so on.

In the selection process of IPng, there were four technical choices:

(1) Replace IPv4 with OSI's CLNP, i.e., TUBA (RFC1347 [36]). TUBA is an abbreviation for TCP and UDP with bigger addresses.

Table 1.3 IP version numbers

Version	Name	Description	Status	RFC
0	TCPv0	Version of March 1977	Obsolete	
1	TCPv1	Version of January 1978	Obsolete	
2	TCPv2	Version A of February 1978	Obsolete	
3	IPv3	Version B of February 1978	Obsolete	
4	IPv4	Version of September 1981	Widely used	RFC791 [15] (Official)
5	ST	Stream protocol	Rarely used	
6	IPv6	IPng candidate, originally named SIP, SIPP	In transition	RFC8507 [30] (SIP) RFC1710 [31] (SIPP) RFC8200 [32] (Official) RFC4291 [33] (Official)
7	CATNIP	IPng candidate, originally named TP/IX	Obsolete	RFC1707 [34] (Experimental)
8	PIP	IPng candidate	Obsolete	RFC1621 [35] (Experimental)
9	TUBA	IPng candidate	Obsolete	RFC1347 [36] (Experimental)
10~15	Unused			

(2) Attempt to reconcile TUBA and IPv4, i.e., CATNIP (RFC1707 [34]). CATNIP is an abbreviation for the common architecture for the Internet. CATNIP attempted to integrate CLNP, IP, and internetwork packet exchange (IPX) protocols at the network layer. For OSI transport protocol class 4, TP4, CLTP, TCP, UDP, IPX, and Sequenced Packet Exchange Protocol (SPX), all provide services at the transport layer.
(3) The radical alternative to IPv4, that is, the Paul's Internet Protocol (PIP) (RFC1621 [35]).
(4) The conservative alternative to IPv4, that is, the Simple Internet Protocol (SIP) (RFC8507 [30]) and Simple Internet Protocol Plus (SIPP) (RFC1710 [31]).

Among the above four technical choices, TUBA and CATNIP were rejected because they almost completely denied the basic design concept of TCP/IP. PIP and SIP have become the basis of today's IPv6 [11].

PIP [35] represents a significant shift in IP, as PIP uses source routing as the basic forwarding mechanism. The addresses in source routing are not global addresses, but more compact locators, which are unique only within a certain area of the network. To implement this scheme, PIP organizes the nodes of the Internet into a hierarchy and defines node names within the hierarchy.

SIP [30] is a more conservative design, including the concept of source routing, but uses global routing names for intermediate nodes.

Internal discussions within the IPng community about IPng led to a compromise called SIPP, which uses SIP syntax but incorporates some advanced semantics from PIP. Of course, the size of the address range is the main motivation to replace IPv4. SIP and SIPP use 64-bit address, which is twice the bit length of IPv4. The final version of IPv6 has a larger address, 128 bits. The choice of 128 bits is not because 2^{64} is too small to address all nodes on the future Internet, but to try to better facilitate the management of the IPv6 address space. The idea is: use the high 64 bits of the 128 bits for network addressing, and the low 64 bits as the extended unique identifier of the interface [11].

1.2.2 The Second Transition: From IPv4 to IPv6

The second transition of the Internet from IPv4 to IPv6 has been going on for over 20 years and is not yet complete. Discussing the problems and solutions of IPv6 transition is the purpose of writing this book.

It needs to be emphasized that: an important idea of the new generation of IPv6 transition technology is to establish a mapping relationship between different network layer protocols, or called "translatable." Recall different versions of IPng, SIP and SIPP are most "translatable" with IPv4 (but not 100% translatable, there are "corner" situations that are untranslatable). The selection of SIPP as the foundation for IPv6 made it technically feasible to enable IPv4/IPv6 interconnection via network layer translation.

Although history cannot be repeated, if the IPng designed at that time was even more "translatable" with IPv4, and stateless translation technology was a mandatory requirement for the IPng deployment (i.e., any new IPv4 address blocks have to be used in an IPv6-only fashion and communicate with IPv4 Internet via stateless translator), then IPv6 could interconnect with IPv4 at the beginning of deployment, thus almost completely eliminating the transition problem.

1.3 Future Internet

1.3.1 Future Internet Protocol

In the long run, IPv6 will not be the final version of the Internet protocol (or more generally: network protocol). Therefore, the research and development of future network protocols must consider transition issues.

The Future Internet Network Design (FIND) and Network Science and Engineering (NetSE) programs in the United States, along with similar initiatives worldwide, have challenged the network research community. These programs ask researchers to envision what the Internet might look like in 15–20 years. They encourage this vision without being limited by today's Internet constraints.

David Clark believes that the potential requirements for future Internet architecture should include [11] the following aspects:

(1) Separation of identifier and locator.
(2) New service models.
(3) Reshaping the role of Internet Service Providers (ISPs), also commonly referred to as network operators.
(4) Analyzing and controlling functional dependencies in network architecture.
(5) Dealing with different network participants, etc.

At present, the global exploration of how to design future Internet protocols is still ongoing.

1.3.2 The Third Transition: From IPv6 to Future Network Protocols

Chapter 16 of this book, "Transition to Future Network Protocols," will summarize the lessons learned from the transition from NCP to TCP/IP, from IPv4 to IPv6, and on this basis, make several suggestions for the "translatable" design of future network protocols.

1.4 Summary

This chapter provides a brief overview of the Internet's history, tracing its origins back to ARPANET, and discusses the first successful transition of the Internet protocol suite (from NCP to TCP/IP). However, the second transition (from IPv4 to IPv6) remains incomplete. Subsequent chapters will delve into this issue and present technical solutions derived from the new generation of IPv6 transition series RFC standards developed by the IETF, in which the author was actively involved.

References

1. APNIC. IPv4 exhaustion. [2022–02–18]. https://www.apnic.net/manage-ip/ipv4-exhaustion.
2. Deering S, Hinden R. RFC1883: Internet protocol version 6 (IPv6) specification. IETF 1995–12.
3. APNIC. IPv6@APNIC. [2022–02–18]. https://www.apnic.net/community/ipv6.
4. Leiner B, Cerf V, Clark D, et al. A brief history of the internet. [2022–02–18]. https://www.internethalloffame.org/brief-history-internet.

5. Li Xing, Bao Congxiao. Review and Reflection on Fifty Years of Internet Technology Innovation and Development. Journal of Shantou University (Humanities and Social Sciences), 2019, 35(12): 5-12 (in Chinese)
6. Li Xing, Bao Congxiao. The Evolutionary Path of Internet Technology: Simplicity is the Ultimate Sophistication - Commemorating the 50th Anniversary of the Birth of ARPANET. China Education Network, 2020, (1): 5, (in Chinese)
7. Baran P. On distributed communications networks. IEEE Transactions on Communications System, 1964, 12(1): 1-9.
8. Lawrence R. Multiple computer networks and intercomputer communications. Proceedings of the first ACM Symposium on Operating System Principles, 1967: 3.1–3.6.
9. Clark D. The design philosophy of the DARPA internet protocols. ACM SIGCOMM Computer Communication Review, 1988, 18(4): 106-114.
10. Network Control Protocol (ARPANET) [2025–01–25]: https://en.wikipedia.org/wiki/Network_Control_Protocol_(ARPANET)#Network_Control_Program
11. Clark D. Designing an Internet- Information Policy. Cambridge: The MIT Press, 2018.
12. Malis A. RFC878: ARPANET 1822L host access protocol. IETF 1983–12.
13. Cerf V, Kahn R. A protocol for packet network intercommunication. IEEE Transactions on Communications, 1974, 22(5): 637-648.
14. Postel J. RFC760: DoD standard internet protocol. IETF 1980–01.
15. Postel J. RFC791: Internet protocol. IETF 1981–09.
16. Postel J. RFC801: NCP/TCP transition plan. IETF 1981–11.
17. Postel J. RFC792: Internet control message protocol. IETF 1981–09.
18. Postel J. RFC793: Transmission control protocol. IETF 1981–09.
19. Postel J. RFC790: Assigned numbers. IETF 1981–09.
20. Postel J. RFC764: Telnet protocol specification. IETF 1980–06.
21. Postel J. RFC765: File transfer protocol specification. IETF 1980–06.
22. Postel J. RFC788: Simple mail transfer protocol. IETF 1981–11.
23. Sluizer S, Postel J. RFC780: Mail transfer protocol. IETF 1981–05.
24. Sluizer S, Postel J. RFC772: Mail transfer protocol. IETF 1981–05.
25. Clark D, Chapin L, Cerf V, et al. RFC1287: Towards the future internet architecture. IETF 1991–12.
26. Gross P, Almquist P. RFC1380: IESG deliberations on routing and addressing. IETF 1992–11.
27. Rekhter Y, Li T. RFC1518: An architecture for IP address allocation with CIDR. IETF 1993–09.
28. Rekhter Y, Moskowitz B, Karrenberg D, et al. RFC1597: Address allocation for private internets. IETF 1994–03.
29. Russell A. Rough consensus and running code and the internet-OSI standards war. IEEE Annals of the History of Computing, 2006, 28(3): 48-61.
30. Deering S, Hinden R. RFC8507: Simple internet protocol (SIP) specification. IETF 2018–12.
31. Hinden R. RFC1710: Simple internet protocol plus white paper. IETF 1994–10.
32. Deering S, Hinden R. RFC8200: Internet protocol version 6 (IPv6) specification. IETF 2017–07.
33. Hinden R, Deering S. RFC4291: IP version 6 addressing architecture. IETF 2006–02.
34. McGovern M, Ullmann R. RFC1707: CATNIP: Common architecture for the internet. IETF 1994–10.
35. Francis P. RFC1621: Pip near-term architecture. IETF 1994–05.
36. Callon R. RFC1347: TCP and UDP with bigger addresses (TUBA), a simple proposal for internet addressing and routing. IETF 1992–06.
37. Saltzer J. RFC1498: On the naming and binding of network destinations. IETF 1993–08.
38. Vecchi M. RFC1686: IPng requirements: A cable television industry viewpoint. IETF 1994–08.
39. Green D, Irey P, Marlow D, et al. RFC1679: HPN working group input to the IPng requirements solicitation. IETF 1994–08.
40. Bellovin S. RFC1681: On many addresses per host. IETF 1994–08.
41. Symington S, Wood D, Pullen J. RFC1667: Modelling and simulation requirements for IPng. IETF 1994–08.

42. Internet Architecture Board. RFC1636: Report of the IAB workshop on security in the internet architecture. IETF 1994–06.

Chapter 2
Design Principles of the Internet

In order to examine the new generation of IPv6 transition technologies, it is essential to review the design principles of IPv4 and IPv6. This will enable the design of IPv6 transition technologies that align with the Internet's evolving trends; accommodate diverse mainstream scenarios; and facilitate distributed, incremental deployment.

Unlike many engineering systems, the Internet does not have a design blueprint, nor was it conceived by individual geniuses, but evolved through trial and error in practice by tens of millions of scientists and engineers in the computer and communication fields worldwide.

However, trial and error need to be carried out under the guidance of certain design principles, otherwise, one will lose direction.

2.1 Concept of Internet Design Principles

A design principle is essentially a belief, a tenant, a concept that you rally behind. It doesn't matter whether you making a specification or if you are making a physical object or a piece of software or a programming language. You will probably find a design principle or multiple design principles behind all good examples of anything that has been built collaboratively. And it's not just from the Internet. Throughout history the design principles are also behind large-scale constructions like countries, societies [1].

Here are a few examples of design principles in the field of information engineering technology.

The inventor of the World Wide Web, Berners-Lee, summarized the following two design principles [2]:

Principles such as simplicity and modularity are the stuff of software engineering; decentralization and tolerance are the life and breath of Internet.

The design philosophy of the UNIX operating system is as follows [3]:

X. Li and C. Bao, *New IPv6 Transition Technology*,
https://doi.org/10.1007/978-981-95-8427-7_2

(1) Do one thing well: Each program should do one thing well, rather than adding new features to existing programs.
(2) Write programs to work together: Programs should be designed to communicate with each other, and the output of one program should be the input of another.
(3) Build a prototype early: Design and build software early, and be willing to throw away parts and rebuild them.
(4) Use tools: Use tools to make programming tasks easier, even if you have to build the tools yourself.

The design philosophy of the HTML5 is as follows [4]:

(1) Avoid needless complexity.
(2) Support existing content.
(3) Be conservative in what you send; be liberal in what you accept.
(4) Solve real problems.
(5) Pave the cowpaths.
(6) Degrade gracefully.
(7) The value of a network is proportional to the square of the number of connected users of the system (n^2).
(8) Design for humans first, machines second.
(9) Rough consensus and running code.

2.2 IPv4 Design Principles

Although the Internet does not have a design blueprint, it does have several important design principles. These design principles have ensured the great success of the Internet, distinguishing it from other networks in history, such as OSI's CLNP technology, the International Telecommunication Union's Integrated Services Digital Network (ISDN) technology, and Asynchronous Transfer Mode (ATM) technology.

From the perspective of Internet technology itself, not all protocols are successful. However, it can be said that the Internet protocols that have achieved great success basically conform to these design principles. IPv6 technology and IPv6 transition technology should not be exceptions.

One of the inventors of the Internet, Vinton Cerf, summarized the design principles of the Internet as follows [5]:

(1) Not designed for any specific applications: just move packets.
(2) Designed to run over any communication technology.
(3) Permit innovation at the edges.
(4) Design to scale.
(5) Open to new protocols, new technologies, and new applications.

The most important protocol of the Internet is IP/ICMP (RFC791 [6]). Figure 2.1 explains the IP/ICMP (as well as IPv6/ICMPv6) in the layered model.

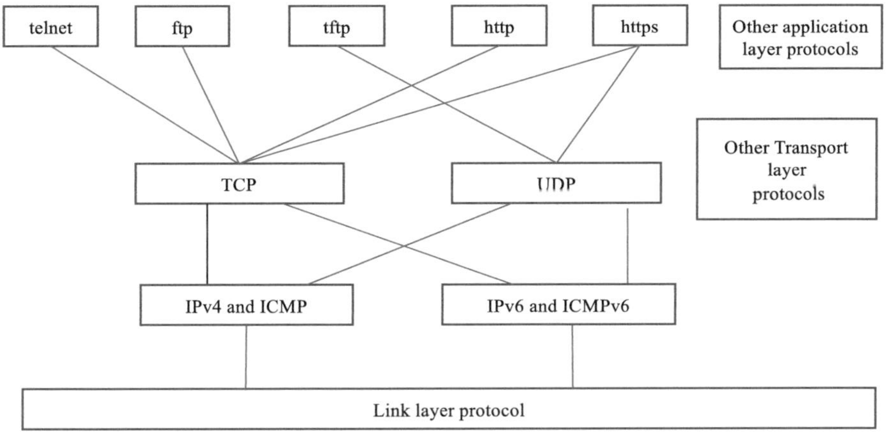

Fig. 2.1 Position of IP and ICMP in the layered model

2.2.1 Basic Design Principles

RFC1958 [7] summarizes 14 basic design principles of the Internet as follows:

(1) Heterogeneity is inevitable and must be supported by design. Multiple types of hardware must be allowed for, e.g., transmission speeds differing by at least seven orders of magnitude, various computer word lengths, and hosts ranging from memory-starved microprocessors up to massively parallel supercomputers. Multiple types of application protocol must also be allowed for, ranging from the simplest such as remote login up to the most complex such as distributed databases.
(2) If there are several ways of doing the same thing, choose one. If a previous design, in the Internet context or elsewhere, has successfully solved the same problem, choose the same solution unless there is a good technical reason not to. Duplication of the same protocol functionality should be avoided as far as possible, without of course using this argument to reject improvements.
(3) All designs must scale readily to very many nodes per site and to many millions of sites.
(4) Performance and cost must be considered as well as functionality.
(5) Keep it simple. When in doubt during design, choose the simplest solution.
(6) Modularity is good. If you can keep things separate, do so.
(7) In many cases, it is better to adopt an almost complete solution now, rather than to wait until a perfect solution can be found.
(8) Avoid options and parameters whenever possible. Any options and parameters should be configured or negotiated dynamically rather than manually.
(9) Be strict when sending and tolerant when receiving. Implementations must follow specifications precisely when sending to the network, and tolerate faulty

input from the network. When in doubt, discard faulty input silently, without returning an error message unless this is required by the specification.

(10) Be parsimonious with unsolicited packets, especially multicasts and broadcasts.

(11) Circular dependencies must be avoided. For example, routing must not depend on lookups in the Domain Name System (DNS), since the updating of DNS servers depends on successful routing.

(12) Objects should be self-describing (include type and size), within reasonable limits. Only type codes and other magic numbers assigned by the Internet Assigned Numbers Authority (IANA) may be used.

(13) All specifications should use the same terminology and notation, and the same bit- and byte-order convention.

(14) And perhaps most important: Nothing gets standardized until there are multiple instances of running code.

2.2.2 Domain Name and Address Issues

DNS is one of the most important infrastructures of the Internet. When designing DNS and network layer protocols, the following points must be noted [7]:

(1) Avoid any design that requires addresses to be hard coded or stored on non-volatile storage (except of course where this is an essential requirement as in a name server or configuration server). In general, user applications should use names rather than addresses.

(2) Addresses must be unambiguous (unique within any scope where they may appear). Upper layer protocols must be able to clearly identify endpoints, and addresses must remain unchanged at the beginning and end of transmission, that is, end-to-end address transparency.

2.2.3 End-To-End Address Transparency

A very important concept of the Internet is "end-to-end address transparency" (RFC2775 [8]). According to the original definition of the Internet, end-to-end address transparency means global unique addressing and also means that the source and destination addresses of the datagram remain unchanged throughout the transmission from source to destination.

The essence of the Internet's "end-to-end" is that: any end-to-end function can only be truly implemented through end systems, for the following reasons:

(1) Any network, no matter how carefully designed, will fail under certain circumstances. Therefore, the best response should be to accept this reality and solve the problem through the end system.

(2) End-to-end security can only be implemented by the end system.

(3) The network system does not need, and is not likely to have, the complete knowledge and ability to solve end-to-end communication problems. Therefore, end-to-end communication problems can only be decided by the end system. Of course, a good network system can improve the transmission performance of the network.

This "end to-end" principle leads to the design concept of "statelessness" on the Internet, that is, the network itself should not maintain state, these states should be maintained by the end nodes. Only when the end system fails will the network function fail. Therefore, connectionless datagrams are superior to virtual circuits. The role of the network is to deliver datagrams as efficiently and flexibly as possible, and other functions should be completed at the end system.

When Louis Pouzin described the initial concept, [9] and Vint Cerf define the Internet [10], they both explicitly define that a single logical address space needs to cover the entire network. This concept leads to two obvious consequences:

(1) The datagram does not change throughout the transmission process.
(2) The source address and destination address can serve as the unique identifiers of the end systems.

Note that, the header of the Internet datagram (IP datagram) will definitely change during the transmission process, for example, the datagram's time to live (TTL), checksum, and fields related to fragmentation may change. However, during the operation of the Internet, the source address and destination address of the datagram remain unchanged.

With the popularization of the Internet, the exhaustion of IPv4 addresses, and the introduction of the concept of Intranet, the use of new technologies disrupted the transparency of end-to-end addresses. Technologies like DHCP and PPP now automate and manage network connections. Firewalls and SOCKS protocols enhance security by controlling traffic flow. Network Address Translation (NAT) allows multiple devices to share a single public IP address. Application Layer Gateways (ALGs) and proxies improve traffic filtering and routing. Caches and split DNS systems optimize resource access and domain resolution.

In the early 1990s, when people considered the evolution from IPv4 to IPng, they hoped to restore the transparency of end-to-end addresses.

From the perspective of end-to-end address transparency, the following conclusions can be drawn:

(1) The originally designed and operated IPv4 Internet (with static address configuration, no NAT, no firewalls, etc.) has end-to-end address transparency.
(2) The introduction of mechanisms such as NAT (network address translation) into the IPv4 Internet has disrupted end-to-end address transparency.
(3) The original intention of IPv6 design was to restore end-to-end address transparency.

The question is, when IPv4 and IPv6 coexist, can end-to-end address transparency still be maintained? Consider the following:

(1) In the case of dual stack without IPv4 NAT, communication between IPv4 hosts has end-to-end address transparency. Communication between IPv6 hosts also has end-to-end address transparency (IPv6 does not have NAT). However, communication between IPv4 and IPv6 hosts obviously does not have end-to-end address transparency, because in the case of dual-stack, IPv4 hosts and IPv6 hosts cannot communicate with each other.
(2) In the case of dual stack with IPv4 NAT, communication between IPv4 hosts does not have end-to-end address transparency. Communication between IPv6 hosts has end-to-end address transparency (IPv6 does not have NAT). However, communication between IPv4 and IPv6 hosts obviously does not have end-to-end address transparency, because in the case of dual stack, IPv4 hosts and IPv6 hosts cannot communicate with each other.
(3) In the case where IPv4-only hosts and IPv6-only hosts communicate with each other through stateless translation technology, they still do not have end-to-end address transparency in the narrow sense, because IPv4 and IPv6 are not compatible. However, if a bidirectional, algorithm-based mapping relationship is established between IPv4 and IPv6 addresses, it can be considered that there is a wide-sense end-to-end address transparency between IPv4 and IPv6. This is the essence of stateless translation technology.

The core idea of the design of stateless translation technology is the wide-sense end-to-end address transparency, which will be elaborated in the following chapters.

2.3 IPv6 Design Principles

To thoroughly understand the features of IPv6 and effectively implement protocol translation and address mapping between IPv4 and IPv6, it is crucial to examine the history and explore the design considerations made by the IETF when developing the IPng protocol (RFC1726 [11]).

2.3.1 Basic Design Principles

1. *Architectural Simplicity*

The simplicity of the IPng architecture does not mean that all possible features have been added, but rather that there are no features that can be removed. IPng continues to maintain the hourglass model of IPv4, any function that can be implemented by a high-level protocol will continue to be implemented by the high-level protocol, and IPng can run on any communication media.

2. *One Protocol to Bind Them All*

The task of the Internet is to provide global IP layer connectivity. The IP layer is the common factor of all nodes on the Internet, and the purpose of the Internet is to provide IP services to everyone.

This does not mean that the Internet must be a single-protocol Internet. Multi-Protocol operations are required to allow for continued testing, experimentation, and development and because service providers' customers clearly want to be able to run protocols such as CLNP, DECNET, and Novell over their Internet connections.

3. *Live Long*

Updating the protocol at the network layer is an extremely difficult task, if not impossible. Therefore, IPng must be able to last at least 20 years without becoming obsolete.

4. *New Functions*

We believe that simply allowing for bigger addresses and more efficient routing is not enough of a benefit to encourage vendors, service providers, and users to switch to IPng, with its attendant disruptions of service, etc. These problems can be solved much more simply with faster routers, balkanization of the Internet address space, and other hacks. IETF believes that there must be positive functional or operational benefits to switching to IPng. In other words, IPng must be able to live for a long time and it must allow the Internet to prosper and to grow to serve new applications and user needs.

5. *Co-Operative Anarchy*

One of the main factors for the success of the Internet is that there is no single, centralized control point or policy issuer for the entire network. This allows each member of the network to customize their own network, applications, environment, and policies according to their needs. This decentralized and decoupled nature must be preserved in IPng, that is, the need for cooperation between members of the network should be minimized. In other words, the entire Internet community can only tolerate the minimum level of centralization and forced cooperation. The benefits of this principle are as follows:

(1) It is easier to test new protocols and services.
(2) It can eliminate single points of failure.
(3) It allows for distributed management.

2.3.2 Features that IPv6 Must Support

1. *Scale*

The IPng protocol must scale to allow the identification and addressing of at least 10^{12} end systems (and preferably much more). The IPng protocol and its associated routing protocols and architecture must allow for at least 10^9 individual networks (and preferably more). The routing schemes must scale at a rate that is less than the square root of the number of constituent networks.

2. *Topological Flexibility*

The routing architecture and protocols of IPng must allow for many different network topologies. The routing architecture and protocols must not assume that the network's physical structure is a tree.

3. *Performance*

A state-of-the-art, commercial-grade router must be able to process and forward IPng traffic at speeds capable of fully utilizing common, commercially available, high-speed media at the time. Furthermore, at a minimum, a host must be able to achieve data transfer rates with IPng comparable to the rates achieved with IPv4, using similar levels of host resources.

4. *Robust Service*

The network service and its associated routing and control protocols must be robust.

5. *Transition*

The protocol must have a straightforward transition plan from the current IPv4. A smooth, orderly, transition from IPv4 to IPng is needed. It is not possible to have a "flag day" form of transition in which all hosts and routers must change over at once. Rather, IPng will need to coexist with IPv4 for some period of time.

6. *Media Independence*

The protocol must work across an internetwork of many different LAN, MAN, and WAN media, with individual link speeds ranging from a ones-of-bits per second to hundreds of gigabits per second. Multiple-access and point-to-point media must be supported, as must media supporting both switched and permanent circuits.

7. *Unreliable Datagram Service*

The protocol must support an unreliable datagram delivery service.

8. *Configuration, Administration, and Operation*

The protocol must permit easy and largely distributed configuration and operation. Automatic configuration of hosts and routers is required.

9. *Secure Operation*

IPng must provide a secure network layer.

10. *Unique Naming*

IPng must assign all IP-Layer objects in the global, ubiquitous, Internet unique names. These names may or may not have any location, topology, or routing significance.

11. *Access*

The protocols that define IPng and its associated protocols (similar to ARP and ICMP in IPv4) must be published as standard track RFCs. The routing protocols (such as OSPF, BGP, and RIP for IPv4) must also be published as standard track RFCs. These protocols must satisfy the requirements specified in RFC1310 [12]. These documents should be as freely available and redistributable as the IPv4 and related RFCs. There must be no specification-related licensing fees for implementing or selling IPng software.

12. *Multicast*

The protocol must support both unicast and multicast packet transmission. Part of the multicast capability is a requirement to be able to send to "all IP hosts on a given subnetwork." Dynamic and automatic routing of multicasts is also required.

13. *Extensibility*

The protocol must be extensible; it must be able to evolve to meet the future service needs of the Internet. This evolution must be achievable without requiring network-wide software upgrades. IPng is expected to evolve over time. As it evolves, it must be able to allow different versions to coexist on the same network. The considerations are as follows:

(1) The algorithms used in processing IPng information should be decoupled from the protocol itself.
(2) The content of packet headers should be extensible.
(3) The fundamental data structures of IPng should not be bound with the other elements of the protocol.
(4) It should be possible to add additional packet types to IPng.

14. *Network Service*

1. The protocol must allow the network (routers, intelligent media, hosts, and so on) to associate packets with particular service classes and provide them with the services specified by those classes.

15. *Support for Mobility*

The protocol must support mobile hosts, networks, and internetworks.

16. *Control Protocol*

The protocol must include elementary support for testing and debugging networks.

17. *Private Networks*

IPng must allow users to build private internetworks on top of the basic Internet Infrastructure. Both private IP-based internetworks and private non-IP-based (e.g., CLNP or AppleTalk) internetworks must be supported.

2.3.3 Things not to Require

1. *Fragmentation*

The technology exists for path MTU discovery. Presumably, IPng will continue to provide this technology. Therefore, IETF believes that IPng fragmentation and reassembly, as provided in IPv4, is not necessary. IETF notes that fragmentation has been shown to be detrimental to network performance and strongly recommend that it be avoided.

2. *IP Header Checksum*

Experience has shown that the IPv4 datagram header checksum does not provide sufficient error protection, but it affects forwarding performance. Therefore, IPng does not set a network layer checksum. The mechanism for error protection is ensured by the link layer's "checksum," i.e., cyclic redundancy check (CRC), and the checksum of the transport layer (such as TCP).

3. *Firewalls*

IPng does not need to consider support for firewalls. Of course, IPng will not prevent the implementation of firewalls.

4. *Network Management*

Network management is not part of the IPng protocol, but a task that needs to be performed separately, such as the Simple Network Management Protocol (SNMP) and Management Information Base (MIB). Network management standards should adapt to the IPng protocol, and not require the IPng protocol to adapt to the needs of network management.

5. *Accounting*

Accounting is not part of the IPng protocol. Accounting standards should adapt to accommodate the IPng protocol, rather than requiring it to adapt to meet accounting needs. Of course, the undeniable source address feature and the globally unified naming capability in IPng can certainly facilitate accounting.

2.3.4 IPv6 Routing Principles

The routing architecture of IPng is an extremely important issue, discussed separately as follows.

1. Scale

First and foremost, the routing architecture must scale to support a very large Internet. Current expectations are for an Internet of about $10^9 \sim 10^{12}$ networks. The routing architecture must be able to deal with networks of this size. Furthermore, the routing architecture must be able to deal with this size without requiring massive, global databases and algorithms. Such databases or algorithms would, in effect, be single points of failure in the architecture (which is not robust), and because of the nature of Internet administration (cooperative anarchy), it would be impossible to maintain the needed consistency.

2. *Policy*

Networks (both transit and non-transit) must be able to set their own policies for the types of traffic that they will admit. The routing architecture must make these policies available to the network as a whole. Furthermore, nodes must be able to select routes for their traffic based on the advertised policies.

3. *QoS*

A key element of the network service criteria is that differing applications wish to acquire differing grades of network service. It is essential that this service information be propagated around the network.

4. *Feedback*

As users select specific routes over which to send their traffic, they must be provided feedback from the routing architecture. This feedback should allow the user to determine whether the desired routes are actually available or not, whether the desired services are being provided, and so forth.

5. *Stability*

Adding additional features (such as routing policies, service quality control, etc.) to the routing system may impair routing stability. However, the routing stability of IPng should be the same as or more stable than IPv4.

6. *Multicast*

Multicast will be more important in IPng than it is today in IPv4. Multicast groups may be very large and very distributed. Membership in multicast groups will be very dynamic. The routing architecture must be able to cope with this. Furthermore, the routing architecture must be able to build multicast routes dynamically, based on factors such as group membership, member location, requested and available qualities of service, and so on.

2.4 Analysis of IPv6 Design Principles

More than 20 years have passed since the IETF published its series of IPv6 standard RFCs. The following reflections are made in conjunction with the design principles of IPv4 and IPv6, particularly the experiences and lessons learned from IPv6 transition technology.

2.4.1 Compatibility Issues Between IPv4 and IPv6

1. *Heterogeneity*

In RFC1958 [7], the first principle of IPv4 design states "Heterogeneity is inevitable and must be supported by design. Multiple types of hardware must be allowed for, e.g., transmission speeds differing by at least 7 orders of magnitude, various computer word lengths, and hosts ranging from memory-starved microprocessors up to massively parallel supercomputers. Multiple types of application protocol must be allowed for, ranging from the simplest such as remote login up to the most complex such as distributed databases."

Discussion

IPv4 and IPv6 have implemented this principle, leading to the great success of the Internet. Since the Internet is a network that allows heterogeneous systems to interconnect, why not consider the interoperability between the two protocols? If the interoperability was fully considered when designing IPv6, there would be no many transition issues with IPv6. From another perspective, IPv4/IPv6 translation technology is to make incompatible IPv4 and IPv6 compatible.

2. *Cost*

In RFC1958 [7], the fourth principle says "Performance and cost must be considered as well as functionality."

Discussion

Chapter 3 of this book "Evolution of IPv6 Transition Technology" compares traditional IPv6 transition technologies. Obviously, the cost of running IPv6-only is lower than running dual stack of IPv6 and IPv4. According to this design principle, it is preferable to deploy an IPv6-only and use translation technology to interconnect with IPv4, rather than using dual-stack technology for IPv6 transition.

3. *Perfection*

In RFC1958 [7], the 7th statement says: "In many cases it is better to adopt an almost complete solution now, rather than to wait until a perfect solution can be found."

Discussion

Given the incompatibility between IPv6 and IPv4, perfect translation is impossible; however, existing translation techniques work well in all but the most minute and inconsequential edge cases.

4. *Multi-Protocol*

The first principle of IPv6 design stated in RFC1726 [11] says: "This does NOT say that the Internet is a One-Protocol Internet. The Internet today, and shall remain in the future, a Multi-Protocol Internet."

Discussion

At the initial design stage of IPng, the decision to support multiple protocols was a pragmatic choice, reflecting the uncertainty about which protocol would ultimately dominate the network landscape. The IPng architecture was intentionally designed to accommodate coexistence and interoperability with existing protocols, enabling gradual migration and testing of new protocols without disrupting legacy systems. However, the long-term vision of IPng was to converge toward a single, unified protocol at the IP layer to simplify implementation, reduce complexity, and ensure universal service. This approach acknowledged that while multi-protocol support was critical during the transition phase, the final outcome would be shaped by market forces and the technical maturity of competing protocols.

Crucially, at that time, the need for IPv4 compatibility was not fully recognized as requiring distinct handling. Since IPv4 had already achieved widespread deployment and heavy usage, allowing it to coexist with IPng protocols would significantly hinder, if not halt, the development of IPng. Therefore, compatibility with IPv4 should be achieved through translation technologies rather than native support. This distinction could ensure that IPng can evolve independently while maintaining backward compatibility without compromising its long-term goals.

5. *Live Long*

The first "General Principle" in RFC1726 [11] says: "It is very difficult to change a protocol as central to the workings of the Internet as IP. Even more problematic is changing such a protocol frequently. This simply cannot be done. We believe that it is impossible to expect the community to make significant, non-backward compatible changes to the IP layer more often than once every 10–15 years."

Discussion

This judgment is correct, but it greatly underestimates the difficulty of updating the "backward incompatible" IP layer protocol. The IPng design guideline RFC1726 [11] has been published for more than 20 years, and the world is still striving to transition the Internet from IPv4 to IPv6. According to the 20-year plan, this should be the update time for an even new version of IP. Therefore, updating the "backward incompatible" IP layer protocol on a system of the scale of the Internet is an extremely difficult task. Therefore, interconnection through stateless translation technology should be one of the design principles of future network layer protocols.

6. *New Functions*

The first "General Principle" in RFC1726 [11] says: "We believe that simply allowing for bigger addresses and more efficient routing is not enough of a benefit to encourage vendors, service providers, and users to switch to IPng, with its attendant disruptions of service, etc. These problems can be solved much more simply with faster routers, balkanization of the Internet address space, and other hacks. We believe that there must be positive functional or operational benefits to switching to IPng. In other words, IPng must be able to live for a long time and it must allow the Internet to prosper and to grow to serve new applications and user needs."

Discussion

Over the past 20 years, apart from solving the problem of address space, IPng (IPv6) has not provided more features than IPv4. People have always been looking for killer applications for IPv6, it started with large-scale videos, followed by peer-to-peer network applications, etc., but these new applications can all run on IPv4. The biggest difficulty in the transition to IPv6 is its incompatibility with IPv4. If IPv6 can interconnect with IPv4 while still providing a larger address space, there is no need for any new killer applications. In other words, the new features of IPng should be able to interconnect with IPv4 with much larger addressing space, which should be the real killer application of IPv6 at this stage. Unfortunately, people realized this too late.

7. *Transition Plan*

RFC1726 [11] mentions: "the protocol must have a straightforward transition plan from the current IPv4," "a smooth, orderly, transition from IPv4 to IPng is needed," "it is not possible to have a 'flag day' form of transition in which all hosts and routers must change over at once," "rather, IPng will need to coexist with IPv4 for some period of time."

Discussion

By comparing the first Internet transition (from NCP to TCP/IP) summarized in Chap. 1 of this book with the author's research on IPv4/IPv6 transition technology over more than 10 years, we highlight the differences between these two transitions. The transition from IPv4 to IPv6 is characterized by entirely different features compared to the earlier transition from NCP to TCP/IP.

(1) Although TCP/IP is incompatible with NCP, TCP/IP has interconnection capabilities that NCP does not have, and NCP does not have a workaround for this. On the other hand, IPv6 is incompatible with IPv4, but apart from the extremely large address space of IPv6 (far beyond the current demand), it does not have any features that IPv4 does not have, and IPv4 has several workarounds such as NAT to solve the address problem.
(2) The transition from NCP to TCP/IP was implemented in a single management domain (ARPANET), which could be enforced, the network scale involved was not large, and the applications that needed to be supported (Telnet, FTP, SMTP, etc.) were not many. On the other hand, the transition from IPv4 to IPv6 needs to be implemented in many different management domains, cannot be enforced, and needs to support a massive number of applications.
(3) The transition from NCP to TCP/IP clearly set a transition period of 1 year. During the transition period, translation services were provided for all applications (i.e., NCP-only hosts and TCP-only hosts could communicate through "relays"), while existing NCP-only hosts had to be upgraded to "dual-stack" hosts that support both NCP and TCP/IP, and new hosts had to be TCP/IP-only. On the other hand, traditional IPv6 transition technology did not put translation technology as a mandatory requirement.

(4) A clear "flag day" was set, and support for NCP was stopped after the "flag day." On the other hand, the transition from IPv4 to IPv6 does not have a "flag day." Traditional IPv6 transition technology bets on dual stack, but does not specify a "flag day" to complete the transition. From an economic perspective, who would be willing to bear the higher cost of deploying dual stack first, without caring about the increased cost of deploying and operating dual stack?

As mentioned above, people's understanding of the transition to IPv6 20 years ago was too idealistic. The current conclusions are as follows:

(1) Only network layer translation technology can truly achieve the transition.
(2) IPv4 will exist for a long time, and may even run forever on some networks and systems.

8. *Security Mechanism*

In RFC1726 [11], the functions that IPv6 Must Support says: "IPng must provide a secure network layer."

Discussion

This implies that the IPv6 must support IPsec. More than 20 years of practice has proven that large-scale deployment of end-to-end IPsec is not feasible. Using higher-level security protocols, such as Transport Layer Security (TLS), HTTPS, and Domain Name System Security Extensions (DNSSEC), is a more feasible security mechanism. Fortunately, this makes the network layer's IPv4/IPv6 translation technology possible.

9. *Fragmentation*

In RFC1726 [11], the features that IPv6 does not need to consider say: "The technology exists for path MTU discovery. Presumably, IPng will continue to provide this technology. Therefore, we believe that IPng Fragmentation and Reassembly, as provided in IPv4, is not necessary. We note that fragmentation has been shown to be detrimental to network performance and strongly recommend that it be avoided."

Discussion

The biggest difficulty in the translation technology of IPv6 and IPv4 is fragmentation processing, which will be discussed in detail in Sect. 5.7

2.4.2 Choice of Stateless and Stateful Technologies

1. *Scalability*

The third item "Scalability" stated in RFC1958 [7] points out: "All designs must scale readily to very many nodes per site and to many millions of sites."

Discussion

This design principle implies a preference for "stateless" technology, because statelessness can fully guarantee scalability, and stateless can perform arbitrary distributed parallel processing without considering state-synchronization issues. In the stateless case, if one translator is not enough, multiple translators can be deployed in a distributed manner; if the bandwidth of one link is not enough, multiple links can easily be added.

2. *Keep It Simple*

The fifth item "Keep it Simple" stated in RFC1958 [7] points out: "When in doubt during design, choose the simplest solution." The sixth item "Modularity" points out: "Modularity is good. If you can keep things separate, do so."

Discussion

These two design principles imply a preference for "stateless" technology.

3. *End-To-End Address Transparency*

RFC1958 [7] points out: "Addresses must be unambiguous (unique within any scope where they may appear)," "Upper layer protocols must be able to identify end points unambiguously. In practice today, this means that addresses must be the same at start and finish of transmission."

Discussion

Stateful technology invalidates the uniqueness of addresses, while stateless technology can ensure end-to-end address transparency.

2.4.3 Other Issues

1. Application Layer Gateway Issues

RFC1958 [7] points out: "Avoid any design that requires addresses to be hard coded or stored on non-volatile storage (except of course where this is an essential requirement as in a name server or configuration server). In general, user applications should use names rather than addresses."

Discussion

Unfortunately, some applications embed addresses instead of domain names into the code, thus cannot use DNS64 or DNS46 for converting IPv4 and IPv6 addresses. This requires the use of double translation technology or Application Layer Gateway (ALG) to ensure interconnection between IPv4 and IPv6. The only exception is in the case of closed systems (such as Apple's iOS or MacOS), where prefix discovery/configuration technology and dedicated application programming interfaces (APIs) can solve these problems.

2. *Host Address Configuration Issues*

In RFC1726 [11], the features that IPv6 must support says: "The protocol must permit easy and largely distributed configuration and operation. Automatic configuration of hosts and routers is required."

Discussion

This requirement leads to Stateless Address Autoconfiguration (SLAAC). The widespread application of Stateless Address Autoconfiguration (SLAAC) technology has brought about the problem of SLAAC not being directly compatible with stateless translation technology.

2.5 Summary

This chapter presents the design principles of the Internet, which have been instrumental in its remarkable success. These principles guide widely used Internet protocol standards, including IPv4 and IPv6. Notably, IPv4's design principles were distilled after its successful deployment, making them particularly insightful. In contrast, IPv6's design principles were initially formulated as a "thought experiment" on a "blank sheet of paper," which proved not entirely accurate in retrospect. The consideration of IPv6 transition largely relied on lessons from the shift from NCP to TCP/IP but overlooked the crucial "flag day" constraint of the first transition.

In summary, the new generation of IPv6 transition technology involves a continuous process of deeply understanding and refining the design principles of the Internet based on real-world needs.

References

1. Keith J. The design of HTML5. [2022–02–23]. https://adactio.com/articles/1704.
2. Berners-Lee T. Principles of design. [2022–02–23]. https://www.w3.org/ DesignIssues/Principles.html.
3. Raymond E. The Art of UNIX Programming. Translated by Jiang Hong, He Yuan, Cai Xiaojun. Beijing: Electronics Industry Press, 2011.
4. Kesteren A V, Stachowiak M. HTML design principles. [2022–02–03]. https://www.w3.org/TR/ html-design-principles/.
5. Li Xing, Bao Congxiao. The Evolution of Internet Technology: The Simplicity of the Great Way - Commemorating the 50th Anniversary of the Birth of ARPANET. China Education Network, 2020, (1): 5, (In Chinese)
6. Postel J. RFC791: Internet protocol. IETF 1981–09.
7. Carpenter B. RFC1958: Architectural principles of the internet. IETF 1996–06.
8. Carpenter B. RFC2775: Internet transparency. IETF 2000–02.
9. Pouzin L. A proposal for interconnecting packet switching networks. Proceedings of EUROCOMP, London, 1974, 5:1023-1036.

10. Cerf V. The catenet model for internetworking. Information Processing Techniques Office, Defense Advanced Research Projects Agency, IEN 48, Washington D.C., 1978: 7.
11. Partridge C F, Kastenholz F. RFC1726: Technical criteria for choosing IP the next generation (IPng). IETF 1994–12.
12. Chapin L. RFC1310: The internet standards process. IETF 1992–03.

Chapter 3
Evolution of IPv6 Transition

The IPv6 header is defined in RFC8200 [1], and the address structure is defined in RFC4291 [2]. The IPv4 header and address structure are defined in RFC791 [3]. Since IPv6 is not compatible with IPv4, there is a transition problem from IPv4 to IPv6.

The development of IPv6 transition technology can be divided into two stages, with the "Montreal co-existence interim meeting" held by IETF in November 2008 (RFC6127 [4]) as the dividing point.

(1) Prior to this meeting, the traditional IPv6 transition was mainly based on dual-stack technology, supplemented by tunneling technology. Although translation technology between IPv4/IPv6 was also defined at that time, the early translation technology had technical defects and could not be truly deployed.
(2) After the meeting, the new generation of IPv6 transition elevated the status of translation technology and established a series of standards centered on translation. People finally realized: translation technology is an indispensable technology for the smooth transition of the Internet to IPv6-only.

3.1 Traditional IPv6 Transition Technology and Standards

According to the type of data path, IPv6 transition technology can be divided into dual stack, encapsulation (tunneling), and translation, as shown in Fig. 3.1.

3.1.1 Dual-Stack Technology

Dual-stack technology (RFC 4213 [5]) is the easiest-to-understand IPv6 transition technology, and it was the one recommended by the IETF in its early days. Dual-stack

X. Li and C. Bao, *New IPv6 Transition Technology*,
https://doi.org/10.1007/978-981-95-8427-7_3

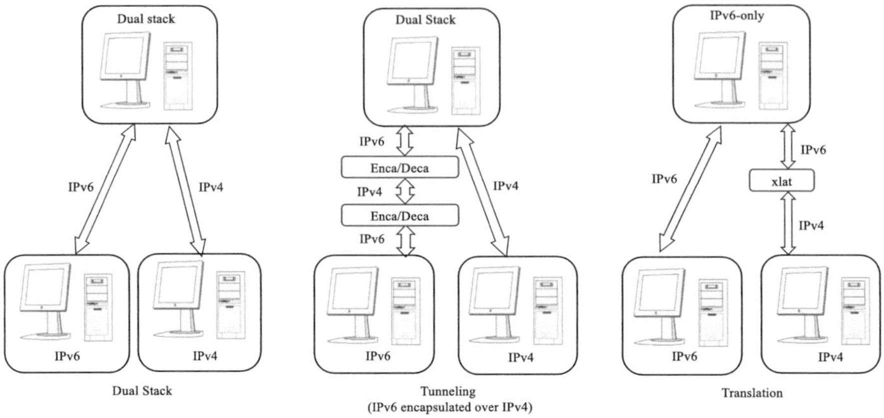

Fig. 3.1 Traditional IPv6 transition technology

technology requires all devices in the network layer (IP layer) on the communication links to support both IPv4 and IPv6, so that IPv4 users can access resources on the IPv4 Internet, while IPv6 users can access resources on the IPv6 Internet. That is, after the network and host are upgraded to dual stack, if the communication peer is IPv6, communication is carried out through IPv6; if the communication peer is IPv4, communication is carried out through IPv4.

In the case of dual stack, network nodes and end systems run both IPv4 and IPv6 protocols at the same time, forming two logically independent networks: the IPv4 network and the IPv6 network. The layered model of the dual-stack network is shown in Fig. 3.2.

Dual-stack technology has completely independent IPv4 and IPv6 protocols at the network layer, which can realize the coexistence of IPv4 and IPv6 networks, but it does not solve the interconnection problem between IPv4 and IPv6.

Fig. 3.2 Dual-stack technology

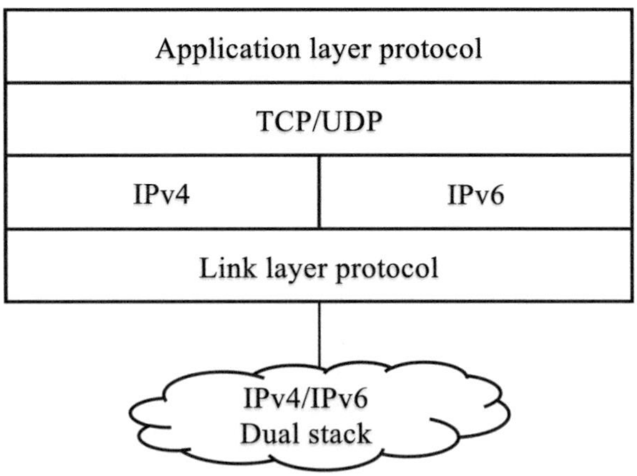

In addition, the amount of IPv4 addresses required by dual-stack technology has not decreased, and the problem of IPv4 address exhaustion has not been truly solved. Because if IPv4 is allowed to use NAT, the shortage of IPv4 addresses can be alleviated to a certain extent by sharing public IPv4 addresses. Due to the strong dependence on IPv4 information resources, operators have no motivation to turn off IPv4 and only open IPv6 services, so the majority of users are still IPv4 users, which makes content providers lack the enthusiasm to deploy IPv6 contents.

When using dual-stack technology, if the IPv6 network communication fails, the timeout mechanism for switching to IPv4 will produce a delay of tens of milliseconds or even close to several seconds, greatly reducing the user's experience of using IPv6. Happy Eyeballs (RFC6555 [6], RFC6556 [7], RFC8305 [8]) can alleviate this problem to some extent, but it can also bring new problems such as poor stability.

According to the "barrel effect" (the amount of water a barrel can hold is determined by the shortest plank), when deploying dual stacks, the overall security of the network system is determined by the weaker security of either IPv4 or IPv6. Therefore, deploying dual stack brings greater security risks than deploying single stack.

All these factors have resulted in a very slow transition process to IPv6.

3.1.2 Encapsulation (Tunneling) Technology

Encapsulation (tunneling) technology (RFC4213 [5]) can connect IPv6 islands through IPv4 in the early stages of transition (as shown in Fig. 3.1), or connect IPv4 islands through IPv6 in the later stages of transition. The basic idea is that when a protocol's datagram needs to traverse another protocol's network, the edge gateway encapsulates the datagram containing the protocol data header in the payload of another protocol's datagram. The datagram is then decapsulated at the edge gateway on the other end. When the two corresponding nodes of the outer protocol used for encapsulation and decapsulation are uniquely determined, it is called a "tunnel." Otherwise, it can be generally referred to as encapsulation.

Tunnel technology uses a message encapsulation mechanism, which can use the IPv4 network to transmit IPv6 messages or use the IPv6 network to transmit IPv4 messages. However, tunnel technology only supports IPv4 to IPv4 communication across the IPv6 network, or IPv6-to-IPv6 communication across the IPv4 network, and cannot support mutual communication between IPv4 and IPv6.

In the early stages of IPv6 deployment, the main requirement was to connect IPv6 islands through the IPv4 Internet. This is shown in Fig. 3.3.

In the middle and especially the later stages of IPv6 deployment, the goal is to build and operate an IPv6-only network, so the main requirement is to connect IPv4 islands through the IPv6 Internet (RFC4925 [9]). This is shown in Fig. 3.4.

Fig. 3.3 IPv6 over IPv4 tunnel technology

Fig. 3.4 IPv4 over IPv6 tunnel technology

Tunnel technology can be divided into the following two types according to its deployment method:

(1) Stateful tunnel (previously called "configured tunnel"), this technology manually or using specific protocol configures tunnel endpoints.
(2) Stateless tunnel (previously called "automatic tunnel"), this technique establishes a mapping relationship between IPv6 addresses and IPv4 addresses, and the tunnel endpoints can be determined using algorithmic methods.

Taking "state characteristics" as the horizontal axis and "protocol internal and external relations" as the vertical axis, we can draw a four-quadrant distribution diagram, representing the characteristics of mainstream tunnel technology in different quadrants, as shown in Fig. 3.5.

1. *Stateful IPv6 over IPv4 Tunnel*

Stateful IPv6 over IPv4 tunnel solves the need to connect IPv6 islands through the IPv4 Internet in the early stages of IPv6 deployment. Some IETF standards are introduced as follows:

1) **Configured Tunnels**

RFC1933 [10] and RFC2893 [11] are early methods for establishing IPv6 standards for IPv4 tunnels.

2) **Tunnel Broker**

An IPv6 tunnel broker sets up IPv6 over IPv4 tunnels through the tunnel setup protocol (TSP) (RFC5572 [12]).

3) **6PE Protocol**

IPv6 provider edge routers (6PE) (RFC4798 [[13]]) connect IPv6 edge networks through the IPv4 backbone network running multi-protocol label switching (MPLS). 6PE uses the multi-protocol border gateway protocol (MP-BGP) on IPv4 to pass MPLS labels.

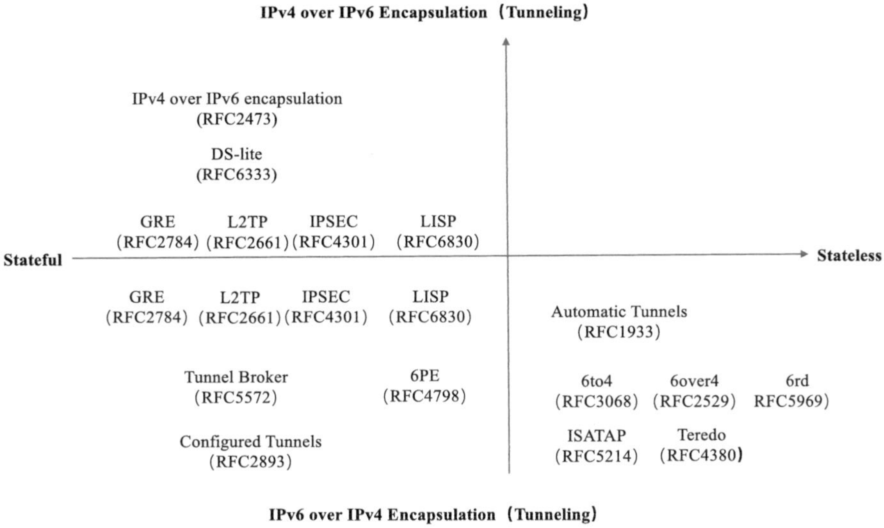

Fig. 3.5 Four quadrants of tunnel technology

4) GRE Protocol

The generic routing encapsulation (GRE) protocol (RFC2784 [14]) is defined above any network layer protocol and encapsulates any network layer protocol. GRE can be used to implement IPv6 over IPv4 tunnels.

5) L2LP

The layer 2 tunneling protocol (L2TP) (RFC2661 [15]) defines a type of encapsulation format using point-to-point protocol. L2TP can be used to implement IPv6 over IPv4 tunnels.

6) IPsec

IPsec protects IP network transmission by encrypting and authenticating IP datagrams. The encapsulating security payload (ESP) (RFC4301 [16]) provides confidentiality, data source authentication, integrity, anti-replay, and limited data flow confidentiality. The authentication header (AH) (RFC4302 [17]) provides connectionless data integrity, message authentication, and replay attack protection for IP datagrams. The Internet key exchange (IKE) (RFC5996 [18]) provides algorithm and key parameters for the security associations required for ESP and AH. AH and ESP support different protocol types, and IPsec can be used to implement IPv6 over IPv4 tunnels.

7) LISP

The locator/ID separation protocol (LISP) (RFC6830 [19]) defines a network layer-based protocol that allows IP addresses to be divided into two new numbering

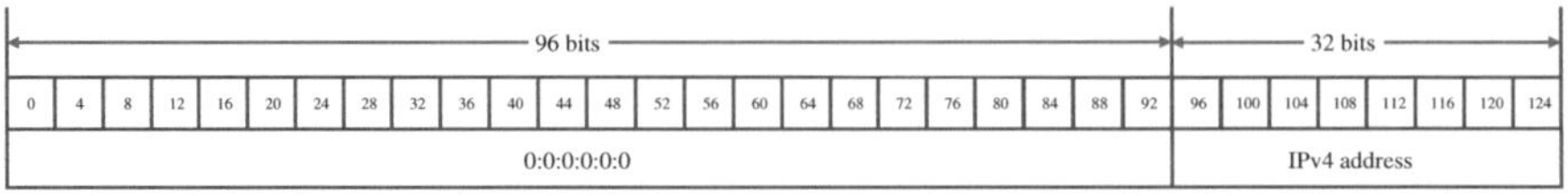

Fig. 3.6 Structure of IPv4-compatible IPv6 addresses

spaces: endpoint identifiers (EID) and routing locators (RLOC). LISP can be used to implement IPv6 over IPv4 tunnels.

2. *Stateless IPv6 over IPv4 Tunnels*

The general method of establishing a stateless IPv6 over IPv4 tunnel mechanism is to define an IPv6 prefix, embed the IPv4 address into the IPv6 prefix, and generate the tunnel endpoint through algorithm. This tunnel mechanism is based on an address mapping algorithm, not through static configuration or dynamic generation, so it is stateless. The encapsulation mode of its IPv6 datagrams can be direct encapsulation, encapsulation through GRE, or encapsulation through UDP, etc.

1) **Automatic Tunnels**

Automatic tunnels (RFC1933 [10], RFC2893 [11]) use a special type of IPv6 address, called an IPv4-compatible address. IPv4-compatible IPv6 addresses have a 96-bit prefix identifier of all zeros and embed the IPv4 address in the lowest 32 bits. The structure of the IPv4-compatible IPv6 address is shown in Fig. 3.6.

IPv4-compatible addresses are assigned to IPv4/IPv6 nodes that support automatic tunneling. Nodes configured with IPv4-compatible addresses can communicate with IPv6 using the full IPv6 address and communicate with IPv4 using the embedded IPv4 address.

2) **6to4**

The 6to4 (RFC3068 [20]) encapsulates IPv6 datagrams directly in IPv4 datagrams, and through the IPv4 address embedded in the IPv6 address, it enables IPv6 to be transmitted over IPv4 networks without the need to configure tunnels and can communicate with native IPv6 networks through relay node. The address format of 6to4 is shown in Fig. 3.7.

Due to significant flaws in the anycast prefix defined by 6to4, this standard was deprecated in 2015 (RFC7526 [21]).

3) **6over4**

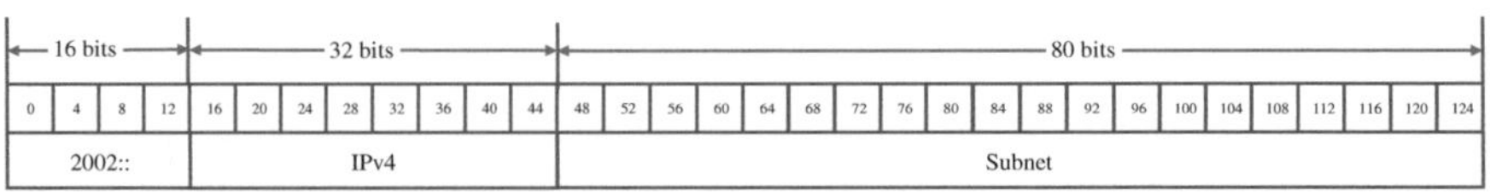

Fig. 3.7 6to4 address format

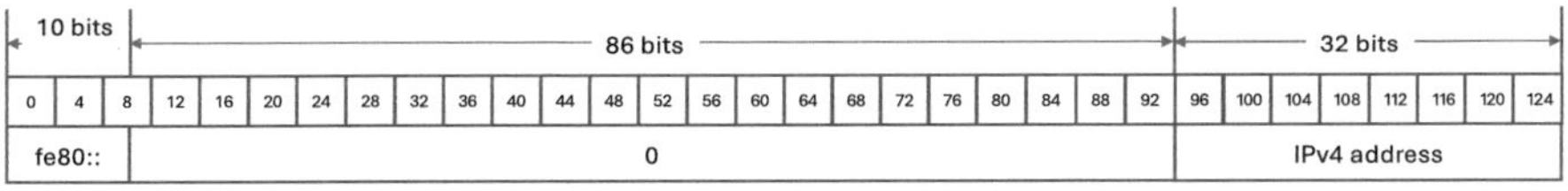

Fig. 3.8 6over4 address format

The 6over4 (RFC2529 [22]) transmits IPv6 datagrams through dual-stack nodes of IPv4 networks that support multicast. 6over4 treats the IPv4 network as a data link layer. 6over4 defines the method of using IPv4 to generate IPv6 link-local addresses, as well as the mechanism for neighbor discovery in the IPv4 network. Any host using 6over4 for IPv6 communication needs to create a corresponding virtual IPv6 interface on the corresponding IPv4 interface. Using the IPv6 local link network prefix fe80::/10, the IPv4 address is embedded on the low bit side of this network prefix, becoming the IPv6 address of this 6over4. The address format of 6over4 is shown in Fig. 3.8.

In order for the "ICMPv6 Neighbor Discovery" mechanism to be available, the IPv4 network must be able to perform multicast access.

4) **6rd**

The fast IPv6 deployment scheme using IPv4 infrastructure (IPv6 rapid deployment on IPv4 infrastructures, 6rd) (RFC5969 [23]) is a technology for Internet service providers to provide IPv6 services to end users through IPv4. It includes automatic IPv6 prefix allocation, stateless resource provisioning, and services. The IP address prefix of 6rd uses the operator's prefix (6rd prefix), as shown in Fig. 3.9.

5) **ISATAP**

The Intra-Site Automatic Tunnel Addressing Protocol (ISATAP) (RFC5214 [24]) allows IPv6 datagrams to be transmitted over an IPv4 network. Unlike 6over4, ISATAP views the IPv4 network as a non-broadcast multi-access network's data link layer, so it does not need to use IPv4 multicast. ISATAP includes a method for generating IPv6 link-local addresses based on IPv4 addresses and a neighbor discovery mechanism based on the IPv4 network. Any host wishing to use ISATAP over a specific IPv4 network can create a virtual IPv6 network interface. ISATAP adds the host's IPv4 address to a specific IPv6 prefix as the interface's IPv6 address, using fe80::0200:5efe: for global unicast addresses and fe80::0000:5efe: for private network addresses. The format is shown in Fig. 3.10.

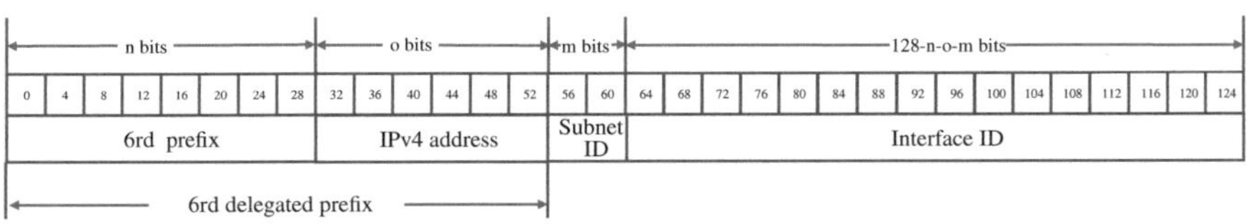

Fig. 3.9 6rd address format

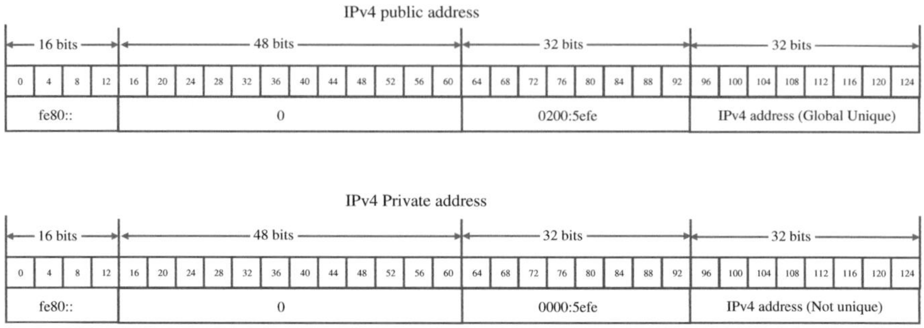

Fig. 3.10 ISATAP address format

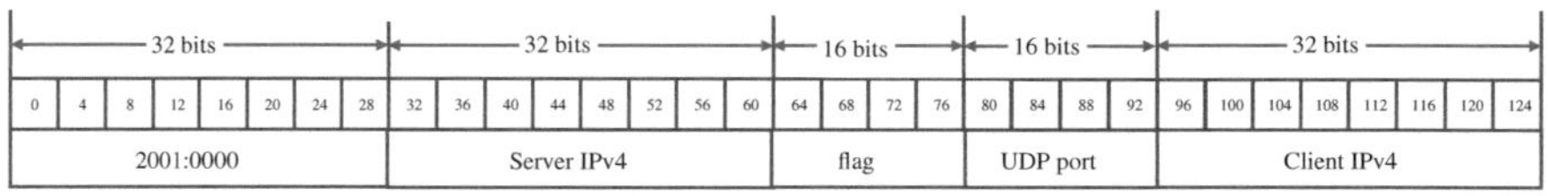

Fig. 3.11 Teredo address format

6) **Teredo**

The Teredo (RFC4380 [25]) provides full IPv6 connectivity for hosts running on the IPv4 Internet. Teredo encapsulates IPv6 datagrams in UDP datagrams, so it can go through NAT. Each Teredo client is assigned a public IPv6 address, the construction of which is shown in Fig. 3.11.

3. *Stateful IPv4 over IPv6 Tunnel*
1) **IPv4 over IPv6 Encapsulation**

The RFC2473 [26] is a general encapsulation definition for IPv6, discussed in detail in Chap. 5 of this book.

2) **DS-Lite Protocol**

Dual-Stack Lite (DS-Lite) (RFC6333 [27]) is an IPv4 over IPv6 tunneling technology based on RFC2473 [26] encapsulation and stateful reuse of public IPv4 addresses, discussed in detail in Chap. 11 of this book.

3) **L2TP**

Already discussed in IPv6 over IPv4, it can also be used for IPv4 over IPv6.

4) **IPsec**

Already discussed in IPv6 over IPv4, it can also be used for IPv4 over IPv6.

5) **LISP**

Already discussed in IPv6 over IPv4, it can also be used for IPv4 over IPv6.

4. *Stateless IPv4 over IPv6 Tunnel*

Traditional IPv6 transition technologies do not have stateless IPv4 over IPv6 tunneling standards.

3.1.3 Translation Technologies

Translation technologies enable communication between IPv4-only nodes and IPv6-only nodes. There are two types of translation technologies. Stateful translation requires static configuration or dynamically generates/maintains the mapping relationship between IPv4 addresses and IPv6 addresses in the translation device by mapping table, while stateless translation establishes the mapping relationship between IPv4 addresses and IPv6 addresses through a pre-set algorithm. The early IPv4/IPv6 translation technologies are RFC2765 [28] and RFC2766 [29].

1. *Stateless Translation Technology*

The early stateless IPv4/IPv6 translation technology is called Stateless IP/ICMP Translation (SIIT) algorithm, defined by RFC2765 [28]. The basic idea is to make IPv6-only host to communicate with IPv4 hosts. Two scenarios were considered at that time: subnet mode and dual-stack mode, as shown in Figs. 3.12 and 3.13, respectively.

In these two scenarios, a stateless translator, called SIIT, is deployed. Through protocol translation, the IPv4 headers and IPv6 headers of the datagrams are translated.

SIIT uses two special types of IPv6 addresses, called IPv4-mapped addresses and IPv4-translated addresses, as shown in Figs. 3.14 and 3.15, respectively.

The IPv6 hosts are configured with IPv4-translated addresses, and the addresses of all IPv4 hosts communicating with the IPv4-translated address are converted into

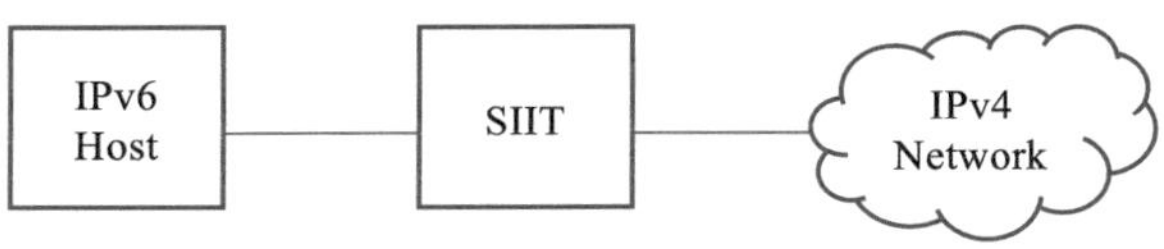

Fig. 3.12 Stateless translation (subnet mode)

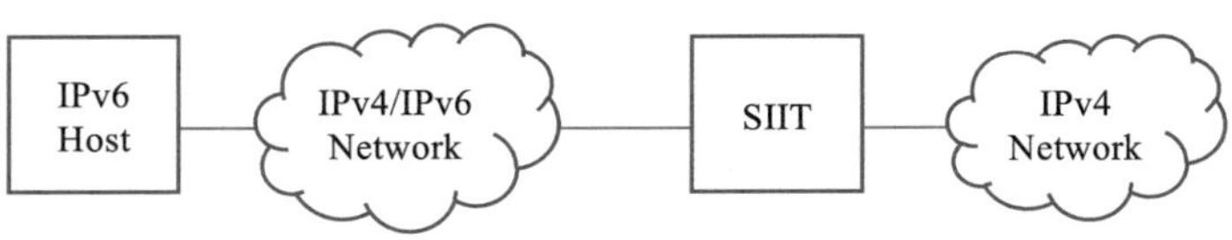

Fig. 3.13 Stateless translation (dual-stack mode)

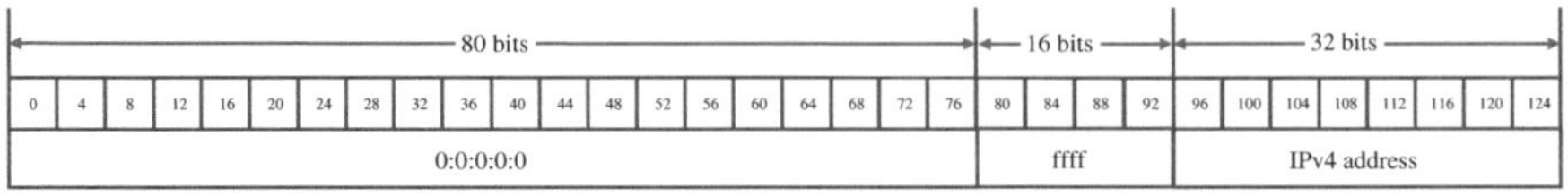

Fig. 3.14 Format of IPv4-mapped IPv6 address

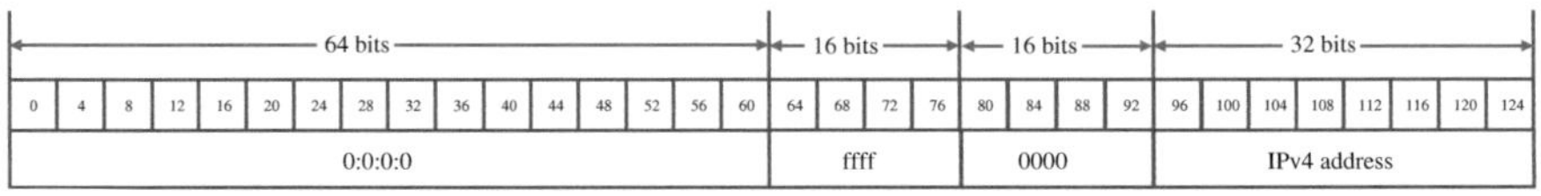

Fig. 3.15 Format of IPv4-translated IPv6 address

IPv4-mapped addresses by translator. The IPv4 address corresponding to the IPv4-translated address is routed to the IPv4 network interface of SIIT in the IPv4 network, and the IPv4-mapped address is routed to the IPv6 network interface of SIIT in the IPv6 network. SIIT translates the IPv4 headers and IPv6 headers of the datagrams.

Note that in this case, IPv4-compatible addresses cannot be used, because IPv4-compatible addresses are designed for automatic tunneling, and network devices perform “tunnel encapsulation” for this type of address format. The comparison of IPv4-compatible addresses, IPv4-mapped addresses, and IPv4-translated addresses is shown in Fig. 3.16.

In summary, this version of stateless translation technology has serious technical flaws in its address definition and can only work within the subnet. The prefixes of IPv4-translated IPv6 address and IPv4-mapped IPv6 address are inconsistent and cannot be routed and forwarded on the Internet, so it is not been deployed practically.

2. *Stateful Translation Technology*

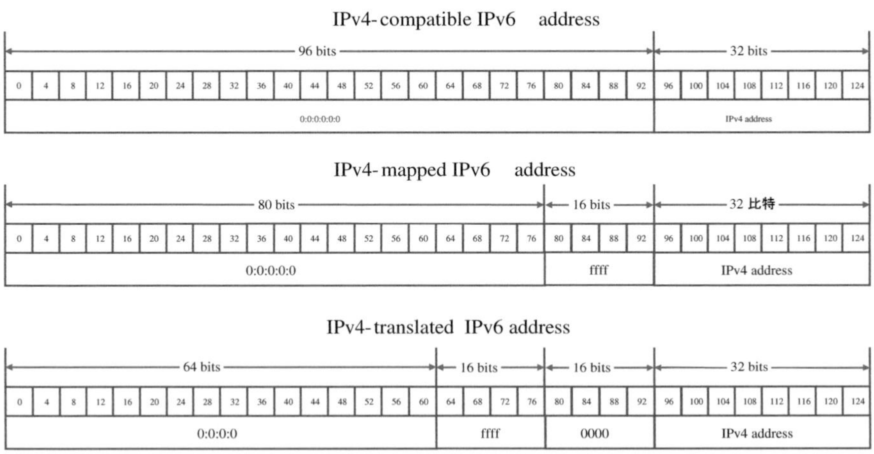

Fig. 3.16 Comparison of IPv4-embedded IPv6 addresses

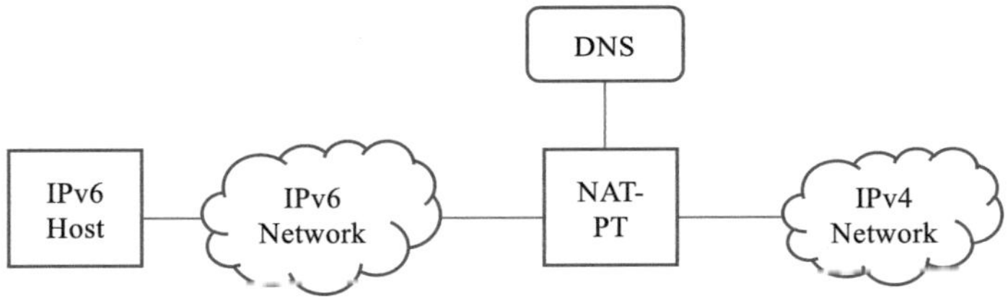

Fig. 3.17 NAT-PT

The early stateful IPv4/IPv6 translation technology is known as Network Address Translation-Protocol Translation (NAT-PT), defined by RFC2766 [29]. NAT-PT dynamically binds IPv4 addresses to IPv6-only hosts on the network. Through translation technology, the IPv4 headers and IPv6 headers in the datagram are translated. To reuse IPv4 addresses, this dynamic binding can also be extended to 5-Tuple (source address, source port, destination address, destination port, and protocol)-based binding, that is, different IPv6-only hosts can share the same IPv4 address by using different ports of the transport layer protocol (TCP or UDP). To cope with the huge gap between IPv4 and IPv6 address spaces, in many cases, a domain name system coupled with the IPv4/IPv6 translator is needed. NAT-PT is shown in Fig. 3.17.

Due to issues such as domain name system coupling, RFC4966 [30] abolished NAT-PT.

3.2 Dilemma and Reflection on Traditional IPv6 Transition Technology

3.2.1 Dilemma of Traditional IPv6 Transition Technology

IPv6 is not compatible with IPv4, so IPv6-only hosts cannot communicate with IPv4-only hosts. At the time of IPv6 design, people did not pay enough attention to the incompatibility between IPv4 and IPv6, and thought that the transition to IPv6 was not difficult. The earliest IPv6 transition technology recommended by IETF was "dual-stack technology" and "tunneling technology," which can be called traditional IPv6 transition technology. Many operators around the world have experimented with IPv6 on different scales through "dual-stack technology" and "tunneling technology." However, despite more than 20 years of effort, the IPv6 transition is still very limited. Although in recent years, the promotion of governments around the world, the "World IPv6 Day" initiated by the Internet Society (ISOC), and the promotion of the industry (such as Google's establishment of an IPv6 website, Apple's AppStore requires applications to support IPv6, etc.) have led to a certain degree of growth in the global deployment of IPv6, overall, the support rate of Internet information resources and operators for IPv6 is still low.

To address the shortage of public IPv4 addresses, many operators have adopted carrier-grade NAT (CGN) technology to provide Internet access services to users in the form of dynamically sharing public IPv4 addresses. IPv4 NAT is a stateful translation technology between public IPv4 addresses and private IPv4 addresses, which is very mature, but it destroys the end-to-end feature, has scalability, security, and user traceability issues, and can only support one-way (client-to-server) initiated communication.

From a practical point of view, due to the exhaustion of IPv4 addresses, it is no longer possible to statically allocate public IPv4 addresses to Internet users. If IPv6 continues to be promoted in the dual-stack mode, it will definitely use IPv6 plus IPv4 NAT technology. Although it can provide IPv6 service, it retains all the disadvantages of IPv4 NAT and cannot really encourage the transition to IPv6 Internet. The difficulty of IPv6 transition lies in the lack of motivation for all parties on the Internet to upgrade. The fundamental reason for this lack of motivation is the incompatibility between IPv6 and IPv4, which prevents IPv6-only hosts and IPv4-only hosts from communicating with each other.

In fact, the entire Internet cannot switch from IPv4 to IPv6 in a short period of time, and there is no "flag day." During the long transition process, a large number of IPv4 applications will still exist. Dual-stack technology cannot enable IPv6 users to access IPv4-only resources, nor can it enable IPv4 users to access IPv6-only resources, which brings great difficulties to the transition to IPv6.

3.2.2 IETF's Considerations on the New Generation of IPv6 Transition Technology

In response to the dilemma of traditional IPv6 transition technology, the IETF held an Interim meeting on IPv6 transition and coexistence in Montreal, Canada in November 2008. The meeting organized reports on several IPv6 transition scenarios and solutions, discussed them in depth, and formed RFC6127 [4] after the meeting. The following is a brief description of the key points of RFC6127.

When IPv6 was initially designed, it was suggested to use dual-stack technology for transition. That is, while continuing to run IPv4, IPv6 is enabled on some network nodes and hosts. Dual-stack technology is still the method promoted by IETF for the popularity of IPv6.

Experience shows that large-scale deployment of IPv6 requires time, energy, and substantial investment. With the exhaustion of the public IPv4 address pool, network operators and Internet service providers are forced to consider no longer supporting end-to-end services using public IPv4 addresses on a large scale. Dual-stack cannot solve the problem of the exhaustion of the public IPv4 address pool, because IPv4 communication is still carried out by IPv4 in the dual stack. In short, the time to finally transition to the IPv6 Internet predicted by the current deployment rate of dual stack is completely inconsistent with the original expectation.

Therefore, the reality requires reconsideration of other IPv6 transition technologies. In particular, it is necessary to consider the adverse effects of the actual situation of large-scale, multi-layer cascading IPv4 NAT on dual-stack deployment. Now IETF needs to re-understand the address and protocol conversion methods that IETF has not paid attention to in the past, and the methods to support IPv4 through IPv6-only, to ensure that IPv6 can coexist with IPv4 and finally complete the IPv6 transition.

The new generation of IPv6 transition technology mainly considers the following five application scenarios:

(1) Users can share scarce public IPv4 addresses to access the IPv4 Internet.
(2) It is necessary to solve the shortage of private IPv4 addresses (RFC1918 [31]) in large networks.
(3) Build and operate an IPv6-only network to reduce complexity and operating costs, but need to be able to continue to access the IPv4 Internet.
(4) Access one or more IPv4-only servers through IPv6.
(5) IPv4-only clients access IPv6-only servers.

The IETF community should solve above scenarios in a short time. Through comprehensive consideration, it is clear that these scenarios require different solutions. Some solutions can rely on existing technologies, while others may require new protocols, or even appropriate changes to the network architecture. There are definitely contradictions in this, which require the entire IETF community to weigh and consider.

Specifically, the IETF will reorganize the Behave working group in the transport field and the Softwire working group in the Internet field to undertake the standardization work of the new IPv6 transition technology. Among them, Behave does the translation work, and Softwire does the tunnel work. At the same time, some auxiliary tools are needed, for example, defining options for the dynamic host configuration protocol version 6 (DHCPv6) to support new protocols.

In view of the urgent situation of the exhaustion of public IPv4 addresses, do not delay the research and development of new technologies with non-mainstream issues. On balance, IETF does not expect any solution to be perfect. When looking for opportunities to deploy IPv6, pursuing perfection too much will lose these opportunities. We need to support the development of various tools to help minimize the current and expected practical problems encountered during the transition to IPv6, in the hope of guiding the Internet onto the best path from here.

Expanding Internet address space and achieving interconnectivity between IPv4 and IPv6 are the key issues that need to be resolved in the transition to IPv6. There should be a type of network device that allows for interconnectivity between incompatible IPv6 and IPv4. With such a device, the following two points can be achieved:

(1) Clients on an IPv6-only network can access servers on the IPv4 Internet.
(2) Servers on an IPv6-only network can provide services for IPv4 clients.

In this case, users on the newly constructed IPv6-only network do not only retain their ability to communicate with the IPv4 Internet but also gain access to the new features offered by IPv6. Consequently, there is no need to concern oneself about when to disable IPv4 in a dual-stack network.

After the IPv6 conference in Montreal, the new generation of IPv6 transition technologies and standards were launched in the IETF's Behave and Softwire working groups, achieving more results than expected in RFC6127 [4].

3.3 New-Generation IPv6 Transition Technology and Standards

3.3.1 Development History

After the Montreal conference, the IETF, based on more than 10 years of IPv6 deployment practice, re-integrated and developed new generation of IPv6 transition technologies. The focus is on standardizing translation technologies (where the translator is referred to as XLAT) that can interconnect IPv6-only and IPv4-only networks, as well as "IPv4 as a Service (IPv4aaS)" technologies that enable IPv4 services to be delivered through an IPv6 network.

Since IPv6 was not designed to be compatible with IPv4, the address spaces of IPv4 and IPv6 are vastly different (IPv4 is 2^{32}, IPv6 is 2^{128}), and the protocol semantics as well as the syntax are incompatible, the following issues must be resolved.

(1) How to establish a mapping relationship between IPv6 addresses and IPv4 addresses, and how to reuse the same IPv4 address for multiple IPv6 addresses.
(2) How to solve the compatibility problem between the IPv6 protocol and the IPv4 protocol.
(3) How to enable each network to independently, manageably, controllably, and traceably incrementally deploy IPv6 without causing a global routing table explosion.
(4) How to support both existing IPv4-only applications and new IPv6 applications, making users unaware of the change in the IP version.
(5) How to provide transition solutions suitable for different scenarios based on the specific conditions of the user's terminal and the network.

Solving above problems involves several areas such as Internet architecture, address planning, routing systems, domain name systems, applications, and network security, and it is a complex system engineering task.

People's understanding of this complex system engineering task is also gradually deepening. Figure 3.18 shows the milestones in the evolution of IPv6 transition technology (including traditional and new-generation IPv6 transition technologies).

(1) Before 1996, the IPv6 standards were gradually established and improved, and several IPv6 test networks (IPv6 islands) had been established worldwide.

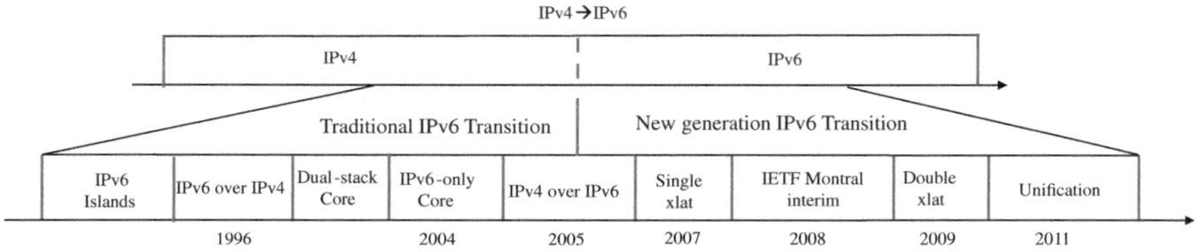

Fig. 3.18 Key nodes in the evolution of IPv6 transition technology

(2) Starting in 1996, IPv6 over IPv4 tunnels were established, represented by the IETF. The IPv6 backbone network (6bone) was released in 1996. 6bone was designed as a global hierarchical IPv6 network, including 6bone top-level transit providers, 6bone sub-top-level transit providers, and 6bone sites as well as other organizations. IPv6 over IPv4 tunnels use the inter-domain routing protocol plus (border gateway protocol plus, BGP+) for interconnection. The author's organization—China Education and Research Network (CERNET)—joined 6bone in 1998. As of June 2009, 260 organizations in 39 countries were connected to 6bone.

(3) After 1996, with the development of 6bone and mainstream router support for IPv6, more and more operators began to upgrade their backbone networks to dual stack.

(4) In 2004, the world's first IPv6-only backbone network appeared. With the support of the China Next Generation Network (CNGI) project, 2nd Generation China Education and Research Network (CERNET2) was built into a multi-autonomous domain IPv6-only backbone network.

(5) In 2005, the IETF established the Softwire Working Group and began the standardization work of IPv4 over IPv6 tunnels.

(6) In 2007, the authors of this book realized that neither IPv6 over IPv4 tunnels nor IPv4 over IPv6 tunnels could solve the interconnection problem between IPv4-only and IPv6-only hosts. Therefore, the authors began to develop a new generation of IPv4/IPv6 translation transition technology.

(7) In 2008, the IETF held an Interim Meeting in Montreal to re-examine the problems of the dual-stack and tunnel technologies, and officially launched the research of the new generation of IPv6 transition technology. It was decided that the Behave Working Group of the IETF Transport Area and the Softwire Working Group of the IETF Internet Area would jointly complete the related tasks. Subsequently, the Behave and the Softwire, in addition to the regular IETF meetings, held several interim meetings to vigorously promote the standardization process of related technologies.

(8) On September 17, 2009, the Behave group held an online meeting to develop the framework, scenarios, and technical modules for translation technology. This effort culminated in the standardization of RFCs related to the new generation of stateless translation (IVI) and stateful translation (NAT64) in 2011 [32].

(9) On September 26, 2011, Softwire held an Interim Meeting at Tsinghua University in Beijing, China. During the meeting, the team clarified and harmonized the concepts of double translation and encapsulation technologies. The standardization of RFCs related to double translation (Mapping of Address and Port using Translation, MAP-T) and tunnel technology (Mapping of Address and Port with Encapsulation, MAP-E) was completed by 2015, resulting in the unification of stateless address and port mapping technology (MAP-T/MAP-E) [33].

The new generation of IPv6 transition technology has addressed key challenges such as IPv4-only and IPv6-only interconnection, IPv4 address sharing, application program-embedded IP addresses, and the unification of stateless double translation and tunnel technologies. It has also developed a series of solutions, including stateless/stateful translation, stateless/stateful double translation, and stateless/partial state/stateful tunnel (encapsulation) technologies.

3.3.2 Classification of IPv6 Transition Technology

With the development of the global Internet, the improvement of application scenarios, and the evolution of technology, the new generation of IPv6 transition technology can be classified into single translation, double translation, and encapsulation technologies, as shown in Fig. 3.19.

1. *Translation Technology (External Characteristics Are Dual Stack)*

Since IPv4 and IPv6 are inherently incompatible, translation technology operates by establishing mirrored virtual counterparts within each network. Specifically, a real

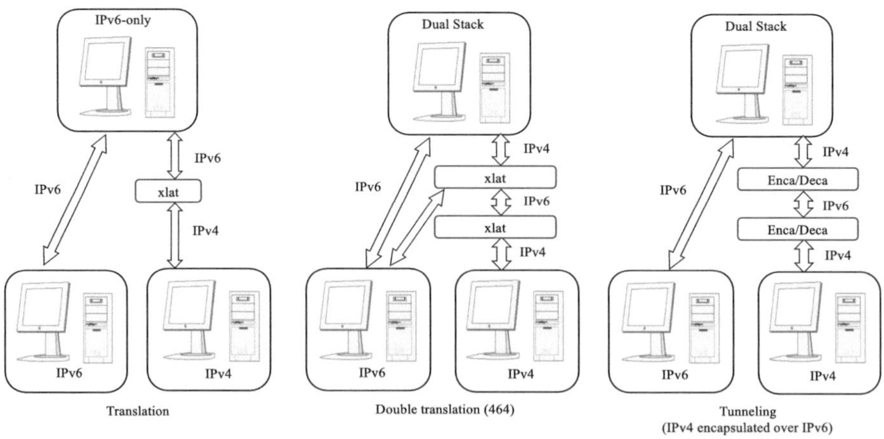

Fig. 3.19 New-generation IPv6 transition technology

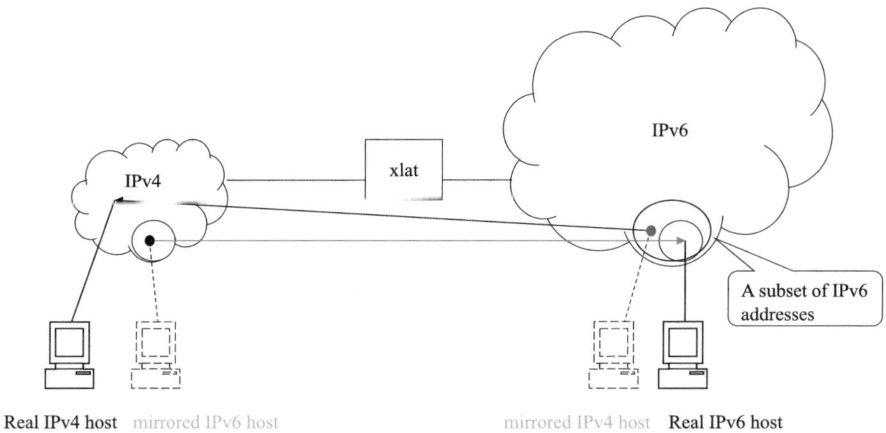

Fig. 3.20 Stateless IPv4/IPv6 translation using mirrored hosts

IPv6 host is mapped to a mirrored virtual IPv4 host within the IPv4 network, while a real IPv4 host is mapped to a mirrored virtual IPv6 host in the IPv6 network. This dual-mirroring mechanism facilitates indirect communication between real IPv4 and IPv6 hosts through their respective mirrored virtual counterparts: the real IPv6 host interacts with the mirrored virtual IPv6 host, and the real IPv4 host communicates with the mirrored virtual IPv4 host, as shown in Fig. 3.20.

Translation technology can be divided into stateless translation and stateful translation technologies (RFC6144 [34]).

Stateless translation maps IPv4/IPv6 addresses (and optionally transport layer ports) via algorithms without maintaining state tables. Similarly, Internet routers operate independently, forwarding each datagram statelessly, enabling high scalability and resilience—key factors in the Internet's success. Stateless translators mimic this behavior, forming a cornerstone of next-generation IPv6 transition technologies.

Stateful translation refers to the mapping relationship between IPv4/IPv6 addresses and transport layer ports dynamically generated according to the 5-tuple of the session, and the device needs to maintain a dynamically generated mapping state table.

There are two perspectives on considering translation technology in relation to its dual-stack external characteristics.

1) **The Internal Network is IPv6-Only, and the External Characteristics Are Dual Stack**

When deploying an IPv4/IPv6 translator at the boundary between the IPv4 Internet and an IPv6 network, the internal network operates as an IPv6-only environment. However, the translator acts as an intermediary, enabling the external interface of the network to support both IPv4 and IPv6 protocols simultaneously. This creates an "external dual-stack" appearance, where the network appears to external systems as a dual-stack network (supporting both IPv4 and IPv6) while internally maintaining

IPv6-only infrastructure. This dual-stack behavior is achieved through protocol translation, address conversion, and seamless communication bridging, as illustrated in Fig. 3.21.

2) **The Network Interface is IPv6-Only, and the API is Dual Stack**

When the computer's operating system supports IPv4/IPv6 translation, the network interface is IPv6-only, and the API of the application system is dual stack, as shown in Fig. 3.22.

2. *Double Translation and Encapsulation Technologies*

When using double translation or encapsulation (tunnel) technologies, the IPv4 datagrams can go through the IPv6-only network, that is, IPv4 as a Service (IPv4aaS or 4aaS).

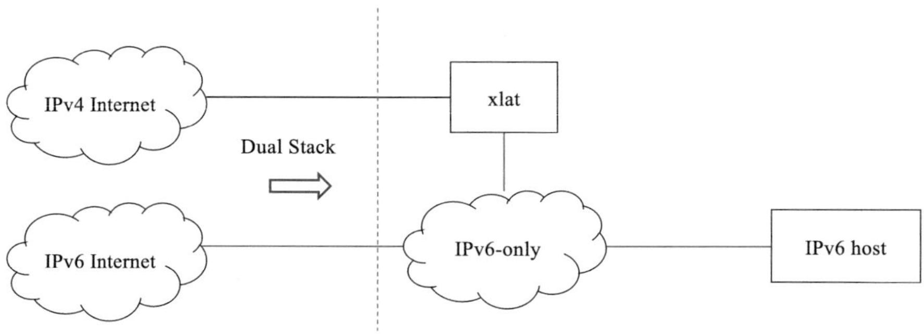

Fig. 3.21 Network behavior of translation technology

Fig. 3.22 Application behavior of translation technology

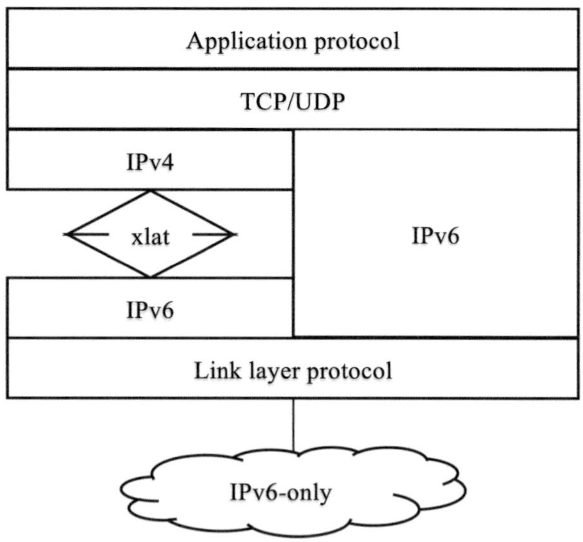

The differences between double translation and encapsulation (tunnel) are as follows:

(1) The maximum allowable datagram payload size is different, and the header overhead of the datagram using double translation is less than encapsulation (tunnel).
(2) On the IPv6 network, the header of the IPv6 datagram using double translation directly contains the address information of the IPv4 end system (in the form of IPv6), while the header of the IPv6 datagram using encapsulation (tunnel) technology is the address of the IPv6 tunnel endpoint.
(3) Encapsulation (tunnel) has better "fidelity," for example, it can retain the option fields in the IPv4 header.
(4) Double translation can degrade into single translation, achieving interconnection between IPv4-only and IPv6-only hosts, and then smoothly transitioning to IPv6-only. However, encapsulation (tunnel) cannot transition to IPv6-only.

3.3.3 IPv6 Transition Technology Standards

Taking "state characteristics" as the horizontal axis and "protocol processing" as the vertical axis, we can draw an extended four-quadrant distribution diagram to represent the new-generation IPv6 transition technology in different quadrants. Note that the translation technologies are further subdivided into single translation and double translation, as shown in Fig. 3.23.

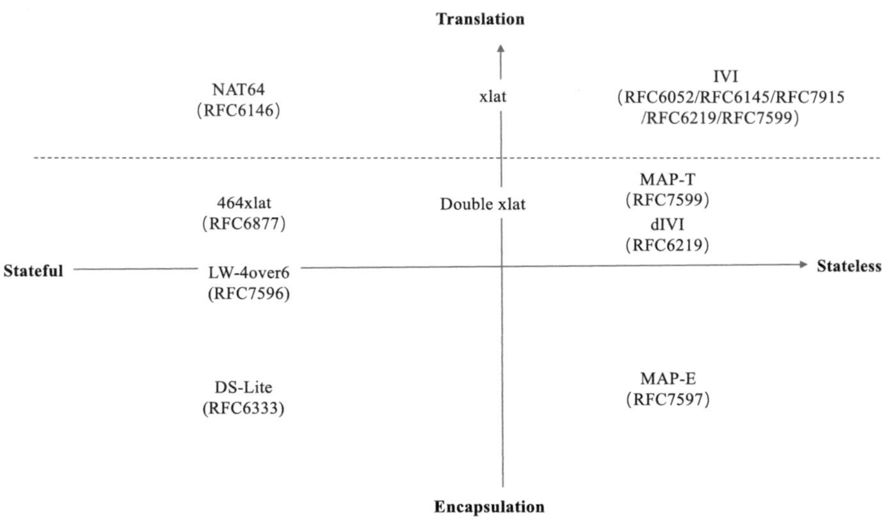

Fig. 3.23 New-generation unified IPv6 transition technology

1. *Stateless Single Translation*

Stateless single translation is the basis of all IPv6 translation technologies, including: ① IVI (Roman numerals use the "subtract left and add right" construction rule, so IV represents 4, VI represents 6, IVI means that IPv4 and IPv6 can talk to each other). In the context of the Internet, IVI represents stateless translation (RFC6052 [35], RFC6145 [36], RFC7915 [37], RFC6219 [38]); ② 1:N IVI (RFC6219 [38], RFC7599 [39]) represents stateless translation with public IPv4 address sharing.

2. *Stateful Single Translation*

Stateful single translation (Network Address Translation 64, NAT64, RFC6146 [40]) adds a session-based dynamic IPv4 transport layer port and IPv6 address mapping module. This technology also has the module of stateless translation technology (RFC6052 [35], RFC6145 [36], RFC7915 [37]).

3. *Stateless Double Translation*

Stateless double translation is an extension of stateless translation technology, and it may add a stateless address and port mapping module. Including: ① double-IVI (double-IVI, dIVI, RFC6219 [38]) and ② mapping of address and port using translation (MAP-T, RFC7599 [39]). This technology also has the module of stateless translation (RFC6052 [35], RFC6145 [36], RFC7915 [37]).

4. *Stateful Double Translation*

Stateful double translation (464 translation, 464XLAT, RFC6877 [41]) is based on stateful translation technology with a cascading stateless translation technology. This technology is jointly supported by stateless translation technology (RFC6052 [35], RFC6145 [36], RFC7915 [37]) and stateful reuse of public IPv4 address translation technology (RFC6146 [40]).

5. *Stateless Tunnel*

Stateless tunnel is based on the same address and port mapping algorithm of the stateless double translation, while in the data plane using IPv4 over IPv6 encapsulation mechanism. The standard is Mapping of Address and Port with Encapsulation (MAP-E, RFC7597 [42]), which is based on encapsulation (RFC2473 [26]).

6. *Stateful Tunnel*

Stateful tunnel is a combination of IPv4 stateful NAT and IPv4 over IPv6 tunnel. It includes ① Dual-Stack Light (DS-Lite, RFC6333 [27]); ② Lightweight 4 over 6 (LW-4o6, RFC7596 [43]), both of them are based on encapsulation (RFC2473 [26]).

3.4 Summary

This chapter introduces traditional IPv6 transition and new-generation IPv6 transition technologies, the watershed of which is the special meeting on IPv6 transition and coexistence held by IETF in Montreal, Canada in November 2008 [4]. The traditional IPv6 transition technology is mainly based on dual stack. However, after more than 20 years of practice, it did not complete the transition to IPv6 before the global IPv4 address pool was exhausted. The new-generation IPv6 transition technology, as the key technology written in this book, is based on translation, which enables IPv6-only and IPv4-only hosts communicating. It is also supplemented by double translation and encapsulation (tunnel) technology. These technologies are the focus of detailed discussion in the subsequent chapters of this book.

References

1. Deering S, Hinden R. RFC8200: Internet protocol version 6 (IPv6) specification. IETF 2017–07.
2. Hinden R, Deering S. RFC4291: IP version 6 addressing architecture. IETF 2006–02.
3. Postel J. RFC791: Internet protocol. IETF 1981–09.
4. Arkko J, Townsley M. RFC6127: IPv4 run-out and IPv4-IPv6 co-existence scenarios. IETF 2011–05.
5. Nordmark E, Gilligan R. RFC4213: Basic transition mechanisms for IPv6 hosts and routers. IETF 2005–10.
6. Wing D, Yourtchenko A. RFC6555: Happy eyeballs: Success with dual-stack hosts. IETF 2012–04.
7. Baker F. RFC6556: Testing eyeball happiness. IETF 2021–04.
8. Schinazi D, Pauly T. RFC8305: Happy eyeballs version 2: Better connectivity using concurrency. IETF 2017–12.
9. Li X, Dawkins S, Ward D, et al. RFC4925: Softwire problem statement. IETF 2007–07.
10. Gilligan R, Nordmark E. RFC1933: Transition mechanisms for IPv6 hosts and routers. IETF 1996–04.
11. Gilligan R, Nordmark E. RFC2893: Transition mechanisms for IPv6 hosts and routers. IETF 2000–08.
12. Blanchet M, Parent F. RFC5572: IPv6 tunnel broker with the tunnel setup protocol (TSP). IETF 2010–02.
13. De Clercq J, Ooms D, Prevost S, et al. RFC4798: Connecting IPv6 islands over IPv4 MPLS using IPv6 provider edge routers (6PE). IETF 2007–02.
14. Farinacci D, Li T, Hanks S, et al. RFC2784: Generic routing encapsulation (GRE). IETF 2000–03.
15. Townsley W, Valencia A, Rubens A, et al. RFC2661: Layer two tunneling protocol "L2TP". IETF 1999–08.
16. Kent S, Seo K. FC4301: Security architecture for the internet protocol. IETF 2005–11.
17. Kent S. RFC4302: IP authentication header. IETF 2005–12.
18. Kaufman C, Hoffman P, Nir Y, P. et al. RFC5996: Internet key exchange protocol version 2 (IKEv2). IETF 2010–09.
19. Farinacci D, Fuller V, Meyer D, et al. RFC6830: The locator/ID separation protocol (LISP). IETF 2013–01.
20. Huitema C. RFC3068: An anycast prefix for 6to4 relay routers. IETF 2001–06.

21. Troan O, Carpenter B. RFC7526: Deprecating the anycast prefix for 6to4 relay routers. IETF 2015–05.
22. Carpenter B, Jung C. RFC2529: Transmission of IPv6 over IPv4 domains without explicit tunnels. IETF 1999–03.
23. Townsley W, Troan O. RFC5969: IPv6 rapid deployment on IPv4 infrastructures (6rd) -- protocol specification. IETF 2010–08.
24. Templin F, Gleeson T, Thaler D. RFC5214: Intra-site automatic tunnel addressing protocol (ISATAP). IETF 2008–03.
25. Huitema C. RFC4380: Teredo: Tunneling IPv6 over UDP through network address translations (NATs). IETF 2006–02.
26. Conta A, Deering S. RFC2473: Generic packet tunneling in IPv6 specification. IETF 1998–12.
27. Durand A, Droms R, Woodyatt J, et al. RFC6333: Dual-stack lite broadband deployments following IPv4 exhaustion. IETF 2011–08.
28. Nordmark E. RFC2765: Stateless IP/ICMP translation algorithm (SIIT). IETF 2000–02.
29. Tsirtsis G, Srisuresh P. RFC2766: Network address translation - protocol translation (NAT-PT). IETF 2000–02.
30. Aoun C E, Davies E. RFC4966: Reasons to move the network address translator - protocol translator (NAT-PT) to historic status. IETF 2007–07.
31. Rekhter Y, Moskowitz B, Karrenberg D, et al. RFC1918: Address allocation for private Internets. IETF 1996–02.
32. Behave W G. IETF Behave WG 2010 Interim Meeting. [2022–11–24]. https://datatracker.ietf.org/doc/minutes-interim-2010-behave-1/.
33. Softwire W G. IETF Softwire WG 2011 Interim Meeting. [2022–11–24]. https://datatracker.ietf.org/doc/agenda-interim-2011-softwire-1/.
34. Baker F, Li X, Bao C, et al. RFC6144: Framework for IPv4/IPv6 translation. IETF 2011–04.
35. Bao C, Huitema C, Bagnulo M, et al. RFC6052: IPv6 addressing of IPv4/IPv6 translators. IETF 2010–10.
36. Li X C, Bao C F, Baker F. RFC6145: IP/ICMP translation algorithm. IETF 2011–04.
37. Bao C, Li X, Baker F, et al. RFC7915: IP/ICMP translation algorithm. IETF 2016–06.
38. Li X, Bao C, Chen M, et al. RFC6219: The China Education and Research Network (CERNET) IVI translation design and deployment for the IPv4/IPv6 coexistence and transition. IETF 2011–05.
39. Li X, Bao C, Dec W, et al. RFC7599: Mapping of address and port using translation (MAP-T). IETF 2015–07.
40. Bagnulo M, Matthews P, Beijnum I. RFC6146: Stateful NAT64: Network address and protocol translation from IPv6 clients to IPv4 servers. IETF 2011–04.
41. Mawatari M, Kawashima M, Byrne C. RFC6877: 464XLAT: Combination of stateful and stateless translation. IETF 2013–04.
42. Troan O, Dec W, Li X, et al. RFC7597: Mapping of address and port with encapsulation (MAP-E). IETF 2015–07.
43. Cui Y, Sun Q, Boucadair M, et al. RFC7596: Lightweight 4over6: An extension to the dual-stack lite architecture. IETF 2015–07.

Chapter 4
IPv6 Transition Scenarios

The incompatibility between IPv4 and IPv6 prevents IPv6-only users from directly accessing IPv4-only resources, and vice versa. This poses significant challenges for deploying IPv6-only networks. IPv4/IPv6 translation technology is essential for enabling interoperability between IPv4-only and IPv6-only networks.

However, due to the vast difference in address space sizes between IPv6 and IPv4, one-to-one mapping is not feasible. This necessitates further refinement of IPv6 transition requirements. This chapter first examines the scenarios defined by RFC6144 [1], which are essential for understanding IPv4/IPv6 translation technology. It then expands and complements these scenarios by introducing IPv4 address sharing and double translation/encapsulation technologies. With a comprehensive and clear scenario definition, readers can naturally select: ① stateless or stateful approaches and ② single translation, double translation, or encapsulation technologies, based on their specific requirements.

First, let's introduce a few concepts.

1. *IPv4 and IPv6*

   Obviously, the transition scenarios of translation technology must distinguish between two protocols: ① IPv4 and ② IPv6.

2. *Network and Internet*

   The transition scenarios of translation technology must distinguish between network and Internet.

   (1) Network refers to the networks owned and operated by providers, university campuses, corporations, and data centers. Within these networks, they possess the ability to do address allocation/assignment, manage DNS, and other related aspects.
   (2) The Internet is a network of networks, a decentralized infrastructure that interconnects diverse networks worldwide. In this book, the term "Internet"

X. Li and C. Bao, *New IPv6 Transition Technology*,
https://doi.org/10.1007/978-981-95-8427-7_4

refers specifically to the global collection of networks that operate independently of individual control. Key components such as address allocation, the Domain Name System (DNS), and routing protocols are not centrally governed.

(3) *Client and Server*

The transition scenarios of translation technology must distinguish between clients and servers.

The client initiates communication to the server actively, while the server passively waits to receive the communication initiated by the clients. The transition scenarios of translation technology can be summarized as: when a client in one protocol family initiates communication to a server in another protocol family through a translator, the situation can be further divided into two types:

(1) IPv6 client initiates access to IPv4 server.
(2) IPv4 client initiates access to IPv6 server.

4.1 Fundamental Scenarios of Translation Technology

There exist eight fundamental scenarios for IPv4/IPv6 translation technology as defined by RFC6144 [1].

4.1.1 Scenario 1: IPv6 Network to IPv4 Internet

The IPv6 clients in the IPv6 network access resources on the global IPv4 Internet, this is a typical deployment scenario known as the green field. For example, to reduce operating costs and complexity, IPv6-only is deployed in campus or corporate networks. In addition, wireless networks (Wi-Fi, 4G/5G/6G) can also be considered in this scenario.

This scenario is shown in Fig. 4.1.

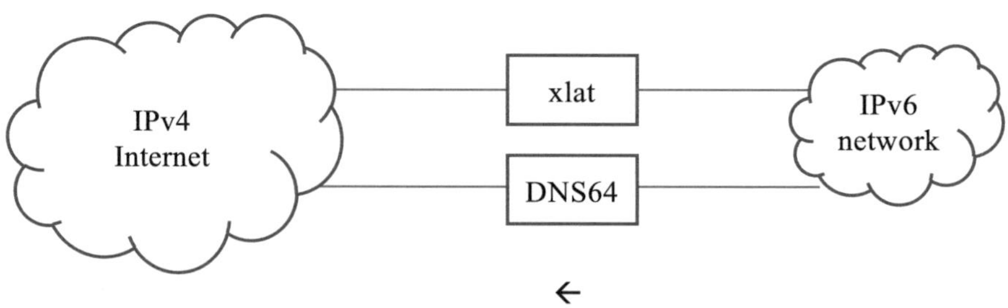

Fig. 4.1 IPv6 network to IPv4 Internet

In addition to the translator (xlat), this scenario requires the deployment of DNS64. When an IPv6-only client queries a recursive DNS, if the target domain name only has an A record (IPv4 address), then DNS64 translates the A record (IPv4 address) into an AAAA record (IPv6 address).

The IPv6 transition technologies that support this scenario include the following:

(1) Stateless single translation IVI (RFC6052 [2], RFC7915 [3], RFC6219 [4]).
(2) Stateless single translation 1: *N* IVI (RFC6219 [4]).
(3) Stateful single translation NAT64 (RFC6146 [5]).

4.1.2 Scenario 2: IPv4 Internet to IPv6 Network

The IPv6 servers in the IPv6 network are accessed by IPv4 clients on the Internet. In this case, the server can transition to IPv6 first, while continuing to provide services to IPv4 users on the Internet through a translator. The workload and operating cost of program development for functions such as address-based access control, pageview statistics, and address tracing for IPv6-only servers are less than those for dual-stack servers to achieve the same functions. At the same time, according to the "barrel effect," the security level of IPv6-only servers is also higher than that of dual-stack servers.

This scenario is shown in Fig. 4.2.

In addition to the translator (xlat), this scenario requires the deployment of DNS46. The AAAA record (IPv6 address) of an IPv6-only server is translated into an A record (IPv4 address) through DNS46. In fact, this process can be achieved through the configuration of authoritative DNS.

The IPv6 transition technologies that support this scenario include the following:

(1) Stateless single translation IVI (RFC6052 [2], RFC7915 [3], RFC6219 [4]).
(2) Stateless single translation 1:*N* IVI (RFC6219 [4]).
(3) Stateful single translation NAT64 (RFC6146 [5]).

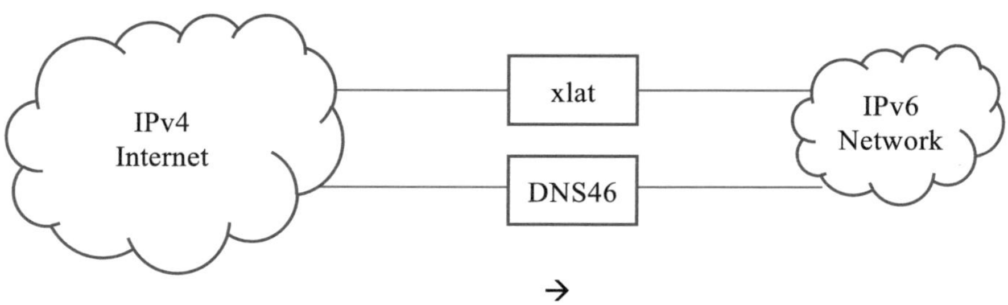

Fig. 4.2 IPv4 Internet to IPv6 network

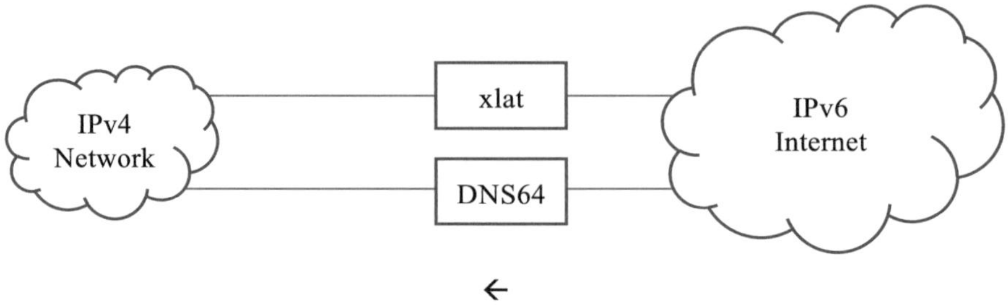

Fig. 4.3 IPv6 Internet to IPv4 network

4.1.3 Scenario 3: IPv6 Internet to IPv4 Network

The IPv4 server in the IPv4 network supports access from IPv6 clients on the global Internet.

This scenario is shown in Fig. 4.3.

In addition to the translator (xlat), this scenario requires the deployment of DNS64. DNS64 translates the A record (IPv4 address) of an IPv4-only server into an AAAA record (IPv6 address) through DNS64. In fact, this process can be achieved by the configuration of authoritative DNS.

The IPv6 transition technologies that support this scenario include the following:

(1) Stateless single translation IVI (RFC6052 [2], RFC7915 [3], RFC6219 [4]).
(2) Stateful single translation NAT64 (RFC6146 [5]).

4.1.4 Scenario 4: IPv4 Network to IPv6 Internet

The IPv4 client in the IPv4 network accesses resources on the global IPv6 Internet.

This scenario is shown in Fig. 4.4.

In addition to the translator (xlat), this scenario requires the deployment of DNS46. When an IPv4-only client queries recursive DNS, if the target domain name only has an AAAA record (IPv6 address), DNS46 translates the AAAA record (IPv6 address)

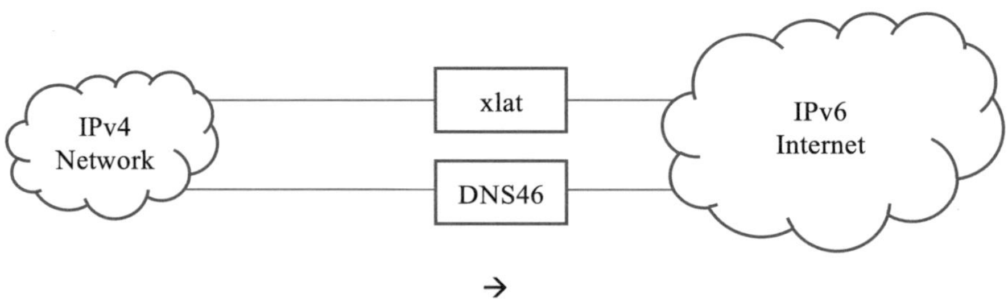

Fig. 4.4 IPv4 network to IPv6 Internet

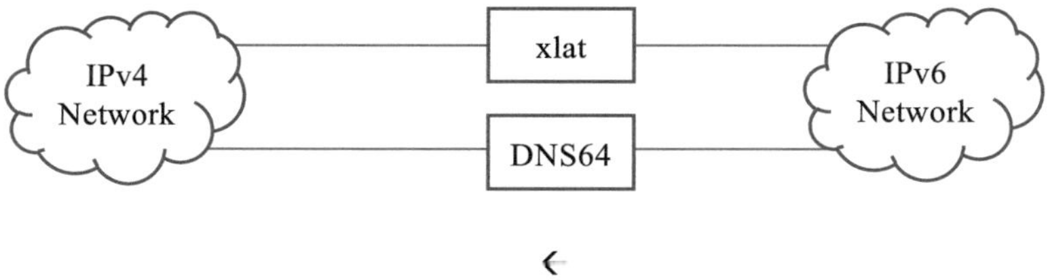

Fig. 4.5 IPv6 network to IPv4 network

into an A record (IPv4 address) based on state or algorithm. Note that in this case, the mapping parameters of DNS are coupled with the mapping parameters of the translator.

The IPv6 transition technologies that support this scenario include the following:

(1) Stateless single translation IVI (RFC6052 [2], RFC7915 [3], RFC6219 [4]).
(2) Stateful single translation NAT64 (RFC6146 [5]).

4.1.5 Scenario 5: IPv6 Network to IPv4 Network

This scenario is a simplified version of Scenario 1, in which the IPv4 network and the IPv6 network belong to the same administrative domain.

This scenario is shown in Fig. 4.5.

In addition to the translator (xlat), this scenario requires the deployment of DNS64. When an IPv6-only client queries recursive DNS, if the target domain name only has A records (IPv4 addresses), then DNS64 translates the A records (IPv4 addresses) into AAAA records (IPv6 addresses). Since the IPv4 network and the IPv6 network belong to the same administrative domain, this process can also be implemented by the configuration of the authoritative DNS.

The IPv6 transition technologies that support this scenario include the following:

(1) Stateless single translation IVI (RFC6052 [2], RFC7915 [3], RFC6219 [4]).
(2) Stateful single translation NAT64 (RFC6146 [5]).

4.1.6 Scenario 6: IPv4 Network to IPv6 Network

This scenario is a simplified version of Scenario 2, in which the IPv4 network and the IPv6 network belong to the same administrative domain.

This scenario is shown in Fig. 4.6.

In addition to the translator (xlat), this scenario requires the deployment of DNS46. When an IPv4-only client queries recursive DNS, if the target domain name only has AAAA records (IPv6 addresses), then DNS46 translates the AAAA records (IPv6 addresses) into A records (IPv4 addresses). Since the IPv4 network and the IPv6

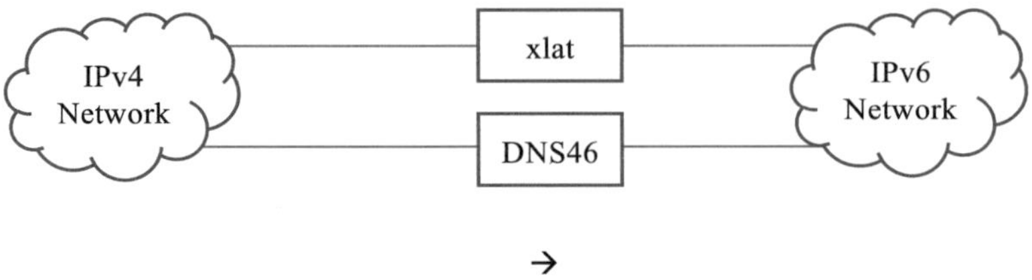

Fig. 4.6 IPv4 network to IPv6 network

network both belong to the same organization, this process can also be implemented by the configuration of the authoritative DNS.

The IPv6 transition technologies that support this scenario include the following:

(1) Stateless single translation IVI (RFC6052 [2], RFC7915 [3], RFC6219 [4]).
(2) Stateful single translation NAT64 (RFC6146 [5]).

4.1.7 Scenario 7: IPv6 Internet to IPv4 Internet

This seems to be the ideal scenario for translation technology, where any IPv6-only client on the global Internet can initiate communication with IPv4 servers on the global Internet through a translator.

This scenario is shown in Fig. 4.7.

Due to the huge difference in address space between IPv4 and IPv6, there is no universal solution for Scenario 7. The only feasible approach to enable Scenario 7 is if all IPv6 networks adopt the translator mechanism described in Scenario 1, which is designed to handle the unique requirements of IPv6-to-IPv4 communication.

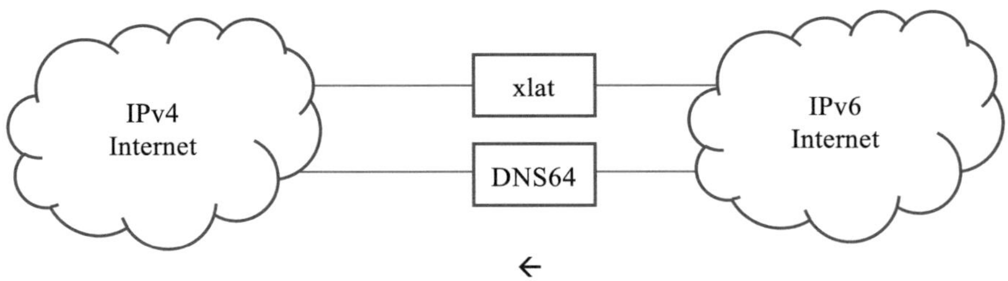

Fig. 4.7 IPv6 Internet to IPv4 Internet

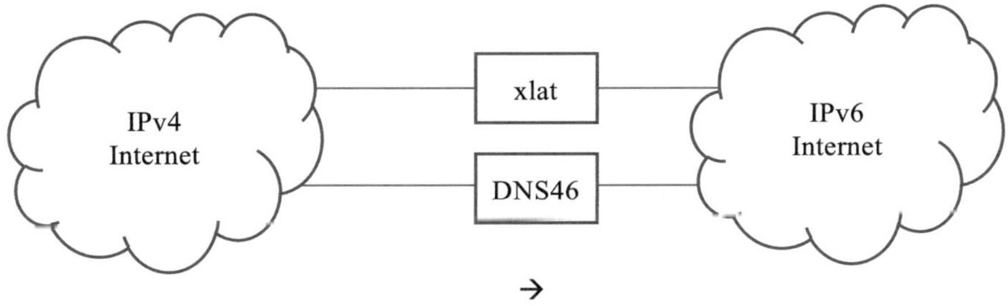

Fig. 4.8 IPv4 Internet to IPv6 Internet

4.1.8 Scenario 8: IPv4 Internet to IPv6 Internet

This also seems to be an ideal scenario for translation technology, where any IPv4-only client on the global Internet can initiate communication with IPv6 servers on the global Internet through a translator.

This scenario is shown in Fig. 4.8.

Due to the huge difference in address space between IPv4 and IPv6, there is no universal solution for Scenario 8. The only feasible approach to enable Scenario 8 is if all IPv6 networks adopt the translator mechanism described in Scenario 2, which is designed to handle the unique requirements of IPv4-to-IPv6 communication.

4.2 Extended Scenarios

4.2.1 1:1 Double Translation (The Extension of Scenario 1)

Scenario 1 is the IPv6 network (client) initiating access to the IPv4 Internet (server). However, when some hosts are IPv4-only, or some applications are IPv4-only, or some applications have embedded IPv4 addresses and try to connect to the network, an extension of Scenario 1 can be made by adding a second translator to translate IPv6 back to IPv4. Note: This double translation can degrade into a single translation (at this time, DNS64 is needed). Therefore, this scenario can degrade into Scenario 1, and finally evolve smoothly into IPv6-only.

This scenario is shown in Fig. 4.9.

The IPv6 transition technology that supports this scenario is simply the cascade of stateless single translators (RFC6052 [2], RFC7915 [3], RFC6219 [4]).

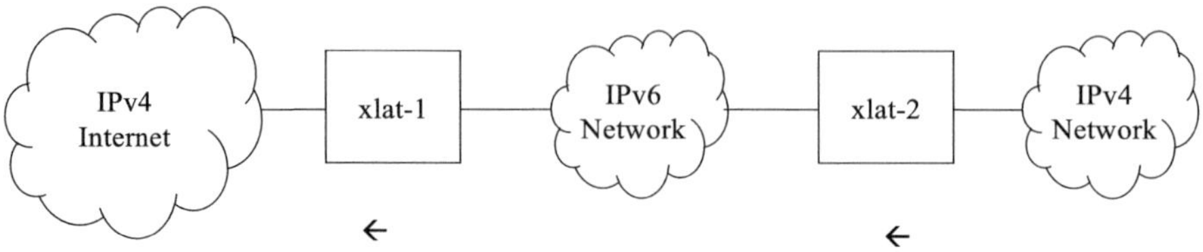

Fig. 4.9 1:1 double translation

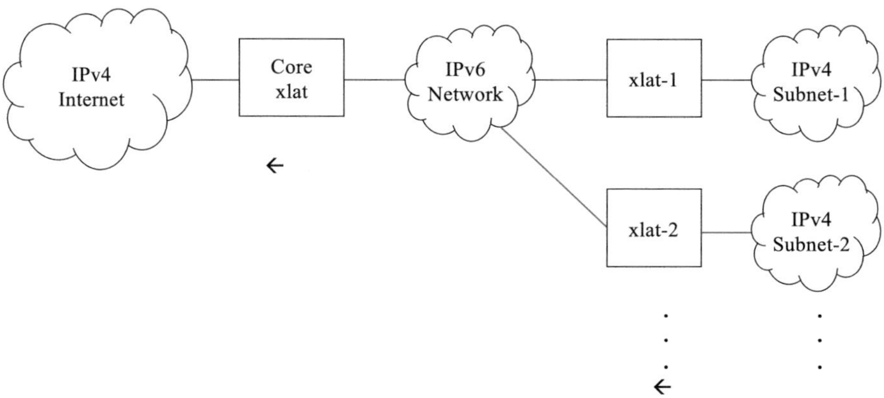

Fig. 4.10 1:*N* double translation

4.2.2 1:N Double Translation (The Extension of Scenario 1)

There is another case of double translation. Considering an IPv4 address can be mapped to different IPv6 addresses by using different transport layer (TCP or UDP) ports, that is, 1:*N* expansion for scenario 1. In this case, scared IPv4 addresses can be multiplexed and the multiple second translators can exist. This double translation can also degrade into single translation (at this time, DNS64 needs to be used). Therefore, this scenario can degrade into Scenario 1, and finally evolve smoothly into IPv6-only.

This scenario is shown in Fig. 4.10.

The IPv6 transition technologies that support this scenario include the following:

(1) Stateless double translation MAP-T (RFC7599 [6]).
(2) Stateless double translation (dIVI, RFC6219 [4]).
(3) Stateful double translation 464XLAT (RFC6877 [7]).

4.2.3 1:N Encapsulation (The Expansion of Scenario 1)

This is similar to above scenario, instead of double translation, the encapsulation (tunnel) technology is used. However, IPv4 over IPv6 tunneling preserves IPv4

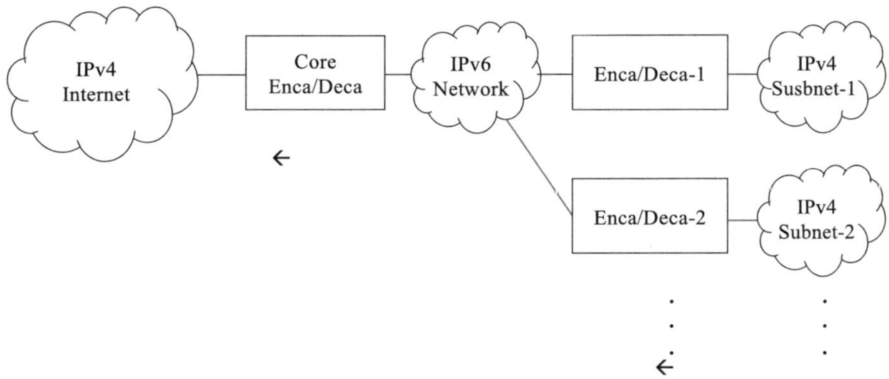

Fig. 4.11 1:*N* encapsulation

addresses and cannot evolve into IPv6-only, unlike translation methods that enable gradual migration.

This scenario is shown in Fig. 4.11.

The IPv6 transition technologies that support this scenario include the following:

(1) Stateless encapsulation MAP-E (RFC7597 [8]).
(2) Stateful encapsulation DS-Lite (RFC6333 [9]).
(3) Partial state encapsulation LW-4o6 (RFC7596 [10]).

4.2.4 1:1 Double Translation (The Expansion of in Scenario 2)

Scenario 2 is the access from the IPv4 Internet (client) to the IPv6 network (server). However, when some hosts on this IPv6 network only support IPv4 or some applications only support IPv4, Scenario 2 can be expanded by adding a second translator to translate IPv6 back to IPv4. This double translation can degrade into single translation (at this time, DNS46 is needed). Therefore, this scenario can degrade into Scenario 2, and finally evolve smoothly into IPv6-only.

The scenario is shown in Fig. 4.12.

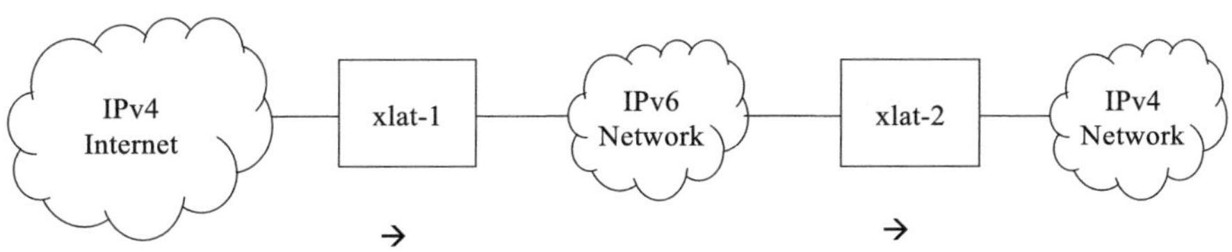

Fig. 4.12 1:1 double translation

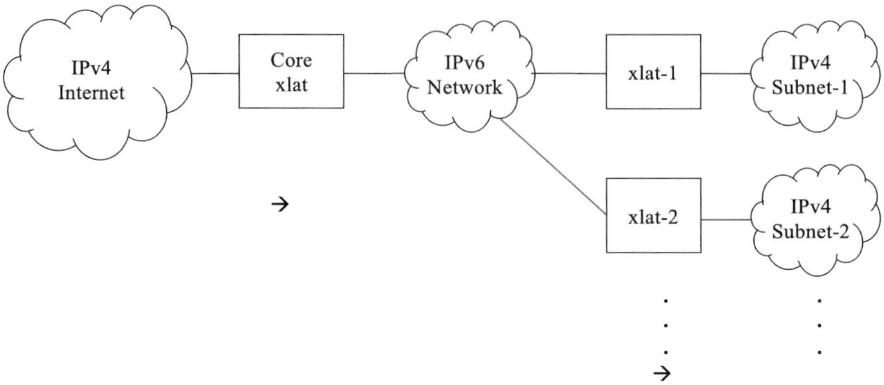

Fig. 4.13 1:*N* double translation

The IPv6 transition technology supporting this scenario is cascade two stateless single translators (RFC6219 [4]).

4.2.5 1:N Double Translation (The Extension of Scenario 2)

There is another case of double translation. Considering, an IPv4 address can be mapped to different IPv6 addresses by using different transport layer (TCP or UDP) ports, that is, 1: *N* expansion for scenario 2. In this case, scared IPv4 addresses can be multiplexed and the multiple second translators can exist. The double translation can degrade into a single translation (at this time, DNS46 is needed). Therefore, this scenario can degrade into scenario 2 and can eventually evolve smoothly into IPv6-only.

The scenario is shown in Fig. 4.13.

The IPv6 transition technologies supporting this scenario include the following:

(1) Stateless double translation MAP-T (RFC7599 [6]).
(2) Cascaded stateless double translation dIVI (RFC6219 [4]).

4.2.6 1:N Encapsulation (The Extension of Scenario 2)

This is similar to above scenario, instead of double translation, the encapsulation (tunnel) technology is used. However, IPv4 over IPv6 tunneling preserves IPv4 addresses and cannot evolve into IPv6-only, unlike translation methods that enable gradual migration.

The scenario is shown in Fig. 4.14.

The IPv6 transition technology supporting this scenario is stateless encapsulation MAP-E (RFC7597 [8]).

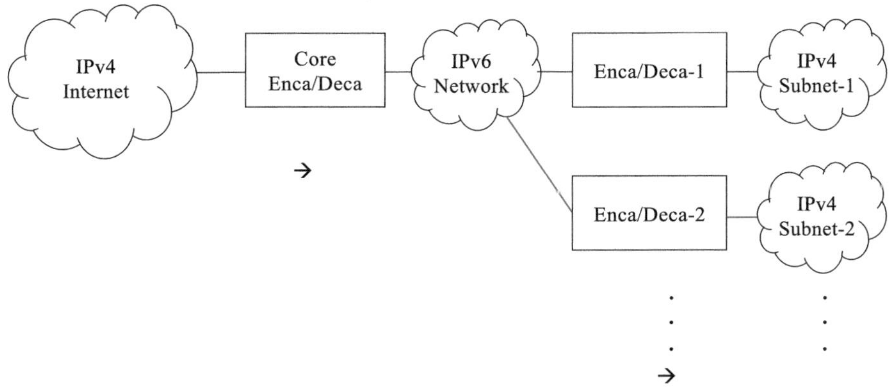

Fig. 4.14 1:*N* encapsulation

4.2.7 1:1 Double Translation (The Extension of Scenario 5)

Scenario 5 is when an IPv6 network (client) initiates access to an IPv4 network (server). However, when some hosts on this IPv6 network only support IPv4, or some applications only support IPv4, or some applications have embedded IPv4 addresses, the scenario 5 can be extended by adding a second translator to translate IPv6 back to IPv4. In this case, it can be further extended, that is, the double translation can span not only an IPv6 network but also the IPv6 Internet. Note: Double translation can degrade into a single translation (at this time, DNS64 needs to be used). Therefore, this scenario can degrade into scenario 5, and finally evolve smoothly into an IPv6-only.

This scenario is shown in Fig. 4.15.

The IPv6 transition technology that supports this scenario is cascaded stateless double translation dIVI (RFC6219 [4]).

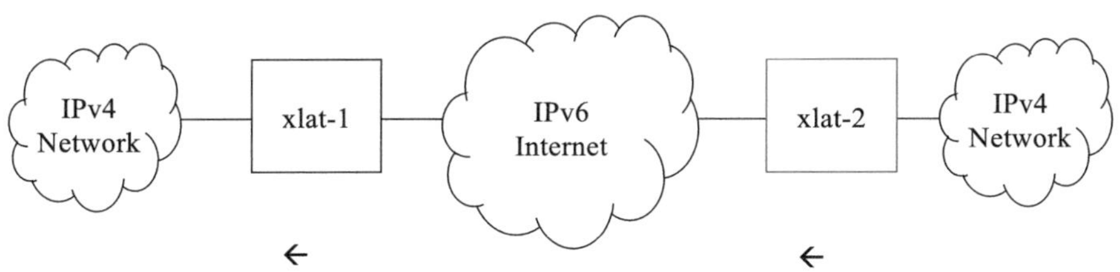

Fig. 4.15 1:1 double translation

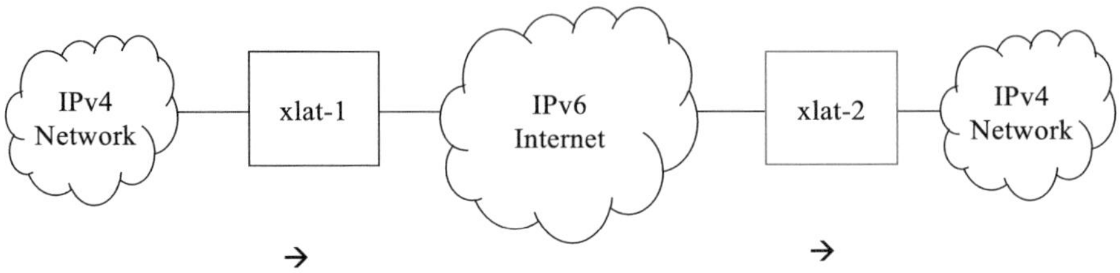

Fig. 4.16 1:1 double translation

4.2.8 1:1 Double Translation (The Extension of Scenario 6)

This is similar to above scenario, but for extension of scenario 6. Note: Double translation can degrade into a single translation (at this time, DNS46 needs to be used). Therefore, this scenario can degrade into the basic application scenario 6 and finally evolve smoothly into IPv6-only.

This scenario is shown in Fig. 4.16.

The IPv6 transition technology that supports this scenario is cascaded stateless double translation dIVI (RFC6219 [4]).

4.3 Framework and Components of Translation Technology

According to the layered model of the network, the network layer serves as the core of the Internet. The essence of translation technology lies in establishing translation rules between IPv4 and IPv6 protocols, which differ in syntax and semantics. Both IPv4 and IPv6 protocols are based on a connectionless mechanism, where the routing and forwarding of individual packets are independent. This implies that routers operate in a stateless manner, also forming the foundation for stateless IPv4/IPv6 translation technology. Consequently, the translation process from IPv4-to-IPv6 packets and vice versa is independent for each individual packet.

The definition of the IPv4 protocol is standardized by RFC791 [18], which provides a detailed description of the IPv4 packet format. Additionally, the definition of IPv4 addresses is also included in RFC791, specifying the 32-bit structure and classification methods of IPv4 addresses.

The standardization of the IPv6 protocol is defined by RFC8200 [19], which comprehensively outlines the IPv6 packet format and extension header mechanisms. The definition of IPv6 addresses is specified in RFC4291 [20], which establishes the 128-bit structure of IPv6 addresses, thereby providing the foundational framework for address planning in IPv6 networks. The specifications of core protocols between IPv4 and IPv6 are illustrated in Fig. 4.17.

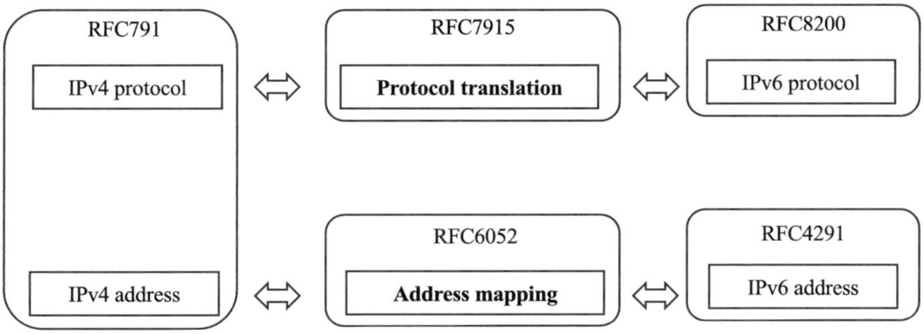

Fig. 4.17 Specifications of core protocols between IPv4 and IPv6

RFC7915 [3] defines the translation rules between IPv4 and IPv6 protocols, aiming to achieve interoperability between IPv4 and IPv6 network layers. RFC6052 [2] specifies the mapping rules between IPv4 and IPv6 addresses, addressing the representation of IPv4 addresses within IPv6 networks. Subsequent chapters of this book will elaborate on the protocols for translation and address mapping. Building upon these foundations, the text will further extend to stateful translation, IPv4 address sharing, and double translation technologies.

To implement translation scenarios, the building blocks of translators, DNS64/DNS46, parameter discovery and configuration modules, and host system support are needed. The framework and components of translation technology are shown in Fig. 4.18 [1].

4.3.1 Translator

Translator is categorized into stateless and stateful translators. Both types share a common protocol processing module and address mapping module. Additionally, stateful translators require an extra state maintenance module.

1. *Protocol Processing Module*

The IPv4 and IPv6 translation interoperability algorithm includes the handling of IPv4 and IPv6 headers, the ICMPv4 and ICMPv6 protocols, the error messages of ICMPErrorv4 and ICMPErrorv6, as well as the handling of checksums in the header of the transport layer protocols such as TCP, UDP (RFC7915 [3]). The biggest challenge in IPv4 and IPv6 interoperability is the fragmentation handling methods. Due to the different lengths of IPv4 and IPv6 headers, the translation from IPv4 to IPv6 usually exceeds the MTU of the data link layer. At the same time, due to the different mechanisms of IPv4 and IPv6 for handling fragmentation, it may cause "black holes." The protocol processing module is discussed in detail in Chap. 5 of this book.

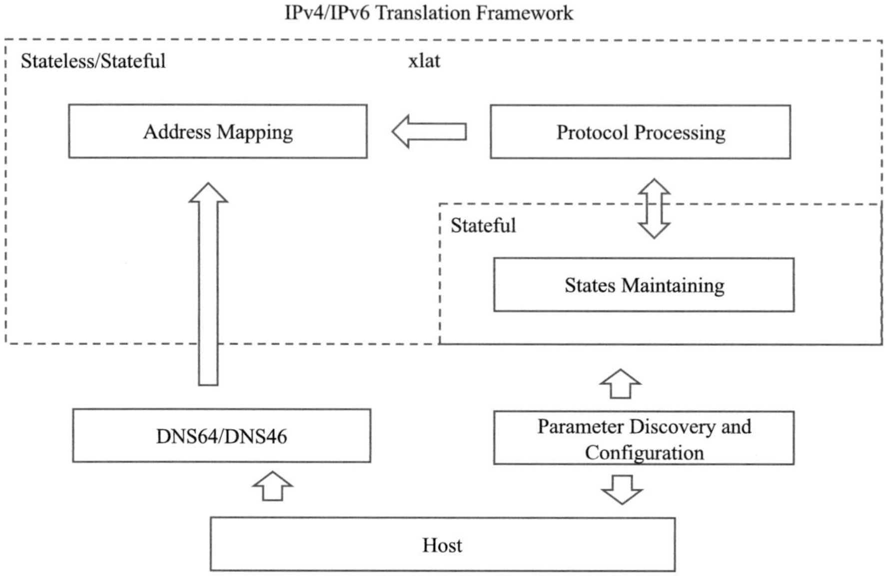

Fig. 4.18 Framework and components of translation technology

2. *Address Mapping Module*

The address mapping of the stateless translator is algorithm-based (RFC6052 [2]), which is discussed in detail in Chap. 6 of this book, including the following content.

(1) **Address Mapping Algorithm and Address Format**

Due to the huge difference between IPv4 and IPv6 address spaces, it is easy to represent IPv4 addresses with IPv6 addresses, but it is difficult to represent IPv6 addresses with IPv4 addresses. The core idea of stateless IPv4/IPv6 address mapping technology is to construct a one-way function to represent IPv6 addresses with IPv4 addresses. At the same time, the IPv6 prefix of the network service provider is used for address mapping, which solves the problems of incremental deployment and potential routing table explosion.

(2) **Suffix Encoding Algorithm**

The traditional method of sharing public IPv4 addresses is to distinguish different host using the same public IPv4 address based on different transport layer port numbers (TCP/UDP, etc.). However, this distinction method is generally based on the state of the address and port binding, which does not support bidirectional initiation of communication and lacks scalability and security features. By embedding the transport layer port identifier (Port Set Identifier, PSID) into the IPv6 address suffix, stateless IPv4 address sharing can be achieved. Using the same IPv4 address and different port ranges, IPv4 and IPv6 can be addressed bidirectionally based on the algorithm (RFC7597 [8], RFC7599 [6]).

(3) **Prefix Encoding Algorithm**

To solve the prefix allocation problem for home users, the method of IPv6 address prefix encoding (Embedded Address bits, EA-bits) can be used (RFC7597 [8], RFC7599 [6]). This method embeds the subnet part of the public IPv4 address and PSID into the prefix of the IPv6 address, so it can uniquely represent the home subnet that reuses the public IPv4 address based on the algorithm while efficiently using the effective length of the IPv6 address.

3. *State Maintenance Module*

Stateful address mapping technology refers to the mapping relationship between IPv4/IPv6 addresses and transport layer ports, which is dynamically generated based on the address-port binding, and the device needs to maintain the mapping state table (RFC6146 [5]). Its principle is consistent with the address conversion technology used in the IPv4 Internet, that is, the source address is dynamically mapped to the combination of public IPv4 address and transport layer (TCP/UDP) port.

4.3.2 Domain Name System (DNS)

The standard addressing method for Internet applications is through DNS. The relationship between domain names and IPv4 addresses is represented by A records and IPv6 addresses is represented by AAAA records. When deploying an IPv4/IPv6 translator, DNS64 is needed to map A records to AAAA records, and DNS46 is needed to map AAAA records to A records (RFC6147 [11]).

DNS64 and DNS46 rely on the parameters of the address mapping algorithm to map between A records and AAAA records. There are two methods to provide DNS64 and DNS46 functions:

(1) Static Configuration: The AAAA record (DNS64) or A record (DNS46) of the DNS authoritative server is statically configured based on the address mapping algorithm.
(2) Dynamic Mapping: For DNS64, according to the AAAA record required by the user, the DNS is recursively queried. If there is no AAAA record, the AAAA record is generated from the A record using the address mapping algorithm and returned to the user. For DNS46, according to the A record required by the user, the DNS is recursively queried. If there is no A record, the A record is generated from the AAAA record using the address mapping algorithm and returned to the user.

The domain name system is discussed in detail in Chap. 7 of this book.

4.3.3 Parameter Discovery and Configuration

Translation technology requires parameters, such as the IPv6 prefix (Pref6) needed for address mapping and the IPv4 address and port range needed for address and port mapping. The methods for obtaining these parameters are as follows:

(1) Static configuration of the required parameters.
(2) Use DNS to discover the IPv6 prefix (RFC7050 [12], RFC8880 [13]).
(3) Use DHCPv6 to configure mechanisms such as the IPv6 prefix, shared IPv4 address, and transport layer (TCP, UDP) port range (RFC7598 [14]).
(4) Use router advertisement option (RA) to configure parameters such as the DNS server address (RFC8106 [15]) and IPv6 prefix (RFC8781 [16]).
(5) Use DHCPv4 option to not assign IPv4 address to IPv6-only capable hosts (RFC8925 [17]). In the IETF, this is referred to as IPv6-mostly.

Chapter 8 of this book has the detailed discussion for these methods.

4.3.4 Host System

When the host itself performs address mapping (rather than relying on an external DNS64 system), or when the host itself needs to implement the IPv4/IPv6 translation function, it needs to implement some or all of the functions of the above components.

4.4 Summary

This chapter explores the scenarios of IPv6 translation technology, examining the incompatibility between IPv4 and IPv6 and the substantial disparity in their address space sizes. It emphasizes the significance of understanding these scenarios for comprehending subsequent chapters and selecting suitable IPv6 transition technologies tailored to specific requirements. To bridge the gap, this chapter also introduces the technical framework and foundational components necessary for implementing these scenarios.

References

1. Baker F, Li X, Bao C, et al. RFC6144: Framework for IPv4/IPv6 translation. IETF 2011–04.
2. Bao C, Huitema C, Bagnulo M, et al. RFC6052: IPv6 addressing of IPv4/IPv6 translators. IETF 2010–10.
3. Bao C, Li X, Baker F, et al. RFC7915: IP/ICMP translation algorithm. IETF 2016–06.

4. Li X, Bao C, Chen M, et al. RFC6219: The China Education and Research Network (CERNET) IVI translation design and deployment for the IPv4/IPv6 coexistence and transition. IETF 2011–05.
5. Bagnulo M, Matthews P, Beijnum I. RFC6146: Stateful NAT64: Network address and protocol translation from IPv6 clients to IPv4 servers. IETF 2011–04.
6. Li X, Bao C, Dec W, et al. RFC7599: Mapping of address and port using translation (MAP-T). IETF 2015–07.
7. Mawatari M, Kawashima M, Byrne C. RFC6877: 464XLAT: Combination of stateful and stateless translation. IETF 2013–04.
8. Troan O, Dec W, Li X, et al. RFC7597: Mapping of address and port with encapsulation (MAP-E). IETF 2015–07.
9. Durand A, Droms R, Woodyatt J, et al. RFC6333: Dual-stack lite broadband deployments following IPv4 exhaustion. IETF 2011–08.
10. Cui Y, Sun Q, Boucadair M, et al. RFC7596: Lightweight 4over6: An extension to the dual-stack lite architecture. IETF 2015–07.
11. Bagnulo M, Sullivan A, Matthews P, et al. RFC6147: DNS64: DNS extensions for network address translation from IPv6 clients to IPv4 servers. IETF 2011–04.
12. Savolainen T, Korhonen J, Wing D. RFC7050: Discovery of the IPv6 prefix used for IPv6 address synthesis. IETF 2013–11.
13. Cheshire S, Schinazi D. RFC8880: Special use domain name 'ipv4only.arpa'. IETF 2020–08.
14. Mrugalski T, Troan O, Farrer I, et al. RFC7598: DHCPv6 options for configuration of softwire address and port-mapped clients. IETF 2015–07.
15. Jeong J, Park S, Beloeil L, et al. RFC8106: IPv6 router advertisement options for DNS configuration. IETF 2017–03.
16. Colitti L, Linkova J. RFC8781: Discovering PREF64 in router advertisements. IETF 2020–04.
17. Colitti, L., Linkova, J., Richardson, M., et al RFC8925: IPv6-Only Preferred Option for DHCPv4 IETF 2020–10.
18. Postel J. RFC791: Internet protocol. IETF 1981–09.
19. Deering S, Hinden R. RFC8200: Internet protocol version 6 (IPv6) specification. IETF 2017–07.
20. Hinden R, Deering S. RFC4291: IP version 6 addressing architecture. IETF 2006–02.

Part II
Technologies

Chapter 5
Protocol Processing

Protocols are the core of the Internet, and the header is the specific embodiment of the protocol. This chapter analyzes in detail the headers involved in IPv4 [1] and IPv6 [2], thereby introducing the processing technology to establish a conversion relationship between incompatible IPv4 and IPv6.

5.1 IPv4

IPv4 is defined by RFC791 [1]. IPv4 is used for the interconnection of the computer systems. IPv4 provides the transmission of datagrams from the source node to the destination node, which are represented by fixed-length addresses. IPv4 also provides fragmentation and reassembly of datagrams when needed.

IPv4 itself does not guarantee the reliability of data transmission, traffic control, and the order of datagrams. If the application has such requirements, these requirements should be provided by other protocols.

IPv4 implements the following two basic functions.

(1) addressing,
(2) fragmentation.

It should be pointed out that IPv6 defined by RFC8200 [2] retains the addressing method consistent with IPv4, but changes the fragmentation method. The change of the fragmentation method by IPv6 is the biggest difficulty in implementing IPv4/IPv6 translation technology.

The IPv4 uses the destination address carried in the header of the datagram to deliver the datagram to the destination node. The process of selecting the transmission path is called routing.

When IPv4 was initially designed, there were many link layer protocols, these link layer protocols have different Maximum Transmission Unit (MTU) restrictions,

X. Li and C. Bao, *New IPv6 Transition Technology*,
https://doi.org/10.1007/978-981-95-8427-7_5

so IPv4 allows fragmentation during transmission, that is, using the fields in the IPv4 header to identify fragments for reassembly in the end system.

All devices at and above the network layer of the Internet must support the processing of IPv4, these devices include routers, layer 3 switches, firewalls, and all end systems (servers, clients, and virtual machines), etc. Processing IPv4 means being able to read and update all fields defined in the IPv4 header (including addressing, fragmentation, etc.) when necessary. At the same time, it must also support the processing of ICMP and the handling of ICMP error messages.

IPv4 treats each datagram as an independent entity unrelated to any other datagram. The transmission of datagrams is connectionless, without the need for any physical or virtual circuits.

IPv4 defines four key mechanisms: service type, time to live, header checksum, and options.

(1) Service Type: It defines the expected quality of service, which is an abstract parameter. Routers can choose a specific path (next hop) based on the service type.
(2) Time to Live: It represents the upper limit of the datagram's lifespan. Set by the sender of the datagram, the value of the time to live decreases gradually as the datagram is transmitted along the path. If the time to live of the datagram has decreased to 0 before it reaches the destination node, the datagram is discarded. Time to live can be considered a self-destructing counter.
(3) Header Checksum: It verifies the correctness of the received datagram. Data may be damaged during transmission, if the header checksum verification fails, the erroneous datagram should be discarded immediately.
(4) Options: They provide some control functions. Options include timestamps, security, and source routing. Datagrams generally do not have options.

In summary, IPv4 is an unreliable communication infrastructure, with neither hop-by-hop acknowledgment nor end-to-end acknowledgment. The verification mechanism for datagrams only has a header checksum, without error control, retransmission, or flow control.

IPv4 can report detected errors through ICMP, which is a module that must be supported in the Internet Protocol.

5.1.1 IPv4 Header Format

The header structure of IPv4 is shown in Fig. 5.1 (RFC791 [1]).

(1) Version: 4 bits. The version number of IPv4 is 4.
(2) Internet Header Length (IHL): 4 bits. The Internet header length is expressed in units of 32 bits words. The minimum value of the IPv4 header length is 5.
(3) Type of Service: 8 bits. It is used to define the expected quality of service, which is an abstract parameter. These parameters are used to select the path

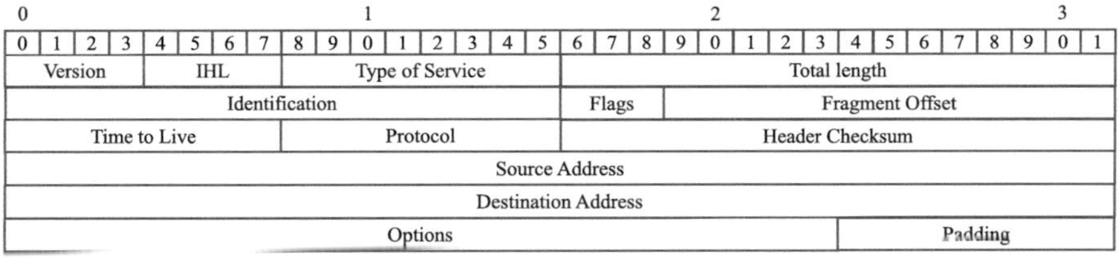

Fig. 5.1 IPv4 header structure

and link layer service parameters. The selection criteria are to balance between low latency, high reliability, and high throughput (RFC1349 [3], RFC2474 [4], RFC2475 [5]).

(4) Total Length: 16 bits. The total length is expressed in octets (octets) to represent the length of the entire datagram (including the data header and data payload). This field allows the maximum length of the datagram to be 65,535 octets. The maximum length of the datagram is not practical for most hosts and networks. All hosts must be able to accept datagrams of 576 octets (whether it is a complete datagram or a fragmented datagram). As the most conservative strategy, it is recommended that hosts only send IPv4 datagrams larger than 576 octets when it is confirmed that the destination node can receive larger datagrams. The reason for choosing the number 576 is that in addition to needing to transmit a reasonably sized data payload, the data header also needs to be transmitted. 576 octets equals 512 octets of data payload plus 64 octets of data header (the maximum IP data header is 60 octets, the typical transport layer data header is 20 octets, and there is a margin of 4 8-bit characters).

(5) Identification: 16 bits. The identification value specified by the source node helps to correctly reassemble the datagram that has been fragmented during transmission (RFC6864 [6]).

(6) Flags: 3 bits. The flag values are as shown in Table 5.1.

(7) Fragment Offset: 13 bits. This field indicates the position of the fragment in the datagram. The fragment offset is measured in units of eight octet (64 bits). The first fragment has offset 0.

(8) Time to Live (TTL): 8 bits. This field indicates the maximum time that this datagram is allowed to exist in the Internet. If this field is 0, the datagram must be discarded immediately. This field must be updated when processing the IP

Table 5.1 Flag values

Bit	Description
Bit 0	Reserved, must be 0
Bit 1(DF)	0: May fragment 1: Don't fragment
Bit 2(MF)	0: Last fragment 1: More fragments

data header. Although the TTL time is in seconds, each module processing the data header must decrease the TTL by 1, so the TTL is only an upper limit, intended to avoid those datagrams that cannot reach the destination node from circulating indefinitely in the network.

(9) Protocol: 8 bits. This field indicates the type of the next Internet protocol in the data. Various protocol types are assigned and registered by IANA, and the values of the currently assigned and registered Internet protocol types are given in Appendix A of this book. In IPv6, this protocol field is renamed as "Next Header" (see Table A.1 in Appendix A).

(10) Header Checksum: 16 bits. A checksum on the header only. Since some header fields change (e.g., time to live), this is recomputed and verified at each point that the Internet header is processed. The checksum algorithm is: The checksum field is the 16 bit one's complement of the one's complement sum of all 16 bit words in the header. For purposes of computing the checksum, the value of the checksum field is 0. This field is removed from IPv6 header.

(11) Source Address: 32 bits, the IP address of the datagram source node.

(12) Destination Address: 32 bits, the IP address of the datagram receiving node.

(13) Options: Variable, the datagram may contain options. All devices capable of processing IP must support the defined options.

(14) Padding: Variable, filled with 0.

5.1.2 Fragmentation

The fragmentation function of IPv4 datagrams is a mandatory option (RFC791 [1]). The source node can send datagrams according to the MTU allowed by the local network (such as MTU = 1500) to improve transmission efficiency. When these datagrams are sent to a network that only allows a smaller MTU (such as MTU = 800), they can only be sent to the destination node through fragmentation.

The mechanism of Internet fragmentation and reassembly can decompose datagrams into arbitrary fragments and reassemble them at the receiving node.

(1) IPv4 datagrams can be marked as "Do Not Fragment (DF = 1)". This kind of datagram that does not allow fragmentation cannot be fragmented under any circumstances. If the MTU of the next hop link interface is smaller than the size of the datagram, it will be discarded.

(2) The "Fragment Offset" field tells the destination node the position of the fragment in the original datagram. The "Fragment Offset" and "Total Length" fields determine the position of this fragment in the original datagram.

(3) The "More Fragments" flag can identify the last fragment. These fields provide the information needed to reassemble the datagram.

(4) The "Identification" field is used to distinguish fragments from different datagrams. The source node of the datagram sets the "Identification" to a pair, that is, the "source address-destination address" pair. This "Identification" is unique

throughout the life cycle of the datagram. The destination node uses the “Identification” field to reassemble the datagram to ensure that fragments from different datagrams have not been mixed.

(5) The “More Fragments” value of the original datagram is set to 0, and the “Fragment Offset” value is also set to 0.

When fragmenting an original datagram, the router creates two new datagrams and copies the datagram header of the original datagram to the two new datagram headers. The original datagram is divided into two parts at the boundary of 64 bits (the second part may not be an integer multiple of 64 bits, but the first one must be). The fragment sequence number is defined as NFB (number of fragment blocks). The first part of the data payload is put into the first datagram, and the “Total Length” is set to the length of the first datagram; the “More Fragments” flag is set to 1 (MF = 1). The second part of the data payload is put into the second datagram, and the “Total Length” is set to the length of the second datagram; the “More Fragments” is the same as the original datagram; the “Fragment Offset” field is set to the value of the original datagram plus NFB.

This process can also be generalized to N fragments, not just the two fragments described.

When reassembling the fragments of a datagram, the destination node combines datagrams with the same values in the fields of “Identification”, “Source address”, “Destination Address”, and “Protocol”.

For the payload part of each fragment, according to the “Fragment Offset” value in the fragment datagram header, the payload is placed in the correct position of the reassembled datagram, thus completing the reassembly. The “Fragment Offset” value of the first fragment is 0, and the “More Fragments” value of the last fragment is 0.

5.1.3 IPv4 Datagram Example

1. *An IPv4 Datagram*

An example of an IPv4 datagram is shown in Fig. 5.2.

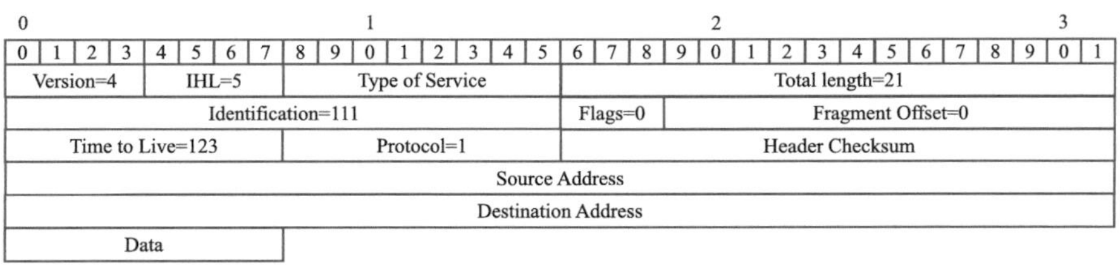

Fig. 5.2 An IPv4 datagram

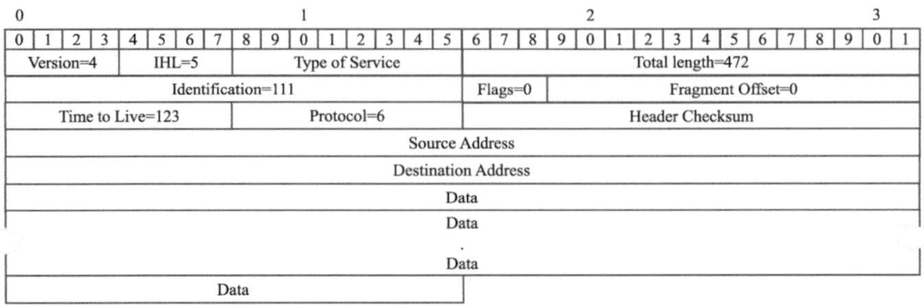

Fig. 5.3 Unfragmented IPv4 datagram header

This is an example of an IPv4 datagram; the datagram header contains five 32-bit fields, with a total length of 21 octets.

2. *Message Fragmentation*

In this example, a medium-sized IPv4 datagram with a payload of 452 octets is shown in Fig. 5.3 (Total length = 20 (IP header) + 452 = 472).

When this IPv4 datagram passes through a transmission channel with MTU = 280, the payload is fragmented into the first fragment (payload length is 256, since the fragment offset is measured in units of eight octet), the second fragment (payload length is 196). Note that 256 + 196 = 452, which is the original payload length.

The first fragment is shown in Fig. 5.4 (Total length = 20 (IP header) + 256 = 276).

The second fragment is shown in Fig. 5.5 (Total length = 20 (IP header) + 196 = 216).

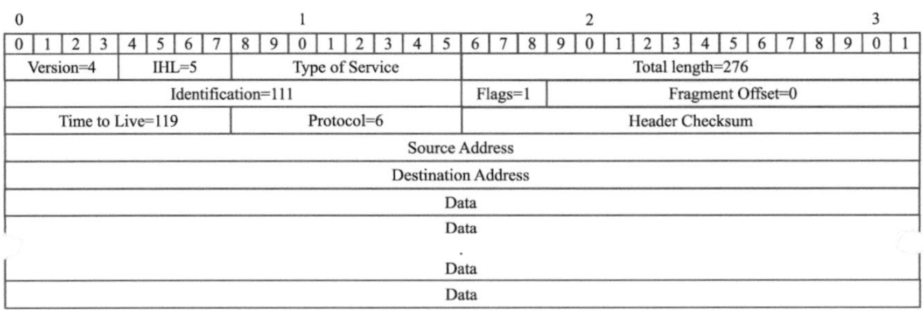

Fig. 5.4 Datagram header of the first fragment after IPv4 fragmentation

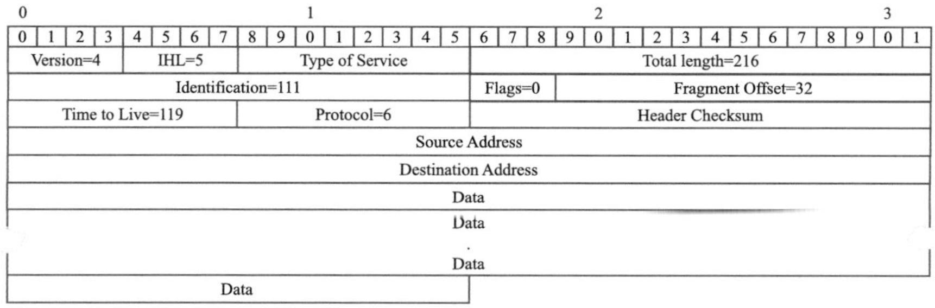

Fig. 5.5 Datagram header of the second fragment after IPv4 fragmentation

5.2 ICMP

RFC792 [7] defines the ICMP for IPv4, with the protocol value Protocol = 1.

5.2.1 IPv4 Control Message Format

IPv4 nodes use ICMP to report encountered errors for proper handling of datagrams, as well as to perform its functions (such as ping). ICMP is a fundamental part of IPv4 (message definitions and required actions), and all IPv4 nodes must fully implement ICMP.

See Appendix H for time-out constants in ICMP.

1. *General Message Format*

Each ICMP message is preceded by an IPv4 datagram header. The ICMP header is identified by the protocol value Protocol = 1 of the IPv4 datagram header.

ICMP messages have a general format, as shown in Fig. 5.6.

(1) Type: 8 bits. This field indicates the type of message, and its value determines the corresponding data format. The types of ICMP messages are shown in Table 5.2.
(2) Code: 8 bits. This field depends on the message type and is used to further describe the message.
(3) Checksum: 16 bits. This field is used to verify the availability of the IPv4 header and data in ICMP.

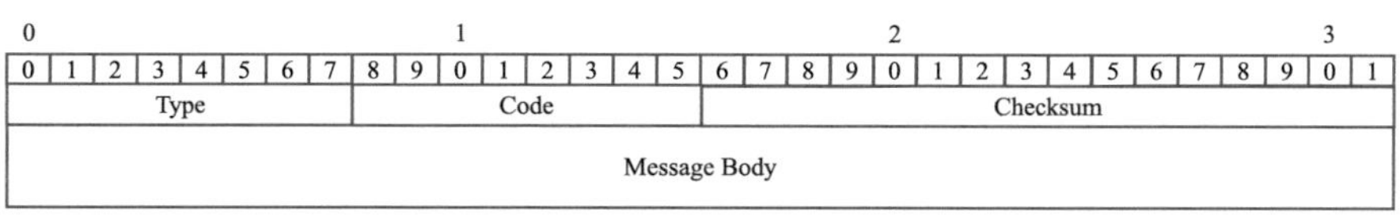

Fig. 5.6 ICMP message format

Table 5.2 ICMP message types

Type	Description
0	Echo reply
3	Destination unreachable
	Code = 4; PTB (RFC1191)
4	Source quench (deprecated, see RFC6633 [8])
5	Redirect
6	Alternative Host Address
8	Echo request
9	ICMP Router Advertisement
10	ICMP Router Solicitation
11	Time exceeded
12	Parameter problem
13	Timestamp (deprecated,
14	Timestamp reply (deprecated,
15	Information request (deprecated, see RFC6918 [9])
16	Information reply (deprecated, see RFC6918 [9])
17	Address Mask Request
18	Address Mask Reply

2. *Determination of Message Source Address and Destination Address*

The source address of the ICMP datagram is the IP address of the router or host that generates the ICMP. Unless specifically designated, it can be any IP address of the router or host.

The destination address of the ICMP datagram is the IP address of the router or host that is expected to receive the datagram.

3. *Calculation of Message Checksum*

The checksum is the 16-bit one's complement of the one's complement sum of the ICMP message starting with the ICMP Type. For computing the checksum, the checksum field should be 0.

It is particularly important to note: The calculation method of the ICMP checksum is different from that of the ICMPv6 checksum, and the ICMPv6 checksum includes the "pseudo-header" field of the IPv6 header.

5.2.2 *ICMP Message Definition*

1. *Destination Unreachable*

"Destination Unreachable" serves as the data part following the IP header, as shown in Fig. 5.7.

(1) Destination Address: The destination address is copied from the source address field of the IP header of the datagram.
(2) Type: The value is 3.
(3) Code: The code value is as shown in Table 5.3.
(4) Unused: This field is not used. The initiator must initialize it to 0, and the receiver should ignore the value of this field. The exception is "DF = 1", where the value of this field is the MTU value of the link to the destination address.
(5) Checksum: The checksum is the 16-bit one's complement of the one's complement sum of the ICMP message starting with the ICMP Type. For computing the checksum, the checksum field should be 0.
(6) The Internet header plus the first 64 bits of the original datagram's data. This data is used by the host to match the message to the appropriate process. If a higher level protocol uses port numbers, they are assumed to be in the first 64 bits of the original datagram's data.

If the router's routing table indicates that the network part of the destination address in the datagram is unreachable (RFC950 [10]), the router can send a "network unreachable message" to the source node of the datagram.

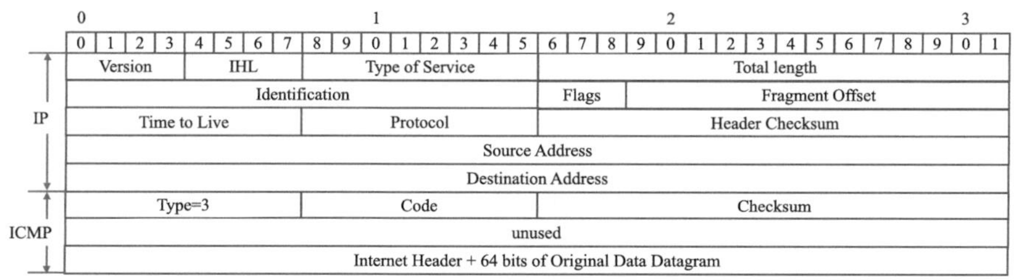

Fig. 5.7 Format of "Destination Unreachable" message with IP header

Table 5.3 Destination unreachable code

Code	Description
0	Network unreachable
1	Host unreachable
2	Protocol unreachable
3	Port unreachable
4	DF = 1, Fragmentation needed (see next section)
5	Source route failed

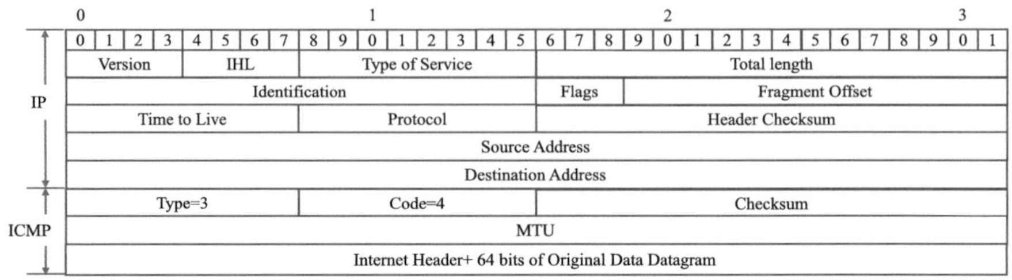

Fig. 5.8 Format of "Packet Too Big" message containing IP header

If the router can determine that the host part of the destination address in the datagram is unreachable, the router can send a "host unreachable message" to the source node of the datagram.

If the protocol module of the destination host is not activated, so that the IP module cannot deliver the datagram to the higher-level protocol, the destination host can send a "protocol unreachable" message to the source node of the datagram.

If the protocol transport layer port of the destination host is not activated, so that the IP module cannot deliver the datagram, the destination host can send a "port unreachable" message to the source node of the datagram.

2. *Packet too Big*

A special scenario arises when "DF = 1", but the MTU of the next hop link interface is smaller than the size of the datagram. In such cases, fragmentation of the datagram is necessary. However, due to the DF = 1, the router is prohibited from fragmenting the packet. Thus, the router must discard the datagram and send back an ICMP message indicating that the datagram is too large for transmission. The error message "Packet Too Big" follows the IP header, as illustrated in Fig. 5.8.

(1) Destination Address: The destination address is copied from the source address field of the IP header of the datagram that generated the message.
(2) Type: The value is 3.
(3) Code: The value is 4.
(4) Maximum Transmission Unit (MTU): The size of the MTU of the next hop link interface.
(5) Checksum: The checksum is the 16-bit one's complement of the one's complement sum of the ICMP message starting with the ICMP Type. For computing the checksum, the checksum field should be 0.
(6) The Internet header plus the first 64 bits of the original datagram's data. This data is used by the host to match the message to the appropriate process. If a higher level protocol uses port numbers, they are assumed to be in the first 64 bits of the original datagram's data.

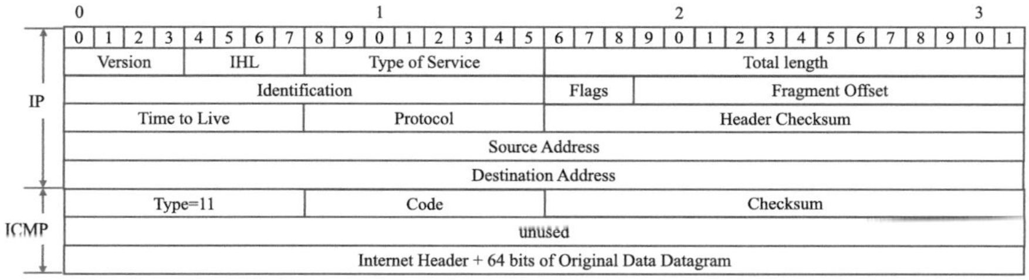

Fig. 5.9 "Timeout" message format containing IP header

Table 5.4 Timeout message code

Code	Description
0	Time to live exceeded in transit
1	Fragment reassembly time exceeded

3. *Timeout Message*

The "Timeout" message serves as the data part after the IP header, as shown in Fig. 5.9.

(1) Destination Address: The destination address is copied from the source address field of the IP header that generates the datagram.
(2) Type: The value is 11.
(3) Code: The code value is as shown in Table 5.4.
(4) Unused: This field is not used.
(5) Checksum: The checksum is the 16-bit one's complement of the one's complement sum of the ICMP message starting with the ICMP Type. For computing the checksum, the checksum field should be 0.
(6) The Internet header plus the first 64 bits of the original datagram's data. This data is used by the host to match the message to the appropriate process. If a higher level protocol uses port numbers, they are assumed to be in the first 64 bits of the original datagram's data.

If the router processing the datagram receives the "time to live" field of the datagram as 0, it must discard the datagram and notify the source node through this timeout message.

If the end system cannot complete the reassembly of the fragmented datagram within a specific time, it must discard the datagram. The host can notify the source node through this timeout message.

If fragment zero is not available then no time exceeded need be sent at all.

4. *Parameter Problem Message*

The "parameter problem" message serves as the data part after the IP header, as shown in Fig. 5.10.

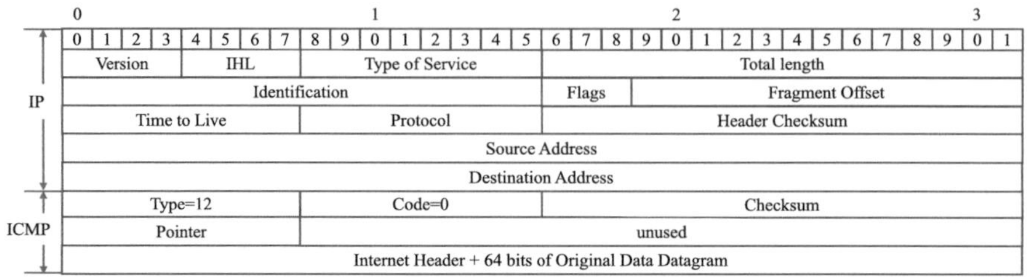

Fig. 5.10 "Parameter Problem" message format containing IP header

(1) Destination Address: The destination address is copied from the source address field of the IP header that generates the datagram.
(2) Type: The value is 12.
(3) Code: The value is 0 (pointer indicates the error).
(4) Pointer: It identifies the octet where an error was detected.
(5) Checksum: The checksum is the 16-bit one's complement of the one's complement sum of the ICMP message starting with the ICMP Type. For computing the checksum, the checksum field should be 0.
(6) The Internet header plus the first 64 bits of the original datagram's data. This data is used by the host to match the message to the appropriate process. If a higher level protocol uses port numbers, they are assumed to be in the first 64 bits of the original datagram's data.

If the router or host processing the datagram finds a parameter problem in the data header that prevents the datagram from being processed, the datagram must be discarded. At this time, the router or host can notify the source node through an ICMP parameter problem message. Note: Parameter problem messages are only sent when the error is serious enough to require discarding the datagram.

The pointer identifies the position of the detected error in the original datagram in units of octets. For example, a pointer of 1 indicates a problem with the service type, and a pointer of 20 indicates a problem with the type code of the first option.

To convey more information, RFC4884 [11] defines ICMP extensions.

5. *Redirect Message*

The "redirect" message serves as the data part after the IP header, as shown in Fig. 5.11.

(1) Destination Address: The destination address is copied from the source address field of the IP header of the originating datagram.
(2) Type: The value is 5.
(3) Code: The code value is as shown in Table 5.5.
(4) Checksum: The checksum is the 16-bit ones complement of the one's complement sum of the ICMP message starting with the ICMP Type. For computing the checksum, the checksum field should be 0.

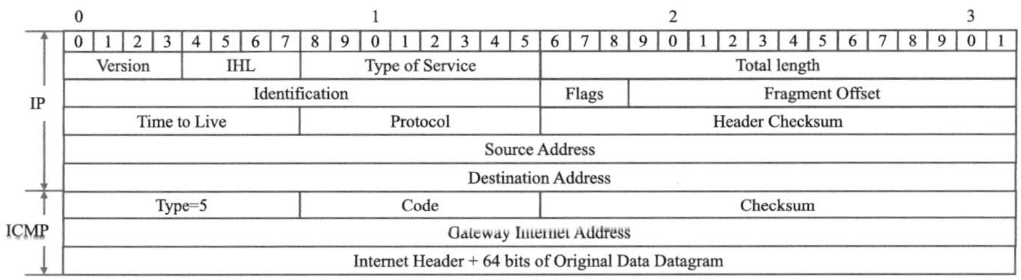

Fig. 5.11 Format of "Redirect" message containing IP header

Table 5.5 Redirect message code

Code	Description
0	Redirect datagrams for the Network
1	Redirect datagrams for the Host
2	Redirect datagrams for the Type of Service and Network
3	Redirect datagrams for the Type of Service and Host

(5) Gateway Internet Address: It specifies the new gateway address to which the redirect is to arrive.
(6) The Internet header plus the first 64 bits of the original datagram's data. This data is used by the host to match the message to the appropriate process. If a higher level protocol uses port numbers, they are assumed to be in the first 64 bits of the original datagram's data.

The gateway sends a redirect message to the host under the following circumstances. The gateway G1 receives a datagram sent by a host on the subnet connected to the gateway. Gateway G1 checks its routing table and obtains another gateway G2, whose address is X. If G2 and the source address of the datagram sent by the host are on the same subnet, it sends a redirect message to the host. The redirect message suggests that the host send traffic directly to X of gateway G2, as this is the shorter path to the destination node.

If there is an IP source route option and the gateway is on the destination address list, even if there is a better route to the destination, a redirect message should not be sent.

6. *Echo Request and Echo Response Messages*

The Echo Request and Echo Response messages serve as the data part following the IP header, as shown in Fig. 5.12.

(1) Source Address and Destination Address: The source address in the Echo Request message is the destination address of the Echo Response message. The Echo Response message swaps the source and destination addresses of the Echo Request message, changes the type code to 0, and recalculates the checksum.

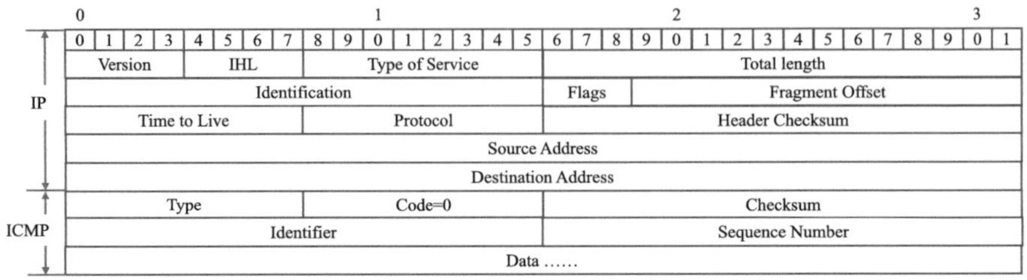

Fig. 5.12 "Echo Request and Echo Response" messages containing IP headers

Table 5.6 Types of echo request and echo response messages

Type	Description
8	Echo request message
0	Echo response message

(2) Type: The type values are as shown in Table 5.6.
(3) Code: The value is 0.
(4) Checksum: The checksum is the 16-bit one's complement of the one's complement sum of the ICMP message starting with the ICMP Type. For computing the checksum, the checksum field should be 0.
(5) Identification: Identification helps the Echo Response message match the corresponding Echo Request message, its value may be 0.
(6) Sequence Number: The sequence number also helps the Echo Response message match the corresponding Echo Request message, its value may be 0.
(7) Data: 0 or more octets of arbitrary data.

If data is received in the Echo Request message, the same data must be returned in the Echo Response message.

Using identification and sequence numbers helps the Echo Response message match the corresponding Echo Request message. Similar to port numbers in TCP or UDP, identification can be used to identify sessions. In consecutive Echo Requests, the sequence number increases by 1 each time, and the Echo Response returns the corresponding sequence number.

5.3 IPv6

IPv6 is the new version of IP, intended to be the successor to IPv4. The IPv6 datagram header is defined by RFC8200 [2], and the changes from the IPv4 datagram header to the IPv6 datagram header can be mainly divided into the following categories.

1. *Expanded Addressing Capability*

IPv6 increases the IP address from 32 to 128 bits, supporting more levels of addressing hierarchy, more addressable nodes, and simpler address autoconfiguration. By adding a "scope" field to the multicast address, the scalability of multicast routing can be improved, and a new type of address called "anycast" is defined, which is used to send datagrams to any node in a group of nodes.

2. *Header Format Simplification*

Several IPv4 datagram header fields have been removed or made optional to reduce the overhead of datagram processing and the bandwidth cost of transmitting the IPv6 datagram header.

3. *Improved Support for Extensions and Options*

IPv6 changes the option and extension method of the IP datagram header to facilitate more efficient forwarding. The new method does not strictly limit the length of options and provides greater flexibility for introducing new options.

4. *Flow Label Function*

IPv6 adds a new feature that can mark the datagrams of the source node as a single stream and process them specifically in the network based on the flow label.

5. *Authentication and Privacy Functions*

IPv6 supports extensions for authentication, data integrity, and (optional) data confidentiality.

5.3.1 IPv6 Header Format

The header structure of IPv6 is shown in Fig. 5.13.

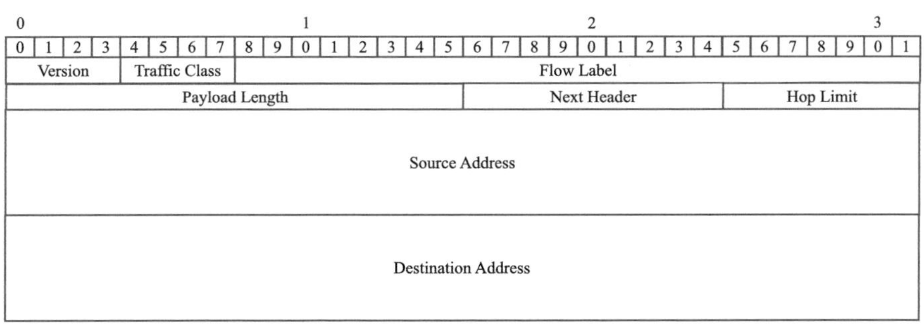

Fig. 5.13 Structure of IPv6 header

(1) Version Number (Version): 4 bits. The version number is 6.
(2) Traffic Type (Traffic Class): 8 bits. The traffic type field is used for network traffic identification and management.
(3) Flow Label: 20 bits. The flow label field is set by the sender and can be used to label different data packets as "flows".
(4) Payload Length: 16-bits unsigned integer. The total length of IPv6 is expressed in octets to represent the length of the effective payload, indicating the length of the remaining data packets after this IPv6 header (note that any extension headers are considered part of the payload and need to be included in the payload length).
(5) Next Header: 8 bits. It identifies the type of header immediately following the IPv6 header, using the same values as the IPv4 protocol field (see Table A.1 in Appendix A).
(6) Hop Limit: 8-bit unsigned integer. Each node forwarding the data packet reduces this value by 1. If the hop limit of the received data packet is 0, or if it is reduced to 0, then this data packet is discarded. The destination node should not discard data packets with a hop limit of 0, but should process them normally.
(7) Source Address: 128 bits. The IP address of the initiator of the data packet.
(8) Destination Address: 128 bits. The IP address of the recipient of the data packet (note: if there is a routing header, the destination address may not be the address of the final recipient).

5.3.2 IPv6 Extension Headers

In the IPv6 header, network layer optional items are encoded in separate headers, which are placed between the IPv6 header and the higher layer headers. There are not many such extension headers, each of which is identified by a different "Next Header" value.

Extension headers are identified by the protocol number defined by IANA, regardless of whether it is IPv4 or IPv6. An IPv6 packet can carry 0, one or more extension headers, each of which is identified by the "Next Header" field of the previous header. When the last "Next Header" value is not an IPv6 extension header, it is a transport layer header (such as TCP or UDP) or a higher layer header (if it is another network layer encapsulation). If there is no transport layer header or higher layer header, it is "No Next Header". Figure 5.14 shows examples of extension headers.

Except for the "Hop-by-Hop Options" header, extended headers are not processed (e.g., modified, inserted, or deleted) by any node on the path of the datagram. Extended headers are only processed when the datagram arrives at the node (or set of nodes in the case of multicast) of the IPv6 destination address.

If a "Hop-by-Hop Options" header is present, it must immediately follow the IPv6 header. Its presence is indicated by a value of 0 in the "Next Header" field of the IPv6 header.

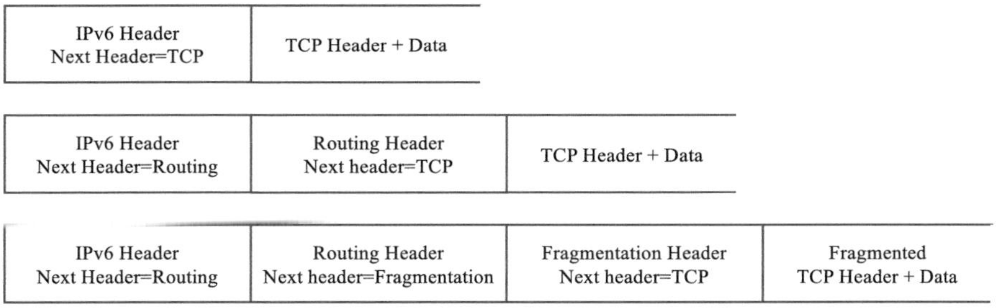

Fig. 5.14 Examples of extended headers

Note: Although the standard requires all nodes to check and process the "Hop-by-Hop Options" header, the current practice is that only nodes explicitly configured to do so will check and process the "Hop-by-Hop Options".

At the destination node, the "Next Header" of the IPv6 header is processed as usual, i.e., the corresponding module is called to process the first extended header, or the higher-level header if there are no extended headers. The content and semantics of each extended header determine whether to continue processing the next header. Therefore, extended headers must be processed strictly in the order they appear in the datagram. The receiving node must not scan the datagram to find a specific type of extended header in an attempt to prioritize processing.

If the destination node needs to process the next header, but the node cannot recognize the value of "Next Header" in the current header, the node should discard the datagram and send an ICMPv6 Parameter Problem message to the source address of the datagram. This Parameter Problem message has a Code value of 1 (unrecognizable "Next Header" type), and the ICMP pointer field should contain the offset to the unrecognizable "Next Header" type value in the original datagram. If the node encounters a value of 0 for "Next Header" in any header other than the IPv6 header, it should take the same action.

Each extension header is an integer multiple of octet long, in order to retain 8-octet alignment for subsequent headers. Multi-octet fields within each extension header are aligned on their natural boundaries.

A complete IPv6 implementation must process the following extended headers:

(1) hop-by-Hop Options,
(2) fragment,
(3) destination Options,
(4) routing,
(5) authentication, and
(6) encapsulating Security Payload.

The first four extended headers are defined in RFC8200.[2]. The authentication header is defined in RFC4302 [12], and the encapsulating security payload is defined in RFC4303 [13]. Appendix A lists the numerical values of the currently defined IPv6 extension headers.

1. *Extension Header Order*

When using multiple extension headers in the same datagram, it is recommended to arrange them in the following order.

(1) IPv6 header,
(2) hop-by-Hop Options,
(3) destination Options (Note 1),
(4) routing,
(5) fragment,
(6) authentication (Note 2),
(7) encapsulating Security Payload (Note 2),
(8) destination Options (Note 3), and
(9) upper-layer Headers (such as TCP and UDP).

Note 1: Process the IPv6 destination address and the destination address list in the subsequent "Routing" header.

Note 2: RFC4303 [13] provides other suggestions on the relative order of the authentication and encapsulating security payload headers.

Note 3: Process the final destination of the datagram.

Except for the "Destination Options" header, each extension header can only appear once. The "Destination Options" header can only appear twice (once before the "Routing" header and once before the "Upper-layer Headers").

If the "Upper-layer Headers" is another IPv6 header (in the case of IPv6 over IPv6 encapsulation/tunneling), then this IPv6 datagram can contain its own extension headers, which follow the same ordering suggestions.

If other extension headers are defined in the future, the position and overall order of the new extension headers relative to the above extension headers must be specified.

IPv6 nodes must be able to process extension headers in any order and consider the situation where extension headers appear repeatedly in the same datagram. However, the "Hop-by-Hop Options" header is limited to appearing after the IPv6 header. Despite this, it is still strongly recommended that the source node of the IPv6 datagram follow the above extension header order to send the datagram (unless subsequent specifications have modified this).

2. *Option Format*

The "Hop-by-Hop Options" header and "Destination Options" header are variable-length "options", as shown in Fig. 5.15.

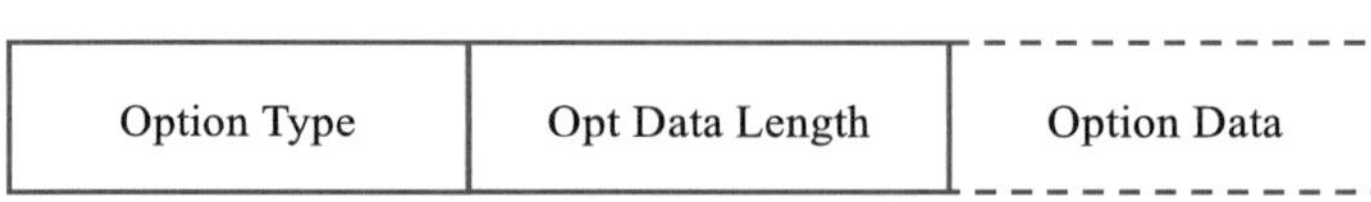

Fig. 5.15 Options

Fig. 5.16 Pad1 option

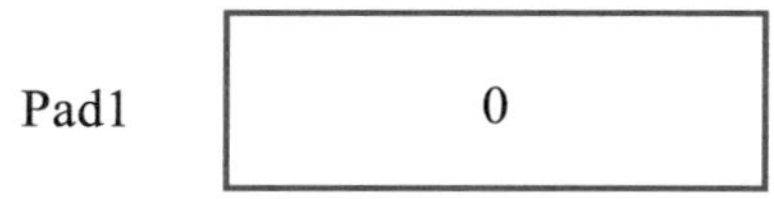

(1) Option Type: 8 bits. This option defines the type identifier of the option.
(2) Option Data Length: 8-bit unsigned integer. This option defines the length of the "Option Data" field, in units of octets.
(3) Option Data: Variable length field. This option defines the data carried by this option type.

The technical details of the Option design are defined in RFC8200.

The examples of the option are Pad1 and PadN.

Pad1 option (alignment requirement: none), as shown in Fig. 5.16.

Note: The format of the Pad1 option is a special case—it does not have length and value fields.

The Pad1 option is used to insert a padding of one octet into the "options" area of the header. If multiple octets need to be padded, the PadN option described below should be used instead of multiple Pad1 options.

PadN option (alignment requirement: none) is shown in Fig. 5.17.

3. *"Hop-by-Hop Options" Header*

The "Hop-by-Hop Options" header is used to carry information that needs to be checked and processed by each node on the path of data packet transmission. The "Hop-by-Hop Options" header is identified by the "Next Header" value in the IPv6 header being 0, and has the following format, as shown in Fig. 5.18.

(1) Next Header: 8 bits. It identifies the type of header immediately following the "Hop-by-Hop Options" header, using the same values as the IPv4 field.
(2) Header Extension Length: 8-bit unsigned integer. The length of the "Hop-by-Hop Options" header in octets, excluding the first octet.
(3) Options: Variable length field. The length makes the complete "Hop-by-Hop Options" header a multiple of octets, containing one or more "Type-Length-Value" (TLV) encoded options.

The only "Hop-by-Hop Option" currently defined is the Pad1 option and the PadN option.

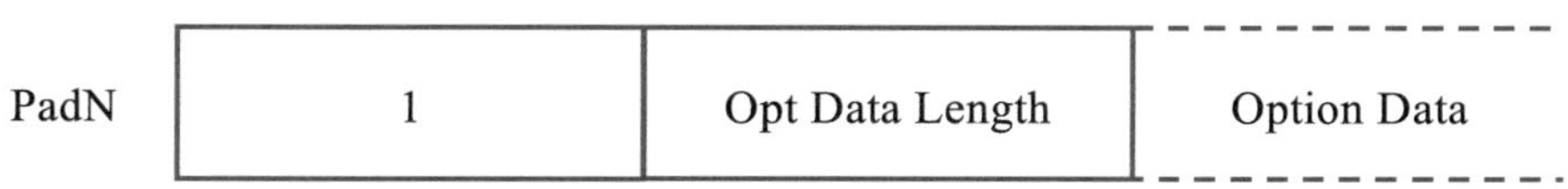

Fig. 5.17 PadN option

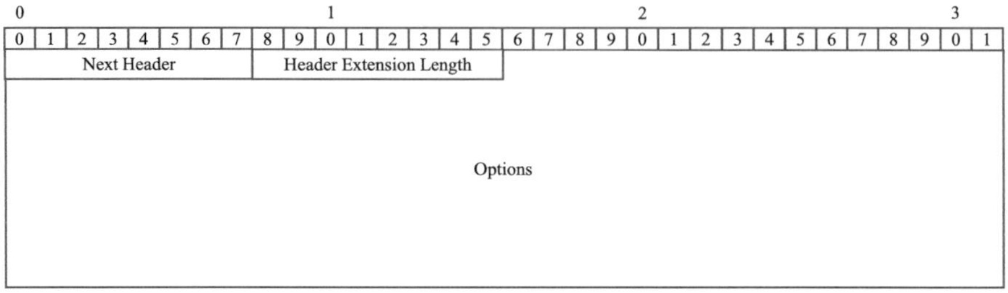

Fig. 5.18 "Hop-by-Hop Options" header

4. *"Routing" Header and IPv6 Segment Routing (SRv6)*

The "source routing" function of IPv6 messages uses the "Routing" header. The "Routing" header lists one or more datagrams that need to be visited before reaching the destination node. This function is very similar to the "Loose Source and Record Route Option" of IPv4. The "Routing" header is identified by the value 43 of the "Next Header" in the previous header, and has the following format, as shown in Fig. 5.19.

(1) Next Header: 8 bits; identifies the type of header immediately following the "Routing" header, see the protocol type definitions in Appendix A of this book.
(2) Header Extension Length: 8 bit unsigned integer; the length of the "Routing" header in octets, excluding the previous octet.
(3) Routing Type: 8 bit identifier; identifies the variable of a specific route.
(4) Segments Left: 8 bit unsigned integer; the number of remaining segments, i.e., the number of intermediate nodes that still need to be visited and are explicitly listed before reaching the final destination. This is essentially a pointer to the next address.
(5) Type-Specific Data: variable-length field; the format and length of the data are determined by the routing type, and the length of the "Routing" header must be a multiple of octets.

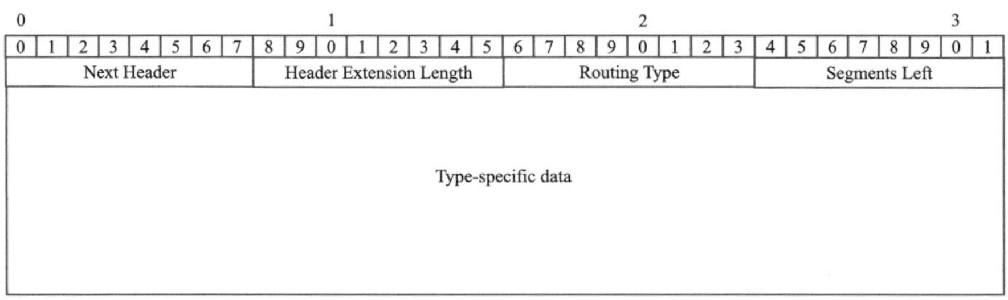

Fig. 5.19 Routing header

If a node encounters an unrecognizable "Routing" header when processing the received message, the behavior of the node is determined by the value of "Segments Left", as described below.

(1) If the value of "Segments Left" is 0, the node must ignore the "Routing" header and continue to process the next header in the datagram, the Type of which is identified by the "Next Header" field in the "Routing" header.
(2) If the value of "Segments Left" is not 0, the node must discard the datagram and send an ICMP Parameter Problem, Code 0 message to the source address of the datagram, with the pointer pointing to the unrecognizable routing type.
(3) If, after processing the "Routing" header of the received message, an intermediate node determines that the message will be forwarded to a link with an MTU smaller than the length of the message, it must discard the datagram. The node must also send an "Internet Control Message Protocol (ICMP) Packet Too Big" message to the source address of the datagram.

The allocation guidelines for the IPv6 "Routing" header can be found in RFC5871 [14].

The IPv6 Segment Routing Header (SRH) is a type of routing extension header as shown in Fig. 5.20 (RFC8402 [15], RFC8754 [16], RFC8986 [17]).

(1) Next Header: 8 bits; identifies the type of header immediately following the "Routing" header, see the protocol type definitions in Appendix A of this book.
(2) Header Extension Length: 8 bits; the length of the "Routing" header in octets, excluding the previous octet.
(3) Routing Type: 8 bits; the value is 4.

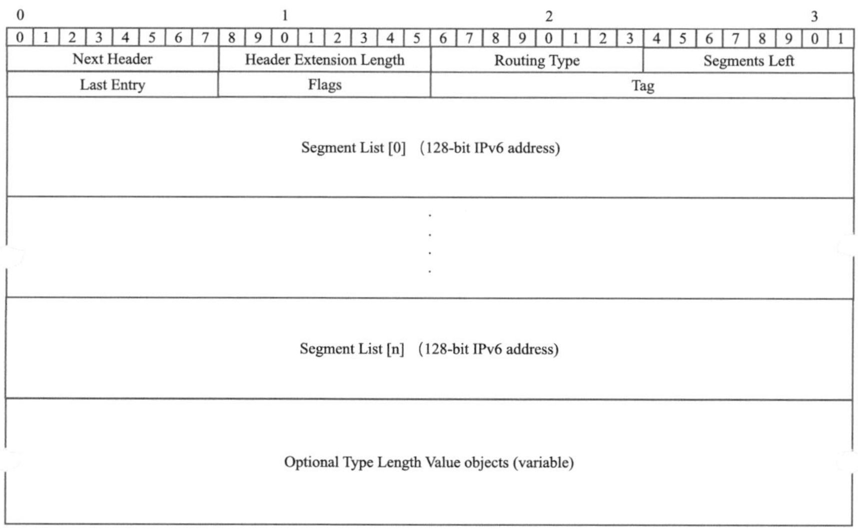

Fig. 5.20 SRH

Fig. 5.21 Flags

0	1	2	3	4	5	6	7
U	U	U	U	U	U	U	U

(4) Segment Left: 8 bits; using the definition of the "Routing" header, as above.
(5) Last Entry: 8 bits; an index starting from 0, pointing to the last entry of the segmented route.
(6) Flags: 8 bits; the currently defined flags are shown in Fig. 5.21.

Where U means unused and reserved; U must be 0 when sent, ignored when received.

(7) Tag: 16 bits; marks the datagram as a certain category, i.e., datagrams sharing the same set of attributes. If the tag is not used, the sender must set the tag to 0. If the tag is not used during the processing of the segmented routing header, it should be ignored. According to the current standard, the tag should not be used when processing the segment identifier (SID) (may be different in the future).
(8) Segment List [0, n]: Variable length, each element is 128 bits, representing the nth 128-bit IPv6 address. The segment list starts from the last IPv6 address. That is, the first element of the segment list (Segment List [0]) is the last source routing policy, the second element (Segment List [1]) is the penultimate source routing policy, and so on.
(9) Optional Type Length Value (TLV) Objects (variable): Variable length; TLV provides metadata for segment processing. The only currently defined TLV is the hash-based message authentication code (HMAC) and "Padding TLV". When processing SID, all TLVs should be ignored unless specifically configured locally. Therefore, support for TLV and HMAC is optional. It should be noted that: if a router or computer supports the processing of TLV, it must support the processing of "Padding TLV". When processing TLV at the endpoints of segmented routing, the TLV must be fully contained within the SRH content determined by the "extended header length". Detection of TLV beyond the boundary of the "extended header length" of SRH needs to generate ICMP parameter problems, code 0.

5. *"Fragment" Header*

The initiator of an IPv6 packet uses the "Fragment" header to send datagrams larger than the path MTU to its destination address (note: unlike IPv4, IPv6 only allows source nodes to fragment datagrams, not routers on the transmission path). The "Fragment" header is identified by the "Next Header" value 44 in the previous header and has the following format, as shown in Fig. 5.22.

(1) Next Header: 8 bits; identifies the type of the fragmentable part of the original datagram of the initial header, using the same value as the IPv4 field.
(2) Reserved: 8 bits; reserved field, initialized to 0 by the sender, ignored when received.

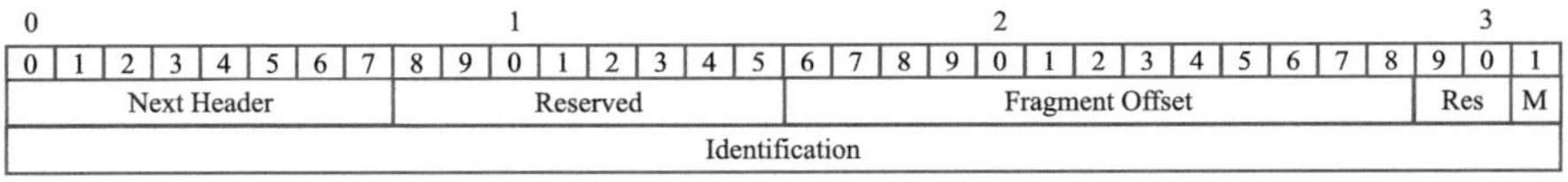

Fig. 5.22 "Fragment" header

(3) Fragment Offset: 13-bit unsigned integer; the offset value is in units of octets, indicating the fragment data relative to the start of this header.
(4) Reserved Field (Res): 2 bits; reserved field, initialized to 0 by the sender, ignored when received.
(5) More Fragments (M): 1 bit; 1 = more fragments, 0 = last fragment.
(6) Identification: 32 bits; see the description below.

To send datagrams larger than the MTU allowed on its path to the target, the source node can fragment the datagram, send each fragment as a separate datagram, and reassemble at the receiving node.

For datagrams to be fragmented, the source node generates an "Identification" value. The "Identification" value must be different from any other datagram recently sent with the same source–destination address pair. If there is a "Routing" header, the destination address here is the destination address of the final destination node. If the waiting time exceeds the transmission time of the datagram from the source node to the destination node or the waiting time for the datagram to be reassembled, it can be considered that this waiting time is not recent. In fact, the source node does not need to know the lifetime of the maximum datagram, but can meet this requirement by using an algorithm with a low reuse frequency (RFC7739 [18]).

The initial unfragmented datagram is called the original datagram, which consists of three parts, as shown in Fig. 5.23.

(1) Common Fragment Headers (Per-Fragment Headers): The "Common Fragment Headers" must include the IPv6 header and any extension headers that must be processed by each node on the path to the destination node, i.e., the headers related to the "Routing" header (if present) and the "Hop-by-Hop Options" header (if present), excluding other extension headers.
(2) Extension and Upper-Layer Headers: The "Extension and Upper-layer Headers" are all other extension headers not included in the "Common Fragment Headers". For this purpose, the Encapsulating Security Payload (ESP) is not considered an extension header. Upper-layer headers include TCP, UDP, IPv4, IPv6, ICMPv6, and ESP, etc.

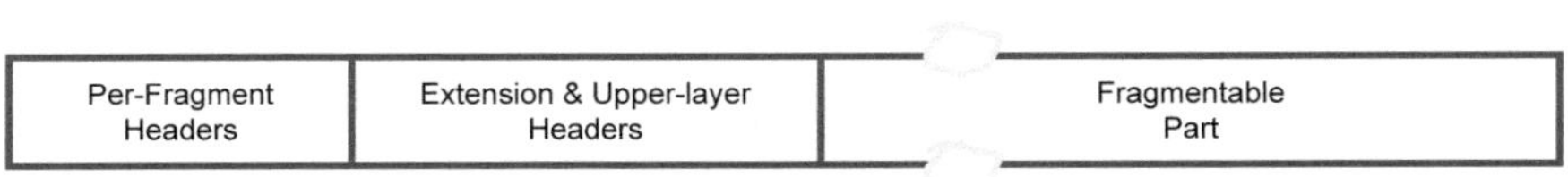

Fig. 5.23 Original data packet

(3) Fragmentable Part: This includes the part after the upper-layer headers, or any part after the "Next Header" value is "No Next Header".

The fragmentable part of the original data packet will be fragmented. The length of the fragment must be chosen so that the resulting fragment packet length is suitable for the MTU along the path to the destination node. Except for the last one ("the rightmost"), each complete fragment is a multiple of octets. Fragments are transmitted in separate fragment packets, as shown in Fig. 5.24 for the original data packet.

The data packet after fragmentation is shown in Fig. 5.25.

The first fragment packet consists of the following parts.

(1) The "Common Fragment Header" of the Original Data Packet: The "payload length" of the original IPv6 header is changed to only include the length of this fragment packet (excluding the length of the IPv6 header itself), and the "next header" field of the "common fragment header" is changed to 44.
(2) The fragment header contains the following parts.

   ① The value of the "Next Header", used to identify the first header after the "common fragment header" of the original data packet.

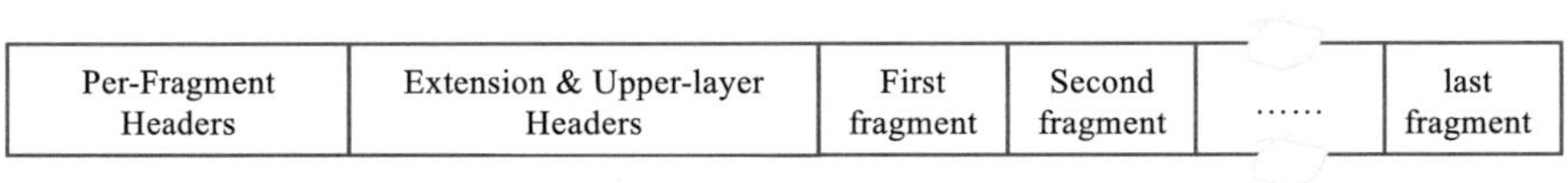

Fig. 5.24 Original data packet (Details)

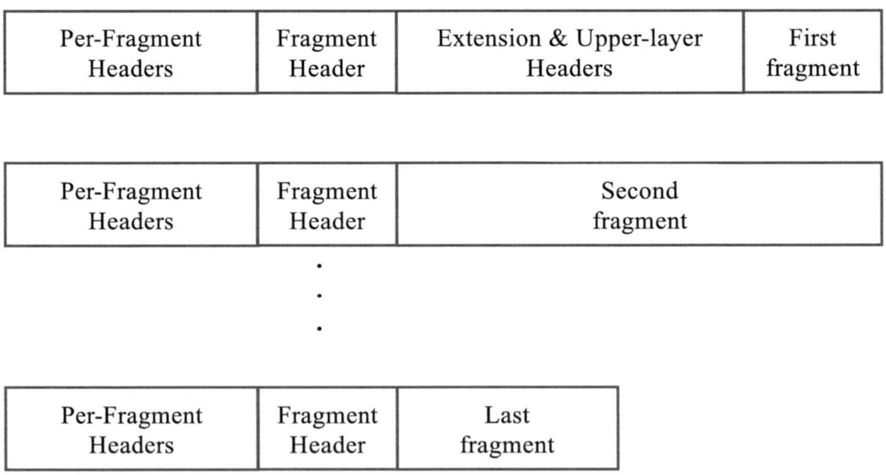

Fig. 5.25 Fragmented datagram (Details)

② "Fragment offset", this is the offset relative to the first fragment of the original data packet, in units of octets, the fragment offset of the first ("leftmost") fragment is 0.
③ flag = 1, because this is the first fragment.
④ The identifier generated for the original data packet.

(3) Extension Headers (if any) and Higher-level Headers: These headers must be located in the first fragment. Note: This will limit the size of the higher-level headers to the smallest MTU on the transmission path.
(4) The Payload Part of the First Fragment: the data payload of the first fragment.

The subsequent fragment packets consist of the following parts.

(1) The "Common Fragment Header" of the Original Packet: The "payload length" of the original IPv6 header is changed to only include the length of this fragment packet (excluding the length of the IPv6 header itself), and the "Next Header" field of the "common fragment header" is changed to 44.
(2) The fragment header contains the following parts.

① The value of the "Next Header", used to identify the first header after the "common fragment header" of the original data packet.
② "Fragment offset", relative to the original data packet, the offset at the beginning of this fragment, in units of octets, the fragment offset of the first ("leftmost") fragment is 0.
③ If the fragment is the last one ("rightmost"), then M flag = 0, otherwise M flag = 1.
④ The identifier generated for the original data packet.

(3) The fragment itself.

No fragment overlapping with any other fragment created from the original data packet should be created. At the destination node, the fragmented datagrams will be reassembled into the original unfragmented form, as shown in Fig. 5.26.

Control the reassembly according to the following rules:

(1) The original data packet is only reassembled for fragmented data packets with the same source address, destination address, and fragmentation identifier.
(2) The "common fragment header" of the reassembled data packet undergoes the following two changes.

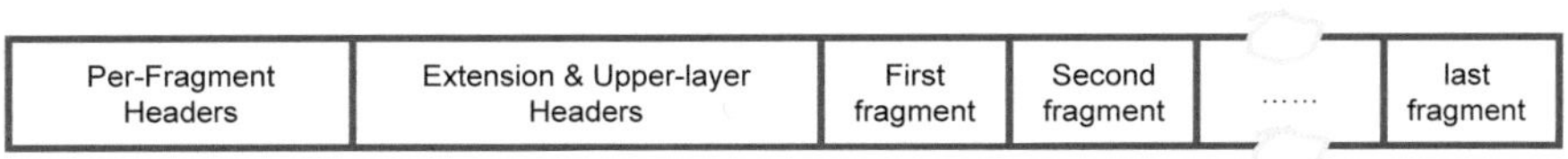

Fig. 5.26 Reassembled original data packet (Details)

① The "Next Header" field of the last header of the "common fragment header" is obtained from the "Next Header" field of the "Fragment header" of the first fragment.

② The "payload length" of the reassembled data packet is calculated based on the length of the "common fragment header" and the length and "fragment offset" of the last fragment. The formula for calculating the payload length of the reassembled original data packet is

$$\text{PL.orig} = \text{PL.first} - \text{FL.first} - 8 + (8 \times \text{FO.last}) + \text{FL.last}$$

where PL.orig is the "payload length" field of the reassembled data packet; PL.first is the "payload length" field of the first fragment packet; FL.first is the fragment length after the fragment header of the first fragment packet; FO.last is the "fragment offset" field of the fragment header of the last fragment packet; FL.last is the fragment length after the fragment header of the last fragment packet.

The "fragmentable part" of the constructed reassembled data packet comes from the fragment after the fragment header in each fragment data packet. The length of each fragment is calculated by subtracting the length of the IPv6 header and the header of the fragment itself from the "payload length" of the packet; their relative positions in the "fragmentable part" are calculated based on the value of the "fragment offset".

(1) The "Fragment" header does not exist in the reassembled data packet.
(2) If the fragment is a complete data packet (i.e., the "fragment offset" field and M flag are 0), then it does not need to be further reassembled and should be treated as a fully reassembled data packet (i.e., update the "Next Header", adjust the "payload length", delete the "fragment header", etc.). Any other fragments matching this data packet (i.e., with the same IPv6 source address, IPv6 destination address, and fragment identifier) should be processed independently.

The following error situations may occur when reassembling fragment data packets.

(1) If the number of fragments received is insufficient to complete the reassembly of the data packet within 60 s after receiving the first data packet, the reassembly of this data packet must be abandoned, and all fragments of this packet must be discarded. If the first fragment (i.e., the fragment with a fragment offset of 0) has been received, an ICMP "fragment reassembly time exceeded" message should be sent to the source address of this fragment.
(2) If the fragment length derived from the "payload length" field is not an integer multiple of octets, and the M flag of this fragment is 1, then the fragment must be discarded. An "ICMP parameter problem" message with a code of 0 should be sent to the source address of the fragment. This message should point to the "payload length" field of the fragment packet. The fragment is invalid due to the mismatch between its length and the M flag.

(3) If the "payload length" of the data packet reassembled from the fragment length and fragment offset exceeds 65,535 octets, then this fragment must be discarded. An "ICMP parameter problem" message with a code of 0 should be sent to the source address of this fragment. The message must point to the "payload length" field of the fragment packet.
(4) If the first fragment does not contain all headers up to the "Upper-layer Header", that fragment must be discarded, and an "ICMP parameter problem" message with a code of 3 should be sent to the source address that sent the fragment. The "pointer" value in this message should be set to 0.
(5) If any fragment of the reassembly overlaps with any other fragment being reassembled for the same datagram, the reassembly of that datagram must be abandoned, all received fragments of that datagram must be discarded, and an ICMP error message should not be sent.
(6) It should be noted that: the network may resend fragments, so these completely identical fragment messages should not be considered as overlapping fragments. In the implementation process, you can choose to detect this situation and discard completely identical duplicate fragment messages, while retaining one of them for reassembly.

The following situations are not expected to occur frequently, but if they do occur, they should not be considered as errors.

(1) The number and content of headers before the fragment headers of different fragments of the same original datagram may be different. Regardless of what headers are stored before the fragment headers in each fragment, they need to be processed before reassembly. Only the headers in the fragment message with a fragment offset of 0 will be retained in the reassembled datagram.
(2) The value of "Next Header" in the fragment headers of different fragments of the same original datagram may be different. Only the headers of the fragment message with a fragment offset of 0 will be retained in the reassembled datagram.

Other fields in the IPv6 header may also change between different fragments during reassembly. If the information provided by the fragment with a fragment offset of 0 is insufficient, these fields may provide other instructions. For example, RFC3168 [19] describes how to combine explicit congestion notification (ECN) bits from different fragments to derive the ECN bits of the reassembled datagram.

6. *Destination Options Header*

The "Destination Options" header is used to carry optional information that only needs to be checked and processed by the destination node of the datagram. If the value of "Next Header" in the current header is 60, then the "Destination Options" header follows. The "Destination Options" header has the following format, as shown in Fig. 5.27.

(1) Next Header: 8 bits; defines the type of header immediately following the "Destination Options" header, using the same values as the IPv4 protocol field.

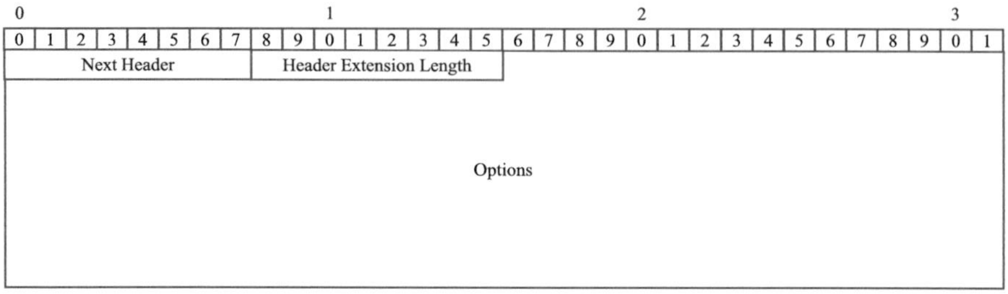

Fig. 5.27 "Destination Options" header format

(2) Header Extension Length: 8-bit unsigned integer; the length of the "Destination Options" header, in octets, excluding the previous octet.
(3) Options: variable length; its length makes the complete "Destination Options" header an integer multiple of octets, containing one or more TLV encoded options.

There are two methods to encode optional destination information in IPv6 datagrams, and the choice of which method to use depends on the operation required by the destination node when it does not understand the optional information.

(1) As a separate extension header. If the required operation is for the destination node to discard the datagram, and an "ICMP Unrecognizable" type message needs to be sent to the source address of the datagram (cannot be sent when the destination address of the datagram is a multicast address), the optional destination information can be used as a separate extension header. The "Fragment" header and "Authentication" header are examples of separate extension headers.
(2) As an option in the "Destination Options" header. If the required operation is for the destination node to discard the datagram, and an "ICMP Unrecognizable" type message needs to be sent to the source address of the datagram (cannot be sent when the destination address of the datagram is a multicast address), the optional destination information can also be encoded as a "Destination Options" header. The encoding of the "Destination Options" header type has the highest 2 bits as 11. The choice may depend on such factors as occupying fewer octets, or producing better alignment or more efficient parsing. Note: If any other operation is required, the optional destination information must be encoded as a "Destination Options" header, with its option type (Option Type) specified in its first and second bits as 00, 01, or 10 to specify the required operation.

7. *No Next Header*

The value 59 in the "Next Header" field of the IPv6 header or any extension header indicates that there is nothing after this header. If the "Payload Length" field of the IPv6 header indicates that there are octets after the header with a "Next Header" field of 59, these octets must be ignored, and in the case of forwarding the message, these octets need to be passed on without change.

5.3.3 Data Packet Size Issue

IPv6 requires that every link in the Internet be able to support an MTU of 1280 octets or larger, known as the IPv6 minimum link MTU. On any link that cannot transmit a 1280 octet packet, fragmentation and reassembly must be provided at a level below IPv6 for that specific link.

Links with configurable MTU (for example, PPP links defined by RFC1661 [20]) must be configured to support an MTU of 1280 octets, and it is recommended to configure an MTU of 1500 octets or larger to accommodate possible encapsulations (i.e., tunnels) without causing fragmentation of IPv6 packets.

An IPv6 node must be able to receive data packets as large as the MTU allowed by each link directly connected to the node.

It is strongly recommended that IPv6 nodes support the Path MTU Discovery Protocol defined by RFC8201 [21] in order to discover and utilize Path MTUs larger than 1280 octets. For the smallest IPv6 implementations (for example, in read-only memory (ROM) used to boot devices), it can simply limit itself to sending packets no larger than 1280 octets and omit the Path MTU Discovery feature.

To send data packets larger than the Path MTU, a node can use the IPv6 Fragmentation Header to fragment the data packet at the sending end and reassemble it at the destination node. However, this fragmentation technique is not encouraged for any application that can adjust its packet size to fit the Path MTU measured (i.e., not less than 1280 octets).

An IPv6 node must be able to receive fragmented data packets, which can reach a size of 1500 octets after reassembly. It is permissible for a node to receive fragmented data packets that exceed 1500 octets after reassembly. However, unless it can be ensured that the destination node has the ability to reassemble larger data packets, the fragmentation of Path MTU data packets should not exceed 1500 octets.

5.3.4 Flow Label

The 20-bit "Flow Label" field in the IPv6 header is used by the sender to mark several data packets that need to be processed in the network as a single flow.

RFC6437 [22] defines the current usage specifications for the IPv6 Flow Label.

5.3.5 Traffic Type

The 8-bit "Traffic Class" field in the IPv6 header is used for network traffic management. Note: The traffic class value of a data packet or data packet fragment received by a node may differ from the value sent by the sender of the data packet.

RFC2474 [4] and RFC3168 [19] specify the current usage specifications for the Traffic Class field for Differentiated Services and Explicit Congestion Notification.

5.3.6 High-Level Protocol

1. *High-Level Checksum*

In order to be used on IPv6, any transport protocol or other high-level protocol that includes the calculation of IP address checksums must be modified to handle 128-bit IPv6 addresses instead of 32-bit IPv4 addresses. Figure 5.28 shows the pseudo headers of TCP (RFC793 [23]) and UDP (RFC768 [24]) containing IPv6 addresses.

The handling of pseudo headers in TCP and UDP is as follows:

(1) If the IPv6 datagram contains a routing header, the destination address used in the pseudo header is the destination address of the final destination. At the initial source node, this address will be in the last element of the routing header. At the destination node, this address is in the "Destination Address" field of the IPv6 header.
(2) The "Next Header" in the pseudo header is used to identify the upper-layer protocol (for example, 6 represents TCP, 17 represents UDP). However, if there is an extension header between the IPv6 header and the "Upper-layer Header", this value is different from the "Next Header" value in the IPv6 header.
(3) The length of the upper-layer message in the pseudo header is the sum of the length of the upper-layer header and the data (for example, the TCP header plus TCP data). Some upper-layer protocols carry their own length information (for example, the length field in the UDP header). For such protocols, the length of the upper-layer message is the length in the pseudo header. For other protocols that do not carry their own length information (such as TCP), in this case, the length information used in the pseudo header is the payload length from the IPv6 header minus the length of any extension headers between the IPv6 header and the upper-layer header.

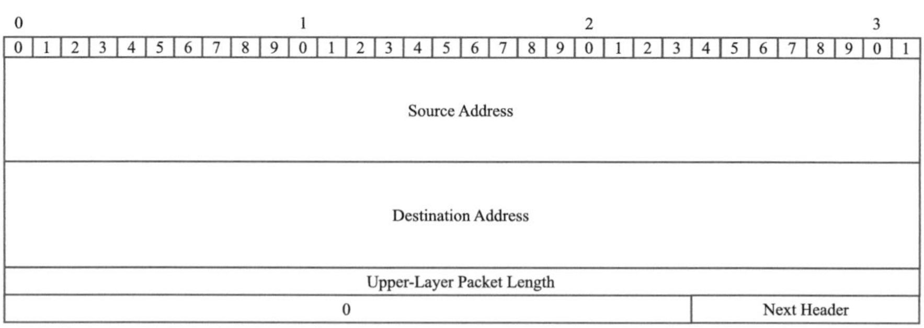

Fig. 5.28 TCP and UDP pseudo header

(4) Unlike IPv4, the default behavior of UDP datagrams initiated by IPv6 nodes is that the "UDP checksum" is mandatory. That is, whenever a UDP datagram is sent, the IPv6 node must calculate the "UDP checksum" on the datagram and pseudo header. If the result of this calculation is 0, it must be changed to hexadecimal FFFF and placed in the UDP header. IPv6 receiving nodes must discard UDP datagrams containing a checksum of 0 and record this error
(5) As an exception to the default behavior, using UDP as a tunnel encapsulation protocol can enable the "UDP checksum" 0 mode for sending and/or receiving on specific ports (or sets of ports). Any node implementing the "UDP checksum" 0 mode must follow the requirements specified in the applicability statement for IPv6 UDP datagrams using the "UDP checksum" 0 mode as defined by RFC6936 [25].

The IPv6 version of ICMP includes the above pseudo header in the calculation of the "checksum". This is a change from the IPv4 version of ICMP, which does not include the pseudo header in its "checksum". The reason for the change in the IPv6 version is to protect ICMP from the impact of transmission errors or corruption in the IPv6 headers it relies on (which is different from IPv4). The value of the "Next Header" field in the ICMP pseudo header is 58, to identify the IPv6 version of ICMP.

2. *Maximum Datagram Lifetime*

Unlike IPv4, IPv6 nodes are not required to enforce a maximum datagram "lifetime". This is why the IPv4 "lifetime" field is renamed "Hop Limit" in IPv6. In practice, there are few IPv4 packets that comply with the datagram "lifetime", so it does not affect actual use. Any higher-level protocols that rely on the Internet layer (whether IPv4 or IPv6) to limit the datagram "lifetime" should be upgraded to provide their own mechanisms to detect and discard outdated datagrams.

3. *Maximum High-Level Payload Size*

When calculating the maximum payload size available for high-level data, high-level protocols must consider the larger IPv6 header relative to the IPv4 header. For example, in IPv4, the "maximum segment size" (MSS) option of TCP is calculated as the maximum datagram size (default value or value known through path MTU discovery) minus 40 octets (20 octets of the minimum length IPv4 header and 20 octets of the minimum length TCP header). When using TCP over IPv6, the MSS must be calculated as the value of the maximum datagram minus 60 octets, because the minimum length IPv6 header (i.e., an IPv6 header without extension headers) is 20 octets larger than the minimum length IPv4 header.

4. *Response to Datagrams with Routing Headers*

When a high-level protocol responds to a datagram containing a routing header and needs to send one or more packets, the response packet must not include a corresponding routing header automatically derived from the received routing header. The only exception to this is when the source address and the integrity and authenticity of the routing header of the received packet have been verified (for example, by using an authenticated header verified received packet). In other words, when responding to a datagram with a routing header, only the following types of packets are allowed to be sent.

(1) Response packets without routing headers.
(2) Response packets with routing headers that are not automatically derived from the received routing headers (for example, routing headers provided by local configuration).
(3) Response packets with routing headers automatically derived from the received routing headers are only allowed to be sent when the node has verified the integrity and authenticity of the datagram source address and routing header.

5.3.7 Security Considerations

From the perspective of basic datagram format and transmission, IPv6 has similar security to IPv4. These security issues include the following.

(1) Eavesdropping, where nodes on the path can observe each IPv6 datagram (including content and metadata).
(2) Replay, where an attacker records a series of datagrams from the network and sends them to the original receiving node.
(3) Datagram insertion, where an attacker forges datagrams with some selected attributes and injects them into the network.
(4) Datagram deletion, where an attacker removes datagrams from the network.
(5) Datagram modification, where an attacker removes datagrams from the line, modifies them, and re-injects them into the network.
(6) Man-in-the-middle (MITM) attacks on communication streams, acting as a receiver for the source node and as a sender for the receiving node.
(7) Denial of service (DoS) attacks, where an attacker sends a large amount of legitimate traffic to the destination node to prevent it from providing normal service.

By using RFC4301 [26] the defined "Security Architecture for the Internet Protocol" can protect IPv6 datagrams from eavesdropping, replay, datagram insertion, datagram modification, and MITM attacks. In addition, higher-level protocols, such as the Transport Layer Security Protocol (RFC8446 [27]) or the Secure Shell (SSH) Protocol (RFC4251 [28]) can be used to protect applications running on IPv6.

There is no mechanism at the IPv6 protocol layer that can prevent DoS attacks.

The IPv6 address space is significantly larger than the IPv4 address space, making it more difficult to scan the address space on the Internet or even on a single network link (for example, a local area network), see RFC7707 [29].

Because IPv6 does not allow the use of address translation technology, it is expected that more IPv6 nodes will be seen on the Internet than IPv4, which will raise some additional privacy issues, such as making it easier to distinguish end nodes, see RFC7721 [30].

The design of the IPv6 extension header architecture, while increasing flexibility, also brings new security challenges. Any new extension header design's security issues need to be carefully studied, including how the new extension headers work and how they are compatible with existing extension headers, see RFC7045 [31].

5.4 ICMPv6

RFC4443 [32] defines the Internet Control Message Protocol (ICMPv6) for IPv6, whose IPv6 "Next Header" value is 58. ICMPv6 is a modification of the IPv4 Internet Control Message Protocol defined by RFC792 [7].

The protocol constants related to time-out in ICMPv6 are seen in Appendix H.

5.4.1 IPv6 Control Message Format

IPv6 nodes use ICMPv6 to report errors encountered in processing datagrams, as well as to perform other IP layer functions, such as diagnostics (ICMPv6 "ping"). ICMPv6 is a component of the basic IPv6 protocol (defining messages and actions to be taken), and all IPv6 nodes must fully implement ICMPv6.

1. *General Message Format*

Each ICMPv6 message is preceded by an IPv6 header and zero or more IPv6 extension headers. The ICMPv6 header is identified by the "Next Header" value of the previous header being 58 (this is different from the value used to identify IPv4 ICMP).

ICMPv6 messages have the following general format, as shown in Fig. 5.29.

(1) Type Field: 8 bits; represents the type of the message, its value determines the format of the corresponding data.
(2) Code Field: 8 bits; depends on the message Type, it is used to further describe the message.

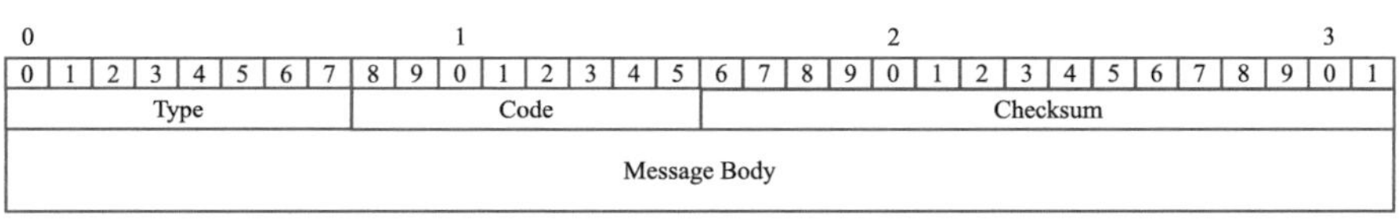

Fig. 5.29 ICMPv6 message format

Table 5.7 ICMPv6 error messages

Type	Description
1	Destination unreachable
2	Packet too big
3	Time exceeded
4	Parameter problem
100	Reserved for internal experiment
101	Reserved for internal experiment
127	Reserved for extension of ICMPv6 error messages

(3) Checksum Field: 16 bits; used to detect the corruption of the IPv6 header and data in ICMPv6.

ICMPv6 messages are divided into two categories: error messages and informational messages. Error messages are identified by the first bit in the "Type" field being 0, so the type values for error messages are 0–127, while the type values for informational messages are 128–255.

The ICMPv6 error messages are shown in Table 5.7.

The ICMPv6 informational messages are shown in Table 5.8

The type field values of 100, 101, 200, and 201 are reserved for internal experiments and are not suitable for general use. Any large-scale deployment should use officially defined values.

The type field values of 127 and 255 are used for future extensions of the Type field. Currently, no special handling is required for datagrams with this field set to 127 and 255.

In summary, the purpose of sending ICMPv6 error messages is to help the higher-level protocol of the sender of the original message that caused the ICMPv6 error message to determine the cause of the error.

2. *Message Source Address Determination*

The node sending the ICMPv6 message must confirm the source and destination addresses in the IPv6 header before calculating the checksum. If the node has multiple unicast addresses, it must choose the source address of the message according to the following requirements.

Table 5.8 ICMPv6 informational messages

Type	Description
128	Echo request
129	Echo reply
200	Reserved for internal experiment
201	Reserved for internal experiment
255	Reserved for extension of ICMPv6 informational messages

(1) If the message is sent to a unicast address of the responding node, the source address of the responding node's reply must be that address.
(2) If the message is sent to any other address, such as a multicast address, an anycast address used by the node, or a unicast address not belonging to the node, the source address of the ICMPv6 datagram sent by the node must be a unicast address belonging to the node. This source address should be selected according to the same rules used to generate other messages for the given destination node. However, it can also use other methods to select the source address of ICMPv6, if this can make the destination address of ICMPv6 communicate better with this source address.

3. *Message Checksum Calculation*

The checksum is the 16-bit one's complement of the one's complement sum of the entire ICMPv6 message, starting with the ICMPv6 message Type field, and prepended with a "pseudo-header" of IPv6 header fields. The Next Header value used in the pseudo-header is 58. Note that the inclusion of a pseudo-header in the ICMPv6 checksum is a change from IPv4.

For computing the checksum, the checksum field is first set to zero.

4. *Message Processing Rules*

The following rules must be followed to process ICMPv6 messages.

(1) If the destination node receives an ICMPv6 error message of an unknown Type, the message must be passed to the higher-level protocol that issued the datagram causing the error, as this can be determined.
(2) If the destination node receives an ICMPv6 informational message of an unknown Type, the message must be silently discarded.
(3) Each ICMPv6 error message (value of the Type field <128) must include as much of the IPv6 datagram causing the error as possible without causing the error message datagram to exceed the minimum IPv6 MTU.
(4) If the network layer protocol is required to pass to the higher-level process through the ICMPv6 error message, the type of the higher-level protocol (contained in the body of the ICMPv6 error message) should be extracted from the original datagram. This extracted information should then be passed to the corresponding higher-level process to handle the related error. If the type of the higher-level protocol cannot be detected from the ICMPv6 message, the ICMPv6 message should be silently discarded after processing at the IPv6 layer.

① An example is when the number of extension headers contained in the ICMPv6 message exceeds the usual situation, the higher-level protocol is discarded to meet the requirements of the minimum IPv6 path MTU.

② Another example is an ICMPv6 message with an ESP extension header. Due to the truncation or the state required to decrypt the datagram is not available, the higher-level protocol cannot be obtained by decrypting the original datagram.

(5) The generation of ICMPv6 error messages is not allowed when the following types of messages are received.

① ICMPv6 error messages.
② ICMPv6 redirect messages.
③ Datagrams sent to IPv6 multicast addresses (this rule has two exceptions: to allow path MTU discovery to apply to IPv6 multicast, when a "Packet Too Big" message is received; when the received ICMPv6 is a parameter problem message, code 2, the highest two bits of its option Type are set to 10, reporting an unrecognized IPv6 option).
④ Datagrams sent as link-layer multicast (this rule has two exceptions: to allow path MTU discovery to apply to IPv6 multicast, when a "Packet Too Big" message is received; when the received ICMPv6 is a parameter problem message, code 2, the highest two bits of its option type are set to 10, reporting an unrecognized IPv6 option).
⑤ Datagrams sent as link-layer broadcast (this rule has two exceptions: to allow path MTU discovery to apply to IPv6 multicast, when a "Packet Too Big" message is received; when the received ICMPv6 is a parameter problem message, code 2, the highest two bits of its option type are set to 10, reporting an unrecognized IPv6 option).
⑥ Datagrams from a single node that cannot be uniquely identified by the source address. For example, from an undefined IPv6 address, an IPv6 multicast address, or an IPv6 anycast address.

(6) In order to limit the overhead of bandwidth and forwarding costs due to the initiation of ICMPv6 error messages, IPv6 nodes must limit the rate of initiating ICMPv6 error messages. The following may occur when the initiating node of the error data message fails to notice that it will generate a flow of ICMPv6 error messages.

① The recommended method to implement rate limiting is to use a token bucket to limit the average transmission rate N. Depending on the specific requirements, N can be "the number of datagrams per second", "the percentage of link bandwidth occupied by datagrams", or "allowing a maximum burst of B error messages".
② It is not recommended to use rate limiting mechanisms that cannot cope with burst traffic (for example, "traceroute"). For example, simply using a timer that limits one error message every T milliseconds (even if T is very small, it is not acceptable).
③ Rate limiting parameters should be configurable. In the case of token bucket implementation, the optimal default value depends on the device to be deployed (for example, whether it is a high-end router or an embedded host). For example, in the case of small/medium devices, possible default values are $B = 10$, $N = 10$ datagrams per second.

5.4.2 *ICMPv6 Error Messages*

1. *Destination Unreachable Message*

   The Destination Unreachable message, as part of the IPv6 header data, is formatted as shown in Fig. 5.30.

   (1) Destination Address: 128 bits; the destination address is copied from the source address field in the IPv6 header of the calling message.
   (2) Type: 8 bits; the value is 1.
   (3) Code: 8 bits; defined as shown in Table 5.9.
   (4) Unused: 32 bits; this field is not used, the sender must initialize it to 0, and it is ignored by the receiver.

   (1) **Description**

   The Destination Unreachable Message should be generated by the router (or other source node) when it cannot deliver to the destination

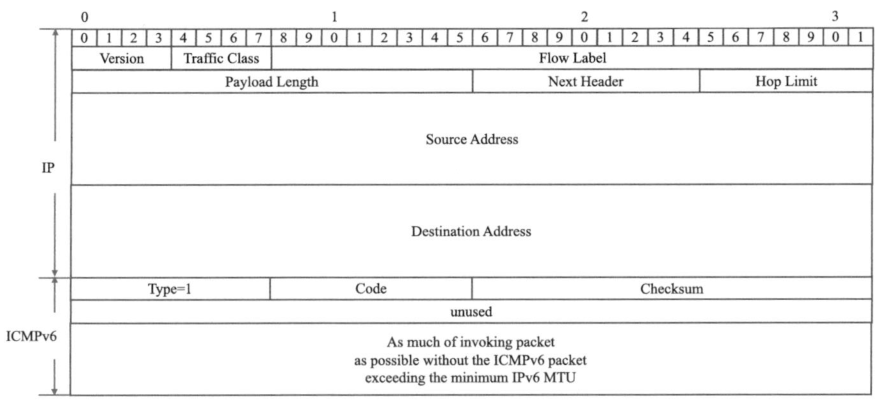

Fig. 5.30 "Destination Unreachable" message containing IPv6 header

Table 5.9 Definition of code

Code	Description
0	No route to destination
1	Communication with destination administratively prohibited
2	Beyond the scope of the source address
3	Address unreachable
4	Port unreachable
5	Source address failed ingress/egress policy
6	Reject route to destination

node for reasons other than line congestion (if datagram discarding is due to line congestion, this type of ICMPv6 message is not allowed).

If the reason for Destination Unreachable Message is the lack of a matching entry in the forwarding node's routing table (this error can only occur when the node's routing does not include the "default route"), the code field is set to 0.

If the reason for Destination Unreachable Message is that communication with the destination node is prohibited by configuration (for example, firewall filtering), the code field is set to 1.

If the reason for Destination Unreachable Message is beyond the range of the source address, the code field is set to 2. This only happens when the range of the source address is smaller than the range of the destination address. For example, the source address of the datagram is a link-local address, and the destination address is a global unicast address. At this point the datagram cannot be delivered to the destination node without leaving the range of the source address.

If the reason for Destination Unreachable Message is that it cannot be mapped to a link layer address, the code field is set to 3. For example, the IPv6 destination address cannot be resolved to the corresponding link address, or there is some link layer specific problem.

A special case of the Destination Unreachable Message code field set to 3 is the router responding to a datagram received from a point-to-point link, although the address belongs to the same subnet, but it is not the router's address. In this case, it is not allowed to resend the message to that link.

When the destination node receives a datagram, but the transport layer protocol (such as UDP) is not listening, and the transport layer protocol has no alternative way to notify the source node, the destination node should initiate a Destination Unreachable Message, and the code field is set to 4.

If the failure is due to the ingress or egress filtering policy for that source address, send Destination Unreachable Message, and the code field is set to 5.

If the reason for failure is that the destination node refuses to accept, send Destination Unreachable Message, and set the code field to 6.

Codes 5 and 6 are more refined subsets of code 1.

For security reasons, some link interfaces can be prohibited from sending ICMP Destination Unreachable Messages.

(2) **Notify the higher-level Protocol**

Nodes that receive the ICMPv6 Destination Unreachable Message, when information from the higher-level protocol can be obtained, must notify the higher-level protocol.

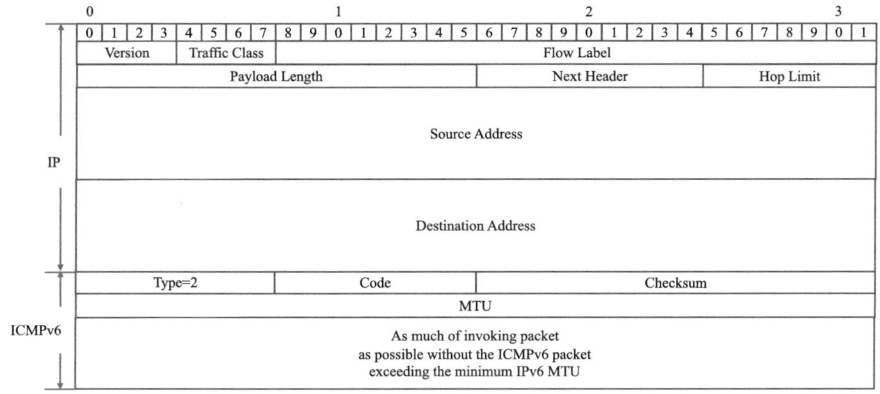

Fig. 5.31 "Packet Too Big" message containing IPv6 header

2. *Packet Too Big Message*

The Packet Too Big Message serves as the data part following the IPv6 header, as shown in Fig. 5.31.

(1) Destination Address: 128 bits; the destination address is copied from the source address field in the invoking packet's IPv6 header.
(2) Type: 8 bits; the value is 2.
(3) Code: 8 bits; the code is set to 0 by the source node and ignored by the receiving node.
(4) Maximum Transmission Unit (MTU): 32 bits; the maximum transmission unit of the next hop link.

(1) **Description**

When the size of the datagram exceeds the MTU of the exit link, the router must send a Packet Too Big Message to respond to the source node of the datagram. This message is used to implement Path MTU Discovery.

The Packet Too Big Message is an exception to the rules for initiating ICMPv6 error messages. Packet Too Big messages need to be sent for the destination address of the received datagram, whether it is a multicast address, link-layer multicast, or link-layer broadcast address.

(2) **Notify the higher-level Protocol**

A node that receives an ICMPv6 Packet Too Big Message must notify the higher-level protocol when information from the higher-level protocol can be obtained.

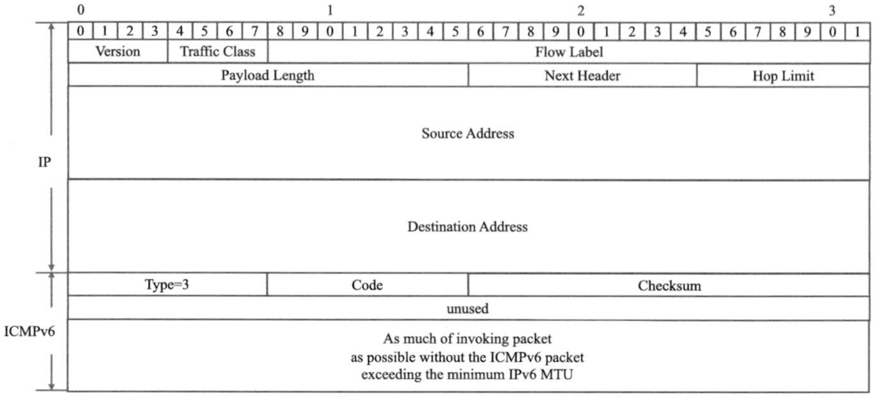

Fig. 5.32 "Time Exceeded" message containing IPv6 header

Table 5.10 "Time Exceeded" message code

Code	Description
0	Hop limit exceeded in transit
1	Fragment reassembly time exceeded

3. *Time Exceeded Message*

The Time Exceeded Message, as the data part following the IPv6 header, is shown in Fig. 5.32.

(1) Destination Address: 128 bits; the destination address is copied from the source address field in the IPv6 header of the invoking packet.
(2) Type: 8 bits; the value is 3.
(3) Code: 8 bits; the code is defined as shown in Table 5.10.

(4) Unused: 32 bits; this field is not used, the code is set to 0 by the source node and ignored by the receiving node.
(1) **Description**

If a router receives a datagram with a "hop limit" of 0, or if the router reduces the "hop limit" of the datagram by 1 to 0, it must discard the datagram and send an ICMPv6 Hop limit exceeded Message with a code of 0 to the node that generated the datagram. This indicates a routing loop or an initial "hop limit" value that is too small.

The ICMPv6 Hop limit exceeded Message of Code 1 indicates "Fragmented Datagram Reassembly" timeout.

(2) **Notify the higher-level Protocol**

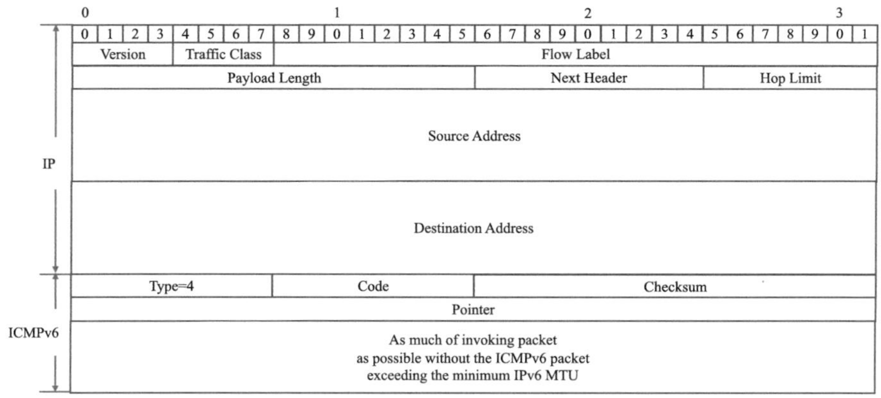

Fig. 5.33 "Parameter Problem" message format containing IPv6 header

The node that receives the ICMPv6 Time Exceeded Message must notify the higher-level protocol when the information of the higher-level protocol can be obtained.

4. *Parameter Problem Message*

The Parameter Problem Message, as the data part following the IPv6 header, is shown in Fig. 5.33.

(1) Destination Address: 128 bits; the destination address is copied from the source address field of the invoking packet's IPv6 header.
(2) Type: 8 bits; the value is 4.
(3) Code: 8 bits; the code is defined as shown in Table 5.11.

(4) Pointer: 8 bits; the detected datagram error location is identified by an octet offset. If the error field exceeds the size of the ICMPv6 error message, the pointer points to the end of the ICMPv6 datagram.
   (1) **Description**

   If an IPv6 node processing a datagram discovers a problem with a field in the IPv6 header or extension header that prevents it from processing the datagram, it must discard the datagram. The node should send an ICMPv6 Parameter Problem Message to the initiating node of the

Table 5.11 "Parameter Problem" message code

Code	Description
0	Erroneous header field encountered
1	Unrecognized next header type encountered
2	Unrecognized IPv6 option encountered

datagram. This message must indicate the type and location of the problem.

Code 1 and Code 2 are more refined subsets of Code 0.

The location of the error in the original datagram detected is identified by an octet offset.

For example, an ICMPv6 message with a "Type" field of 4, a "Code" field of 1, and a "Pointer" field of 40 indicates that the IPv6 extension header message following the original data IPv6 header contains an unrecognizable "Next Header" field value.

(2) **Notify higher-level Protocol**

The node that receives the ICMPv6 Parameter Problem Message must notify the higher-level protocol when the higher-level protocol information can be obtained.

5.4.3 *ICMPv6 Informational Messages*

1. *Echo Request Message*

The Echo Request Message serves as the data part following the IPv6 header, as shown in Fig. 5.34.

(1) Destination Address: 128 bits; the destination address can be any valid IPv6 address.
(2) Type: 8 bits; the value is 128.
(3) Code: 8 bits; the value is 0.
(4) Identification: 16 bits; the identification helps to match an Echo Response to an Echo Request, its value may be 0.

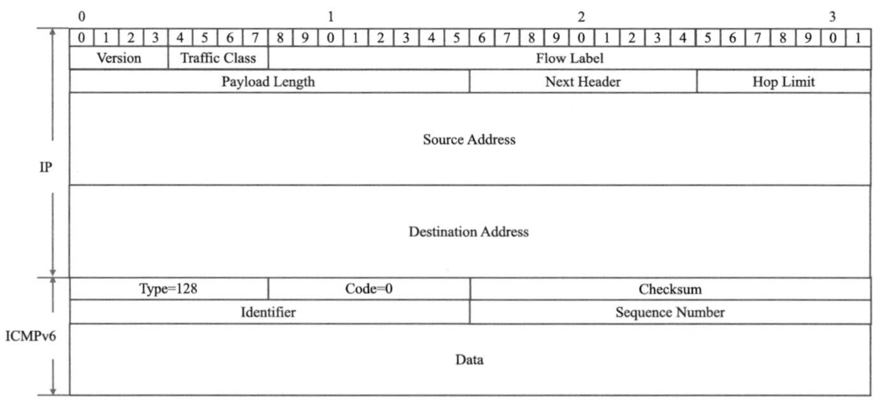

Fig. 5.34 "Echo Request" message with IPv6 header

(5) Sequence Number: 16 bits; the sequence number helps to match an Echo Response to an Echo Request, its value may be 0.
(6) Data: variable length; 0 or more octets of arbitrary data.
    (1) **Description**

    Each node must implement an ICMPv6 function that receives an Echo Request Message and initiates a corresponding Echo Response Message. Each node should implement an application layer interface that initiates an Echo Request for diagnostic purposes and receives an Echo Response.

    (2) **Notify higher-level Protocols**

    The Echo Request Message can be passed to the process receiving ICMP messages.

2. *Echo Response Message*

The Echo Response Message serves as the data part following the IPv6 header, as shown in Fig. 5.35.

(1) Destination Address: 128 bits; the destination address is copied from the source address field of the IPv6 header of the Echo Request message.
(2) Type: 8 bits; the value is 129.
(3) Code: 8 bits; the value is 0.
(4) Identification: 16 bits; comes from the identifier of the Echo Request Message.
(5) Sequence Number: 16 bits; comes from the sequence number of the Echo Request Message.
(6) Data: Variable length; comes from the data of the Echo Request Message.

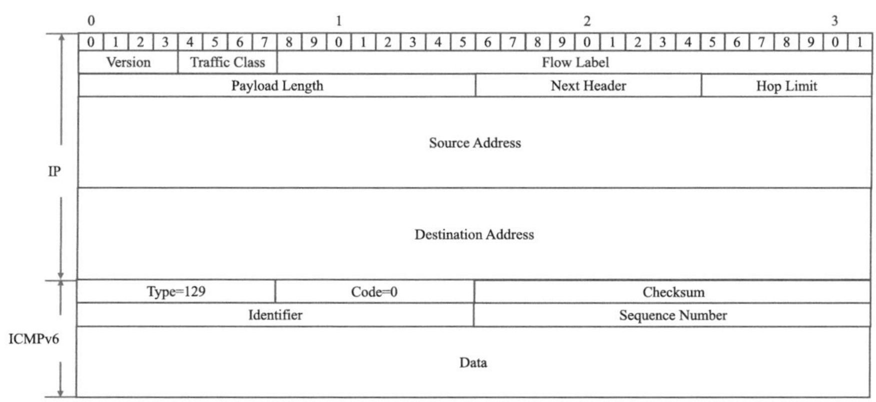

Fig. 5.35 "Echo Response" message with IPv6 header

(1) **Description**

Each node must implement the ICMPv6 function of receiving Echo Request Message and initiating the corresponding Echo Response Message. Each node should implement an application layer interface for initiating Echo Request and receiving Echo Response for diagnostic purposes.

The source address of the Echo Response Message responding to the Echo Request Message sent by the unicast address must be the same as the destination address of that Echo Request Message.

The source address of the Echo Response Message responding to the Echo Request Message sent by the multicast or anycast address must be the unicast address of the link interface that received that Echo Request Message.

The data received from the ICMPv6 Echo Request Message must be returned intact and unmodified in the Echo Response.

(2) **Notify the higher-level Protocol**

Each received Echo Response Message must be passed to the process that initiated the Echo Request Message. However, note that it is also possible to receive an Echo Response Message in the absence of a process that initiated an Echo Request Message.

Note: There is no limit to the amount of data that can be put into Echo Request and Echo Response Messages.

5.4.4 Security Considerations

1. *Authentication and Confidentiality of ICMP Messages*

The authenticity of ICMP is ensured by the IP authentication (AUTH) header or the IP ESP header. The confidentiality of ICMP can be ensured using the IP ESP header.

2. *ICMP Attacks*

ICMP messages may be subject to various attacks, a brief discussion of these attacks and their prevention is as follows:

(1) ICMP messages may be misled, causing the receiving node to believe that the source of the message is a source address different from the actual source node. This type of problem can be solved by applying the IP AUTH header.
(2) ICMP messages or responses may be misled, causing the source node to send the message or response to a destination address different from the actual one needed. This type of problem can be solved by applying the IP AUTH header or IP ESP header. AUTH provides protection against changing the source and destination addresses in the message. ESP does not provide this protection, but the calculation of the ICMP checksum includes the source and destination

addresses, and ESP protects the checksum. Therefore, the combination of the ICMP checksum and ESP can provide this protection. Note that the protection provided by ESP is not as strong as that provided by AUTH.

(3) Changes may occur in the message fields of ICMP messages, and AUTH or ESP can prevent such operations.
(4) A large number of reciprocally generated ICMP messages may be used for Denial of Service (DoS) attacks, and correctly following traffic control specifications to limit the mechanism of ICMP error messages can solve this problem.
(5) Malicious nodes can send multicast messages, which maliciously force the setting of unknown target options, but use a valid multicast source's IPv6 source address. In this way, a large number of destination nodes will send "ICMP parameter problem" messages to the multicast source, leading to DoS attacks. When forwarding multicast, routers require nodes to be on the correct multicast path, that is, close to the multicast source. Note: This type of attack can only be avoided by protecting multicast traffic. Be careful when the multicast source sends forced setting of unknown target options, because if the target option is unknown to a large number of destination nodes, the multicast source itself will become the target of a DoS attack.
(6) When ICMP messages are passed to higher-level processes, attacks may be formed on higher-level protocols (for example, TCP and UDP). It is recommended that higher-level protocols (using the information contained in the ICMP message payload) respond after some form of verification of the ICMP message. Using IPsec to protect higher-level processes can mitigate these attacks.
(7) ICMP error messages indicate that there was a problem with the network processing Internet datagrams. Note: In many cases, it cannot be expected that the error will be resolved quickly.
(8) Therefore, the consideration of ICMP error messages may need to take into account not only the received error type and code but also additional factors. These factors include the time of receiving the error message, previous network error reports, and the networking situation of the node receiving the error message.

5.5 UDP

UDP is a transport layer protocol above the IP layer, providing datagram services, defined by RFC768 [24].

This protocol provides an application with a mechanism to send messages to other programs with the least overhead. UDP is transaction-oriented and cannot guarantee the reliability and correctness of transmission. Applications that need reliable data stream transmission should use the Transmission Control Protocol.

The protocol number of UDP is 17, see Table A.1 in Appendix A.

The UDP header format is shown in Fig. 5.36.

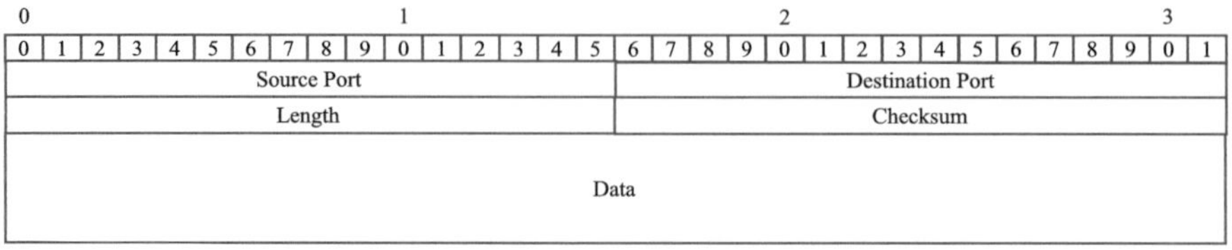

Fig. 5.36 UDP header format

(1) Source Port: 16 bits; optional field. When meaningful, it represents the port number of the sending process. The reply datagram should be sent to this port number. If not used, set to all zeros.
(2) Destination Port: 16 bits; has a meaning within the context of a particular Internet destination address.
(3) Length: 16 bits; the length of the user datagram in octets, including the UDP header and data part (this means that the minimum value of the length is 8).
(4) Checksum: 16 bits; checksum is the 16-bit one's complement of the one's complement sum of a pseudo header of information from the IP header, the UDP header, and the data, padded with zero octets at the end (if necessary) to make a multiple of two octets. This information can prevent datagrams from being routed incorrectly. This checksum process is the same as the one used in TCP.
(5) Data: variable length; data carried by UDP.

In UDP, when the port number (source port or destination port) takes a value between 0 and 1023, it is called a service port, see Table G.1 in Appendix G.

For protocol constants related to time in UDP, see Appendix H.

5.6 TCP

TCP is a transport layer protocol above the IP layer, providing a service of reliable transmission of data streams in the correct sequence, defined by RFC793 [23] and subsequent RFCs.

The protocol number of TCP is 6, see Appendix A.

5.6.1 TCP Header Format

The TCP header format is shown in Fig. 5.37.

(1) Source Port: 16 bits; source port number.
(2) Destination Port: 16 bits; destination port number.

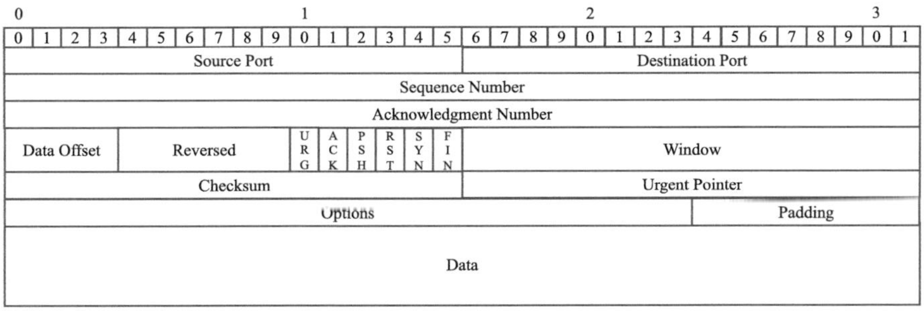

Fig. 5.37 TCP header format

(3) Sequence Number: 32 bits; the sequence number of the first data octet in this segment (except when SYN is present). If SYN is present the sequence number is the initial sequence number (ISN) and the first data octet is ISN + 1.
(4) Acknowledgment Number: 32 bits; if the ACK control bit is set this field contains the value of the next sequence number the sender of the segment is expecting to receive. Once a connection is established this is always sent.
(5) Data Offset: 4 bits; the number of 32 bit words in the TCP Header. This indicates where the data begins. The TCP header (even one including options) is an integral number of 32 bits long.
(6) Reserved: 6 bits, reserved for future use; must be 0.
(7) Control Bits: 6 bits (from left to right).

① URG: Urgent Pointer field significant
② ACK: Acknowledgment field significant
③ PSH: Push Function
④ RST: Reset the connection
⑤ SYN: Synchronize sequence numbers
⑥ FIN: No more data from sender

(8) Window: 16 bits; the number of data octets beginning with the one indicated in the acknowledgment field which the sender of this segment is willing to accept.
(9) Checksum: A 16-bit complement, composed of the sum of the pseudo header consisting of the IP header, TCP header, and data, plus the octet of padding 0, and its complement (note: padding must be done when necessary to form an even number of octets). When calculating the checksum, the "checksum" field is set to 0. The pseudo header contains the source address, destination address, protocol, and TCP length. This information can prevent misrouted datagrams. The TCP length is the length of the user datagram in units of octets, including the TCP header and data part.
(10) Urgent Pointer: 16 bits; this field passes the current value of the urgent pointer as the positive offset of the sequence number in this segment. The urgent pointer

points to the sequence number of the urgent data in the following octets. This field is only valid when URG is 1 in the segment.

(11) Options: Variable length; options may occupy the space at the end of the TCP header and are multiples of octets in length. The calculation of the checksum includes options.

(12) Padding: Variable length; filled with 0.

(13) Data: Variable length; data carried by TCP.

In TCP, port numbers (source port or destination port) are referred to as service ports when their values range from 0 to 1023, see Table G.1 in Appendix G.

Protocol constants related to time in TCP are seen in Appendix H.

5.6.2 TCP State

Theoretically, TCP is an event-driven finite state machine. Events include user OPEN, SEND, RECEIVE, CLOSE, ABORT; states include ABORT, SYN, ACK, RST, and FIN flags, as well as timeouts.

The state transitions of TCP are shown in Fig. 5.38. Note that this state diagram only explains the state changes, the operations causing events and results, and does not explain error conditions or operations unrelated to state changes. In the figure, TCB stands for transmission control block.

The finite state machine of TCP is maintained by the end system, so routers and stateless translators do not need to maintain TCP state. However, stateful translators need to maintain state in order to dynamically generate and destroy mappings between IPv4 and IPv6 addresses and TCP ports based on TCP state.

5.7 Protocol Translation

RFC7915 [33] defines the IPv4/IPv6 translation rules.

5.7.1 IPv4/IPv6 Translation Model

The translation model includes two or more network domains, connected by at least one translator for different protocols, as shown in Fig. 5.39.

1. *Applicability of the Translation Model*

The expected behavior of the translation model is as follows:

(1) The translator needs to strictly follow the conversion algorithm between IPv4 datagrams and IPv6 datagrams.

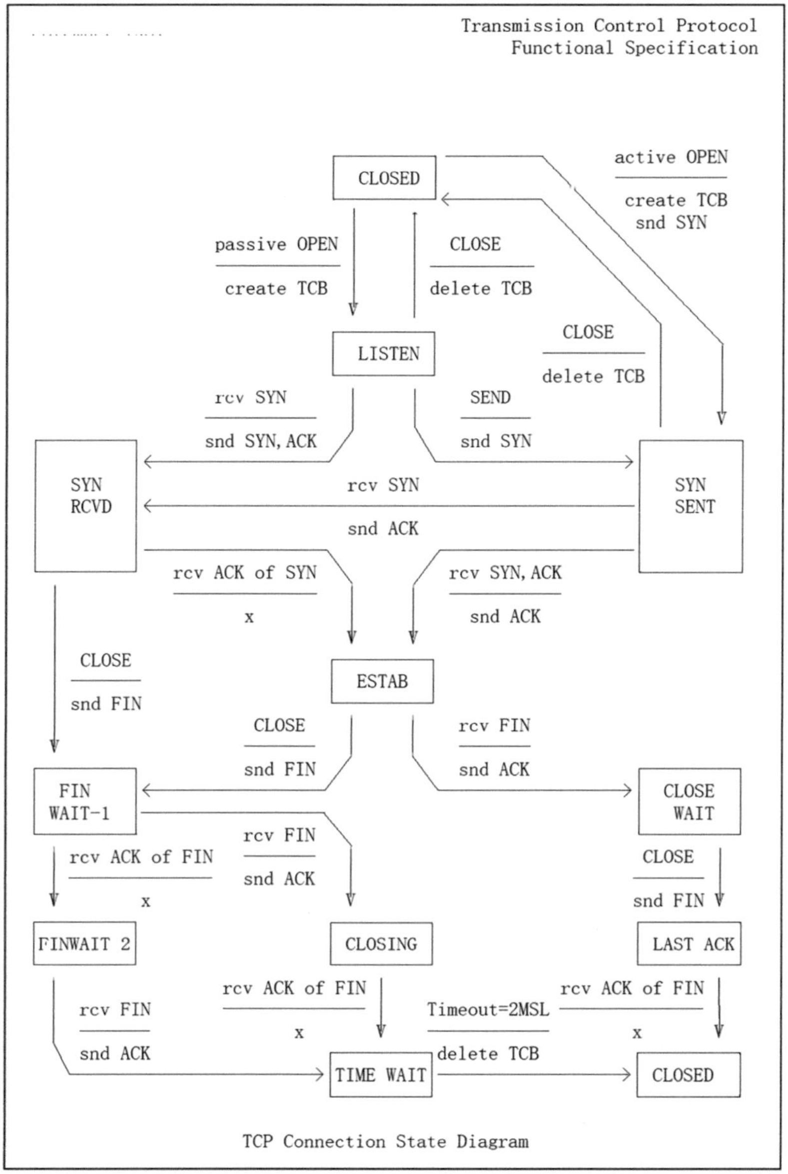

Fig. 5.38 TCP state transitions

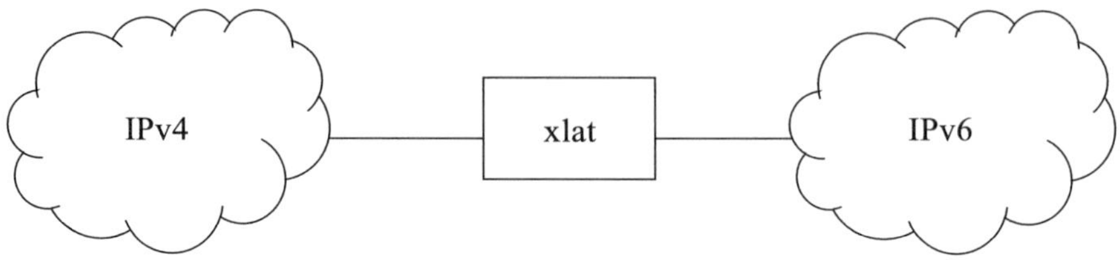

Fig. 5.39 IPv4/IPv6 translation model

(2) The conversion algorithm does not translate any IPv4 options, nor does it convert any IPv6 extension headers other than the fragment header.
(3) Because the translator's address translation for IPv4 and IPv6 usually does not satisfy the checksum neutral condition, it is necessary to recalculate the checksum at the transport layer (TCP, UDP, etc.) based on the pseudo header. Stateful translators need to handle TCP state, so the translator must comply with the TCP datagram processing algorithm specified in RFC5382 [34].
(4) IPv4 UDP fragment datagrams that do not contain a UDP checksum (i.e., the UDP checksum field is 0) do not have significant use on the Internet and do not normally need to be translated and forwarded by the translator. Note: Depending on the needs of network operation, the translator can be configured to translate and forward such datagrams.
(5) The translator will not translate and forward fragmented ICMP/ICMPv6 datagrams.
(6) The unicast datagram header translation rules can also be used for the translation and forwarding of multicast datagram headers. However, the current address mapping standard (RFC6052 [35]) only defines unicast address mapping rules, so the IPv4 multicast addresses defined by RFC5771 [36] cannot be mapped to the multicast addresses defined by RFC3307 [37]. If there is a need for multicast translation, RFC6219 [38] provides an experimental example of multicast address mapping.

2. *Stateless and Stateful Modes*

The translator has two operating modes: stateless translator and stateful translator. In both cases, it is assumed that a system (node or application) has an IPv4 address but no IPv6 address, and is communicating with another system that has an IPv6 address but no IPv4 address.

In stateless mode, the translator uses configuration information to map IPv4 addresses and IPv6 addresses based on the datagram itself using a deterministic algorithm. The default behavior defined in RFC6052 [35] is as follows:

(1) A specific IPv6 address range (IPv4-converted IPv6 address) represents the entire public IPv4 address domain.
(2) The address of the IPv6 system (IPv4-translatable IPv6 address) is mapped to a subset of the operator's public IPv4 address through an algorithm.

Stateless translators do not retain any dynamic session or binding state, so there is no need to couple all messages belonging to a single data stream with a specific translator.

In stateful mode, the translator needs to maintain state, and the default behavior defined in RFC6052 [35] is as follows:

(1) A specific IPv6 address range (IPv4 to IPv4 address) represents the entire public IPv4 address domain.
(2) IPv6 nodes use any IPv6 address outside this range.

Stateful translators need to maintain a dynamic conversion table binding IPv4 addresses (which may include transport layer port numbers) and IPv6 addresses. Therefore, all datagrams belonging to a specific data stream must be handled by the same translator.

3. *Path MTU Discovery and Fragmentation*

Since the IPv4 header is composed of 20 or slightly more than 20 octets, and the IPv6 header is composed of 40 octets, handling the maximum datagram is crucial for the operation of the IPv4/IPv6 translator. In Internet standards, there are three mechanisms to handle this problem.

(1) Use the path maximum transmission unit discovery (PMTUD) mechanism defined by RFC4821 [39].
(2) Use the "IPv4 fragmentation" and "IPv6 fragmentation" mechanisms defined by RFC791 [1] and RFC8200 [2] respectively.
(3) Use the "Transport Layer Negotiation, such as TCP Maximum Segment Size (MSS) Option" mechanism defined by RFC6691 [40].

The translator is a special type of router, that is, when the size of the translated datagram exceeds the MTU of the next hop interface, the translator must send a "Packet Too Big" error message to the source node of the datagram, or fragment the datagram.

5.7.2 From IPv4 to IPv6

To convert from IPv4 to IPv6, the translator follows these steps:

(1) Receive an IPv4 datagram for a destination node in the IPv6 address domain.
(2) Translate the IPv4 header of the datagram into an IPv6 header.
(3) Remove the original IPv4 header and replace it with the IPv6 header.
(4) Recalculate the transport layer checksum.
(5) The data part of the datagram remains unchanged.
(6) Forward datagrams according to the IPv6 destination address.

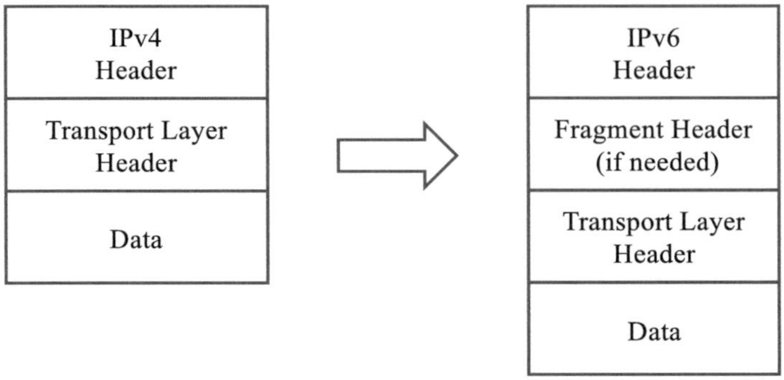

Fig. 5.40 Translation from IPv4 to IPv6

The conversion methods are shown in Fig. 5.40.

IPv6 devices must support PMTUD, but this is optional in IPv4. IPv6 routers are not allowed to fragment datagrams, only the source node can fragment.

When an IPv4 node chooses path MTU discovery (by setting the "Do not Fragment bit", i.e., DF = 1), end-to-end path MTU discovery across the translator can be achieved. In this case, IPv4 or IPv6 routers (including translators) may send back "Packet Too Big" ICMP messages to the source node. When an IPv6 router sends an ICMPv6 error message, the translator converts the ICMPv6 error message into an ICMP message that IPv4 can understand. Therefore, the IPv6 fragment extension header only exists when the IPv4 message has already been fragmented.

However, when the IPv4 source node does not set the "Do not Fragment bit", i.e., DF = 0, the translator must ensure that the size of the datagram does not exceed the path MTU allowed by the IPv6 side. This is achieved by fragmenting the IPv4 datagram (including the fragment extension header) to conform to the smallest IPv6 path MTU, which is 1280 octets. There have been cases where the IPv6 fragment extension header may not pass through a firewall with incomplete functionality. Therefore, in the case where the network and the translator belong to the same operator, the translator must provide a configuration function to allow the system administrator to increase the MTU value to meet the requirements of the network environment (greater than 1280 octets). This adjustment will help reduce the probability of IPv6 datagrams containing fragment extension headers.

When the IPv4 source node does not set the DF bit, the translator must not insert a fragment extension header into the unfragmented datagram.

To ensure that whether the source node or the IPv4 router generates datagram fragments, the lower 16 bits of the fragment identifier are end-to-end unique to ensure that the datagram can be correctly reassembled.

In addition to fragment processing and path MTU discovery requiring special rules, special processing is also required for ICMPv4 error messages and the addition of ICMPv6 pseudo-header checksums.

The translator should ensure that datagrams belonging to the same stream leave the translator in the same order as they arrive.

The processing of the datagram header is defined by the following rules.

1. *Convert the IPv4 Header to the IPv6 Header*

If the DF flag is not set (i.e., DF = 0) and the size of the IPv4 datagram will cause the IPv6 datagram to be larger than the user-defined size (referred to as "low-IPv6-MTU", default is 1280 octets), the datagram should be fragmented so that the generated IPv6 datagram (including the added fragment extension header) is less than or equal to the low-IPv6-MTU. For example, if the datagram has already been fragmented before translation, the IPv6 datagram should be fragmented so that their length, excluding the IPv4 header, is at most 1232 octets (1280 octets minus the 40 octets of the IPv6 header and the octet of the fragment extension header). The translator must provide a configuration function. If the actual minimum IPv6 MTU of the network is known, the threshold of the minimum IPv6 MTU can be adjusted to a value greater than 1280 octets. These fragmented datagrams are translated independently according to the following logic.

If the DF flag is set (i.e., DF = 1) and the MTU of the next hop link interface is less than the total length of the IPv4 datagram plus 20 octets, the translator must send an ICMPv4 "Fragmentation Needed" error message to the IPv4 source address.

The header conversion involved in this scenario is shown in Fig. 5.41 (refer to the detailed explanations in Figs. 5.1 and 5.14, respectively).

The IPv6 header fields are set as follows:

(1) Version: Set to 6.
(2) Traffic Class:

   ① By default, copy the octet from the IP service type (type of service, TOS) to the traffic class. According to RFC2474 [4], the bit semantics of this field are identical in IPv4 and IPv6.
   ② In some IPv4 environments, these fields may use the old semantics of service type and precedence. The implementation of the translator should support administrator configuration, i.e., ignore the IPv4 TOS value and always set the IPv6 traffic class to 0.
   ③ If the translator is at the boundary of network management, refer to the filtering and updating considerations defined by RFC2475 [5].

(3) Flow Label: The value is 0 (all bits are 0).

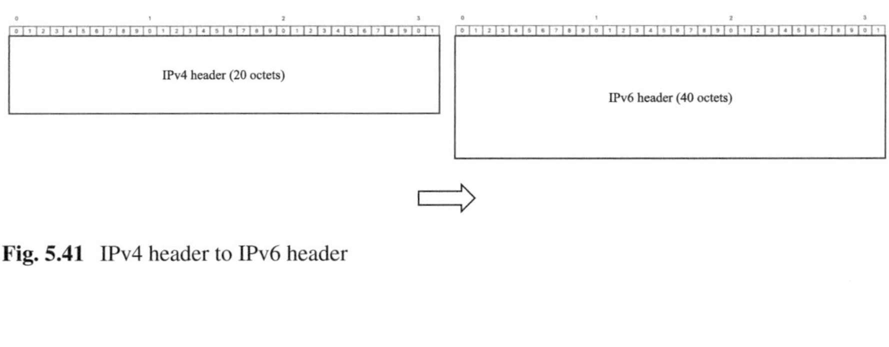

Fig. 5.41 IPv4 header to IPv6 header

(4) Payload Length: The total length value of the IPv4 header minus the size of the IPv4 header and IPv4 options (if any).
(5) Next Header:

① For ICMPv4 (value is 1), change to ICMPv6 (value is 58).
② Otherwise, copy the Protocol field in the IPv4 header.

(6) Hop Limit: The hop limit originates from the TTL value in the IPv4 header.

① Since the translator is a router, as part of forwarding, the translator needs to decrement the TTL in the IPv4 header (before translating the datagram), or the Hop Limit in the IPv6 header (after translating the datagram).
② As part of reducing TTL or Hop Limit, the translator (like any router) must check this value. If it is 0, send an ICMPv4 "TTL Exceeded" or ICMPv6 "Hop Limit Exceeded" error message.

(7) Source Address: Map the IPv4 address to the IPv6 address according to the algorithm.

① If the translator finds that the source address is an illegal address (for example, 0.0.0.0, 127.0.0.1, etc.), the translator should silently discard the datagram (RFC1812 [41]).
② When translating ICMPv4 error messages into ICMPv6 error messages, it is necessary to translate "illegal" source addresses to help troubleshoot errors.

(8) Destination Address: Map the IPv4 address to the IPv6 address according to the algorithm.
(9) If there is an unexpired source route option: Discard the datagram and send an ICMPv4 "Destination Unreachable, Source Route Failed" (Type 3, Code 5) error message to the source node of the datagram.
(10) If there are any other IPv4 options in the IPv4 datagram: Ignore these options.

When the datagram itself is fragmented, or the DF bit is not set (i.e., DF = 0), and the size of the datagram exceeds the low-IPv6-MTU configured by the translator, a fragment extension header needs to be added, as shown in Fig. 5.42.

The above rules can still be used, but the following IPv6 fields need to be specially handled.

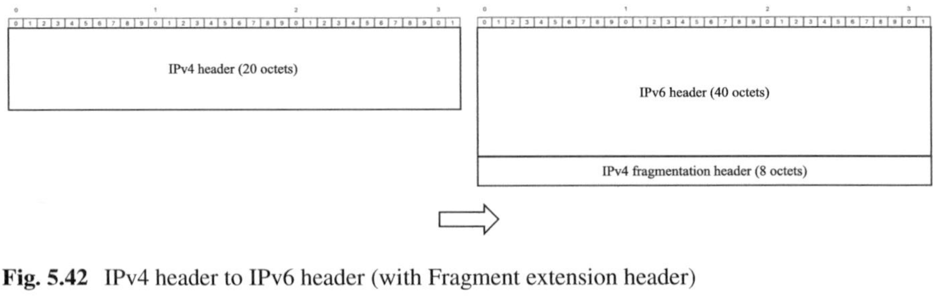

Fig. 5.42 IPv4 header to IPv6 header (with Fragment extension header)

(1) Payload Length of IPv6 Header: The total length value of the IPv4 header plus the value of the Fragment Extension Header, minus the size of the IPv4 header and IPv4 options (if any).
(2) Next Header of IPv6 Header: Fragment Extension Header (44).
(3) Next Header of the Fragment Extension Header: ① For ICMPv4 (value is 1), change to ICMPv6 (value is 58); ② Otherwise, copy the Protocol field in the IPv4 header.
(4) Fragment Offset of the Fragment Extension Header: Copy the "Fragment Offset" field in the IPv4 header.
(5) M flag of the Fragment Extension Header: Copy the "MF" bit in the IPv4 header.
(6) Identification of the Fragment Extension Header: Copy the lower 16 bits of the "Identification" field in the IPv4 header, and set the upper 16 bits to 0.

2. *Converting ICMPv4 Header to ICMPv6 Header*

Unlike ICMPv4, ICMPv6 has a pseudo-header checksum similar to UDP and TCP. Therefore, all ICMPv4 messages that need to be translated must calculate the checksum during the translation process.

In addition, it is necessary to translate the "Type" field of all ICMPv4 datagrams, and translate the IP header contained in the ICMPv4 error message.

The conversion of the ICMPv4 header to the ICMPv6 header is shown in Fig. 5.43.

The translation rules for ICMPv4 messages are as follows.

ICMPv4 query messages:

(1) Echo Request/Echo Response (type 8 and type 0): Adjust to 128 and 129 respectively, change according to Type, include ICMPv6 pseudo-header, and recalculate checksum.
(2) Information Request/Information Response (Type 15 and Type 16): Already deprecated in the ICMPv6 header, should be silently discarded.
(3) Timestamp Request/Timestamp response (Type 13 and Type 14): Already deprecated in the ICMPv6 header, should be silently discarded.
(4) Address Mask Request/Address Mask Reply (Type 17 and Type 18): Already deprecated in the ICMPv6 header, should be silently discarded.
(5) ICMP Router Advertisement (Type 9): single-hop message, should be silently discarded.

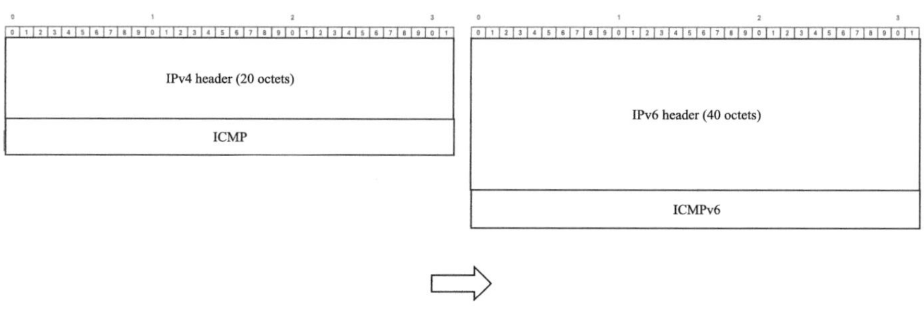

Fig. 5.43 ICMPv4 header to ICMPv6 header

(6) ICMP Router Request (type 10): single-hop message, should be silently discarded.
(7) Unknown ICMPv4 type: Should be silently discarded.

IGMP Messages.

The current IETF standard (which may change in the future) stipulates that all multicast listener discovery (MLD) messages defined by RFC2710 [42], RFC3590 [43], and RFC3810 [44] correspond to the IPv4 Internet Group Management Protocol (IGMP) defined by RFC3376 [45]. All "normal" IGMP messages are single-hop messages and should be silently discarded. If other types of IGMP messages are received, they should be silently discarded, as in most cases this is due to configuration errors.

ICMPv4 Error Messages.

(1) Destination Unreachable (Destination Unreachable) (Type 3): Set the Type to 1, and adjust the ICMP checksum according to the Type change (including ICMPv6 pseudo header). The translation rules for Code are as follows:

① Code 0, 1 (Network Unreachable, Host Unreachable): Set the Code to 0 (No route to the destination node).
② Code 2 (Protocol Unreachable): Convert to ICMPv6 Parameter Problem (Type 4, Code 1) and generate a pointer pointing to the Next Header field of IPv6.
③ Code 3 (Port Unreachable): Set the Code to 4 (Port Unreachable).
④ Code 4 (Fragmentation Needed and DF Set): Translate to ICMPv6 Packet Too Big message (Type 2), set Code to 0. The MTU field must be adjusted according to the difference in size between the IPv4 header and the IPv6 header, but it must never be set to less than the minimum IPv6 MTU value (1280 bytes). That is, it should be set to

$$\max(1280,\ \min(\mathrm{PTB} + 20,\ \mathrm{MTU\_of\_IPv6\_nexthop},\ \mathrm{MTU\_of\_IPv4\_nexthop} + 20))$$

Note: If an IPv4 router sets the MTU field to 0 (indicating it has not implemented RFC1191 [46]), the translation process must use the value specified by RFC1191 to determine the path MTU. The translation should use this RFC1191-derived value as the path MTU in the ICMPv6 datagram. This value must be less than the total length field of the returned datagram but greater than or equal to 1280.
⑤ Code 5 (Source Route Failed): Set the Code to 0 (No route to the destination node). Note: This error is unlikely to occur because the source route will not be translated.
⑥ Code 6, 7, 8: Set the Code to 0 (No route to the destination node).
⑦ Code 9, 10 (Communication with Destination Host is Administratively Prohibited): Set the Code to 1 (Communication with Destination Host is Administratively Prohibited).

⑧ Code 11, 12: Set the Code to 0 (No route to the destination node).
⑨ Code 13 (Communication Administratively Prohibited): Set the Code to 1 (Communication with Destination Node is Administratively Prohibited).
⑩ Code 14 (Host Precedence Violation): Should be silently discarded.
⑪ Code 15 (Precedence Cutoff in Effect): Set the Code to 1 (Communication with Destination Node is Administratively Prohibited).
⑫ Other Code values: Should be silently discarded.

(2) Redirect (Type 5): Single hop message, should be silently discarded.
(3) Alternative Host Address (Type 6): Should be silently discarded.
(4) Source Quench (Type 4): Deprecated in ICMPv6, should be silently discarded.
(5) Time Exceeded (Type 11): Set the Type to 3, and adjust the ICMP checksum according to the Type change (including ICMPv6 pseudo header). The Code remains unchanged.
(6) Parameter Problem (Type 12): Set the Type to 4, and adjust the ICMP checksum according to the Type change (including ICMPv6 pseudo header). The translation rules for Code are as follows.

① Code 0 (Pointer indicates error): Set the Code to 0 (Encountered an erroneous datagram header field) and update the pointer according to Table 5.12 (If the original IPv4 does not list the pointer value, or the translated IPv6 pointer value is listed as "n/a", it should be silently discarded).

Table 5.12 Pointer update

Original IPv4 pointer value		Translated IPv6 pointer value	
0	Version/Header length (Version/IHL)	0	Version/Traffic class (Version/Traffic Class)
1	Type of Service (Type of Service)	1	Traffic Class/Flow Label (Traffic Class/Flow Label)
2, 3	Total Length (Total Length)	4	Payload Length (Payload Length)
4, 5	Identification (Identification)	Undefined (n/a)	
6	Flags/Fragment Offset (Flags/Fragment Offset)	Undefined (n/a)	
7	Fragment Offset (Fragment Offset)	Undefined (n/a)	
8	Time to Live (Time to Live)	7	Hop Limit (Hop Limit)
9	Protocol (Protocol)	6	Next Header (Next Header)
10, 11	Header Checksum (Header Checksum)	Undefined (n/a)	
12–15	Source Address (Source Address)	8	Source Address (Source Address)
16–19	Destination Address (Destination Address)	24	Destination Address (Destination Address)

② Code 1 (Missing Required Option): Should be silently discarded.
③ Code 2 (Incorrect Length): Set the Code to 0 (encountered an error in the header field) and update the pointer. If the original IPv4 does not list the pointer value, or the translated IPv6 pointer value is listed as "n/a", it should be silently discarded, as shown in Table 5.12.
④ Other Code Values: Should be silently discarded.

(7) Unknown ICMPv4 Type: Should be silently discarded.

ICMP Error Payload: If the received ICMPv4 datagram contains an ICMPv4 extension field (RFC4884 [11]), translating the ICMPv4 datagram will cause the ICMPv6 datagram to change in length. In this case, the ICMPv6 extension length attribute must be adjusted accordingly (for example, the translation from IPv4 address to IPv6 address causes the datagram to lengthen). If the size of the ICMPv6 message after translating the ICMPv4 extension exceeds the MTU of the next hop link interface, the ICMPv4 extension should be truncated.

For extensions not defined in RFC4884 [11], the translator should treat the extensions as opaque bit strings, and there is no need to translate any IPv4 address information that may be contained in these strings, although this may cause problems for subsequent processing of ICMP extensions.

3. *Converting ICMPv4 Error Messages to ICMPv6*

ICMP error messages containing erroneous datagrams must be translated into IPv6 datagrams (excluding the TTL value of the internal IPv4/IPv6 datagram). If the translation of this error message changes the length of the datagram, the total length field of the external IPv6 header must be updated. The conversion process is shown in Fig. 5.44.

The translation of the internal IP header can be accomplished by calling the translation function of the external IP header, but this is limited to the first embedded IP header, more embedded headers must be discarded.

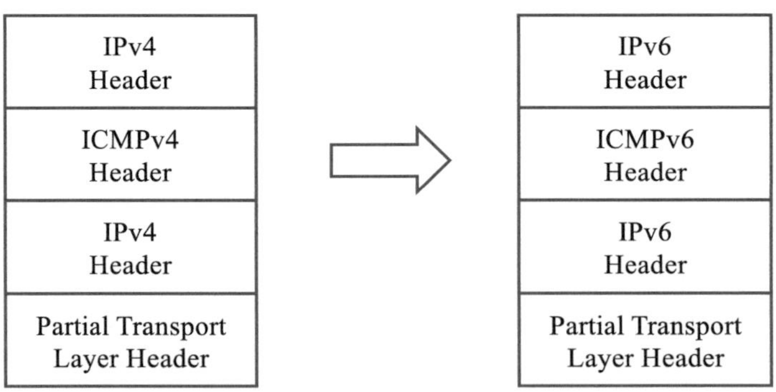

Fig. 5.44 Conversion of ICMP error messages from IPv4 to IPv6

4. *Generating ICMPv4 Error Messages*

If the translator discards the IPv4 datagram, an ICMPv4 error message should be sent to the original sender of the datagram, unless the discarded datagram itself is also an ICMPv4 error message.

The "Type" in the ICMPv4 message format must be 3 (destination unreachable), and the "Code" must be 13 (administratively prohibited). The translator should allow the decision to be made through configuration: send ICMPv4 error messages, send at a certain rate limit, or not send at all.

5. *Transport Layer Header Translation*

If the address translation algorithm is not "checksum neutral", the transport layer header containing the pseudo header must be recalculated and updated. The translator must perform this operation for TCP, ICMP, and UDP datagrams with UDP checksums (i.e., the UDP "checksum" field is not 0).

For UDP datagrams without a UDP checksum (i.e., the UDP "checksum" field is 0), the translator should provide a configuration function to allow the following operations.

(1) discard the datagram and generate a system management event that at least specifies the IP address and port number,
(2) calculate the IPv6 checksum and forward the datagram (affects performance).

Stateless translators cannot calculate the checksum of UDP fragmented datagrams, so if a stateless translator receives the first fragment of an IPv4 UDP datagram with a "checksum" field of 0, the translator should discard the datagram and generate a system management event that at least specifies the IP address and port number.

The method for the stateful translator to handle received IPv4 UDP datagrams with a "checksum" field of 0 is referred to in RFC6146 [47].

Other transport layer protocols, such as the Datagram Congestion Control Protocol (DCCP [48]), translators may choose to support. For ease of debugging and troubleshooting, the translator must forward all transport layer protocols.

6. *Whether to Translate*

If the translator also provides normal routing function, the rules for choosing translation or routing forwarding are as follows:

(1) If the destination IPv4 address has a "longer prefix match IPv4 route", the translator must directly forward, not translate the datagram.
(2) Otherwise, if the translator receives an IPv4 datagram, and its IPv4 destination address is in the IPv6 domain, the translator must translate the datagram into an IPv6 datagram.

5.7.3 From IPv6 to IPv4

The steps for the translator to convert from IPv6 to IPv4 are as follows:

(1) Receive an IPv6 datagram with a destination node in the IPv4 domain.
(2) Translate the IPv6 header of the datagram into an IPv4 header.
(3) Remove the original IPv6 header and replace it with an IPv4 header.
(4) The headers of ICMPv6 (RFC4443 [32]), TCP (RFC793 [23]), UDP (RFC768 [24]), and DCCP (RFC4340 [48]) include checksums that cover the IP header. If the address mapping algorithm is related to the checksum, it must be checked before translation. The ICMP and transport layer headers must be updated during the translation process.
(5) The data part of the datagram remains unchanged and the datagram is forwarded according to the IPv6 destination address.

Its conversion method is shown in Fig. 5.45.

The translator must fully consider the differences between IPv6 and IPv4 in handling fragmentation and minimum link MTU. The MTU of an IPv6 link must be 1280 octets or larger, while the limit for IPv4 is 68 octets. The translator must correctly handle the "Packet Too Big" ICMP messages received and processed by the IPv6 host.

The translator handles the minimum MTU as follows:

(1) When translating an ICMPv4 "Fragmentation Needed" packet, the MTU marked in the ICMPv6 "Packet Too Big" should not be less than 1280 octets. This ensures that the IPv6 node will never encounter or handle a path MTU value smaller than the minimum IPv6 link MTU (1280 octets).
(2) When the generated IPv4 datagram is less than or equal to 1260 octets, the translator must set DF = 0 for the generated datagram; if not, the translator must set DF = 1 for the generated datagram.

This method allows for end-to-end path MTU discovery for paths with an MTU not less than 1280 (minimum IPv6 MTU) (corresponding to an MTU of 1260 octets in

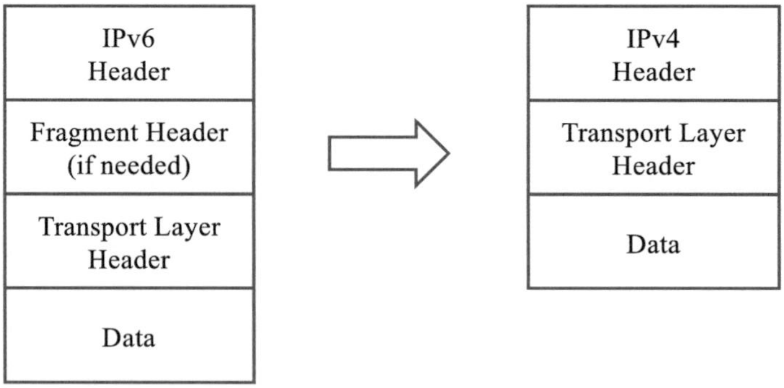

Fig. 5.45 Translation from IPv6 to IPv4

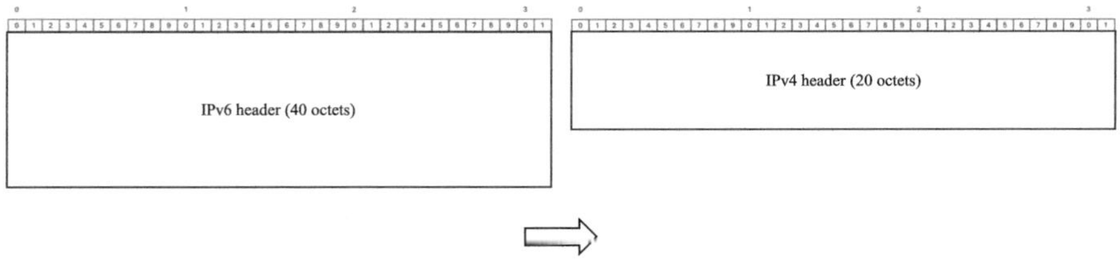

Fig. 5.46 IPv6 header to IPv4 header

the IPv4 domain). When there is an MTU < 1260 on the path, IPv4 routers connected to these links will fragment the datagrams according to the method of RFC791 [1].

In addition to special rules for fragmentation and path MTU discovery, the actual processing of datagram headers is defined by the following rules. Furthermore, special handling is required for translating ICMPv4 error messages and adding checksums to ICMPv6 pseudo headers.

The translator should ensure that datagrams belonging to the same stream leave the translator in the same order as they arrive.

1. *Convert IPv6 Headers to IPv4 Headers*

If there is no IPv6 fragment header, the datagram header conversion is as shown in Fig. 5.46.

The IPv4 header fields are set as follows:

(1) Version: Set to 4.
(2) IP Header Length (IHL): Set to 5 (no IPv4 options).
(3) Type of Service:

 ① By default, copy the IPv6 Traffic Class (all 8 bits), according to RFC2474 [4], the semantics of these bits are the same in IPv4 and IPv6.
 ② The translator implementation should support administrator configuration, i.e., ignore the IPv6 Traffic Class and always set the IPv4 Type of Service to a specified value.
 ③ If the translator is at the boundary of network management, refer to the filtering and updating considerations defined by RFC2475 [5].

(4) Total Length: The payload length value from the IPv6 header plus the size of the IPv4 header.
(5) Identification: Set in the translator based on the fragment identifier.
(6) Flags:

 ① If the translated IPv4 datagram is less than or equal to 1260 octets, the DF flag is set to 0.
 ② In other cases, the DF flag is set to 1.

(7) Fragment Offset: Set to all 0 s.

(8) Time to Live: The Time to Live originates from the Hop Limit value in the IPv6 header.

① Since the translator is a router, as part of forwarding, the translator needs to decrement the "Hop Limit" in the IPv6 header (before datagram translation), or the "Time to Live" in the IPv4 header (after datagram translation).
② As part of reducing the "Time to Live" or "Hop Limit", the translator (like any router) must check this value, and if it is 0, send an ICMPv4 "TTL Exceeded" or ICMPv6 "Hop Limit Exceeded" error message.

(9) Protocol:

① The handling of the IPv6-Frag (value 44) header is discussed separately.
② ICMPv6 (value 58) is changed to ICMPv4 (value 1), and it needs to come with a translation that handles the payload.
③ IPv6 header HOPOPT (value 0), IPv6 Route (value 43), and IPv6 Opts (value 60) are skipped during processing because they have no meaning in IPv4.
④ For the first "Next Header" that does not match the above conditions, its "Next Header" value (including the transport layer protocol number) is copied to the "Protocol" field in IPv4. This means that all transport layer protocols will be translated. Note: Some protocols cannot be translated, for example, if the address mapping is not "checksum irrelevant", the IPsec authentication header (value 51) and the "checksum" verification of some other protocols will not pass. That is, for these protocols, the translator cannot recalculate the checksum.

(10) Header Checksum: Calculated after creating the IPv4 header.
(11) Source Address: The IPv6 address is mapped to the IPv4 address according to the algorithm. If the source address of the message obtained by the translator is an illegal address, such as the "localhost loopback address" (::1), the translator should silently discard this datagram.
(12) Destination Address: The IPv6 address is mapped to the IPv4 address according to the algorithm.
(13) Extension Headers:

① If there are any IPv6 "Hop-by-Hop Header", "Destination Option Header", or "Routing Header" where the remaining segments (Segments Left) field equals 0 in the IPv6 datagram, these IPv6 extension headers must be ignored (i.e., do not attempt to translate extension headers), and the datagram is translated as usual. Note that the "total length" field and the "protocol" field need to be adjusted accordingly to "skip" these Extension Headers.
② If there is a "Routing Header" where the remaining segments (Segments Left) field does not equal 0, the translator does not translate the datagram, but sends an ICMPv6 parameter problem/error message to the source node of this datagram. The "error message" is of Type 4, Code 0, and the

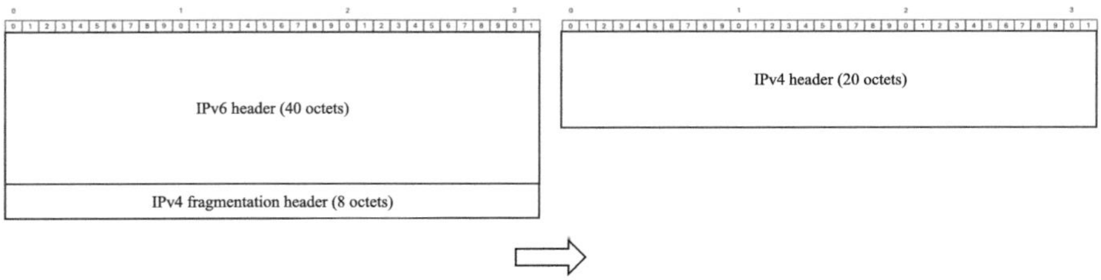

Fig. 5.47 IPv6 header (with Fragment extension header) to IPv4 header

"pointer" field points to the position of the first octets of the "remaining segments".

If the IPv6 datagram contains a fragment header, the header conversion involved in this case is shown in Fig. 5.47.

If the IPv6 datagram contains a Fragment Header, the following fields must be specially handled.

(1) Total Length:

① If the "Next Header" field of the Fragment Header is an Extension Header (except ESP, but including the Authentication Header), the datagram should be discarded and logged.

② For other cases, the "total length" must be set to the "payload length" from the IPv6 header minus the length of other Extension Headers up to the Fragment Header, minus the size of the Fragment Header (its value is 8), and finally add the size of the IPv4 header.

(2) Identification: Copied from the lower 16 bits of the "identification" field in the fragment extension header.

(3) Flags:

① The IPv4 More Fragments (MF) flag is copied from the M flag in the IPv6 Fragment Header.

② Set DF = 0, thus allowing this datagram to be further fragmented by IPv4 routers.

(4) Fragment Offset:

① If the "next header" field of the Fragment Header is not an Extension Header (except ESP), then the "fragment offset" must be copied from the "fragment offset" field of the IPv6 Fragment Header.

② If the "next header" field of the Fragment Header is an Extension Header, the datagram should be discarded and logged.

(5) Protocol:

① Change ICMPv6 (value 58) to ICMPv4 (value 1).

② Besides this, ignore the Extension Headers and copy the "Next Header" field from the last IPv6 Extension Header.

If the translated IPv6 datagram that is less than or equal to 1280 octets is still larger than the MTU of the next hop link interface of the IPv4 datagram, the translator must fragment the IPv4 to enable it to be transmitted on the MTU-limited link.

2. *Convert ICMPv6 Header to ICMPv4 Header*

If the "checksum-independent" mapping address is not used, ICMPv4 should update its "checksum" field, noting that ICMPv4 does not have a pseudo-header.

The translator must translate the ICMP datagram corresponding to ICMPv6, that is, the translator must translate not only the header but also the IPv4 header in the ICMP error message contained in the datagram.

The conversion of the ICMPv6 header to the ICMPv4 header is shown in Fig. 5.48.

The operations required to translate various ICMPv6 messages are as follows.

ICMPv6 Query Messages:

(1) Echo Request/Echo Response (Type 8 and Type 0): Adjust the type values to 128 and 129 respectively, and exclude the ICMPv6 pseudo-header based on the Type change.
(2) MLD Multicast Listener Query/Report/Done (Type 130, 131, 132): single-hop messages, should be silently discarded.
(3) Neighbor Discovery Messages (Type 133–137): single-hop messages, should be silently discarded.
(4) Unknown Informational Messages: Should be silently discarded.

ICMPv6 Error Messages:

(1) Destination Unreachable (Type 1): Set the Type to 3, then exclude the ICMPv6 pseudo-header and update the "checksum" based on the translated "Type/Code". The Code translation rules are as follows:

   ① Code 0 (No Route to Destination Node): Set the Code to 1 (Host unreachable).
   ② Code 1 (Communication with Destination Host Administratively Prohibited): Set the Code to 10 (Communication with destination host administratively prohibited).

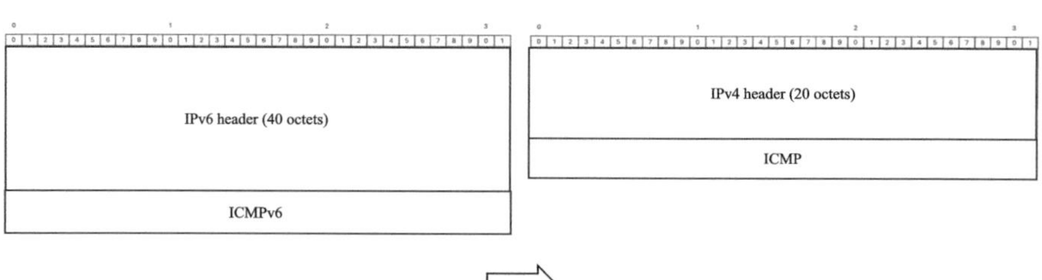

Fig. 5.48 ICMPv6 header to ICMPv4 header

③ Code 2 (Beyond Source Address Scope): Set the Code to 1 (Host unreachable). Note: This error is unlikely to occur because the source address of the translatable IPv4 is usually a global IPv4 unicast address.
④ Code 3 (Address Unreachable): Set the Code to 1 (Host unreachable).
⑤ Code 4 (Port Unreachable): Set the Code to 3 (Port unreachable).
⑥ Other Code Values: Should be silently discarded.

(2) Packet Too Big (Type 2): Translate to ICMPv4 Destination Unreachable (Type 3), Code 4, and recalculate the ICMPv4 checksum after excluding the ICMPv6 pseudo-header based on the Type change. The MTU field must be calculated considering the difference in size between the IPv4 and IPv6 headers and whether the erroneous datagram includes a fragment extension header. Its calculation formula is

$$\text{MTU} = \min(\text{PTB} - 20,\ \text{MTU\_of\_IPv4\_nexthop},\ \text{MTU\_of\_IPv6\_nexthop} - 20)$$

(3) Time Exceeded (Type 3): Set the Type to 11, then update the "checksum" (excluding the ICMPv6 pseudo-header) based on the translated "Type/Code". The Code remains unchanged.
(4) Parameter Problem (Type 4): Translate "Type/Code" according to the rules below, then update the "checksum" based on the translated "Type/Code" (excluding ICMPv6 pseudo header). The Code translation rules are as follows:

① Code 0 (Encountered an error in the header field): Set the Type to 12, the Code to 0, and update the pointer according to Figs. 5.10 and 5.41. If the original IPv6 pointer value is not listed, or the translated IPv4 pointer value is "n/a", silently discard the packet, as shown in Table 5.13.
② Code 1 (Encountered an Unrecognizable "Next Header" Type): Translate to ICMPv4 protocol unreachable (Type 3, Code 2).
③ Code 2 (Encountered an Unrecognizable IPv6 Option): The packet should be silently discarded.
④ Unknown Error Message: The packet should be silently discarded.

Table 5.13 Pointer update

Original IPv6 pointer value		Translated IPv4 pointer value	
0	Version/Traffic class	0	Version/IHL, Type of service
1	Traffic class/Flow label	1	Type of service
2, 3	Flow label	(n/a)	Undefined
4, 5	Payload length	2	Total length
6	Next header	9	Protocol
7	Hop limit	8	Time to live
8–23	Source address	12	Source address
24–39	Destination address	16	Destination address

ICMP Error Payload: If the received ICMPv6 datagram contains an ICMPv6 extension field (RFC4884 [11]), the translation of ICMPv6 will result in a change in the length of the ICMPv4 datagram. When this happens, the ICMPv6 extension length attribute must be adjusted accordingly (for example, the translation from IPv6 address to IPv4 address results in a shortening of the datagram).

For extensions not defined in RFC4884 [11], the translator treats the extensions as opaque bit strings, so there is no need to translate any IPv6 address information that may be contained in these strings, although this can cause problems for subsequent processing of ICMP extensions.

3. *ICMPv6 Error Messages Converted to ICMPv4*

ICMP error messages containing erroneous datagrams must be translated into IPv4 datagrams (excluding the "time to live"/"hop limit" values of the internal IPv4/IPv6 datagrams). If the translation of this "error message" changes its length, the "total length" field in the external IPv6 header must be updated.

The conversion process is shown in Fig. 5.49.

The translation of the internal IP header can be accomplished by calling the translation function of the external IP header, but only for the first embedded IP header, more embedded headers must be discarded.

4. *Generating ICMPv6 Error Messages*

If the translator discards an IPv6 datagram, it should send an ICMPv6 error message to the original sender of the datagram, unless the discarded datagram itself is also an ICMPv6 error message.

The ICMPv6 message must be of Type 1 (destination node unreachable) and Code 1 (communication with the destination host is administratively prohibited). The translator should allow configuration to decide: send ICMPv4 error messages, send at a certain rate limit, or not send at all.

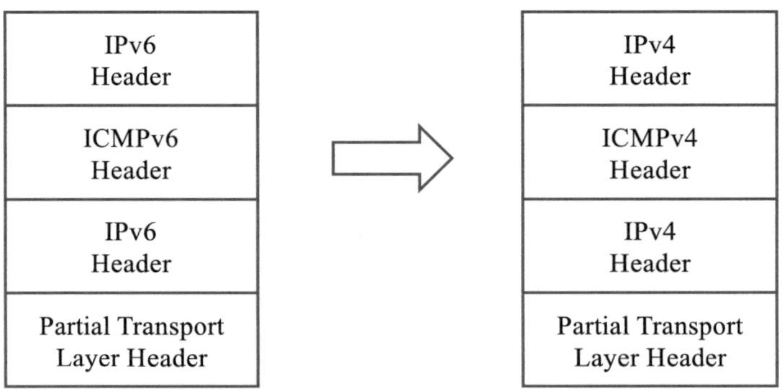

Fig. 5.49 IPv6 to IPv4 ICMP error message conversion

5. *Transport Layer Header Conversion*

If the address translation algorithm is not "checksum-independent", the transport layer header containing the pseudo-header must be recalculated and updated. The translator must perform this operation for TCP, ICMP, and UDP datagrams.

Other transport layer protocols, such as DCCP [48], the translator can choose to support. For ease of debugging and troubleshooting, the translator must forward all transport layer protocols.

6. *Whether to Translate*

If the translator also provides normal routing forwarding function, the rules for translation or routing forwarding are as follows:

(1) When the destination IPv6 address has a "longer prefix match IPv6 route", the translator must directly forward, rather than translate the message.
(2) Otherwise, when the translator receives an IPv6 datagram, if its IPv6 destination address is in the IPv4 domain, the datagram must be translated into IPv4.

7. *Special Considerations for ICMPv6 Datagrams too Large*

Research shows that the network's behavior of discarding "ICMPv6 Packet Too Big" error messages is not uncommon. This kind of message discarding can cause PMTUD black holes (RFC2923 [49]), this problem can be solved by using the packetization layer path MTU discovery (PLPMTUD) mechanism defined by RFC4821 [39].

5.7.4 Key Points of IP Address Mapping

The translator must support the stateless address mapping algorithm defined in RFC6052 [35]. Note: RFC7136 [50] updated RFC4291 [51], allowing the U-bit of unicast addresses not to be used, as long as they are not derived from the address of the media access control (MAC) sublayer protocol of the IEEE. Therefore, the address mapping algorithm defined in RFC6219 [38] also conforms to the IPv6 address architecture.

Stateless translators should support the explicit address mapping algorithm defined in RFC7757 [52].

Stateless translators should support RFC6791 [53] to handle ICMP/ICMPv6 datagrams.

Specific implementations of protocol translators can support stateless and stateful translation modes (for example, NAT64 defined by RFC6146 [47]).

Specific implementations of protocol translators can support stateless NAT64 functions (for example, MAP-T customer edge (CE) or MAP-T border relay (BR) defined by RFC7599 [54]).

5.7.5 Security Considerations

Stateless IP/ICMP translators do not bring any new security issues beyond those already existing in the IPv4 and IPv6 protocols.

Deriving IPv4 addresses from IPv6 addresses may pose potential security issues (especially broadcast addresses, loopback addresses, or addresses that do not conform to the "IPv4-converted IPv6 address" defined in Chap. 6).

The IPsec authentication header defined by RFC4302 [12] cannot be used for translation Network Address Translation.

Like IPv4 to IPv4 network address translation, ESP datagrams in tunnel mode can be translated because tunnel mode ESP does not depend on the header fields before ESP header encapsulation. Similarly, unless addresses irrelevant to the checksum are used, transport mode ESP cannot be translated. In both cases, IPsec ESP endpoints usually detect whether there is a translator in the path and encapsulate ESP in UDP datagrams (RFC3948 [55]).

5.8 ICMP Source Address Processing

The translation algorithm defined by RFC7915 [33] states: "The IPv6 address in the IPv6 header may not be an 'IPv4-translatable IPv6 address' and cannot be directly translated into an IPv4 address." In this case, the translation can use stateful translation, or the method defined by RFC6791 [53].

Considering the case where ICMP messages travel cross a translator (xlat) as illustrated in Fig. 5.50.

Host2 employs an IPv4-translatable IPv6 address, while Host1 utilizes an IPv4 address. Through the translator (xlat), Host1 perceives Host2's address as the corresponding IPv4 address of the IPv4-translatable IPv6 address. However, when R62

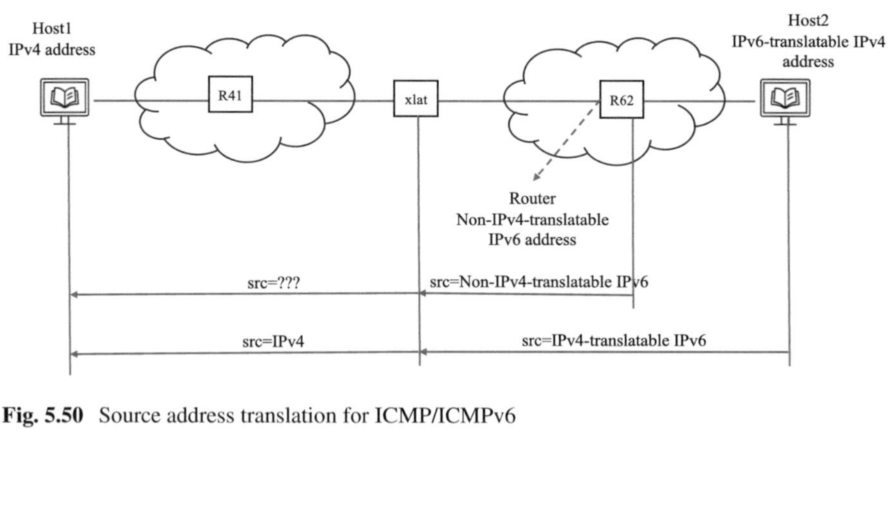

Fig. 5.50 Source address translation for ICMP/ICMPv6

detects issues with the datagram and sends an ICMPv6 message to Host1, R62's IPv6 address is not an IPv4-translatable IPv6 address, thereby lacking a corresponding IPv4 address. In such a scenario, the translator xlat requires special handling for the source address (src) during the translation from ICMPv6 to ICMP.

Therefore, when a stateless translator receives a "Packet Too Big" ICMPv6 message, its destination address usually comes from an "IPv4-translatable IPv6 address", but the source address may be any IPv6 address (non-"IPv4-translatable IPv6 address"), and the translator needs to choose a source address to generate the ICMP message. This source address needs to meet the following conditions.

The source address used should not cause the ICMP datagram to be dropped, it should not come from the address space defined by RFC1918 [56] or RFC6598 [57], because this address space is likely to be filtered by unicast reverse path forwarding (uRPF) (RFC3704 [58]).

One of the purposes of IPv4/IPv6 translation is to address the scarcity of public IPv4 addresses, so it is unrealistic to configure a public IPv4 address for each node that may generate ICMPv6 messages.

Another consideration in choosing the source address is that the recipient of the ICMP message should be able to distinguish to some extent the ICMPv6 messages generated by different IPv6 network nodes (for example, the traceroute diagnostic program can provide different IPv6 network source addresses after traversing the IPv4/IPv6 translator). This consideration means that the IPv4/IPv6 translator needs to have an IPv4 address pool to map the source addresses of ICMPv6 datagrams generated from different sources. Internet operational practices show that currently only traceroute and mtr use ICMPv6 source addresses for path tracing.

The currently recommended source address selection method is to use a public IPv4 address (or a small public IPv4 address pool) as the source address to translate ICMP messages, and to use the ICMP extension defined by RFC5837 [59] to treat the IPv6 address as the interface IP address sub-object.

5.8.1 ICMP Extension

For a public IPv4 address (IPv4 interface address or translator's loopback address) or public IPv4 address pool, the translator should implement the ICMP extension defined by RFC5837 [59].

The ICMP message should copy the IPv6 source address included in the original ICMPv6 to the interface IP address sub-object of the ICMP extension. As part of the data following the IPv4 header, its data structure is shown in Fig. 5.51.

The parameters defined by RFC792 [7] are as follows:

(1) Destination Address: 32 bits; the destination address is copied from the source address field of the calling message.
(2) Type: The value is 11.
(3) Code: The code is as shown in Table 5.14.

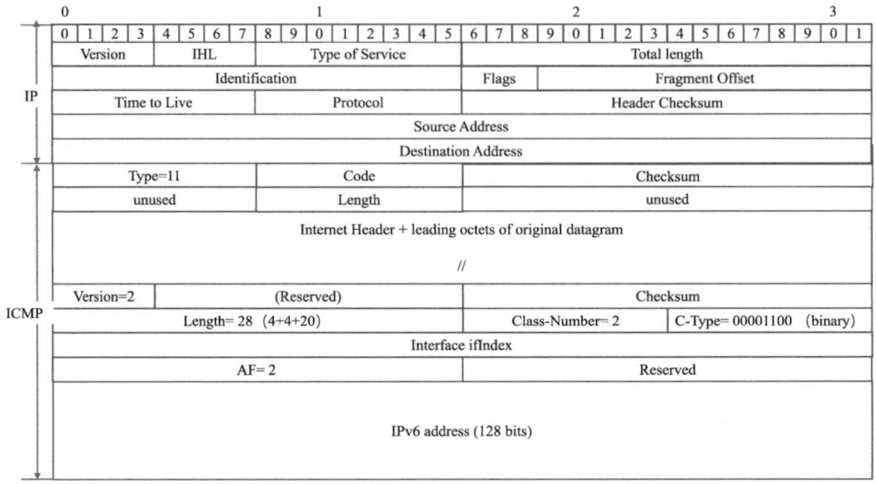

Fig. 5.51 ICMP extension format with IPv4 header

Table 5.14 Code

Code	Description
0	Time exceeded
1	Fragment reassembly time exceeded

(4) Unused: This field is not used.
(5) Checksum: The checksum is the 16-bit complement of the sum of the ICMP message starting with the ICMP type. To calculate the checksum, the "Checksum" field is first set to 0.
(6) Internet Header + Leading Octets of Original Datagram: This data is used by the host processing. If higher-level protocols use port numbers, they are assumed to be located in the first 64 bits of the original datagram.

The parameters defined by RFC4884 [11] are as follows:

(1) Version: 4 bits; the value is 2 (ICMP extension).
(2) Reserved: 12 bits; the code is set to 0 by the source node and ignored by the receiving node.
(3) Checksum: 16 bits; a value of all zeros indicates that the checksum was not transmitted.
(4) Length: 16 bits; set to 28, the length of the object, in octets, including the object header and object payload.
(5) Class-Number: 8 bits; set to 2, identifying the object category.
(6) C-Type (Subclass Number): 8 bits; set to 12, description of the network interface.

The parameters defined by RFC7915 [33] are as follows:

(1) Interface Index: 32 bits; the network interface index defined by RFC2863 [60].
(2) AF (Address Family): 16 bits; set to 2 (IPv6).

(3) Reserved: 16 bits; this field is not used. The code is set to 0 by the source node and ignored by the receiving node.
(4) IPv6 Address: 128 bits; the IPv6 address of this network interface.

When using an enhanced traceroute application, the real IPv6 source address in the ICMPv6 message can be extracted. Therefore, it can improve the visibility of the IPv6 network. In the future, a new ICMP extension can be considered to indicate that the datagram has been translated and its source address belongs to the translator, not the initiating node.

5.8.2 *Stateless Address Mapping Algorithm*

If a public IPv4 address pool is configured on the translator, it is recommended to randomly select the IPv4 source address. Random selection can reduce the probability of receiving two ICMP messages with the same source address from the same traceroute application, thereby avoiding misunderstandings caused by routing loops. The enhanced traceroute application supporting RFC5837 [59] extension will display the real IPv6 source address in the ICMPv6 message.

5.9 Protocol Encapsulation

5.9.1 *IPv6 Tunnel*

RFC2473 [61] defines the IPv6 tunnel, which is a technique for establishing a "virtual link" between two IPv6 nodes for transmitting datagrams as payloads. One node of the tunnel encapsulates the datagrams received from other nodes or itself and forwards them through the tunnel. The other node decapsulates the received datagrams and forwards the original datagrams to the original destination address.

A bidirectional tunnel is achieved by combining two unidirectional tunnels, i.e., configuring two tunnels, where the entrance node of one tunnel is the exit node of the other tunnel, as shown in Fig. 5.52.

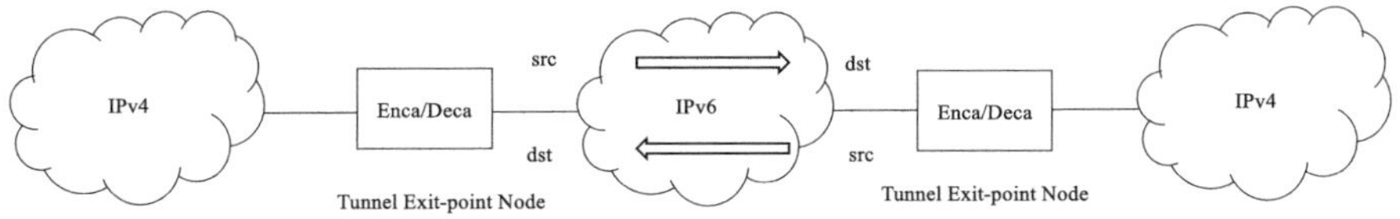

Fig. 5.52 Bidirectional tunnel mechanism

1. *IPv6 Datagram Encapsulation*

IPv6 encapsulation encapsulates the original datagram into a new IPv6 header (including IPv6 extension headers), collectively referred to as the tunnel IPv6 header. When the original datagram is forwarded to the entrance node of the virtual link, the original datagram is forwarded according to the protocol forwarding rules. For example, if the original datagram is.

(1) An IPv6 datagram, then the "hop limit" of the IPv6 original header is reduced by 1.
(2) An IPv4 datagram, then the "time to live" of the IPv4 original header is reduced by 1.

During encapsulation, the source address of the tunnel IPv6 header is the IPv6 address of the tunnel entrance node, and the destination address is the IPv6 address of the tunnel exit node. The encapsulation structure is shown in Fig. 5.53.

The tunnel extension header should be arranged in the order suggested by RFC8200 [2].

As the pre-information of the datagram entering this node, the tunnel entrance node can (determined by configuration) insert the "Tunnel Encapsulation Limit" option. The "Tunnel Encapsulation Limit" option uses the "Destination Options Header", located between the encapsulated IPv6 header and the header of the original IPv6 datagram (depending on the configuration of the information tunnel entrance node, other IPv6 extension headers can appear before or after the "Destination Options Header").

The tunnel encapsulation protocol allows multiple encapsulations, so it is necessary to define the "Tunnel Encapsulation Limit" option. This option specifies (excluding the "Tunnel Encapsulation Limit" itself) the number of times the datagram can be further encapsulated. For example, a "Tunnel Encapsulation Limit" extension header with a limit value of 0 indicates that the datagram is not allowed to be further encapsulated before exiting the current tunnel.

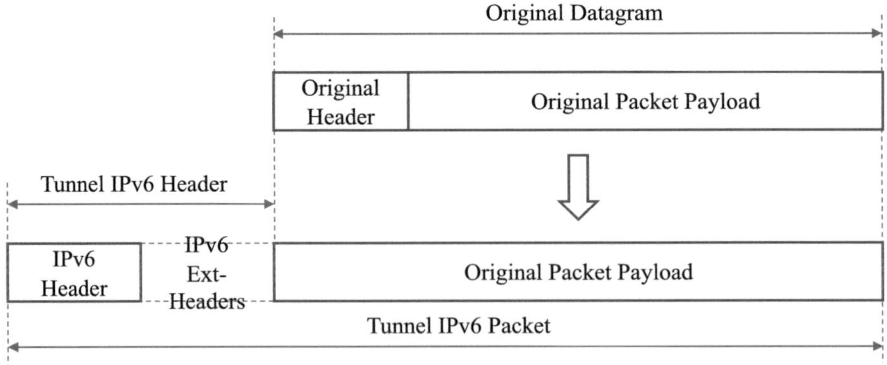

Fig. 5.53 Encapsulated datagram

The "Tunnel Encapsulation Limit" option is only meaningful for the tunnel entrance node. The tunnel entrance node needs to perform the following process for each datagram entering the tunnel of this node.

(1) Check the datagram to see if there is a "Tunnel Encapsulation Limit" option behind the IPv6 header. The content after the IPv6 header must be strictly checked in the order of "from left to right" until one of the following headers is encountered and then stop.

① Contains the "Tunnel Encapsulation Limit" option.
② Another IPv6 header.
③ Non-IP extension headers, such as TCP, UDP, or ICMP.
④ A header that cannot be resolved because it is encrypted or the type is unknown.

Note: This requirement is an exception to the processing flow of the "Destination Options Header", because usually the "Destination Options Header" only needs to be checked at the destination node. A more "standard" workaround is to use the "Hop-by-Hop Header", but this will add extra processing load to each IPv6 node on the tunnel path and increase latency.

(2) If the datagram entering the tunnel entrance node contains the "Tunnel Encapsulation Limit" extension header and the limit value is 0, discard the datagram and send an ICMP parameter problem message to the previous tunnel entrance node. The Code field is 0 (erroneous header field encountered), and the Pointer field points to the third octets option of the "Tunnel Encapsulation Limit" extension header (i.e., the octets containing the limit value of 0).
(3) If the datagram entering the tunnel entrance node contains the "Tunnel Encapsulation Limit" extension header and the limit value is not 0, as part of adding the encapsulation header at this tunnel entrance node, another "Tunnel Encapsulation Limit" option extension header must be added. The limit value of this "Tunnel Encapsulation Limit" is the limit value of the previous "Tunnel Encapsulation Limit" minus 1.
(4) If the datagram entering the tunnel entrance node does not contain the "Tunnel Encapsulation Limit" extension header, but this tunnel entrance node has set the "Tunnel Encapsulation Limit" parameter, as part of adding the encapsulation header at this tunnel entrance node, a "Tunnel Encapsulation Limit" extension header must be added. The limit value of this "Tunnel Encapsulation Limit" is the "Tunnel Encapsulation Limit" parameter set by this tunnel entrance node.
(5) If the datagram entering the tunnel entrance node does not contain the "Tunnel Encapsulation Limit" extension header, and this tunnel entrance node has not set the "Tunnel Encapsulation Limit" parameter, then do not insert the "Tunnel Encapsulation Limit" option extension header.

The "Tunnel Encapsulation Limit" extension header added by the tunnel entrance node will be removed as part of the decapsulation process at the tunnel exit node.

The source node of the original datagram and the node that encapsulates this datagram at the tunnel entrance can be the same node.

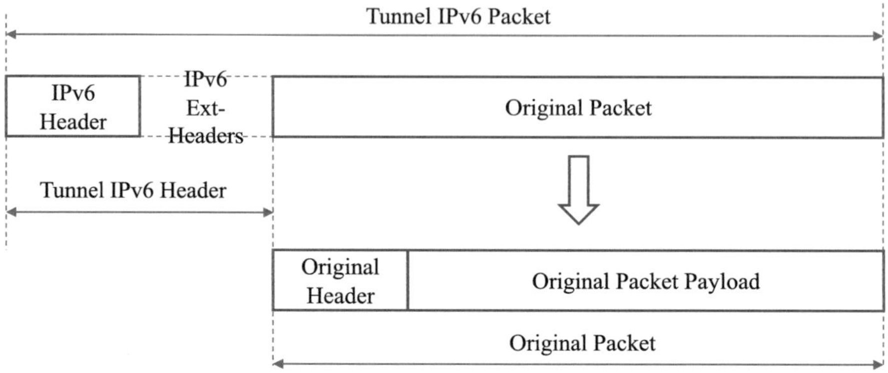

Fig. 5.54 Tunnel datagram decapsulation

2. *IPv6 Datagram Processing in IP Tunnels*

Nodes in the tunnel process IPv6 tunnel datagrams according to IPv6.

(1) The tunnel "Hop-by-Hop Options Header" is processed by each receiving node of the tunnel.
(2) The tunnel routing extension header is used to identify the intermediate processing nodes of the tunnel, to control the forwarding of tunnel datagrams through the tunnel path with finer granularity.
(3) The tunnel "Destination Options Header" is processed at the exit node of the tunnel.

3. *IPv6 Datagram Decapsulation*

The decapsulation of tunnel datagrams is shown in Fig. 5.54.

When the tunnel exit node receives an IPv6 datagram with the destination address being the tunnel exit node, it processes the tunnel header strictly according to the left-to-right processing rules of IPv6. When the processing is completed, check the "Next Header" field of the last header. If this field is marked as "Tunnel", discard the tunnel header and further process the original datagram.

If the "Next Header" field is still the numerical value of the IPv6 tunnel protocol, the generated original datagram needs to continue to be processed by the IPv6 protocol layer.

The node that decapsulates the datagram at the tunnel exit and the destination node can be the same node.

5.9.2 IPv6 Tunnel Header

The tunnel entrance node fills in the main tunnel IPv6 header as follows:

(1) Version: 4 bits; the value is 6.

(2) Traffic Class: 8 bits; determined by the configuration of the tunnel entrance node, the traffic class can be set to the traffic class of the original datagram or a pre-configured value.
(3) Flow Label: 20 bits; determined by the configuration of the tunnel entrance node, the flow label can be set to a pre-configured value. The typical value is 0.
(4) Payload Length: 16 bits; the length of the original datagram, plus the length of the tunnel encapsulation, and the length of the IPv6 extension header (if any).
(5) Next Header: 8 bits; determined by the formal protocol type.

   ① If the original datagram is an IPv6 datagram, the tunnel entrance node sets this parameter to 41.
   ② If it is a "Hop-by-Hop Options Header", then set it to 0.
   ③ If it is a "Destination Options Header", then set it to 60.

(6) Hop Limit: 8 bits.

   ① The "hop limit" of the tunnel IPv6 packet is set to a pre-configured value.
   ② The default value for the host is the "hop limit" declared by the neighbor discovery protocol.
   ③ The default value for the router is the default IPv6 hop limit value (64).

(7) Source Address: 128 bits; configured as the IPv6 address of the tunnel entrance node.
(8) Destination Address: 128 bits; configured as the IPv6 address of the tunnel exit node.

Depending on the configuration parameters of the IPv6 node, the tunnel entrance node can attach one or more IPv6 extension headers to the tunnel IPv6 header, such as the "Hop-by-Hop Options header", the "Routing Header", or other extension headers.

To limit the number of nested encapsulations of datagrams, the "Destination Options Header" of the tunnel can be configured. If this option is the only one present in the "Destination Options Header", it has the following content format, as shown in Fig. 5.55.

(1) Next Header: 8 bits; identifies the type of the original datagram header. If the original datagram is an IPv6 datagram, the next header protocol value is set to 41.
(2) Header Extension Length: 8 bits; the length of the extension header is in octets, excluding the first octet, the tunnel entry node needs to set this field to 0.
(3) Option Type: 8 bits; set to 4.

0										1										2										3	
0	1	2	3	4	5	6	7	8	9	0	1	2	3	4	5	6	7	8	9	0	1	2	3	4	5	6	7	8	9	0	1
Next Header								Header Extension Length=0								Option Type= 4								Option Data Length=1							
Tunnel Encapsulation Limit								PadN Option Type=1								Option Data Length=1								Option Data Length=0							

Fig. 5.55 Tunnel IPv6 extension header

(4) Option1 Data Length: 8 bits; set to 1.
(5) Tunnel Encapsulation Limit: 8-bit unsigned integer; determined according to requirements.
(6) PadN Option Type: 8 bits; set to 1, used to align this header.
(7) Option2 Data Length: 8 bits; set to 1 (option data is an octet).
(8) Option Data Length: 8 bits; set to 0 (all 0).

5.9.3 Tunnel Datagram Fragmentation

1. *IPv6 Tunnel Datagram Fragmentation*

When the original IPv6 datagram enters the tunnel, if the original datagram exceeds the tunnel MTU (i.e., the MTU of the path between the tunnel entry and exit nodes minus the size of the tunnel encapsulation header), the following processing is performed.

(1) If the original IPv6 datagram is larger than the IPv6 minimum link MTU, the tunnel entry node discards the datagram and sends an ICMPv6 "Packet Too Big" message to the source address of the original datagram. The recommended MTU size field is set to the larger of the tunnel MTU or the IPv6 minimum link MTU, i.e.,

$$\max(\text{tunnel MTU, IPv6 minimum link MTU})$$

(2) If the original IPv6 datagram is equal to or smaller than the IPv6 minimum link MTU, the tunnel entrance node encapsulates the original datagram, then divides the generated IPv6 tunnel datagram into fragments that do not exceed the tunnel MTU path to the IPv6 tunnel exit node.

2. *IPv4 Tunnel Datagram Fragmentation*

When the original IPv4 datagram enters the tunnel, if the original datagram exceeds the tunnel MTU (i.e., the MTU of the path between the tunnel entrance node and exit node minus the size of the tunnel encapsulation header), the following processing is performed.

(1) If $DF = 1$ in the original IPv4 datagram, the tunnel entrance node discards the datagram and sends an ICMP "Packet Too Big" message to the source address of the original datagram. The ICMP message Type is "unreachable", the Code is "Packet Too Big", and the recommended MTU field is set to the size of the tunnel's MTU.
(2) If $DF = 0$ in the original IPv4 datagram, the tunnel entrance node encapsulates the original datagram, then divides the generated IPv6 tunnel datagram into fragments that do not exceed the tunnel MTU path to the IPv6 tunnel exit node.

5.9.4 IPv6 Tunnel Error Reporting and Handling

The tunnel ICMP messages reported to the source node of the original datagram are as follows:

(1) Hop Limit Exceeded

① The tunnel has an incorrectly configured hop limit, or contains a routing loop, preventing the datagram from reaching the tunnel exit node.
② This issue is reported to the tunnel entrance node, which can reconfigure the tunnel hop limit to a higher value.
③ This issue will be further reported to the source node of the original datagram.

(2) Unreachable Node

① A node in the tunnel does not exist or is unreachable.
② This issue is reported to the tunnel entrance node, which should reconfigure the valid path between the tunnel entrance and exit nodes.
③ This issue will be further reported to the source node of the original datagram.

(3) Parameter Problem

① The ICMP parameter problem message points to the "Tunnel Encapsulation Limit" in the "Destination Options Header", where the "Tunnel Encapsulation Limit" field is set to 1, indicating that the tunnel message exceeds the maximum allowed encapsulation number.
② This issue will be further reported to the source node of the original datagram.

(4) The above three issues are detected within the tunnel, and their causes are tunnel configuration and topology issues. This issue is reported to the source node of the original IPv6 datagram as a problem of "inaccessibility" caused by "link failure" in the tunnel.
(5) Packet Too Big: The tunnel datagram exceeds the tunnel path MTU. The handling method for the information carried by such ICMP messages is as follows:

① The tunnel entrance node sets or adjusts the tunnel MTU.
② The tunnel entrance node notifies the source node of the datagram of the MTU size of this tunnel, so that it sends IPv6 datagrams of an appropriate size to the tunnel entrance node.

1. *ICMPv6 Messages of the Original IPv6 Datagram*

The ICMP messages sent by the tunnel entrance node to the source node of the original datagram are as follows:

(1) Source Address of the IPv6 Header: A valid IPv6 unicast address of the sending link interface.
(2) Destination Address of the IPv6 Header: The source address field is copied from the original IPv6 header.

For the following ICMP error messages: ① Hop Limit Exceeded; ② Unreachable Node; ③ Parameter Problem, the handling method is to first point the pointer to the valid "Tunnel Encapsulation Limit" in the "Destination Options" extension header, and set the "Tunnel Encapsulation Limit" field to 0.

(1) Type: The value is 1 (unreachable node).
(2) Code: Value is 3 (Address inaccessible).

The handling method for the ICMP error message "Packet Too Big" is.

(1) Type: Value is 2 (Packet Too Big).
(2) Code: Value is 0.
(3) Tunnel MTU: The MTU field in the ICMP message minus the length of the tunnel header.

Only when the original datagram is larger than the minimum link MTU of IPv6, the "Packet Too Big" message is sent to the source node of the original datagram.

2. *ICMP Messages of IPv4 Original Datagrams*

The ICMP message sent by the tunnel entrance node to the source node of the original datagram is as follows.

(1) Source Address of the IPv4 Header: The valid IPv4 unicast address of the sending link interface.
(2) Destination Address of the IPv4 Header: Copy the source address field from the original IPv4 header.

For the following ICMP error messages: ① Hop Limit Exceeded; ② Unreachable Node; ③ Parameter Problem, the handling method is to point to the valid "Tunnel Encapsulation Limit Header", and set the "Tunnel Encapsulation Limit" field to 0.

(1) Type: Value is 3 (Unreachable node).
(2) Code: Value is 1 (Host unreachable).

The handling method for the ICMP error message "Packet Too Big" is.

(1) Type: Value is 3 (Packet Too Big).
(2) Code: Value is 4.
(3) Tunnel MTU: The MTU field in the ICMP message minus the length of the tunnel header.

Only when the original datagram DF = 1, the "Packet Too Big" message is sent to the source node of the original datagram.

5.9.5 *Security Considerations*

The security of the tunnel entrance and exit nodes of the IPv6 tunnel can be protected by protecting the IPv6 path between the IPv6 tunnels, that is, one or more security headers that comply with RFC4302 [12], RFC4303 [13], RFC4835 [62] are used as the pre-headers of the tunnel. At the exit node of the secure IPv6 tunnel, the tunnel security header is processed using security algorithms that comply with RFC4302 [12], RFC4303 [13], RFC4835 [62]. After processing the tunnel header, discard the tunnel IPv6 security header and other tunnel headers.

The strength of integrity, authentication, and confidentiality depends on the type of security header, such as authentication or encryption ESP, and the parameters of the secure tunnel configuration. There is no direct relationship and interaction between the security level of the original datagram and the security level of the secure IPv6 tunnel, because the original datagram is just the valid payload of the secure IPv6 tunnel.

5.10 Summary

Protocols are the core of the Internet, and datagram headers are the specific embodiment of protocols. This chapter has analyzed the datagram headers of the main protocols involved in IPv4 and IPv6 technologies, and on this basis, the translation algorithms and encapsulation algorithms between IPv4 and IPv6 datagram headers have been given.

References

1. Postel J. RFC791: Internet protocol. IETF 1981–09.
2. Deering S, Hinden R. RFC8200: Internet protocol version 6 (IPv6) specification. IETF 2017–07.
3. Almquist P. RFC1349: Type of service in the internet protocol suite. IETF 1992–07.
4. Nichols K, Blake S, Baker F, et al. RFC2474: Definition of the differentiated services field (DS field) in the IPv4 and IPv6 headers. IETF 1998–12.
5. Blake S, Black D, Carlson M, et al. RFC2475: An architecture for differentiated services. IETF 1998–12.
6. Touch J. RFC6864: Updated specification of the IPv4 ID field. IETF 2013–02.
7. Postel J. RFC792: Internet control message protocol. IETF 1981–09.
8. Gont F. RFC6633: Deprecation of ICMP source quench messages. IETF 2015–10.
9. Gont F, Pignataro C. RFC6918: Formally deprecating some ICMPv4 message types. IETF 2013–04.
10. Mogul J, Postel J. RFC950: Internet standard subnetting procedure. IETF 1985–08.
11. Bonica R, Gan D, Tappan D, et al. RFC4884: Extended ICMP to support multi-part messages. IETF 2007–04.
12. Kent S. RFC4302: IP authentication header. IETF 2005–12.
13. Kent S. RFC4303: IP encapsulating security payload (ESP). IETF 2005–12.

14. Arkko J, Bradner S. RFC5871: IANA allocation guidelines for the IPv6 routing header. IETF 2010–05.
15. Filsfils C, Previdi S, Ginsberg L, et al. RFC8402: Segment routing architecture. IETF 2018–07.
16. Filsfils C, Dukes D, Previdi S, et al. RFC8754: IPv6 segment routing header (SRH). IETF 2020–03.
17. Filsfils C, Camarillo P, Leddy J, et al. RFC8986: Segment routing over IPv6 (SRv6) network programming. IETF 2021–02.
18. Gont F. RFC7739: Security implications of predictable fragment identification values. IETF 2016–02.
19. Ramakrishnan K, Floyd S, Black D. RFC3168: The addition of explicit congestion notification (ECN) to IP. IETF 2001–09.
20. Simpson W. RFC1661: The point-to-point protocol (PPP). IETF 1994–07.
21. McCann J, Deering S, Mogul J, et al. RFC8201: Path MTU discovery for IP version 6. IETF 2017–07.
22. Amante S, Carpenter B, Jiang S, et al. RFC6437: IPv6 flow label specification. IETF 2011–11.
23. Postel J. RFC793: Transmission control protocol. IETF 1981–09.
24. Postel J. RFC768: User datagram protocol. IETF 1980–08.
25. Fairhurst G, Westerlund M. RFC6936: Applicability statement for the use of IPv6 UDP datagrams with zero checksums. IETF 2013–04.
26. Kent S, Seo K. RFC4301: Security architecture for the internet protocol. IETF 2005–11.
27. Rescorla E. RFC8446: The transport layer security (TLS) protocol version 1.3. IETF 2018–08.
28. Ylonen T, Lonvick C. RFC4251: The secure shell (SSH) protocol architecture. IETF 2006–01.
29. Gont F, Chown T. RFC7707: Network reconnaissance in IPv6 networks. IETF 2016–03.
30. Cooper A, Gont F, Thaler D. RFC7721: Security and privacy considerations for IPv6 address generation mechanisms. IETF 2016–03.
31. Carpenter B, Jiang S. RFC7045: Transmission and processing of IPv6 extension headers. IETF 2013–12.
32. Conta A, Deering S, Gupta M. RFC4443: Internet control message protocol (ICMPv6) for the internet protocol version 6 (IPv6) specification. IETF 2006–03.
33. Bao C, Li X, Baker F, et al. RFC7915: IP/ICMP translation algorithm. IETF 2016–06.
34. Guha S, Biswas B, Ford S, et al. RFC5382: NAT behavioral requirements for TCP. IETF 2008–10.
35. Bao C, Huitema C, Bagnulo M, et al. RFC6052: IPv6 addressing of IPv4/IPv6 translators. IETF 2010–10.
36. Cotton M, Vegoda L, Meyer D. RFC5771: IANA guidelines for IPv4 multicast address assignments. IETF 2010–03.
37. Haberman B. RFC3307: Allocation guidelines for IPv6 multicast addresses. IETF 2002–08.
38. Li X, Bao C, Chen M, et al. RFC6219: The China Education and Research Network (CERNET) IVI translation design and deployment for the IPv4/IPv6 coexistence and transition. IETF 2011–05.
39. Mathis M, Heffner J. RFC4821: Packetization layer path MTU discovery. IETF 2007–03.
40. Borman D. RFC6691: TCP options and maximum segment size (MSS). IETF 2012–07.
41. Baker F. RFC1812: Requirements for IP version 4 routers. IETF 1995–06.
42. Deering S, Fenner W, Haberman B. RFC2710: Multicast listener discovery (MLD) for IPv6. IETF 1999–10.
43. Haberman B. RFC3590: Source address selection for the multicast listener discovery (MLD) protocol. IETF 2003–09.
44. Vida R, Costa L. RFC3810: Multicast listener discovery version 2 (MLDv2) for IPv6. IETF 2004–06.
45. Cain B, Deering S, Kouvelas I, et al. RFC3376: Internet group management protocol, version 3. IETF 2002–10.
46. Mogul J, Deering S. RFC1191: Path MTU discovery. IETF 1990–11.
47. Bagnulo M, Matthews P, Beijnum I. RFC6146: Stateful NAT64: Network address and protocol translation from IPv6 clients to IPv4 servers. IETF 2011–04.

48. Kohler E, Handley M, Floyd S. RFC4340: Datagram congestion control protocol (DCCP). IETF 2006–03.
49. Lahey K. RFC2923: TCP problems with path MTU discovery. IETF 2000–09.
50. Carpenter B, Jiang S. RFC7136: Significance of IPv6 interface identifiers. IETF 2014–02.
51. Hinden R, Deering S. RFC4291: IP version 6 addressing architecture. IETF 2006–02.
52. Anderson T, Popper A. RFC7757: Explicit address mappings for stateless IP/ICMP translation. IETF 2016–02.
53. Li X, Bao X, Wing D, et al. RFC6791: Stateless source address mapping for ICMPv6 packets. IETF 2012–11.
54. Li X, Bao C, Dec W, et al. RFC7599: Mapping of address and port using translation (MAP-T). IETF 2015–07.
55. Huttunen A, Swander B V, Volpe V, et al. RFC3948: UDP encapsulation of IPsec ESP packets. IETF 2005–01.
56. Rekhter Y, Moskowitz B, arrenberg D, et al. RFC1918: Address allocation for private internets. IETF 1996–02.
57. Weil J, Kuarsingh V, Donley C, et al. RFC6598: IANA-reserved IPv4 prefix for shared address space. IETF 2012–04.
58. Baker F, Savola P. RFC3704: Ingress filtering for multihomed networks. IETF 2004–03.
59. Atlas A, Bonica R, Pignataro C, et al. RFC5837: Extending ICMP for interface and next-hop identification. IETF 2010–04.
60. McCloghrie K, Kastenholz F. RFC2863: The interfaces group MIB. IETF 2000–07.
61. Conta A, Deering S. RFC2473: Generic packet tunneling in IPv6 specification. IETF 1998–12.
62. Manral V. RFC4835: Cryptographic algorithm implementation requirements for encapsulating security payload (ESP) and authentication header (AH). IETF 2007–04.

Chapter 6
Address Mapping

Addressing is the core component of the Internet. This chapter provides a detailed analysis and comparison of the address structures of IPv4 and IPv6, and derives a stateless mapping algorithm between IPv4 and IPv6 addresses (and transport layer port numbers, if required).

6.1 IPv4 Address Structure

IP provides datagram transmission from the source node to the destination node, which are represented by fixed-length addresses. The Internet Protocol uses the address carried in the datagram header to deliver the Internet datagram to the destination node. The process of selecting the transmission path is called routing. The Internet Protocol treats each datagram as an independent entity that is unrelated to any other datagram. It is connectionless at the network layer and does not require the existence of physical or virtual circuits. The address in the Internet datagram is global unique address, and both end systems (servers, clients) and links (routers) use unified addressing (see the content of Sect. 2.2.3 of this book). However, in recent years, with the exhaustion of IPv4 addresses and the introduction of IPv4 address translation technology, the uniqueness of the entire Internet's addressing structure has been changed. In short, servers on the Internet still maintain the uniqueness of the global IP address, while the vast majority of clients use private IPv4 addresses and do not have the uniqueness of the global IP addresses.

The originally designed IPv4 address uses a classful mode, defined by RFC791 [1]. It is assumed that there are three types of networks in the world.

(1) A small number of large networks, each with tens of millions of hosts.
(2) A medium number of medium-sized networks, each with tens of thousands of hosts.
(3) Numerous small networks, each with hundreds of hosts.

X. Li and C. Bao, *New IPv6 Transition Technology*,
https://doi.org/10.1007/978-981-95-8427-7_6

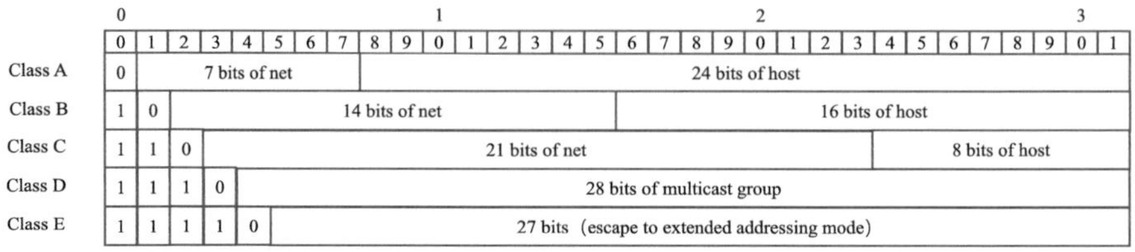

Fig. 6.1 Classful IPv4 address

Large, medium, and small networks are distinguished by the leading bits of the address, as shown in Fig. 6.1.

The total length of the IPv4 address is 32 bits, represented as 4 segments, each segment is an octet, which is represented by a decimal from 0 to 255, called dotted decimal, that is, an IPv4 address is represented by 4 numbers from 0 to 255, such as 192.168.1.1.

The classification of IPv4 addresses and the range of network numbers are as follows.

(1) Class A address.

① The first bit of the first octet is 0.
② The first octet is the network address, and the other three octets are the host address.
③ Class A address range: 1.0.0.0 to 127.255.255.255.
④ The 127.X.X.X in Class A address is the loopback address.
⑤ Class A address is a unicast address.

(2) Class B address.

① The first two bits of the first octet are 10.
② The first and second octets are the network address, the other two octets are the host address.
③ The range of Class B addresses: 128.0.0.0~191.255.255.255.
④ The 169.254.X.X of Class B addresses is a reserved address.
⑤ Class B addresses are unicast addresses.

(3) Class C addresses.

① The first 3 bits of the first octet are 110.
② The first, second, and third octets are the network address, the fourth octet is the host address.
③ The range of Class C addresses: 192.0.0.0~223.255.255.255.
④ Class C addresses are unicast addresses.

(4) Class D addresses.

① The first 4 bits of the first octet are 1110.
② There is no distinction between network address and host address.

③ The range of Class D addresses: 224.0.0.0~239.255.255.255.
④ Class D addresses are multicast addresses.

(5) Class E addresses.

① The first 5 bits of the first octet are 11110.
② There is no distinction between network address and host address.
③ The range of Class E addresses: 240.0.0.0~255.255.255.255.
④ Class E addresses are defined as experimental addresses, but they have not been activated to date.

6.1.1 Classless IPv4 Address Structure

In the late 1980s, the expansion of academic networks and the commercialization of the Internet led to many new organizations joining the Internet. Each new organization needed to allocate addresses according to the Class A/B/C address plan, and the demand for network addresses (especially in Class B space) grew exponentially. Therefore, researchers in the field of network operations and network engineering began to consider how to improve the Class A/B/C address system to meet the needs of long-term scalability. In November 1991, the IETF created the ROAD working group. This group identified three major issues in January 1992.

(1) Exhaustion of Class B network addresses: One fundamental reason for this problem is the lack of a network category suitable for medium-sized organizations. Class C has a maximum of 254 host addresses, which is too few. Class B allows up to 65534 host addresses, which is too many for most organizations. However, Class B addresses are most suitable for subnetting, i.e., one Class B address can be divided into 256 subnets of Class C address size.
(2) Routing table explosion problem: The size of the routing table exceeded the ability of the hardware, software, and personnel to effectively process and manage at that time.
(3) Address exhaustion problem: The eventual exhaustion of the 32-bit IPv4 address space.

Between 1993 and 1995, the growth of the Internet at that time made the first two problems critically important. In 1990, the ROAD working group introduced the concept of "supernet" (RFC1338 [2]), and later published RFC1518 [3] and RFC1519 [4], introducing the concept of classless inter-domain routing (CIDR).

CIDR (RFC4632 [5]) was defined with the design and deployment purpose of slowing down the growth of the global routing table and reducing the consumption rate of the IPv4 address. The ROAD working group did not attempt to solve the third problem, as it is a longer-term issue. Instead, the ROAD working group worked to address the difficulties faced in the short and medium term, allowing the Internet to continue to function effectively while making progress on a longer-term solution.

Since then, the IETF has not recommended the use of the A/B/C class-based address allocation system, but instead uses "classless" hierarchical IP address blocks, known as prefixes. The allocation of prefixes is intended to roughly follow the actual Internet topology, so that clustered addresses can be used to simplify the growth of the global routing table. One implication of this strategy is that prefix allocation and address aggregation are usually based on the "provider-subscriber" relationship, as this is the basis for determining the Internet topology.

When initially proposed in RFC1338 [2] and RFC1519 [4], CIDR was intended to solve short-term problems of 3–5 years. In fact, this address allocation mechanism has far exceeded its expected lifespan and has become a medium-term solution to the above problems.

In the simplest sense, the change from A/B/C class network addresses to classless prefixes is to clarify which bits in the 32-bit IPv4 address are interpreted as network addresses (prefixes), and which bits are used to address individual hosts within the network. In CIDR notation, the prefix is displayed as "dotted decimal", just like traditional IPv4 addresses, followed by a "/" (slash) character, then followed by a decimal value from 0 to 32, which describes the number of bits of the prefix.

For example, the traditional B-class network 172.16.0.0 with an implied network mask of 255.255.0.0 is defined as the prefix 172.16.0.0/16, where "/16" indicates that the network part (high 16 bits) of the 32-bit mask used to extract the prefix is "1", and the host part (low 16 bits) is "0". Similarly, the traditional C-class network number 192.168.99.0 is defined as the prefix 192.168.99.0/24; the network part (high 24 bits) is "1", and the host part (low 8 bits) is "0".

Using classless prefixes with explicit prefix lengths allows for more flexible matching of address space as needed. Previously, only three types of networks, A/B/C, could be allocated. The new classless prefix address model can flexibly define address spaces of size 2 to the power of n, where n ranges from 0 to 32.

The IPv4 address pool is managed by IANA (see Tables B.1 in Appendix B, C.1 in Appendix C, and D.1 in Appendix D).

IANA allocates IPv4 address blocks from the global IPv4 address pool to Regional Internet Registries (RIRs). These allocations are made in bit blocks of 2^{24} addresses (i.e., /8). RIRs allocate smaller address blocks to Local Internet Registries (LIRs) or ISPs. These entities can directly use the aforementioned IPv4 address blocks for "allocation" (usually the case for ISPs. Currently, the size of IPv4 allocations is /24 or shorter prefix lengths, for IPv6 it is /48 or shorter prefix lengths) or further "subdivide" the addresses (assignment) (this will be handled by the ISP's internal routing, no uniform regulation is required) to their customers. These RIR address allocations vary according to the needs of each ISP or LIR. For example, a large ISP can be allocated an address block of 2^{17} addresses (/15 prefix), while a small ISP can be allocated an address block of 2^{11} addresses (/21 prefix).

The CIDR table provides information on all CIDR prefix sizes, showing the number of possible addresses in each prefix and the number of such size prefixes that can be in the 32-bit IPv4 address space, as shown in Fig. 6.2.

notation	addrs/block	# blocks	Notes
n.n.n.n/32	1	4294967296	Host
n.n.n.x/31	2	2147483648	Point-to-Point link
n.n.n.x/30	4	1073741824	
n.n.n.x/29	8	536870912	
n.n.n.x/28	16	268435456	
n.n.n.x/27	32	134217728	
n.n.n.x/26	64	67108864	
n.n.n.x/25	128	33554432	
n.n.n.0/24	256	16777216	Class C
n.n.x.0/23	512	8388608	
n.n.x.0/22	1024	4194304	
n.n.x.0/21	2048	2097152	
n.n.x.0/20	4096	1048576	
n.n.x.0/19	8192	524288	
n.n.x.0/18	16384	262144	
n.n.x.0/17	32768	131072	
n.n.0.0/16	65536	65536	Class B
n.x.0.0/15	131072	32768	
n.x.0.0/14	262144	16384	
n.x.0.0/13	524288	8192	
n.x.0.0/12	1048576	4096	
n.x.0.0/11	2097152	2048	
n.x.0.0/10	4194304	1024	
n.x.0.0/9	8388608	512	
n.0.0.0/8	16777216	256	Class A
x.0.0.0/7	33554432	128	
x.0.0.0/6	67108864	64	
x.0.0.0/5	134217728	32	
x.0.0.0/4	268435456	16	
x.0.0.0/3	536870912	8	
x.0.0.0/2	1073741824	4	
x.0.0.0/1	2147483648	2	
0.0.0.0/0	4294967296	1	Default route

Fig. 6.2 CIDR table

(1) *n* is the decimal representation of an octet value.
(2) *x* is a value of 1 to 7 bits, based on the prefix length, forming network bits as "1", non-network bits as "0", and bitwise "and" with the IPv4 address, and then converted to decimal form.

The initial development of classless addressing was mainly to improve the scalability of routing on the global Internet. Since the scalability of routing is closely coupled with the way addresses are used, the deployment of CIDR has a significant impact on the way addresses are allocated. The only way to reduce the number of routing states on the Internet is through address aggregation. Generally speaking, the topology of the network is determined by the ISP that builds the network, so address allocation with topological significance is necessarily ISP-oriented.

For a network connected to an ISP, aggregation is simple: the network uses the address space allocated by its ISP, which is a subset of the ISP's address space. The network does not need explicit routing. The ISP broadcasts an aggregated block. This route is declared to provide routing reachability for all customers of the ISP. However, there are three situations that can reduce the effect of aggregation.

(1) Multihomed networks: Multihomed networks must announce address blocks to each ISP, which typically prevents them from aggregating their routing information into any of these ISP's address spaces. The network can still use a subset of the ISP's address space, but in most cases, the route to that subset of the ISP's address space should be explicitly announced by all ISPs.
(2) Therefore, the global routing cost of multihomed networks is the same as before the adoption of CIDR.
(3) Networks that change ISPs but do not renumber: This creates a "punching" effect in the original ISP's cluster route announcement. CIDR handles this situation by requiring the new ISP to announce a more specific address block. This announcement takes precedence over the cluster address block because it is a longer match. To maintain the efficiency of aggregation, it is recommended that networks that change ISPs eventually use address prefixes obtained from the new ISP's address space.
(4) Traffic engineering: To implement traffic engineering, it is usually necessary to "punch" in the ISP's aggregated address announcement. This announcement takes precedence over the aggregated address block because it is a longer prefix match. Therefore, even if a network uses the ISP's address space, the global routing cost is about the same as before the adoption of CIDR in the case of implementing traffic engineering.

The routing announcement rules on the Internet through BGP are as follows:

(1) Rule One: Forwarding on the Internet is based on "longest prefix match". That is, the address prefixes of multihomed networks must always be explicitly announced (cannot be aggregated). If a network is multihomed, then all paths entering the "higher network hierarchy" must be known in that level.
(2) Rule Two: Routers that generate aggregated-address block should not discard datagrams that match any more specific routes. In other words, the "next hop" of the aggregated route should be an empty destination node. This is to prevent forwarding loops when some addresses covered by the aggregation cannot be accessed.

Note that during network failures, it may happen that some datagrams are routed to a network that obtains address space from one ISP but can only access the Internet through another ISP (i.e., the network has changed ISPs). In this case, such datagrams will be forwarded along the path announced by the cluster route. Rule Two will cause

ISPs that only announce aggregated routes to discard such datagrams to prevent erroneous delivery.

All routing destination nodes can accept any network address and mask, the only constraint is that the mask must remain continuous. Note that the aggregated route with a prefix of 0.0.0.0/0 is used as the default route. To prevent the default route from being broadcasted through inter-domain protocols, this route is only allowed to be published to another routing domain when the router is explicitly configured, and it should not be used as a "default" option.

CIDR technology supports multi-level hierarchical address aggregation, but at the final subnet level, there are the following restrictions on the use of IPv4 addresses.

(1) The first unicast address with a value of 0 in the IPv4 subnet is the network identifier of the subnet and cannot be used by the hosts on the subnet.
(2) The last address of the IPv4 subnet is the broadcast address and cannot be used by the hosts on the subnet.
(3) The total number of addresses that can be assigned to the hosts on the IPv4 subnet is the total number of addresses for the host on the subnet minus 3, because the router acting as the default route also needs to be assigned an address.

6.1.2 *Special IPv4 Addresses*

There are some reserved special addresses in the network as shown below, special IPv4 unicast addresses are shown in Table 6.1.

Special IPv4 multicast addresses are shown in Table 6.2.

These special addresses must be handled separately during the translation process between IPv4/IPv6.

Table 6.1 Special IPv4 unicast addresses

Address	Purpose
0.0.0.0	Undefined address
255.255.255.255	Broadcast address
127.x.x.x	Loopback address, for local use

Table 6.2 Special IPv4 multicast addresses

Address	Purpose
224.0.0.1	All hosts in the subnet
224.0.0.2	Every router in the network with multicast capability
224.0.0.0–224.0.0.255	For use within the subnet
239.0.0.0–239.255.255.255	For use within the organization

6.1.3 Private and Shared Address Spaces

1. *Private Address Space*

The development of the Internet has exceeded everyone's expectations, and its continuous exponential growth rate has brought new challenges.

(1) The first challenge is the exhaustion of the global IPv4 address space. IPv4 addresses have been exhausted, and it is almost impossible to obtain new IPv4 address segments from regional Internet address registration organizations, except for IPv4 address transactions.
(2) Another challenge is the explosion of the IPv4 routing table. In order to control the growth of the routing table, ISPs obtain a segment of address space from RIRs (such as the Asia Pacific Network Information Center (APNIC), etc.) and then allocate subsets of this address space to customers according to demand. In this case, through address aggregation technology, this address space only appears in a single routing entry in the global routing table (RFC1518 [3], RFC1519 [4]). However, given the current scale and growth rate of the Internet, it is not realistic to assign a globally unique public IPv4 address to each host connected to the Internet. Furthermore, it is also unrealistic to dynamically assign addresses to hosts in an organization that temporarily need to connect to the Internet using common address allocation and configuration techniques.

Based on the above reasons, the IETF has classified the devices used for TCP/IP networking within an enterprise.

(1) First category.

① No need to access hosts of other enterprises or the global Internet.
② The IP addresses used by hosts in this category are unique within the enterprise, but meaningless to other enterprises.

(2) Second category.

① Need partial access (for example, email, FTP, network news, remote login) to servers of other enterprises or hosts of the global Internet. These accesses can be handled through intermediate gateways (for example, Network Address Translation (NAT) or application layer gateway (ALG)). For these hosts, unrestricted external access (through IP connections) is unnecessary and should be avoided for privacy/security reasons.

② The IP addresses used by these hosts are clear within the enterprise, but meaningless to other enterprises.

(3) Third category.

① Need network layer (provided through IP connections) access to servers of other enterprises or hosts of the global Internet. Public servers of their own enterprise, allowing clients of other enterprises or hosts of the global Internet to access.
② These hosts need to access hosts of other enterprises or the global Internet through globally unique public IP addresses, or be accessed by them.

Therefore, the first and second category hosts are called "private", while the third category hosts are called "public".

For example, for security reasons, many enterprises use application layer gateways to connect their internal networks to the Internet. The internal network usually does not directly access the Internet, so only one or more gateways are visible on the Internet. In this case, the hosts of the internal network are "private" and can use non-global-unique Internet addresses, while the gateways visible on the Internet are "public" and need to use globally unique public Internet addresses.

IANA has reserved three private IPv4 address space blocks (RFC1918 [6]), as shown in Table 6.3.

Enterprises can use the above address blocks without approval from IANA and/or RIR, so they can be used by any number of enterprises. However, these private address spaces are only unique within the enterprise (or between coordinated enterprises). Any enterprise that needs a globally unique address space needs to obtain a public IPv4 address from the Internet address registration authority.

The following points should be noted when using private address spaces:

(1) According to the classification method of devices using TCP/IP networking within the enterprise, private addresses are configured for the first and second types of devices, and public addresses are configured for the third type of devices. For the second type of devices, limited access to the outside is provided through NAT or ALG.

Table 6.3 Private IPv4 addresses

Address range	Prefix	Host address	Class identified
10.0.0.0–10.255.255.255	Prefix 10/8	24 bits	1 Class A address
172.16.0.0–172.31.255.255	Prefix 172.16/12	20 bits	16 consecutive Class B addresses
192.168.0.0–192.168.255.255	Prefix 192.168/16	16 bits	256 consecutive Class C addresses

(2) When changing a host from the first/second type to the third type, it involves changing the IP address, changing the corresponding DNS entries, and modifying the configuration files of the machine or related devices. The same process is required for the reverse.
(3) Because private addresses do not have a global meaning, the routing information of private addresses should not be announced outside the enterprise domain. The boundary routers of the enterprise network, especially the boundary routers of the ISP, should not announce and receive routing information containing private addresses.
(4) Similar to the boundary routers of the enterprise network, the boundary routers of the ISP should not send and receive datagrams with private addresses as the destination address and source address.
(5) Indirect references to such addresses should be restricted within the enterprise. A prominent example of this reference is the DNS resource authority record. ISPs should take measures to prevent the leakage of this internal information of the enterprise.
(6) The use of private addresses can greatly save public IPv4 address resources.
(7) The use of private addresses can give enterprises flexibility in network design (including address allocation, routing configuration, security management, and sustainability).
(8) One disadvantage of using private address spaces is that when enterprises merge, multiple private address interwoven internal networks may be interconnected, in which case it is necessary to renumber the addresses, re-allocate addresses, and reconfigure the parameters of the networking devices.

2. *Shared Address Space*

Simply defining private IPv4 address space is not enough, because the IPv4 address space is almost exhausted. However, before the transition to IPv6 is completed, ISPs must continue to support the growth of IPv4. For this reason, many ISPs deploy carrier-grade NAT (CGN) devices described in RFC6264 [7]. Since CGN is deployed on the network side of the ISP, it usually needs to use public IPv4 addresses. In this case, using private IPv4 addresses will cause operational failures, so ISPs need to obtain new IPv4 address blocks. These types of address blocks are called "shared IPv4 addresses" and are used to connect CGN devices to customer premise equipment (CPE).

On the other hand, the shared IPv4 addresses are not globally routable IPv4 addresses, similar to the private IPv4 addresses defined in RFC1918 [6]. However, shared IPv4 addresses and the private IPv4 addresses defined in RFC1918 [6] are different. According to the definition of RFC6598 [8], the shared address space can only be used for ISP's infrastructure (the routers and other network devices).

The shared IPv4 address range allocated by IANA is shown in Table 6.4.

Shared IPv4 addresses are mainly used for CGN deployment. Shared IPv4 addresses can also be used as non-globally routable addresses, forwarding datagrams using the same private IPv4 addresses between different interfaces of the router (through NAT).

Table 6.4 Shared IPv4 addresses

Address range	Prefix	Host address	Traditional naming
100.64.0.0–100.127.255.255	100.64/10 prefix	22 bits	64 Class B addresses

Datagrams using shared IPv4 addresses as destination or source addresses cannot be forwarded on the ISP's border router. Internet service providers must filter such datagrams on the ingress link, the only exception being for CGN hosting services.

When running a single DNS infrastructure, Internet Content Providers (ICPs) should not configure ZONE files containing shared IPv4 addresses. When running a mixed DNS infrastructure, ICPs should not publish ZONE files containing shared IPv4 addresses.

Reverse DNS queries for shared IPv4 addresses are not allowed to be forwarded to the global DNS (DNS providers should filter out recursive requests for reverse DNS queries to the shared IPv4 address space). In doing so, mechanisms similar to AS112.net (defined by RFC6304 [9] and RFC1918 [6] for private IPv4 address space reverse DNS queries) can be avoided.

6.2 IPv6 Address Structure

6.2.1 IPv6 Address

The IPv6 address is defined by RFC4291 [10], as a 128-bit identifier for an interface/interface set. There are three types of IPv6 addresses.

(1) Unicast: A single interface identifier. Datagrams sent to a unicast address are delivered to the interface configured with that unicast address.
(2) Anycast: A set of interface identifiers (usually belonging to different nodes). Datagrams sent to an anycast address are delivered to one of the "nearest" interfaces configured with that anycast address ("nearest" is measured by the distance of the routing protocol).
(3) Multicast: A set of interface identifiers (usually belonging to different nodes). Datagrams sent to a multicast address are delivered to all interfaces that have joined that multicast address.

There are no broadcast addresses in IPv6, their function is replaced by multicast addresses.

The allocation of IPv6 addresses is shown in Table E.1 in Appendix E and Table F.1 in Appendix F.

1. *IPv6 Addressing Model*

All types of IPv6 addresses belong to interfaces, not nodes. An IPv6 unicast address refers to a single interface. The interface belongs to a single node, so any unicast address of that node can serve as the identifier for that node.

All interfaces must have at least one link local class unicast address. A single interface can also have multiple IPv6 addresses of any type or range (unicast, anycast, and multicast).

For interfaces that do not need to send or receive IPv6 datagrams, it is not necessary to configure a unicast address beyond the link local range. This is more convenient for point-to-point interfaces. There is one exception to this addressing model: if multiple physical interfaces are used as a logical interface in the implementation, a unicast address (or a set of them) can be assigned to multiple physical interfaces. This is useful for load balancing across multiple physical interfaces.

Currently, IPv6 continues to use the IPv4 addressing model, that is, a subnet prefix is associated with a link. But multiple subnet prefixes can be assigned to the same link.

2. *Text Representation of Addresses*

IPv6 addresses are represented as three types of strings.

(1) Preferred form: x:x:x:x:x:x:x:x, where "x" is 1 to 4 hexadecimal characters, i.e., an IPv6 address contains eight 16-bit addresses separated by ":".
Example:
2001:db8:0:0:8:800:200c:417a
Note that it is not necessary to write leading 0s in a domain.
(2) "Compressed form: A group or multiple groups of 16-bit 0 s can be represented as "::" "::" can only appear once in an IPv6 address. "::" can be used to compress leading or trailing 0 s in an IPv6 address.
Example:
2001:db8::8:800:200c:417a (unicast address)
ff01::101 (multicast address)
::1 (loopback address)
:: (undefined address)
(3) Combined form of IPv4 and IPv6: x:x:x:x:x:x:d.d.d.d, where "x" is 6 high-bit hexadecimal addresses and "d" is 4 low-bit decimal addresses (standard IPv4 representation).
Example:
::13.1.68.3
::ffff:129.144.52.38

3. *Representation of Prefix*

Similar to the representation of IPv4 prefixes, the IPv6 prefix is represented as: IPv6 address/prefix length.

(1) The IPv6 address is a valid IPv6 address as mentioned above.
(2) The prefix length is a decimal value that specifies the number of consecutive bits from the left that include the prefix.
Example:
2001:db8:0:cd30::/60

4. *Address Type Identification*

The type of IPv6 address is identified by the high bits, as shown in Table 6.5.

Anycast addresses are taken from the unicast address space (can be any unicast address), and semantically, anycast addresses cannot be distinguished from unicast addresses.

The general format of global unicast addresses is described below. Some special use subtypes of global unicast addresses include IPv6 addresses that embed IPv4 addresses. Future standard specifications may redefine one or more subranges of global unicast space. Current IPv6 implementations must use any of the prefixes listed above as global unicast addresses.

5. *Unicast Address*

IPv6 unicast addresses can be aggregated by any prefix length, similar to CIDR in IPv4.

IPv6 has the following types of unicast addresses.

(1) Global unicast.
(2) Site-local unicast (obsolete, not recommended for use).
(3) Link-local unicast.

Table 6.5 IPv6 address types

Address type	Binary prefix representation	IPv6 representation
Undefined	00…0(128 bits)	::/128
Loopback	00…1(128 bits)	::1/128
Multicast	11111111	ff00::/8
Link local	1111111010	ff80::/10
Global unicast	Other	2000::/3

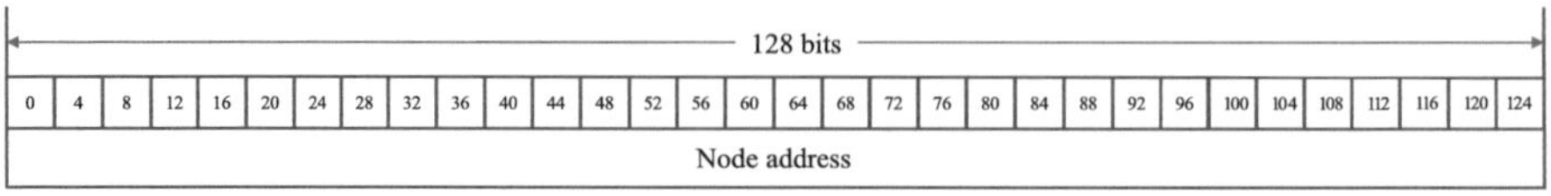

Fig. 6.3 Basic understanding of the IPv6 addresses by nodes

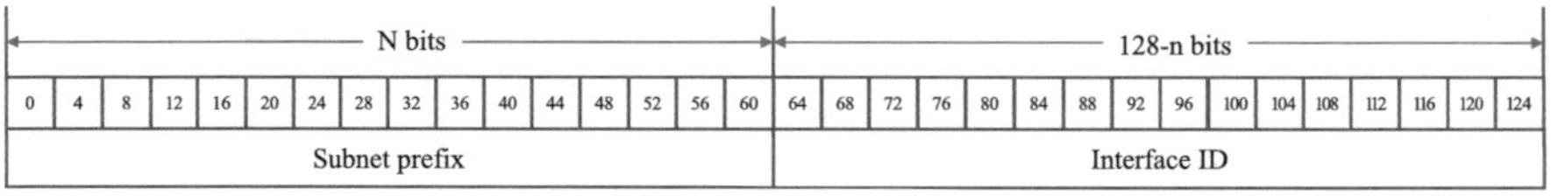

Fig. 6.4 In-depth understanding of the IPv6 addresses by nodes

There are also some special use subtypes of global unicast addresses, such as IPv6 addresses that embed IPv4 addresses. In the future, other types of unicast addresses or subtypes of unicast may be defined.

Depending on the role of the node (for example, host or router), IPv6 nodes may have different understandings of the internal structure of IPv6 addresses.

(1) The node can consider the unicast address (including its own address) as having no internal address structure, as shown in Fig. 6.3.
(2) A slightly more complex host (but still quite simple) may understand the subnet prefix length of its own network link interface, where different addresses may have different n, as shown in Fig. 6.4.

Although routers may not need to interpret the internal structure of IPv6 unicast addresses, routers must have one or more hierarchical network prefix information to run routing protocols. Depending on the position of the router in the routing hierarchy, different routers have different knowledge of network prefix information.

In addition to the above network boundary knowledge, nodes should not make any assumptions about the structure of IPv6 addresses.

Nodes need to treat the following IPv6 addresses specially.

1) **Undefined address**

The address 0:0:0:0:0:0:0:0 is called an undefined address, which should never be assigned to any node, indicating no address. The source address field of any message sent by an IPv6 host before address initialization is 0:0:0:0:0:0:0:0.

Undefined addresses are not allowed to be used as the destination address of an IPv6 datagram or an address in an IPv6 routing header. IPv6 routers are not allowed to forward IPv6 datagrams whose source address is 0:0:0:0:0:0:0:0.

2) **Loopback Address**

The unicast address 0:0:0:0:0:0:0:1 is known as the loopback address. Nodes can use this address to send IPv6 datagrams to themselves. The loopback address cannot be

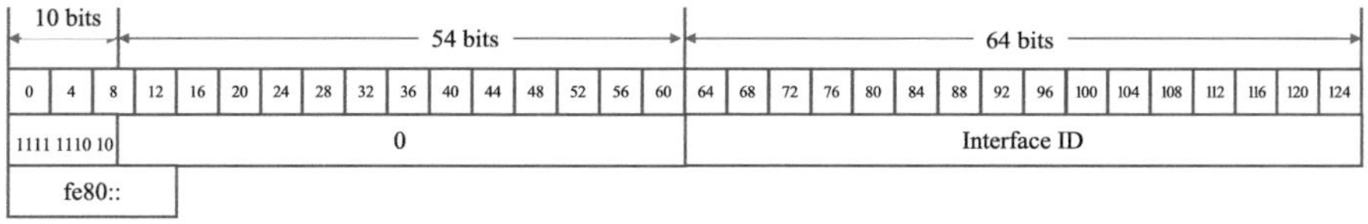

Fig. 6.5 Link-local address

assigned to any physical interface. It has a local link scope and can be considered as the unicast address of the local link virtual interface (commonly referred to as the "loopback" interface).

The loopback address cannot be used as the source address for datagrams sent outside this node. Datagrams with the loopback address as the destination address cannot be sent outside this node, IPv6 routers are not allowed to forward these datagrams, but must discard them.

3) **IPv6 Addresses Embedding IPv4**

Originally there are three types of IPv6 addresses that embed IPv4 addresses in the lower 32 bits, named IPv4-compatible IPv6 address, IPv4-mapped IPv6 address, and IPv4-translated IPv6 address. These type of addresses are historical and will not be used. The address format of these IPv6 addresses is in Chap. 3 of this book. The new IPv4 address embedding formats are in the later Sections of this Chapter.

4) **Link-Local Address**

The link-local address is used for a single link. The link-local address has the following format, as shown in Fig. 6.5.

The link-local address is used for automatic address configuration, neighbor discovery, and other purposes on a single link, or for communication between nodes on this link in the absence of a router.

Routers must not forward datagrams with the link-local address as the source or destination address on links other than this link.

5) **Site-Local Address**

The original consideration of the site-local address was to address within the site without the need for a global prefix, but the IETF has deprecated the site-local address.

The site-local address has the following format, as shown in Fig. 6.6.

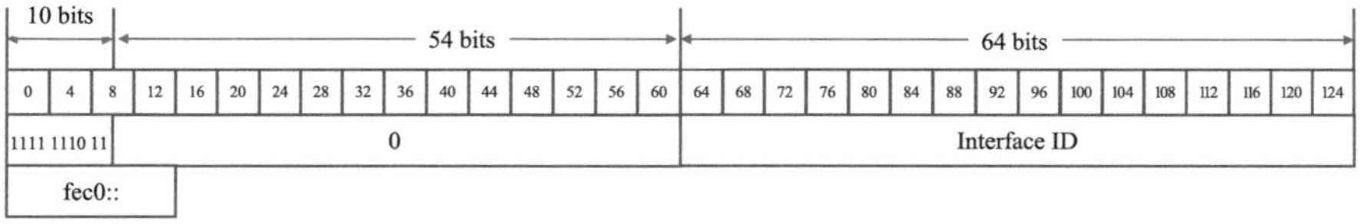

Fig. 6.6 Site-local address

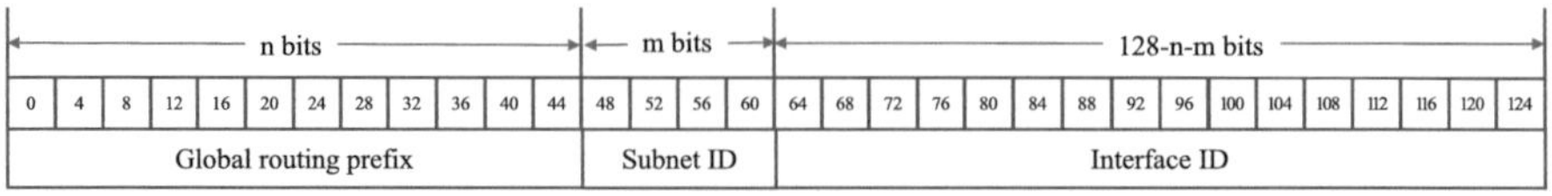

Fig. 6.7 Global unicast address

New implementations do not need to support the special behavior of this prefix defined by RFC3513 [12] (i.e. new implementations must treat this prefix as a global unicast address). Existing implementations and deployments can continue to use the prefix of the site-local address.

6) **Global Unicast Address**

The global routing prefix is a hierarchical structure of IPv6 addresses and prefix lengths assigned to a site (a collection of subnets/links). The subnet ID is the "link identifier" within the site, and the interface ID is the "interface identifier".

The general format of the IPv6 global unicast address is shown in Fig. 6.7.

All global unicast addresses not starting with binary 000 need to have a 64-bit "interface identifier" field, i.e.,

$$n + m = 64$$

Global unicast addresses starting with binary 000 do not have this restriction for the "interface identifier" field.

6. *Anycast Address*

An IPv6 anycast address is an address assigned to multiple interfaces (usually belonging to different nodes). Data packets sent to an anycast address are delivered to one of the "nearest" interfaces configured with that anycast address ("nearest" is measured by the distance of the routing protocol).

Anycast addresses are allocated from the unicast address space and can use any unicast address format. Therefore, anycast addresses cannot be semantically distinguished from unicast addresses. When a unicast address is assigned to more than one interface, this address becomes an anycast address, and the node where the address is located must be explicitly configured to know that this is an anycast address.

For any anycast address, there is a longest prefix "P" of this anycast address to identify the topological range of the service provided. Within the area identified by "P", the anycast address must exist as a separate route in the routing table (usually called a "host" route). Outside the area identified by "P", the anycast address can be clustered into the routing entry of prefix "P".

Note: The prefix "P" of the anycast address can be an empty prefix, i.e., the serviced members may not have topological locality. In this case, the anycast address must maintain a separate routing entry throughout the Internet, which will lead to scalability issues, i.e., how many such anycasts can appear in the global Internet at most. Therefore, global anycasts are not scalable.

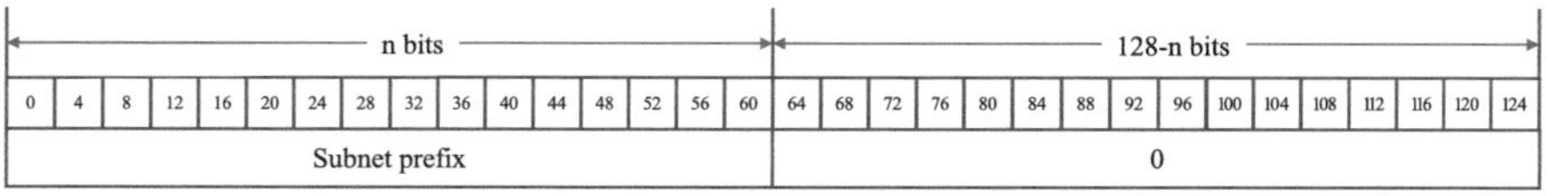

Fig. 6.8 Router subnet prefix anycast address

Examples of using anycast addresses are as follows:

(1) Identify a group of routers providing Internet access. These addresses can be used as intermediate addresses in the IPv6 routing extension header, identifying a particular service provider or a group of service providers.
(2) Identify a group of routers connected to a specific subnet, or a group of routers providing access to a specific routing domain.
(3) Identify DNS servers at all levels, especially root servers (DNS root).

The router subnet prefix anycast address is predefined, as shown in Fig. 6.8.

The subnet prefix anycast address is used to identify the prefix of a specific link. Semantically, this anycast address is the same as the "interface identifier" of the link interface subnet prefix with a value of 0.

Data packets sent to the router subnet prefix anycast address will be delivered to a router on the subnet. All router link interfaces need to support the router subnet prefix anycast address. The router subnet prefix anycast address is intended to allow applications to communicate with a router in a group of routers.

Therefore, for a specific IPv6 subnet, the first unicast address with a value of 0 is the anycast address of the router interface and cannot be assigned to other hosts on the subnet.

CIDR technology supports multi-level hierarchical address aggregation, but at the final subnet level, the use of IPv6 addresses has the following restrictions.

(1) The first unicast address with a value of 0 in the IPv6 subnet is the anycast address of the router subnet and cannot be assigned for use by hosts on the subnet.
(2) IPv6 does not require broadcasting (multicasting is used to implement the corresponding function), so the last address of the subnet can be assigned for use by hosts on the subnet.

7. *Multicast Address*

An IPv6 multicast address is an identifier for a set of link interfaces (usually on different nodes). A link interface can belong to any number of multicast groups. An IPv6 address starting with binary 11111111 is a multicast address.

RFC3306 [13], RFC3956 [14], and RFC7371 [15] have extended the definition of original multicast format, as shown in Fig. 6.9.

1) **Flag 1 (ff1): 4 bits**

(1) The high bit flag was initially reserved and must be initialized to 0.

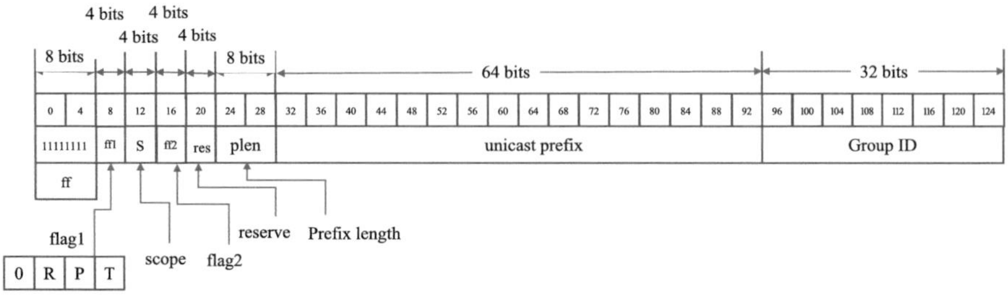

Fig. 6.9 Multicast address format

(2) R rendezvous point flag, defined by RFC3956 [14]. Where R = 0 indicates that the rendezvous point address is not embedded; R = 1 indicates that the IPv6 unicast address of the rendezvous point is embedded.
(3) P prefix flag, defined by RFC3306 [13]. Where P = 0 indicates no prefix information; P = 1 indicates prefix information.
(4) T transient flag. T = 0 indicates a permanently assigned ("well-known") multicast address, assigned by IANA. T = 1 indicates a non-permanent ("transient" or "dynamic") multicast address.

2) **Scope: 4 bits**

Multicast scope: used to define the multicast domain, its values are as shown in Table 6.6.

3) **Flag 2 (ff2): 4 bits**

The flag is reserved, its value must be set to all 0 s.

4) **Reserved (reserve, res): 4 bits**

Reserved for future expansion, its value must be set to all 0 s.

5) **Embedded IPv6 Unicast Address Prefix Length (plen): 8 bits**

Only to be used when an IPv6 unicast address is embedded in the multicast address, otherwise its value must be set to all zeros.

6) **Group Identifier (group ID): 112 bits or 32 bits**

The structure of the "group identifier" field is defined by RFC3306 [13], including "permanent" or "transient" multicast groups within a given range.

(1) Permanently assigned multicast addresses are independent of the scope.
(2) For example, if the Network Time Protocol (NTP) group has a permanent multicast address, and its group ID is 101 (hexadecimal), then ff01:0:0:0:0:0:0:101 represents all NTP servers on the same node and the same interface; ff02:0:0:0:0:0:0:101 represents all NTP servers on the same link; ff05:0:0:0:0:0:0:101 represents all NTP servers within the same site; ff0e:0:0:0:0:0:0:101 represents all NTP servers on the Internet.

Table 6.6 Definition of domains

Value	Definition	Description
0	Reserved	–
1	Local interface scope	The local interface scope is limited to a single interface of a node and is only used for multicast transmission of loopback addresses
2	Local link scope	The local link scope is the same as the unicast scope that spans the same topological area
3	Reserved	–
4	This management scope	This management scope must be the smallest configuration management scope, and cannot be automatically derived from physical connections or non-multicast configurations
5	Local site scope	The local site scope is limited to a single site
6	(Unassigned)	Can be used by administrators to define other multicast areas
7	(Unassigned)	Can be used by administrators to define other multicast areas
8	This organization scope	Limited to multiple sites belonging to one organization
9	(Unassigned)	Can be used by administrators to define other multicast areas
A	(Unassigned)	Can be used by administrators to define other multicast areas
B	(Unassigned)	Can be used by administrators to define other multicast areas
C	(Unassigned)	Can be used by administrators to define other multicast areas
D	(Unassigned)	Can be used by administrators to define other multicast areas
E	Global scope	Across the entire Internet
F	Reserved	–

(3) Non-permanently assigned multicast addresses only make sense within a given range. For example, the group identified by the non-permanently assigned site-local multicast address ff15:0:0:0:0:0:0:101 has the following characteristics: ① Groups from different sites are unrelated; ② Groups from different ranges are unrelated; ③ They are unrelated to permanently assigned groups.

Multicast addresses must not be used as the source address in an IPv6 datagram or appear in any routing extension headers.

Routers must not forward any multicast datagrams beyond the "scope" field indicated in the multicast address.

Nodes must not send datagrams to multicast addresses whose "scope" field contains a value of 0. If such a datagram is received, it must be silently discarded.

"Nodes should not send datagrams to multicast addresses whose "scope" field contains a reserved value of "F". If such a datagram is sent or received, it must be treated as if the same datagram was sent to a multicast address with a global scope.

The following well-known multicast addresses are predefined and have explicit scope significance.

When the flag T is 0, these group IDs are not allowed to be used for any other scope.

Reserved multicast addresses are as follows:

ff00:0:0:0:0:0:0:0
ff01:0:0:0:0:0:0:0
ff02:0:0:0:0:0:0:0
ff03:0:0:0:0:0:0:0
ff04:0:0:0:0:0:0:0
ff05:0:0:0:0:0:0:0
ff06:0:0:0:0:0:0:0
ff07:0:0:0:0:0:0:0
ff08:0:0:0:0:0:0:0
ff09:0:0:0:0:0:0:0
ff0a:0:0:0:0:0:0:0
ff0b:0:0:0:0:0:0:0
ff0c:0:0:0:0:0:0:0
ff0d:0:0:0:0:0:0:0
ff0e:0:0:0:0:0:0:0
ff0f:0:0:0:0:0:0:0

The above multicast addresses are reserved and will never be assigned to any multicast group.

All nodes addresses are as follows:

ff01:0:0:0:0:0:0:1
ff02:0:0:0:0:0:0:1

The above multicast address identifies all IPv6 nodes, where: ff01 represents the local interface scope; ff02 represents the local link scope.

All router addresses:

ff01:0:0:0:0:0:0:2
ff02:0:0:0:0:0:0:2
ff05:0:0:0:0:0:0:2

The above multicast address identifies all IPv6 routers, where: ff01 represents the local interface scope; ff02 represents the local link scope; ff05 represents the local site scope.

Solicited node address:

ff02:0:0:0:0:1:ffXX:XXXX

The "solicited node" multicast address is calculated as a function of a node's unicast and anycast addresses. A solicited node's multicast address is formed by obtaining the lower 24 bits of the address (unicast or anycast), appended to the ff02:0:0:0:0:1:ff00::/104 prefix, between ff02:0:0:0:0:1:ff00:0000 and ff02:0:0:0:0:1:ffff:ffff.

For example, the multicast address of the "solicited node" corresponding to the IPv6 address 4037::01:800:200e:8c6c is ff02::1:ff0e:8c6c. In the case where multiple IPv6 prefixes are configured, the IPv6 addresses only differ in the prefix part (i.e., the high bits), and these different IPv6 prefix addresses can map to the same "solicited node" multicast address, thereby reducing the number of multicast addresses that the node must join.

Networked nodes need to calculate the "solicited node" multicast address and join all the "solicited node" multicast addresses corresponding to the unicast and anycast addresses configured on the node (manually or automatically) on the corresponding interface.

7) **Several Special Multicast Addresses**

For IPv6 multicast extensions, see: RFC3306 [13], RFC3956 [14], RFC7371 [15], RFC7346 [16], and RFC4489 [17] etc.

(1) Unicast prefix-based IPv6 multicast address format. RFC3306 [13] stipulates a dynamic allocation method for IPv6 multicast addresses—unicast prefix-based IPv6 multicast addresses. This type of IPv6 multicast address includes the unicast address prefix of its multicast source network, and allocates globally unique multicast addresses in this way. Its structure is shown in Fig. 6.10.

Where, ff1 is 4 bits, where the first bit is defined as R bit (R = 0), the second bit is defined as P bit (P = 1), the third bit is defined as T bit (T = 1), and the fourth bit is undefined. This 4-bit combination represents the identifier of the multicast address based on the unicast address prefix; S is 4 bits, determined according to the scope; ff2 is 4 bits, a reserved field, must be 0; res is 4 bits, a reserved field, must be 0; plen is 8 bits, indicating the effective length of the

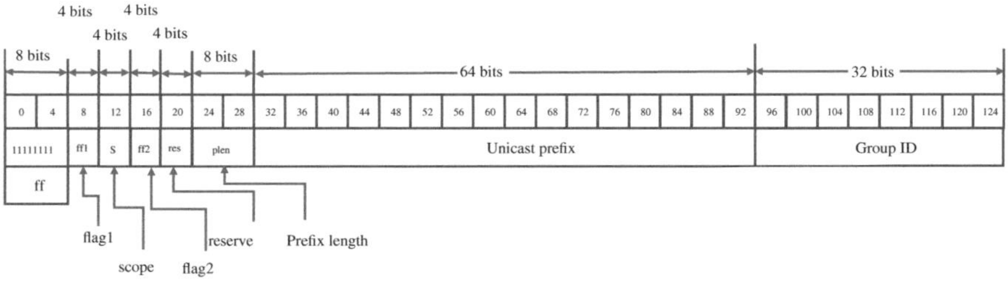

Fig. 6.10 Unicast prefix-based IPv6 multicast address format

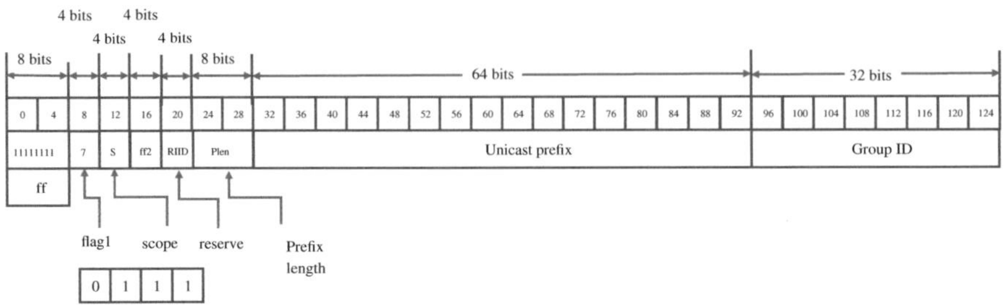

Fig. 6.11 Format of IPv6 multicast address with embedded rendezvous point

network prefix (in bits); the unicast prefix is 64 bits, indicating the unicast prefix of the subnet to which this multicast address belongs.

For example, the network with a unicast prefix of 3ffe:ffff:1::/48 assigns a multicast address based on the unicast prefix of ff3X:30:3ffe:ffff:1::/96 (X represents any legal "scope").

(2) Embedded Rendezvous Point (RP) IPv6 multicast address format: This format incorporates an IPv6 multicast address with an embedded RP address, enabling multicast routers to directly parse the RP address from the address itself (RFC3956 [14]). The embedded RP is part of IPv6 PIM, which employs a unique RP discovery mechanism. As illustrated in Fig. 6.11, this mechanism allows multicast routers to identify and utilize the RP address without additional lookups.

Here, ff1 is 4 bits, where the first bit is defined as R bit (R = 1), the second bit is defined as P bit (P = 1), the third bit is defined as T bit (T = 1), and the fourth bit is undefined. This 4-bit combination represents the identifier of the IPv6 multicast address with an embedded rendezvous point (RP); S is 4 bits, determined by the range; ff2 is 4 bits, a reserved field, must be 0; RIID is 4 bits, representing the interface identifier of the RP address; plen is 8 bits, representing the effective length of the network prefix (in bits); the unicast prefix is 64 bits, representing the unicast prefix of the subnet to which this multicast address belongs.

Suppose the network administrator wants to set the RP in the 2001:db8:beef:feed::/64 segment, then the IPv6 multicast address with the embedded RP address is ff7X:Y40:2001:db8:beef:feed::/96, which can allocate 32 bits of group identification, and the embedded RP address is 2001:db8:beef:beed::Y/64.

(3) Source-specific multicast address format. RFC3306 [13] also defines IPv6 source-specific multicast (SSM), and the multicast address also uses the IPv6 multicast address format based on the unicast prefix, where the plen field and the unicast prefix field are both 0. The range of IPv6 SSM multicast addresses is ff3X::/32 (X represents any legal "range"). The source-specific multicast address format is shown in Fig. 6.12.

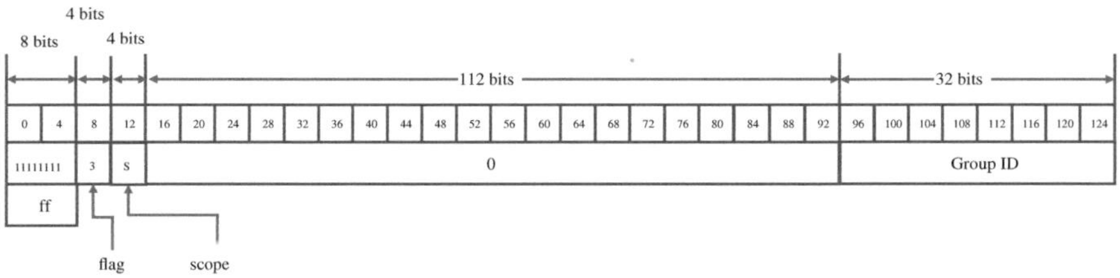

Fig. 6.12 Source-specific multicast address format

8. *Interface Identifier*

The interface identifier in the IPv6 unicast address is used to identify the link interface, which must be unique within the subnet. It is recommended not to assign the same interface identifier to different nodes on the link. Of course, the interface identifier may also be unique in a larger range. In some cases, the interface identifier can be directly generated from the link layer address of the interface. The same interface identifier can be used on multiple interfaces connected to different subnets on a single node.

Note: The uniqueness of the interface identifier is unrelated to the uniqueness of the IPv6 address. For example, a global unicast address can be created by a local interface identifier, and a link-local address can also have a global interface identifier.

Except for the address value starting with binary 000, the interface identifier of all unicast addresses must be 64 bits, which may be created by the 64-bit extended unique identifier (EUI-64).

EUI-64 can be generated by a universal token (for example, the 48-bit MAC address of IEEE 802 or IEEE EUI-64). When there is no global token (for example, serial links, tunnel endpoints, etc.), or when you do not want to use a global token (for example, privacy temporary tokens), a local token can be used.

An example of a modified EUI-64 is created as follows.

Converting IEEE EUI-64 to an interface identifier involves inverting the "u" bit. The following is the IEEE EUI-64, as shown in Fig. 6.13.

Where, "c" stands for "company identifier" (company_id) bits; "0" stands for "global/local" bits (u); "g" stands for "group identifier" bits (g); "m" stands for "manufacturer extension identifier" bits.

The corresponding IPv6 interface identifier is shown in Fig. 6.14.

The only change is the reversal of the "global/local" bit (u) value.

0					1					2					3					4					5					6	
0	2	4	6	8	0	2	4	6	8	0	2	4	6	8	0	2	4	6	8	0	2	4	6	8	0	2	4	6	9	0	2
c	c	c	0	c	c	c	c	c	c	c	c	m	m	m	m	m	m	m	m	m	m	m	m	m	m	m	m	m	m	m	m
c	c	c	g	c	c	c	c	c	c	c	c	m	m	m	m	m	m	m	m	m	m	m	m	m	m	m	m	m	m	m	m

Fig. 6.13 IEEE EUI-64

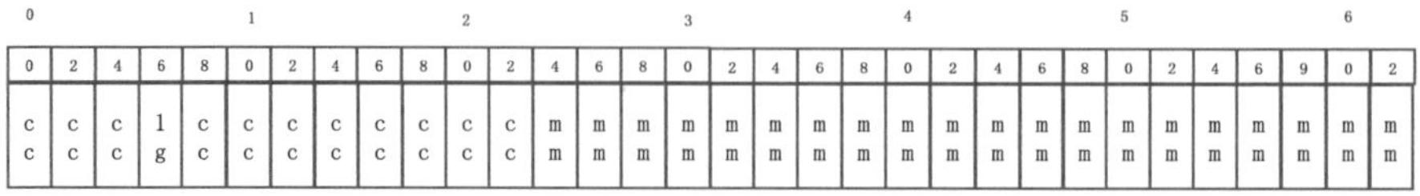

Fig. 6.14 Modified EUI-64

The motivation for reversing the "u" bit in the IEEE EUI-64 is that system administrators can conveniently configure the improved EUI-64 when there is no hardware token (for example, using a physical link or tunnel). If not reversed, the standard address format would be 0200:0:0:1, 0200:0:0:2, instead of the simpler 0:0:0:1, 0:0:0:2, etc.

IPv6 nodes do not need to verify the uniqueness of the improved EUI-64 in the global scope when the "u" bit is 1.

The "global/local" bit identifier of the improved EUI-64 is used to develop an IPv6 address format that can use a global hardware token, as shown in Fig. 6.15.

Because MAC addresses are globally unique, the modified EUI-64 is also globally unique, which leads to serious user privacy leakage issues. Therefore, RFC7136 [18] updated RFC4291 [10], the new standard allows IPv6 addresses not generated by the IEEE MAC address to be free from the "u" bit constraint. RFC3041 [19], RFC4941 [20] RFC8981 [21], RFC8064 [22] introduced and improved the privacy mechanism of the address, making the interface identifier a variable of time.

The interface identifier is one of the most confusing concepts in IPv6. Here are some key points summarized according to the IETF's RFC standards (which are inherently contradictory).

(1) Unicast addresses do not have an internal address structure, so an interface identifier is not needed.
(2) The prefix length of IPv6 routing can be 0 –128 bits, so an interface identifier is not needed.
(3) Except for addresses starting with the binary value 000, the interface identifier of all unicast addresses must be 64 bits (recommended to be EUI-64).
(4) EUI-64 is formed by reversing the "u" bit in the IEEE EUI-64. The "u" bit being 1 indicates global uniqueness; the "u" bit being 0 indicates local scope.
(5) IPv6 nodes do not need to verify the global uniqueness of the interface identifier when the "u" bit is 1. (And there is no unified scheme to verify the global uniqueness of the interface identifier).

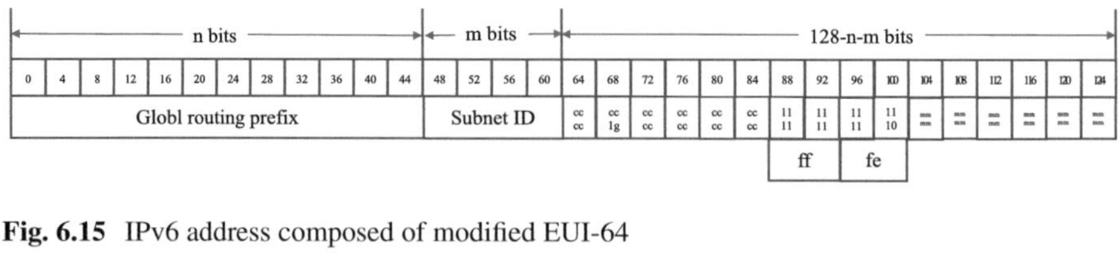

Fig. 6.15 IPv6 address composed of modified EUI-64

(6) IPv6 addresses not generated by the IEEE MAC address are not subject to the "u" bit constraint.
(7) Stateless address configuration SLAAC, must use a 64-bit interface identifier.
(8) The introduction of privacy addresses makes the interface identifier changing over time.

Despite the above contradictory requirements, the semantic consensus for the address of the new generation of IPv6 transition technology is:

(1) In order to support as wide a range of IPv6 terminal systems as possible, the IPv6 configuration technology using the SLAAC mechanism should be adopted, so the prefix length of the terminal access subnet must be 64 bits.
(2) In addition, IPv6 addresses do not need to consider any restrictions on interface identifiers (i.e., any length of prefix length can be used, "u" bits can be any value).
(3) In order to support the mechanism of the mainstream operating systems discovering translator prefixes through DNS (RFC7050 [23]), the prefix length of "IPv4-converted IPv6 address" is recommended to be 96 bits (see Chap. 8 of this book). Note that IETF also tries to put RFC7050 obsolete.

9. *Addresses Required by IPv6 Nodes*

An IPv6 host needs to recognize the following addresses.

(1) The link-local address required for each interface.
(2) Any other existing (manually or automatically configured) unicast and anycast addresses of the node interface.
(3) Loopback address.
(4) All node multicast addresses.
(5) The "node request" multicast address corresponding to each unicast and anycast address of the node.
(6) Other multicast addresses that the node belongs to.

An IPv6 router needs to recognize all the addresses that the host needs to recognize, as well as the following addresses.

(1) The subnet anycast address of all router interfaces.
(2) All other anycast addresses configured by the router.
(3) All router multicast addresses.

6.2.2 Unique Local IPv6 Unicast Addresses

Similar to private IPv4 addresses (RFC1918 [6] addresses), RFC4193 [24] defines IPv6 "private addresses". Unlike private IPv4 addresses, the massive address space of IPv6 allows organizations to define non-overlapping "private addresses" (i.e., no need for unified registration, but globally unique IPv6 unicast addresses), known as Unique Local Addresses (ULAs). These addresses are not expected to be globally

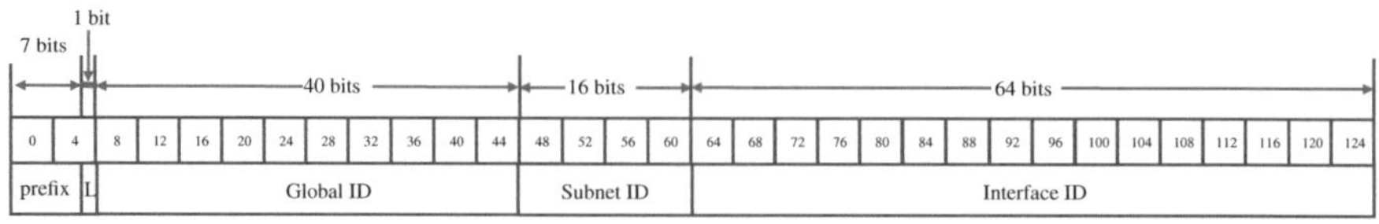

Fig. 6.16 ULA format

routable, but are routable within a limited area, such as within a corporate network, or even between corporate networks where there is a demand for communication.

ULA have the following characteristics.

(1) The prefix is globally unique (with a very low probability of conflict).
(2) They have a well-known prefix, which facilitates filtering at the network boundary.
(3) They allow for combination or private interconnection without causing address conflicts, thus eliminating the need for renumbering.
(4) They are independent of ISPs and do not need to be connected to the global Internet.
(5) Even if they are accidentally leaked to the outside world through routing or domain names, they will not conflict with other addresses.
(6) Applications can treat these addresses as IPv6 global unicast addresses.

1. *Format*

ULA use pseudorandom numbers to create a global identifier (Global ID), with the following format, as shown in Fig. 6.16.

(1) Prefix: 7 bits; the fc00::/7 prefix is used to identify unique local IPv6 unicast addresses.
(2) L: 1 bit; if the prefix is locally assigned, it is set to 1. Future use scenarios for 0 can be defined.
(3) Global Identifier (Global ID, ID): 40 bits; Global identifier used to create a globally unique prefix.
(4) Subnet ID: 16 bits; Subnet identifier within the site.
(5) Interface ID: 64 bits; Interface ID.

Reason for choosing /7: The prefix /7 corresponds to a 41-bit global ID space (including L bits), which can provide 22 trillion address prefix allocations, while only occupying 0.8% of the total IPv6 address space.

2. *Pseudo-random Global ID Algorithm*

The algorithm described below is used to generate a global ID locally. In each case, the generated global ID is used for prefix generation.

(1) Obtain the current time in 64-bit NTP format.

(2) Obtain the EUI-64 from the system running this algorithm. If EUI-64 does not exist, a 48-bit MAC address can be created. If EUI-64 cannot be obtained or created, a unique identifier of this node (for example, the system serial number) should be used.
(3) Concatenate the time with the system-specific identifier to create a key.
(4) Calculate the digest according to the SHA-1 algorithm, the result value is 160 bits.
(5) Use the least significant 40 bits as the global ID.
(6) Use the fc00::/7 prefix, set the L bit to 1, and then concatenate the above 40-bit global ID to generate the local IPv6 prefix (/48).

This algorithm will generate a unique global ID and can be used to create a local IPv6 prefix.

By default, the range of these addresses is global. Its limitation lies in the routability of the prefix (limited to one network, or with explicit routing protocols with other networks).

3. *Configuration Guide*

ULA are routed within the site in the same way as other types of unicast addresses, and any IPv6 routing protocol can be used.

ULA will share the same subnet ID with global unicast IPv6 addresses.

The default configuration of the network management domain boundary routing protocol should be not to receive or send routes within the range of the fc00::/7 prefix. Network administrators can configure to allow receiving and sending longer prefixes of fc00::/7 when needed, in order to interconnect between specific networks through ULA.

If BGP is used at the boundary with the Internet Service Provider, the default BGP configuration must filter the sending and receiving of prefixes within the range of fc00::/7. If interconnection is needed, a /48 or longer routing prefix can be configured.

For link-state-based interior gateway protocols (IGP), it is recommended to include prefixes using unique local IPv6 unicast addresses in the IGP domain or areas, in order to control the distribution of prefixes.

Use ULA for communication within the site, so that it is not necessary to change the global address when changing ISPs.

When merging multiple sites, using ULA is less likely to require address changes, because all addresses are (almost) unique, so only the corresponding routes need to be configured.

When a host using a ULA needs to communicate with the Internet, there are two options.

(1) Hosts that need to communicate with the Internet configure a permanent or temporary global unicast IPv6 address while configuring a unique local IPv6 unicast address.
(2) Use IPv6 Network Prefix Translation (NPTv6), see Chap. 12 of this book.

4. *DNS Issues*

It is recommended not to configure ULA in the global DNS.

Reverse domain name queries for ULA should not be sent to global domain name servers. The recommended method is for the domain name resolution server to assume an authoritative server for an empty d.f.ip6.arpa domain when it receives such queries, and return the DNS error code "non-existent record" (NXDOMAIN, CODE = 3).

5. *High-Level Protocols and Applications*

For ULA, applications and other high-level protocols can be processed in the same way as other types of global unicast IPv6 addresses, without the need for special treatment.

6.3 Address Mapping Technology

6.3.1 IPv4-Embedded IPv6 Address

1. *Address Format Evolution and Design Requirements*

The core of IPv4/IPv6 translation technology is to formulate translation rules for IPv4 headers and IPv6 headers. The mapping of IPv4 addresses and IPv6 addresses is one of the main components of header translation.

(1) Stateless translation technology for mapping from IPv4 addresses to IPv6 addresses and from IPv6 addresses to IPv4 addresses is algorithm-based, without the need to dynamically establish a mapping table through a client-initiated session.
(2) Stateful translation technology for mapping from IPv4 addresses to IPv6 addresses is still stateless (and thus algorithm-based), but mapping from IPv6 addresses to IPv4 addresses is stateful, requiring a client-initiated session to dynamically establish a mapping table.

In addition, translation technology defines two types of IPv6 addresses, which are used as follows:

(1) "IPv4-translatable IPv6 address": This address is an IPv6 address that has a mapping relationship with an IPv4 address and is configured for real IPv6 hosts within the IPv6 domain. This address can be seen as an upgraded version of the IPv4 translated address defined by RFC4291 [10].
(2) "IPv4-converted IPv6 address": Used to represent real IPv4 hosts in the IPv6 network in a mirrored form. This address can be seen as an upgraded version of the IPv4 mapped address defined by RFC4291 [10].

A summary of special IPv6 addresses for traditional IPv6 transition technology and new-generation IPv6 transition technology is shown in Fig. 6.17

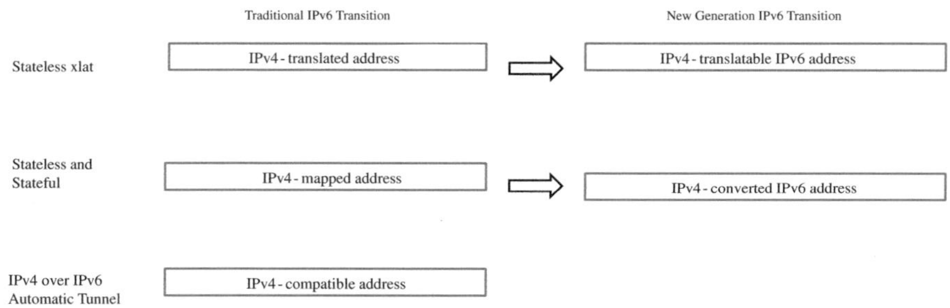

Fig. 6.17 Special IPv6 addresses for IPv6 transition technology

The uses of these addresses are shown in Table 6.7.

The design requirements for the IPv6 addresses involved in the new generation of stateless IPv4/IPv6 translation technology are as follows:

(1) Embed the IPv4 address in the IPv6 address.
(2) Unify the format and parameters of "IPv4-translatable IPv6 address" and "IPv4-converted IPv6 address" where possible.
(3) Redefine prefix properties, including "Network Specific Prefix" and "Well-Known Prefix".
(4) Introduce flexibility in prefix length.
(5) Expand the mapping algorithm for the prefix and suffix when necessary.

2. *"IPv4-Embedded IPv6 Address" Format*

RFC6052 [11] defines "IPv4-translated IPv6 address" and "IPv4-converted IPv6 address", both of which follow the same format, called "IPv4-embedded IPv6 address". It consists of a variable length prefix, an embedded IPv4 address, and a variable length suffix.

The format of "IPv4-embedded IPv6 address" is shown in Fig. 6.18.

Where, the prefix length is specified by "PL". In addition, the unique octet (u-oct) is set to 0, for compatible with the interface identifier in the IPv6 addressing architecture defined by RFC4291 [10]. That is, depending on the prefix length, the

Table 6.7 IPv6 addresses used for transition technology

Translation mechanism	IPv6 address configured for real IPv6 host	Representing real IPv4 host in IPv6 network in mirrored form
Stateless translator (Current)	IPv4-translatable IPv6 address	IPv4-converted IPv6 address
Stateful translator (Current)	Any IPv6 address	
Stateless translator (Historical)	IPv4 translated address	IPv4 mapped address
Stateful translator (Historical)	Any IPv6 address	
Automatic tunnel (Historical)	IPv4 compatible address	

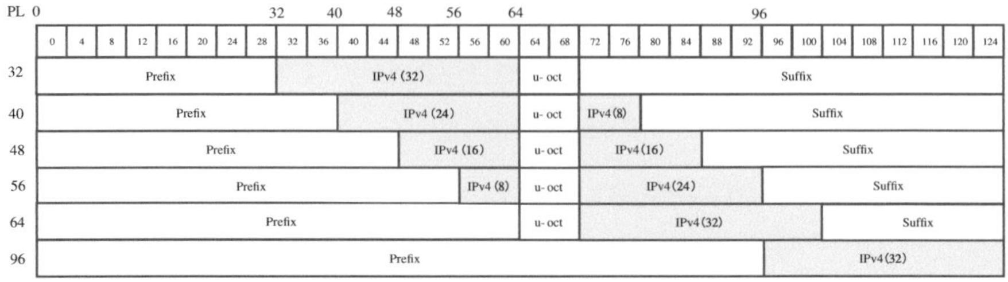

Fig. 6.18 Format of IPv4-embedded IPv6 address (including u-oct)

four octets of IPv4 address may be separated by "u-oct" of all zeros. Especially in the following cases.

(1) The prefix length is 32 bits, and the IPv4 address encoding is located at 32–63 bits.
(2) The prefix length is 40 bits, the first 24 bits of the IPv4 address are encoded at 40–63 bits, and the remaining 8 bits are at 72–79 bits.
(3) The prefix length is 48 bits, the first 16 bits of the IPv4 address are encoded at 48–63 bits, and the remaining 16 bits are at 72–87 bits.
(4) The prefix length is 56 bits, the first 8 bits of the IPv4 address are encoded at 56–63 bits, and the remaining 24 bits are at 72–95 bits.
(5) The prefix length is 64 bits, and the IPv4 address encoding is located at 72–103 bits.
(6) The prefix length is 96 bits, and the IPv4 address encoding is located at 96–127 bits.

If the prefix length is 96 bits, then there are no remaining bits, so there is no suffix. In other cases, the remaining bits of the address form the suffix. These bits are reserved for expansion and should currently be set to 0. When the translator receives a message containing an "IPv4-embedded IPv6 address" with a suffix not equal to 0, it should ignore these non-zero values and continue execution as if these bits were 0 (this behavior after expansion is different).

RFC7136 [18] updated RFC4291 [10], allowing the "u" bit to be ignored for IPv6 addresses generated from non-IEEE MAC layer addresses. Therefore, the new "IPv4-embedded IPv6 address" can maintain the continuity of the IPv4 address embedded in the IPv6 address, as shown in Fig. 6.19.

To consider compatibility, the implementation of the translator must support both formats without u-oct and with u-oct (completed by configuration commands), it is recommended:

(1) The format without u-oct is the default format;
(2) The format with u-oct is specified by the configuration.

It should be noted that the "IPv4-embedded IPv6 address" defined by RFC6219 [25] is a special case without u-oct. For operators with a /32 or larger IPv6 prefix,

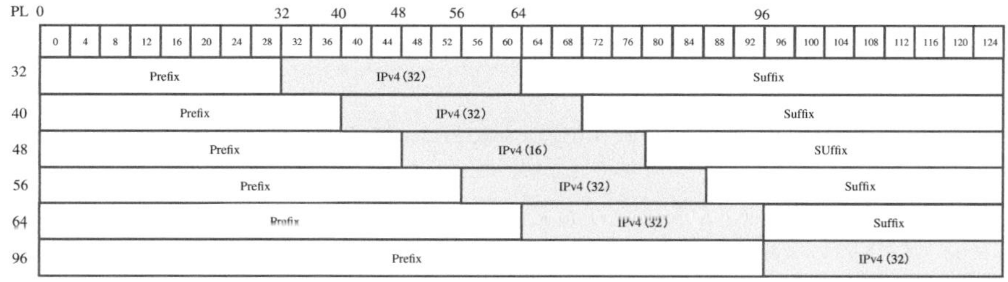

Fig. 6.19 Format of IPv4-embedded IPv6 address (without u-oct)

it is recommended to use its last /40 as IPv4 translation, which has the following features.

(1) The IPv6 address has explicit translation semantics, identified by the ff bit from 32 to 39 (for example, 2001:db8: ff00::/40).
(2) The traditional IPv4 /24 subnet corresponds to the IPv6 interface identifier length /64.
(3) A single IPv4 address /32 corresponds to IPv6 /72.

The "IPv4-embedded IPv6 address" defined by RFC6219 [25] is shown in Fig. 6.20.

3. *Address Converting Algorithm*

Generate "IPv4-embedded IPv6 address" according to the following algorithm.

(1) Combine the IPv6 prefix, IPv4 address, and suffix to generate a 128-bit IPv6 address.
(2) When configuring the format with u-oct, if the prefix length is less than 96 bits, insert an 8-bit "u-oct" of all zeros at the appropriate position (64–71 bits).

Extract the IPv4 address from the "IPv4-embedded IPv6 address" according to the following algorithm.

(1) When u-oct is not configured, obtain the 32-bit IPv4 address and suffix according to the IPv6 prefix length.

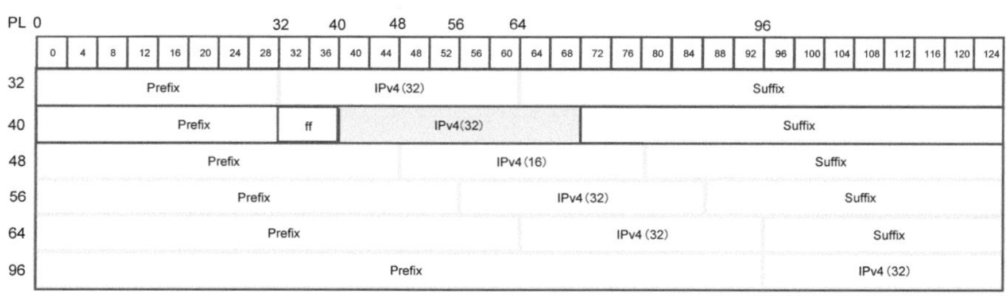

Fig. 6.20 "IPv4-embedded IPv6 address" (RFC6219)

(2) When configuring the u-oct format, if the prefix length is 96 bits, extract the IPv4 address from the last 32 bits; for other prefix lengths, delete the 8-bit u-oct byte, obtain a 120-bit sequence (move the valid bits from 72–127 bits to 64–119 bits), and then extract the 32-bit IPv4 address and suffix after the IPv6 prefix.

6.3.2 IPv6 Prefix Category

The “IPv4-embedded IPv6 address” requires an IPv6 prefix, which is divided into two categories.

(1) Network Specific Prefix (NSP).
(2) Well-Known Prefix (WKP).

The IPv6 prefix length when using NSP is 32 bits, 40 bits, 48 bits, 56 bits, 64 bits, or 96 bits. The IPv6 prefix length when using the WKP can only be 96 bits.

1. *Network Specific Prefix*

The NSP is a subset of the overall IPv6 prefix used by the ISP, specifically for IPv4/IPv6 translation. The NSP can be directly aggregated to the overall IPv6 prefix used by the ISP, without the need to announce the routing information separately outside the ISP’s aggregated prefix (except for the purpose of traffic engineering). Therefore, routing policy can be configured according to the standard Internet routing principle, based on the “longest match principle”, which will not affect the global routing table.

For IPv6 (when the “IPv4-converted IPv6 address” and the “IPv4-translatable IPv6 address” use the same NSP):

(1) The “IPv4-translatable IPv6 address” is a subset of the “IPv4-converted IPv6 address”.
(2) The “IPv4-converted IPv6 address” is a subset of the aggregated IPv6 prefix used by the operator.
(3) The aggregated IPv6 prefix used by the operator is a subset of the global IPv6 address.

For IPv4:

(1) The IPv4 address corresponding to the “IPv4-translatable IPv6 address” is the IPv4 address used by the operator for translation purposes, which is a subset of IPv4 addresses owned by the operator.
(2) The IPv4 address corresponding to the “IPv4-converted IPv6 address” is the global public IPv4 address.

These relationships are shown in Fig. 6.21.

Note: The following various addresses have containment and correspondence relationships.

(1) Smallest set of IPv4 addresses: The IPv4 address IVI4(i) corresponding to an ISP’s “IPv4-translatable IPv6 address”.

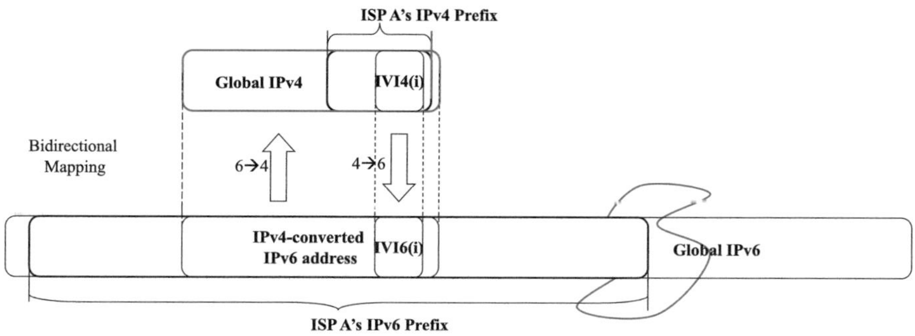

Fig. 6.21 Relationship between IPv4 address space and IPv6 address space (1)

(2) Intermediate set of IPv4 addresses: An ISP's IPv4 address.
(3) Largest set of IPv4 addresses: Global IPv4 address.
(4) Smallest set of IPv6 addresses: An ISP's "IPv4-translatable IPv6 address" IVI6(i).
(5) Intermediate set of IPv6 addresses: An ISP's "IPv4-converted IPv6 address".
(6) Larger set of IPv6 addresses: An ISP's IPv6 address.
(7) Largest set of IPv6 addresses: Global IPv6 address.

The mapping relationship (correspondence relationship) based on the algorithm is shown in Table 6.8.

It should be noted that different ISPs will definitely use different NSPs, so the following conclusions can be drawn.

(1) The "IPv4-converted IPv6 address" of each ISP corresponds to an overlapping IPv4 address space.
(2) The "IPv4-translatable IPv6 address" of each ISP corresponds to a non-overlapping IPv4 address space.

Figure 6.22 shows the relationship between the IPv4 address space and the IPv6 address space when two ISPs use their own NSP.

Pay attention to the inclusion, mutual exclusion, and mapping relationships of the following addresses.

(1) The IPv4 address IVI4(i) corresponding to the "IPv4-translatable IPv6 address" of ISP(i).
(2) The IPv4 address of ISP(i).

Table 6.8 Mapping relationship

IPv6	Mapping	IPv4
IPv4-translatable IPv6 address: IVI6(i)	←→	IVI4(i)
IPv4-converted IPv6 address	←→	Global IPv4 address

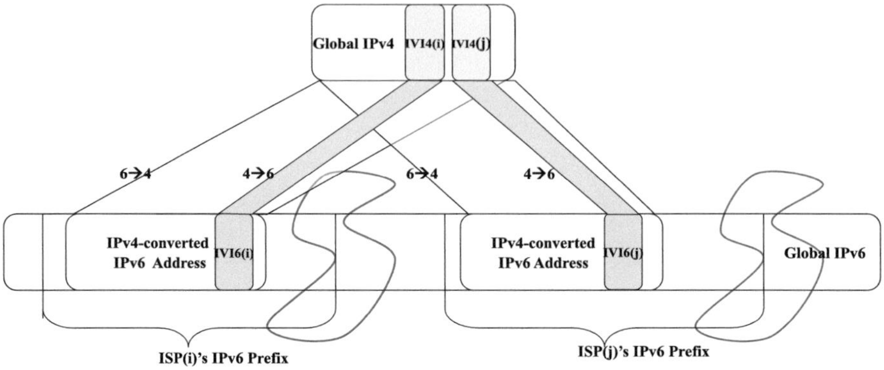

Fig. 6.22 Relationship between IPv4 address space and IPv6 address space (2)

(3) The IPv4 address IVI4(j) corresponding to the "IPv4-translatable IPv6 address" of ISP(j).
(4) The IPv4 address of ISP(j).
(5) The global IPv4 address.
(6) The "IPv4-translatable -IPv6 address" IVI6(i) of ISP(i).
(7) The "IPv4-converted IPv6 address" of ISP(i).
(8) The IPv6 address of ISP(i).
(9) The "IPv4-translatable IPv6 address" IVI6(j) of ISP(j).
(10) The "IPv4-converted IPv6 address" of ISP(j).
(11) The IPv6 address of ISP(j).
(12) The global IPv6 address.

The mapping relationship based on the algorithm is shown in Table 6.9.

In summary, the network reachability matrix using NSP is shown in Fig. 6.23.

The "IPv4-translatable IPv6 address" (IVI address) using NSP establishes an algorithm-based mapping relationship between IPv4 and IPv6, which can achieve interconnection.

The deployment of the "IPv4-translatable IPv6 address" (IVI address) using NSP can be divided into three stages.

1) **Single Deployment**

Table 6.9 Mapping relationship

IPv6	Mapping	IPv4
IPv4-translatable IPv6 address: IVI6(i)	←→	IVI4(i)
IPv4-converted IPv6 address of ISP(i)	←→	The global IPv4 address
IPv4-translatable IPv6 address: IVI6(j)	←→	IVI4(j)
IPv4-converted IPv6 address of ISP(j)	←→	The global IPv4 address

	Global IPv4	IVI	Global IPv6
Global IPv4	OK	OK	NO
IVI	OK	OK	OK
Global IPv6	NO	OK	OK

Fig. 6.23 Reachability matrix

Single deployment refers to only one ISP deploying "IPv4-translatable IPv6 address" and an IPv4/IPv6 translator (xlat), as shown in Fig. 6.24.

(1) B is a real IPv4 host, B' is the "IPv4-converted IPv6 address" in the IPv6 network.
(2) A' is the "IPv4-translatable IPv6 address", A is the corresponding IPv4 address.
(3) IPv6 host A' can communicate with the entire IPv4 Internet through the translator and the entire IPv6 Internet directly.

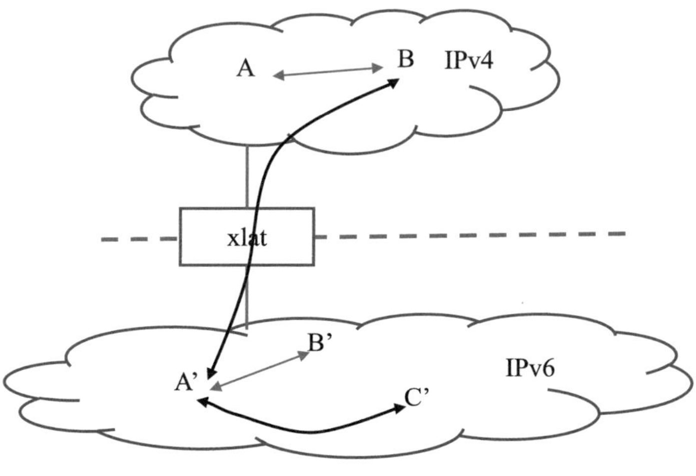

Fig. 6.24 Single deployment

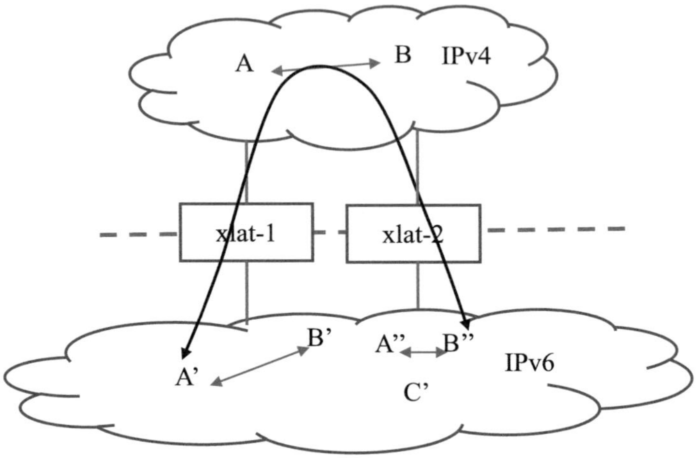

Fig. 6.25 Independent deployment

2) **Independent Deployment**

Independent deployment refers to two ISPs independently setting up "IPv4-translatable IPv6 address" and translators (xlat-1 and xlat-2), as shown in Fig. 6.25.

(1) A' is the "IPv4-translatable IPv6 address", A is the corresponding IPv4 address.
(2) B" is the "IPv4-translatable IPv6 address", B is the corresponding IPv4 address.
(3) For A', B' is the "IPv4-converted IPv6 address", but in fact, it is the mirror of B" (IPv4-translatable IPv6 address).
(4) For B", A" is the "IPv4-converted IPv6 address", but in fact, it is the mirror of A' (IPv4-translatable IPv6 address).
(5) Through two translations (xlat-1 and xlat-2), A' and B" can communicate with each other.
(6) IPv6 hosts A' and B" can communicate with the entire IPv4 Internet through the translator and the entire IPv6 Internet directly.

3) **Direct Communication**

In the above cases, A' and B" can communicate directly without the need for translators, as shown in Fig. 6.26.

The "IPv4-translatable IPv6 address" A' and "IPv4-translatable IPv6 address" B" can communicate directly, since they are IPv6 hosts.

2. *Well-Known Prefix*

The advantage of the Well-Known Prefix (WKP) is that it can be used as a default configuration (default). The IPv4 mapping prefix defined in RFC2765 [26] is::ffff:0:0/96. However, for several versions of Mac OS and Windows systems, the IPv4 mapping prefix is used to generate IPv4 datagrams, not to send IPv6 datagrams. If::ffff:0:0/96

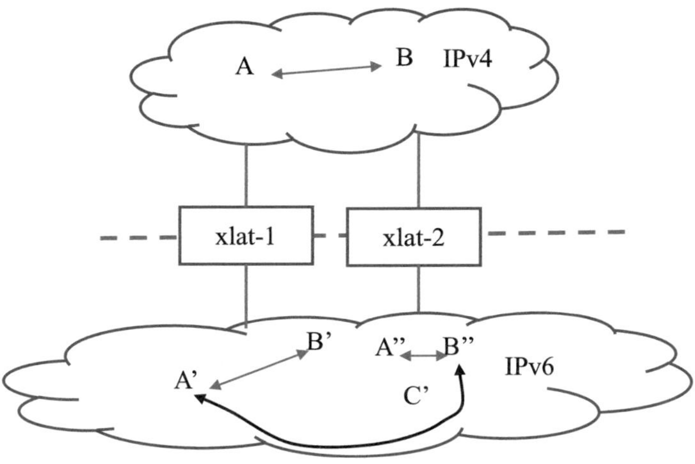

Fig. 6.26 Direct communication

is used, these operating systems will not be able to support translation technology without upgrading, so the WKP cannot use::ffff:0:0/96.

Considering the IPv6 address representation format defined in RFC4291 [10], the dotted decimal can only appear on the far right. The /96 prefix is compatible with this specification. This representation makes the address format easier to use and the log files easier to read. Therefore, the prefix length of WKP should be /96.

The WKP should ideally have the characteristic of being "checksum independent". The sum of the hexadecimal numbers 0064 and ff9b is ffff, that is, the complement of 1 equals the value of 0. The "IPv4-embedded IPv6 address" constructed using this prefix will have the same complement checksum as the embedded IPv4 address.

Considering the above, RFC6052 [11] defines the WKP used for the address mapping algorithm. The value of this IPv6 prefix is shown in Fig. 6.27.

3. *Extended Well-Known Prefix*

RFC8215 [27] extends the range of the well-known prefix, which can be used by multiple IPv4/IPv6 translators within a domain. The extended WKP is shown in Fig. 6.28.

The specific explanations are as follows.

1) **Length of the Extended WKP**

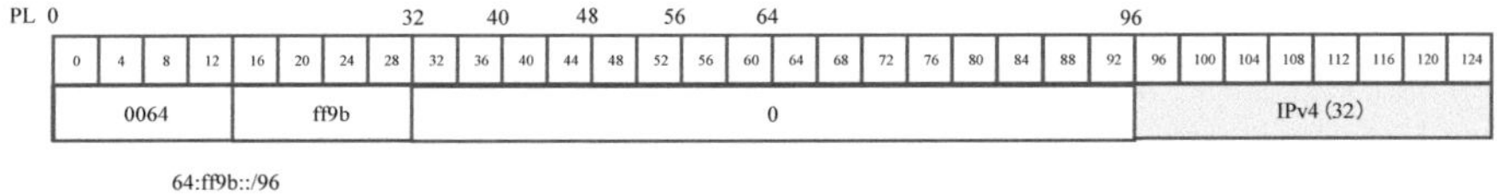

Fig. 6.27 Well-known prefix

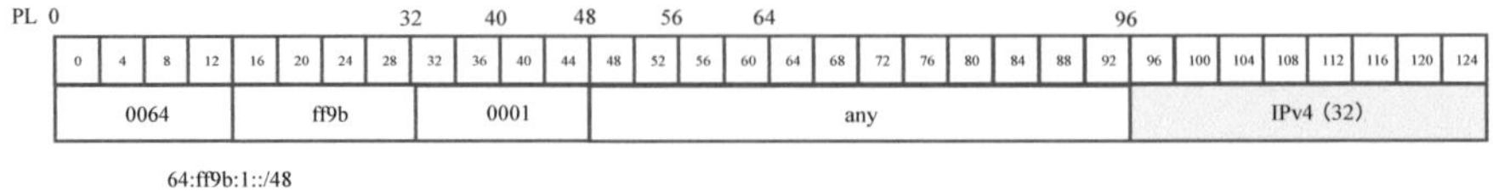

Fig. 6.28 Extended well-known prefix

In order to deploy multiple different WKPs within a domain, the prefix length of the new well-known prefix must be able to contain multiple /96 s. At the same time, for clarity, the prefix length should be a multiple of 16, so it can be distinguished by ":". The other longest prefix length given in RFC6052 [11] is 64, to meet the requirement of being a multiple of 16, choosing /48 is appropriate.

2) **Value of the Extended WKP**

In order to minimize the additional "pollution" of the unallocated IPv6 address space, engineers can choose an address space adjacent to the already defined WKP 64:ff9b::/96. Given that we have decided to use a prefix length of /48, we can only choose 64:ff9a:ffff::/48 or 64:ff9b:1::/48. The advantage of 64:ff9a:ffff::/48 is that it is completely adjacent to 64:ff9b::/96, while 64:ff9b:1::/48 is not completely adjacent to 64:ff9b::/96. However, if we choose 64:ff9a:ffff::/48, the address space clustered with 64:ff9a:ffff::/48 and 64:ff9b::/96 is 64:ff9a::/31, which would waste a relatively large address space. In addition, when choosing 64:ff9b:1::/48, the address space wasted due to not being adjacent to 64:ff9b::/96 is 64:ff9b::/47. Therefore, 64:ff9b:1::/48 is the choice that least"pollutes" the unallocated IPv6 address space. Finally, 64:ff9b:1::/48 is shorter in text representation than 64:ff9a:ffff::/48, making it easier to input.

3) **Deployment Considerations for the Extended Well-Known Prefix**

The following points should be noted when using the extended WKP.

(1) 64:ff9b:1::/48 is a general reserved address range, and operators can freely choose any one or more /96 from /48 in their own management domain for different IPv4/IPv6 translators.
(2) By default, IPv6 nodes and applications should treat 64:ff9b:1::/48 the same as other global unicast addresses. In particular, no assumptions should be made about the syntax or attributes of the address (such as the existence and location of embedded IPv4 addresses) or the type of related translation mechanisms (such as stateful or stateless).
(3) 64:ff9b:1::/48 or any longer prefix can only be used for intra-domain routing.
(4) Note that 64:ff9b:1::/48 (or any longer prefix) does not overlap with 64:ff9b::/96. Therefore, there can be different restriction ranges.
(5) If operators attempt to use the aggregate prefix 64:ff9b::/47, they must be aware that this aggregate prefix includes unallocated address ranges, so the IETF may use this address range for completely different purposes in the future.

4) **Irrelevant to Checksum**

Using 64:ff9b:1::/48 itself does not guarantee irrelevance to checksum, for discussions on checksum neutrality, see RFC6052 [11].

Below are several examples of checksum-neutral prefixes (not exhaustive):

64:ff9b:1:fffe::/96

64:ff9b:1:fffd:1::/96

64:ff9b:1:fffc:2::/96

64:ff9b:1:abcd:0:5431::/96

6.3.3 *Mapping Examples*

The mapping examples and text representation of "IPv4-embedded IPv6 address" are as follows. According to RFC4291 [10], the WKP or NSP with /96 can also be represented in dotted decimal notation.

The examples of operator prefixes originate from the "Document IPv6 Prefix" reserved in RFC3849 [28]. The IPv4 address 192.0.2.33 originates from a part of the "Document 192.0.2.0/24 subnet" reserved in RFC5735 [29]. The representation of the IPv6 address is compatible with the standard defined in RFC5952 [30].

1. *Examples using NSP*

1) **Use of NSP Without u-oct**

Examples of using NSP without u-oct are shown in Table 6.10.

2) **Use of NSP with u-oct**

Examples of using NSP with u-oct are shown in Table 6.11.

2. *Examples using WKP*

1) **Examples of Using WKP**

Table 6.10 Examples of using NSP without u-oct

Operator prefix	IPv4 address	IPv4-embedded IPv6 address (without u-oct)
2001:db8::/32	192.0.2.33	2001:db8:c000:221::
2001:db8:100::/40	192.0.2.33	2001:db8:1c0:2:2100::
2001:db8:122::/48	192.0.2.33	2001:db8:122:c000:221::
2001:db8:122:300::/56	192.0.2.33	2001:db8:122:3c0:2:2100::
2001:db8:122:344::/64	192.0.2.33	2001:db8:122:344:c000:221::
2001:db8:122:344::/96	192.0.2.33	2001:db8:122:344::192.0.2.33

Table 6.11 Examples of using NSP with u-oct

Operator prefix	IPv4 address	IPv4-embedded IPv6 address" (with u-oct)
2001:db8::/32	192.0.2.33	2001:db8:c000:221::
2001:db8:100::/40	192.0.2.33	2001:db8:1c0:2:21::
2001:db8:122::/48	192.0.2.33	2001:db8:122:c000:2:2100::
2001:db8:122:300::/56	192.0.2.33	2001:db8:122:3c0:0:221::
2001:db8:122:344::/64	192.0.2.33	2001:db8:122:344:c0:2:2100::
2001:db8:122:344::/96	192.0.2.33	2001:db8:122:344::192.0.2.33

Table 6.12 Examples of using basic well-known prefix

Well-known prefix	IPv4 address	IPv4-embedded IPv6 address
64:ff9b::/96	192.0.2.33	64:ff9b::192.0.2.33

Table 6.13 Examples of using extended Well-Known prefix

Extended WKP	IPv4 address	IPv4-embedded IPv6 address
64:ff9b:1:fffe::/96	192.0.2.33	64:ff9b:1:fffe::192.0.2.33

Examples of using WKP are shown in Table 6.12.

2) **Examples of Using Extended WKP**

Examples of using extended WKP are shown in Table 6.13.

6.3.4 Deployment Guide

1. *Prefix Selection for Stateless Translator Deployment*

When deploying a stateless translator in an ISP, campus network, or enterprise network, the internal IPv6 nodes of the network are configured with "IPv4-translatable IPv6 addresses", enabling them to be accessed by IPv4. The IPv4 addresses of the IPv4 Internet are represented as "IPv4-converted IPv6 addresses".

Specific suggestions are as follows:

(1) Networks deploying stateless IPv4/IPv6 translators should configure NSP.
(2) "IPv4-translatable IPv6 addresses" and "IPv4-converted IPv6 addresses" must be constructed in the format of "IPv4-embedded IPv6 address".
(3) "IPv4-translatable IPv6 addresses" must use NSP.
(4) Unless there is a special reason, "IPv4-translatable IPv6 addresses" and "IPv4-converted IPv6 addresses" should use the same NSP.

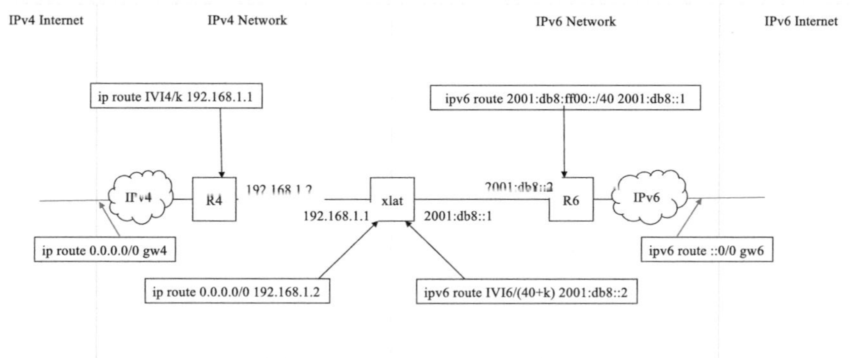

Fig. 6.29 Stateless translator routing configuration example

Figure 6.29 is a routing configuration example.

In this case, the IPv4 network is connected to the IPv4 Internet, while the IPv6 network is connected to the IPv4 Internet through an IPv4/IPv6 translator (xlat) and connected to the IPv6 Internet directly.

The hosts on the IPv6 network are configured with "IPv4-translatable IPv6 addresses", their corresponding public IPv4 address prefix is IVI4/k, and the prefix length is k, then "IPv4-translatable IPv6 address" is IVI6/(40 + k). The NSP is 2001:db8:ff00::/40.

The routes that need to be configured for the IPv4 network are as follows:

(1) Default route to the IPv4 Internet 0.0.0.0/0.
(2) The IPv4 route corresponding to the translator's "IPv4-translatable IPv6 address" is IVI4/*k*.

The routes that need to be configured for the IPv6 network are as follows:

(1) Default route to the IPv6 Internet ::0/0.
(2) The route to the translator's IPv4 Internet is "IPv4-converted IPv6 address" (2001:db8:f00::/40).

The routes that need to be configured for the translator (xlat) are as follows:

(1) Default route to the IPv4 Internet 0.0.0.0/0.
(2) The route to the user subnet "IPv4-translatable IPv6 address" is IVI6/(40 + *k*).

1) **The Issue of "IPv4-translatable IPv6 address" and "IPv4-converted IPv6 address" Using the Same IPv6 Prefix**

Using the same IPv6 prefix can ensure that the "IPv4-translatable IPv6 address" has the optimal route within the operator's network. Specifically, if an IPv6 host wants to access another host's IPv4 address, and the actual host using this IPv4 address is an IPv6 host (using IPv4-translatable IPv6 address), then constructing the "IPv4-converted IPv6 address" and "IPv4-translatable IPv6 address" with the same

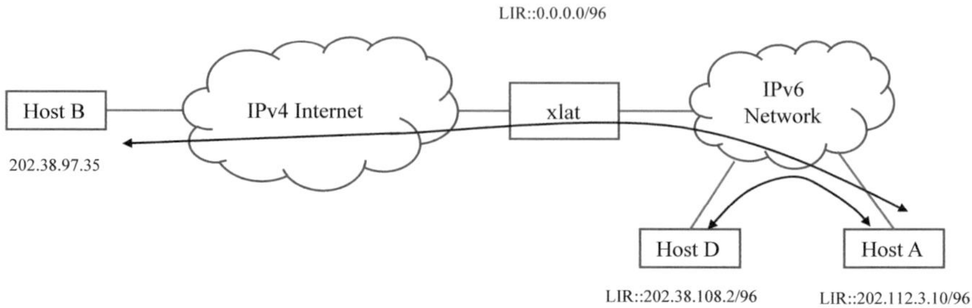

Fig. 6.30 Optimal routing

operator prefix is the optimal route. The principle of Internet routing (i.e., longest prefix matching) can ensure direct communication between the two hosts without the need for processing by the translator, as shown in Fig. 6.30.

Assuming the translator is located between the IPv6 network and the IPv4 Internet, and has configured the corresponding routes according to the rules in the example above.

(1) The IPv6 prefix belongs to the LIR prefix.
(2) Host B is an actual IPv4 host (address is 202.38.97.35).
(3) Hosts A and D are IPv6 hosts, each configured with "IPv4-translatable IPv6 addresses" located on different IPv6 subnets (LIR::202.112.3.10 and LIR::202.38.108.2).

In this case, communication between Host A and Host B needs to go through the translator, because Host A is on the IPv6 network, while Host B is on the IPv4 Internet.

However, communication between Host A and Host D does not need to go through the translator, because the IPv6 network has a longer IPv6 prefix for the subnets where Host A and Host D are located on the IPv6-only side of the translator (LIR).

It should be noted that there can be exceptions to the rule of configuring the same IPv6 prefix for "IPv4-translatable IPv6 address" and "IPv4-converted IPv6 address".

(1) When implementing stateless double translation across different administration domains, Internet routing policies usually do not allow the announcement of longer prefixes from other operators. In this case, different IPv6 prefixes must be configured for "IPv4-translatable IPv6 address" and "IPv4-converted IPv6 address".
(2) In the case of stateless double translation, where the home gateway shares the IPv4 address, the IPv6 address of the home gateway is used by both the "IPv4-translatable IPv6 address" and other IPv6-only hosts served by the home gateway. This usage leads to an overlap with the "IPv4-converted IPv6 address". In this case, different IPv6 prefixes must be configured for "IPv4-translatable IPv6 address" and "IPv4-converted IPv6 address" (Example is MAP-T in Chap. 10 of this book).

2) **Issues with Routing Configuration for "IPv4-translatable IPv6 addresses" Longer than /64 Interface Identifiers**

Intra-domain routing protocols must be able to deliver datagrams to nodes served by "IPv4-translatable IPv6 addresses". This may require routing for "IPv4-embedded IPv6 addresses" (usually longer than /64 interface identifiers). At the same time, for security reasons, routers need to use some form of reverse path check to verify the validity of the source of "IPv4-translatable IPv6 addresses".

3) **Suffix Selection Issues**

(1) Checksum neutral. In the case of stateless translation, if both "IPv4-translatable IPv6 addresses" and "IPv4-converted-IPv6 addresses" are constructed using methods of the checksum neutral, there is no need to recalculate the checksum (IPv6 addresses have the same checksum as the embedded IPv4 addresses). In the case of stateful translation, checksum neutral cannot be achieved during the translation process, because only one of the two addresses has the property of "checksum neutral". The IETF once considered reserving 16 bits in the suffix for achieving checksum neutral. But this method was not adopted because it is still invalid for stateful translation. Meanwhile, checksum neutral can be achieved by adjusting the prefix (i.e., choosing a prefix whose complement checksum equals 0 or 0xffff).
(2) Port range encoding. The extension of the suffix can be used to represent the transport layer port encoding of stateless translation, allowing multiple IPv6 hosts to share an IPv4 address, i.e., each IPv6 host uses a different port range.
(3) Non-zero values. When using a /32 prefix, a full zero suffix will lead to a full zero interface identifier. This conflicts with the provisions of RFC4291 [10], i.e., the full zero interface identifier has been used for router anycast addresses. But in actual use, a /64 subnet only contains one "IPv4-translatable IPv6 address", and the semantics will not cause confusion. Therefore, this specification retains the full zero suffix. This problem does not exist for prefixes greater than 32 bits (for example, the recommended /40, /56, /64, and /96).

4) **In-depth Discussion of Instances of Stateless Address Mapping Configuration**

Consider an IPv6 network with the prefix 2001:db8:122::/48, where the network administrator chooses the operator prefix 2001:db8:122:344::/64 to implement stateless translation. The IPv4 subnet is 192.0.2.0/24, and the corresponding "IPv4-translatable IPv6 address" prefix is 2001:db8:122:344:c0:2::/96. In this network, host A is assigned an "IPv4-translatable IPv6 address", which is 2001:db8:122:344:c0:2:2100::, and the corresponding IPv4 address is 192.0.2.33. The address of host A is configured manually or by DHCPv6.

In this example, host A is not directly connected to the translator, but through router R, which is configured to forward datagrams of 2001:db8:122:344:c0:2:2100:: to host A. At the same time, router R uses intra-domain routing protocols to announce the prefix 2001:db8:122:344:c0:2:2100::/104. If this topology includes multiple

"IPv4-translatable IPv6 addresses" exported from the same IPv4 subnet, a shorter IPv6 routing prefix can be announced. If a datagram with a destination address of 192.0.2.33 arrives at the translator, the destination address will be mapped to 2001:db8:122:344:c0:2:2100::, and the IPv6 datagram will be routed to R, and finally reach A.

Now suppose that host B in the same domain gets the IPv4 address of host A (through application-specific recommendations). If B has the ability to perceive the existence of the translator, B can use the operator prefix 2001:db8:122:344::/64 and the IPv4 address 192.0.2.33 to form the IPv6 destination address 2001:db8:122:344:c0:2:2100::. The IPv6 datagram sent by host B will be forwarded to router R, then forwarded to host A, thus avoiding protocol translation.

The efficiency of forwarding and reverse path checking depends on the combination of IPv6 prefixes and IPv4 addresses. Theoretically, routers can route and forward any length of IPv6 prefix, but in practice, the efficiency of routing and forwarding on IPv6 prefixes longer than 64 bits may be lower. However, routing and forwarding efficiency is not the only consideration when choosing the length of an IPv6 prefix. The availability of shorter IPv6 prefixes and the impact of all-zero identifiers also need to be considered when using stateless translators. If a /32 IPv6 prefix is used, all routing bits are contained within the first 64 bits of the IPv6 address, resulting in excellent routing characteristics. However, these prefixes may be difficult to obtain, and allocating a /32 to small chunks of "IPv4-translatable IPv6 addresses" may be seen as wasteful. Additionally, a /32 IPv6 prefix and a suffix of zero will result in an all-zero interface identifier, which may pose problems. Choosing a medium-length prefix (e.g., /40, /48, or /56) is a compromise. In this case, only shared IPv4 bits are part of the /64 prefix. This has some effect on reverse path checking, but only for the most significant bits of the IPv4 address. In this case, deception of external IPv4 addresses can be reduced, but deception of internal IPv6 nodes impersonating "IPv4-translatable IPv6 addresses" is ineffective. A compromise is to use a prefix of an organization's IPv6 address that does not exceed 1/256 for the IPv4/IPv6 translator. For example, for operators who obtain /32 or shorter IPv6, a /40 prefix can be chosen for translation services. For a /48 access network, a /56 prefix can be chosen for translation services, or all "IPv4-translatable IPv6 addresses" share the same link, using a /96 prefix. The choice of prefix length is related to the deployment scenario. Stateless translation can be used for scenarios 1, 2, 5, and 6. For different scenarios, the prefix length recommendations are as follows:

(1) For scenario 1 (IPv6 network (client) initiating access to the IPv4 Internet (server)) and scenario 2 (IPv4 Internet (client) initiating access to the IPv6 network (server)), operators holding /32 prefixes should use /40 prefixes, and nodes holding /48 should use /56 prefixes.
(2) For scenario 5 (IPv6 network (client) initiating access to the IPv4 network (server)) and scenario 6 (IPv4 network (client) initiating access to the IPv6 network (server)), /64 or /96 prefixes should be used. When the IPv4/IPv6 translation service uses the operator's prefix, the prefix of the "IPv4-translatable IPv6 address" used by the stateless translator must be aggregated and published

to the Internet. Similarly, if the translator has configured multiple operator prefixes, these prefixes must be published to the IPv6 Internet after appropriate aggregation.

2. *Prefix Selection for Stateful Translation Deployment*

ISP, campus networks, or enterprise networks deploy stateful translators to provide translation services. In this deployment, the NSP or the WKP can be used. When using these services, IPv6 nodes can configure any IPv6 address, and IPv4 nodes are represented by "IPv4-converted IPv6 addresses". When a network deploys multiple stateful translators, stability issues may arise. That is, if several translators use the same prefix, there is a risk that datagrams belonging to the same session will be routed to different translators when the internal routing state changes. This problem can be solved by configuring different prefixes for different translators or by synchronizing states between translators. Stateful translation can be used for scenario 1 (IPv6 network (client) initiating access to IPv4 Access to the Internet (server), Scenario 3 (IPv6 Internet (client) initiated to IPv4 network (server) access) and Scenario 5 (IPv6 network (client) initiated to IPv4 network (server) access). The well-known prefix should generally be used, but there are two exceptions.

(1) In all scenarios, for management reasons, the NSP can be used.
(2) The WKP should not be used for Scenario 3 (IPv6 Internet (client) initiated to IPv4 network (server) access), as this will result in non-global IPv4 addresses embedded in the well-known prefix. In this case, the operator prefix must be used (for example, /96 prefix).

The WKP should not be used to represent non-global IPv4 addresses, such as those defined in RFC1918 [6] and RFC5735 [29]. Translators should not translate datagrams composed of WKP and non-global IPv4 addresses, but should discard them. The WKP should not be used to construct "IPv4-translatable IPv6 addresses". Nodes configured with "IPv4-translatable IPv6 addresses" should be able to communicate directly with the global IPv6, without the need for any protocol conversion device. Only "IPv4-translatable IPv6 addresses" can be used for inter-domain routing, and longer prefix routes of the WKP are not allowed for inter-domain routing. In this case, only the operator prefix can be used.

The WKP can be used to deploy translation services for enterprise networks.

If the operator provides IPv4/IPv6 translation services for its peering partners, the WKP can appear in the inter-domain routing table. The upstream (and/or) downstream operators announcing the WKP should be able to use BGP policy (RFC4271) [31] to control the inter-domain release of the WKP. Networks that announce the WKP must provide IPv4/IPv6 translation services.

When the IPv4/IPv6 translator uses the WKP, the prefix length of the "IPv4-embedded IPv6 address" exceeding the WKP should not be announced via BGP (especially not via eBGP) (RFC4271 [31]). Because this will lead to the introduction of the IPv4 routing table into the IPv6 table, causing routing scalability issues. Network administrators of BGP nodes should configure BGP filtering policies to discard prefixes exceeding the length of the "IPv4-embedded IPv6 address" of the well-known prefix.

6.3.5 Security Considerations

1. *Preventing Deception*

The IPv4/IPv6 translator can be considered a special router, with the same security risks as a router, and the same solutions can be implemented. The exception is deception from IPv6 addresses embedded with IPv4 addresses.

Attackers can use IPv6 addresses embedded with IPv4 as the source address of malicious datagrams. After translation, the datagram will appear to come from an IPv4 source address, which may be difficult to trace further. If no measures are taken, malicious IPv6 nodes may deceive any IPv4 address.

The solution is to implement reverse path checking and allow IPv6 datagrams to only come from authorized nodes.

2. *Secure Configuration*

IPv6 nodes use the address mapping prefix to send datagrams to the IPv4/IPv6 translator. Attackers can try to interfere with IPv6 nodes, DNS gateways, and IPv4/IPv6 translators using incorrect parameters, leading to network interruptions, denial of service, and possible information leakage. To avoid such attacks, network administrators need to ensure the security of prefix configuration.

3. *Firewall Configuration*

Firewalls and other security devices filter traffic based on IPv4 addresses. Attackers may attempt to disrupt the normal operation of the firewall by exploiting IPv6 packets that are ultimately translated into IPv4 by the translator. If such an attempt is successful, this type of traffic, which should be blocked, will pass through the firewall.

In all these scenarios, network administrators should ensure that datagrams sent or received with "IPv4-embedded IPv6 addresses" are treated the same as datagrams sent or received with their original IPv4.

6.4 Address Mapping Technology Extension

Address mapping technology defines "IPv4-translatable IPv6 addresses" and "IPv4-converted IPv6 addresses", establishing a one-to-one mapping relationship between IPv4 addresses and IPv6 addresses. If this mapping rule had been introduced at the inception of IPv6, the history of IPv6 transition technology would have been rewritten. In the 1990s, only half of the public IPv4 address pool was allocated. If network operators applying for new IPv4 addresses at that time were required to commit to using public IPv4 addresses in the form of "IPv4-translatable IPv6 addresses" (i.e., through stateless translators, enabling IPv6-only hosts to interconnect with the IPv4 Internet), then by the time the public IPv4 address pool was fully allocated, at least half of the hosts worldwide would have transitioned to IPv6, surpassing the critical mass of IPv6. The transition could be completed by gradually switching the already used IPv4 addresses to “IPv4-translatable IPv6 addresses”. If history could be replayed, the two stages of IPv6 transition would be as shown in Fig. 6.31.

Unfortunately, history cannot be replayed. The new generation of IPv6 transition technology was invented when the global IPv4 address pool was already exhausted. Under these circumstances, it is no longer feasible to establish a one-to-one mapping relationship between IPv4 addresses and IPv6 addresses on a large scale. Therefore, a one-to-many mapping relationship needs to be established between IPv4 addresses and IPv6 addresses. Similar to IPv4 NAT, IPv4 address sharing technology needs to use transport layer (TCP, UDP) port number to identify different internal hosts (RFC6269 [32]).

The differences from IPv4 NAT are as follows:

(1) The vast majority of IPv4 NATs are stateful. In this case, the private IPv4 address plus transport layer port of the internal network are dynamically mapped to the public IPv4 address plus transport layer port.
(2) The IPv4/IPv6 translator can be stateless, and the IPv6 address plus transport layer port of the IPv6 network are mapped based on algorithm to the public IPv4 address plus transport layer port.

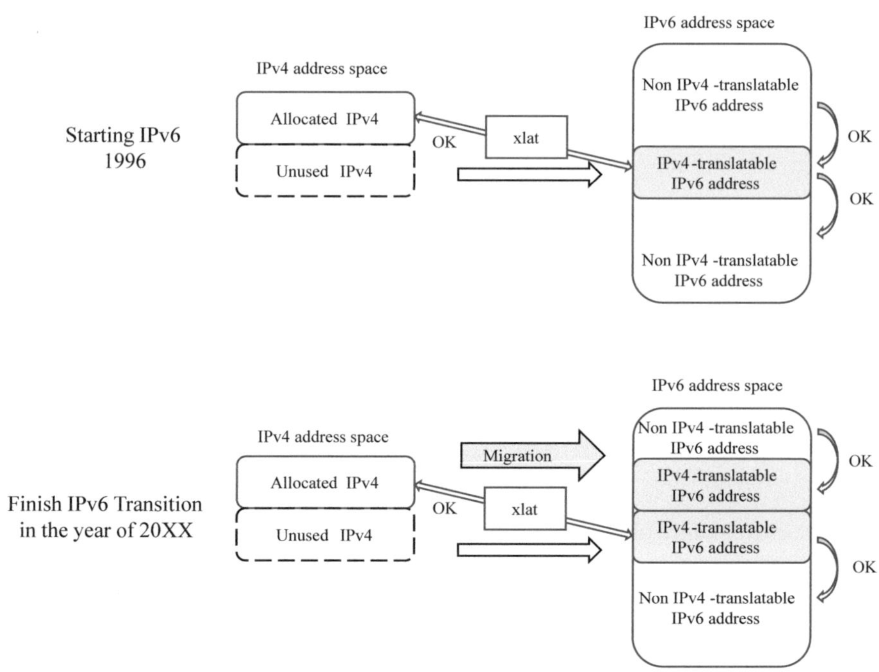

Fig. 6.31 If history could be replayed, the two stages of IPv6 transition

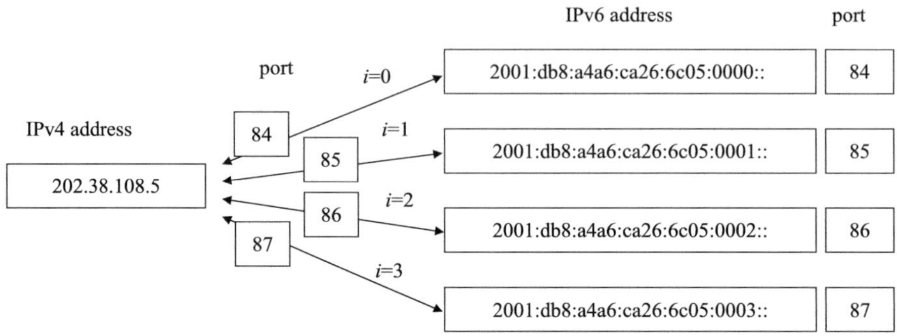

Fig. 6.32 4 IPv6 hosts sharing a single public IPv4 address

For example, a public IPv4 address, when converted to an "IPv4-translatable IPv6 address", all odd transport layer ports are used by the first IPv6 host, and all even transport layer ports are used by the second IPv6 host. This can achieve a multiplexing ratio of 2.

Following the same logic, using a "modular operator", an example with a multiplexing ratio of 4 is shown in Fig. 6.32.

The parameters are as follows:

(1) IPv6 prefix: 2001:db8:a4a6::/48.
(2) Public IPv4 address: 202.38.108.5/32.
(3) The "IPv4-translatable IPv6 address" (without u-oct): 2001:db8:a4a6:ca26:6c05::/80.
(4) Multiplexing ratio: 4.
(5) Port encoding bits: 80 ~ 95.

The following conclusions can be drawn.

(1) The first IPv6 host: 2001:db8:a4a6:ca26:6c05:0000::.
Available ports are: 0, 4, 8, 12, ..., 84, ..., 65532.
(2) The second IPv6 host: 2001:db8:a4a6:ca26:6c05:0001::.
Available ports are: 1, 5, 9, 13, ..., 85, ..., 65533.
(3) The third IPv6 host: 2001:db8:a4a6:ca26:6c05:0002::.
Available ports are: 2, 6, 10, 14, ..., 86, ..., 65534.
(4) The fourth IPv6 host: 2001:db8:a4a6:ca26:6c05:0003::.
Available ports are: 3, 7, 11, 15, ..., 87, ..., 65535.

The corresponding algorithm is as follows:

(1) For a given host k, the range of ports P that the host is allowed to use is

$$P = Rj + k$$

where $j = 0,1,2,..., N\text{-}1$

(2) For any given port P, the corresponding host k is

$$k = P\%N$$

where % is the modulus operator.

Note:

① k is the port set identifier (PSID), which determines the mapping algorithm between the 16-bit transport layer port number (including ICMP, ICMPv6 identifiers) and the IPv6 host identifier;
② How to embed the PSID into the IPv6 address is another issue completely independent of the above mapping algorithm.

In summary, the suffix extension of "IPv4-embedded IPv6 address" can be used to represent the transport layer port encoding of stateless translation, allowing multiple IPv6 hosts to share an IPv4 address (each IPv6 host uses a different port range).

6.4.1 Port Mapping Algorithm

1. *Mathematical Representation of the General Modular Algorithm*

The essence of the transport layer port mapping algorithm is to encode the 16-bit port number of TCP or UDP (including ICMP, ICMPv6 identifiers). Theoretically, the simplest algorithm is to directly use the 16-bit port number, but this is not a good method because an IP address usually uses multiple concurrent transport layer ports. The essence of the transport layer port mapping algorithm should define a set of transport layer ports for an IPv6 host. Therefore, a Port Set Identifier (PSID) is defined for the port mapping algorithm.

Different transport layer port mapping algorithms can be designed, but different algorithms will have different advantages, disadvantages, and best application scenarios. Since different PSIDs must have non-overlapping port ranges, there are two extreme cases.

(1) Modular operation: For each PSID, the transport layer ports that can be used are discontinuous, evenly distributed throughout the entire port range (0–65535).
(2) Division operation: For each PSID, the transport layer ports that can be used are continuous, some at the low end of the transport layer port, and some at the high end.

The "General Modular Algorithm" is a unification of the above two algorithms, which can flexibly meet the general scenarios including these two extreme cases.

For a given multiplexing ratio (R: a group of IPv6 addresses share a single IPv4 address) and the maximum continuous port (M) that a PSID can use, the General Modulo Algorithm is defined as follows.

(1) When PSID (k) is given, the corresponding port number (P) is determined by the following formula:

$$P = RMj + Mk + i, k = 0 \sim R - 1, j = \frac{\frac{1024}{M}}{R}, \ldots, \frac{\frac{65536}{M}}{R} - 1$$

(2) When the port number (P) is given, PSID (k) is determined by the following formula:

$$k = \left(\text{floor}\left(\frac{P}{M}\right)\right)\%R$$

where, % is the modular operation; floor (arg) is a "floor function", that is, it returns the smallest integer greater than arg.

2. *Bit Representation of the Generalized Modular Algorithm*

The bit representation of the generalized modular algorithm is called the "infix" encoding algorithm. Given the multiplexing rate ($R = 2^k$) and the maximum number of consecutive ports ($M = 2^m$), for any transport layer port-set identifier PSID (k), the available ports (P) can be represented in bit form, as shown in Fig. 6.33.

Where, j and i are the port range index and the port continuity index, respectively.

The reason it is called the "infix" encoding algorithm is that the PSID has a fixed position within the 16-bit port range, in other words, the PSID is embedded as an "infix" in the 16-bit port range.

(1) Although multiplication and division operations are introduced in the generalized modulo algorithm, for any transport layer port value, the corresponding PSID can be obtained by bit operations on the "infix". Therefore, the generalized modular algorithm does not introduce computational complexity.

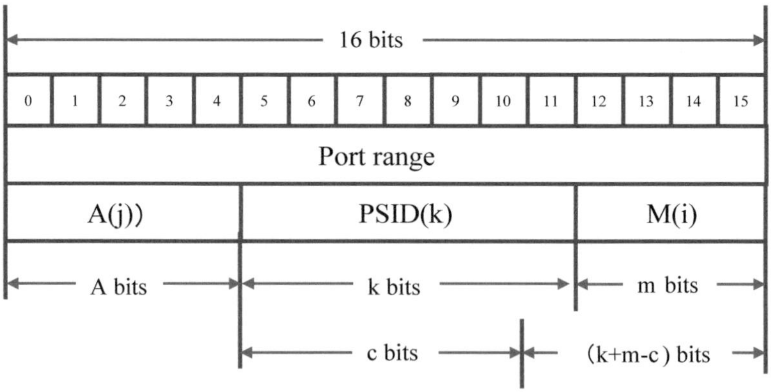

Fig. 6.33 Bit representation of the generalized modular algorithm

(2) There is a PSID "infix" length (c), so the PSID also has the aggregation feature of CIDR, that is, if the embedding format is properly defined, when a node needs a larger transport layer port range, multiple PSIDs ($c < k$) can be allocated to that node.
(3) When $m = 0$, the generalized modular algorithm degenerates into "modular operation". When $a = 0$, the generalized modular algorithm degenerates into "division operation".

3. *Algorithm Example*

1) **Example of PSID with Fixed Prefix Length**

For $R = 128$ $(k = 7)$, $M = 4$ $(m = 2)$, as shown in Fig. 6.34.

2) **PSID with Variable Prefix Length**

PSID with different prefix lengths (c), as shown in Fig. 6.35.

4. *Features of the Generalized Modulo Algorithm*

The generalized modular algorithm has the following characteristics.

(1) Apart from the Well-Known port range (0~1023), no transport layer ports are wasted.
(2) The algorithm is flexible and can be used flexibly according to the multiplexing ratio (R), the maximum continuous port range (M) and the PSID prefix length (c).

	Port range-1	Port rang-2	Port
PSID=0	1024, 1025, 1026, 1027,	1536, 1537, 1538, 1539,	2048
PSID=1	1028, 1029, 1030, 1031,	1540, 1541, 1542, 1543,	....
PSID=2	1032, 1033, 1034, 1035,	1544, 1545, 1546, 1547,	....
PSID=3	1036, 1037, 1038, 1039,	1548, 1549, 1550, 1551,	....
...			
PSID=127	1532, 1533, 1534, 1535,	2044, 2045, 2046, 2047,	....

Fig. 6.34 PSID with fixed prefix length

Host	PSID prefix	Number of ports
Host0	000/2	2x8192
Host1	010/3	1x8192
Host2	011/3	1x8192
Host3	100/1	4x8192

Fig. 6.35 PSID with different prefix lengths

(3) It does not introduce algorithmic complexity.
(4) It allows operators to define the IPv4 address multiplexing ratio, with theoretical values ranging from 1:1 to 1:65536.
(5) It supports differentiated port range deployment for different translators.
(6) For the same translator, it supports different nodes using different sizes of port ranges.
(7) It supports the use of different algorithms to allocate the Well-Known port range (0~1023).
(8) It can support protocols that require continuity of transport layer ports, such as the Real-time Transport Protocol (RTP)/Real-time Transport Control Protocol (RTCP), which both require the use of adjacent transport layer ports.

6.4.2 PSID Suffix Encoding Format

The above generalized modulo algorithm gives the relationship between the transport layer port range and PSID. The PSID suffix encoding format is discussed below. Taking "IPv4-embedded IPv6 address" (without u-oct format) as an example, as shown in Fig. 6.26.

The suffix encoding involves two important parameters of the generalized modulo algorithm: the port multiplexing ratio (R) and the port continuity parameter (M).

(1) Port multiplexing ratio (R): Determined by the amount of public IPv4 addresses owned by the operator, the Quality of Service (QoS) guarantee for users, security tracing requirements, etc. it can be adjusted for different situations.
(2) Port maximum continuity parameter (M): Selected according to best practices, generally not specially adjusted.

In practice, three different PSID suffix encoding formats have been defined and used, which are discussed separately below.

1. *Fixed-Length Right-Aligned PSID Suffix Encoding with Multiplexing Ratio Parameter*

This is the initial design, as shown in Fig. 6.36.

(1) R: 4 bits; represents the multiplexing ratio, which is 1~4096.
(2) PSID: 12 bits; represents the port set identifier.

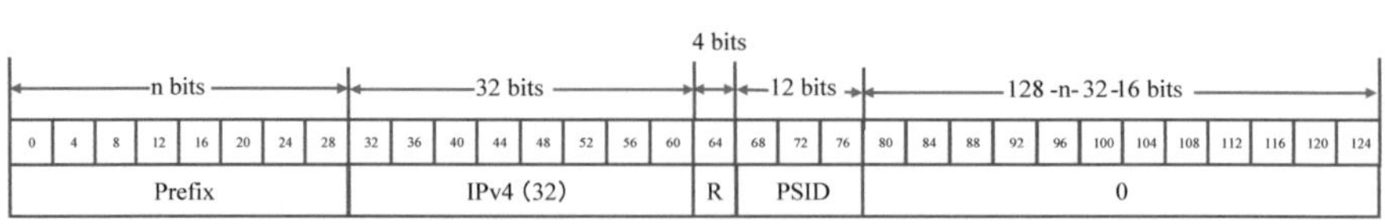

Fig. 6.36 Fixed-length PSID right-aligned suffix with ratio identifier

(PSID bits)	Range(16 bits)	Ratio	# of Ports
0	0000-0000	1	65, 536
1	1000-1001	2	32, 768
2	2000-2003	4	16, 384
3	3000-3007	8	8, 192
4	4000-400f	16	4, 096
5	5000-501f	32	2, 048
6	6000-603f	64	1, 024
7	7000-707f	128	512
8	8000-80ff	256	256
9	9000-91ff	512	128
10	a000-a3ff	1, 024	64
11	b000-b7ff	2, 048	32
12	c000-cfff	4, 096	16

Fig. 6.37 Encoding list (1)

This suffix encoding is called “fixed-length right-aligned PSID with multiplexing ratio parameter”. Figure 6.37 gives the PSID bits, the possible values of PSID, the corresponding multiplexing ratio (*R*), and the number of available concurrent ports.

The advantages of this suffix encoding are as follows:

(1) The multiplexing ratio (*R*) is self-descriptive in the address.
(2) PSID in the address conforms to thinking habits.

Its disadvantages are as follows:

(1) The maximum multiplexing ratio (*R*) is limited to 4096.
(2) PSID encoding contains invalid values.

2. *Fixed-Length Right-Aligned PSID Suffix Encoding*

For MAP-T (RFC7599 [33]) and MAP-E (RFC7597 [34]), the suffix format defined by the stateless transport layer port mapping algorithm is shown in Fig. 6.38.

This suffix encoding is called “Fixed-length Right-aligned PSID suffix encoding”, Fig. 6.39 gives the PSID bits, the possible values of PSID, the corresponding multiplexing ratio (*R*), and the available concurrent port numbers.

The advantages of this suffix encoding are as follows:

(1) The maximum multiplexing ratio (*R*) can reach the theoretical value (65536).
(2) PSID in the address conforms to thinking habits.

The disadvantage is: PSID encoding contains invalid values.

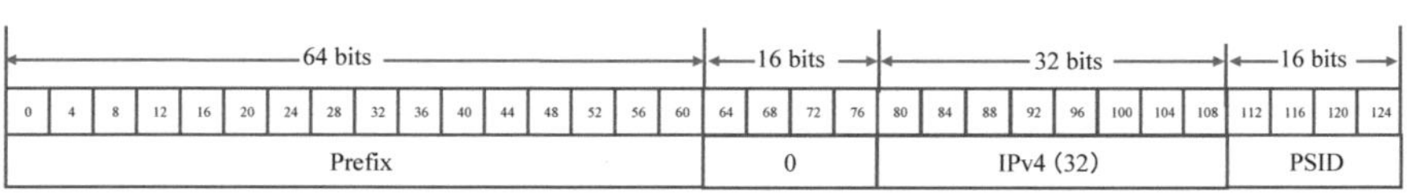

Fig. 6.38 Address right-aligned, fixed-length PSID right-aligned suffix encoding

(PSID bits)	Range(16 bits)	Ratio	# of Ports
0	0000-0000	1	65, 536
1	0000-0001	2	32, 768
2	0000-0003	4	16, 384
3	0000-0007	8	8, 192
4	0000-000f	16	4, 096
5	0000-001f	32	2, 048
6	0000-003f	64	1, 024
7	0000-007f	128	512
8	0000-00ff	256	256
9	0000-01ff	512	128
10	0000-03ff	1, 024	64
11	0000-07ff	2, 048	32
12	0000-0fff	4, 096	16
13	0000-1fff	8, 192	8
14	0000-3fff	16, 384	4
15	0000-7fff	32, 768	2
16	0000-ffff	65, 536	1

Fig. 6.39 Encoding list (2)

3. *Variable-Length Left-Aligned PSID Suffix Encoding*

The suggested suffix format defined by the stateless transport layer port mapping algorithm is shown in Fig. 6.40.

This suffix encoding is called "Variable-length Left-aligned PSID suffix encoding", Fig. 6.41 gives the PSID bits, the possible values of PSID, the corresponding multiplexing ratio (*R*) and the available concurrent port numbers.

The advantages of this suffix encoding are as follows:

(1) The maximum multiplexing ratio (*R*) can reach the theoretical value (65536).
(2) PSID encoding is continuous.

The disadvantage is: PSID in the address is not intuitive.

Using a similar approach, we can define "Unified Address and Port Set Identifier Prefix Length Representation". That is, extending "IPv4-translatable IPv6 address" to 48 bits (IPv4 address 32 bits, maximum port multiplexing ratio is 16 bits (65536)), then the IPv4 address corresponding to the "extended IPv4-translatable IPv6 address" can be represented as

$$u.v.w.x.y.z/k$$

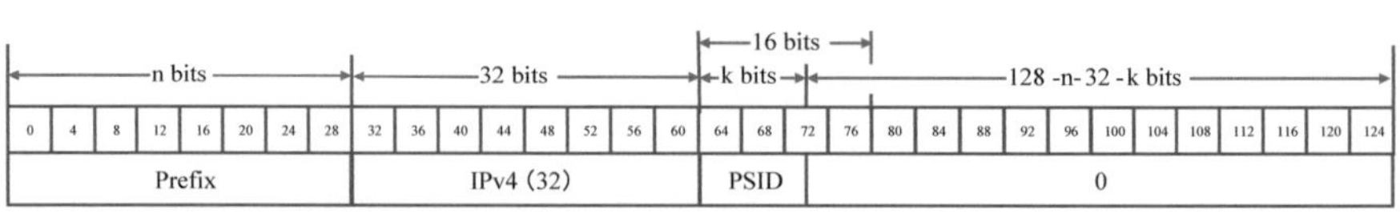

Fig. 6.40 Variable-length PSID left-aligned suffix encoding

(PSID bits)	Range (variable bits)	Ratio	# of Ports
0	–	1	65, 536
1	0000, 8000	2	32, 768
2	0000, 4000, 8000, c000	4	16, 384
3	0000, 2000, 4000, ···, e000	8	8, 192
4	0000, 1000, 2000, ···, f000	16	4, 096
5	0000, 0800, 1000, ···, f800	32	2, 048
6	0000, 0400, 0800, ···, fc00	64	1, 024
7	0000, 0200, 0400, ···, fe00	128	512
8	0000, 0100, 0200, ···, ff00	256	256
9	0000, 0080, 0100, ···, ff80	512	128
10	0000, 0040, 0080, ···, ffc0	1, 024	64
11	0000, 0020, 0040, ···, ffe0	2, 048	32
12	0000, 0010, 0020, ···, fff0	4, 096	16
13	0000, 0008, 0010, ···, fff8	8, 192	8
14	0000, 0004, 0008, ···, fffc	16, 384	4
15	0000, 0002, 0004, ···, fffe	32, 768	2
16	0000, 0001, 0002, ···, ffff	65, 536	1

Fig. 6.41 Encoding list (3)

where, u.v.w.x is the IPv4 address; y, z are PSID; *k* is the prefix length represented by CIDR. The extended IPv4 CIDR table is shown in Fig. 6.42.

Directly embedding the corresponding "IPv4-translatable IPv6 address" into the IPv6 prefix can form a "Variable-length Left-aligned PSID suffix encoding" address.

Here are a few examples.

Example 1 The IPv6 prefix is 2001:da8:ff00::/40, the public IPv4 address is 1.2.3.0/24, and the multiplexing ratio is $R = 1$, then the address format and the number of available ports are shown in Fig. 6.43.

Example 2 The IPv6 prefix is 2001:da8:ff00::/40, the public IPv4 address is 1.2.4.2/32, and the multiplexing ratio is $R = 256$, then the address format and the number of available ports are shown in Fig. 6.44.

Example 3 The IPv6 prefix is 2001:da8:ff00::/40, the public IPv4 address is 1.2.4.3/32, and the multiplexing ratio is $R = 2048$, then the address format and the number of available ports are shown in Fig. 6.45.

Example 4 The parameters are the same as in Example 2, the IPv6 prefix is 2001:da8:ff00::/40, the public IPv4 address is 1.2.4.3/32, and the multiplexing ratio is $R = 2048$, but PSID = 0 and 1 are combined into $(0 + 1)$, then the address format and the number of available ports are shown in Fig. 6.46.

Example 5 The parameters are the same as in Example 2, the IPv6 prefix is 2001:da8:ff00::/40, the public IPv4 address is 1.2.4.3/32, and the multiplexing ratio is $R = 2048$, but PSID = 0 is split into 00 and 01, then the address format and the number of available ports are shown in Fig. 6.47.

notation	addrs/block	# blocks	notes/# ports
n.n.n.n.y.z/48	1/65536	65536*4294967296	1
n.n.n.n.y.z/47	1/32768	32768*4294967296	2
n.n.n.n.y.z/46	1/16384	16384*4294967296	4
n.n.n.n.y.z/45	1/8192	8192*4294967296	8
n.n.n.n.y.z/44	1/4096	4096*4294967296	16
n.n.n.n.y.z/43	1/2048	2048*4294967296	32
n.n.n.n.y.z/42	1/1024	1024*4294967296	64
n.n.n.n.y.z/41	1/512	512*4294967296	128
n.n.n.n.y.z/40	1/256	256*4294967296	256
n.n.n.n.y.z/39	1/128	128*4294967296	512
n.n.n.n.y.z/38	1/64	64*4294967296	1024
n.n.n.n.y.z/37	1/32	32*4294967296	2048
n.n.n.n.y.z/36	1/16	16*4294967296	4096
n.n.n.n.y.z/35	1/8	8*4294967296	8192
n.n.n.n.y.z/34	1/8	4*4294967296	16384
n.n.n.n.y.z/33	1/2	2*4294967296	32786
n.n.n.n.y.z/32	1	1*4294967296	65536
n.n.n.n/32	1	4294967296	"host route"
n.n.n.x/31	2	2147483648	"p2p link"
n.n.n.x/30	4	1073741824	
n.n.n.x/29	8	536870912	
n.n.n.x/28	16	268435456	
n.n.n.x/27	32	134217728	
n.n.n.x/26	64	67108864	
n.n.n.x/25	128	33554432	
n.n.n.0/24	256	16777216	legacy "Class C"
n.n.x.0/23	512	8388608	
n.n.x.0/22	1024	4194304	
n.n.x.0/21	2048	2097152	
n.n.x.0/20	4096	1048576	
n.n.x.0/19	8192	524288	
n.n.x.0/18	16384	262144	
n.n.x.0/17	32768	131072	
n.n.0.0/16	65536	65536	legacy "Class B"
n.x.0.0/15	131072	32768	
n.x.0.0/14	262144	16384	
n.x.0.0/13	524288	8192	
n.x.0.0/12	1048576	4096	
n.x.0.0/11	2097152	2048	
n.x.0.0/10	4194304	1024	
n.x.0.0/9	8388608	512	
n.0.0.0/8	16777216	256	legacy "Class A"
x.0.0.0/7	33554432	128	
x.0.0.0/6	67108864	64	
x.0.0.0/5	134217728	32	
x.0.0.0/4	268435456	16	
x.0.0.0/3	536870912	8	
x.0.0.0/2	1073741824	4	
x.0.0.0/1	2147483648	2	
0.0.0.0/0	4294967296	1	"default route"

Fig. 6.42 Extended IPv4 CIDR table

Serial number	IPv4 prefix	IPv6 prefix	# of ports
	1.2.3.0/24	2001:da8:ff01:0203::/64	
0	1.2.3.0/24	2001:da8:ff01:0203:0000::/64	65536
1	1.2.3.1/24	2001:da8:ff01:0203:0100::/64	65536
2	1.2.3.2/24	2001:da8:ff01:0203:0200::/64	65536
……			
255	1.2.3.255/24	2001:da8:ff01:0203:ff00::/64	65536

Fig. 6.43 R = 1

PSID	1.2.4.2.0.0/40	2001:da8:ff01:0204:0200:0000::/80	# of ports
0	1.2.4.2.0.0/40	2001:da8:ff01:0204:0200:0000::/80	256
1	1.2.4.2.1.0/40	2001:da8:ff01:0204:0200:0100::/80	256
2	1.2.4.2.2.0/40	2001:da8:ff01:0204:0200:0200::/80	256
	……		
255	1.2.4.2.255.0/40	2001:da8:ff01:0204:0200:ff00::/80	256

Fig. 6.44 R = 256

PSID	1.2.4.3.0.0/43	2001:da8:ff01:0204:0300:0000::/83	# of ports
0	1.2.4.3.0.0/43	2001:da8:ff01:0204:0300:0000::/83	32
1	1.2.4.3.8.0/43	2001:da8:ff01:0204:0300:0800::/83	32
2	1.2.4.3.16.0/43	2001:da8:ff01:0204:0300:1000::/83	32
	……		
2047	1.2.4.3.255.248/43	2001:da8:ff01:0204:03ff:f800::/83	32

Fig. 6.45 R = 2048

PSID	1.2.4.3.0.0/43	2001:da8:ff01:0204:0300:0000::/83	# of ports
(0+1)	1.2.4.3.0.0/42	2001:da8:ff01:0204:0300:0000::/82	64
2	1.2.4.3.16.0/43	2001:da8:ff01:0204:0300:1000::/83	32
	……		
2047	1.2.4.3.255.248/43	2001:da8:ff01:0204:03ff:f800::/83	32

Fig. 6.46 R = 2048, combined

PSID	1.2.4.3.0.0/43	2001:da8:ff01:0204:0300:0000::/83	# of ports
00	1.2.4.3.0.0/44	2001:da8:ff01:0204:0300:0000::/83	16
01	1.2.4.3.0.0/44	2001:da8:ff01:0204:0300:0400::/83	16
1	1.2.4.3.8.0/43	2001:da8:ff01:0204:0300:0800::/83	32
2	1.2.4.3.16.0/43	2001:da8:ff01:0204:0300:1000::/83	32
	……		
2047	1.2.4.3.255.248/43	2001:da8:ff01:0204:03ff:f800::/83	32

Fig. 6.47 R = 2048, split

6.4.3 Prefix Encoding Format—EA-Bits

Considering a new problem: assigning different IPv6 prefixes to users who share public IPv4 addresses without state, i.e., not only encoding the IPv4 address and PSID into the suffix of IPv6, but also encoding the IPv4 address and PSID into the prefix of IPv6. This type of encoding is used for MAP-T (RFC7599 [33]) and MAP-E (RFC7597 [34]).

Theoretically, the encoding method of the suffix can be applied to the IPv6 prefix encoding, but in practice, there may be a problem of insufficient bit numbers of the IPv6 prefix. Because the maximum length of the IPv4 address and PSID may reach 48 bits, if the standard 64 bits of the IPv6 interface identifier are retained, the larger prefix that meets the conditions is IPv6/16. Obviously, it is unrealistic to assign IPv6/16 to each operator.

From another perspective, simply encoding the PSID into the IPv6 prefix encoding cannot meet the demand, because for a service domain of an operator, it usually does not share only one public IPv4 address, but shares a public IPv4 address pool represented in CIDR form. Therefore, simply encoding the PSID into the IPv6 prefix cannot distinguish different public IPv4 addresses in this address pool.

Considering comprehensively, define "Embedded Address Bits (EA-bits)" as: variable length, identifying the subnet part of the IPv4 prefix and PSID.

1. *EA-Bits Mapping Algorithm*

The EA-bits field corresponds to specific IPv4 address pool and PSID, with the following characteristics.

(1) The EA-bits field is unique for a given IPv6 prefix, containing a complete or partial IPv4 address, and in the case of shared IPv4 addresses, it also includes the PSID.
(2) The length of the IPv6 prefix plus the length of the EA-bits must be less than or equal to the length of the IPv6 prefix assigned to the end user.
(3) If only a shared IPv4 address/prefix is encoded by EA-bits, the full IPv4 address/prefix must be configured by using other methods.

Figure 6.48 shows the structure of a complete IPv6 address containing EA-bits.

(1) *r* is the length of the IPv4 prefix (not shown in Fig. 6.48).
(2) *o* is the length of the EA-bits field.

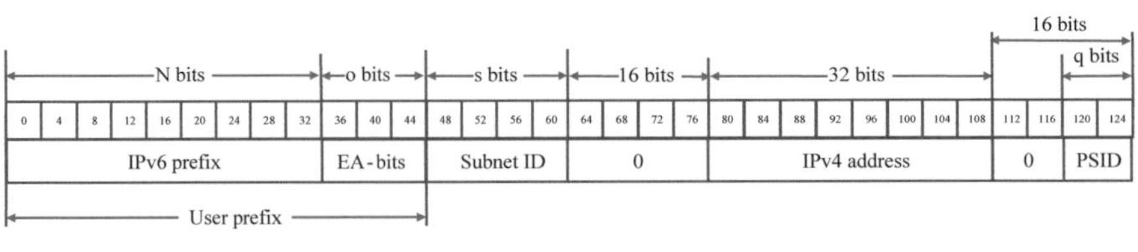

Fig. 6.48 IPv6 address format containing EA-bits

(3) p is the length of the IPv4 suffix contained in the EA-bits. The offset of the EA-bits field in the IPv6 address is equal to the length of the IPv6 prefix (included in the o bit in Fig. 6.48).

The length of the EA-bits field (o) can be 0 ~ 48:

① A length of 48 means that the full IPv4 address and port are embedded in the end user's IPv6 prefix (assigning a single port);
② A length of 0 means that any part of the IPv4 address or port is not an embedded address.

(1) $o + r < 32$: Assign IPv4 prefix, as shown in Fig. 6.49.
(2) $o + r = 32$: Assigning a full IPv4 address, as shown in Fig. 6.50.
(3) $o + r > 32$: Assigning a shared IPv4 address, as shown in Fig. 6.51.

In the case of assigning a shared IPv4 address, the EA-bits are constructed from the 32-bit IPv4 address and the 16-bit port number, as shown in Fig. 6.52.

EA-bits are composed of a part of the IPv4 address and PSID.

2. *Case of Constructing an IPv6 address with EA-bits*

Here is an example of an IPv6 address with EA-bits.

The IPv6 prefix assigned to the end user is: 2001:db8:0012:3400::/56.

The operator defines the basic mapping rule: {2001:db8:0000::/40 (IPv6 prefix), 192.0.2.0/24 (IPv4 prefix), 256 (IPv4 address sharing rate), 16 (EA-bits length)}.

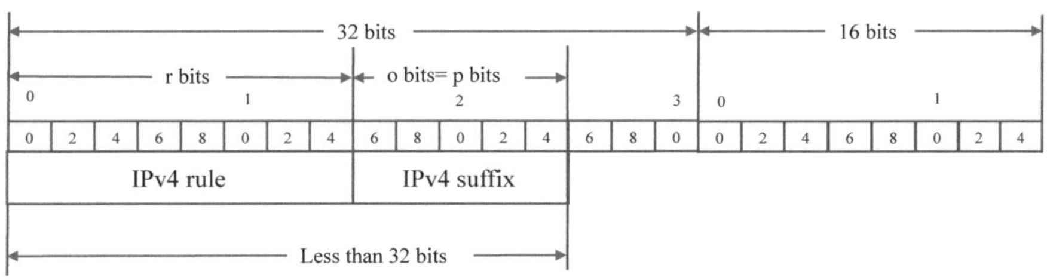

Fig. 6.49 Contains IPv4 prefix (o + r < 32)

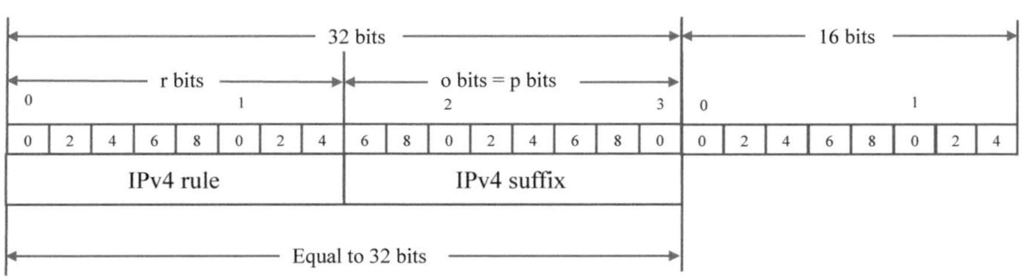

Fig. 6.50 Contains a full IPv4 address (o + r = 32)

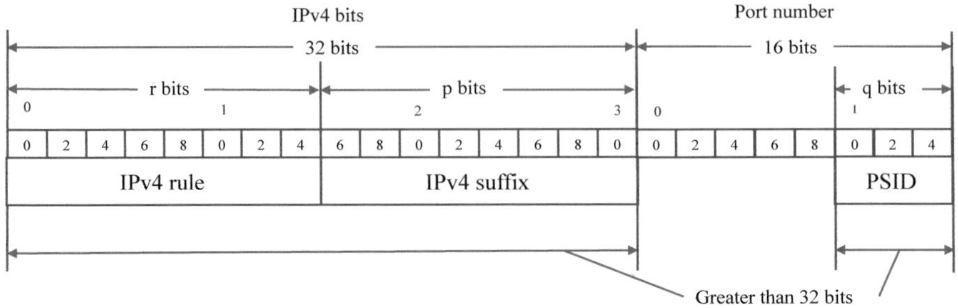

Fig. 6.51 Contains a shared IPv4 address (o + r > 32)

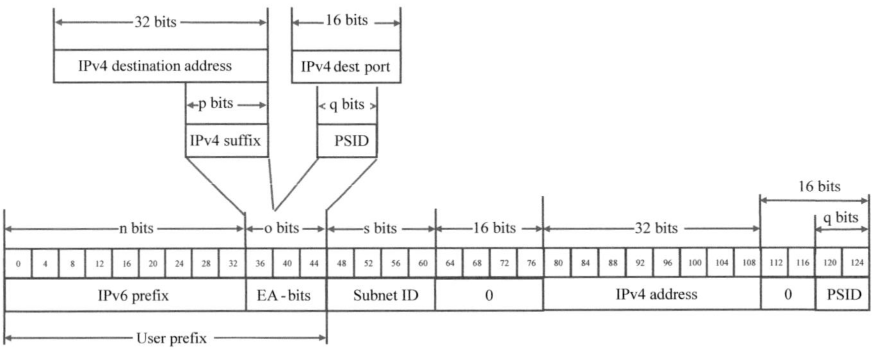

Fig. 6.52 Derivation of IPv6 address

Based on the above conditions, the PSID offset can be calculated as 6 (default); thus, the IPv4 address and port set can be determined as follows:

EA-bits offset: 40.

IPv4 suffix bits (p): IPv4 address length (32) - IPv4 prefix length (24) = 8.

IPv4 address: 192.0.2.18 (0xc0000212).

PSID starting bit: 40 + p = 40 + 8 = 48.

PSID length: o – p = (56 – 40) – 8 = 8.

PSID: 0 × 34.

Available ports (63 ranges): 1232 – 1235, 2256 – 2259, ..., 63696 – 63699, 64720 – 64723.

Finally, the IPv6 address is obtained: 2001:db8:0012:3400:0000:c000:0212:0034 (Table 6.14).

Table 6.14 Range of IPv6 addresses

Sequence	IPv4 address	PSID	IPv6 address
1	192.0.2.0	0	2001:db8:0000:3400:0000:c000:0200:0000
2	192.0.2.0	1	2001:db8:0000:3400:0000:c000:0200:0001
3	192.0.2.0	2	2001:db8:0000:3400:0000:c000:0200:0002
...	192.0.2.0	...	...
256	192.0.2.0	255	2001:db8:0001:3400:0000:c000:0200:00ff
257	192.0.2.1	0	2001:db8:0001:3400:0000:c000:0201:0000
258	192.0.2.1	1	2001:db8:0001:3400:0000:c000:0201:0001
259	192.0.2.1	2	2001:db8:0001:3400:0000:c000:0201:0002
...	192.0.2.1	...	...
512	192.0.2.1	255	2001:db8:0001:3400:0000:c000:0201:00ff
513	192.0.2.2	255	2001:db8:0002:3400:0000:c000:0202:0000
514	192.0.2.2	0	2001:db8:0002:3400:0000:c000:0202:0001
515	192.0.2.2	1	2001:db8:0002:3400:0000:c000:0202:0002
516	192.0.2.2	2	2001:db8:0002:3400:0000:c000:0202:0003
...	192.0.2.2	...	...
768	192.0.2.2	255	2001:db8:0002:3400:0000:c000:0202:00ff
...	...	...	...
65280	192.0.2.255	255	2001:db8:00ff:0000:0000:c000:02ff:0000
65281	192.0.2.255	0	2001:db8:00ff:0100:0000:c000:02ff:0001
65282	192.0.2.255	1	2001:db8:00ff:0200:0000:c000:02ff:0002
65283	192.0.2.255	2	2001:db8:00ff:0300:0000:c000:02ff:0003
...	192.0.2.255	...	...
65536	192.0.2.255	255	2001:db8:00ff:ff00:0000:c000:02ff:00ff

6.4.4 Mapping Extended "IPv4-Translatable IPv6 Addresses" to RFC1918 Space

Through the sharing algorithm of the aforementioned IPv4 public addresses, IPv4 public addresses and PSID can be mapped to extended "IPv4-translatable IPv6 addresses". Further considering, public IPv4 addresses and PSID can also be partially mapped to private IPv4 address space (RFC1918 [6] address space). In this case, a public IPv4 address can be mapped to several private IPv4 addresses for IPv4 nodes to use based on the algorithm. In other words, its external characteristics are similar to IPv4 NAT, but its mapping algorithm is stateless, with stateless scalability, traceability, and security.

	1.2.4.3.0.0/43	10.3.0.0/27	# of ports
0	1.2.4.3.0.0/43	10.3.0.0/27	32
1	1.2.4.3.0.8/43	10.3.0.8/27	32
2	1.2.4.3.0.16/43	10.3.0.16/27	32
	……		
2047	1.2.4.3.255.248/43	10.3.255.248/27	32

Fig. 6.53 $R = 2048$, represented by 10.0.0.0/8

The example uses the private IPv4 address 10.0.0.0/8 as an example, the first segment reserves 10, the second segment is replaced with the fourth segment of the public IPv4 address 1.2.4.3, and the third and fourth segments of the private IPv4 address are 10.3.PS.ID/16, as shown in Fig. 6.53.

6.5 Explicit Address Mapping Extension

In addition to the stateless IPv4 and IPv6 mapping algorithm defined by RFC6052 [11], RFC7757 [35] defines another stateless mapping algorithm, called the explicit address mapping extension. The main idea is embedding part of the IPv4 address in IPv6 prefix to simplify the IPv6 address structure. However, the hairpin function is required in the translator. More details are presented in RFC7757 [35].

6.6 Multicast Address Mapping

The stateless translation technology can be used not only for unicast datagrams but also for multicast datagrams. The processing of multicast datagrams involves the following steps.

(1) Protocol translation: Consistent with unicast, it is processed using the algorithm based on RFC7915 [36] introduced in Chap. 5 of this book.

(2) Handling of special multicast protocols.

① The traditional Internet multicast protocol is Protocol Independent Multicast-Sparse Mode (PIM-SM), which requires support for PIM-SM protocol penetration in the translator on both IPv4 and IPv6 sides of the translator. In addition, the source address in IPv6 must be an "IPv4-translatable IPv6 address" to execute PIM, as PIM-SM requires support for Reverse Path Forwarding (RPF).

② Multicast includes Any Source Multicast (ASM) and Source Specific Multicast (SSM). ASM is more complex, especially in cross-domain situations. For IPv4 ASM, the Multicast Source Discovery Protocol (MSDP)

IPv4 Group Address	IPv6 Group Address
232.0.0.0/8 232.255.255.255/8	ff3e:0:0:0:0:0:f000:0000/96 ff3e:0:0:0:0:0:f0ff:ffff/96

Fig. 6.54 SSM multicast group address mapping

is needed, and for IPv6 ASM, techniques such as Embedded Rendezvous Point (embedded-RP) are required. Therefore, the IPv4/IPv6 translator is more suitable for handling SSM.

③ The protocol for a host to join a "multicast group" is IGMP for IPv4 and Multicast Listener Discovery (MLD) for IPv6. These two protocols are generally used within a subnet, so translation is not required.

Translation of IPv4 and IPv6 multicast addresses. As mentioned above, only the translation of SSM addresses is considered. IPv4 SSM will have 2^{24} group addresses. Correspondingly, IPv6 PIM-SM SSM group addresses (PIM-SSM) (RFC5771 [37], RFC3569 [38], RFC4607 [39]) and the mapping algorithm can be defined, as shown in Fig. 6.54.

6.7 Summary

Addressing is the core component of the Internet. This chapter has analyzed and compared the address structures of IPv4 and IPv6 in detail, and on this basis, it has provided a stateless mapping algorithm between IPv4 addresses and IPv6 addresses. This includes the following points.

(1) IPv4-embedded IPv6 address format.
(2) Generalized modular algorithm.
(3) IPv6 address suffix encoding.
(4) IPv6 address prefix encoding.

References

1. Postel J. RFC791: Internet protocol. IETF 1981-09.
2. Fuller V, Li T, Yu J, et al. RFC1338: Supernetting: An address assignment and aggregation strategy. IETF 1992-06.
3. Rekhter Y, Li T. RFC1518:An architecture for IP address allocation with CIDR. IETF 1993-09.

4. Fuller V, Li T, Yu J, et al. RFC1519: Classless inter-domain routing (CIDR): An address assignment and aggregation strategy. IETF 1993-09.
5. Fuller V, Li T. RFC4632: Classless inter-domain routing (CIDR): The internet address assignment and aggregation. IETF 2006-08.
6. Rekhter Y, Moskowitz B, Karrenberg D, et al. RFC1918: Address allocation for private internets. IETF 1996-02.
7. Jiang S, Guo D, Carpenter B. RFC6264:An incremental carrier-grade NAT (CGN) for IPv6 transition. IETF 2011-06.
8. Weil J, Kuarsingh V, Donley C, et al. RFC6598: IANA-reserved IPv4 prefix for shared address space. IETF 2012-04.
9. Abley J, Maton W. RFC6304: AS112 nameserver operations. IETF 2011-07.
10. Hinden R, Deering S. RFC4291: IP version 6 addressing architecture. IETF 2006-02.
11. Bao C, Huitema C, Bagnulo M, et al. RFC6052: IPv6 addressing of IPv4/IPv6 translators. IETF 2010-10.
12. Hinden R, Deering S. RFC3513: Internet protocol version 6 (IPv6) addressing architecture. IETF 2003-04.
13. Haberman B, Thaler D. RFC3306:Unicast-prefix-based IPv6 multicast addresses. IETF 2002-08.
14. Savola P, Haberman B. RFC3956: Embedding the rendezvous point (RP) address in an IPv6 multicast address. IETF 2004-11.
15. M, Venaas S. RFC7371: Updates to the IPv6 multicast addressing architecture. IETF 2014-09.
16. Droms R. RFC7346: IPv6 multicast address scopes. IETF 2014-08.
17. Park J, Shin M, Kim H. RFC4489: A method for generating link-scoped IPv6 multicast addresses. IETF 2006-04.
18. Carpenter B, Jiang S. RFC7136: Significance of IPv6 interface identifiers. IETF 2014-02.
19. Narten T, Draves R. RFC3041: Privacy extensions for stateless address autoconfiguration in IPv6. IETF 2001-01.
20. Narten T, Draves R, Krishnan S. RFC4941: Privacy extensions for stateless address autoconfiguration in IPv6. IETF 2007-09.
21. Gont F, Krishnan S, Narten T, et al. RFC8981: Temporary address extensions for stateless address autoconfiguration in IPv6. IETF 2021-02.
22. Gont F, Cooper A, Thaler D, et al. RFC8064: Recommendation on stable IPv6 interface identifiers. IETF 2017-02.
23. Savolainen T, Korhonen J, Wing D. RFC7050: Discovery of the IPv6 prefix used for IPv6 address synthesis. IETF 2013-11.
24. Hinden R, Haberman B. RFC4193: Unique local IPv6 unicast addresses. IETF 2005-10.
25. Li X, Bao C, Chen M, et al. RFC6219: The China Education and Research Network (CERNET) IVI translation design and deployment for the IPv4/IPv6 coexistence and transition. IETF 2011-05.
26. Nordmark E. RFC2765: Stateless IP/ICMP translation algorithm (SIIT). IETF 2000-02.
27. Anderson T. RFC8215: Local-use IPv4/IPv6 translation prefix. IETF 2017-08.
28. Huston G, Lord A, Smith P. RFC3849: IPv6 address prefix reserved for documentation. IETF 2004-07.
29. Cotton M, Vegoda L. RFC5735:Special use IPv4 addresses. IETF 2010-01.
30. Kawamura S, Kawashima M. RFC5952: A recommendation for IPv6 address text representation. IETF 2010-08.
31. Rekhter Y, Li T, Hares S. RFC4271: A border gateway protocol 4 (BGP-4). IETF 2006-01.
32. Ford M, Boucadair M, Durand A, et al. RFC6269: Issues with IP address sharing. IETF 2011-06.
33. Li X, Bao C, Dec W, et al. RFC7599: Mapping of address and port using translation (MAP-T). IETF 2015-07.

34. Troan O, Dec W, Li X, et al. RFC7597: Mapping of address and port with encapsulation (MAP-E). IETF 2015-07.
35. Anderson T, Popper A. RFC7757: Explicit address mappings for stateless IP/ICMP translation. IETF 2016-02.
36. Bao C, Li X, Baker F, et al. RFC7915: IP/ICMP translation algorithm. IETF 2016-06.
37. Cotton M, Vegoda L, Meyer D. RFC5771: IANA guidelines for IPv4 multicast address assignments. IETF 2010-03.
38. Bhattacharyya S. RFC3569: An overview of source-specific multicast (SSM). IETF 2003-07.
39. Holbrook H B, Cain B. RFC4607: Source-specific multicast for IP. IETF 2006-08.

Chapter 7
DNS Support

Internet applications are using DNS, a distributed database that maps between domain names and IPv4 or IPv6 addresses, for users to access the Internet. The mapping between names and IPv4 addresses is represented by A records, and the mapping between names and IPv6 addresses is represented by AAAA records. Therefore, when deploying an IPv4/IPv6 translator, DNS64 is used to map A records to AAAA records, and DNS46 is used to map AAAA records to A records, as shown in Fig. 7.1.

If the function of DNS64 or DNS46 is for servers in this management domain, it is generally implemented on the "DNS authority server". If the function of DNS64 or DNS46 is for clients to access the Internet, it must be implemented on the "recursive resolver". Authority servers generally use algorithm-based static configuration, while domain name recursive resolver uses algorithm-based dynamic mapping.

According to whether the DNS service is implemented as IPv4 accessing IPv6 or IPv6 accessing IPv4, and whether the DNS service is based on authoritative servers or recursive resolver, four scenarios can be shown in Fig. 7.2.

7.1 DNS64

7.1.1 Introduction to DNS64

DNS64 is defined by RFC6147 [1], which is a mechanism for synthesizing AAAA records from A Resource Records (RR). The AAAA records created by DNS64 use the same name as the A records, but map to IPv6 addresses instead of IPv4 addresses. This IPv6 address is synthesized by DNS64 based on the A record of the domain authoritative server, using an address mapping algorithm. In other words, DNS64 synthesizes AAAA records of "IPv4-converted IPv6 address" or "IPv4-translatable IPv6 address" based on the A record, and returns it to the user.

X. Li and C. Bao, *New IPv6 Transition Technology*,
https://doi.org/10.1007/978-981-95-8427-7_7

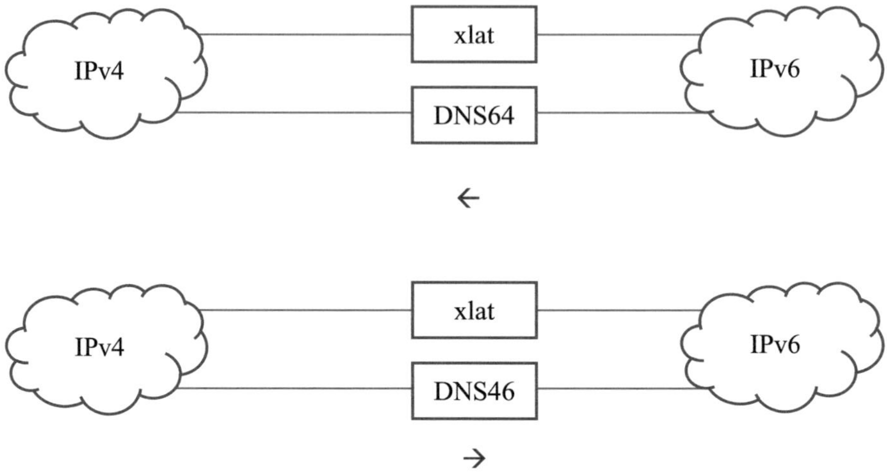

Fig. 7.1 Application scenarios of DNS64 and DNS46

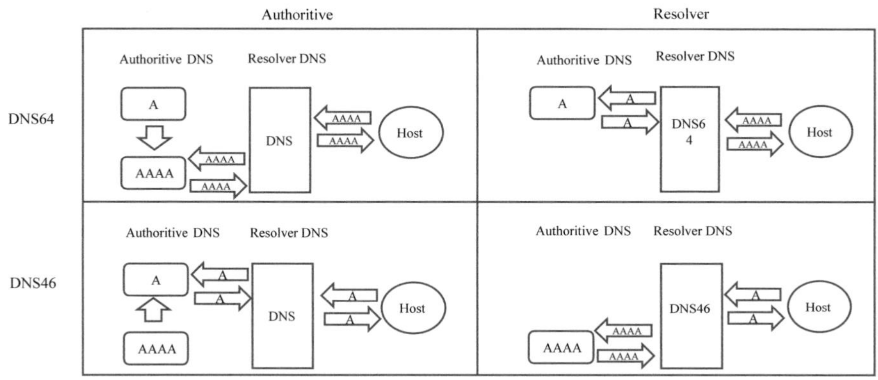

Fig. 7.2 Relationship of DNS64, DNS46, authoritative and resolving servers

DNS64, together with the IPv4/IPv6 translator, enables IPv6-only clients to communicate with IPv4 servers based on the server's fully qualified domain name (FQDN). These mechanisms play an important role in the coexistence and transition period from IPv4 to IPv6. Due to the exhaustion of IPv4 addresses, many IPv6-only clients need to communicate with IPv4 servers. DNS64 is needed when an IPv6 client initiates access to an IPv4 server in an IPv6-only network configured with an IPv4/IPv6 translator.

DNS64 first tries to request AAAA records. If no AAAA record is found for the destination node, DNS64 performs an A record query. For each A record, the corresponding AAAA record is synthesized.

The configuration of DNS64 requires information of the "IPv6 prefix". The IPv4/IPv6 translator and DNS64 must be configured with the same "IPv6 prefix". This prefix is necessary for generating "IPv4-converted IPv6 address" (AAAA record) from the IPv4 address (A record). This "IPv6 prefix" is represented as: Pref64::/*n*.

RFC6052 [2] defines the Pref64::/*n* prefix and its use scenarios; there are two types of prefixes.

(1) Well-Known Prefix (WKP): 64:ff9b::/96, etc.
(2) Network Specific Prefix (NSP).

The main difference between these two prefixes is: NSP is a prefix assigned by the operator itself, which can represent "IPv4-translatable IPv6 address" and "IPv4-converted IPv6 address", and is fully controllable. The WKP is a default prefix, only used to represent "IPv4-converted IPv6 address".

DNS64 function can be executed in the following three places.

(1) The first option is to locate the DNS64 function at the DNS authoritative server.

  ① In this case, the DNS authoritative server statically synthesizes AAAA records (IPv4-converted IPv6 address) from A records.
  ② This situation is generally used for the scenario 3 "IPv6 Internet (client) initiates access to IPv4 network (server)" in Chap. 4 of this book, and can also be used for scenario 5 "IPv6 network (client) initiates access to IPv4 network (server)".
  ③ In this case, the IPv4/IPv6 translator and DNS64 are deployed at the boundary between IPv4 and IPv6 networks.

(2) The second option is to locate the DNS64 function at the DNS resolver.

  ① In this case, the DNS resolver dynamically synthesizes AAAA records. When an IPv6 host queries the DNS resolver for a domain name, if the domain name only has an A record and no AAAA record, DNS64 dynamically synthesizes an "IPv4-converted IPv6 address" based on the queried A record.
  ② This situation is generally used in the scenario 1 "IPv6 network (client) initiates access to the IPv4 Internet (server)" in Chap. 4 of this book, and can also be used in scenario 5 "IPv6 network (client) initiates access to the IPv4 network (server)".
  ③ In this case, the IPv4/IPv6 translator and DNS64 are deployed at the boundary between IPv4 and IPv6 networks.
  ④ The advantage of this mode is that it does not require any modifications or upgrades to the host.

(3) The third choice is to place the DNS64 function in the end system.

  ① In this case, the host itself dynamically synthesizes AAAA records from A record. When the end system queries a domain name, if the domain name only has an A record and no AAAA record, the DNS64 function in the end system dynamically synthesizes an "IPv4-converted IPv6 address" based on the queried A record.

② This situation is generally used in the scenario 1 ”IPv6 network (client) initiates access to the IPv4 Internet (server)” in Chap. 4 of this book, and can also be used in scenario 5 “IPv6 network (client) initiates access to the IPv4 network (server)”.
③ In this case, the IPv4/IPv6 translator is deployed at the boundary between IPv4 IPv6 networks. The DNS64 is deployed in the end system itself.
④ The advantage of this method is that it is compatible with the domain name system security extensions (DNSSEC).
⑤ The disadvantage of this mode is its deployability, as it requires upgrades and modifications to the end system.

7.1.2 DNS64 Specification

DNS64 is a mapping function that synthesizes AAAA records from A records. The DNS64 function can be implemented in end systems, domain name resolvers, or domain name authority servers. In addition to the function of synthesizing AAAA records from A records, DNS64 must comply with the regular DNS server functions defined by RFC1034 [3] and RFC1035 [4].

DNS64 should support mapping different IPv4 address ranges to different IPv6 prefixes. This function can allow the handling of special-purpose IPv4 addresses defined by RFC5735 [5].

DNS messages contain several parts, and the DNS message changed by DNS64 is the answer part. This part is combined with other parts to create the return response of the DNS query.

DNS64 also needs to respond to pointer (PTR) queries, returning any IPv6 prefixes used for synthesizing AAAA records.

7.1.3 AAAA Query and Answer

When DNS64 receives an AAAA record query, it first queries the non-synthetic record, that is, it directly performs the query (or directly queries the database in the case of a domain name authority server). If there is a local cache, its result can be obtained locally. DNS64 must have the functions and behaviors of a regular DNS.

1. *Response When There is AAAA Data*

If there is one or more AAAA records in the domain name query result, these AAAA records should be directly returned to the client querying the domain name, that is, DNS64 should not include synthesized AAAA records in the response. The only exception is the handling of special IPv4 addresses, which can synthesize AAAA records according to configuration rules. By default, when there are real AAAA records, DNS64 must never synthesize AAAA records.

2. *Response When an Error Occurs*

If the response code (RCODE) obtained from the query is not 0 (no error condition), there are two possibilities.

(1) RCODE = 3 (Domain Error), this situation should be handled according to normal DNS operations (usually returning the error to the client). This stage occurs before any synthesis, so the response returned to the client does not need any special handling, consistent with usual DNS behavior.
(2) Any other RCODE should be treated as RCODE = 0. This is because a large number of domain servers currently deployed, when requesting AAAA records, but AAAA records do not exist, these domain servers have various behaviors. Many domain servers can replace with RCODE = 0 when receiving AAAA queries without AAAA records (RFC4074 [6]). Note that this means, from a practical perspective, several types of DNS error messages are caused by the queried domain not having AAAA records.

It should be pointed out that: there are still some domain servers that, when querying AAAA records, even if the domain's A record exists, will generate RCODE = 3 response. These servers clearly violate the definition of RCODE = 3, and it is expected to decrease with the promotion of IPv6.

3. *Handling Timeouts*

If the query does not receive any answers before the timeout, it will be treated as RCODE = 2 (Server Failure).

4. *Special Exclusion Set for AAAA Records*

Some IPv6 addresses cannot be used by IPv6-only hosts. If such IPv6 addresses are returned to IPv6-only hosts as AAAA records, it will cause user communication failures. For example, AAAA records belong to the::ffff:0:0/96 address range. Therefore, DNS64 implementation should provide a mechanism to exclude special IPv6 prefix ranges (within this range, an empty answer should be returned). For example, the default configuration includes special handling of the::ffff/96 network, otherwise when the client queries DNS64, it may prevent dual-stack hosts from communicating with these hosts.

When DNS64 performs its initial AAAA query, if it only receives AAAA records containing the above exclusion address range, it must be treated as an empty answer, and subsequent operations are based on this. If at least one AAAA record outside the exclusion address range is received, this AAAA record should be used by default. DNS64 must never return AAAA records within the exclusion address range.

5. *Handling CNAME and DNAME*

If the response contains a canonical name (CNAME) or non-terminal DNS name redirection (DNAME), the query should follow along the CNAME or DNAME chain until the first A record or AAAA record is obtained. This may require DNS64 to request an A record, in case there are no AAAA records, but only CNAME or DNAME for the original AAAA query. The handling of the obtained AAAA record or A record is the same as the handling of any other AAAA record or A record obtained by other means.

When summarizing the answer section, any query chain of CNAME or DNAME, including the synthesized AAAA record, should be included as an answer.

6. *Synthesis Required Data*

If the query does not report an error, but the query result of the AAAA record is empty, then DNS64 should try to query the A record in the domain (perform another query, or query the database in the case of the DNS authoritative server). If this new A record query result is empty or an error, the empty result or error code should be returned to the client. If one or more A records are returned, then DNS64 should synthesize AAAA records based on the A records. DNS64 returns the synthesized AAAA records in the answer section, deleting the A records.

7. *Performing Synthesis*

The steps to synthesize AAAA records from A records are as follows:

(1) The NAME field is set to the NAME field in the A record.
(2) The TYPE field is set to 28 (AAAA).
(3) The CLASS field is set to CLASS = 1. Under this specification, DNS64 does not define any CLASS fields other than 1.
(4) The TTL field is set to the original A record query domain and the start of the authority (start of authority, SOA) record, the smaller value in TTL. To obtain the TTL of the SOA record, DNS64 does not need to perform a new query, but can use the TTL value of the SOA record of the negative answer when querying AAAA. If the SOA record does not provide a negative answer to the AAAA query, then DNS64 should use the smaller of the original A record's TTL or 600 s. Of course, the SOA record can also be queried separately and use the query result, but this will increase the query burden.
(5) The RDLENGTH field is set to 16.
(6) The RDATA field is set to the IPv6 representation of the IPv4 address from the RDATA field of the A record. DNS64 must check each A record according to the configured IPv4 address range and select the IPv6 prefix corresponding to the synthesized AAAA record.

8. *Parallel Query*

DNS64 can perform parallel queries of AAAA records and A records to reduce latency.

Note: Parallel queries will result in unnecessary A record queries when there is no need to synthesize AAAA records. A possible trade-off is to implement serial queries with very short intervals.

9. *Generating IPv6 Representation of IPv4 Address*

DNS64 supports using multiple algorithms to generate "IPv4-converted IPv6 addresses", but the following restrictions should be noted.

(1) The algorithm that DNS64 uses to synthesize AAAA records (IPv4-converted IPv6 addresses) from A records (IPv4 addresses) must be consistent with the algorithm of the IPv4/IPv6 translator.
(2) The algorithm must be reversible, i.e., it must be able to derive the IVI4 from the IPv6 address.
(3) The input of the algorithm must only depend on the IPv4 address, "IPv6 prefix" (represented as Pref64::/*n*), and a set of stable parameters; for Pref64::/*n*, *n* must be less than or equal to 96. If one or more Pref64::/*n* are configured in DNS64, the default algorithm must use these prefixes (instead of using the WKP). If there is no available prefix, the algorithm must use the WKP 64:ff9b::/96 defined in RFC6052 [2].

DNS64 must support the IPv6 address generation algorithm defined by RFC6052 [2] as the default algorithm of DNS64.

7.1.4 Processing Other Resource Records and Additional Resources

1. *PTR Resource Record*

If the DNS64 server receives a query for a PTR record in the "IP6.ARPA" domain, it must strip the "IP6.ARPA" label from the QNAME, reverse assemble the address part using the encoding scheme defined by RFC3596 [7], and check whether the prefix of the reassembled address is Pref64::/*n* or the default WKP. DNS64 has two schemes to respond to such PTR queries. The DNS64 server must provide one of the responses, and cannot provide both responses at the same time, unless different IP6.ARPA domains need to answer different classes.

(1) The first choice is for the DNS64 server to respond as an authoritative server for this prefix. If the address prefix matches any Pref64::/*n* used in this network, whether Pref64::/*n* is a NSP or a WKP (64:ff9b::/96), the DNS server can use locally resolved data (resolved data, RDATA) to reply to the query. Note: The premise of adopting this algorithm is that it must match any Pref64::/*n* used in the network, not just the locally configured Pref64::/*n*. This is because end users may query the PTR records of any address (including those not returned by this DNS64), and when this policy is in effect, these queries will not be sent to the global DNS. The advantage of this policy is that end users can understand that the answer is generated by DNS64; the disadvantage is that DNS64 cannot provide reverse tree information for global domain names.
(2) The second choice is for the DNS64 server to synthesize CNAME records that map the IP6.ARPA namespace to the corresponding "IN-ADDR.ARPA" name. In this case, DNS64 should ensure that the "IN-ADDR.ARPA" name can correspond to the PTR's RDATA record, and there

is no duplicate CNAME. This is to avoid synthesizing a longer CNAME or pointing to an empty set. The rest of the response will be normal DNS processing. If necessary, CNAME can be generated on the spot. The advantage of this method is that DNS64 can provide reverse tree information for global domain names. The disadvantage is that it increases the additional load on DNS64 (because it must synthesize a matching Pref64::/*n* CNAME for each PTR query).

If the address prefix does not match any Pref64::/*n*, the DNS64 server must handle it like any other query. That is, the DNS resolver must attempt any other (non-A record/non-AAAA record) queries, and must reply in an authoritative server manner, or give a referral.

2. *Processing Additional Parts*

DNS64 must never synthesize any records in the additional part of the answer. DNS64 must keep the additional part unchanged.

Note: On the surface, synthesizing the additional part of the answer seems to reduce the number of times DNS queries are re-executed. But due to the uncertainty of the additional part, this brings potential risks.

3. *Other Resource Records*

All other records of the query results must remain unchanged, including the reply to query A records.

7.1.5 Assembling Synthetic Responses into AAAA Query Answers

DNS64 uses multiple data to build the response returned to the query client.

The query results used for synthesis include errors, answers, or empty sets, etc. If it is an empty set, then DNS64 directly returns the result to the query terminal; otherwise, the response is assembled as follows.

Depending on the role of DNS64, the "header" field is set according to the usual rules of the DNS resolver or the DNS authoritative server. The "question part" is copied from the original data of the query. The "answer part" is generated according to the above rules. The "authority part" and other parts are copied from the final query result of DNS64, used as the basis for synthesis.

The final response of DNS64 will be subject to all DNS standard rules, including truncation (RFC1035 [4]) and EDNS0 processing (RFC2671 [8]).

7.1.6 Deployment Schemes and Examples

In all the examples below, the IPv4/IPv6 translator interconnects the IPv4 network and the IPv6 network, and DNS64 also accesses both the IPv4 and IPv6 networks. In addition, the IPv4/IPv6 translator and DNS64 configure the same "IPv6 prefix". This section discusses the following scenarios.

1. *IPv6 Network (Client) Initiates Access to IPv4 Internet (Server)*
   Since the servers on the IPv4 Internet are uncontrollable, this scenario can only use the method of dynamically generating AAAA records from A records.

   The topology when using a stateless translator is shown in Fig. 7.3.

   (1) IPv6 client: H1, configured with "IPv4-translatable IPv6 address" 2001:da8::203.0.113.1.
   (2) IPv4 server: H2, FQDN = h2.example.com, IPv4 address = 192.0.2.1.
   (3) IPv6 prefix: Using the NSP = 2001:db8::/96 (configured for both DNS64 and Stateless xlat).

The steps for H1 and H2 to establish communication are as follows:

(1) H1 queries the DNS record of h2.example.com. H1 sends a request for the AAAA record to the DNS resolver with DNS64 functionality.
(2) The DNS resolver performs a recursive query and finds that h2.example.com does not have an AAAA record.
(3) The DNS resolver performs a recursive query for the A record of H2 and finds that its A record is a single IPv4 address 192.0.2.1. Then, the DNS resolver synthesizes an AAAA record. The IPv6 address in the AAAA record includes the IPv6 prefix and the IPv4 address 2001:db8::192.0.2.1.
(4) H1 receives the synthesized AAAA record and sends an IPv6 datagram to H2. The source address of the IPv6 datagram is 2001:da8::203.0.113.1, and the destination address is 2001:db8::192.0.2.1.
(5) The IPv6 datagram is routed to the IPv6 interface of Stateless xlat, translated into an IPv4 datagram, the source address of the IPv4 datagram is 203.0.113.1 (stateless translation mode), and the destination address is 192.0.2.1.

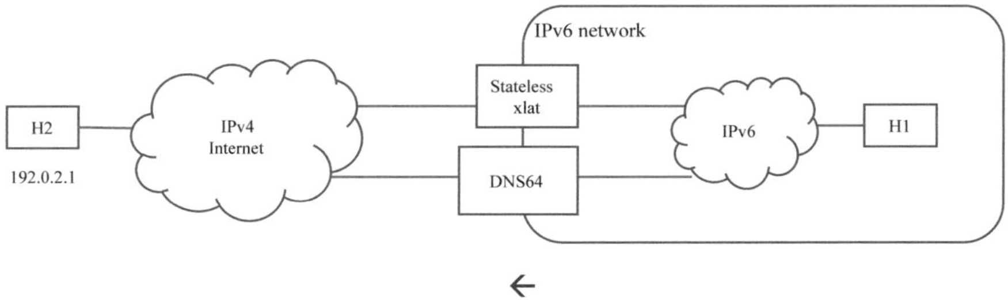

Fig. 7.3 Using stateless translator

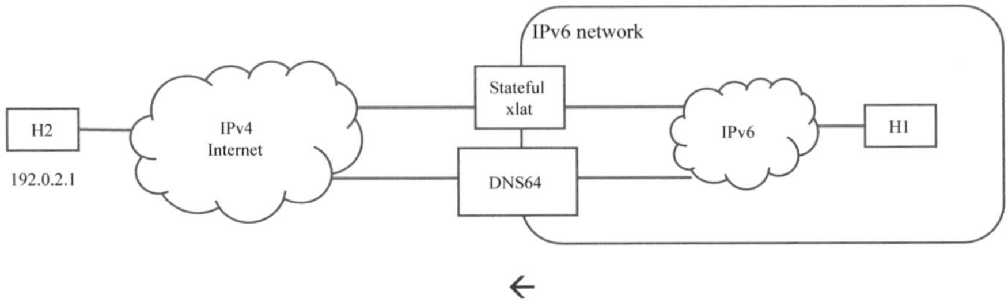

Fig. 7.4 Using stateful translator

The topology when using a stateful translator is shown in Fig. 7.4.

(1) IPv6 client: H1, IPv6 address = 3ffe:3200::1.
(2) IPv4 server: H2, FQDN = h2.example.com, IPv4 address = 192.0.2.1.
(3) IPv6 prefix: Using the WKP = 64:ff9b::/96 (configured for both DNS64 and Stateful xlat).
(4) The IPv4/IPv6 translator has IPv4 address 203.0.113.1 in the pool.

The steps for H1 and H2 to establish communication are as follows:

(1) H1 queries the DNS record of h2.example.com. H1 sends a request for the AAAA record to the DNS resolver with DNS64 functionality.
(2) The DNS resolver performs a recursive query and finds that h2.example.com does not have an AAAA record.
(3) The DNS resolver performs a recursive query for the A record of H2 and finds that its A record is a single IPv4 address 192.0.2.1. Then, the DNS resolver synthesizes an AAAA record. The IPv6 address in the AAAA record includes the IPv6 prefix and the IPv4 address 64:ff9b::192.0.2.1.
(4) H1 receives the synthesized AAAA record and sends an IPv6 datagram to H2. The source address of the IPv6 datagram is 3ffe:3200::1, and the destination address is 64:ff9b::192.0.2.1.
(5) The IPv6 datagram is routed to the IPv6 interface of the Stateful xlat, translated into an IPv4 datagram, the source address of the IPv4 datagram is 203.0.113.1 (stateful translation mode), and the destination address is 192.0.2.1.

2. *IPv6 Internet (client) Initiating Access to IPv4 Network (server)*

Since the servers on the IPv4 network are controllable, this scenario can either directly configure AAAA records on the authoritative domain name server, or the authoritative DNS server can dynamically generate AAAA records from A records.

This scenario generally uses a stateful translator.

Using authoritative DNS static configuration is shown in Fig. 7.5.

(1) IPv6 client: H1, IPv6 address = 3ffe:3200::1.
(2) IPv4 server: H2, FQDN = h2.example.com, IPv4 address = 192.0.2.1.

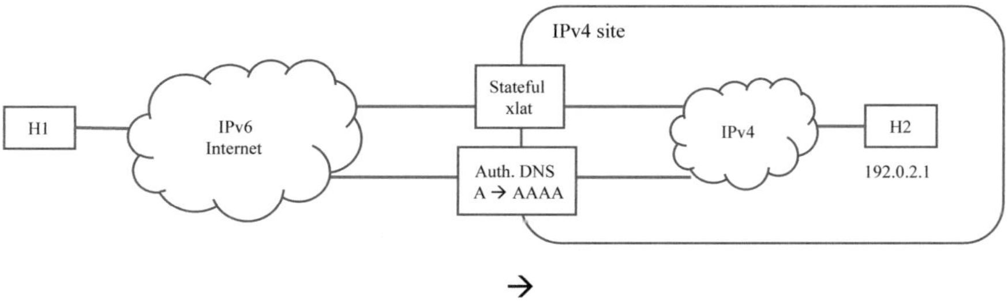

Fig. 7.5 Method of using authoritative domain name configuration

(3) IPv6 prefix: Use the operator prefix 2001:db8::/96 (configured for Stateful xlat).
(4) Authoritative DNS server configuration: A = 192.0.2.1, AAAA = 2001:db8::192.0.2.1.
(5) The Stateful xlat has configured a public IPv4 address pool: 203.0.113.1.

In this scenario, the function of DNS64 is directly manifested as the authoritative DNS server is not only configuring an A record, but also configuring an AAAA record that complies with the Stateful xlat rule. Note: In this case, the IPv4 address can be either a public IPv4 address or a private IPv4 address, because at this time, the IPv6 clients in the IPv6 Internet is accessing the IPv4 server via operator's "IPv6 prefix", and therefore it will not cause ambiguity.

The steps for H1 and H2 to establish communication are as follows:

(1) H1 queries the DNS record of h2.example.com. H1 sends a request for the AAAA record to the DNS resolver, and received AAAA = 2001:db8::192.0.2.1.
(2) H1 sends a data packet to H2. The source address of the IPv6 packet is 3ffe:3200::1, and the destination address is 2001:db8::192.0.2.1.
(3) The IPv6 packet is routed to the IPv6 interface address of Stateful xlat, translated into an IPv4 packet, the source address of the packet is 203.0.113.1 (stateful translation mode), and the destination address is 192.0.2.1.

Using dynamic domain name generation is shown in Fig. 7.6.

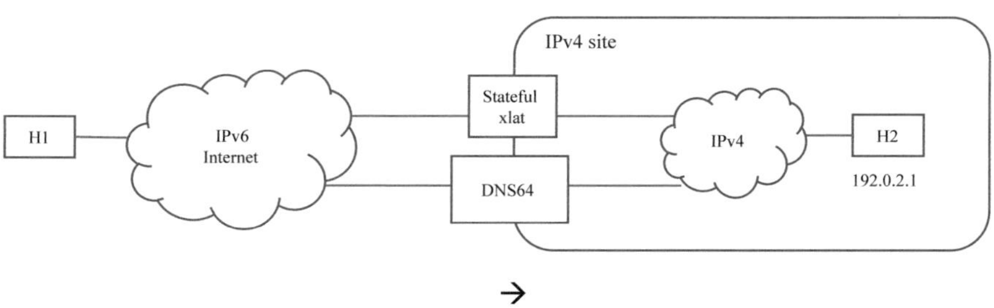

Fig. 7.6 Method of using dynamic domain name generation

(1) IPv6 client: H1, IPv6 address = 3ffe:3200::1.
(2) IPv4 server: H2, FQDN = h2.example.com, IP address = 192.0.2.1.
(3) IPv6 prefix: Use NSP of 2001:db8::/96 (configured for both DNS64 and Stateful xlat).
(4) The Stateful xlat has configured a public IPv4 address: 203.0.113.1.

When using dynamic domain name updates defined by RFC2136 [9], AAAA records can be generated based on the A records of the authoritative DNS server, according to the policy.

The steps for H1 and H2 to establish communication are as follows:

(1) H1 queries the DNS record of h2.example.com. H1 sends a request for the AAAA record through the DNS resolver. This request reaches the authoritative DNS server of h2.example.com.
(2) The authoritative DNS server of h2.example.com does not have an AAAA record.
(3) According to the local policy of the authority DNS server, the AAAA records should be generated based on A records (192.0.2.1), the DNS server synthesizes the AAAA records, which contains the IPv6 prefix and the IPv4 address as 2001:db8::192.0.2.1.
(4) H1 receives the synthesized AAAA record and sends an IPv6 datagram to H2. The source address of the IPv6 datagram is 3ffe:3200::1, and the destination address is 2001:db8::192.0.2.1.
(5) The IPv6 datagram is routed to the IPv6 interface address of Stateful xlat and translated into an IPv4 datagram. The source address of the IPv4 datagram is 203.0.113.1 (stateful translation mode), and the destination address is 192.0.2.1.

7.2 DNS46

7.2.1 Introduction to DNS46

DNS46 is a mechanism that synthesizes A records from AAAA records. The A records created by DNS46 use the same name as the original AAAA records, but map to an IPv4 address instead of an IPv6 address. This IPv4 address is synthesized by DNS46 based on the AAAA records of the authority DNS server using an address mapping algorithm.

DNS46, together with the IPv4/IPv6 translator, enables IPv4-only clients to communicate with IPv6-only servers based on the server's fully qualified domain name (FQDN). These mechanisms will play a key role in the coexistence and transition period from IPv4 to IPv6. As IPv4 addresses are exhausted, but the transition to IPv6 is lengthy, IPv6-only servers need to provide services for IPv4 users. In a IPv4-only network with an IPv4/IPv6 translator configured, DNS46 is needed when an IPv4 client initiates access to an IPv6 server.

DNS46 first tries to request A records. If no A records are found, then DNS46 performs an AAAA record query. For each AAAA record, the corresponding A record is synthesized.

The configuration of DNS46 requires information of the "IPv6 prefix". The IPv4/IPv6 translator and DNS46 must be configured with the same "IPv6 prefix". This "IPv6 prefix" is represented as Pref64::/*n*.

RFC6052 [2] defines the Pref64::/*n* prefix and the scenarios. For DNS46, only the Pref64::/*n* operator prefix is allowed.

There are two choices for implementing DNS46 functionality.

(1) The first choice is to locate the DNS46 function at the authority DNS server.

① In this case, the authority DNS server statically synthesizes A records from AAAA records (the IPv4 address corresponding to the "IPv4-translatable IPv6 address").

② This situation is generally used for scenario 2 "IPv4 Internet (client) initiates access to IPv6 network (server)" in Chap. 4 of this book, and can also be used for scenario 6 "IPv4 network (client) initiates access to IPv6 network (server)".

③ In this case, the IPv4/IPv6 translator and DNS46 are deployed at the boundary of the IPv4 network and the IPv6 network.

(2) The second choice is to locate the DNS46 function at the DNS resolver.

① In this case, the DNS resolver dynamically synthesizes A records. When an IPv6 host queries a DNS resolver, if the domain name only has AAAA records and no A records, then DNS46 dynamically synthesizes an IPv4 address based on the queried AAAA record.

② This situation is generally used for Scenario 4 "IPv4 Network (Client) Initiates Access to IPv6 Internet (Server)", and can also be used in Scenario 6 "IPv4 Network (Client) Initiates Access to IPv6 Network (Server)".

③ In this case, the IPv4/IPv6 translator and DNS46 are deployed at the boundary of the IPv4 and IPv6 networks.

7.2.2 DNS46 Specification

DNS46 is a logical function that synthesizes A records from AAAA records. The function of DNS46 can be implemented in the DNS resolver or in the authority DNS server. In addition to the function of synthesizing A records from AAAA records, DNS46 must comply with the regular DNS server functions defined by RFC1034 [3] and RFC1035 [4].

The DNS message contains several parts, and the DNS message changed by DNS46 is the answer part. This part is combined with other parts to create the actual message that is returned as a response to the DNS query.

7.2.3 A Query and Response

When DNS46 receives a query of type A record, it first queries this type of non-synthetic record, that is, it directly performs the A query (or in the case of an authority DNS server, queries the database). Its answer can be obtained from the local cache (if any). DNS46 must have the function and behavior of a regular DNS.

1. *Response When There is an A Record*

If there is one or more A records in the domain name query result, these A records should be directly returned to the client querying the domain name, that is, DNS46 should not include synthetic A records in the response. By default, when a real A record exists, DNS46 should never synthesize an A record.

2. *Response When an Error Occurs*

If the RCODE of the query response is not 0 (no error condition), then RCODE = 3 (domain name error) should be set. This situation is a normal DNS operation handling (usually returning the error to the client). This stage occurs before any synthesis, so the response returned to the client does not need any special handling and is consistent with the behavior of a regular DNS.

3. *Handling Timeouts*

If no answer is received before the query times out, it will be considered as RCODE = 2 (server failure).

4. *Handling CNAME and DNAME*

If the response contains CNAME or DNAME, the query chain along the CNAME or DNAME should be followed until the first A record or AAAA record is obtained. This may require DNS46 to request an A record, in case there is no A record for the original A query, but only CNAME or DNAME. The handling of the obtained A record or AAAA record is the same as the handling of any other A record or AAAA record obtained by any other means.

When summarizing the answer part, any CNAME or DNAME query chain should be included as part of the answer, including the synthesized A record.

5. *Data Required for Synthesis*

If the query does not report an error, but the query result of the A record is empty, then DNS46 should try to query the AAAA record in the domain name (by performing another query, or querying the database in the case of an authority DNS server). If the result of this new AAAA record query is empty or an error occurs, the empty result or error code should be returned to the client. On the contrary, if one or more AAAA records are queried, DNS46 should synthesize A records based on the AAAA records. DNS46 returns the synthesized A record in the answer part and deletes the AAAA record.

6. *Performing Synthesis*

The steps to synthesize A records from AAAA records are as follows:

(1) The NAME field is set to the NAME field in the AAAA record.
(2) The TYPE field is set to 1 (A).
(3) The CLASS field is set to CLASS = 1. Under this specification, DNS46 does not define any CLASS field other than 1.
(4) The TTL field is set to the smaller of the original AAAA record's TTL and the SOA record's TTL. To obtain the TTL of the SOA record, DNS46 does not need to perform a new query, it can use the TTL of the SOA record obtained from the negative response to the A record query. If the SOA record does not provide a negative response to the A record query, then DNS46 should use the smaller of the original AAAA record's TTL or 600 s. Of course, it can also query the SOA record separately and use the result of that query, but this will increase the query load.
(5) The RDLENGTH field is set to 4.
(6) The RDATA field is set to the IPv4 representation of the IPv6 address from the RDATA field of the AAAA record. DNS46 must check each AAAA record according to the configured IPv6 address range and synthesize the corresponding A record.

7. *Parallel Query*

DNS46 can perform parallel queries of A records and AAAA records to minimize latency.

Note: Parallel queries can lead to unnecessary AAAA record queries when there is no need to synthesize A records. A possible trade-off is to perform serial queries with very short intervals.

8. *Generating IPv4 Representation of IPv6 Address*

DNS46 supports using multiple algorithms to generate IPv4 addresses. The following limitation should be noted: The algorithm that DNS46 uses to synthesize A records of IPv4 addresses from the IPv6 addresses of AAAA records must be consistent with the algorithm of the IPv4/IPv6 translator.

7.2.4 Processing Other Resource Records and Additional Resources

1. *Processing Additional Section*

DNS46 must never synthesize any records in the additional section of the answer. DNS46 must keep the additional section unchanged.

Note that, on the surface, synthesizing the additional section of the answer seems to reduce the number of times DNS queries need to be performed again. However, due to the uncertainty of the additional section, this can bring potential risks.

2. *Other Resource Records*

All other records from the query results must remain unchanged, including the obtained AAAA records.

7.2.5 Assembling Synthesized Response into a Query Answer

DNS46 uses multiple data to construct the response returned to the query client.

The query results used for synthesizing the response include several situations such as errors, answers, or empty sets. If it is an empty set, then DNS46 directly returns the result to the query terminal; otherwise, the process of synthesizing the response is as follows.

Depending on the role of DNS46, the "header" field is set according to the usual rules of the domain name resolution server or the authoritative domain name server. The "question section" is copied from the original data of the query. The "answer section" is generated according to the above rules. The "authority section" and other sections are copied from the final query result of DNS46, used as the basis for synthesis.

The final response of DNS46 should be subject to all DNS standard rules, including truncation (RFC1035 [4]) and EDNS0 processing (RFC2671 [8]).

7.2.6 Deployment Schemes and Examples

In all the examples below, the IPv4/IPv6 translator interconnects the IPv4 network and the IPv6 network, and DNS46 also connects to both the IPv4 network and the IPv6 network. In addition, the IPv4/IPv6 translator and DNS46 are configured with the same "IPv6 prefix".

The scenario 2 of the translation technology in Chap. 4 of this book is discussed here: IPv4 Internet (client) initiates access to the IPv6 network (server) (stateless translation).

This case implements the access (authoritative domain name configuration) from IPv4-only clients in the IPv4 Internet to IPv6-only servers in the IPv6 network, as shown in Fig. 7.7.

(1) IPv4 client: H1, IPv4 address = 1.2.3.4.
(2) IPv6 server: H2, FQDN = h2.example.com, address = 2001:db8::192.0.2.1.
(3) IPv6 prefix: Use the operator prefix 2001:db8::/96 (Stateless xlat configuration).

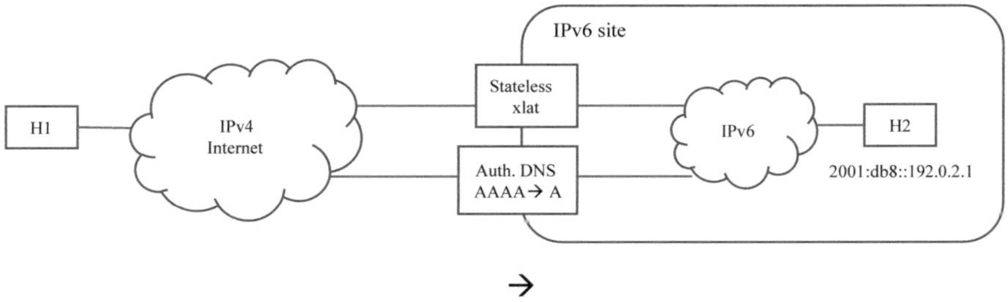

Fig. 7.7 Using authoritative domain name configuration

(4) Authoritative domain name server: AAAA = 2001:db8::192.0.2.1, A = 192.0.2.1.

The function of DNS46 is directly manifested as the authoritative DNS server not only configures the AAAA record of the IPv6-only server, but also configures the A record that complies with the Stateless xlat and DNS46 rules.

The steps for H1 and H2 to establish communication are as follows:

(1) H1 queries the DNS record of h2.example.com. H1 sends a request for the A record to the DNS resolver and receives A = 192.0.2.1.
(2) H1 sends a datagram to H2. The source address of the IPv4 datagram is 1.2.3.4, and the destination address is 192.0.2.1.
(3) The IPv4 datagram is routed to the IPv4 interface of Stateless xlat, translated into an IPv6 datagram, the source address of the IPv6 datagram is 2001:db8::1.2.3.4 (stateless translation mode), and the destination address is 2001:db8::192.0.2.1.

7.3 DNSSEC Processing

DNSSEC (Domain Name System Security Extensions, RFC4033 [10], RFC4034 [11], RFC4035 [12]) poses a special challenge to DNS64 or DNS46 because DNSSEC aims to detect security issues with DNS changing answers, but DNS64 or DNS46 will change the answers from the authoritative domain name server.

7.3.1 DNSSEC Scenarios

Recursive resolvers can be security-aware or security-oblivious. In addition, security-aware recursive resolvers can "verify" or "not verify" the security of the domain name according to the operator's policy. In the following cases, the. DNS resolver is also performing the function of DNS64 or DNS46 and has a local policy of "verifying security". This general situation is called vDNS64 or vDNS46.

DNSSEC provides the following indicator bits:

(1) If a query with the "DNSSEC OK" (DO) bit arrives at vDNS64 or vDNS46, it indicates that the query initiator understands DNSSEC. The DO bit does not mean that the query initiator will verify the response, but only indicates that the query initiator can understand the response containing DNSSEC data. Conversely, if DO is not set, it indicates that the query initiator does not understand DNSSEC.
(2) If a query with the "checking disabled" (CD) bit arrives at vDNS64 or vDNS46, it indicates that the query initiator needs to verify all data so that he can check it himself. According to local policy, vDNS64 or vDNS46 can still verify, but regardless of the verification result, all data must be returned to the query initiator.

The following are possible scenarios.

(1) DNS64 or DNS46 receives DO = 0: In this case, DNSSEC is not a problem because the query initiator does not understand DNSSEC. According to local policy, DNS64 or DNS46 can verify the response for DNSSEC.
(2) DNS64 or DNS46 that does not support DNSSEC receives DO = 1: In this case, DNSSEC is not supported.
(3) "Security-aware" and "non-validating" DNS64 or DNS46 receives DO = 1, CD = 0: In this case, there is no need to validate DNSSEC.
(4) "Security-aware" and "non-validating" DNS64 or DNS46 receives DO = 1, CD = 1: In this case, DNS64 or DNS46 should pass all the data obtained to the query initiator. This situation does not apply to DNS64 or DNS46 unless the query initiator itself has the functionality of DNS64 or DNS46. If DNS64 or DNS46 modifies the record, the query initiator will receive the returned data and attempt to validate it, ending with a validation failure.
(5) "Security-aware" and "validating" DNS64 or DNS46 receives DO = 0, CD = 0: In this case, the resolver validates the data. If it fails, it returns RCODE 2 (server failure); otherwise, it returns the answer. This is the ideal situation for DNS64 or DNS46, i.e., the resolver validates the data, then synthesizes a new record and passes it to the query initiator.
(6) "Security-aware" and "validating" DNS64 or DNS46 receives DO = 1, CD = 0: In this case, there is no need to validate DNSSEC, but it is necessary to set the "authentic data" (AD) bit, AD = 1.
(7) "Security-aware" and "validating" DNS64 or DNS46 receives DO = 1, CD = 1: In this case, DNS64 or DNS46 should pass all the data obtained to the query initiator. This situation does not apply to DNS64 or DNS46 unless the query initiator itself has the functionality of DNS64 or DNS46. If DNS64 or DNS46 modifies the record, the query initiator will receive the returned data and attempt to validate it, ending with a validation failure.

7.3.2 *DNSSEC Behavior of DNS64 or DNS46*

DNS64 or DNS46 should handle local policies that need to support DNSSEC as follows.

(1) If DO = 0, CD = 0, then DNS64 (or DNS46) should perform validation and synthesis as needed. In this case, DNS64 (or DNS46) must never set AD = 1 in any response.

(2) If DO = 1, CD = 0, then DNS64 (or DNS46) should perform validation. When DNS64 (or DNS46) performs validation, it must first verify that there is no valid AAAA (or A) record, then query the A (or AAAA) record and validate it, and implement the function of DNS64 (or DNS46) on this basis, synthesizing the AAAA (or A) record. Otherwise, attackers will use DNS64 (or DNS46) as a tool to evade DNSSEC validation. Similarly, DNS46 (or DNS46) also needs to handle this. Note: In the case of successful validation, AD = 1 should be set in the response to the query initiator. This is acceptable because RFC4035 [12] points out that AD = 1 can be set only when all records are validated. If validation fails, then DNS64 or DNS46 must respond with RCODE = 2 (server failure).

(3) If DO = 1, CD = 1, then DNS64 (or DNS46) can perform validation, but must never perform synthesis, and must return data to the query initiator (like a regular domain name resolver), relying on the query initiator itself for validation and synthesis. This method means that the functionality of DNS64 (or DNS46) cannot be provided, but this is the price to ensure the security of domain name queries.

7.4 Summary

Domain names are a key infrastructure of the Internet and play an important role in the IPv4/IPv6 translation process (single translation). This chapter discusses in detail the application scenarios, technical details, and cases of DNS64 and DNS46 deployment. DNSSEC is an important measure to ensure the security of the Internet infrastructure, but there is a contradiction between DNSSEC and the functionality of DNS64 or DNS46. This chapter provides related trade-off strategies.

References

1. Bagnulo M, Sullivan A, Matthews P, et al. RFC6147: DNS64: DNS extensions for network address translation from IPv6 clients to IPv4 servers. IETF 2011-04.
2. Bao C, Huitema C, Bagnulo M, et al. RFC6052: IPv6 addressing of IPv4/IPv6 translators. IETF 2010-10.
3. Mockapetris P. RFC1034: Domain names—concepts and facilities. IETF 1987-11.

4. Mockapetris P. RFC1035: Domain names—implementation and specification. IETF 1987-11.
5. Cotton M, Vegoda L. RFC5735: Special use IPv4 addresses. IETF 2010-01.
6. Morishita Y, Jinmei T. RFC4074: Common misbehavior against DNS queries for IPv6 addresses. IETF 2005-05.
7. Thomson S, Huitema C, Ksinant V, et al. RFC3596: DNS extensions to support IP version 6. IETF 2003-10.
8. Vixie P. RFC2671: Extension mechanisms for DNS (EDNS0). IETF 1999-08.
9. Vixie P, Thomson S, Rekhter Y, et al. RFC2136: Dynamic updates in the domain name system (DNS UPDATE). IETF 1997-04.
10. Arends R, Austein R, Larson M, et al. RFC4033: DNS security introduction and requirements. IETF 2005-03.
11. Arends R, Austein R, Larson M, et al. RFC4034: Resource records for the DNS security extensions. IETF 2005-03.
12. Arends R, Austein R, Larson M, et al. RFC4035: Protocol modifications for the DNS security extensions. IETF 2005-03.

Chapter 8
IPv6 Parameter Discovery and Configuration

When adopting the new-generation IPv6 transition technology, in addition to perform the protocol translation, address mapping, and domain name mapping, other supporting technologies and standards are also needed. Specifically, for IPv6-only networks, when an IPv6 client initiates access to an IPv4 server, it must synthesize an IPv6 address from an IPv4 address. Therefore, parameters such as "IPv6 prefix" (RFC6052 [1], RFC7597 [2]), public IPv4 address multiplexing ratio (RFC7597 [2]) are needed. This chapter discusses the discovery and configuration techniques of these parameters, including the following points.

(1) IPv6 prefix discovery method based on "Well-Known IPv4-only Name."
(2) Configuration method of IPv6 prefix and other parameters based on DHCPv6 extension.
(3) DNS resolver configuration method based on RA.
(4) IPv6 prefix configuration method based on RA.
(5) DHCPv4 Option 108 (so-called IPv6-mostly).
(6) Considerations for the BGP extension of translation technology.

8.1 IPv6 Prefix Discovery Technique

When an IPv6-only client initiates access to an IPv4 server, the IPv4/IPv6 translator and DNS64 need to work together. DNS64 uses the A record (IPv4 address) and "IPv6 prefix," follows the address mapping algorithm (RFC6052 [1]) to synthesize the AAAA record (i.e., "IPv4-converted IPv6 address"). The IPv6 client initiates access to the "IPv4-converted IPv6 address," routes to the IPv4/IPv6 translator, and the translator translates the IPv6 datagram into an IPv4 datagram to achieve communication between IPv6 and IPv4.

X. Li and C. Bao, *New IPv6 Transition Technology*,
https://doi.org/10.1007/978-981-95-8427-7_8

However, DNS64 cannot provide services for applications that do not use DNS (for example, some IPv6 applications using embedded IPv4 address). If there is a mechanism to discover the IPv6 prefix, then the client can directly synthesize the "IPv4-converted IPv6 address" following the address mapping algorithm.

Furthermore, DNS64 cannot provide DNS64 services for client machines that have enabled DNSSEC verification. For these hosts that have enabled DNSSEC verification, the host must first perform DNSSEC verification on the A record, and after passing, synthesize the "IPv4-converted IPv6 address" itself. Therefore, the host must be able to discover the "IPv6 prefix."

The above two situations require the host (or application system) to discover the "IPv6 prefix" parameter defined by RFC6052 [1], represented as Pref64::/*n*.

RFC7050 [3] and RFC8880 [4] describe a method for hosts to use a "best effort" strategy to detect the existence of DNS64. When DNS64 exists, the host is instructed to obtain the IPv6 prefix configured by the IPv4/IPv6 translator. This allows the host to synthesize the "IPv4-converted IPv6 address" itself or perform DNSSEC verification. Obtaining the synthesized "IPv4-converted IPv6 address" related information can also help dual-stack networks or hosts with multiple network interfaces, these hosts can choose to communicate directly via IPv4 or via the IPv4/IPv6 translator. Note: This is a "best effort" method, which has a gap with the robustness, security, and good behavior of end-to-end IPv6-only communication. Therefore, this is a transitional solution, and it is strongly recommended to prefer end-to-end IPv6-only communication.

8.1.1 Prefix Discovery Method

RFC7050 [3] defines the "Well-Known Name" (WKN) and the "Well-Known Address" (WKA) corresponding to the "Well-Known Name." Be careful not to confuse it with the "Well-Known Prefix" defined by RFC6052 [1]. In addition, it is necessary to pay attention to the relationship between these definitions and the "IPv6 prefix (Pref64::/*n*)."

(1) WKN: ipv4only.arpa (this domain name only has an A record: WKA).
(2) WKA: 192.0.0.170/32 and 192.0.0.171/32.
(3) WKP: 64:ff9b::/96.
(4) NSP with /32, /40, /48, /56, /64, /96 (a subset of the operator's IPv6 address space).
(5) IPv6 prefix: Pref64::/*n* (including WKP and NSP).

When the host needs to verify whether the IPv4/IPv6 translator exists, and tries to discover one or more Pref64::/*n* corresponding to the translator, it can send a DNS query for the AAAA record of the WKN (ipv4only.arpa). This DNS query of the host can be implemented in an IPv6-only network or in a dual-stack network, as shown in Fig. 8.1.

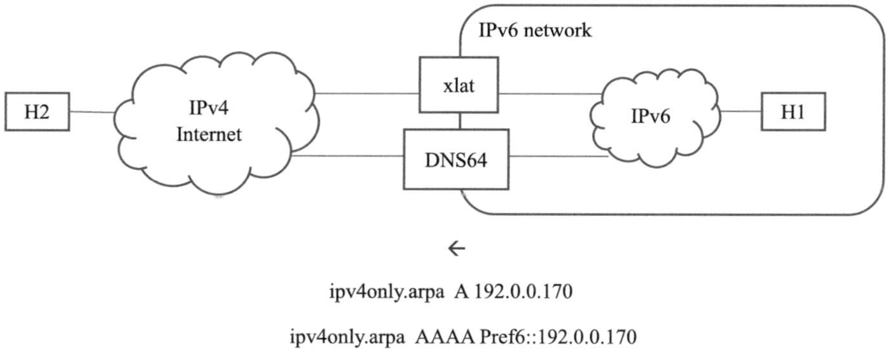

Fig. 8.1 Discovering Pref64::/n through DNS

When querying the AAAA record for ipv4only.arpa, the CD bit must be set to 0; otherwise, DNS64 will not perform IPv6 address synthesis, causing the host to be unable to obtain the IPv6 prefix Pref64::/*n* used for synthesizing the "IPv4-converted IPv6 address."

If the host receives a DNS reply with one or more AAAA records, it indicates that the access network provides the synthesis service of "IPv4-converted IPv6 address" (with DNS64 function). But in some scenarios, for example, when there is a "forced portal" (captive portals), "Domain does not exist" (NXDOMAIN) hijacking, or "No data" (NODATA) hijacking may lead to false alarms. One method to detect such hijacking is to query a potentially non-existent domain (usually returning an empty or error response) and see if it returns valid records. In fact, as long as the hijacked domain does not return an AAAA record in the format defined by RFC6052 [1], it does not affect the discovery process of Pref64::/*n*.

The host must verify all returned AAAA records to get all Pref64::/*n*. These Pref64::/*n* may include the WKP of 64:ff9b::/96, one or more NSPs. The host should search for the IPv4 address corresponding to the WKN in the AAAA records (IPv6 addresses). The host should allow searching for these IPv4 addresses at all possible locations defined by RFC6052 [1]. The host must check the octet boundaries to ensure that the 32-bit IPv4 address corresponding to the WKN only appears once in the IPv6 address. Note that some versions of Apple's iOS and Mac OS support RFC7050 [3], but they may only support the discovery of IPv6 prefixes of length / 96 in RFC6052 [1].

If there is only one Pref64::/*n* in the DNS response, the host should use this Pref64::/*n* for local "IPv4-converted IPv6 address" synthesis.

If there are multiple Pref64::/*n* in the DNS response, the host needs to determine whether other IPv6 addresses are synthesized "IPv4-converted IPv6 addresses," that is, traverse all these Pref64::/*n*. The host must synthesize "IPv4-converted IPv6 addresses" in the order these Pref64::/*n* are received. That is, when the host is providing locally synthesized "IPv4-converted IPv6 addresses" to the upper layer protocol, this list must be given in the order received, all Pref64::/*n* synthesized "IPv4-converted IPv6 addresses."

If the IPv4 address corresponding to the WKN cannot be found at the location defined by RFC6052 [1], it indicates that the access network did not use the standard address format. Alternatively, the access network may have failed to use the IPv4 address corresponding to the WKN when synthesizing the AAAA record. In these cases, it becomes impossible to determine Pref64::/n.

If the host does not receive the AAAA record of the query WKN, the host can query the A record of the WKN. Receiving this A record indicates that the DNS resolver does not have DNS64 capability.

If the host receives a negative response (NXDOMAIN, NODATA) or DNS query timeout, it means that there is no DNS64 service on the access network, or the security policy filters out the query of the WKN, or the DNS resolution fails. All these unsuccessful situations will cause the host to be unable to synthesize "IPv4-converted IPv6 addresses" locally. In the case of timeout, the host should retransmit the DNS query like any other DNS (RFC1035 [5]). In the case of a negative response (i.e., NXDOMAIN, NODATA response), the host must resend the AAAA query under the condition of obeying the TTL parameter (RFC1035 [5]). The host can monitor DNS replies containing WKP in the IPv6 addresses and use this WKP for "IPv4-converted IPv6 address" synthesis.

To minimize the consumption of Internet resources, the host should only perform the discovery of Pref64::/*n* when necessary. The process (for example, when local synthesis of "IPv4-converted IPv6 address" is needed, when a new network interface is activated, etc.). The host should cache Pref64::/*n*, and repeat the Pref64::/*n* discovery process 10 s before the TTL of the WKN expires.

1. *Verification of Discovered Pref64::/n*

If the host uses an insecure network with the DNS64 server or the DNS64 server is untrustworthy, attackers can intervene in the discovery process of Pref64::/*n*, modify data, leading to Denial of Service (DoS) attacks, redirection attacks, man-in-the-middle attacks, or other attacks. To avoid attacks, the host should communicate with the trusted DNS64 server through a secure channel or use DNSSEC. The provider of NAT64 should have mechanisms to protect the discovery service of Pref64::/*n* through a secure channel and/or using DNSSEC.

DNSSEC can only verify that the discovered Pref64::/*n* belongs to the domain of the IPv4/IPv6 translator. That is, DNSSEC verification cannot confirm that the host is definitely located within the network providing the Pref64::/*n* service. In addition, DNSSEC cannot verify the WKP.

2. *Network Configuration Requirements to Use DNSSEC*

   If the operator chooses to use DNSSEC to verify Pref64::/*n*, the provider of the IPv4/IPv6 translator must make the following configurations.

   (1) Have one or more FQDNs (hereinafter referred to as NAT64 FQDN) belonging to the IPv4/IPv6 translator. In a network with multiple Pref64::/*n* (for load balancing), the network administrator selects a single NAT64 FQDN to map to multiple Pref64::/*n*, or each Pref64::/*n* corresponds to a different NAT64 FQDN.

(2) Each NAT64 FQDN must configure one or more AAAA records containing Pref64::WKA (Pref64::/*n* combined with WKA).
(3) Each Pref64::WKA must have a PTR record pointing to the corresponding NAT64 FQDN.
(4) Sign the AAAA record (IPv4-converted IPv6 address) and A record of the NAT64 FQDN using DNSSEC.

3. *Host Configuration Requirements to Use DNSSEC*

Where possible, the host should communicate with the DNS64 server through a secure channel. In addition, hosts that support DNSSEC can use the following process to verify the discovered Pref64::/*n*.

Discover Pref64::/*n* by requesting the AAAA record of ipv4only.arpa, the IPv6 address (IPv4-converted IPv6 address) of this AAAA record is composed of Pref64::/*n* combined with WKA, that is, Pref64::WKA. For each Pref64::/*n* that the host wants to verify, the host performs the following steps.

(1) Query the PTR record (based on the ".ip6.arpa." tree) for the IPv6 address (Pref64::WKA, i.e., "IPv4-converted IPv6 address") obtained from the above AAAA record. According to the steps stipulated in RFC1034 [6], RFC1035 [5], and RFC6672 [7], considering the cases of CNAME and DNAME, one or more NAT64 FQDNs are obtained.
(2) The host should compare the queried NAT64 FQDN domain with a list of trusted domains of a group of hosts, and select the matching NAT64 FQDN. This means that the host is testing a specific domain. If there is no trusted domain, then the discovery process of Pref64::/*n* is not secure and cannot continue to execute the following steps.
(3) Query the AAAA record of the NAT64 FQDN.
(4) Verify whether the AAAA record contains Pref64::WKA. There may be multiple AAAA records for the NAT64 FQDN. In this case, the host must check whether it matches the address obtained in step (1). The host must ignore other responses and not use them for the synthesis of local IPv6 addresses.
(5) Perform DNSSEC verification of the received AAAA record.

After the host successfully completes the above five steps, it can be considered that Pref64::/*n* has passed the verification.

8.1.2 Connectivity Check

After obtaining Pref64::/*n*, the host should perform a connectivity check to ensure that this Pref64::/*n* is operating normally. Factors affecting normal operation include: the IPv6 route of the IPv4/IPv6 translator is unreachable, the translator stops running, the route from the translator to IPv4 is unreachable, etc.

There are mainly two methods to check the connectivity of this Pref64::/*n*. The first method is to perform a dedicated connectivity check. The second method is to simply try to use the obtained Pref64::/*n*. Both methods have their pros and cons, such as bringing additional network traffic, or users may feel a noticeable delay. Which method to implement should be decided after weighing the pros and cons according to different applications and network situations.

The host should use a dedicated server and a specific protocol for connectivity testing. If this is not feasible, the host can query the PTR record of Pref64::WKA to obtain the NAT64 FQDN. Then the host queries the A record of the NAT64 FQDN, which will return zero or more A records, pointing to the operator's connectivity check server. A negative response to a PTR or A record query means that there is no available connectivity check server. Operators providing IPv4/IPv6 translation services should configure one or more A records for the NAT64 FQDN, pointing to the connectivity check server. This connectivity check method is only suitable for scenarios where Pref64::/*n* is the NSP, because it is not possible to register different A records for each different domain using a WKP.

If there are multiple connectivity check servers available for use, the host will choose the first one, so it is recommended to prefer a specific protocol's connectivity check server.

The default protocol for the connectivity check server pointed to by the A record of the NAT64 FQDN is ICMPv6 (RFC4443 [8]). Therefore, network operators must disable ICMPv6 rate limiting for connectivity check messages.

When the host performs a connectivity check, the host sends an ICMPv6 Echo Request message (whose destination address is "IPv4-converted IPv6 address") to the check server synthesized with Pref64::/*n* and the IPv4 address. This will test the IPv6 route from the host to the IPv4/IPv6 translator, the operation of the translator, and the IPv4 route from the translator to the connectivity check server. If the host does not receive a reply to the ICMPv6 Echo Request, the host should send another ICMPv6 Echo Request after 1 s. If there is still no reply, the host should send a third ICMPv6 Echo Request after 2 s.

If ICMPv6 Echo Response is received, this confirms that the communication between the host and the connectivity check server is normal. If no ICMPv6 Echo Response is received after three tests and a 3 s timeout, the Pref64::/*n* may not function properly. The host can choose another different Pref64::/*n* (if available) for testing. Note: Failure to receive an ICMPv6 response does not mean that the network cannot transmit anything other than ICMPv6 messages. If a separate connectivity check is not performed before the local "IPv4-converted IPv6 address" synthesis, the host can monitor the connection status of the locally synthesized "IPv4-converted IPv6 address." Based on the connection status and possible ICMPv6 error messages, such as Destination Unreachable, the host can pause the local "IPv4-converted IPv6 address" synthesis and restart the discovery process of Pref64::/*n*.

1. *Regulations for ipv4only.arpa*

The host is not allowed to perform connectivity checks on the IPv4 addresses returned by querying ipv4only.arpa. This is because, by regulation, this address does not have a corresponding server. Similarly, network operators should not configure these IPv4 addresses for any server. The reason for not using this address for connectivity checks is: for IPv4/IPv6 translators that work normally but do not have a configured connectivity check server, they should be able to provide normal access services for IPv6 clients to initiate to IPv4 servers. Conversely, looking up additional DNS records for connectivity checks can ensure that datagrams do not unnecessarily leak to the Internet and reduce failures caused by connectivity check errors.

2. *FQDN Replacement*

Some applications, operating systems, devices, or networks may run their own DNS infrastructure to perform the function of ipv4only.arpa, but use different A records. The main advantage of doing this is to ensure the availability and controllability of the DNS infrastructure. For example, a company named Example can run its specific application to query ipv4only.example.com. In this case, the remaining steps are the same except for the need to query different DNS records.

8.1.3 Flowchart

The following is a flowchart for discovering and verifying Pref64::/*n*. In this example, the DNS64 server provides three Pref64::/*n* prefixes.

(1) The first Pref64::/n uses NSP: 2001:db8:42::/96; Pref64:: WKA is 2001:db8:42::192.0.0.170.
(2) The second Pref64::/n uses NSP: 2001:db8:43::/96; Pref64:: WKA is 2001:db8:43::192.0.0.170.
(3) The third Pref64::/n uses WKP; Pref64:: WKA is 64:ff9b::192.0.0.170.

The DNS64 server can also return a synthesized address containing 192.0.0.171. Note that, according to IETF standards, there is no need to verify the WKP. The verification process is shown in Fig. 8.2.

8.1.4 Operational Considerations for Hosting the IPv4-Only WKN

The authoritative DNS server for the WKN (ipv4only.arpa) should set the TTL to at least 60 min to improve the effectiveness of DNS caching. The authoritative server for the WKN (ipv4only.arpa) must use DNSSEC signatures.

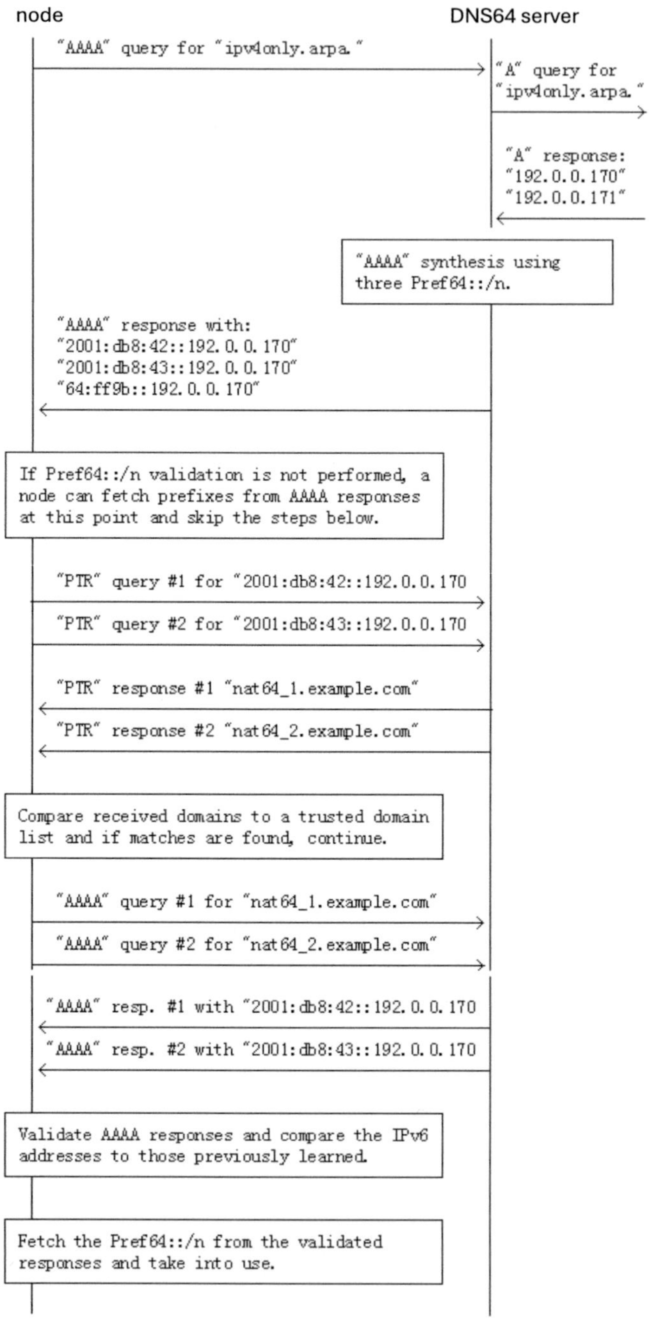

Fig. 8.2 Discovery and verification process of Pref64::/n

8.1.5 Operational Considerations for DNS64 Operators

Operators of DNS64 servers can optimize network behavior by managing the responses of DNS64.

If the network operator wants the host to use multiple Pref64::/*n* prefixes, the operator needs to make the DNS64 server provide multiple synthesized AAAA records.

There is no mechanism to guarantee which Pref64::/n the host will ultimately use. If the operator wants the host to use only a specific Pref64::/n or to change it periodically for reasons such as load balancing, the only guaranteed method involves configuring the DNS64 server to return only one synthesized AAAA record. Properly setting the TTL ensures the host periodically repeats the discovery of Pref64::/n, maintaining the desired behavior. Apart from setting Pref64::/n and TTL, the DNS64 server should not perform any other operations on the WKN.

8.1.6 IANA Parameters

1. *Well-Known Domain Name*

The WKN is: ipv4only.arpa.

2. *IPv4 Address Corresponding to WKN*

The WKN needs to be mapped to two different global IPv4 addresses, as shown in Table 8.1.

Table 8.1 IPv4 address corresponding to the well-known domain name

Attribute	Value
Address block	192.0.0.170/32 192.0.0.171/32
Name	NAT64/DNS64 discovery
Allocation time	February 2013
Term of use	Long-term
As source address	No
As destination address	No
Global	No
Purpose	Reserved for internet protocol

8.2 DHCPv6 Parameter Configuration Technology

The new-generation IPv6 transition technologies, including single translation technology, double translation technology, and tunneling technology, have the feature of being able to share public IPv4 addresses. For operational automation, parameter configuration methods represented by DHCPv6 series technologies (assigning IPv6 addresses, prefix lengths, and DNS resolvers, etc.) need to be expanded.

The structure of DHCPv6 is shown in Fig. 8.3.

Its workflow is: the DHCPv6 client sends a message, requesting the DHCPv6 server to assign it an IPv6 address and network configuration parameters. The DHCPv6 server replies with a message, notifying the client of the address and network configuration parameters it can assign.

This chapter takes RFC7598 [9] as an example to discuss the DHCPv6 extension for MAP series, including stateless double translation (MAP-T), stateless encapsulation (MAP-E), and lightweight 4over6 (LW-4o6). The MAP-T and MAP-E are discussed in Chap. 10 of this book, and the LW-4o6 technology is discussed in Chap. 11.

The MAP series technology solution is responsible for stateless forwarding between the MAP IPv6 domain and the IPv4 Internet by one or more MAP relay routers (border router, BR). At the same time, one or more MAP edge (customer edge, CE) devices are configured to forward between the MAP IPv6 network domain and the user's IPv4/IPv6 network, as shown in Fig. 8.4.

In general, both the MAP BR and MAP CE in the same MAP domain need to configure related parameters (called Softwire46 parameters), so a unified DHCPv6 parameter configuration extension mechanism can be formed. These parameters mainly include the following.

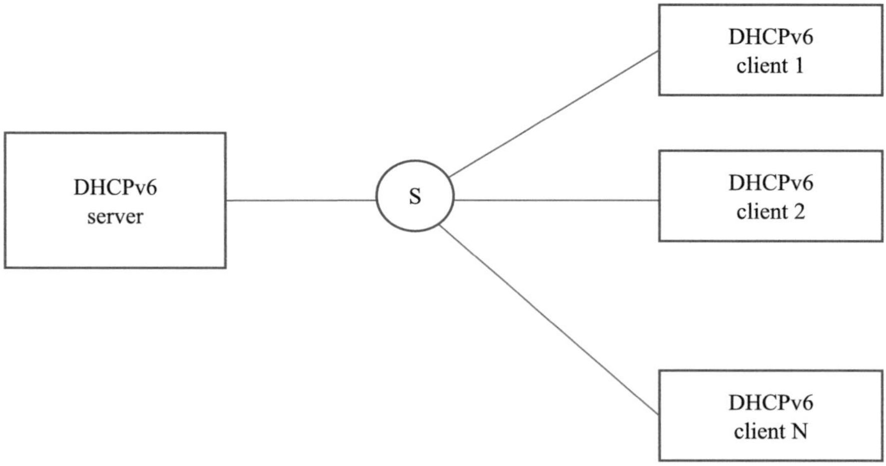

Fig. 8.3 DHCPv6

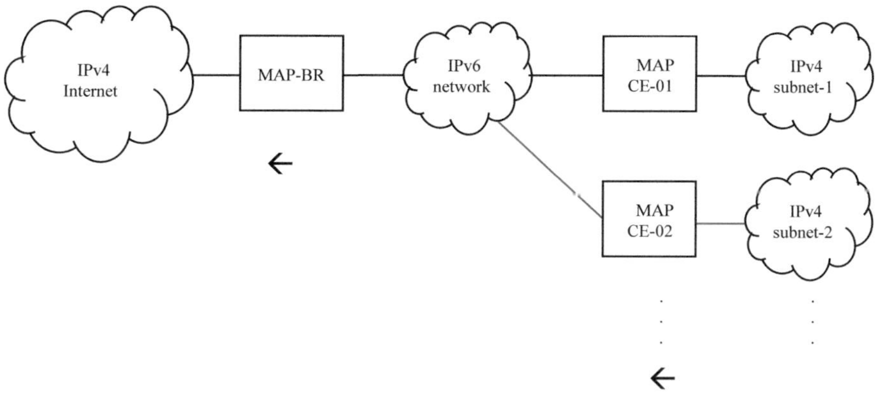

Fig. 8.4 Schematic diagram of MAP series technology

(1) Public IPv4 address.
(2) Transport layer port range.
(3) Operating mode (translation or encapsulation).

The configuration of these parameters is defined by RFC7598 [9] and is implemented through the DHCPv6 options defined by RFC3315 [10]. This method can configure parameters for home gateways (MAP CE) or directly for end systems.

8.2.1 Softwire46 Overview

The MAP series transition technologies provide IPv4 services for CE routers through an IPv6-only access network. MAP-T [11] and MAP-E [2] can embed part of the IPv4 address in the IPv6 prefix, thus supporting the configuration of parameters for many users and supporting the mesh (direct CE to CE) mode. MAP-T CE and MAP-E CE also support the hub-and-spoke mode, as well as the mode that does not share public IPv4 addresses (no embedded address bits). The difference between MAP-T and MAP-E is that MAP-T is a double translation (RFC7915 [12]), while MAP-E is an encapsulation (RFC2473 [13]). LW-4o6 [14] is a hub-and-spoke mode IPv4 over IPv6 tunneling mechanism (RFC2473 [13]), with completely independent IPv4 and IPv6 addressing (zero embedded address bits).

The DHCPv6 option (Softwire46) binds the relevant configuration parameters (including IPv4 services) of the MAP series to the full lifecycle of the IPv6 prefix assigned to the user. That is, the IPv4 address or IPv4 prefix or shared IPv4 address, transport layer port range, and any parameters related to authorization and auditing of Softwire46 are all bound to the full lifecycle of the user's IPv6 prefix.

In order to support multiple mechanisms and switching between mechanisms, the DHCPv6 "Option Request Option" (ORO) defined by RFC3315 [10] is used. Each mechanism has a corresponding DHCPv6 container option. The DHCPv6 client can request the required parameters using the specific ORO container option code. The parameters of this mechanism can be completed by embedding their respective container options in the option format.

This method means that configuration options can only be included in the container options. If the Softwire46 DHCPv6 client receives configuration options that are not encapsulated in the container, these options must be ignored.

8.2.2 Common Softwire46 DHCPv6 Options

Softwire46 CE uses the DHCPv6 protocol to configure parameters. The MAP CE is a DHCPv6 client, and the DHCPv6 server provides DHCPv6 options according to the server-side policy.

Each CE needs to configure enough information to calculate its IPv4 address, IPv4 prefix, or shared IPv4 address.

In addition, the CE also needs to get the BR's IPv6 address or IPv6 prefix. In the case of needing to share the IPv4 public address, the CE also needs to get the parameters of the port range algorithm and the port set. The collection of these parameters is as follows:

(1) MAP-E and MAP-T use the OPTION_S46_RULE option.
(2) LW-4o6 uses the OPTION_S46_V4V6BIND option. The CE also needs the BR's IPv6 address or IPv6 prefix.
(3) MAP-E and LW-4o6 use the OPTION_S46_BR option.
(4) MAP-T uses the OPTION_S46_DMR option. The CE also needs the parameters of the port range algorithm and the port set.
(5) All mechanisms can include the OPTION_S46_PORTPARAMS option.

Softwire46 options use addresses instead of FQDNs.

1. *OPTION_S46_RULE Option*

Figure 8.5 shows the OPTION_S46_RULE option, which is used to configure the basic mapping rule (BMR) and forwarding mapping rule (FMR).

The behavior of this rule is defined by RFC3315 [10]. The client can send options encapsulated in the corresponding container options, carrying specific values, as

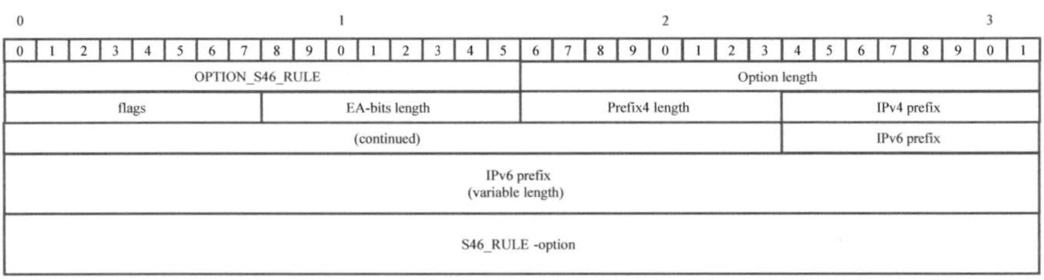

Fig. 8.5 OPTION_S46_RULE option

Fig. 8.6 S46 rule flags

0	1	2	3	4	5	6	7
Reserved							F

"hints" to the DHCPv6 server. Depending on the policy configuration of the DHCPv6 server, these "hints" can be accepted or ignored. The client must be able to handle received values that are different from the "hint" values previously sent by the client.

(1) Option code (OPTION_S46_RULE): 16 bits; set to 89.
(2) Option length: 16 bits; this length does not include the option code and option length fields, but includes all encapsulated lengths, represented in units of octets.
(3) Flags: 8 bits; flags applicable to this rule.
(4) Embedded length (EA-bit length): 8 bits; the length of the embedded address (EA), with an allowable range of 0–48.
(5) IPv4 prefix length (Prefix4 length): 8 bits; the IPv4 prefix specified in the IPv4 prefix field, with an allowable range of 0–32.
(6) IPv4 prefix: 32 bits; the prefix of the IPv4 S46 rule. The bits in the prefix after the Prefix4 length are reserved bits. The source node must set the reserved bits to 0, and the receiving node must ignore the reserved bits.
(7) IPv6 prefix length (Pref6-len): 8 bits; the IPv6 prefix specified in the IPv6 prefix field, with an allowable range of 0–128.
(8) IPv6 prefix: variable length; the IPv6 prefix of the S46 rule domain. If Pref6-len is not a multiple of 8 bits, this field needs to be padded with 0 on the right.
(9) Rule options (S46_RULE-options): variable length; S46_RULE-options extension, can contain 0 or more options. The OPTION_S46_PORTPARAMS option is currently defined.

The format of the S46 Rule Flags field is shown in Fig. 8.6.

(1) Reserved: 7 bits; reserved.
(2) F: 1 bit; if set, this rule is also used as a forwarding rule, based on the longest prefix match principle, comparing the user (IPv6 prefix/length) and (IPv6 prefix/Pref6-len). If not set, this rule is only used as a BMR and cannot be used for forwarding.

In typical mesh deployment scenarios, a single BMR can be set, and by setting F = 1, the BMR can also serve as an FMR.

2. *OPTION_S46_BR Option*

Figure 8.7 shows the OPTION_S46_BR option, which is used to configure the IPv6 address of the BR.

(1) Option code (OPTION_S46_BR): 16 bits; set to 90.
(2) Option length: 16 bits; represented in units of octets.
(3) BR's IPv6 address (BR IPv6 address): 128 bits; the IPv6 address of S46 BR.

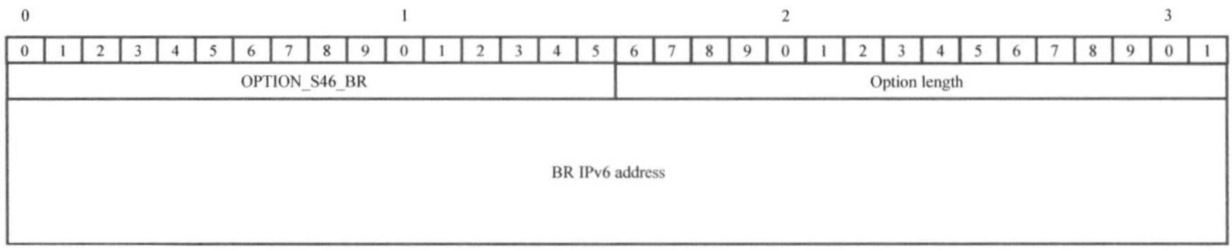

Fig. 8.7 OPTION_S46_BR

The redundancy of BR can be achieved by using the BR IPv6 address as an anycast address. Of course, multiple OPTION_S46_BR option containers can also be included.

3. *OPTION_S46_DMR Option*

Figure 8.8 shows the OPTION_S46_DMR option, which is used to configure the default mapping rule (DMR).

(1) Option code (OPTION_S46_DMR): 16 bits; set to 91.
(2) Option length: 16 bits; in units of octet, 1 + length of DMR IPv6 prefix.
(3) Length of DMR's IPv6 prefix (DMR prefix6 length): 8 bits; length of DMR IPv6 prefix, allowable range is 0–128.
(4) DMR's IPv6 prefix (DMR IPv6 prefix): variable length; DMR's IPv6 prefix. If the DMR prefix6 length is not a multiple of 8 bits, this field needs to be padded with 0 on the right.

4. *OPTION_S46_V4V6BIND Option*

Figure 8.9 shows the OPTION_S46_V4V6BIND option, which is used to configure the CE's full IPv4 address or shared IPv4 address. The IPv6 prefix field is used for the CE as a tunnel source.

(1) Option code (OPTION_S46_V4V6BIND): 16 bits; set to 92.
(2) Option length: 16 bits; includes all encapsulated lengths, represented in units of octets (the length of the option code and option length fields is not included here).
(3) IPv4 Address (IPv4 address): 32 bits; IPv4 address.
(4) Bind IPv6 Prefix Length (Bindprefix6 length): 8 bits; The length of the IPv6 prefix in the Bind IPv6 prefix field, with an allowable range of 0–128.

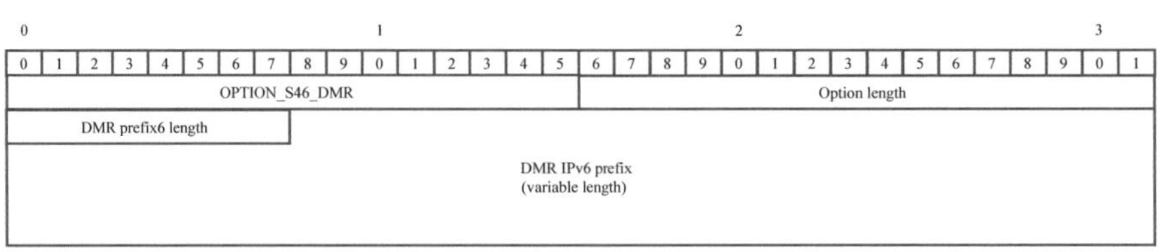

Fig. 8.8 OPTION_S46_DMR option

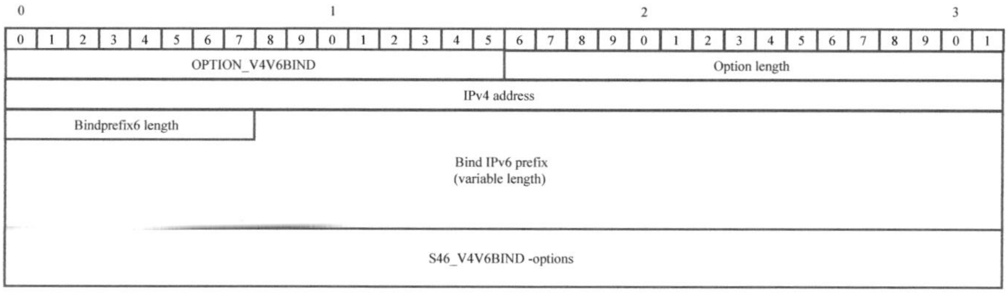

Fig. 8.9 OPTION_S46_V4V6BIND option

(5) Bind IPv6 Prefix (Bind IPv6 prefix): Variable length; Bind IPv6 prefix or IPv6 address. If the Bindprefix6 length is not a multiple of 8 bits, this field needs to be right-padded with 0.
(6) S46_V4V6BIND Options (S46_V4V6BIND-options): Variable length; OPTION_S46_V4V6BIND extension, can contain 0 or more options. OPTION_S46_PORTPARAMS is currently defined.

5. *OPTION_S46_PORTPARAMS Option*

Figure 8.10 shows the OPTION_S46_PORTPARAMS option, used for configuring the information of the transport layer port set of the CE (RFC7597 [2]).

(1) Option code (OPTION_S46_PORTPARAMS): 16 bits; set to 93.
(2) Option length: 16 bits; the value is 4.
(3) Offset: 8 bits; defines the offset bit number (a-bits) of the S46 algorithm excluding the port range, according to RFC7597 [2], the allowable range is 0–15.
(4) Port set identifier length (PSID length): 8 bits; defines the valid bits of PSID ("*k*" value). When set to 0, the PSID field will be ignored. After the "a" field, there are *k* bits representing the port number of this PSID value. The address multiplexing ratio is.
(5) Port set identifier (PSID): 16 bits; PSID defines the set of transport layer ports (port range) assigned to CE. The first *k* bits on the left of this field contain the binary value of PSID. The remaining $16 - k$ bits on the right are filled with 0.

① When S46 CE receives the PSID defined by the OPTION_S46_PORTPARAMS option, it must use the transport layer port range defined by this explicit PSID.
② When S46 CE receives an IPv4 prefix (IPv4 prefix), not a full IPv4 address, it must discard the transport layer port range defined by this explicit PSID.

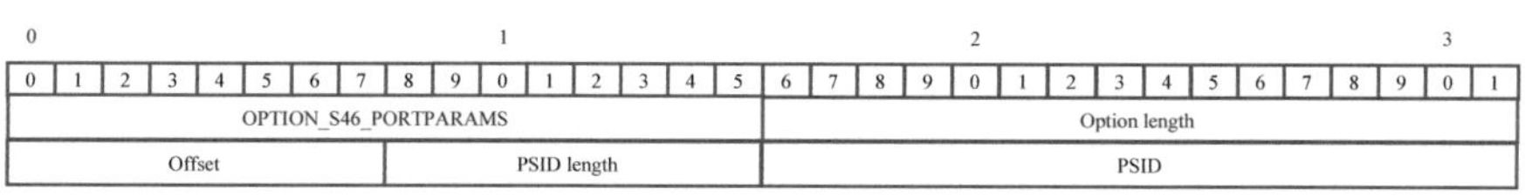

Fig. 8.10 OPTION_S46_PORTPARAMS option

In addition, the OPTION_S46_PORTPARAMS option must be included in the OPTION_S46_RULE option or OPTION_S46_V4V6BIND option.

8.2.3 *Softwire46 Container*

1. *S46 MAP-E Container Option*

S46 The MAP-E container option (OPTION_S46_CONT_MAPE) is used to encapsulate all MAP-E related rules and port parameter options for a specific service domain, as shown in Fig. 8.11.

(1) Option code (OPTION_S46_CONT_MAPE): 16 bits; set to 94.
(2) Option length: 16 bits; expressed in units of octets.
(3) Encapsulated options: variable length; Softwire46 options of the MAP-E domain.

The Encapsulated options field contains options specific to OPTION_S46_CONT_MAPE. Currently, there are two encapsulated options: OPTION_S46_RULE (at least one) and OPTION_S46_BR (at least one).

① Other encapsulated options may be defined in the future.
② A DHCPv6 message may contain multiple OPTION_S46_CONT_MAPE options (representing multiple domains).

2. *S46 MAP-T Container Option*

The S46 MAP-T Container Option (OPTION_S46_CONT_MAPT) is used to encapsulate all MAP-T related rules and port parameter options for a specific service domain, as shown in Fig. 8.12.

(1) Option code (OPTION_S46_CONT_MAPT): 16 bits; set to 95.
(2) Option length: 16 bits; expressed in units of octets.

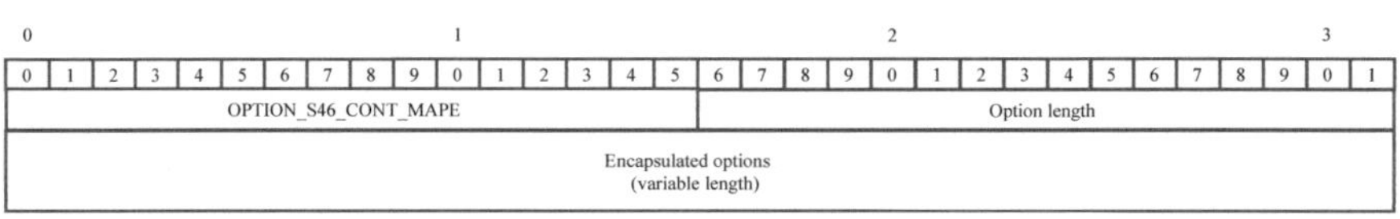

Fig. 8.11 S46 MAP-E container option

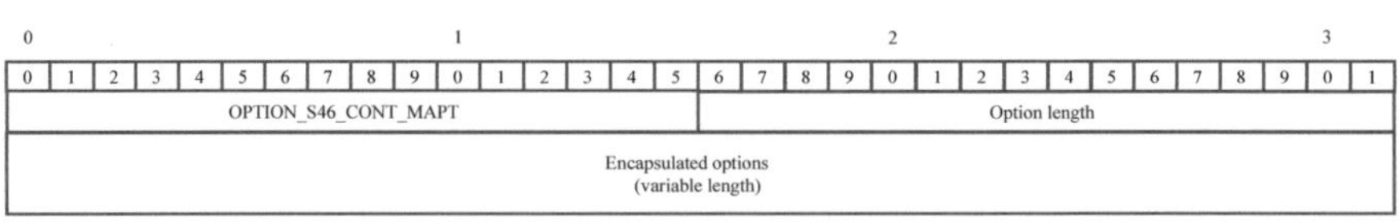

Fig. 8.12 S46 MAP-T container option

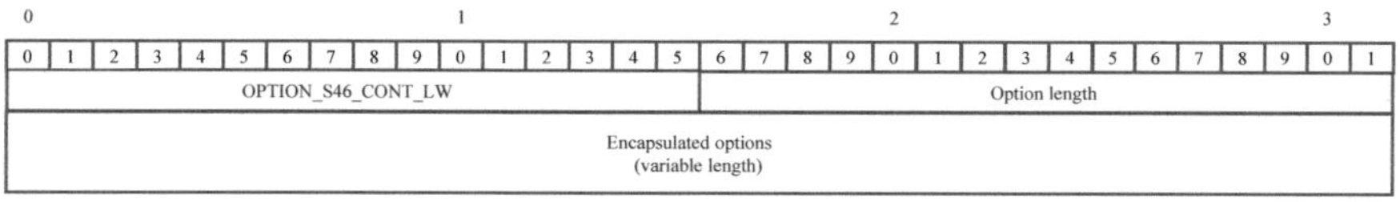

Fig. 8.13 OPTION_S46_CONT_LW container option

(3) Encapsulated options: variable length; Softwire46 options of the MAP-T domain.

The Encapsulated options field contains OPTION_S46_CONT_MAPT specific options. There are currently two encapsulated options: OPTION_S46_RULE (at least one) and OPTION_S46_DMR (only one).

3. *S46 LW-4o6 Container Option*

The S46 LW-4o6 Container Option (OPTION_S46_CONT_LW) is used to encapsulate all LW-4o6 related rules and port parameter options for a specific service domain, as shown in Fig. 8.13.

(1) Option code (OPTION_S46_CONT_LW): 16 bits; set to 96.
(2) Option length: 16 bits; expressed in units of octets.
(3) Encapsulated options: variable length; Softwire46 options of the LW-4o6 domain.

The Encapsulated options field contains options specific to OPTION_S46_CONT_LW. There are currently two encapsulated options: OPTION_S46_V4V6BIND (at most one) and OPTION_S46_BR (at least one).

8.2.4 Softwire46 Option Encapsulation

Table 8.2 shows which encapsulated options are required, optional, or not allowed for different defined container options.

When a container that violates the above rules is received, the corresponding Softwire46 DHCPv6 client must ignore these container options.

Table 8.2 Container options

Option	MAP-E	MAP-T	LW-4o6
OPTION_S46_RULE	Required	Required	Not allowed
OPTION_S46_BR	Required	Not allowed	Required
OPTION_S46_PORTPARAMS	Optional	Optional	Optional
OPTION_S46_DMR	Not allowed	Required	Not allowed
OPTION_S46_V4V6BIND	Not allowed	Not allowed	Optional

8.2.5 DHCPv6 Server Behavior

RFC3315 [10] describes the way DHCPv6 clients and servers use ORO to negotiate configurations. That is, by default, if the client does not explicitly request a certain Softwire46 container option in the ORO, the server will not actively provide it.

The CE router can support some (or all) mechanisms defined for Softwire46. When the client requests multiple mechanisms through ORO, the server should reply with the corresponding Softwire46 container options for which the server has configuration information.

8.2.6 DHCPv6 Client Behavior

The S46 CE acting as a DHCPv6 client will send requests to the DHCPv6 server located in the IPv6 network. The S46 CE uses the following DHCPv6 messages, using the ORO mechanism, to request S46 container options.

(1) SOLICIT.
(2) REQUEST.
(3) RENEW.
(4) REBIND.
(5) INFORMATION-REQUEST.

When processing the received S46 container options, the client should have the following behaviors.

(1) The client must support processing multiple OPTION_S46_RULE received in the OPTION_S46_CONT_MAPE or OPTION_S46_CONT_MAPT containers.
(2) When the client receives unsupported S46 options or invalid parameter values, it should discard the related S46 container and log it.
(3) Like all DHCPv6 derived configuration states, there is a possibility of a man-in-the-middle attack during actual operation. Therefore, security facilities such as IPv6 firewalls must be configured.

8.2.7 IANA Parameters

IANA has assigned the following DHCPv6 option codes, as shown in Table 8.3.

Table 8.3 Examples using basic public prefix

Code	Description
89	OPTION_S46_RULE
90	OPTION_S46_BR
91	OPTION_S46_DMR
92	OPTION_S46_V4V6BIND
93	OPTION_S46_PORTPARAMS
94	OPTION_S46_CONT_MAPE
95	OPTION_S46_CONT_MAPT
96	OPTION_S46_CONT_LW

8.3 DNS Resolver Address Configuration via RA

The address configuration modes of IPv6 include "stateless address allocation" using SLAAC and "stateful address allocation" using DHCPv6 technology. Since only SLAAC is supported by all operating systems (Android does not support DHCPv6), in the case of IPv6-only scenario, the IPv6 Router Advertisement (RA) option must be extended (DNS RA option). Its purpose is to allow IPv6 routers to announce the DNS resolver address and the DNS host search list (DNS search list, DNSSL). This extension is defined by RFC8106 [15].

8.3.1 Background

The IPv6 neighbor discovery (ND) protocol and IPv6 SLAAC provide mechanisms for configuring fixed or one or more IPv6 addresses, default routers, and other parameters (RFC4861 [16], RFC4862 [17]). One of its core components is RA, the structure of which is shown in Fig. 8.14.

RA periodically sends message or responds to requests. Routers report their existence and provide the information the nodes need to configure themselves.

When a mobile host (such as a laptop) connects to a subnet, it is not possible to manually configure it each time. Although one-time static configuration is possible, it is not feasible in practice.

DNS information can be provided via DHCPv6 (RFC3315 [10], RFC3736 [18], RFC3646 [19]). However, when the host only uses SLAAC, it must also be able to get DNS resolver address. This problem is not urgent in dual-stack networks because IPv4 can obtain the IPv4 address of the DNS resolver through DHCP, and resolve the AAAA record through the IPv4 DNS resolver.

RFC8106 [15] defines the mechanism of DNS RA options, so it can be used for IPv6-only hosts that only support SLAAC to automatically configure the address of the DNS resolver.

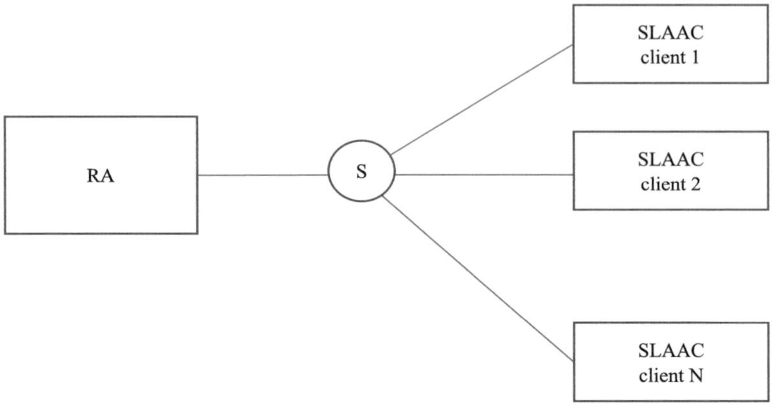

Fig. 8.14 RA

The DNS configuration of RA can enable the host to obtain a complete Internet parameter configuration under SLAAC without using DHCPv6. However, for situations that need to obtain more parameters through DHCPv6, it is recommended to still obtain DNS parameters through DHCPv6, instead of using DNS configuration based on RA.

DNS configuration based on RA allows IPv6 hosts to directly obtain DNS configuration (i.e., DNS resolver address and DNSSL) through the network interface. Note: In this case, the host obtains the IPv6 prefix, default gateway, and DNS information from the same RA source.

RFC4339 [20] discusses the advantages and disadvantages of obtaining DNS parameters through DHCPv6, through "any known multicast address" and based on RA.

8.3.2 Coexistence of DNS RA Options and DHCP Options

There are currently two protocols to configure the DNS parameters of the host, namely RA options and DHCPv6 (Dynamic Host Configuration Protocol IPv6) options (RFC3646 [19]), these two mechanisms can be used together. RFC4861 [16] stipulates the selection mechanism of the host state configuration mechanism. Hosts that comply with this specification must extract DNS information from RA messages, unless the user specifies static DNS configuration. If the host obtains DNS parameters from multiple RAs (and/or) DHCPv6, the host must maintain a list of the usage order of this information.

8.3.3 Extension of RA's Neighbor Discovery

The DNS RA option is an ND option called "RDNSS option," which contains the addresses of RDNSSes. In addition, there is an ND option of "DNSSL option," which contains DNSSL. This is to be consistent with DHCPv6 options to ensure the ability to determine search domains.

The DNS RA option uses existing ND messages (i.e., RA) to carry. An IPv6 host can configure one or more IPv6 addresses of RDNSS through RA messages. When using the prefix information option of the ND protocol (RFC4861 [16], RFC4862 [17]), through the RDNSS and DNSSL options, the IPv6 host can configure the network IPv6 address and DNS information without needing DHCPv6 at all.

Note that this method requires manual configuration or through an automatic configuration mechanism (such as DHCPv6 or proprietary configuration mechanisms of suppliers) to configure DNS information for routers providing RA functions.

1. *Domain Name Resolution Server Options*

The RDNSS option contains one or more IPv6 addresses of RDNSSes, all of which share the same lifetime. If different addresses need to have different lifetime values, multiple RDNSS options can be used. Figure 8.15 shows the format of the RDNSS option.

(1) Type: 8 bits; IANA assigned value is 25 (assigned to RDNSS option type).
(2) Length: 8-bit unsigned integer; the length of the option (including "Type" and "Length" fields) is in units of eight octets. If there is only one IPv6 address, the minimum value is 3. Each additional RDNSS address will increase the length by 2. The receiving node determines the number of IPv6 addresses contained in this option through the length.
(3) Reserved: 16 bits; for future expansion, it can currently be filled with all 0 s.
(4) Lifetime: 32 bits (unsigned integer). The lifetime (in seconds) corresponds to the time when the datagram is received. These RDNSS IPv6 addresses are the addresses of the domain name resolution servers. By default, the value of the lifetime should be at least 3 × MaxRtrAdvInterval, where MaxRtrAdvInterval is the maximum RA interval defined by RFC4861 [16]. Note: All 1 s (0xffffffff) represent infinity, and all 0 s mean that the RDNSS address must no longer be used.

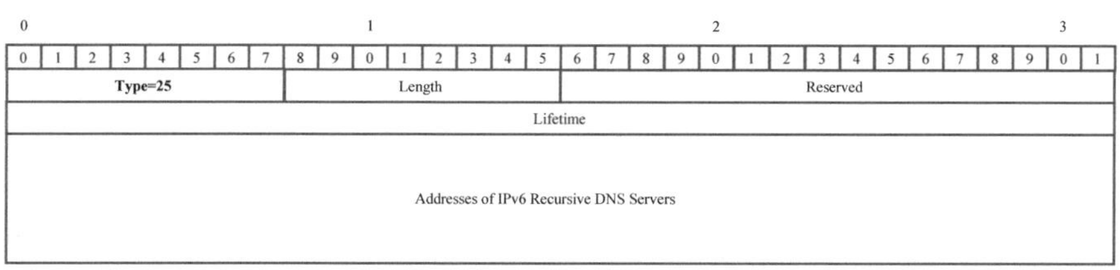

Fig. 8.15 RDNSS option

(5) Addresses of IPv6 Recursive DNS Servers: variable length; one or more 128-bit IPv6 addresses of RDNSSes. The number of these addresses is determined by the length field. That is, the number of addresses = (length − 1)/2.

Note: The address of RDNSSes in the RDNSS option can be a link-local address. At this time, this link-local address should be registered in the resolution repository together with the network interface domain to mark the network interface that received the RDNSS option (RFC4007 [21]). When the resolver sends a DNS query message to the link-local address, the corresponding network interface must be used.

The basic principle of selecting the default value of the lifetime field is as follows: the router lifetime field, set by AdvDefaultLifetime, has the default value specified in 3 × MaxRtrAdvInterval (RFC4861 [16]). The reason is that even if the network interface has a high packet loss rate, such or larger default values can allow DNS resolution to continue in the case of RA loss. Note: The ratio of AdvDefaultLifetime to MaxRtrAdvInterval is the number of unsolicited RA multicast messages sent by the router. Since the DNS option entry allows up to three consecutive RA datagrams to be lost, the default lifetime value can make the DNS option survivable in a packet loss environment.

2. *DNSSL Option*

The DNSSL option contains one or more DNS domain suffixes, all of which share the same lifetime. If different lifetime values are needed, multiple DNSSL options can be used. Figure 8.16 shows the format of the DNSSL option.

(1) Type: 8 bits; IANA assigned value is 31 (assigned to DNSSL option type).
(2) Length: 8-bit unsigned integer; the length of the option (including "Type" and "Length" fields) is in units of eight octets. If there is only one domain name, the minimum value is 2. The "Length" field is set to an integer multiple of eight octets to accommodate all the names in the "Domain Names of DNS Search List" field.
(3) Reserved: 16 bits; for future expansion use, currently can be filled with all 0 s.
(4) Lifetime: 32 bits (unsigned integer). The lifetime (in seconds) corresponds to the time when the datagram is received. These DNSSL domain names can be used for name resolving. By default, the value of the lifetime should be at least 3 × MaxRtrAdvInterval, where MaxRtrAdvInterval is the maximum RA interval

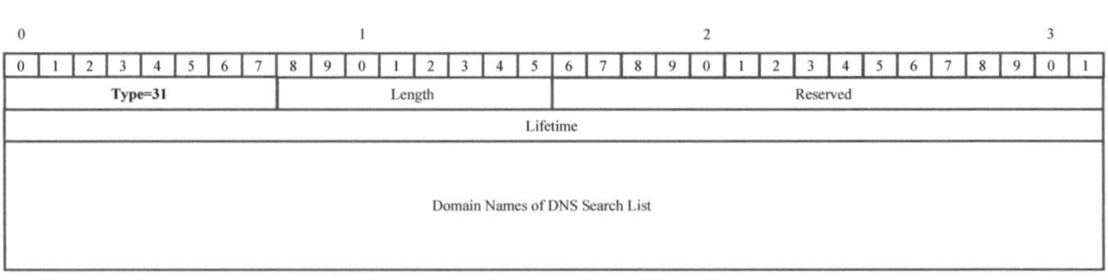

Fig. 8.16 DNSSL option

defined by RFC4861 [16]. Note: all 1 s (0xffffffff) represent infinity, and all 0 s mean that the RDNSS address must no longer be used.

(5) Domain Names of DNS Search List: variable length. DNSSL contains one or more domain names, which must be encoded according to the description of RFC1035 [5]. The key point is: each domain name ends with an octet of all 0 s. The sequence of labels at the end of the byte is defined as the domain name identifier. For multiple domain names, cascade according to the above encoding. Note that the domain name must not use the compression format defined by RFC1035 [5]. Also, since the size of this field must be eight octets, it must be filled with all 0 s when necessary.

8.3.4 The Order of the DNS Configuration

Configure the RDNSS and DNSSL options according to the ND option configuration method defined by RFC4861 [16].

1. *Configuration Process of IPv6 Host*

When the IPv6 host receives the DNS options (RDNSS option, DNSSL option) through the RA message, its processing flow is as follows:

(1) Use the "Length" field to check the validity of the DNS options, that is, the value of the "Length" field in the RDNSS option is greater than or equal to the minimum value (which is 3) and meets the requirement (Length − 1)/2 = 0. The value of the "Length" field in the DNSSL option is greater than or equal to the minimum value (which is 2). In addition, the validity check of the RDNSS option should also include that the IPv6 address in the "IPv6 Domain Name Resolution Server Address" field is a unicast address.

(2) If the DNS options are valid, the host should copy the relevant information to the DNS repository and the resolver repository at once. Otherwise, the host must discard these options.

When the DNS information of RDNSS and DNSSL is obtained from multiple sources (such as RA and DHCPv6), the IPv6 host should retain some DNS options from all sources. Unless its discovery mechanism explicitly stipulates, the exact number of IPv6 addresses and domain names to be retained belongs to the local configuration policy. However, in the case of multiple sources, it is recommended to store at least three RDNSS addresses (or DNSSL domain names). The DNS options from RA and DHCPv6 should be stored in the DNS repository and the resolver repository, with the order being DHCPv6 priority; that is, the DNS information from DHCPv6 is prioritized over the DNS information from RA. In addition, for DNS options announced by RA, use the Secure Neighbor Discovery (SEND) protocol (RFC3971 [22]). The DNS information announced by RA using SEND takes precedence over the DNS information announced by RA without using SEND. In addition, the DNS options announced by RA through SEND must take precedence over those announced by unauthenticated DHCPv6 (RFC3118 [23]).

2. *DNS Option Configuration Warnings*

There are two warnings for DNS option configuration.

(1) DNS options come from multiple sources.
(2) DNS options come from multiple network interfaces.

In the case where DNS options come from multiple sources (for example, RA and DHCPv6), an IPv6 host can configure its IPv6 address from these sources. However, in this case, it is impossible to control how the host uses DNS information. Therefore, network administrators need to carefully configure different DNS options among various mechanisms to minimize the problems caused by this impact. If different network interfaces provide different DNS information, it may also lead to inconsistent behavior. The solutions can be found in RFC6418 [24], RFC6419 [25], and RFC6731 [26].

8.3.5 Implementation Considerations

The following issues need to be considered during implementation.

(1) DNS repository management.
(2) Synchronization between RDNSS server list and resolver repository.
(3) Synchronization between DNSSL and resolver repository.

1. *DNS Repository Management*

For DNS repository management, the following two data structures should be synchronized with the resolver repository.

(1) Save the RDNSS address list.
(2) Save the DNSSL search domain name list.

Each entry in the two lists consists of an RDNSS address (or DNSSL domain name) and an expiration time.

(1) RDNSS address of the DNS server list: The IPv6 address of RDNSS is used to announce the address of the DNS resolver in the network through the RDNSS option.
(2) DNSSL domain name: Use the DNS domain name suffix provided by DNSSL to perform DNS query searches for short, unqualified domain names.
(3) Expiration time of the DNS server list (or DNSSL): After this time, the corresponding RDNSS (or DNSSL) information is invalid. The expiration time is set to the "lifetime" field of the RDNSS option or DNSSL option plus the current time. When the same network interface receives a new RDNSS option with the same address (or a new DNSSL option with the same domain name), it is updated to the new expiration time. If the current time is greater than the expiration time, this entry is considered expired and should not continue to be used.

Please note that DNS does not need to delete the information of the RDNSS and DNSSL options whose lifetime has expired, because these options have a lifetime use value.

2. *Synchronization Between RDNSS Server List and Resolver Repository*

When an IPv6 host receives multiple RDNSS information in the network (such as campus network or enterprise network) through RA messages with RDNSS options, it needs to store the RDNSS addresses in the DNS server list and resolver repository. The processing of RDNSS includes the following two items.

(1) Process the RDNSS options contained in the RA message.
(2) Process expired RDNSS options.

The processing flow is as follows:

(1) Receive and parse the RDNSS option. For each RDNSS address in the RDNSS option, perform steps (2) to (4).
(2) For each RDNSS address, check the following: If the address already exists in the DNS server list and the "Lifetime" field of the RDNSS option is 0, the corresponding RDNSS entry is deleted from the DNS server list and the resolver repository. This deletion prevents misuse of the RDNSS entry due to network management actions. Examples of such actions include terminating RDNSS service or re-planning IPv6 addresses. That is, when the machine running RDNSS intentionally or unintentionally stops the RDNSS service, it can exit. In addition, when re-planning IPv6 addresses, the IPv6 address of RDNSS has changed, so any previous RDNSS address should not continue to be used. In this case, stop processing RDNSS. Otherwise, go to step (3).
(3) For each RDNSS address, if it already exists in the DNS server list and the "Lifetime" field of the RDNSS option is not 0, update the "Expiration Time" field. Otherwise, go to step (4).
(4) For each RDNSS address, if it does not exist in the DNS server list, register the RDNSS address and corresponding lifetime in the DNS server list, and then insert it as the first RDNSS address in the resolver repository. If this DNS server list is full, delete the entry with the shortest lifetime from the DNS server list. The corresponding RDNSS address also needs to be deleted from the resolver repository. Note: The first RDNSS address in the RDNSS option should be positioned as the first address in the resolver repository, the second RDNSS address as the second address in the repository, and so on. This sorting allows the RDNSS addresses in the RDNSS option to be prioritized according to their order in the DNS's RDNSS option.

The processing of expired RDNSS is as follows: Whenever an entry in the DNS server list expires, the expired entry will be deleted from the DNS server list, and the corresponding RDNSS address entry will be deleted from the resolver repository.

3. *Synchronization Between DNSSL and the Resolver Repository*

When an IPv6 host receives multiple DNSSL information through an RA message with an RDNSS option, it needs to store the DNSSL addresses in the DNS server list and the resolver repository in order. The processing of DNSSL includes the following points.

(1) Process the DNSSL option included in the RA message.
(2) Process the expired DNSSL option.

The processing of the DNSSL option is the same as the processing of the RDNSS option.

8.3.6 Security Considerations

Attackers can mislead IPv6 hosts to use illegal DNS servers by sending fraudulent RA messages with illegal RDNSS addresses. Similarly, attackers can use illegal DNSSL options to make IPv6 hosts use fraudulent DNSSL to resolve hostnames without DNS suffixes. These attacks are similar to the ND attacks described in RFC4861 [16], which redirect traffic to malicious addresses using redirect or neighbor announcement messages.

It is recommended to use the SEND protocol defined by RFC3971 [22] as the security mechanism for ND. In this case, ND can use SEND to digitally sign all ND options (including RDNSS and DNSSL options).

Similar to configuring network device interfaces to prevent unauthorized DHCPv6 services (RFC7610 [27]), security can also be enhanced by configuring network device interfaces to prevent unauthorized RA services. The specific method is to prevent unauthorized hosts from sending RDNSS and DNSSL options (RFC6105 [28], RFC6104 [29]).

Attackers may provide forged DNSSL options, causing victims to use illegal domain suffixes when querying non-fully qualified domain names. For these types of attacks, the DNS resolver in the IPv6 host can handle them by implementing the methods defined by RFC1535 [30], RFC1536 [31], and RFC3646 [19].

8.4 IPv6 Prefix Configuration via RA

When an IPv6-only host accesses the IPv4 Internet through an IPv4/IPv6 translator, it needs to map the IPv4 address to an IPv6 address (IPv4-converted IPv6 address) using the mechanism defined by RFC6052 [1]. In this case, the following methods can be used.

(1) DNS64 defined by RFC6147 [32].
(2) IPv6 prefix discovery mechanism defined by RFC7050 [3].
(3) RA Pref64 extension defined by RFC8781 [33].

DNS64 usually uses manually configured IPv6 prefixes (referred to as NAT64 Prefix), while RFC7050 [3] and RFC8781 [33] are automatic discovery and configuration mechanisms for NAT64 Prefix. Note that if DNS64 is used on an IPv6 host, an automatic configuration mechanism for the IPv6 prefix is also needed.

The advantages of using the RA Pref64 extension defined by RFC8781 [33] are as follows:

(1) Supports DNSSEC.
(2) Supports DNS over TLS (DOT) and DNS over HTTPS (DOH).
(3) Supports applications directly embedding IPv4 addresses.
(4) Supports "fate sharing," that is, through RA declaration, IPv6-only hosts can directly obtain the networked IPv6 prefix, default gateway, domain name resolution server address (RFC8106 [15]), and IPv6 prefix for IPv4/IPv6 translation.
(5) Supports "atomic configuration," that is, all network configuration parameters are completed through a single datagram (RA), eliminating incompleteness.
(6) Supports updatability, that is, it can be changed at any time.
(7) Supports deployability, all IPv6 hosts and networks need to support the neighbor discovery protocol defined by RFC4861 [16].

8.4.1 Extension Format

Figure 8.17 shows the NAT64 Prefix option format.

(1) Type: 8 bits; IANA assigns it as 38 (Pref64 option type).

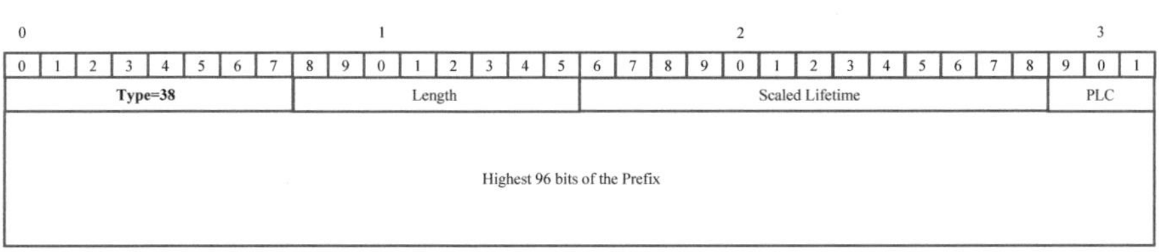

Fig. 8.17 NAT64 prefix option format

(2) Length: 8-bit unsigned integer; the length of the option (including the "Type" and "Length" fields) in units of eight octets. The sender must set the length to 2. If the value of the "Length" field is not 2, the receiver must ignore the Pref64 option.
(3) Scaled Lifetime: 13 bits (unsigned integer); the maximum lifetime in units of 8 s, during which this NAT64 Prefix can be used.
(4) Prefix Length Code (PLC): 3 bits (unsigned integer); this field encodes the NAT64 Prefix length defined in RFC6052 [1]. The allowed values for this field are 0, 1, 2, 3, 4, and 5, corresponding to NAT64 Prefix lengths of 96 bits, 64 bits, 56 bits, 48 bits, 40 bits, and 32 bits, respectively. If the PLC field is any other value, the receiver must ignore the Pref64 option.
(5) Highest 96 bits of the Prefix: 96 bits (unsigned integer); contains the 0–95 bits of the NAT64 prefix.

8.4.2 Extended Lifetime Handling

It is strongly recommended that the lifetime of the NAT64 prefix should not be shorter than the router lifetime defined by RFC4861 [16] (represented by a 16-bit unsigned integer), otherwise the NAT64 prefix will expire before the next unrequested RA arrives. Therefore, this extension encodes the lifetime of the NAT64 prefix in units of 8 s. The receiver must multiply the scaled lifetime value by 8 (through logical left shift) to calculate the maximum available time of the NAT64 prefix (unit: second). Therefore, the longest lifespan of the NAT64 prefix is 65528 s. This ensures that the NAT64 prefix does not expire before the default router lifetime. When using this option, it is not recommended that the default router lifetime exceeds 65528 s. A lifetime of 0 indicates that the NAT prefix is no longer in use.

By default, the value of the "Scaled Lifetime" field should be set to the smaller of 3 $\times$ MaxRtrAdvInterval divided by 8 or 8191 (RFC4861 [16]).

Router vendors should allow administrators to specify non-zero lifetime values that cannot be divided by 8. In this case, the router should round the provided value to the nearest integer that can be divided by 8 and is less than 65,536, then divide the result by 8 (or logical right shift 3 bits) and set the "Scaled Lifetime" field accordingly. If the non-zero lifetime value divided by 8 is less than 8, the "Scaled Lifetime" field should be set to 1. This ensures that lifetimes less than 8 s are encoded as non-zero extended lifetimes.

8.4.3 Configuration Guide

This option specifies the same NAT64 prefix for all IPv4 destination nodes. If a network operator wants to route different IPv4 address spaces to different NAT64 devices, this can be achieved by routing longer sub-prefixes. For example, suppose the network operator uses the internal address space 10.0.0.0/8 defined by RFC1918 [34]. The operator wants to translate the 10.0.0.0/8 address segment through NAT64 device A and the rest of the IPv4 address space through NAT64 device B. If the operator's NAT64 prefix is 2001:db8:a:b::/96, then the operator can route 2001:db8:a:b:a00:0/104 to NAT64 A, 2001:db8:a:b:/96 to NAT64 B.

This option may appear multiple times in the RA (for example, when renumbering the network from one NAT64 prefix to another NAT64 prefix).

Note that this option should only be used for IPv6-only networks and is not applicable to dual-stack networks.

In some cases, the host may receive multiple NAT64 prefixes from different sources. Possible situations include but are not limited to the following.

(1) The host can use multiple mechanisms to discover Pref64 prefixes. Currently includes the Port Control Protocol (PCP) defined by RFC7225 [35], the method defined by RFC7050 [3] through IPv4-only domain names, and the Pref64 RA option defined by RFC8781 [33] and so on.
(2) The Pref64 option can appear multiple times in a single RA.
(3) The host receives multiple RAs with different Pref64 prefixes on a given network interface.

When the host obtains multiple Pref64s through the RA Pref64 option (appearing multiple times in a single RA or receiving multiple RAs), the host should follow the recommendations given in RFC7050 [3] to synthesize IPv6 addresses.

When discovering different Pref64s using multiple mechanisms, the host should only select one information source. The recommended priority is as follows.

(1) Prefix discovered through PCP [35] (if supported).
(2) Pref64 discovered through RA [33] option.
(3) Pref64 generated through RFC7050 [3].

It is recommended to use the method defined in RFC4861 [16] to check RA messages to ensure that all routers announce consistent information on the link. If inconsistent, the router should record it.

8.4.4 Security Considerations

Since all IPv6 host auto-configuration schemes require RA, RA must be protected. For example, deploying RA protection (RFC6105 [28]).

If an incorrect NAT64 prefix is provided to the host, the IPv6 host will not be able to communicate with the IPv4 destination address. If an attacker can send a malicious RA, it may result in a Denial of Service (DoS) attack or a man-in-the-middle attack (RFC6104 [29]).

8.5 IPv6-Mostly Configuration

8.5.1 *Background*

One of the major challenges in deploying an IPv6 LAN is that such networks need to provide network services for different hosts and operating systems. Although modern operating systems support full-function operation under IPv6-only, and through network-side deployment of IPv4/IPv6 translation technologies discussed earlier (such as IVI, 464XLAT for Android systems, and IPv6 prefix discovery techniques like RFC7050 [3] or RA extension for Apple systems RFC8781 [33]) in this book, they can still access the IPv4 Internet.

However, some other operating systems may not fully support IPv6 access or cannot handle embedded IPv4 addresses in applications (e.g., URL containing IPv4 addresses instead of domain names).

Therefore, traditional methods often involve deploying dual stack within the LAN, i.e., assigning IPv4 addresses via DHCPv4 and IPv6 addresses via RA (SLAAC) or DHCPv6. In this case, every host in the LAN will be assigned an IPv4 address; even though techniques like Happy Eyeball can prioritize IPv6 access for hosts, they do not reduce the workload of IPv4 address allocation and security management.

For wireless LANs, a workaround is to configure different SSIDs, encouraging users with modern operating systems to connect to the IPv6-only SSID, while other users connect to the dual-stack SSID. In practice, however, most users will default to connecting to the dual-stack SSID. It's worth noting that this technique cannot be used for wired LANs.

The ideal scenario is for traditional operating systems to run in a dual-stack environment within the LAN (with the extreme case being some operating systems running on IPv4-only, although this would mean they couldn't access IPv6). To achieve this goal:

(1) Disabling IPv4 on modern operating systems is not feasible because the operating system must still be able to run in IPv4-only networks.
(2) Modern operating systems detect whether the network only provides IPv6 services and if so, stop using IPv4. However, this method is impractical as when a host connects to a network, it doesn't know whether the network is IPv4-only, dual stack, or IPv6-only. To ensure connectivity, the host will immediately start configuring both IPv4 and IPv6. After confirming IPv6 accessibility, it releases IPv4, which could cause visible errors since it might have already started using applications assigned with IPv4 addresses.

RFC8925 [36] provides a solution by using a new DHCPv4 option that indicates to clients whether the network provides IPv6-only services (including IPv4/IPv6 translation functionality), and thus no IPv4 is needed. That is to say: If specific subnets provide IPv4 as-needed, IPv4 addresses will not be offered to these types of clients. Note that this method requires updating DHCP server behavior according to RFC2563 [37] (i.e., the DHCPOFFER packet includes the IPv6-only Preferred option).

Corresponding to the IPv6-only discussed in this book, this technology is referred to as IPv6-mostly.

8.5.2 *IPv6-Only Preferred Option*

1. *Option Format*

The extended DHCP option is shown in Fig. 8.18.

(1) Code: 8-bit identifier of the IPv6-Only Preferred option code as assigned by IANA: 108. The client includes the Code in the Parameter Request List in DHCPDISCOVER and DHCPREQUEST messages.
(2) Length: 8-bit unsigned integer. The length of the option, excluding the Code and Length Fields. The server MUST set the length field to 4. The client MUST ignore the IPv6-Only Preferred option if the length field value is not 4.
(3) Value: 32-bit unsigned integer. The number of seconds for which the client should disable DHCPv4 (V6ONLY_WAIT configuration variable). If the server pool is explicitly configured with a V6ONLY_WAIT timer, the server MUST set the field to that configured value. Otherwise, the server MUST set it to zero. The client MUST process that field.

The client never sets this field, as it never sends the full option but includes the option code in the Parameter Request List.

2. *DHCPv4 Client Behavior*

The following are the configuration and deployment notes of the DHCPv4 client:

(1) A DHCPv4 client should allow a device administrator to configure IPv6-only capability either for a specific interface (to indicate that the device is IPv6-only capable if connected to a NAT64 network via that interface) or for all interfaces. The DHCPv4 client on an IPv4-requiring host must not include the IPv6-only Preferred option code in the Parameter Request List of any DHCPv4 packets and must ignore that option in packets received from DHCPv4 servers.
(2) DHCPv4 clients running on IPv6-only-capable hosts should include the IPv6-only Preferred option code in the Parameter Request List in DHCPDISCOVER and DHCPREQUEST messages for interfaces so enabled and follow the processing as described below on a per-enabled-interface basis.

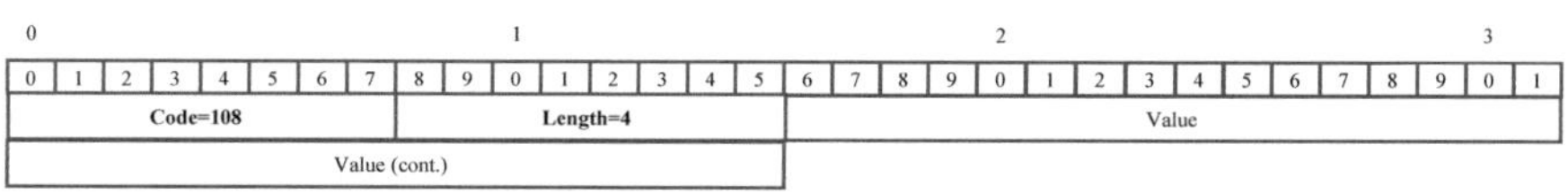

Fig. 8.18 DHCP option format

(3) If the client did not include the IPv6-Only Preferred option code in the Parameter Request List in the DHCPDISCOVER or DHCPREQUEST message, it must ignore the IPv6-only Preferred option in any messages received from the server.
(4) If the client includes the IPv6-only Preferred option code in the Parameter Request List and the DHCPOFFER message from the server contains a valid IPv6-only Preferred option, the client should not request the IPv4 address provided in the DHCPOFFER.
(5) If the client includes the IPv6-only Preferred option code in the Parameter Request List and the server responds with a DHCPOFFER message without a valid IPv6-only Preferred option, the client must proceed as normal with a DHCPREQUEST.

3. *DHCPv4 Server Behavior*

The following are the configuration and deployment notes of the DHCPv4 server:

(1) The DHCPv4 server should be able to configure all or individual pools to include the IPv6-only Preferred option in DHCPv4 responses if the client included the option code in the Parameter Request List.
(2) The server must not include the IPv6-only Preferred option in the DHCPOFFER or DHCPACK message if the selected pool is not configured as IPv6-mostly. The server must not include the IPv6-only Preferred option in the DHCPOFFER or DHCPACK message if the option was not present in the Parameter Request List sent by the client.
(3) If the IPv6-only Preferred option is present in the Parameter Request List received from the client and the corresponding DHCPv4 pool is explicitly configured as belonging to an IPv6-mostly network segment, the server must include the IPv6-only Preferred option when responding with the DHCPOFFER or DHCPACK message.

8.5.3 Workflow

The deployment for IPv6-mostly (Option 108) is illustrated in Fig. 8.19.

In addition to the standard RA functionality for SLAAC configuration, the router provides RDNSS and offers IPv6 prefix (PREF64) information aligned with the translator (xlat) configuration. It also supports DHCPv4 proxy functionality.

For hosts (Host-1 through Host-n), SLAAC is the default behavior for IPv6 address assignment, while IPv4 address configuration via DHCPv4 is optional.

(1) If the host supports Option 108, the DHCPv4 server does not assign an IPv4 address. In this scenario, the host operates as IPv6-only. Communication with the IPv6 Internet is direct, whereas IPv4 Internet access requires translation via the translator (xlat).
(2) If the host does not support Option 108, the DHCPv4 server assigns an IPv4 address to the host. This case has two sub-cases:

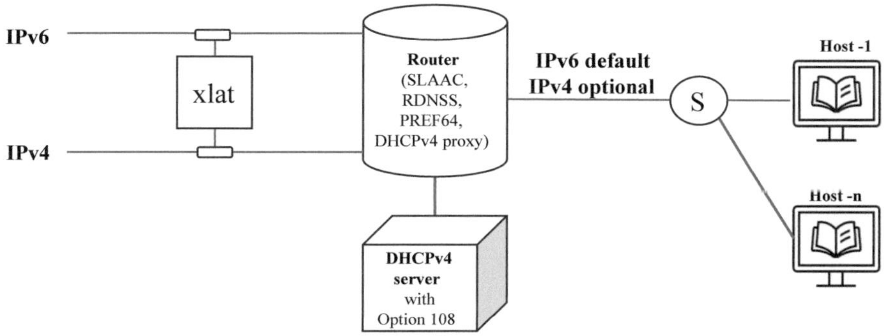

Fig. 8.19 Deployment for IPv6-mostly (option 108)

① Sub-case A: If the host supports SLAAC, it operates as a dual-stack host (IPv4/IPv6).
② Sub-case B: If the host does not support SLAAC, it operates as IPv4-only.

8.5.4 Security Considerations

An attacker might send a spoofed DHCPOFFER containing an IPv6-Only Preferred option with the value field set to a large number, such as 0xffffffff, effectively disabling DHCPv4 on clients supporting the option. If the network is IPv4-only, such clients would lose connectivity, while on a dual-stack network without NAT64 service, only connectivity to IPv4-only destinations would be affected. Recovery from such an attack would require triggering a network attachment event.

It should be noted that disabling IPv4 on a host upon receiving the IPv6-only Preferred option from the DHCPv4 server protects the host from IPv4-related attacks and therefore could be considered a security feature, as it reduces the attack surface.

8.5.5 Remarks

Although DHCPv4 Option 108 presented here is neither the configuration of IPv6 address, nor the discovery of IPv6 prefix, but rather for the IPv4 address configuration. It bridges the gap between dual stack and IPv6-only, as IPv6-mostly. This is why the title of this book is "IPv6 Transition Technology—IPv6-only, IPv6-mostly and IPv4aaS."

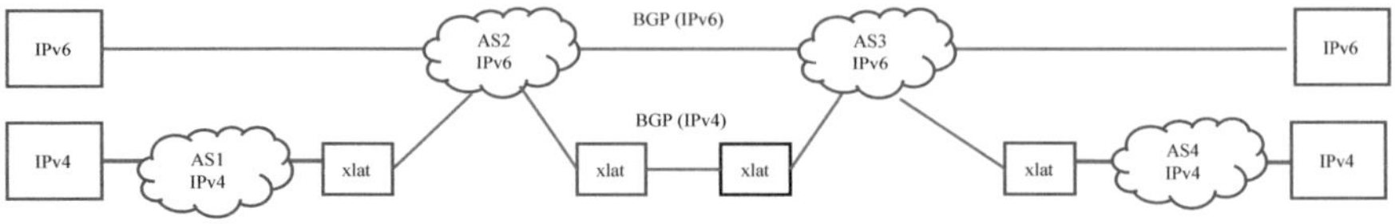

Fig. 8.20 Two IPv6-only networks doing IPv4 peering

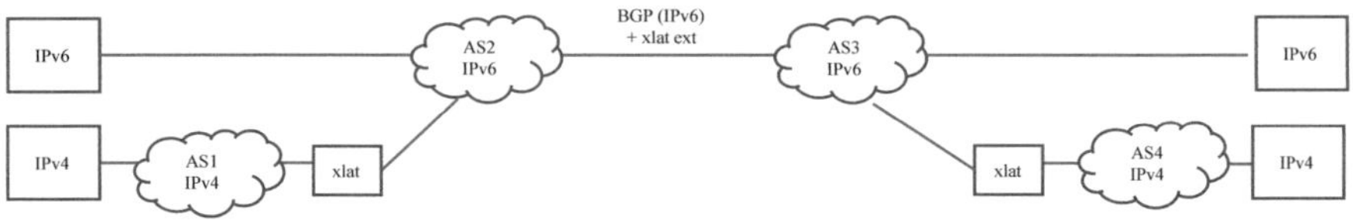

Fig. 8.21 Two IPv6-only networks doing IPv4 peering using IPv6 BGP extension

8.6 Considerations for the BGP Extension of Translation Technology

8.6.1 Background

This book provides a detailed discussion on IPv6 transition technologies that enable incremental deployment based on stateless translation. This allows each ISP to independently deploy IPv6-only networks while maintaining interconnection with the global IPv4 Internet via translators. However, as more ISPs implement this plan, new challenges arise, as illustrated in Fig. 8.20.

Since AS2 provides IPv4 service to downstream AS1, and AS3 also provides IPv4 service to downstream AS4, aside from performing IPv6 BGP peering at the boundaries between AS2 and AS3, each must establish translators (xlats) to convert IPv6 packets into IPv4 packets for IPv4 BGP peering. However, this is unnecessary in the data plane since both AS2 and AS3 are IPv6-only networks. Consequently, if IPv6 BGP were extended to include IPv6 prefix information for translation purposes along with all IPv4 BGP attributes (AS paths, communities, etc.), then AS2 and AS3 would only need to perform extended IPv6 BGP peering, as shown in Fig. 8.21.

8.6.2 Work in Progress

This work is currently under discussion in IETF [38, 39].

8.7 Summary

This chapter discusses the automatic discovery and configuration methods of parameters required by several translation technologies. Including using DNS to discover IPv6 prefixes, using DHCPv6 to configure IPv6 prefixes, the transport layer (TCP, UDP) port range when sharing IPv4 addresses, and using RA to configure DNS resolver addresses and IPv6 prefixes for the IPv6 translators. Additionally, this chapter introduces the recently developed DHCPv4 extension (option 108), which facilitates not configuring IPv4 addresses specifically for modern operating systems. Lastly, it examines the IPv6 Border Gateway Protocol (BGP) extension.

References

1. Bao C, Huitema C, Bagnulo M, et al. RFC6052: IPv6 addressing of IPv4/IPv6 translators. IETF 2010-10.
2. Troan O, Dec W, Li X, et al. RFC7597: Mapping of address and port with encapsulation (MAP-E). IETF 2015-07.
3. Savolainen T, Korhonen J, Wing D. RFC7050: Discovery of the IPv6 prefix used for IPv6 address synthesis. IETF 2013-11.
4. Cheshire S, Schinazi D. RFC8880: Special use domain name 'ipv4only.arpa'. IETF 2020-08.
5. Mockapetris P. RFC1035: Domain names - implementation and specification. IETF 1987-11.
6. Mockapetris P. RFC1034: Domain names - concepts and facilities. IETF 1987-11.
7. Rose S, Wijngaards W. RFC6672: DNAME redirection in the DNS. IETF 2012-06.
8. Conta A, Deering S, Gupta M. RFC4443: Internet control message protocol (ICMPv6) for the Internet protocol version 6 (IPv6) specification. IETF 2006-03.
9. Mrugalski T, Troan O, Farrer I, et al. RFC7598: DHCPv6 options for configuration of softwire address and port-mapped clients. IETF 2015-07.
10. Droms R, Bound J, Volz B, et al. RFC3315: Dynamic host configuration protocol for IPv6 (DHCPv6). IETF 2003-07.
11. Li X, Bao C, Dec W, et al. RFC7599: Mapping of address and port using translation (MAP-T). IETF 2015-07.
12. Bao C, Li X, Baker F, et al. RFC7915: IP/ICMP translation algorithm. IETF 2016-06.
13. Conta A, Deering S. RFC2473: Generic packet tunneling in IPv6 specification. IETF 1998-12.
14. Cui Y, Sun Q, Boucadair M, et al. RFC7596: Lightweight 4over6: An extension to the dual-stack lite architecture. IETF 2015-07.
15. Jeong J, Park S, Beloeil L S, et al. RFC8106: IPv6 router advertisement options for DNS configuration. IETF 2017-03.
16. Narten T, Nordmark E, Simpson W, et al. RFC4861: Neighbor discovery for IP version 6 (IPv6). IETF 2007-09.
17. Thomson S, Narten T, Jinmei T. RFC4862: IPv6 stateless address autoconfiguration. IETF 2007-09.
18. Droms R. RFC3736: Stateless dynamic host configuration protocol (DHCP) service for IPv6. IETF 2004-04.
19. Droms R. RFC3646: DNS configuration options for dynamic host configuration protocol for IPv6 (DHCPv6). IETF 2003-12.
20. Jeong J. RFC4339: IPv6 host configuration of DNS server information approaches. IETF 2006-02.
21. Deering S, Haberman B, Jinmei T, et al. RFC4007: IPv6 scoped address architecture. IETF 2005-03.

22. Arkko J, Kempf J, Zill B, et al. RFC3971: Secure neighbor discovery (SEND). IETF 2005-03.
23. Droms R, Arbaugh W. RFC3118: Authentication for DHCP messages. IETF 2001-06.
24. Blanchet M, Seite P. RFC6418: Multiple interfaces and provisioning domains problem statement. IETF 2011-11.
25. Wasserman M, Seite P. RFC6419: Current practices for multiple-interface hosts. IETF 2011-11.
26. Savolainen T, Kato J, Lemon T. RFC6731: Improved recursive DNS server selection for multi-interfaced nodes. IETF 2012-12.
27. Gont F, Liu W, Velde G. RFC7610: DHCPv6-shield: Protecting against rogue DHCPv6 servers. IETF 2015-08.
28. Abegnoli E, Velde G, Popoviciu C, et al. RFC6105: IPv6 router advertisement guard. IETF 2011-02.
29. Chown T, Venaas S. RFC6104: Rogue IPv6 router advertisement problem statement. IETF 2011-02.
30. Gavron E. RFC1535: A security problem and proposed correction with widely deployed DNS software. IETF 1993-10.
31. Kumar A, Postel J, Neuman C, et al. RFC1536: Common DNS implementation errors and suggested fixes. IETF 1993-10.
32. Bagnulo M, Sullivan A, Matthews P, et al. RFC6147: DNS64: DNS extensions for network address translation from IPv6 clients to IPv4 servers. IETF 2011-04.
33. Colitti L, Linkova J. RFC8781: Discovering PREF64 in router advertisements. IETF 2020-04.
34. Rekhter Y, Moskowitz B, Karrenberg D G, et al. RFC1918: Address allocation for private internets. IETF 1996-02.
35. Boucadair M. RFC7225: Discovering NAT64 IPv6 prefixes using the port control protocol (PCP). IETF 2014-05.
36. L. Colitti, J. Linkova, M. Richardson, et al. RFC8925: IPv6-Only Preferred Option for DHCPv4, IETF 2020-10.
37. R. Troll, RFC2563: DHCP Option to Disable Stateless Auto-Configuration in IPv4 Clients. IETF 1999-05.
38. Xie C. Ma C, Li X, et al. Framework of Multi-domain IPv6-only Underlay Network and IPv4-as-a-Service, IETF draft https://datatracker.ietf.org/doc/draft-ietf-v6ops-framework-md-ipv6only-underlay/
39. Xie C, Dong G, Li X, et al. MP-BGP Extension and the Procedures for IPv4/IPv6 Mapping Advertisement, IETF draft: https://datatracker.ietf.org/doc/draft-ietf-idr-mpbgp-extension-4map6/

Chapter 9
Single Translation

The IPv4/IPv6 single translation techniques include stateless translation (1:1 IVI), stateless translation with IPv4 address sharing (1:*N* IVI), and stateful translation (NAT64).

This chapter discusses these technologies in detail from the perspectives of research and development ideas, basic principles, deployment configuration, security considerations, and case analysis.

9.1 Stateless Translation

Stateless translation (1:1 IVI) uses algorithm-based mapping to perform IPv4/IPv6 translation (RFC6052 [1], RFC7915 [2], and RFC6219 [3]). It also requires DNS64 or DNS46. 1:1 IVI is commonly referred to as IVI (in Roman numerals, "IV" represents 4, "VI" represents 6, so "IVI" represents IPv4/IPv6 conversion). The topology of 1:1 IVI is shown in Fig. 9.1.

9.1.1 Background

The past 20 years of IPv6 deployment experience show that supporting communication between IPv4-only hosts and IPv6-only hosts is an important requirement. However, the first generation of IPv6 transition technology could not effectively support this (RFC4213 [4]). For example, dual-stack hosts can communicate with both IPv4 hosts and IPv6 hosts, but single-stack hosts can only communicate with hosts of the same address family. IPv4 over IPv6 tunneling technology (RFC3056 [5], RFC5214 [6], RFC4380 [7]) can connect IPv6 islands through the IPv4 network, but it cannot provide communication between IPv4-only hosts and IPv6-only hosts.

X. Li and C. Bao, *New IPv6 Transition Technology*,
https://doi.org/10.1007/978-981-95-8427-7_9

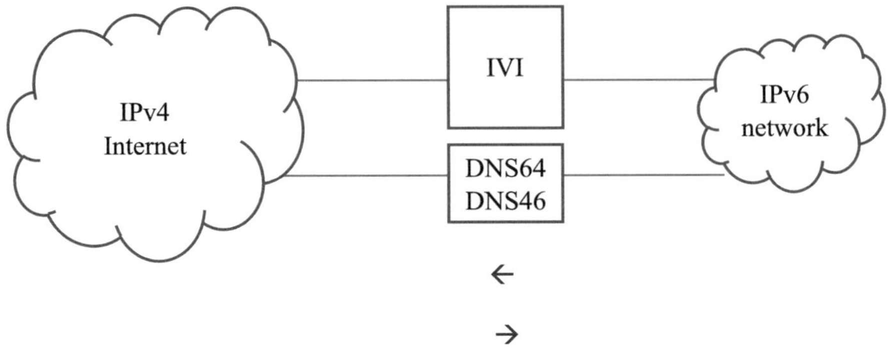

Fig. 9.1 Topology of 1:1 IVI

The translation technology defined by RFC2765 [8], RFC2766 [9], RFC3142 [10], and RFC2775 [11] enables hosts in IPv4 and IPv6 networks to communicate with each other. However, its design at the time had operational, scalability, and security issues, and it could not support the "end-to-end address transparency" of the Internet.

Because IPv4 and IPv6 are not compatible, they have different address spaces and different structures of datagram headers; they cannot directly communicate with each other and must go through translation technology. In traditional transition technologies, several RFCs have been specified to implement translation.

(1) IP/ICMP conversion algorithm (SIIT) defined by RFC2765 [8]. SIIT provides a conversion mechanism between IPv4 and IPv6 datagram headers (including ICMP headers) without the need to maintain connection status. However, SIIT does not specify address allocation and routing schemes (RFC2766 [9]). For example, SIIT uses "IPv4-mapped IPv6 address" (::ffff:ipv4-addr/96) and "IPv4-translated IPv6 address" (::ffff:0:ipv4-address/96) for address mapping, but these addresses violate the aggregation principle of IPv6 routing (RFC4291 [12]).
(2) Network Address Translation—Protocol Translation (NAT-PT) as defined by RFC2766 [9]. NAT-PT is a stateful translation technology coupled with DNS. Its main problems are as follows [13]:

① NAT-PT does not support application layer protocols with embedded IP addresses.
② The mechanism of NAT-PT leads to the loss of "end-to-end address transparency." "End-to-end address transparency" means the addressing capability of a global address space, maintaining the uniqueness of the end-to-end address of the datagram throughout the network transmission process, and the ability to use the source address and destination address as unique identifiers (RFC2775 [11]).
③ The semantic incompatibility between IPv4 headers and IPv6 headers may lead to information loss.

④ In NAT-PT technology, DNS is tightly coupled with the translator, lacking the persistence of address mapping (RFC4966 [13]).
⑤ NAT-PT has difficulty supporting "referrals" because hosts outside of NAT-PT do not have information processed internally by NAT-PT, so they may not understand what the "referral" address represents.
⑥ Stateful translation technology can lead to issues such as scalability, multi-homing, and load balancing.

Due to serious technical and operational problems with NAT-PT, IETF has deprecated it (RFC4966 [13]).

Based on the above analysis, the design ideas of stateless IPv4/IPv6 translation technology IVI are as follows:

(1) For clients and servers in an IPv6-only network, they should support communication initiated by IPv6 clients in an IPv6-only network to servers on the IPv4 Internet, as well as communication initiated by clients on the IPv4 Internet to IPv6 servers in an IPv6-only network.
(2) Current best practices for IPv4 and IPv6 routing should be followed, without dramatically increasing the size of the IPv4 and IPv6 global routing tables.
(3) Support for incremental deployment.
(4) It should be able to use IPv4 addresses efficiently to address the problem of IPv4 address exhaustion.
(5) To achieve scalability, the translator should be stateless in the backbone.
(6) DNS functionality should be decoupled from the translator.

9.1.2 Basics of Stateless Translation

The IVI is a stateless translation technology, which utilizes the Network Specific Prefix (NSP) and can be independently implemented by each ISP. The core idea of IVI design is to embed a subset of the ISP's IPv4 prefix into IPv6 Network Specific Prefix (NSP), such addresses are defined as "IPv4-translatable IPv6 addresses" in RFC6052 [1]. At the same time, public IPv4 addresses on the Internet are embedded into the same NSP, such addresses are defined as "IPv4-converted IPv6 addresses" in RFC6052 [1]. In this way, the ISP's hosts using "IPv4-translatable IPv6 addresses" can communicate directly with the global IPv6 Internet, and also communicate with the global IPv4 Internet through a stateless translator. These communications can be initiated by either IPv6 or IPv4. The implementation topology of IVI stateless IPv4/IPv6 translation technology, which includes the interconnection relationship between IPv6-only network and IPv6 Internet, is shown in Fig. 9.2.

To achieve translation between IPv4 and IPv6, the IVI translator creates mirrored hosts in both IPv4 and IPv6. Specifically, a real IPv6 host is mapped to a mirrored IPv4 host within the IPv4 network, while a real IPv4 host is mapped to a mirrored IPv6 host in the IPv6 network. The IPv6 mirrored hosts use IPv6 addresses from a

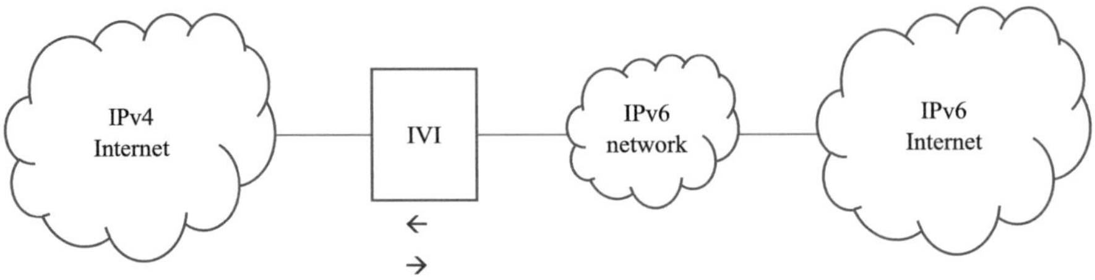

Fig. 9.2 IVI topology

subset of the ISP's IPv6 prefix, while the IPv4 mirrored hosts use IPv4 addresses from a subset of the ISP's IPv4 prefix.

1. *Representing IPv4 Address with IPv6*

   The IPv4 address is 32 bits, and the IPv6 address is 128 bits, so any IPv6 prefix shorter than 96 bits (/96) can be chosen from the ISP's IPv6 prefix to represent the entire IPv4 Internet, as shown in Fig. 9.3.

   (1) Prefix: Network Specific Prefix (NSP, the length should be shorter then /96).
   (2) IPv4 Address: Global IPv4 address space.
   (3) Suffix: All zeros.

   This type of address is defined as "IPv4-converted IPv6 address" in RFC6052 [1].

2. *Representing IPv6 Address with IPv4*

   To represent an IPv6 address in IPv4, each ISP can "borrow" a portion of their public IPv4 addresses, embed these IPv4 addresses into their (as chosen above) IPv6 prefix shorter than /96, and form an IPv6 address for their own IPv6 host, as shown in Fig. 9.4.

   (1) Prefix: Network Specific Prefix (NSP).
   (2) IPv4 Address: A portion of the ISP's own public IPv4 addresses, which is a subset of the global IPv4 address space.
   (3) Suffix: All zeros (can be expanded in the future).

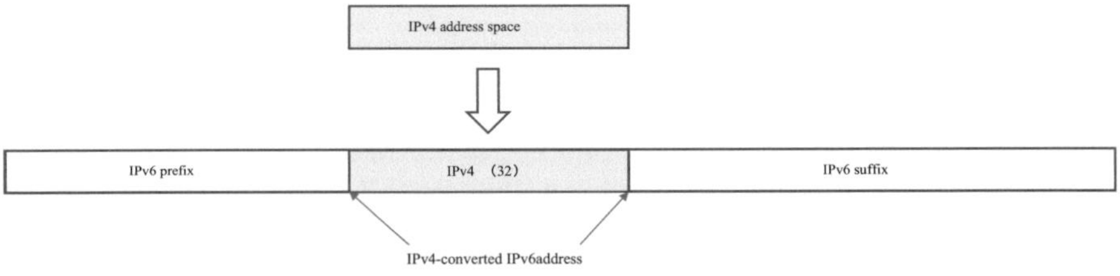

Fig. 9.3 IPv6 address representing IPv4

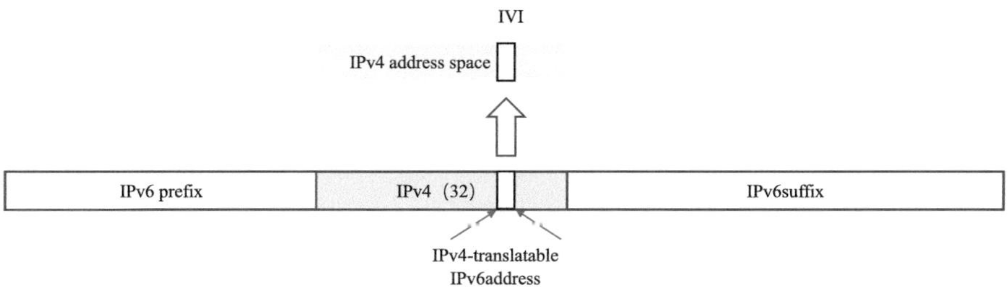

Fig. 9.4 IPv4 address representing IPv6

This type of address is defined as "IPv4-translatable IPv6 Address" in RFC6052 [1].

3. *Address Mapping*

Address mapping is defined in RFC6052 [1], discussed in Chap. 6 of this book, as shown in Fig. 6.25. It is recommended to use the format without u-oct, as shown in Fig. 6.26.

4. *Prefix Length Selection*

The Prefix Length is selected according to RFC6052 [1], discussed in Chap. 6 of this book.

5. *"IPv4-converted IPv6 address" and " IPv4-translatable IPv6 address" use the same or different IPv6 prefixes*

According to RFC6052 [1], "IPv4-converted IPv6 address" and "IPv4-translatable IPv6 address" should use the same IPv6 prefix, as discussed in Chap. 6 of this book.

6. *Protocol Translation*

Protocol translation is carried out according to the rules discussed in Chap. 5 of this book and defined by RFC7915 [2].

7. *Multicast Translation Function*

The IVI mechanism can support specific source protocol independent multicast (PIM-SSM: RFC5771 [14], RFC3569 [15], RFC4607 [16]) translation and communication between IPv4 and IPv6. The mapping relationship between IPv4 and IPv6 SSM group addresses is shown in Fig. 6.54.

The interoperability of the IPv4 PIM-SM multicast protocol and the IPv6 PIM-SM multicast protocol can be achieved through an application layer gateway (ALG), or by statically joining the corresponding group in the IPv4 network and the IPv6 network. In IPv4, it is the Internet Group Management Protocol Version 3 (IGMPv3), and in IPv6, it is the Multicast Listener Discovery Version 2 (MLDv2) protocol (RFC4604 [17]).

9.1.3 Stateless Translation Configuration

1. *Routing and Forwarding*

   The routing configuration of the stateless single translation technology IVI is shown in Fig. 6.29.

   (1) The stateless translator (xlat) can be regarded as a special dual-stack router with two link interfaces (IPv4 and IPv6). Its routing configuration can be statically configured or dynamically configured by routing protocols.
   (2) The router R4 routes the ISP's IPv4 prefix corresponding to "IPv4-translatable IPv6 address" to xlat's IPv4 interface 192.0.2.1. This IPv4 prefix is announced to the IPv4 Internet after being aggregated to the ISP's IPv4 prefix.
   (3) The router R6 routes Network Specific Prefix (NSP) to xlat's IPv6 interface 2001:db8::1 (RFC6219 [3], RFC6052 [1], RFC7915 [2]). This IPv6 prefix is announced to the IPv6 Internet after being aggregated to the ISP's IPv6 prefix.
   (4) The stateless translator (xlat) routes the "IPv4-translatable IPv6 address" to R6's IPv6 interface 2001:db8::2.
   (5) The stateless translator (xlat) routes the IPv4 default route (0.0.0.0/0) to the R4's IPv4 interface 192.0.2.2.

The stateless translator (xlat) can learn/announce the above routes by running dynamic routing protocols (IGP or BGP) on R4 and/or R6.

The IPv4 prefix and IPv6 prefix used for stateless translation technology are announced to the Internet after being aggregated by the ISP's IPv4 prefix and IPv6 prefix, respectively. Therefore, it will not affect the IPv4 and IPv6 global routing tables (RFC4632 [18]).

Due to the stateless nature of IVI technology, it can support multi-homing and multi-translator load balancing.

Since IVI translation technology can be independently deployed by each ISP using their own IPv4 prefix and IPv6 prefix as needed, it can enable the global Internet to be transparently and smoothly deployed to IPv6 step by step.

2. *Application Layer Gateway*

Due to the reversible, one-to-one mapping relationship established between IPv4 addresses and a subset of IPv6 addresses by stateless single translation technology, it can support the vast majority of existing application protocols. However, some application protocols identify application layer entities with IP addresses (such as FTP, H.323, etc.). In these cases, application layer gateways should be used. Typically, stateless translators can integrate commonly used application layer gateways as needed.

However, application layer gateways are bound to specific application layer protocols and lack universality. Therefore, double translation technologies such as DIVI, MAP-T, and 464XLAT are better choices. Currently, Apple's iOS and Mac

OS systems, Google's Android, and Microsoft's Windows 10 Enterprise Edition have integrated the stateless translation technology defined by RFC6052 [1] and RFC7915 [2], along with the prefix discovery/configuration technologies (RFC7050 [19], etc.) into operating system themselves, so these operating systems can support any application program.

3. *Host Configuration*

   Because the "IPv4-translatable IPv6 address" has a special address format. For example, 192.0.2.1/32 corresponds to 2001:db8:ffc0:2:100::/72 (NSP = 2001:db8:ff00::/40). Therefore, the host IPv6 address must be configured manually or through stateful DHCPv6, not via the SLAAC mechanism.

   (1) The host can be manually configured: "IPv4-translatable IPv6 address," the IPv6 prefix length of this subnet, the IPv6 default gateway address, and the IPv6 address of the DNS64 resolver.
   (2) The host can be configured through stateful DHCPv6: DHCPv6 configures the "IPv4-translatable IPv6 address," the IPv6 prefix length of this subnet and the IPv6 address of the DNS64 resolver. In this case, the host must obtain the IPv6 default gateway address from the router (RA).

Each IPv6 host may have multiple addresses, but when the host communicates with the IPv4 host through the translator, it must use the "IPv4-translatable IPv6 address" as the IPv6 source address (RFC6724 [20]).

4. *DNS Configuration for IPv6 Server*

The stateless IPv4/IPv6 translator provides the ability for IPv4 users to access IPv6 server. In order to support access to this server through the DNS, DNS46 function must be provided. The most direct method is to configure an A record for the authoritative DNS server, alone with the AAAA record. The A record is the IVI4 address corresponding to the "IPv4-translatable IPv6 address" and the AAAA record is the "IPv4-translatable IPv6 address" itself.

5. *DNS Resolution Service Configuration of IPv6 Client*

When an IPv6-only host acts as a client, in order to access the IPv4 Internet, the DNS resolver used by the client must have DNS64 functionality (RFC6147 [21]). When the IPv6 client queries a domain name, DNS64 first queries the AAAA record. If the AAAA record does not exist, it queries the A record and maps it to the AAAA record according to the translator's IPv6 prefix, and returns it to the IPv6-only client. Note that the DNS64 server must be connected to a dual-stack environment (interconnected with the IPv4 Internet and IPv6 Internet) to ensure the completeness of the DNS recursive resolution chain.

9.1.4 Security Considerations

1. *IPsec and its NAT traversal technology*

IVI technology maintains the end-to-end transparency of the address and can support IPsec whether NAT traversal technology is used or not.

2. *DNSSEC*

For IPv6 servers, both AAAA records and A records of authoritative DNS can be signed with DNSSEC, so there is no DNSSEC problem.

For IPv6 clients:

(1) The IPv6 client itself cannot implement DNSSEC verification for the AAAA record synthesized by DNS64 according to the translation rules. In this case, the host can perform DNSSEC verification on the A record according to the translation rules. For related discussions, see RFC6147 [21].
(2) If a secure DNS protocol is running between the client and the DNS resolver, there is no security problem, because DNS64 can implement DNSSEC verification for A records and synthesize AAAA records.

3. *Firewall filtering rules*

Since IVI technology is stateless, it establishes a reversible, one-to-one mapping relationship between the IPv4 address and a subset of the IPv6 address, maintaining the end-to-end address transparency. Therefore, firewall filtering rules can be implemented directly or mapped to another address domain and implemented there based on the address mapping algorithm.

9.1.5 Stateless Translation Example

The topology and data flow of the IVI example are shown in Fig. 9.5. In the figure, the left side is the topology, and the right side is the source address and destination address of the datagram on this link.

1. *Scenario*

(1) IPv6 network (client H1) initiates access to the IPv4 Internet (server H2).
(2) IPv4 Internet (client H2) initiates access to the IPv6 network (server H1).

2. *IVI Parameters*

(1) IPv6 prefix: 2001:db8:100::/40.
(2) IPv6 address format: has u-oct (RFC6052 [1]).

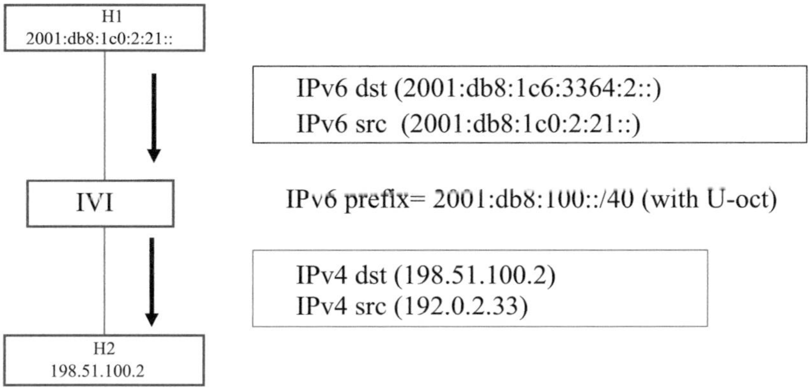

Fig. 9.5 IVI example

3. *Host Address*

   (1) H1: An IPv6 host in the IPv6 network uses the "IPv4-translatable IPv6 address," that is, 2001:db8:1c0:2:21:: (the IVI4 address is 192.0.2.33).
   (2) H2: An IPv4 host in the IPv4 Internet, that is, 198.51.100.2.

4. *Address Mapping Relationship*

   (1) "IPv4-translatable IPv6 address ":

$$(192.0.2.33) \longleftrightarrow (2001 : db8 : 1c0 : 2 : 21 ::)$$

(2) "IPv4-converted IPv6 address":

$$(198.51.100.2) \longleftrightarrow (2001 : db8 : 1c6 : 3364 : 2 ::)$$

9.2 1:*N* Stateless Translation

1:*N* stateless translation (1:*N* IVI) adopts the IPv4/IPv6 address mapping algorithm using NSP (RFC6052 [1], RFC7915 [2] and RFC6219 [3]). At the same time, it efficiently uses public IPv4 address by embedding transport layer ports identifier in the IPv6 address. It requires the support of DNS64/DNS46. The topology of 1:*N* IVI is shown in Fig. 9.6

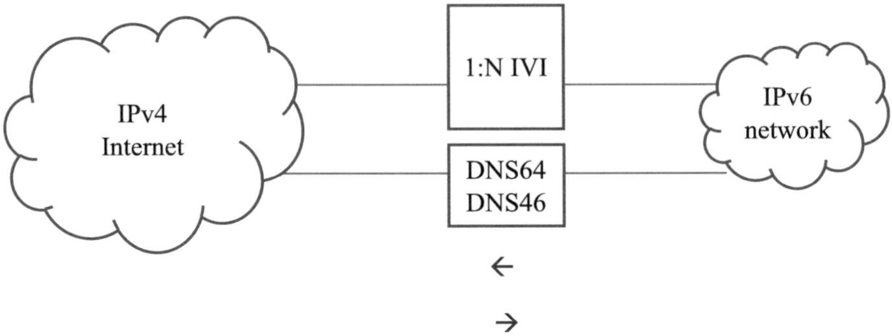

Fig. 9.6 1:*N* IVI topology

9.2.1 Background

1:1 IVI has good scalability, security, can maintain end-to-end address transparency, supports bidirectional initiated communication, but it requires a one-to-one correspondence between IPv4 addresses and IPv6 addresses.

Facing the problem of global exhaustion of public IPv4 addresses, a very natural idea is: Can we invent an extension mechanism that maintains the above characteristics of stateless IPv4/IPv6 translation technology (1:1 IVI) and can also share the scarce public IPv4 address resources? This is the 1:*N* IVI technology. Its core idea is to use the port number of the transport layer protocol (TCP, UDP) to establish an algorithm-based mapping relationship between a public IPv4 address and a group (individual) IPv6 addresses. Note that unlike the IPv4 NAT technology, the above mapping is not dynamically generated, but is algorithm-based. This algorithm embeds the PSID [22, 23] into the IPv6 address through suffix encoding technology.

It should be noted that:

(1) When the 1:*N* IVI mechanism is used for IPv6-only servers, each server reusing the same public IPv4 address can only serve specific service ports defined by the PSID, and the whole process is stateless.
(2) When the 1:*N* I IVI mechanism is used for IPv6-only clients, the transport layer source port of the datagram initiated by the client is randomly generated by the operating system, so it is necessary to map the randomly generated transport layer source port to a port range defined by PSID. For the return message of the same session, it is also necessary to map the target port back to the original random port. In this case, the mapping between IPv4 addresses and IPv6 addresses is stateless, but the mapping of transport layer ports needs to maintain state, which can also be called partial state. This state maintenance needs to be implemented on one of the following devices.

① Client operating system. That is, the client randomly generates the source port of the transport layer according to the range specified by the given IPv6 address (including PSID). In this case, the 1:*N* IVI translator is stateless.
② Home gateway. That is, the home gateway keeps the IPv6 source address and IPv6 destination address unchanged, but according to the IPv6 address assigned to the client, it maps the transport layer source port randomly generated by the client to the port range defined by PSID. For the return message of the same session, it maps the target port back to the original random port. In this case, the 1:*N* IVI translator is stateless.
③ 1:*N* IVI translator. That is, the 1:*N* IVI translator maps the transport layer source port randomly generated according to the IPv6 address assigned to the client to the port range defined by this PSID. For the return message of the same session, it maps the target port back to the original random port. In this case, the 1:*N* IVI translator is partially stateful.

The 1:*N* IVI has the following advantages.

(1) It can share scarce public IPv4 addresses, and compared with NAT64, it can greatly reduce the complexity of maintaining state.
(2) It supports bidirectional initiated communication (communication initiated by IPv6 clients in IPv6-only networks to servers on the IPv4 Internet, and communication initiated by clients on the IPv4 Internet to IPv6 servers in IPv6-only networks).
(3) It can greatly reduce the cost of storage and management of logs brought by management needs such as traceability.

9.2.2 *Basics of 1:*N *Stateless Translation*

In order to enable *N* IPv6 hosts to share an IPv4 address, transport layer port multiplexing technology is used; that is, these *N* IPv6-only hosts can only concurrently use a subset of the transport layer port space ($2^{16} = 65{,}536$). In the case of uniform distribution, for the multiplexing ratio *N*, the number of available ports is:

For example, if the port multiplexing ratio $N = 128$, then each IPv6 host can concurrently use 512 ports when communicating with the IPv4 Internet via TCP and UDP. Note: These IPv6 hosts have no port restrictions when communicating with other IPv6 hosts in the IPv6 Internet, and can concurrently use 65,536 ports. More discussions are in Chap. 6 of this book.

The 1:*N* IVI topology is shown in Fig. 9.7.

In Fig. 9.7, Host-0, Host-1, etc., share the same IPv4 address, but different hosts have non-overlapping transport layer port numbers.

1. *Transport layer port mapping algorithm*

The generalized modulus algorithm is recommended for the transport layer port mapping algorithm. More discussions are in Chap. 6 of this book.

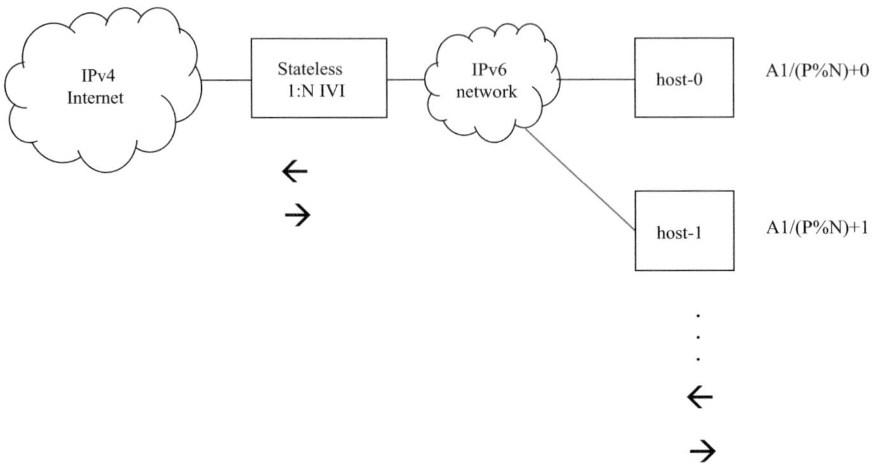

Fig. 9.7 1:*N* IVI topology (details)

2. *"IPv4-translatable IPv6 address" format*

It is recommended to use the no u-oct format for encoding, as shown in Fig. 6.26. More discussions are in Chap. 6 of this book.

3. *PSID format*

It is recommended to use variable length PSID left-aligned suffix encoding, as shown in Fig. 6.47. More discussions are in Chap. 6 of this book.

4. *Address and transport layer port mapping algorithm*

For 1:*N* IVI, IPv6-only hosts using "IPv4-translatable IPv6 addresses" need to follow the algorithm-specified transport layer port range to send and receive datagrams.

(1) **1:*N*IVI**

The 1:*N* IVI's handling algorithm for IPv4 (address/port) and IPv6 (address/port) is as follows:

(1) From IPv6 to IPv4: Check the source (address and port) of the IPv6 datagram. If it falls within the port range defined by the 1:*N* "IPv4-translatable IPv6 address" PSID, then map it to the corresponding IPv4 address of the "IPv4-translatable IPv6 address," with the source port unchanged; map the destination address to the "IPv4-converted IPv6 address," with the destination port unchanged. If it does not fall within the port range defined by the 1:*N* "IPv4-translatable IPv6 address" PSID, then discard the datagram.

(2) From IPv4 to IPv6: Map the IPv4 source address of the datagram to the "IPv4-converted IPv6 address," with the source port unchanged; calculate the PSID based on the mapping algorithm, and generate "IPv4-translatable IPv6 address," with the destination port unchanged.

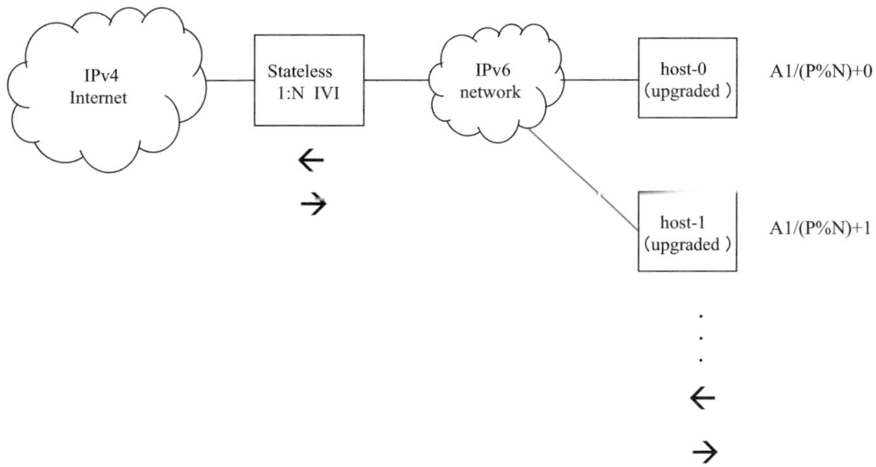

Fig. 9.8 1:*N* IVI (modified hosts)

If a 1:*N* IVI's IPv6 host is used as a server, then well-known ports (such as 80, 443, etc.) will be provided by the IPv6 host of the corresponding PSID.

If 1:*N* IVI's IPv6 host is used as a client, then the client operating system must generate the source port according to the value of the PSID. In this case, the stateless feature can be fully maintained. Its topology is shown in Fig. 9.8.

(2) **Partial-state 1:*N*IVI**

The partial-state 1:*N* IVI's processing algorithm for IPv4 (address/port) and IPv6 (address/port) is as follows:

(1) From IPv6 to IPv4: Check the source (address and port) of the IPv6 datagram. If it falls within the port range defined by the 1:*N* "IPv4-translatable IPv6 address" PSID, then map it to the corresponding IPv4 address of the "IPv4-translatable IPv6 address," with the source port unchanged; map the destination address to the "IPv4-converted IPv6 address," with the destination port unchanged. If it does not fall within the port range defined by the 1:*N* "IPv4-translatable IPv6 address" PSID, map the source port to the port range specified by the PSID, and maintain a port mapping table.
(2) From IPv4 to IPv6: Map the IPv4 source address of the datagram to the "IPv4-converted IPv6 address," with the source port unchanged; calculate the PSID according to the mapping algorithm, generate "IPv4-translatable IPv6 address," and map the destination port back to the original port according to the port mapping table.

A 1:*N* partial-state translator needs to maintain three session tables: TCP, UDP, and ICMP. The TCP and UDP session tables contain addresses and transport layer ports. The ICMP session table contains addresses and identifiers, and each entry in the session table saves the state of each session.

(1) The TCP session table is based on the port mapping algorithm and the TCP finite state machine. When the finite state machine reaches the termination state, the TCP session will be deleted.
(2) The UDP session table is based on the port mapping algorithm and the UDP session timer. When the timer expires, the UDP session will be deleted.
(3) The ICMP session table is based on the identifier mapping algorithm and the ICMP session timer. When the timer expires, the ICMP session will be deleted.

The reason it is called partial state is as follows:

(1) Address mapping is entirely based on algorithm, with no need to maintain any state.
(2) If the source port of the IPv6 to IPv4 datagram is within the range specified by the "IPv4-translatable IPv6 address," there is no need to create a session table.

Partial State Deployment 1:N IVI enables IPv6 clients to operate with unmodified operating systems, as illustrated in Fig. 9.9.

5. *"IPv4-converted IPv6 address" and "IPv4-translatable IPv6 address" use the same or different IPv6 prefixes*

According to RFC6052 [1], "IPv4-converted IPv6 address" and "IPv4-translatable IPv6 address" should use the same IPv6 prefix. Using the same IPv6 prefix can ensure that the "IPv4-translatable IPv6 address" has the optimal routing path within the network. Specifically, if an IPv6 node wants to access another node's IPv4 address, and the actual node using this IPv4 address is an IPv6 node, then using the same NSP to construct the "IPv4-converted IPv6 address" and "IPv4-translatable IPv6 address" can guarantee the optimal route, because the principle of Internet routing (i.e., "longest prefix wins") can ensure direct communication between the two nodes, without the need for processing by the translator (hairpin function).

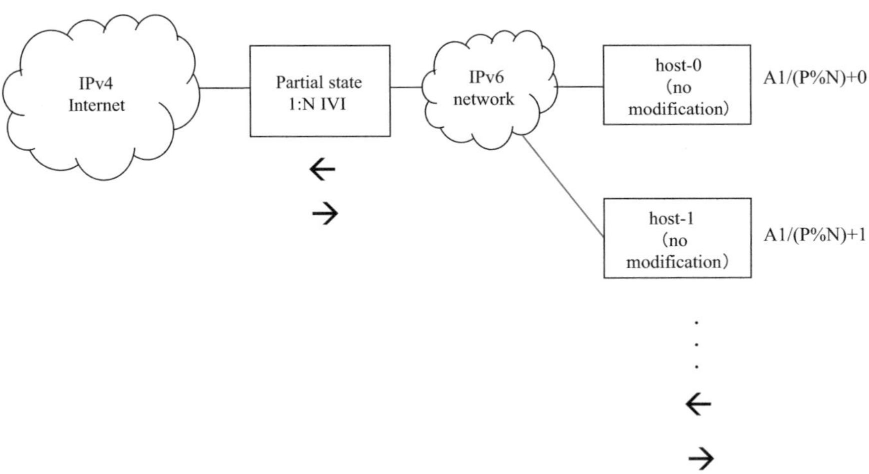

Fig. 9.9 Partial-state 1:*N* IVI

6. *Protocol Translation*

Protocol translation is carried out according to the rules defined by RFC7915 [2]. More discussions are in Chap. 5 of this book.

9.2.3 *1:*N *Stateless Translation Configuration*

1. *Routing and Forwarding*

   1:*N* IVI's routing configuration principle is consistent with 1:1 IVI.

2. *Application Layer Gateway*

   1:*N* IVI's application layer gateway requirements are consistent with 1:1 IVI.

3. *Host Address Configuration*

   1:*N* IVI's host address configuration method is the same as 1:1 IVI.

4. *DNS Configuration of IPv6 Server*

   The DNS configuration method for 1:*N* IVI's IPv6 server is the same as 1:1 IVI.

5. *DNS Resolution Service Configuration of IPv6 Client*

   The DNS configuration method for 1:*N* IVI's IPv6 client is the same as 1:1 IVI.

9.2.4 *1:*N *Stateless Translation Cascade Deployment*

1:*N* IVI can also be deployed in a cascade mode, that is, the first translator deploys 1:1 IVI, the second translator deploys 1:1 "IPv4-translatable IPv6 address" to 1:*N* "IPv4-translatable IPv6 address," as shown in Fig. 9.10.

9.2.5 *1:*N *Stateless Translation Example*

The topology and data flow of the 1:*N* IVI example are shown in Fig. 9.11. The left side is the topology, and the right side is the source address and destination address of the datagram on this link.

1. *Scenario*

   (1) IPv6 network (client H1) initiates access to the IPv4 Internet (server H2).
   (2) IPv4 Internet (client H2) initiates access to the IPv6 network (server H1).

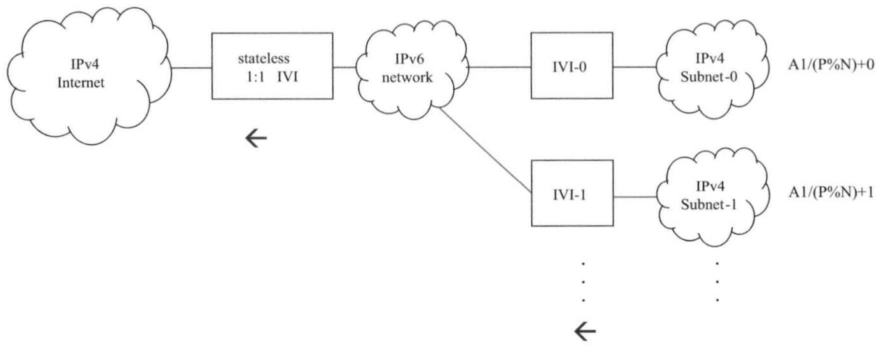

Fig. 9.10 1:*N* IVI cascade deployment

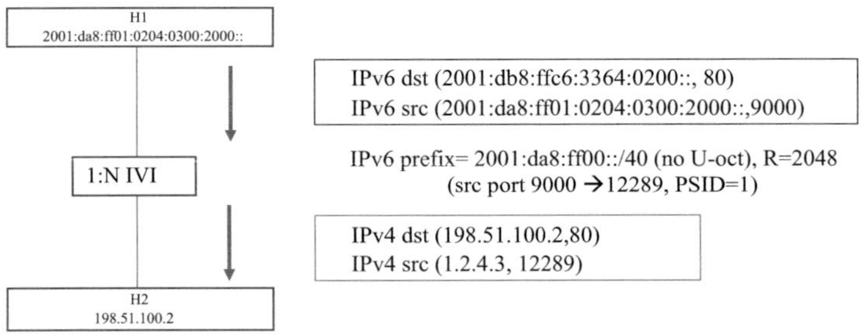

Fig. 9.11 1:*N* IVI example

2. *1: N IVI Parameters*

   (1) IPv6 prefix: 2001:db8:100::/40.
   (2) IPv6 address format: no u-oct (RFC7915 [2] updates RFC6052 [1]).
   (3) IPv4 address sharing ratio: 2048.

3. *Host Address*

   (1) H1: An IPv6 host in the IPv6 network uses the "IPv4-translatable IPv6 address," that is, 2001:da8:ff01: 0204:0300:2000:: (the IVI4 address is 1.2.4.3).
   (2) H2: An IPv4 host in the IPv4 Internet, that is, 198.51.100.2.

4. *Address and Port Mapping Relationship Annotation*

Since it is a 1:*N* mapping, the multiplexing ratio $R = 2048$, the IPv4 in this example is 1.2.3.4, PSID = 1, therefore the port range available for this IPv6 host is

$$\begin{aligned} kR + \text{PSID} \quad & (k = 0, 1, \cdots, 31) \\ = 2048k + 1 \quad & (k = 0, 1, \cdots, 31) \end{aligned}$$

The available ports are 1, 2049, 6144, 8192, 10,241, 12,289, …, 63,488.

Since the source port (9000) sent by H1 is not within the range allowed by PSID = 1, the 1:*N* IVI translator establishes a session table (TCP, UDP, or ICMP), mapping 9000 to 12,289.

Although it is a 1:*N* mapping, as long as it is within the range allowed by the PSID, it has end-to-end address transparency and supports bidirectional communication initiation.

(1) *"IPv4-translatable IPv6 address"*

$$(1.2.4.3, 9000) \longleftrightarrow (2001 : \text{da8} : \text{ff01} : 0204 : 0300 : 2000 ::, 12289)$$

(2) "IPv4-converted IPv6 address"

$$(198.51.100.2, 80) \longleftrightarrow (2001 : \text{db8} : \text{ffc6} : 3364 : 0200 ::, 80)$$

9.3 Stateful Translation

In this book, stateful translation specifically refers to NAT64 technology. Currently, IPv4 widely uses NAT technology, which dynamically maps the private IPv4 addresses and transport numbers of the local hosts to the public IPv4 address and transport numbers to reach the global Internet. Applying similar principles, NAT64 dynamically maps the IPv6 addresses and transport numbers of the local host to the public IPv4 address and transport numbers to reach the global IPv4 Internet. NAT64 uses the protocol translation rules defined by RFC6052 [1] and RFC7915 [2], and requires the support of DNS64/DNS46 technology. The difference between NAT64 and stateless IPv4/IPv6 translation technology lies in address mapping mechanism. The specific technical description of NAT64 is divided into two scenarios.

(1) The IPv6 host in an IPv6 network initiates communication with the IPv4 Internet, as shown in Fig. 9.12.
(2) The IPv6 host in the IPv6 Internet initiates communication with the IPv4 network, as shown in Fig. 9.13.

9.3.1 Background

NAT64 is defined by RFC6146 [24]. NAT64 is a stateful IPv4/IPv6 transition and coexistence mechanism. When used in conjunction with DNS64 (RFC6147 [21]), NAT64 allows IPv6-only clients to initiate communication with IPv4 servers. When using NAT traversal technologies such as interactive connectivity establishment (ICE) (RFC5245 [25]), NAT64 can also support peer-to-peer communication.

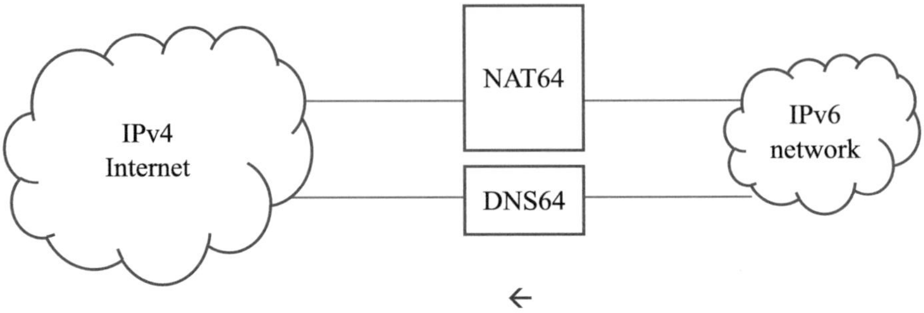

Fig. 9.12 NAT64(1)

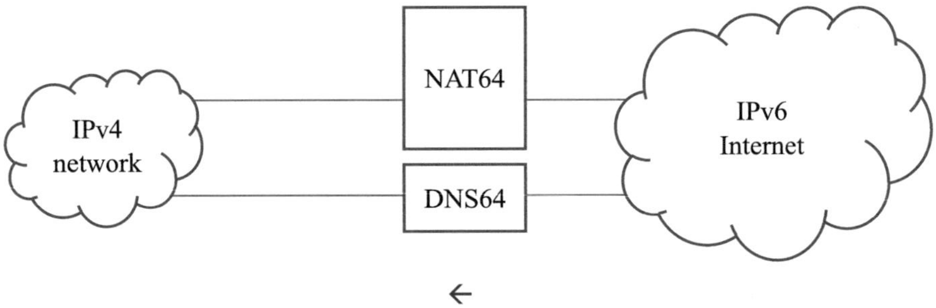

Fig. 9.13 NAT64(2)

Stateful NAT64 also supports communication initiated by IPv4 clients with statically configured IPv6-only servers. The header translation between IPv4 and IPv6 is defined by RFC7915 [2], and the translation of the IPv4 server's address to the IPv6 address (IPv4-converted IPv6 address) is defined by RFC6052 [1]. The IPv6 address of the IPv6 client is converted to a shared public IPv4 address (its sharing mechanism is implemented through transport layer port mapping) through network address and protocol translation (NAPT) (RFC3022 [26]). The current standard only defines the conversion of TCP, UDP, and ICMP unicast datagrams through stateful NAT64.

DNS64 is a mechanism for synthesizing AAAA records from DNS A records, and its synthesis algorithm is defined by RFC6052 [1].

To implement basic NAT64 functionality, a stateful NAT64 needs to be deployed between a IPv4 network and an IPv6-only network, as well as a DNS resolver with DNS64 functionality. The relevant scenarios are defined by RFC6144 [27]. Stateful IPv4/IPv6 translation technology (NAT64) can efficiently share public IPv4 addresses among IPv6 hosts, but only supports communication initiated by IPv6 client. At the same time, there are issues of scalability and security.

NAT64 has the following functions.

(1) NAT64 only handles TCP, UDP, and ICMP, and should have characteristics similar to Network Address Translation 44 (NAT44: UDP: RFC4787 [28], TCP: RFC5382 [29], and ICMP: RFC5508 [30]). Therefore, NAT64 supports endpoint-independent mappings, as well as endpoint-independent and address-dependent filtering. NAT64 is compatible with current NAT traversal technologies (ICE: RFC5245 [25], etc.).
(2) Similar to NAT44, there is no pre-existing state in NAT64, so it only supports IPv6-only clients initiating communication with IPv4 servers.
(3) Depending on the filtering policy used (endpoint independent or address dependent), NAT64 can support limited communication initiated by IPv4-only clients to IPv6-only servers. This includes the following two situations: ① The IPv6 node has recently initiated a session to the same or another IPv4 node (NAT traversal technology); ② Static configuration of the IPv6 node for mapping.
(4) NAT64 supports multiple IPv6-only nodes sharing a single public IPv4 address to access the IPv4 Internet.
(5) Currently, the NAT64 standard only supports TCP, UDP, and ICMP.

9.3.2 Basics of Stateful Translation

In the mechanism of NAT64, IPv6 datagrams enter NAT64 and are converted into IPv4 datagrams. IPv4 datagrams enter NAT64 and are converted into IPv6 datagrams. The conversion of NAT64 is asymmetric. In order to perform the conversion from IPv6 datagrams to IPv4 datagrams, NAT64 needs to maintain a state table. The state table contains bindings of IPv6 addresses and TCP/UDP ports to IPv4 addresses and TCP/UDP ports.

This binding state can be statically configured, or dynamically generated (the first IPv6 datagram establishes session state). After the binding state is created, bidirectional datagrams from IPv6 to IPv4 and from IPv4 to IPv6 can be converted through NAT64. Therefore, in general, NAT64 only supports IPv6-only clients initiating access to IPv4 servers. Static configuration or ICE can support communication initiated by IPv4-only nodes to IPv6-only nodes.

The main components of NAT64 include address translation and protocol conversion. Protocol conversion is defined by RFC7915 [2].

NAT64 has two address pools: an "IPv6 address pool" representing IPv4 addresses in the IPv6 network and an "IPv4 address pool" representing IPv6 addresses in the IPv4 network.

The IPv6 address pool is one or more IPv6 prefixes assigned to NAT64, represented as Pref64::/*n*. NAT64 will use Pref64::/*n* to construct the "IPv4-converted IPv6 address" defined by RFC6052 [1]. Due to the massive IPv6 address space, each Pref64::/n can cover the entire IPv4 address space. Therefore, every IPv4 address is allowed to map to an IPv6 address (RFC6052 [1]).

The IPv4 address pool is a set of public IPv4 addresses allocated by the local administrator. Because the IPv4 address space is a scarce resource, the IPv4 address pool is usually small and cannot establish a permanent one-to-one mapping with IPv6 addresses. Therefore, apart from the mapping between specific IPv4 addresses and IPv6 addresses created statically, the IPv4 address pool can only be created and released dynamically according to demand. Therefore, similar to NAT44, NAT64 shares IPv4 addresses (using transport layer ports) instead of directly mapping IPv6 addresses to IPv4 addresses. This means that NAT64 needs to perform address and port translation.

Since the mapping from IPv6 addresses to IPv4 addresses is dynamic, and the mapping from IPv4 addresses to IPv6 addresses is static, the communication initiated by IPv6 nodes to IPv4 nodes is based on the algorithm defined by RFC6052 [1]. However, the communication initiated by IPv4 nodes to IPv6 nodes is relatively complex (such as through static configuration or must be initiated dynamically by IPv6 nodes).

Using the DNS64 mechanism, IPv6-only clients obtain IPv6 addresses of IPv4 servers. The IPv6-only client sends IPv6 datagrams to this IPv6 address.

The datagram is routed to the NAT64 device, where its IPv6 source address and transport layer source port is associated with a specific address and port in the public IPv4 address pool. This association creates a binding state, enabling the return datagram of the same session to be mapped back to the original initiating client of the datagram.

When the session is in progress, this mapping maintains the binding. Once the session stops or the timer runs out, the public IPv4 address and the bound transport layer port return to the IPv4 address pool for reuse in other sessions.

The above DNS64 function is defined by RFC6147 [21], used to synthesize AAAA records from DNS's A records. The synthesized AAAA record contains the Pref64::/*n* assigned to NAT64 and the A record of the IPv4 server. The synthesized AAAA record is returned to the IPv6-only client for sending IPv6 datagrams with the AAAA record as the destination address.

To ensure security, NAT64 can create rules to filter IPv6 datagrams, binding tables, and session tables as needed by management. Filtering can prevent denial of service attacks that exhaust IPv4 addresses, ports, memory, and CPU resources.

The filtering of IPv4 datagrams is closely coupled with the state of NAT64 and should follow the recommendations of RFC4787 [28] and RFC5382 [29]. Therefore, NAT64 supports "endpoint independent filtering" and "address-dependent filtering" for TCP, UDP, and ICMP.

If NAT64 implements "endpoint-independent filtering" on the incoming IPv4 datagram, the IPv4 datagram will be discarded unless there is an address and port binding table for the destination address in NAT64.

If NAT64 implements "address-dependent filtering" on the incoming IPv4 datagram, the IPv4 datagram will be discarded unless there is an address and port binding table for the destination address in NAT64, and it has the same source address.

9.3.3 Stateful Translation Algorithm

NAT64 devices need to configure IPv6 link interfaces and IPv4 link interfaces. Each NAT64 device must have at least one IPv6 prefix, represented as Pref64::/*n*. NAT64 must maintain a public IPv4 address pool.

NAT64 includes the following data structures.

(1) UDP binding information library.
(2) UDP session table.
(3) TCP binding information library.
(4) TCP session table.
(5) ICMP query binding information library.
(6) ICMP query session table.

NAT64 has three Binding Information Bases (BIB): TCP, UDP, and ICMP. In the case of UDP and TCP, each entry in the BIB describes the following mapping:

$$\left(X',\ \mathrm{x}\right) \longleftrightarrow (\mathrm{T},\ \mathrm{t})$$

where X' is an IPv6 address; T is an IPv4 address; x and t are transport layer ports. T is an address from the IPv4 address pool assigned to NAT64. The BIB has two columns: (X', x), (T, t). A given IPv6 (address/port) or IPv4 (address/port) can appear in at most one entry in the BIB. For example, (2001:db8::17, 49,832) can only appear once in TCP. Note: TCP and UDP have independent BIBs because TCP and UDP port spaces do not overlap.

In the case of the ICMP BIB, each ICMP BIB entry specifies a mapping between (IPv6 address, ICMPv6 identifier) and (IPv4 address, ICMPv4 identifier).

$$\left(X',\ \mathrm{i1}\right) \longleftrightarrow (\mathrm{T},\ \mathrm{i2})$$

where X' is an IPv6 address; T is an IPv4 address; i1 and i2 are identifiers for ICMPv6 and ICMPv4 respectively. T is an address from the IPv4 address pool assigned to NAT64. The BIB has two columns: (X', i1), (T, i2). A given IPv6 (address/identifier) or IPv4 (address/identifier) can appear in at most one entry in the ICMP BIB.

Any entry in the three BIBs can be dynamically created by a datagram or manually created by an administrator. The NAT64 device should support manual configuration of any entry in the three BIBs. When the session table ends, the associated BIB table should also be deleted. Dynamically created entries will delete the corresponding session table BIB entry when the last session associated with the BIB is deleted. Manually configured BIBs will not automatically delete related entries, regardless of whether there is a corresponding session table, and can only be manually deleted by the administrator.

NAT64 also has three session tables: TCP, UDP, and ICMP. Each entry retains session status. In the case of UDP and TCP, each session table entry describes the following mapping:

$$(X', \text{ x}), (Y', \text{ y}) \longleftrightarrow (\text{T}, \text{ t}), (\text{Z}, \text{ z})$$

where X' and Y' are IPv6 addresses; T and Z are IPv4 addresses; x, y, z, and t are transport layer ports. T is an address from the IPv4 address pool assigned to NAT64. Y' is the "IPv4-converted IPv6 address" of IPv4 address Z. y is always equal to z.

Each TCP or UDP session table entry (STE) has five columns, representing the conversion of incoming IPv6 datagrams into outgoing IPv4 datagrams.

(1) The IPv6 source (address/port) of the STE: (X', x).
(2) The IPv6 target (address/port) of the STE: (Y', y).
(3) The IPv4 source (address/port) of the STE: (T, t).
(4) The IPv4 target (address/port) of the STE: (Z, z).
(5) The lifetime of the STE.

In the case of the ICMP session table, each entry of the ICMP session specifies the mapping between the 3-Tuple (IPv6 source address, IPv6 destination address, ICMPv6 identifier) and the 3-Tuple (IPv4 source address, IPv4 destination address, ICMPv4 identifier).

$$(X', Y', \text{ i1}) \longleftrightarrow (\text{T}, \text{ Z}, \text{ i2})$$

where X' and Y' are IPv6 addresses; T and Z are IPv4 addresses; i1 is the ICMPv6 identifier; i2 is the ICMPv4 identifier. T is an address from the IPv4 address pool assigned to NAT64. Y' is the "IPv4-converted IPv6 address" of the IPv4 address Z.

Each ICMP session table entry has seven.

(1) STE's IPv6 source address: X'.
(2) STE's IPv6 destination address: Y'.
(3) STE's ICMPv6 identifier: i1.
(4) STE's IPv4 source address: T.
(5) STE's IPv4 destination address: Z.
(6) STE's ICMPv4 identifier: i2.
(7) STE's lifespan.

NAT64 uses "session state information" to determine whether the session has been completed and performs "address-related filtering." A session can be uniquely identified by the input or output tuple.

For each TCP or UDP session, there is a corresponding BIB entry, uniquely specified by the IPv6 source (address/port) (IPv6 to IPv4 direction) or IPv4 destination (address/port) (IPv4 to IPv6 direction). For each ICMP, there is a corresponding BIB entry, uniquely specified by the IPv6 source address and ICMPv6 identifier (IPv6 to IPv4 direction) or IPv4 destination address and ICMPv4 identifier (IPv4 to IPv6 direction). For all BIBs, a single BIB entry can correspond to multiple sessions. If the BIB entry is dynamically created, delete the BIB entry when the last session is deleted.

NAT64 performs the following steps when processing incoming datagrams.

(1) Determine the input tuple.
(2) Filter and update binding and session information.
(3) Calculate the output tuple.
(4) Convert the datagram.
(5) Handle hairpins.

1. *Determine the input tuple*

In the case of TCP and UDP, the datagram is a 5-Tuple: source address, source port, destination address, destination port, and protocol. In the case of ICMP, the datagram is a 3-Tuple: source address, destination address, and ICMP identifier.

If the input IP datagram is a complete (unfragmented) UDP or TCP packet, extract the 5-Tuple from the datagram.

If the input datagram is a complete (unfragmented) ICMP message (ICMPv4 or ICMPv6), extract the 3-Tuple from the datagram.

If the input datagram contains a complete (unfragmented) ICMP error message containing a UDP or TCP datagram, extract the 5-Tuple from the TCP or UDP datagram of the ICMP error message. Note: At this time, the source and destination should be swapped; that is, the embedded source (address/port) is converted to the destination (address/port), and the embedded destination (address/port) is converted to the source (address/port). If the 5-Tuple cannot be determined, the datagram must be discarded.

If the input datagram contains a complete (unfragmented) ICMP error message with an internal embedded error message, the datagram must be discarded.

If the input data packet contains a complete (unfragmented) ICMP error message, which internally embeds an ICMP message, then extract the 3-Tuple from the ICMP packet of the ICMP error message. Note: At this time, the source and target should be swapped; that is, the embedded source (address/port) is converted to the target (address/port), and the embedded target (address/port) is converted to the source (address/port). If the 3-Tuple cannot be determined, the data packet must be discarded.

If the input data packet contains fragments, further processing must be carried out. NAT64 must be able to handle fragmentation. In particular, NAT64 must be able to handle out-of-order fragments.

(1) NAT64 must be able to limit the device resources used for storing fragments to prevent DoS attacks.
(2) As long as NAT64 has available device resources, NAT64 must allow fragments to arrive over a period of time. The time interval should be configurable, and the default value must be at least FRAGMENT_MIN.
(3) NAT64 requires that UDP, TCP, or ICMP headers are fully contained in fragments with an offset equal to 0 (the first fragment).

For input data packets carrying TCP or UDP fragments, and the checksum is not 0, NAT64 can choose to cache the fragments when they arrive and then translate all fragments. In this case, the processing of the 5-tuple or 3-tuple fragments of the input data packet is consistent with the processing method of the unfragmented data packet mentioned above. NAT64 can also process subsequent fragments in real-time based on the 5-tuple or 3-tuple information extracted from the first fragment when the fragment arrives. Note: In the second case, it must be considered that subsequent fragments may arrive before the first fragment.

For input IPv4 carrying 0 checksum UDP data packets, if NAT64 has sufficient device resources, it must reassemble the data packets and calculate the checksum. If NAT64 does not have enough resources, it must discard the data packet (RFC7915 [2]).

To improve the security of the network, when deploying NAT64, one should understand the attacks on data packet fragmentation discussed in RFC1858 [31] and RFC3128 [32], and take corresponding measures. In addition, one should understand the problems brought about by high-speed reassembly of data packets discussed in RFC4963 [33].

If the value of the last "next header" of the input IPv6 packet is not TCP, UDP, or ICMPv6, the IPv6 packet should be discarded. If the security policy allows, NAT64 should send an ICMPv6 "destination unreachable error message" when discarding this IPv6 packet, with the specific parameter being "Code 4: port unreachable" (Code 4: Port Unreachable) to the source address of this IPv6 packet. Note: In the future, in addition to TCP, UDP, and ICMPv6, it may also include the stream control transmission protocol (SCTP) or the datagram congestion control protocol (DCCP).

If the value of the "protocol" of the input IPv4 packet is not TCP, UDP, or ICMP, the IPv4 packet should be discarded. If the security policy allows, NAT64 should send an ICMP "destination unreachable error message" when discarding this IPv4 packet, with the specific parameter being "Code 2: protocol unreachable" (Code 2: Protocol Unreachable) to the source address of this IPv4 packet. Note: In the future, in addition to TCP, UDP, and ICMPv6, it may also include SCTP or DCCP.

2. *Filtering and updating binding and session information*

The filtering and updating of NAT64 are related to the protocol (UDP, TCP, or ICMP). Note: ICMP error messages should not change the BIB or session table.

Regardless of the transport protocol used, NAT64 must discard input IPv6 packets with a source address containing Pref64::/*n* to prevent hairpinning loops. In addition, NAT64 must only process destination addresses containing Pref64::/*n*. The input IPv6 datagram. Similarly, NAT64 must only process incoming IPv4 datagrams with a destination address that includes the NAT64 IPv4 pool.

(1) UDP Session Processing

Store the following state information for UDP sessions.

(1) Binding relationship:

$$(X',\ \mathrm{x}),\ (Y',\ \mathrm{y}) \longleftrightarrow (\mathrm{T},\ \mathrm{t}),\ (\mathrm{Z},\ \mathrm{z})$$

(2) Lifecycle: Set a timer to track the remaining lifecycle of the UDP session. When the timer expires, the UDP session will be deleted. If all dynamically

created UDP sessions are deleted, then delete the corresponding entry in the UDP BIB.

The handling of UDP's BIB and sessions depends on counters, the details of which can be found in RFC6146 [24]. In summary: NAT64 searches the UDP BIB for an entry that matches the IPv6 source (address/port). If such an entry does not exist, NAT64 will attempt to create a new one. NAT64 searches the session table for a 5-Tuple that matches the incoming datagram. If no such entry is found, NAT64 will attempt to create a new one. NAT64 sets (or resets) the timer in the session table entry to the maximum session lifetime. The maximum session lifetime can be manually configured, and by default should be at least UDP_DEFAULT. This maximum session lifetime must not be less than UDP_MIN. If an appropriate IPv4 (address/port) cannot be allocated or a BIB entry cannot be created, the datagram is discarded. NAT64 should send an ICMPv6 "Destination Unreachable Error Message" (Code 3: Address Unreachable).

(2) *TCP Session Processing*

NAT64's handling of TCP is based on a finite state machine, storing the following state information for TCP sessions.

(1) Binding relationship:

$$\left(X', \text{ x}\right), \left(Y', \text{ y}\right) \longleftrightarrow (\text{T}, \text{ t}), (\text{Z}, \text{ z})$$

(2) Lifecycle: Set a timer to track the remaining lifecycle of the TCP session. When the timer expires, the TCP session will be deleted. If all dynamically created TCP sessions are deleted, then delete the corresponding entry in the TCP BIB.

According to RFC5382 [29], the setting for the inactive lifetime of a TCP session should be at least 124 min, so each entry in the TCP session table corresponds to an existing TCP session. For this, a finite state machine is needed to track all TCP sessions.

The states are defined as follows:

(1) CLOSED: Similar to the definition in RFC793 [34], CLOSED is a fictitious state, representing that a 5-Tuple does not exist, so there is no connection.
(2) V4 INIT: NAT64 has received an IPv4 datagram containing a TCP SYN, implying that a TCP connection is being attempted from the IPv4 side. NAT64 is waiting for a matching IPv6 datagram containing a TCP SYN from the opposite direction.
(3) V6 INIT: NAT64 has received, translated, and forwarded an IPv6 datagram containing a TCP SYN, implying that a TCP connection is being initiated from the IPv6 side. NAT64 is waiting for a matching IPv4 datagram containing a TCP SYN from the opposite direction.
(4) ESTABLISHED: Represents a working connection, data can be transmitted in both directions.

(5) V4 FIN RCV: NAT64 has received an IPv4 datagram containing a TCP FIN, data can still be transmitted in the connection. NAT64 is waiting for a matching IPv6 datagram containing a TCP SYN from the opposite direction.
(6) V6 FIN RCV: NAT64 has received an IPv6 datagram containing a TCP FIN, data can still be transmitted in the connection. NAT64 is waiting for a matching IPv4 datagram containing a TCP SYN from the opposite direction.
(7) V6 FIN + V4 FIN RCV: NAT64 has received a TCP FIN's IPv4 datagram and IPv6 datagram. NAT64 still maintains the connection status in a short time, in order to forward the remaining datagrams (especially ACK) in both directions.
(8) TRANS: NAT64 has received the TCP RST datagram or due to the connection's lifecycle decreasing to the remaining TCP_TRANS minutes. In this case, the lifecycle of the connection status is set to TCP_TRANS minutes. If there are no new datagrams, NAT64 will maintain this connection for TCP_TRANS minutes, then terminate.

NAT64 uses a finite state machine to handle TCP sessions. The state changes of the TCP finite state machine are driven by the datagrams received by NAT64 from the IPv6 and IPv4 link interfaces. Each TCP session (TCP's 5-tuple) has a corresponding TCP finite state machine. When NAT64 is initialized, all states of the TCP finite state machines are CLOSED. For details on NAT64's handling of TCP, see RFC6146 [24]. The state transition of the simplified TCP finite state machine is shown in Fig. 9.14.

(3) *ICMP Session Handling*

Store the following state information for ICMP sessions.

(1) Binding relationship:

$$\left(X', \ Y', \ \text{i1}\right) \longleftrightarrow (\text{T}, \ \text{Z}, \ \text{i2})$$

(2) Lifecycle: Set a timer to track the remaining lifecycle of the ICMP session. When the timer expires, the ICMP session will be deleted. If all dynamically created ICMP sessions are deleted, then delete this entry from the ICMP BIB.

The handling of ICMP's BIB and sessions depends on counters, for details see RFC6146 [24]. In summary: NAT64 searches the ICMP BIB, looking for entries that match the IPv6 source (address/port). If such an entry does not exist, NAT64 will try to create a new one. NAT64 searches the session table, looking for the 3-Tuple of the incoming datagram. If no such entry is found, NAT64 will try to create a new one. NAT64 sets (or resets) the timer in the session table entry to the maximum session lifetime. The maximum session lifetime can be manually configured. If it is not possible to allocate an appropriate IPv4 (address/port) or create a BIB entry, then discard the datagram. If the datagram is discarded, NAT64 should send an ICMP error message, with type 3 (destination node unreachable) and code 13 (communication administratively prohibited).

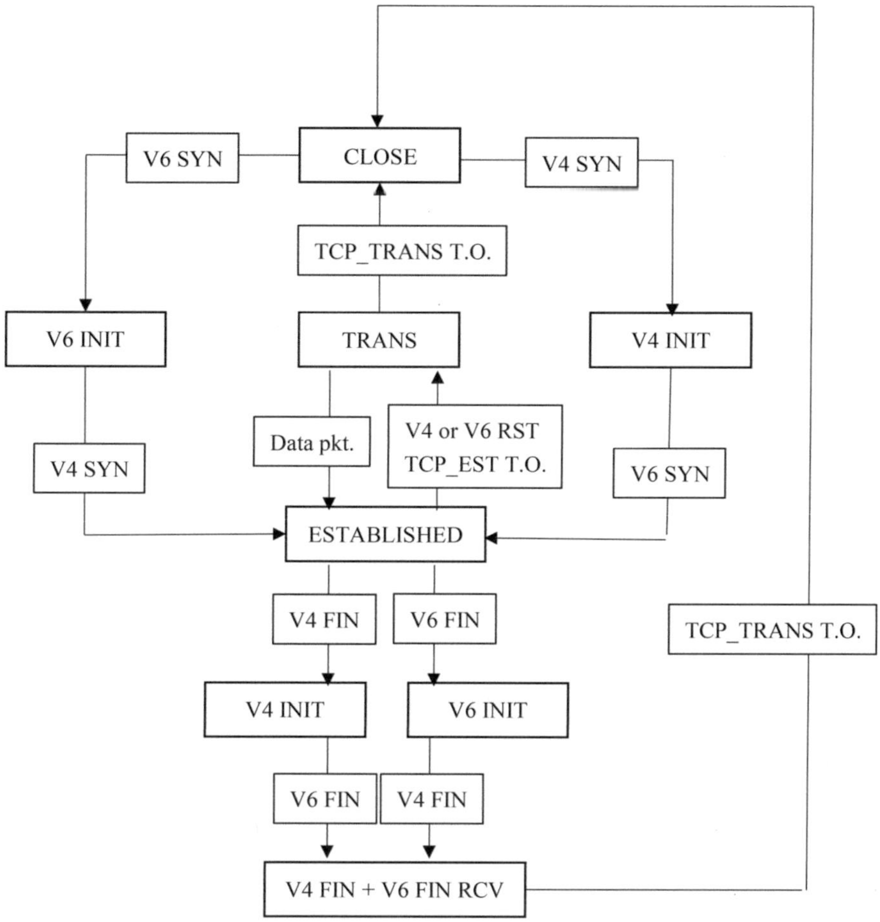

Fig. 9.14 NAT64's TCP finite state machine

3. *Calculate Output 5-tuple or 3-tuple*

This step generates the output datagram's 5-tuple (or 3-tuple) by using the BIB to transform the input datagram's 5-tuple (or 3-tuple). Note: Not all (addresses and ports) use BIB for transformation. BIB entries are used to convert the IPv6 source (address and port) to the IPv4 source (address and port), and to convert the IPv4 target (address and port) to the IPv6 target (address and port). For details on calculating the output 5-tuple (or 3-tuple), see RFC6146 [24].

4. *Transform Datagram*

The protocol conversion of the datagram is carried out according to the algorithm defined in RFC7915 [2]. More discussions are in Chap. 6 of this book.

5. *Handle Hairpinning*

   If the destination address of the IPv4-converted datagram belongs to NAT64's IPv4 address pool, then this datagram is a hairpinning datagram, and the handling method is as follows:

   (1) The output 5-tuple is changed to the input 5-tuple.
   (2) The datagram is considered as a datagram received by the output link interface.

Then process this datagram according to the above "Filtering and Updating Binding and Session Information."

9.3.4 Security Considerations

Any protocol that relies on IP header information is incompatible with NAT64. This means that end-to-end IPsec AH verification fails (tunnel mode and transport mode) and ESP verification fails (transport mode). The use of UDP encapsulation can restore end-to-end IPsec transmission, see RFC3948 [35].

When using NAT64, refer to RFC4787 [28] to configure security filtering rules. Furthermore, NAT64 devices themselves may become victims of network attacks, especially victims of DoS attacks. This includes exhaustion of the limited public IPv4 address pool, exhaustion of fragment reassembly resources, and exhaustion of binding table resources.

9.3.5 Stateful Translation Example

The topology and data flow of the NAT64 example are shown in Fig. 9.15. The left side is the topology, and the right side is the source and destination addresses of the datagrams on this link.

1. *Scenario*

   An IPv6 network (client H1) initiates access to the IPv4 Internet (server H2).
2. *NAT64 Parameters*

   (1) IPv6 prefix: 64:ff9b::/96 (well-known prefix).
   (2) IPv4 address pool: 203.0.113.0/24.

3. *Host Address*

   (1) H1: An IPv6 host (2001:db8::1) in the IPv6 network.
   (2) H2: An IPv4 host (192.0.2.1) in the IPv4 Internet.

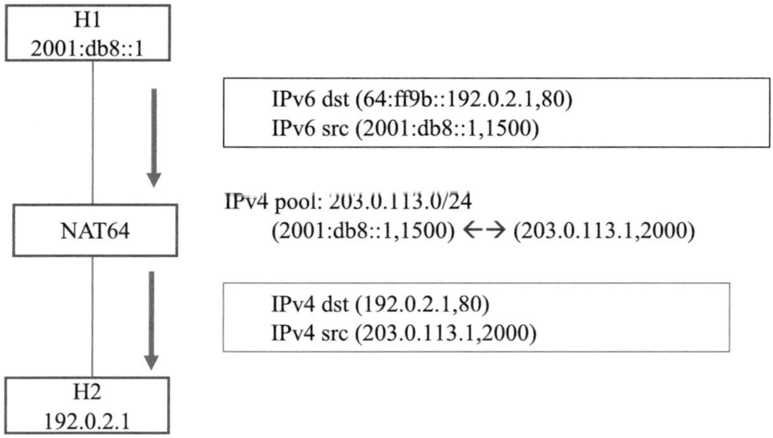

Fig. 9.15 NAT64 example

4. *Address and Port Mapping Relationship Notes*

   (1) Establish a session table (TCP or UDP or ICMP):

$$(203.0.113.1,\ 2000) \longleftrightarrow (2000 : \mathrm{db8} :: 1,\ 1500)$$

   (2) "IPv4-converted IPv6 address":

$$(192.0.2.1,\ 80) \longleftrightarrow (64 : \mathrm{ff9b} :: 192.0.2.1,\ 80)$$

9.4 Summary

This chapter introduces the core translation technologies for achieving IPv4 and IPv6 intercommunication, including stateless single translation (IVI), stateless single translation with IPv4 address multiplexing (1:*N* IVI), and stateful single translation (NAT64).

References

1. Bao C, Huitema C, Bagnulo M, et al. RFC6052: IPv6 addressing of IPv4/IPv6 translators. IETF 2010-10.
2. Bao C, Li X, Baker F, et al. RFC7915: IP/ICMP translation algorithm. IETF 2016-06.
3. Li X, Bao C, Chen M, et al. RFC6219: The China Education and Research Network (CERNET) IVI translation design and deployment for the IPv4/IPv6 coexistence and transition. IETF 2011-05.
4. Nordmark E, Gilligan R. RFC4213: Basic transition mechanisms for IPv6 hosts and routers. IETF 2005-10.

5. Carpenter B, Moore K. RFC3056: Connection of IPv6 domains via IPv4 clouds. IETF 2001-02.
6. Templin F, Gleeson T, Thaler D. RFC5214: Intra-site automatic tunnel addressing protocol (ISATAP). IETF 2008-03.
7. Huitema C. RFC4380: Teredo: Tunneling IPv6 over UDP through network address translations (NATs). IETF 2006-02.
8. Nordmark E. RFC2765: Stateless IP/ICMP translation algorithm (SIIT). IETF 2000-02.
9. Tsirtsis G, Srisuresh P. RFC2766: Network address translation - protocol translation (NAT-PT). IETF 2000-02.
10. Hagino J, Yamamoto K. RFC3142: An IPv6-to-IPv4 transport relay translator. IETF 2001-01.
11. Carpenter B. RFC2775: Internet transparency. IETF 2000-02.
12. Hinden R, Deering S. RFC4291: IP version 6 addressing architecture. IETF 2006-02.
13. Aoun C, Davies E. RFC4966: Reasons to move the network address translator - protocol translator (NAT-PT) to historic status. IETF 2007-07.
14. Cotton M, Vegoda L, Meyer D. RFC5771: IANA guidelines for IPv4 multicast address assignments. IETF 2010-03.
15. Bhattacharyya S. RFC3569: An overview of source-specific multicast (SSM). IETF 2003-07.
16. Holbrook H, Cain B. RFC4607: Source-specific multicast for IP. IETF 2006-08.
17. Holbrook H, Cain B, Haberman B. RFC4604: Using internet group management protocol version 3 (IGMPv3) and multicast listener discovery protocol version 2 (MLDv2) for source-specific multicast. IETF 2006-08.
18. Fuller V, Li T. RFC4632: Classless inter-domain routing (CIDR): The internet address assignment and aggregation. IETF 2006-08.
19. Savolainen T, Korhonen J, Wing D. RFC7050: Discovery of the IPv6 prefix used for IPv6 address synthesis. IETF 2013-11.
20. Thaler D, Draves R, Matsumoto A, et al. RFC6724: Default address selection for internet protocol version 6 (IPv6). IETF 2012-09.
21. Bagnulo M, Sullivan A, Matthews P, et al. RFC6147: DNS64: DNS extensions for network address translation from IPv6 clients to IPv4 servers. IETF 2011-04.
22. Troan O, Dec W, Li X, et al. RFC7597: Mapping of address and port with encapsulation (MAP-E). IETF 2015-07.
23. Li X, Bao C, Dec W, et al. RFC7599: Mapping of address and port using translation (MAP-T). 2015-07.
24. Bagnulo M, Matthews P, Beijnum I. RFC6146: Stateful NAT64: Network address and protocol translation from IPv6 clients to IPv4 servers. IETF 2011-04.
25. Rosenberg J. RFC5245: Interactive connectivity establishment (ICE): A protocol for network address translator (NAT) traversal for offer/answer protocols. IETF 2010-04.
26. Srisuresh P, Egevang K. RFC3022: Traditional IP network address translator. IETF 2001-01.
27. Baker F, Li X, Bao C, et al. RFC6144: Framework for IPv4/IPv6 translation. IETF 2011-04.
28. Audet F, Jennings C. RFC4787: Network address translation (NAT) behavioral requirements for unicast UDP. IETF 2007-01.
29. Guha S, Biswas K, Ford B, et al. RFC5382: NAT behavioral requirements for TCP. IETF 2008-10.
30. Srisuresh P, Ford B, Sivakumar S, et al. RFC5508: NAT behavioral requirements for ICMP. IETF 2009-04.
31. Ziemba G, Reed D, Traina P. RFC1858: Security considerations for IP fragment filtering. IETF 1995-10.
32. Miller I. RFC3128: Protection against a variant of the tiny fragment attack (RFC 1858). IETF 2001-06.
33. Heffner J, Mathis M, Chandler B. RFC4963: IPv4 reassembly errors at high data rates. IETF 2007-07.
34. Postel J. RFC793: Transmission control protocol. IETF 1981-09.
35. Huttunen A, Swander B, Volpe V, et al. RFC3948: UDP encapsulation of IPsec ESP packets. IETF 2005-01.

Chapter 10
Stateless Double Translation and Encapsulation

In order to maintain as much interconnectivity with the IPv4 Internet as possible, while solving problems such as the embedding of IP addresses at the application layer, double translation technology can be used. Since the stateless double translation and encapsulation technology can use the same address format, this chapter discusses the solutions of stateless double translation and encapsulation technologies together, including stateless double translation dIVI and MAP-T, as well as stateless encapsulation MAP-E.

10.1 Stateless Double Translation—Base Case

Stateless double translation technology (double IVI, dIVI) implements cascading single translations, i.e., from IPv4 to IPv6, and then from IPv6 to IPv4. Using the protocol translation and address mapping defined by RFC6219 [1], RFC6052 [2], and RFC7915 [3], there is no need for DNS64 and DNS46. The topology is as shown in Fig. 10.1.

10.1.1 Background

Stateless IPv4/IPv6 translation technology has better scalability and security, can maintain end-to-end address transparency, and supports bidirectional initiated communication (communication initiated by IPv6 clients in IPv6-only networks to servers on the IPv4 Internet, and communication initiated by clients on the IPv4 Internet to IPv6 servers in IPv6-only networks). However, some application layer protocols use IP addresses to identify application layer entities (such as FTP, H.323, etc.). In these cases, an Application Layer Gateway (ALG) is needed. But the ALG is

X. Li and C. Bao, *New IPv6 Transition Technology*,
https://doi.org/10.1007/978-981-95-8427-7_10

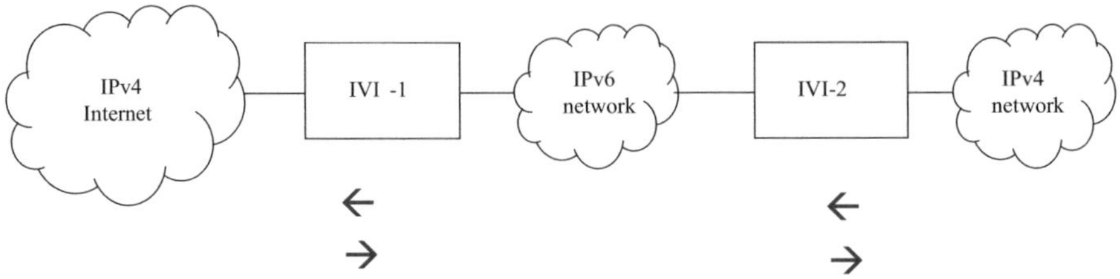

Fig. 10.1 Stateless double translation (dIVI)

bound to a specific application layer protocol, and different ALGs must be developed for different applications. For proprietary and encrypted applications, it is impossible to develop a corresponding ALG.

To address this issue, double translation technology is considered. Since double translation is from IPv4 to IPv6 and then back to IPv4, it can support any application layer protocol that can penetrate IPv4 NAT. In addition, even if the application does not have an IPv6 version, double translation technology can also be used.

Although double translation shares similarities with IPv4 over IPv6 tunneling, it can transition into a single translation, enabling interoperability between IPv4 and IPv6.

The characteristics of double translation are summarized as follows:

(1) It can support IPv4 services across the IPv6 network, and also support interconnection and interoperability between IPv4 and IPv6.
(2) The network can directly implement ACL and rate-limiting according to the IPv6 5-tuple without decapsulation.
(3) It does not require DNS64 and DNS46.

10.1.2 Basics of Stateless Double Translation

Stateless double translation (dIVI) can simply be regarded as the cascading of two stateless translation (IVI) translators, due to the introduction of two translators, it has greater flexibility for configuring addresses.

1. *Address Format*

Similar to IVI, the dIVI is recommended to use the address format without u-oct, as shown in Fig. 6.26. More discussion is in Chap. 6 of this book.

2. *Prefix Length Selection*

According to RFC6052 [2], the IPv6 prefixes lengths can be /32, /40, /48, /56, /64 and /96.

3. *IPv4-converted IPv6 address and IPv4-translatable IPv6 address use the same or different IPv6 prefixes*

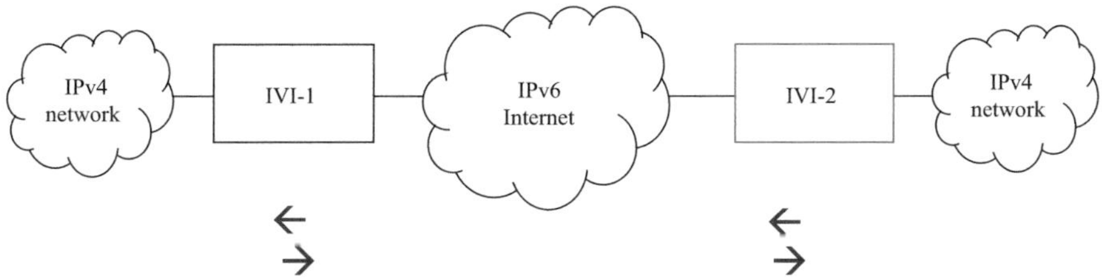

Fig. 10.2 dIVI (464VPN)

According to RFC6052 [2] "The 'IPv4-converted IPv6 address' and 'IPv4-translatable IPv6 address' should use the same IPv6 prefix."

However, there are exceptions to the rule of configuring the same IPv6 prefix for the "IPv4-translatable IPv6 address" and "IPv4-converted IPv6 address." When implementing cross-domain double translation, Internet routing policies usually do not allow the announcement of longer prefixes from other operators. In this case, different IPv6 prefixes must be configured for the "IPv4-translatable IPv6 address" and "IPv4-converted IPv6 address."

4. *Protocol Translation*

Protocol translation is carried out according to the rules defined by RFC7915 [3]. More discussion is in Chap. 5 of this book.

5. *464 Virtual Private Network (464VPN)*

For double translation technology, an important scenario is to build an IPv4-IPv6-IPv4 Virtual Private Network (464VPN) using private IPv4 addresses through the IPv6 Internet, as shown in Fig. 10.2.

In this scenario, different IPv6 prefixes must be configured for the "IPv4-translatable IPv6 address" and "IPv4-converted IPv6 address."

In this scenario, IPv4 addresses can use the private IPv4 addresses defined by RFC1918 [4], that is, using private IPv4 addresses to generate "IPv4-embedded IPv6 address" ("IPv4-translatable IPv6 address" and "IPv4-converted IPv6 address"). Therefore, it can be considered that dIVI technology extends the IPv4 private network to any place reachable by the IPv6 Internet.

When the "IPv4-translatable IPv6 address" is generated using the private IPv4 addresses defined by RFC1918 [4], an IPv4 NAT can be deployed at the IPv4 network to convert public IPv4 addresses to private IPv4 addresses, thus having similar characteristics to deploying traditional IPv4 NAT.

The characteristics of implementing 464VPN with dIVI are as follows:

(1) Applications do not need to be upgraded to IPv6, maintaining complete consistency with the original system.
(2) The original IPv4 security devices, mechanisms, and policies can continue to be used.

(3) The IPv6 Internet carries the standard IPv6 datagrams (no encapsulation or tunnel), so traffic engineering techniques can be used without decapsulation.
(4) When necessary, it can degrade to a single translation, but still retains the characteristics of a "private network," that is, only between "IPv4-translatable IPv6 addresses" can communicate.
(5) Compatible with high-level security protocols.

10.1.3 Stateless Double Translation Configuration

1. *Routing and Forwarding*

The routing configuration principle of dIVI is consistent with that of IVI.

Note: Dynamic routing protocols (such as BGP) can be configured to make IPv4 routing cross IPv6 networks, which is called 464BGP.

2. *Application Layer Gateway*

Double translation does not require ALG. In other words, any application layer protocol that can penetrate IPv4 NAT can penetrate dIVI.

3. *DNS Configuration*

Double translation does not require DNS64 and DNS46.

10.1.4 Stateless Double Translation Example

The topology and data flow of the dIVI example are shown in Fig. 10.3. The left side is the topology, and the right side is the source address and destination address of the datagram on this link.

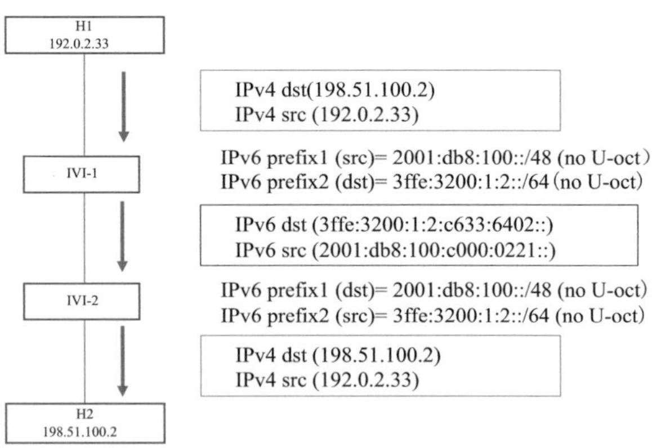

Fig. 10.3 dIVI example

1. *Scenario*

   (1) The IPv4 network (client H1) initiates access to the IPv4 Internet (server H2) through the IPv6 network.
   (2) The IPv4 Internet (client H2) initiates access to the IPv4 network (server H1) through the IPv6 network.

2. *dIVI Parameters*

   (1) Source IPv6 prefix of translator IVI-1: 2001:db8:100::/48.
   (2) Destination IPv6 prefix of translator IVI-1: 3ffe:3200:1:2::/64.
   (3) Destination IPv6 prefix of translator IVI-2: 2001:db8:100::/48.
   (4) Source IPv6 prefix of translator IVI-2: 3ffe:3200:1:2::/64.
   (5) IPv6 address format: no u-oct (RFC7915 [3] updates RFC6052 [2]).

3. *Host Address*

   (1) H1: An IPv4 host (192.0.2.33) in the IPv4 network.
   (2) H2: An IPv4 host (198.51.100.2) in the IPv4 Internet.

4. *Address Mapping*

   (1) "IPv4-translatable IPv6 address":

$$(192.0.2.33) \longleftrightarrow (2001:db8:100:c000:0221::)$$

   (2) "IPv4-converted IPv6 address":

$$(198.51.100.2) \longleftrightarrow (3ffe:3200:1:2:c633:6402::)$$

10.2 Stateless Double Translation—MAP-T

Stateless double translation with IPv4 address sharing (MAP-T) is defined in RFC7599 [5]. MAP-T does not require DNS64 and DNS46. The topology of MAP-T is shown in Fig. 10.4.

10.2.1 Background

In recent years, Internet service providers have provided new deployment experiences based on stateless IPv4/IPv6 translation technology (such as RFC6219 [1]), indicating that the communication between IPv6-only host and existing IPv4 hosts can be ensured without the need to deploy end-to-end IPv4/IPv6 dual stacks. Therefore, it is possible to deploy IPv6-only networks without losing connectivity to the

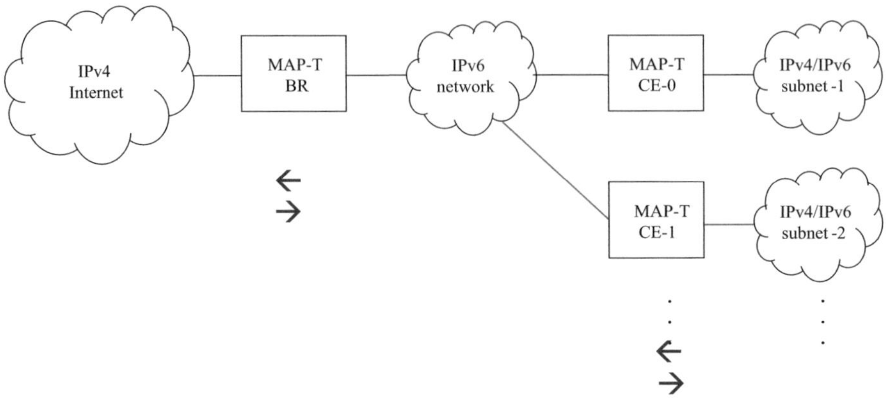

Fig. 10.4 MAP-T

IPv4 Internet. However, due to the exhaustion of public IPv4 addresses, it is necessary to extend RFC6052 [2] and RFC7915 [3] to support shared IPv4 addresses. At the same time, to solve the problem of application layer gateways, it is recommended to use double IPv4/IPv6 translation technology for this scenario.

At the same time, in order to achieve better scalability and security goals, researchers consider introducing stateless technology into IPv4 over IPv6 tunnels. This ultimately led to the IETF's unified stateless 464 technology, including the stateless double translation (MAP-T, RFC7599 [3, 5]) and the stateless encapsulation (MAP-E, RFC7597 [6, 7]. Both technologies support mesh and hub and spoke topology.

The advantages of translation technology are as follows:

(1) Less overhead compared to encapsulation.
(2) Standard IPv6 processing technology can be used for ACL and rate-limiting without decapsulation.
(3) IPv4-only clients can communicate with IPv6-only servers.
(4) In the later stages of the migration from IPv4 to IPv6, IPv6 networks will be very common, but users will still need to access some remaining IPv4 hosts. Therefore, MAP-T can degrade from double translation to single translation, achieving interconnection and interoperability between IPv4 and IPv6.

RFC7598 [8] defines the DHCPv6 options for configuring MAP-T parameters, and the technical details are referred to in Chap. 8 of this book.

The stateful double translation technology is called 464XLAT, defined by RFC8683 [1, 9], and its technical details are referred to in Chap. 11 of this book.

10.2.2 Basics of MAP-T

MAP-T is deployed in an IPv6-only network, but providing IPv4/IPv6 dual-stack services. In this way, service providers can transition to IPv6 first, regardless of whether users turn off IPv4. In addition, the newly built IPv6-only network can continue to provide IPv4 services (IPv4aaS) using MAP-T technology.

According to the above requirements, the MAP-T mechanism also supports users using shared IPv4 addresses, full IPv4 addresses, or IPv4 prefixes.

MAP-T is constructed using existing standard components.

(1) The NAPT function defined by RFC2663 [10] is used on CE to limit the range of transport layer TCP/UDP port numbers, ICMP identifiers, and fragment identifiers. For datagrams issued from a private IPv4 network, the built-in NAPT function of the CE must transform the transport layer port numbers (for example, TCP and UDP port numbers) to be within the port range designated for that CE. This process is consistent with MAP-E defined by RFC7597 [6].
(2) NAPT must be connected to the IPv4/IPv6 stateless translation function of the CE, using the function defined by RFC7915 [3] to translate datagrams (including IPv4/IPv6 addresses and transport layer TCP/UDP ports).

The MAP-T architecture requires that shared IPv4 addresses can only be used as the external global address of the NAPT running on the CE, and must never be used to identify network interfaces. Theoretically, if the ISP's protocol stack and application system support the use of restricted transport layer ports, the shared IPv4 address could also serve as the host interface address. However, this would bring significant changes and potential risks to the IP model defined by RFC6250 [11], so it should not be handled this way at present.

For full IPv4 addresses or IPv4 prefixes, the IP model defined by RFC6250 [11] remains unchanged. In this case, the full IPv4 address or IPv4 prefix can be used as it is now (for example, to identify network interfaces or as the IPv4 address pool for DHCP). Furthermore, in this case, there is no need to use NAPT to limit the transport layer ports of datagrams obtained through mapping.

Internet service providers assign a regular IPv6 prefix to each MAP-T CE. Based on the configuration rules of the MAP-T domain, the MAP-T IPv6 address and the corresponding IPv4 address can be calculated. To share IPv4 addresses, the port numbers of transport layer protocols (TCP, UDP) must be used, so the MAP-T CE also needs to configure PSID. Each MAP-T CE is responsible for forwarding traffic between datagrams generated by the user's private IPv4 address and datagrams generated by the IPv6 address of the MAP-T domain. This forwarding is based on stateless translation technology (RFC7915 [3]).

The MAP-T BR connects one or more MAP-T domains to the external IPv4 Internet; that is, it forwards traffic between IPv6 datagrams of the MAP-T domain and IPv4 datagrams. This forwarding is based on stateless translation technology (RFC7915 [3]).

Compared with the encapsulation technology of IPv4 over IPv6 used by MAP-E, MAP-T uses translation technology for two purposes: firstly, to reduce encapsulation overhead and allow the use of regular IPv6 network tools, such as ACL, rate-limiting, etc., to control IPv4 traffic; secondly, to allow IPv4-only nodes to communicate directly with IPv6-only servers (using the "IPv4-translatable IPv6 address" defined by RFC6052 [2]) in the MAP-T domain.

10.2.3 MAP-T Mapping Algorithm

MAP-T nodes are configured with one or more mapping rules.

According to the functions that need to be implemented, MAP-T can be configured with different mapping rules. Each MAP-T node must be configured with basic mapping rules, and can also be configured with additional mapping rules. Basic mapping rules are used to configure IPv4 addresses, IPv4 prefixes, or shared IPv4 addresses. Basic mapping rules can also be used for forwarding, that is, mapping the IPv4 address and (optional) port to the IPv6 address. Additional forwarding mapping rules allow direct communication between different IPv4 subnets within a MAP-T domain. If its IPv4 address does not match either the "basic mapping rule" or the "additional mapping rule" (using the longest prefix match algorithm), it is considered external traffic to the MAP-T domain and is forwarded to the MAP-T's BR by default.

MAP-T defines two types of mapping rules.

(1) Basic Mapping Rule (BMR): Mandatory, used for address mapping and forwarding. A CE can configure multiple IPv6 prefixes for end users. Each end user's IPv6 prefix can only be configured with one basic mapping rule. However, all end users of the CE who have the same mapping rule after aggregation can share the same basic mapping rule. Combined with the end user's IPv6 prefix, the basic mapping rule is used to configure the IPv4 prefix, IPv4 address or shared IPv4 address and PSID assigned to the CE.
(2) Forwarding Mapping Rule (FMR): Optional, used for forwarding. Basic mapping rules can also serve as forwarding mapping rules. Each forwarding mapping rule will establish an entry for the IPv4 prefix rule in the rule library. Given the IPv4 destination address and transport layer port within the MAP-T domain, the MAP-T node routes the datagram according to the matching FMR and forwards it to the target network corresponding to the IPv4 destination address and transport layer port. FMR is not required in hub-and-spoke mode.

BMR and FMR share the same parameters.

(1) IPv6 prefix (including prefix length).
(2) IPv4 prefix (including prefix length).
(3) EA-bits length (number of bits).

The MAP-T node finds the end user's IPv6 prefix in the BMR by executing the longest match algorithm, which is used for the allocation of the IPv4 prefix, IPv4 address, or shared IPv4 address. The IPv6 address of MAP-T is generated by the IPv6 prefix defined by BMR. This IPv6 address must be assigned to the network interface of the MAP-T node, serving as the IPv4/IPv6 translation node for MAP-T traffic. Port-restricted IPv4 routing also exists in all FMRs, and the default route exists in the MAP-T BR.

FMR is used for direct communication between MAP-T CEs, known as mesh mode. In hub-and-spoke mode, an independent FMR is not required, and all traffic must be sent directly to the MAP-T BR. Although FMR is optional, meaning that a MAP CE can configure 0 or more FMRs, all MAP-T CEs must implement support for both BMR and FMR.

1. *Port Mapping Algorithm*

The port mapping algorithm is used for the MAP-T domain with shared IPv4 addresses which is defined in Chap. 6 of this book [5, 6, 12]. The relationship between PSID and transport layer ports is shown in Fig. 6.40.

2. *Basic Mapping Rules*

The basic mapping rules are mandatory, and the configuration of MAP-T BR and MAP-T CE is as follows:

(1) IPv6 prefix (including prefix length).
(2) IPv4 prefix (including prefix length).
(3) EA-bits length (number of bits).

MAP-T CE also needs to configure IPv4 address or shared IPv4 address.

Figure 6.55 shows the full MAP-T IPv6 address format. More discussion is in Chap. 6 of this book.

All CEs using the same BMR need to configure the same IPv6 prefix.

(1) The EA-bits field represents the parameters of the IPv4 address and transport layer port corresponding to this MAP-T CE.
(2) The EA-bits field is unique for the IPv6 prefix and can contain a full IPv4 address or shared IPv4 address. In the case of shared IPv4 addresses, it also contains PSID.
(3) An EA-bits field length of 0 means that all relevant MAP-T's IPv4 address information is directly passed in the BMR, not derived from the EA-bits field in the end-user IPv6 prefix.

The IPv6 address of MAP-T is composed by combining the end-user IPv6 prefix, MAP-T subnet ID, and the specified interface identifier.

The MAP subnet identifier is defined as the first subnet, i.e., $s = 0$.

Definition: $r =$ IPv4 prefix length given by BMR; $o =$ EA-bits field length given by BMR; $p =$ IPv4 suffix length contained in the EA-bits field, $p = o - q$.

If the length of r is 0, the full IPv4 address or prefix will be encoded with EA-bits. If EA-bits only contains shared IPv4 address, the IPv4 prefix is provided to the CE in other ways (such as DHCPv6 options). The IPv4 prefix (r) and the IPv4 suffix in EA-bits (p) are concatenated into an IPv4 address or IPv4 prefix.

The offset of the EA-bits field in the IPv6 address is equal to the prefix length of IPv6 in the BMR. The length of the EA-bits field (o) is given by the length of EA-bits in the BMR, with a value of 0 ~ 48. A length of 48 means that the full IPv4 address and transport layer port (only a single port assigned) are embedded in the end-user IPv6 prefix. A length of 0 means that no IPv4 address or transport layer port is embedded in the end-user IPv6 prefix. The sum of the IPv6 prefix length and EA-bits length must be less than or equal to the length of the end-user IPv6 prefix.

(1) If $o + r < 32$ (the length of the IPv4 address in bits), it means that an IPv4 prefix is assigned, as shown in Fig. 6.49
(2) If $o + r = 32$, then it means a full IPv4 address has been assigned. This address is formed by combining the IPv4 prefix and EA-bits, as shown in Fig. 6.50.
(3) If $o + r > 32$, then it means a shared IPv4 address has been assigned. The number of IPv4 address suffix bits in the EA-bits is $p = 32 - r$. The PSID bit field is used to create a port set. The length of the PSID bit field in the EA-bits is $q = o - p$, as shown in Fig. 6.51.

The length of r can be 32, which means that the IPv4 address is not embedded in the EA-bits. This means that there is no dependency between the IPv4 address and the IPv6 address. In addition, the length of o can be 0 (no EA-bits are embedded in the end-user IPv6 prefix), which means that other mechanisms (such as DHCPv6) need to be used to configure the PSID.

3. *Forwarding Mapping Rules*

Forwarding mapping rules are optional and are only used in mesh mode to implement direct communication from CE to CE.

Adding forwarding mapping rules will add IPv4 routes in the IPv4 prefix in the rule table, as shown in Fig. 6.52. More discussion is in Chap. 6 of this book.

4. *Default Route*

The default route refers to its datagram's destination address being the entire Internet outside the MAP-T domain.

The IPv4 traffic sent by the MAP-T node is converted into IPv6 traffic within the MAP-T domain. The source address of the IPv6 datagram is the source node's MAP-T IPv6 address derived from the basic mapping rules, and the destination address of the IPv6 datagram is the receiving node's MAP-T IPv6 address derived from the forwarding mapping rules.

The IPv4 destination address outside the MAP-T domain is the "IPv4-converted IPv6 address" derived from RFC6052 [2] and the MAP-T BR IPv6 prefix. When the MAP-T CE sends traffic to any such destination address, the source address of the IPv6 datagram is the IPv6 address of MAP-T, and the destination address is the "IPv4-converted IPv6 address." Note that this address mapping follows the MAP-T DMR, whose IPv6 prefix is the IPv6 prefix of the MAP-T BR. A typical MAP-T CE will configure an IPv4 default route using the DMR. The MAP-T BR will convert datagrams with external IPv4 source addresses to the IPv6 domain of MAP-T.

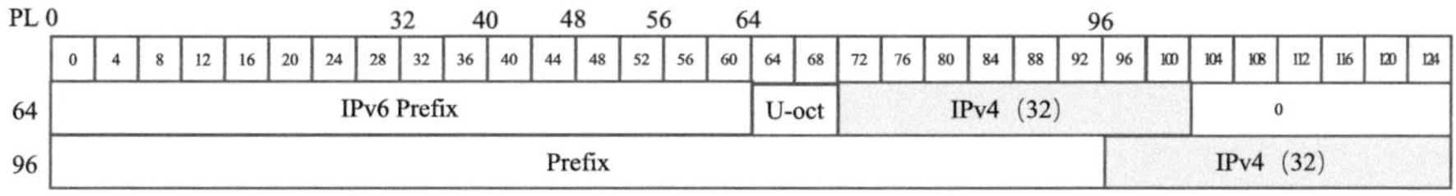

Fig. 10.5 DMR address format (with u-oct)

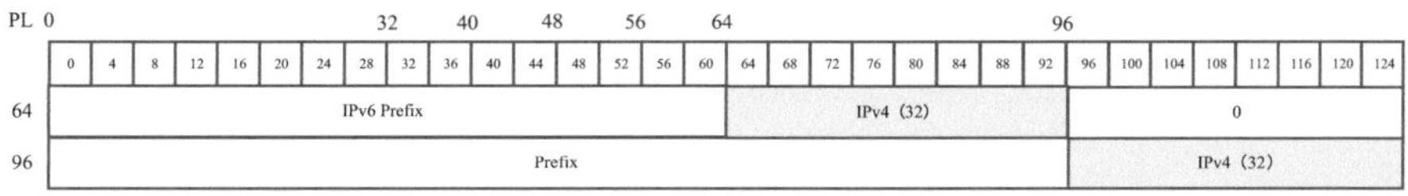

Fig. 10.6 DMR address format (without u-oct)

By default, the DMR IPv6 prefix length should be 64 bits and should not exceed 96 bits in any case. The mapping rule for the "IPv4-converted IPv6 address" defaults to following RFC6052 [2] with a /64 suffix of 0×0. The recommended DMR address format (you can choose a 64-bit prefix length with or without u-oct, or a 96-bit prefix length) is shown in Fig. 10.5.

Considering the update of RFC7915 [3] to RFC6052 [2], the recommended DMR address format (you can choose a 64-bit prefix length without u-oct, or a 96-bit prefix length) is shown in Fig. 10.6.

5. *IPv6 Interface Identifier*

The interface identifier format of the MAP-T node is shown in Fig. 10.7.

For the IPv4 prefix, the IPv4 address field is right-padded with 0 (total 32 bits), and the PSID field is left-padded with 0 (total 16 bits). For the IPv4 prefix or the full IPv4 address, the PSID field is 0.

If the final user's IPv6 prefix length is greater than 64 bits, the left side of the interface identifier will be overwritten by the part of the IPv6 prefix that exceeds 64 bits.

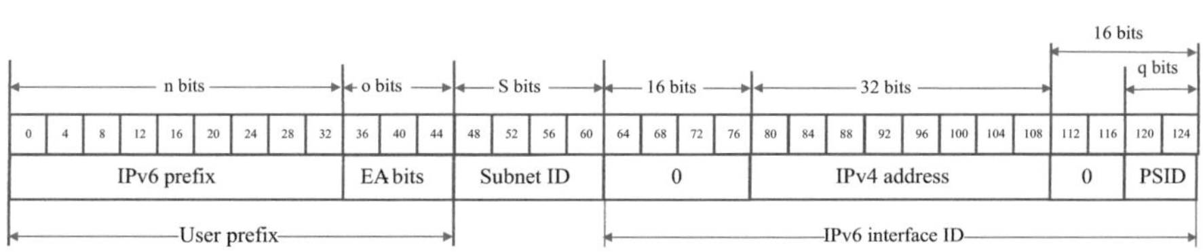

Fig. 10.7 IPv6 interface identifier

10.2.4 MAP-T Configuration

For a given MAP-T domain, both BR and CE must configure the parameters specified by this MAP-T domain.

(1) Basic mapping rules and (optional) forwarding mapping rules, including IPv6 prefix, IPv4 prefix, and EA-bits length.
(2) Choose to use hub-and-spoke mode (all traffic is sent to BR) or mesh mode (supporting direct communication from CE to CE).
(3) Use IPv4/IPv6 stateless translation technology (RFC7915 [3]).
(4) Configure the IPv6 prefix used in DMR by BR.

1. *MAP-T CE*

   In the same MAP-T domain, all CE parameter configurations must be consistent. There are currently several ways to configure parameters.

   (1) Through IPv6 DHCPv6 option extension (RFC7598 [8]).
   (2) Based on the Broadband Forum's "TR-69" standard.
   (3) XML-based objects retrieved after establishing an IPv6 connection.
   (4) Manual configuration by the administrator.
   (5) Others.

In addition to the MAP-T configuration parameters, MAP-T CE also needs an IPv6 prefix. This is the final user's IPv6 prefix, used to access the IPv6 Internet. This IPv6 prefix configuration should also use the above methods.

The relevant configuration parameters of MAP-T (including IPv4 services) need to be bound to the full lifecycle of the IPv6 prefix assigned to the user. That is, the IPv4 address of MAP-T, or IPv4 prefix, or shared IPv4 address; transport layer port range; and any parameters related to authorization and audit, are all bound to the full lifecycle of the user's IPv6 prefix.

A single MAP-T CE can also connect to multiple MAP-T domains, just like any router may have multiple upstream IPv4 service providers (the IPv4 address of each network interface is assigned by their respective DHCP). Each MAP-T domain requires a specific final user IPv6 prefix. The network interface corresponding to the CE corresponds to different MAP-T domains, gets the corresponding MAP-T parameters, and generates the corresponding IPv4 prefix, IPv4 address, or shared IPv4 address.

2. *MAP-T BR*

The MAP-T BR must configure the mapping rules of this MAP-T domain.

For increased reliability and load balancing, the BR IPv6 prefix MAY be shared across a given MAP domain. As MAP is stateless, any BR may be used for forwarding to/from the domain at any time.

Since MAP-T uses the address space of the ISP, there is no need to publish refined routes of IPv6 or IPv4 to external networks through BGP. Note that if the MAP-E BR uses an anycast IPv6 address, the corresponding anycast address must be announced in the ISP's IGP.

10.2.5 Data Plane Processing Considerations

The end-to-end data packet forwarding in MAP-T involves MAP-T CE and MAP-T BR, from IPv4 to IPv6 or from IPv6 to IPv4, which will be discussed separately below.

1. *IPv4 to IPv6 in MAP-T CE*

When MAP-T CE receives an IPv4 packet, it should perform network address port translation 44 (NAPT44) and create a NAPT44 binding. The source address and transport layer source port range of the data packet generated by NAPT44 must be consistent with the source address and transport layer source port assigned to the MAP-T CE by the basic mapping rules of MAP-T.

IPv4 packets determine the parameters of the IPv4/IPv6 stateless translation function according to MAP-T rules and the longest prefix match principle (matching the IPv4 destination address plus port set identifier). By default, all traffic matches with DMR and performs IPv4/IPv6 stateless translation according to DMR parameters. Data packets may match (optional) forwarding mapping rules and perform IPv4/IPv6 stateless translation according to FMR parameters. In all cases, the IPv6 address of the MAP-T CE is the source address of the data packet.

MAP-T CE must support basic mapping rules and should support one or more forwarding mapping rules.

2. *IPv6 to IPv4 in MAP-T CE*

When MAP-T CE receives an IPv6 packet, it performs its regular IPv6 operations (filtering, pre-routing, etc.). Only the data packets whose destination address is the IPv6 address of MAP-T CE and whose source address matches DMR or FMR based on the longest prefix match principle are processed by MAP-T CE. MAP-T CE must check the transport layer target port number of each received data packet to see if it is within the range allowed by BMR configuration. MAP-T CE must discard any unqualified data packets and count them. When MAP-T CE receives an IPv6 packet with address that matches FMR via the longest prefix match principle, it must first check the transport layer source port number. If the port number is outside the allowed range, the CE discards the packet and replies with an ICMPv6 Destination Unreachable message. This message indicates a violation of the ingress/egress policy, specifying parameters: Type = 1, Code = 5.

For each data packet processed by MAP-T, the IPv4/IPv6 translation function of MAP-T CE must calculate the corresponding IPv4 destination address and IPv4 source address. The IPv4 destination address extracts relevant information from the IPv6 address through BMR parameters. The IPv4 address is extracted from the IPv6 address by matching DMR or FMR based on the longest prefix match principle. Then the data packet is processed using IPv4/IPv6 translation technology.

The generated IPv4 packet is then forwarded to the NAPT44 function of MAP-T CE. The IPv4 destination address and transport layer target port number must be mapped to the original values of the data stream.

3. *IPv6 to IPv4 in MAP-T BR*

When MAP-T BR receives an IPv6 packet, it must select a matching rule on MAP-T BR for its address based on the longest prefix match principle. Based on the transport layer port set identifier obtained from the source address, the selected matching rule enables MAP-T BR to check whether its IPv4 address and transport layer port are legal. Therefore, MAP-T BR must check the legality of the data packet source address. If the transport layer source port of the data packet is not within the allowed range, MAP-T BR must discard the data packet, count it, and reply with ICMPv6 Destination Unreachable, indicating "source address does not comply with ingress/egress policy," with specific parameters: Type = 1, Code = 5.

When constructing an IPv4 packet, MAP-T BR must generate an IPv4 source address and IPv4 destination address, translate the header according to RFC7915 [3], and perform regular IPv4 forwarding with the resulting output.

4. *IPv4 to IPv6 in MAP-T BR*

When the MAP-T BR receives an IPv4 datagram, it uses the longest prefix match method to match the destination IPv4 address and transport layer port, finding the corresponding FMR and DMR for this MAP-T domain. The MAP-T BR must calculate the IPv6 destination address and transport layer port based on the selected FMR, the IPv4 destination address, and the transport layer port. The MAP-T BR must also calculate the source address of the IPv6 datagram (IPv4-converted IPv6 address) based on the source address of the IPv4 datagram and the IPv6 prefix of the MAP-T BR. When constructing the IPv6 datagram, the MAP-T BR must generate the IPv6 source address and IPv6 destination address, translate the header according to RFC7915 [3], and then perform regular IPv6 forwarding.

Note: When there is no sharing of IPv4 addresses, MAP-T is just a regular stateless IPv4/IPv6 translator.

5. *ICMP Processing*

Both MAP-T CE and MAP-T BR must follow the ICMP/ICMPv6 translation rules defined by RFC7915 [3]. Unlike TCP and UDP protocol ports (which have two 16-bit fields to identify the source port and target port), the headers of ICMP and ICMPv6, defined by RFC792 [13] and RFC4443 [14] respectively, only have one 16-bit identification field. Therefore, after receiving an IPv4 ICMP message, the MAP-T CE must rewrite the ICMP identification field calculated from the transport layer port set.

When the MAP-T BR receives an ICMP message with a shared IPv4 address, it must use its identification to replace the transport layer target port number to determine the IPv6 destination address. In all other cases, the MAP-T BR does not need identification information when calculating the destination IPv6 address.

6. *Fragmentation Handling and Path MTU Discovery*

Due to the different sizes of IPv4 and IPv6 headers, any device installed between IPv4 and IPv6 networks must have the ability to handle MTU. There are three mechanisms to address this issue.

(1) Path MTU Discovery (PMTUD).
(2) Fragmentation.
(3) Transport layer negotiation, such as the TCP MSS option defined by RFC879 [15].

MAP-T uses the above three mechanisms to handle different situations.

Note: The protocol translation mechanism defined by RFC7915 [3] is not completely lossless. For example, when communication initiated by IPv4 traverses double translation, any ICMP independent path MTU discovery originating from IPv4 (RFC4821 [16]) will not be entirely reliable. This is because the combination of DF = 1/MF = 1 defined in RFC4821 [16] will result in DF = 0/MF = 1 after double translation.

(1) Fragmentation handling within the MAP-T domain. Encapsulating IPv4 datagrams in the MAP-T domain will increase their size (usually by 20 octets). Therefore, it is strongly recommended to properly manage MTU in the MAP-T domain, i.e., by configuring the MAP-T CE WAN interface to avoid fragmentation.
(2) For IPv4 packets entering the MAP-T domain, fragmentation is handled according to the rules of RFC7915 [3].
(3) Receiving IPv4 fragments at the boundary of the MAP-T domain. IPv4 datagrams received from outside the MAP-T domain require the IPv4 destination address and transport layer target port. However, transport layer protocol information is only available in the first fragment of the received datagram. So as with RFC6346 [17], it is stated that when a MAP-T node receives IPv4 datagram fragments from the outside, it must reassemble them before sending the datagram to the MAP-T link. If the first datagram fragment received by the MAP-T node contains transport layer protocol information, it can use a cache and forward subsequent fragments of the same datagram based on the information in the cache. Users of MAP-T should be aware of the fact that there are attacks against datagram fragmentation (RFC1858 [18], RFC3128 [19]). Users of MAP-T should also be aware of other issues with high-speed reassembly of datagrams (RFC4963 [20]).
(4) Sending IPv4 fragments to the outside. If IPv4 hosts inside two different MAP-T CEs with the same IPv4 address send datagram fragments to the same external IPv4 destination host, these hosts may use the same IPv4 fragment identifier, resulting in fragment reassembly errors at the IPv4 destination host. Given that the IPv4 fragment identifier is also a 16-bit field, it can be analogous to the

transport layer port range. Therefore, compared to the rate of sending fragments, if the fragment identifier space is large enough, then MAP-T CE can rewrite the IPv4 fragment identifier to the numerical range defined by PSID. However, this method increases the probability of conflicts during fragment reassembly (RFC6864 [21]).

10.2.6 NAT44 Considerations

The NAT44 implemented in MAP-T CE should comply with the behaviors defined in RFC4787 [22], RFC5508 [23], RFC5382 [24]. In the IPv4 address sharing mode of MAP-T, NAT44 must limit the transport layer port number range according to the basic mapping rules.

10.2.7 Other Considerations

1. *EA-bits length is 0*

The MAP-T solution supports a configuration where the length of EA-bits is 0, which means that the user's IPv6 prefix and IPv4 address (and/or) transport layer port range are independent of each other. In this case, the PSID information can be obtained from the BMR. The constraint for this use case is that each MAP-T domain can only have one MAP-T CE. The MAP-T BR provides services for multiple MAP-T domains, each with only one MAP-T CE. Note: The MAP-T BR must configure an FMR for each MAP-T CE to associate the given MAP-T CE's IPv6 prefix and IPv4 address + optional PSID.

2. *Mesh and Hub-Spoke Modes*

In the hub-spoke mode, all traffic sent by the MAP-T CE is forwarded through the MAP-T BR; while in the mesh mode, the MAP-T CE can directly forward traffic to another MAP-T CE. By default, the MAP-T CE only has a BMR, so it only supports the hub-spoke mode. To support the mesh mode, the corresponding FMR needs to be configured.

3. *Communication with IPv6-only Servers in the MAP-T Domain*

By default, MAP-T supports any communication between IPv4 and IPv4, as well as between IPv6 and IPv6, and it also supports communication between IPv4 and IPv6 under "specific circumstances." The "specific circumstances" here refer to the IPv6 server configured with an "IPv4-translatable IPv6 address." This address uses the IPv6 prefix of the MAP-T domain DMR. Such IPv6-only servers (for example, HTTP servers or web content caching devices) can serve both IPv6-only users and IPv4-only users in this MAP-T domain. These IPv6-only servers should not only configure AAAA records in the authoritative DNS, but also configure A records.

When these IPv6-only servers need to communicate with the IPv4 Internet, they need to use DNS64 (RFC6147 [25]).

4. *Compatibility with Other IPv4/IPv6 Translation Technologies*

The IPv4/IPv6 translator in MAP-T CE can interconnect with the stateful IPv4/IPv6 translator (NAT64: RFC6146 [26]) deployed in network operators. In this case, the DMR prefix of MAP-T CE is the corresponding prefix of the NAT64 device. This effectively allows MAP-T CE to utilize NAT64 devices, playing the role of client translation (CLAT) defined by RFC6877 [27]. In other words, the default mode of MAP-T CE is to communicate with MAP-T BR, but when necessary, it can switch to the IPv6 prefix of NAT64 and use NAT64 to communicate with IPv4 devices.

10.2.8 Security Considerations

Spoofing attacks: By checking the consistency between IPv4 and IPv6 data sources at MAP-T nodes, MAP-T does not introduce new deception attacks.

Denial of Service (DoS) Attacks: Any IPv4 address sharing mechanism carries the risk of DoS attacks. It is recommended to accelerate the deployment of IPv6 to reduce the use of IPv4 address sharing mechanisms.

Routing Loop Attacks: Routing loop attacks may exist in the "automatic tunneling" mechanism (RFC6324 [28]), but MAP-T can avoid routing loop attacks because each MAP-T BR checks the source address of the received IPv6 datagram according to the "forwarding rules."

Attacks facilitated by restricted port set: For hosts that have not performed input filtering (RFC2827 [29]), attackers can inject deceptive datagrams into the host using the transport layer ports of existing outbound connections (RFC4953 [30], RFC5961 [31], RFC6056 [32]). The success of the attack depends on whether the attacker can guess which transport layer ports the host is currently using. To reduce such attacks, the NAT44 of MAP-T CE can be configured with "address-dependent filtering" (RFC4787 [1]). In addition, it is recommended that MAP-T CE use DNS transport proxy (RFC5625 [33]) to handle DNS queries, that is, through IPv6-only, not through the IPv4 of MAP-T domain restricted transport layer ports for DNS queries. RFC6269 [34] outlines other issues and considerations with IPv4 address sharing.

10.2.9 MAP-T Example

The topology and data flow of the MAP-T example are shown in Fig. 10.8. The left side is the topology, and the right side is the source and destination addresses of the datagrams on this link.

1. *Scenario*

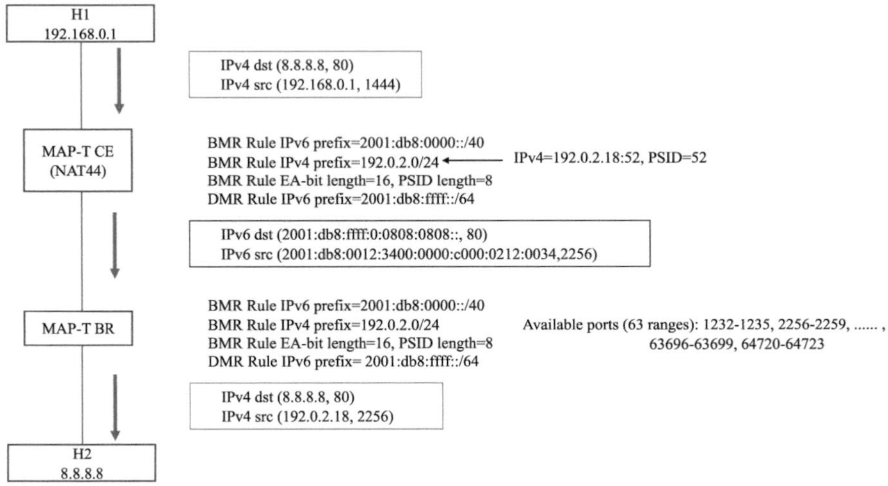

Fig. 10.8 MAP-T example

An IPv4 network (client H1) initiates access to the IPv4 Internet (server H2) through the IPv6 network.

2. *MAP-T Parameters*

(1) Basic mapping rules.
① Rule IPv6 prefix: 2001:db8:0000::/40.
② Rule IPv4 prefix: 192.0.2.0/24.
③ Rule EA-bit length: 16.
④ PSID length: 8 (multiplexing ratio of 256); PSID offset: 6 (default).
(2) Default mapping rule: 2001:db8:ffff::/64.

3. *Host Address*

(1) H1: An IPv4 host in the IPv4 network (192.168.0.1).
(2) H2: An IPv4 host in the IPv4 Internet (8.8.8.8).

4. *Address Mapping*

(1) EA-bits offset: 40.
(2) IPv4 suffix bits (p): IPv4 address length (32)—IPv4 prefix length (24) = 8.
(3) PSID start: $40 + p = 40 + 8 = 48$.
(4) PSID length (q): (User prefix length—Rule IPv6 prefix length) $-p = (56-40) - 8 = 8$.
(5) Available port range (63): 1232~1235, 2256~2259, ..., 63,696~63,699, 64,720~64,723.
The IPv4 address in this example: 192.0.2.18 (0xc0000212).
The PSID in this example: 0x34.
(6) User IPv6 prefix: 2001:db8:0012:3400::/56.
(7) MAP CE IPv6 address: 2001:db8:0012:3400:0000:c000:0212:0034.

10.3 Stateless Tunnel—MAP-E

Stateless tunnel (encapsulation) (MAP-E) implements IPv4 over IPv6 encapsulation and decapsulation in the process of transmitting datagrams from source to destination, and has address and port mapping, as defined by RFC7597 [6]. MAP-E does not require domain name extension, and the topology is shown in Fig. 10.9.

10.3.1 Background

The mechanism used by MAP-E can be traced back to the mid-1990s (RFC1933 [35], RFC4213 [36]). RFC1933 [35] first described the "automatic tunnel" mechanism, which assigns a host an IPv6 address composed of an IPv6 "well-known prefix" and an embedded host IPv4 address. Since the IPv4 address is embedded in the IPv6 destination address, any node can automatically establish an IPv6 over IPv4 tunnel by extracting the IPv4 address to transmit IPv6 datagrams to the IPv4 tunnel endpoint.

This idea has led to many different technologies, such as 6over4 defined by RFC2529 [37], 6to4 defined by RFC3056 [38], ISATAP defined by RFC5214 [39], and 6rd defined by RFC5969 [40].

These IPv6 over IPv4 mechanisms all have the following characteristics.

(1) Automatically configure IPv6 addresses or prefixes for hosts or sites.
(2) Automatically or implicitly configure IPv4 addresses for tunnel endpoints. Given an IPv6 destination address, the IPv4 tunnel endpoint address can be calculated.
(3) Embed all or shared IPv4 addresses into the IPv6 address.

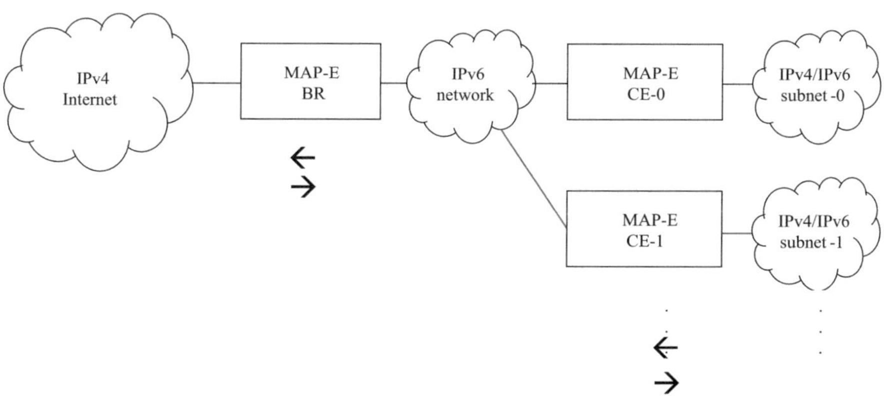

Fig. 10.9 MAP-E

For IPv4 over IPv6, a similar method can be used, that is, to establish an algorithm-based mapping relationship between the IPv4 prefix, the full IPv4 address, or the shared IPv4 address and the IPv6 address.

The external characteristics of the stateless double translation technology are enabling IPv4 to cross IPv6 networks. This led to the IETF releasing the unified stateless 464 technology, which includes the MAP-T stateless double translation technology (RFC7599 [5]) and the MAP-E stateless encapsulation technology (RFC7597 [6]). Both technologies support mesh and hub-and-spoke topology.

The advantage of encapsulation technology is that it can completely transmit special information in the IPv4 header, such as the IPv4 option. However, encapsulation technology has a larger header overhead than double translation, and it cannot use standard IPv6 processing technology for ACL and rate-limiting, nor can it degrade into a single translation technology; thus, it cannot achieve interconnection and intercommunication between IPv4 and IPv6.

RFC7598 [8] defines the DHCPv6 option for configuring MAP-E parameters, and the technical details are referred to in Chap. 8 of this book.

The stateful tunnel technology is called DS-Lite, defined by RFC6333 [41], and the technical details are referred to in Chap. 11 of this book.

10.3.2 Basics of MAP-E

MAP-E is based on an IPv6-only network and provides IPv4/IPv6 dual-stack access services. In this way, operators can transit the network infrastructure to IPv6 first and can still provide IPv4 services (IPv4aaS) using MAP-E technology.

According to the above requirements, the MAP-E mechanism supports users using shared IPv4 addresses, full IPv4 addresses, or IPv4 prefixes.

Similar to MAP-T, MAP-E is constructed using existing standard components.

(1) The NAPT function defined by RFC2663 [10] is used on the CE to limit the transport layer port number.
(2) NAPT must be connected to the CE's IPv4 over IPv6 forwarding function, using the function defined by RFC2473 [7, 42] to encapsulate/decapsulate datagrams.

The MAP-E architecture requires that shared IPv4 addresses can only be used as the external global address of the NAPT running on the CE, and must never be used to identify network interfaces.

For the full IPv4 address or IPv4 prefix, the IP model defined by RFC6250 [11] remains unchanged.

Internet service providers assign a regular IPv6 prefix to each MAP-E CE. Based on the configuration rules of the MAP-E domain, the MAP-E IPv6 address and the corresponding IPv4 address can be calculated. To share IPv4 addresses, port numbers of the transport layer protocol (TCP, UDP) must be used, so MAP-E CE also needs to configure PSID. Each MAP-E CE is responsible for forwarding traffic between datagrams generated by the user's private IPv4 address and datagrams generated by the IPv6 address of the MAP-E domain. This forwarding is based on IPv4 over IPv6 encapsulation (RFC2473 [7]).

The MAP-E BR connects one or more MAP-E domains to the external IPv4 Internet; that is, it forwards traffic between IPv6 datagrams of the MAP-E domain and IPv4 datagrams. This forwarding is based on IPv4 over IPv6 encapsulation (RFC2473 [7]).

10.3.3 MAP-E Mapping Algorithm

The MAP-E node is configured with one or more mapping rules.

Depending on the functionality to be implemented, MAP-E can configure different mapping rules. Each MAP-E node must configure a basic mapping rule and can also configure additional mapping rules. The basic mapping rule is used to configure IPv4 addresses, IPv4 prefixes, or shared IPv4 addresses. The basic mapping rule can also be used for forwarding, that is, mapping the IPv4 destination address and (optional) target port to the IPv6 address. Additional mapping rules allow multiple different IPv4 subnets to exist within a MAP-E domain, and traffic forwarding between these IPv4 subnets can be optimized according to the additional mapping rules. If its IPv4 destination address does not match the above basic mapping rules and additional mapping rules (using the longest prefix match algorithm), it is considered external traffic to the MAP-E domain and is forwarded to the MAP-E BR by default.

MAP-E defines the following two types of mapping rules.

(1) Basic mapping rule: mandatory, used for address mapping and forwarding. A CE can configure multiple IPv6 prefixes for end users. Each end user's IPv6 prefix can only configure one basic mapping rule. However, the IPv6 prefixes of all end users clustered by the CE with the same mapping rules can share the same basic mapping rule. Combined with the end user's IPv6 prefix, the basic mapping rule is used to export the IPv4 prefix, IPv4 address, or shared IPv4 address and PSID assigned to the CE.
(2) Forwarding mapping rule: optional, used for forwarding. The basic mapping rule can also serve as a forwarding mapping rule. Each forwarding mapping rule will establish an entry for the IPv4 prefix rule in the rule library. Given the IPv4 destination address and transport layer port within the MAP-E domain, the MAP-E node routes and forwards the datagram to the network target corresponding to the IPv4 destination address and transport layer port according to the matching FMR. No FMR is required in hub-and-spoke mode.

The BMR and FMR mapping rules share the same parameters: ① IPv6 prefix (including prefix length); ② IPv4 prefix (including prefix length); ③ EA-bits length (number of bits).

The MAP-E node finds the end user's IPv6 prefix in the BMR by executing the longest match algorithm, the result of which is used for the allocation of the IPv4 prefix, full IPv4 address, or shared IPv4 address. The IPv6 address of MAP-E is generated by the IPv6 prefix defined by BMR. This IPv6 address must be assigned to the network interface of the MAP-E node, serving as the encapsulation/decapsulation node for MAP-E traffic. Port-restricted IPv4 routing exists in all FMRs, and the default route exists in the MAP-E BR.

FMR is used for direct communication between MAP-E CEs, known as mesh mode. In hub-and-spoke mode, no independent FMR is required, and all traffic must be sent directly to the MAP-E BR. Although FMR is optional, i.e., a MAP CE can configure 0 or more FMRs, all MAP-E CEs must implement support for BMR and FMR.

1. *Port Mapping Algorithm*

The port mapping algorithm of MAP-E is identical to that of MAP-T, see Sect. 10.2.3.

2. *Basic Mapping Rules*

The basic mapping rules of MAP-E are identical to that of MAP-T, see Sect. 10.2.3.

3. *Forwarding Mapping Rules*

The forwarding mapping rules of MAP-E are identical to that of MAP-T, see Sect. 10.2.3.

4. *Default Route*

The default route of MAP-E differs from MAP-T.

Within a MAP-E domain, all IPv4 traffic between nodes is encapsulated in IPv6 datagrams, with the IPv6 address of the sending MAP-E node as the source address and the IPv6 address of the receiving MAP-E node as the destination address. For IPv4 destination addresses outside the MAP-E domain, their traffic is also encapsulated in IPv6 datagrams, in which case the IPv6 address of the MAP-E BR is the destination address.

On a MAP-E CE, the path to the BR can be represented as a point-to-point IPv4 over IPv6 tunnel defined by RFC2473 [7], with the IPv6 address of the MAP-E CE as the tunnel source address and the IPv6 address of the BR as the tunnel endpoint address. When MAP-E is enabled, a typical CE router will automatically configure the IPv4 default route to the BR. The BR will send the IPv4 traffic received from outside the MAP-E domain to the designated CE according to the MAP-E forwarding rules.

5. *IPv6 Interface Identifier*

The interface identifier of the MAP-E node is identical to that of MAP-T, see Sect. 10.2.3.

10.3.4 MAP-E Configuration

For a given MAP-E domain, both BR and CE must configure the parameters specified by this MAP-E domain.

(1) Basic mapping rules and (optional) forwarding mapping rules, including IPv6 prefix rules, IPv4 prefix rules, and EA-bits length.
(2) Hub-and-spoke mode (all traffic is sent to the BR) or mesh mode (supporting direct communication from CE to CE).
(3) All MAP-E CEs must configure the IPv6 address of the MAP-E BR.

1. *MAP-E CE*

   In the same MAP-E domain, all CE parameters must be configured consistently. There are currently several parameter configuration methods.

   (1) Through IPv6 DHCPv6 option extension (RFC7598 [8]).
   (2) Based on the Broadband Forum's "TR-69" standard.
   (3) XML-based objects retrieved after establishing an IPv6 connection.
   (4) Manual configuration by the administrator.
   (5) Others.

In addition to MAP-E configuration parameters, MAP-E CE also needs an IPv6 prefix. This is the end user's IPv6 prefix, used to access the IPv6 Internet. This IPv6 prefix configuration should also use the above methods.

The relevant configuration parameters of MAP-E (including IPv4 services) need to be bound to the full lifecycle of the user-assigned IPv6 prefix. That is, the IPv4 address or IPv4 prefix or shared IPv4 address, transport layer port range of MAP-E, and any parameters related to authorization and auditing, are all bound to the full lifecycle of the user's IPv6 prefix.

A single MAP-E A CE can also connect to multiple MAP-E domains, just as any router may have multiple upstream IPv4 service providers (the IPv4 address of each network interface is assigned by their respective DHCP). Each MAP-E domain requires a specific end-user IPv6 prefix. The CE corresponding network interface corresponds to different MAP-E domains, gets the corresponding MAP-E parameters, and generates the corresponding IPv4 prefix, IPv4 address, or shared IPv4 address.

2. *MAP-E BR*

The MAP-E BR must configure the mapping rules of this MAP-E domain.

To improve reliability and achieve load balancing, the MAP-E BR IPv6 address can be an anycast address within a given MAP-E domain. Based on the stateless nature of MAP-E, the MAP-E CE can use any MAP-E BR with any anycast IPv6 address at any time. If the MAP-E BR IPv6 address is an anycast address, then the MAP-E BR must use this anycast IPv6 address as the source address for the datagram sent to the MAP-E CE.

Since MAP-E uses the address space of the ISP, there is no need to announce specific routes of IPv6 or IPv4 to external networks through BGP. Note that if the MAP-E BR uses an anycast IPv6 address, the corresponding anycast address must be announced in the ISP's IGP.

10.3.5 Data Plane Processing Considerations

MAP-E uses the encapsulation mode defined by RFC2473 [7, 42]. More discussion is in Chap. 5 of this book.

1. *Sending Rules*

For shared IPv4 addresses, the MAP-E CE first performs the NAT44 function for the IPv4 datagram received from the LAN and creates the appropriate NAT44 binding. The IPv4 datagram generated by this binding must contain the IPv4 source address and the source port range specified by the transport layer port identifier specified by the MAP-E CE parameter configuration. The MAP-E CE encapsulates the IPv4 datagram into IPv4 over IPv6, and the source and destination addresses of the IPv6 datagram must be generated according to the method defined by the MAP-E address mapping rules.

2. *Receiving Rules*

The MAP-E CE first decapsulates the received IPv6 datagram and forwards the generated IPv4 datagram to the NAT44 function of the MAP-E CE for processing according to the NAT44 conversion table.

The MAP-E BR first uses the longest match algorithm for the IPv6 address of the received IPv6 datagram and the rules within the MAP-E domain, as well as for the IPv6 destination address and the MAP-E BR's IPv6 address for comparison and selection. The EA-bits are determined from the source IPv6 address according to the selected MAP-E mapping rule.

To prevent spoofing of IPv4 addresses, any MAP-E node (CE and BR) must perform the following verification on the received datagram.

(1) The embedded IPv4 address or IPv4 prefix, as well as the PSID (if any), which determine the legitimate source address and source port range of the IPv4 datagram, must be extracted from the source address of the IPv6 datagram according to the MAP-E rules.
(2) The node extracts the source IPv4 address and port of the IPv4 datagram encapsulated in the IPv6 datagram. If it is found that they exceed the above-mentioned legitimate range, the datagram must be discarded, and the counter must be incremented to indicate that a potential spoofing attack may be underway. For datagrams whose source IPv6 address is the IPv6 address of the MAP-E BR, this source address verification is not performed.

By default, the MAP-E CE router must discard the MAP-E virtual interface (i.e., after the IPv6 datagram is decapsulated) generated, the destination node is not the shared IPv4 address, full IPv4 address, or IPv4 prefix defined by this MAP-E CE.

3. *ICMP Processing*

ICMP messages should be supported in the MAP-E domain. Therefore, the NAT44 function in the MAP-E CE must have the ICMP processing method defined by RFC5508 [23].

If the MAP-E CE receives an ICMP message with an "Identifier" field in the ICMP header, the NAT44 in the MAP-E CE must rewrite this field with a specific value allowed by the port set according to the MAP-E mapping rules. After the MAP-E BR and other MAP-E CEs receive the ICMP message, they must handle the ICMP Identifier field in a manner similar to handling ports in TCP/UDP headers.

If a MAP-E node receives an ICMP error message detected within an IPv6 tunnel, and this ICMP error message does not have an ICMP Identifier field, the MAP-E node should relay the ICMP error message to the original source (RFC2473 [7]).

4. *Fragmentation Processing and Path MTU Discovery*

Due to the different sizes of IPv4 headers and IPv6 headers, any device installed between IPv4 networks and IPv6 networks must have the ability to handle MTU. There are three mechanisms to address this issue.

(1) Path MTU Discovery (PMTUD).
(2) Fragmentation.
(3) Transport layer negotiation, such as the TCP MSS option defined by RFC879 [15].

MAP-E uses these three mechanisms to handle different situations.

(1) **Fragmentation handling within the MAP-E domain**

Encapsulating IPv4 datagrams in the MAP-E domain will increase their size (usually by 40 octets). Therefore, it is strongly recommended to properly manage the MTU in the MAP-E domain, i.e., through configuration, to prevent the MAP-E CE WAN interface from fragmenting.

For IPv4 packets entering the MAP-E domain, fragmentation is handled according to the rules of RFC2473 [7].

Using anycast source addresses may result in ICMP error messages generated on the transmission path being sent to different MAP-E BRs, which means that it may cause a path MTU discovery (PMTUD) black hole on the IPv6 path (RFC2473 [7]). Therefore, when the MAP-E BR uses anycast IPv6 source addresses, PMTUD across the MAP-E domain should not be enabled.

Multiple MAP-E BRs using the same anycast source address can simultaneously send datagram fragments to the same MAP-E CE. If datagram fragments from different MAP-E BRs happen to use the same datagram fragment ID, reassembly errors may occur (RFC4459 [43]).

(2) **Receiving IPv4 fragments at the boundary of the MAP-E domain**

IPv4 datagrams received from outside the MAP-E domain require an IPv4 destination address and a transport layer destination port. However, transport layer protocol information is only available in the first fragment of the received datagram, so as described in RFC6346 [17], MAP-E nodes must reassemble the datagram before sending it to the MAP-E link when receiving IPv4 datagram fragments from outside. If the first datagram fragment received by the MAP-E node contains transport layer protocol information, it can forward subsequent fragments of the same datagram using cached information. It should be recognized that MAP-E is susceptible to attacks against datagram fragmentation (RFC1858 [18], RFC3128 [19]), and other issues with high-speed reassembly of datagrams should also be known (RFC4963 [20]).

(3) **Sending IPv4 fragments to the outside**

If IPv4 fragments are located in two different MAP-E CE, the internal IPv4 hosts send fragmented datagrams to the same external IPv4 destination host; these hosts may use the same IPv4 fragmentation identifier, leading to fragmentation reassembly errors in the IPv4 destination host. Given that the IPv4 fragmentation identifier is also a 16-bit field, it can be analogous to the transport layer port range. Therefore, compared to the rate of sending fragments, if the fragmentation identifier space is large enough, then MAP-E CE can rewrite the IPv4 fragmentation identifier as the numerical range defined by PSID. However, this method will increase the probability of conflicts during fragment reassembly (RFC6864 [21]).

10.3.6 NAT44 Considerations

The NAT44 implemented in MAP-E CE should comply with the behaviors defined by RFC4787 [22], RFC5508 [23], and RFC5382 [24]. In the IPv4 address sharing mode of MAP-E, NAT44 must limit the transport layer port number range according to the basic mapping rules.

10.3.7 Security Considerations

Spoofing attacks: By checking the consistency between IPv4 and IPv6 data sources at MAP-E nodes, MAP-E does not introduce new spoofing attacks.

Denial of service (DoS) attacks: Any IPv4 address sharing mechanism carries the risk of DoS attacks. It is recommended to accelerate the deployment of IPv6 to reduce the use of IPv4 address sharing mechanisms.

Routing loop attacks: Although routing loop attacks may exist in the "automatic tunneling" mechanism (RFC6324 [28]), MAP-E can avoid them. This is because each MAP-E BR will check the source address of the received IPv6 datagram according to the "forwarding rules."

Restricted port set attacks: For hosts that have not performed input filtering (RFC2827 [29]), attackers can inject spoofed datagrams into the host using the currently existing outbound connection's transport layer ports (RFC4953 [30], RFC5961 [31], RFC6056 [32]). The success of the attack depends on whether the attacker can guess which transport layer ports the host is currently using. To reduce such attacks, the NAT44 of MAP-E CE can configure "address-dependent filtering" (RFC4787 [22]). In addition, it is recommended that MAP-E CE use DNS transport proxy (RFC5625 [33]) to handle DNS queries, that is, through IPv6-only, rather than through MAP-E domain restricted transport layer port's IPv4 to perform DNS queries. RFC6269 [34] outlines other issues and considerations of IPv4 address sharing.

10.3.8 MAP-E Example

The topology and data flow of the MAP-E example are shown in Fig. 10.10. The left side is the topology, and the right side is the source and destination addresses of the datagrams on this link.

1. *Scenario*
   IPv4 network (client H1) initiates access to the IPv4 Internet (server H2) through the IPv6 network.
2. *MAP-E Parameters*
   (1) Basic mapping rules.
      ① Rule IPv6 prefix: 2001:db8:0000::/40.

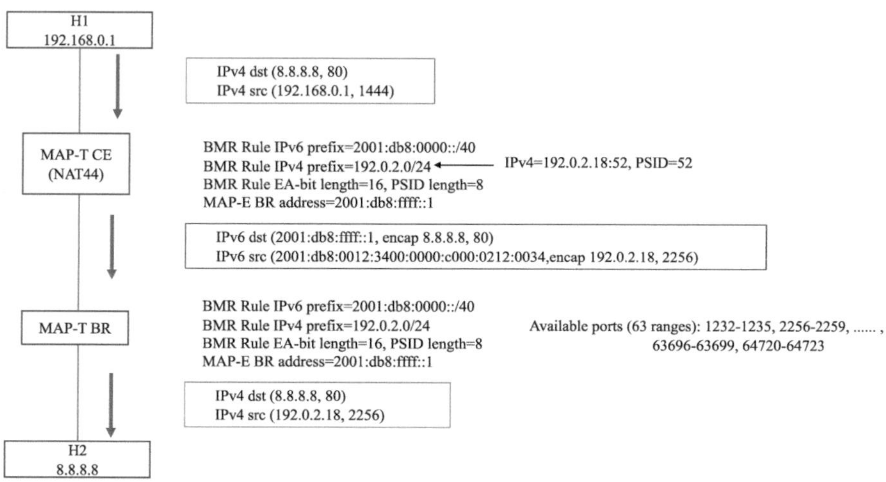

Fig. 10.10 MAP-E example

② Rule IPv4 prefix: 192.0.2.0/24.
③ Rule EA-bits length: 16.
④ PSID length: 8 (multiplexing ratio is 256); PSID offset: 6 (default).
MAP-E BR IPv6 address: 2001:db8:ffff::1.

3. *Host Address*

(1) H1: An IPv4 host in the IPv4 network (192.168.0.1).
(2) H2: An IPv4 host in the IPv4 Internet (8.8.8.8).

4. *Address Mapping*

(1) EA-bits offset: 40.
(2) IPv4 suffix bits (p): IPv4 address length (32)—IPv4 prefix length (24) = 8.
(3) PSID starts: $40 + p = 40 + 8 = 48$.
(4) PSID length (q): (User prefix length–Rule IPv6 prefix length) $-p =$ (56–40) $- 8 = 8$.
(5) Available port range (63): 1232 ~ 1235, 2256 ~ 2259, …, 63,696 ~ 63,699, 64,720 ~ 64,723.
This example IPv4 address: 192.0.2.18 (0xc0000212).
This example PSID: 0x34.
(6) User IPv6 prefix: 2001:db8:0012:3400::/56.
(7) MAP CE IPv6 address: 2001:db8:0012:3400:0000:c000:0212:0034.

10.4 Mixed MAP-T/MAP-E

The CE and BR can be configured in different modes. For example CE can be configured in translation mode, and BR can be configured in encapsulation mode, as shown in Fig. 10.11

The reason is that the forwarding mode is only required in the IPv4 to IPv6 direction, while it can be automatically identified by checking the value of the next header in the IPv6 packets in the IPv6 to IPv4 direction. This feature provides great flexibility to the users and operators to select the desired forwarding mode without dropping a single packet in a different forwarding mode.

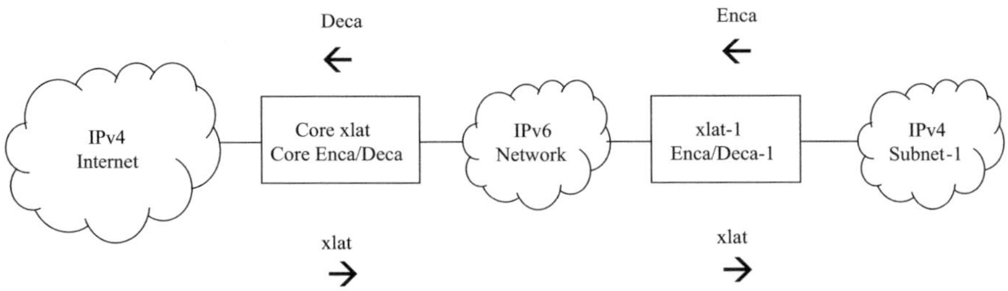

Fig. 10.11 Mixed MAP-T and MAP-E

Therefore, a unified MAP CE can support MAP-T, MAP-E, mixed MAP-T/MAP-E, and backward compatible with NAT64 and dual-stack lite.

10.5 Summary

This chapter introduces stateless double translation (dIVI and MAP-T) and stateless encapsulation (MAP-E). Among them, dIVI and MAP-T can flexibly degrade to a single translation technology application scenario as needed in the middle and later stages of the transition from IPv4 to IPv6.

dIVI is suitable for deployment in campus networks and corporate networks, while MAP-T is suitable for deployment in home broadband environments. From another perspective, MAP-E is also suitable for deployment in home broadband environments. MAP-E has the advantage of preserving all IPv4 datagram header information, but it cannot smoothly transition to IPv6-only.

References

1. Li X, Bao C, Chen M, et al. RFC6219: The China Education and Research Network (CERNET) IVI translation design and deployment for the IPv4/IPv6 coexistence and transition. IETF 2011-05.
2. Bao C, Huitema C, Bagnulo M, et al. RFC6052: IPv6 addressing of IPv4/IPv6 translators. IETF 2010-10.
3. Bao C, Li X, Baker F T, et al. RFC7915: IP/ICMP translation algorithm. IETF 2016-06.
4. Rekhter Y, Moskowitz B, Karrenberg D, et al. RFC1918: Address allocation for private internets. IETF 1996-02.
5. Li X, Bao C, Dec W, et al. RFC7599: Mapping of address and port using translation (MAP-T). IETF 2015-07.
6. Troan O, Dec W, Li X, et al. RFC7597: Mapping of address and port with encapsulation (MAP-E). IETF 2015-07.
7. Conta A, Deering S. RFC2473: Generic packet tunneling in IPv6 specification. IETF 1998-12.
8. Mrugalski T, Troan O, Farrer I, et al. RFC7598: DHCPv6 options for configuration of softwire address and port-mapped clients. IETF 2015-07.
9. Martinez J. RFC8683: Additional deployment guidelines for NAT64/464XLAT in operator and enterprise networks. IETF 2019-11.
10. Srisuresh P, Holdrege M. RFC2663: IP network address translator (NAT) terminology and considerations. IETF 1999-08.
11. Thaler D. RFC6250: Evolution of the IP model. IETF 2011-05.
12. Fuller V, Li T. RFC4632: Classless inter-domain routing (CIDR): The internet address assignment and aggregation. IETF 2006-08.
13. Postel J. RFC792: Internet control message protocol. IETF 1981-09.
14. Conta A, Deering S, Gupta M. RFC4443: Internet control message protocol (ICMPv6) for the internet protocol version 6 (IPv6) specification. IETF 2006-03.
15. Postel J. RFC879: The TCP maximum segment size and related topics. IETF 1983-11.
16. Mathis M, Heffner J. RFC4821: Packetization layer path MTU discovery. IETF 2007-03.
17. Bush R. RFC6346: The address plus port (A+P) approach to the IPv4 address shortage. IETF 2011-08.

18. Ziemba G, Reed D, Traina P. RFC1858: Security considerations for IP fragment filtering. IETF 1995-10.
19. Miller I. RFC3128: Protection against a variant of the tiny fragment attack (RFC1858). IETF 2001-06.
20. Heffner J, Mathis M, Chandler B. RFC4963: IPv4 reassembly errors at high data rates. IETF 2007-07.
21. Touch J. RFC6864: Updated specification of the IPv4 ID field. IETF 2013-02.
22. Audet F, Jennings C. RFC4787: Network address translation (NAT) behavioral requirements for unicast UDP. IETF 2007-01.
23. Srisuresh P, Ford B, Sivakumar S, et al. RFC5508: NAT behavioral requirements for ICMP. IETF 2009-04.
24. Guha S, Biswas K, Ford B, et al. RFC5382: NAT behavioral requirements for TCP. IETF 2008-10.
25. Bagnulo M, Sullivan A, Matthews P, et al. RFC6147: DNS64: DNS extensions for network address translation from IPv6 clients to IPv4 servers. IETF 2011-04.
26. Bagnulo M, Matthews P, Beijnum I. RFC6146: Stateful NAT64: Network address and protocol translation from IPv6 clients to IPv4 servers. IETF 2011-04.
27. Mawatari M, Kawashima M, Byrne C. RFC6877: 464XLAT: Combination of stateful and stateless translation. IETF 2013-04.
28. Nakibly G, Templin F. RFC6324: Routing loop attack using IPv6 automatic tunnels: Problem statement and proposed mitigations. IETF 2011-08.
29. Ferguson P, Senie D. RFC2827: Network ingress filtering: Defeating denial of service attacks which employ IP source address spoofing. IETF 2000-05.
30. Touch J. RFC4953: Defending TCP against spoofing attacks. IETF 2007-07.
31. Ramaiah A, Stewart R, Dalal M. RFC5961: Improving TCP's robustness to blind in-window attacks. IETF 2010-08.
32. Larsen M, Gont F. RFC6056: Recommendations for transport-protocol port randomization. IETF 2011-01.
33. Bellis R. RFC5625: DNS proxy implementation guidelines. IETF 2009-08.
34. Ford M, Boucadair M, Durand A, et al. RFC6269: Issues with IP address sharing. IETF 2011-06.
35. Gilligan R, Nordmark E. RFC1933: Transition mechanisms for IPv6 hosts and routers. IETF 1996-04.
36. Nordmark E, Gilligan R. RFC4213: Basic transition mechanisms for IPv6 hosts and routers. IETF 2005-10.
37. Carpenter B, Jung C. RFC2529: Transmission of IPv6 over IPv4 domains without explicit tunnels. IETF 1999-03.
38. Carpenter B, Moore K. RFC3056: Connection of IPv6 domains via IPv4 clouds. IETF 2001-02.
39. Templin F, Gleeson T, Thaler D. RFC5214: Intra-site automatic tunnel addressing protocol (ISATAP). IETF 2008-03.
40. Townsley W, Troan O. RFC5969: IPv6 rapid deployment on IPv4 infrastructures (6rd) -- Protocol specification. IETF 2010-08.
41. Durand A, Droms R, Woodyatt J, et al. RFC6333: Dual-stack lite broadband deployments following IPv4 exhaustion. IETF 2011-08.
42. Nichols K, Blake S, Baker F, et al. RFC2474: Definition of the differentiated services field (DS Field) in the IPv4 and IPv6 headers. IETF 1998-12.
43. Savola P. RFC4459: MTU and fragmentation issues with in-the-network tunneling. IETF 2006-04.
44. Cotton M, Eggert L, Touch J, et al. RFC6335: Internet assigned numbers authority (IANA) procedures for the management of the service name and transport protocol port number registry. IETF 2011-08.

Chapter 11
Stateful Double Translation and Encapsulation

This chapter discusses solutions for stateful double translation and stateful encapsulation technologies, including 464XLAT, DS-Lite, and LW-4o6.

11.1 Stateful Double Translation

In this book, stateful double translation specifically refers to 464XLAT technology. 464XLAT uses the building block of stateless single translation technology, with the addition of stateful address mapping and double translation technology. Stateful double translation technology is known as 464XLAT, defined by RFC6877 [1], as shown in Fig. 11.1.

11.1.1 Background

The idea of using stateless double translation technology is to keep the core network devices stateless. When reusing public IPv4 addresses, the user's home gateway (the 2nd translator) performs transport layer port mapping. Naturally, researchers also considered deploying a stateful translator (NAT64) in the core network and a 2nd translator (stateless) on user devices. The advantage is that the user device implementation is relatively simple, and the complexity of maintaining the state is done by the core devices. 464XLAT only supports the IPv4 client/server model, where the server needs to have a public IPv4 address. This means that 464XLAT is not suitable for IPv4 peer-to-peer communication or as a server-side solution.

The main features of 464XLAT are as follows:

X. Li and C. Bao, *New IPv6 Transition Technology*,
https://doi.org/10.1007/978-981-95-8427-7_11

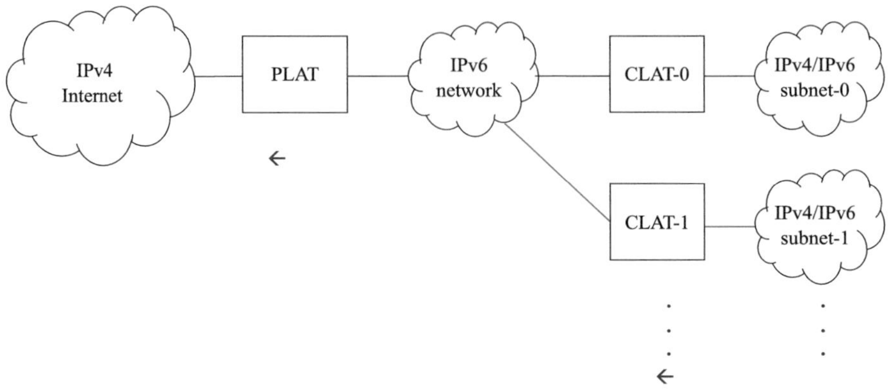

Fig. 11.1 464XLAT

(1) 464XLAT only requires a minimal pool of public IPv4 addresses; thus, it can more flexibly reuse public IPv4 addresses (but loses the ability to initiate bidirectional communication, increasing the cost of traceability).
(2) No new protocols are needed, allowing for quick deployment.
(3) IPv6-only networks are simpler, cheaper, and easier to operate than dual-stack networks.
(4) 464XLAT can directly use standard IP monitoring and traffic engineering tools, without the need for decapsulation processes when using tunnels.

11.1.2 Basics of Stateful Double Translation

464XLAT combines the stateful IPv4/IPv6 translation technology defined by RFC6146 [2] and the stateless IPv4/IPv6 translation technology standard defined by RFC7915 [3]. 464XLAT does not require DNS64 defined by RFC6147 [4] because IPv4 clients send IPv4 datagrams containing DNS requests, these IPv4 datagrams are translated into IPv6 datagrams by the client-side translator (CLAT), and then retranslated into IPv4 datagrams by the provider-side translator (PLAT). Of course, 464XLAT can also use DNS64, thus supporting direct use of the stateful IPv4/IPv6 single translation defined by RFC6146 [2] instead of double translation.

Although the 464XLAT architecture can be used for the wired network in the form of a home gateway, currently, it is mainly used for the 3G/4G/5G and Wi-Fi mobile devices. The architecture is shown in Fig. 11.2.

The CLAT function on the user equipment (UE) provides the local ISP's protocol stack with private IPv4 address support (RFC1918 [5]). Applications on the UE can thus use the private IPv4 address to communicate with hosts on the global IPv4 Internet through double translation (CLAT and PLAT). In addition, the UE (including the "IPv4-converted IPv6 address" resolved by DNS64) can communicate directly with hosts on the global IPv6 Internet (including the global IPv4 Internet translated

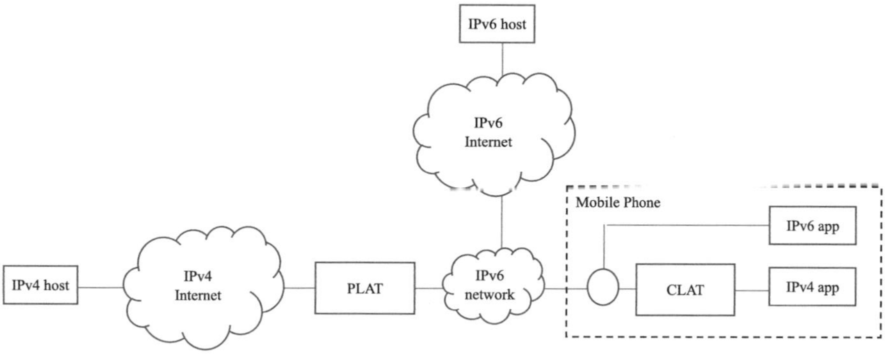

Fig. 11.2 464XLAT wireless network architecture

by PLAT) without the need for CLAT participation. Note: When the UE acts as a hotspot, it provides access services for hosts on the hotspot network by providing private IPv4 addresses through NAT44, similar to the wired network architecture mode.

11.1.3 Stateful Double Translation Algorithm

1. *IPv6 Address Format*

The IPv6 address format in 464XLAT is defined by RFC6052 [6].

2. *IPv4/IPv6 Address Mapping Process*

464XLAT (RFC6877 [1]) consists of PLAT and CLAT. PLAT is stateful IPv4/IPv6 translation, while CLAT is stateless translation. The client obtains the IPv6 prefix through the IPv6 prefix assignment mechanism (such as the IPv6 dynamic host configuration protocol with prefix delegation, DHCPv6-PD, defined by RFC3633 [7]), thus having a dedicated IPv6 prefix for translation.

For communication initiated by the IPv4 client, its IPv4 source address and IPv4 destination address are converted by CLAT through stateless translation technology (RFC6052 [6], RFC7915 [3]) into "IPv4-translatable IPv6 address" and "IPv4-converted IPv6 address," and then reach PLAT through the IPv6-only network. PLAT uses stateful translation technology (RFC6146 [2]) to convert the "IPv4-translatable IPv6 address" into an address in the public IPv4 address pool (shared), and convert the "IPv4-converted IPv6 address" into the original IPv4 destination address. For the returned datagram, reverse processing is performed.

3. *IPv6 Prefix Processing*

In the default state, CLAT needs to use two IPv6 prefixes.

First, CLAT must know its own IPv6 prefix. CLAT should obtain its own upstream IPv6 link interface's /64 prefix, all downstream link interfaces' IPv6/64 prefixes, and a dedicated /64 prefix for sending and receiving stateless translation datagrams. When there is no DHCPv6-PD defined by RFC3633 [7] running, it is impossible to obtain a dedicated /64 prefix for sending and receiving stateless translation datagrams. CLAT can perform NAT44 for all IPv4 LAN datagrams, ensuring that all IPv4 datagrams initiated by the LAN originate from a single IPv4 address. This IPv4 address is then converted into an "IPv4-translatable IPv6 address" using stateless translation technology. The conversion utilizes the IPv6 interface address prefix as defined in RFC 6052 [6]. This IPv6 address is generated by the CLAT using the Neighbor Discovery Protocol (NDP) and validated through Duplicate Address Detection (DAD).

Secondly, CLAT must know the IPv6 prefix used by the PLAT side. CLAT will use this IPv6 prefix to generate the "IPv4-converted IPv6 address" to translate the datagram into an IPv4 datagram through PLAT to access the IPv4 Internet. The IPv6 prefix used by the PLAT side can be discovered using the prefix discovery technology of RFC7050 [8] or other mechanisms, such as using RA options, etc., which is discussed in Chap. 8 of this book.

4. *DNS Proxy Implementation*

The CLAT should implement the DNS proxy defined by RFC5625 [9]. IPv4-only nodes querying the IPv4 DNS server behind the CLAT should be avoided, as in this case each DNS query has to go through a double translation by the CLAT and PLAT. The CLAT should set itself up as a DNS resolver to provide DNS query services for IPv4/IPv6 clients within the LAN. Note: IPv4-only clients should be allowed to query the IPv4 DNS server via the CLAT and PLAT.

5. *CLAT in the Gateway*

The CLAT function can be implemented in a general home gateway or a mobile device with network sharing capabilities (such as a smartphone). A router with CLAT capabilities should also provide general router services, such as assigning private IPv4 addresses (RFC1918 [5]) via DHCP, DHCPv6, NDP with router announcements, and DNS services.

6. *CLAT-to-CLAT Communication*

464XLAT is a hub-and-spoke architecture that supports IPv4 services over an IPv6-only network. The interactive connectivity establishment (ICE) protocol defined by RFC5245 [10] can be used to support point-to-point communication within the 464XLAT network.

7. *Processing Mode in 464XLAT Architecture*

Table 11.1 outlines the processing modes in the 464XLAT architecture.

Table 11.1 Processing modes in 464XLAT architecture

Server	Application	Type	Translator location
IPv6	IPv6	IPv6 end-to-end	None
IPv4	IPv6	Stateful NAT64	PLAT
IPv4	IPv4	464XLAT	PLAT/CLAT

11.1.4 Deployment Considerations

Traffic engineering independent of the PLAT provider can still be achieved even if the end user's network provider is different from the PLAT provider (for example, another ISP).

(1) The end user's network provider can directly know the IPv4 destination address from the IPv6 header, so it can implement traffic engineering based on the IPv4 destination address using existing IPv6 tools (monitoring, access control lists, traffic throttling, etc.). Any encapsulation (tunneling) method does not have this advantage, because to achieve the same functionality, decapsulation operations must be performed.

(2) If the network provider can assign more /64 IPv6 prefixes to each user device, the 464XLAT architecture can use one /64 to support direct communication of IPv6 datagrams, and another /64 to support IPv4 datagrams, using 464XLAT double translation communication. Therefore, it can identify "native IPv6 datagrams" and "IPv4/IPv6 translation datagrams," and by differentiating the handling of different IPv6 prefixes, it can achieve traffic engineering that distinguishes between IPv6 and IPv4.

11.1.5 Security Considerations

The deployment of 464XLAT should consider the security considerations discussed in RFC6052 [6], RFC7915 [3] and RFC6146 [2], and take corresponding measures.

11.1.6 Stateful Double Translation Example

The topology and data flow of the 464XLAT example are shown in Fig. 11.3. The left side is the topology, and the right side is the source and destination addresses of the datagrams on this link.

1. Scenario

IPv4 network (client H1) initiates access to the IPv4 Internet (server H2) through the IPv6 network.

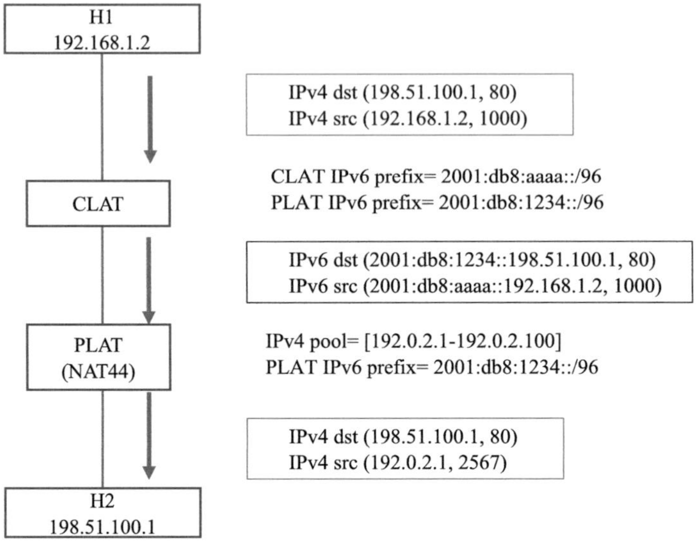

Fig. 11.3 464XLAT example

2. 464XLAT Parameters

   (1) CLAT IPv6 prefix: 2001:db8:aaaa::/96.
   (2) PLAT IPv6 prefix: 2001:db8:1234::/96.
   (3) IPv4 address pool: 192.0.2.1–192.0.2.100.

3. Host Addresses

   (1) H1: An IPv4 host (192.168.1.2) in the IPv4 network.
   (2) H2: An IPv4 host (198.51.100.1) in the IPv4 Internet.

4. Notes on Address and Port Mapping

CLAT for stateless translation:

(1) "IPv4-translatable IPv6 Address":
(192.168.1.2, 1000) ← → (2001:db8:aaaa::192.168.1.2, 1000)
(2) "IPv4-converted IPv6 address":
(198.51.100.1, 80) ← → (2001:db8:1234::198.51.100.1, 80)

PLAT for stateful translation:

(1) Establish session table (TCP or UDP or ICMP):
(192.0.2.1, 2567) ← → (2001:db8:aaaa::192.168.1.2, 1000)
(2) "IPv4-converted IPv6 address":
(198.51.100.1, 80) ← → (2001:db8:1234::198.51.100.1, 80)

11.2 Stateful Tunneling

Stateful tunneling technology, known as DS-Lite (RFC6333 [11]), consists of stateful IPv4/IPv6 address and transport layer port mapping and IPv4 over IPv6 protocol encapsulation technology, as shown in Fig. 11.4.

11.2.1 Background

RFC6333 [11] introduced the Dual-Stack Lite (DS-Lite) technology. This technology aims to optimize the cost–benefit ratio for network service providers during the transition to IPv6. DS-Lite uses two mature technologies (IPv4 over IPv6 and NAT) to share public IPv4 addresses and provide services through an IPv6-only access network. In a DS-Lite service domain, there is an Address Family Transition Router (AFTR) and numerous Basic Bridging Broad Band (B4) devices, i.e., home gateways.

DS-Lite does not rely on cascaded IPv4 NAT, but uses IPv4 over IPv6 tunnels across the ISP's IPv6-only access network, allowing users to share public IPv4 addresses through the operator-level IPv4-IPv4 NAT (AFTR) network. This method has several advantages.

(1) Network operators can transit their access networks (up to customer premises equipment or CPE) to IPv6-only, reducing costs.
(2) Network operators use IPv6-only with a massive address space to build and manage access networks, providing IPv4 access services to numerous users, which is more cost-effective than managing overlapping private IPv4 address spaces for the same number of users.
(3) Since tunnels can terminate anywhere in the ISP's network, they help with horizontal scaling and provide flexibility in traffic load.

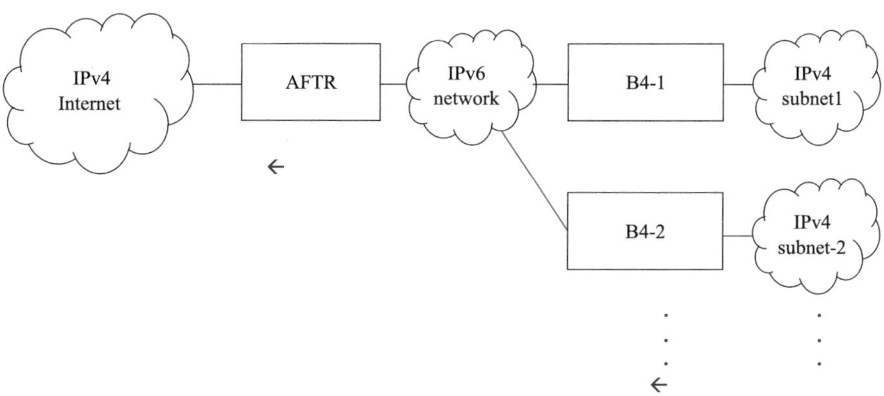

Fig. 11.4 DS-Lite

(4) Since the tunnel provides a direct connection between the core device AFTR and the access device B4, users and their applications can control the AFTR's NAT function when needed.

Since DS-Lite technology uses tunnels, it is essentially still a dual-stack operation mode, i.e., IPv4 and IPv6 operate independently. The advantage is that the two protocols do not affect each other, but the disadvantage is that it cannot achieve interconnection between IPv4 and IPv6. Therefore, it is difficult to transition to IPv6-only.

11.2.2 Basics of Stateful Tunneling

The typical deployment of DS-Lite is for the CPE's uplink (the WAN interface of B4 device) to be IPv6-only, and the downlink to be IPv4 or dual-stack, providing services to hosts in the local area network.

DS-Lite CPE should not provide NAT functionality between the B4 device WAN interface and the downlink. Its IPv4 NAT function is provided by the core device (AFTR) operated by the ISP. That is, double IPv4 NAT operation should be avoided.

DS-Lite CPE should run a DHCP server to distribute RFC1918 [5] addresses (for example, 192.168.0.0/16) to hosts in the home. DS-Lite CPE should be the IPv4 default gateway and DNS server. In addition, as a DNS server, it needs to run a DNS proxy so that hosts in the home can accept DNS requests for IPv4 datagrams and send them to the Internet service provider's DNS resolver using IPv6 datagrams. Note: If hosts in the home decide to use other IPv4 DNS servers, DS-Lite CPE will forward these DNS requests through the B4 interface. However, each DNS request will create a NAT binding in the AFTR. A large number of DNS requests may directly impact the AFTR's NAT.

DS-Lite CPE also supports the RA function of IPv6 and has IPv6 routing capabilities. Therefore, hosts in the home that support IPv6 can directly access the IPv6 Internet. It will not go through the tunnel, nor will it translate datagrams.

There are two specific implementations of the DS-Lite architecture: home gateway architecture as shown in Fig. 11.5 and the host architecture (almost no implementation) [12].

This architecture is designed for broadband deployment for home users, but it also adapts to other user devices when they are IPv4-only.

The DS-Lite deployment scenarios based on the home gateway architecture are as follows:

(1) The WAN interface of the CPE is IPv6-only.
(2) The CPE assigns RFC1918 [5] defined IPv4 addresses (IPv6-only or dual-stack user hosts) to the LAN via DHCP. Global IPv6 unicast addresses (dual-stack user hosts) are assigned via RA or DHCPv6.
(3) The CPE provides a DNS resolver function for the LAN.

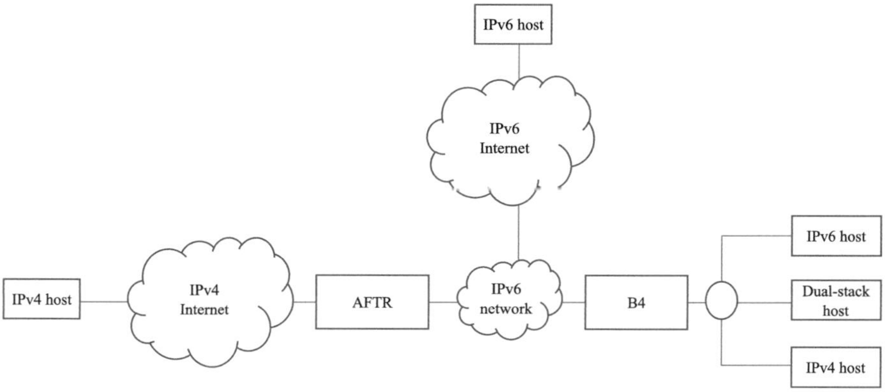

Fig. 11.5 DS-Lite home gateway architecture

When the user host accesses the IPv6 Internet, the user host will use the global IPv6 address obtained from the CPE as the source address, and send the IPv6 datagram to the CPE. The CPE routes the IPv6 datagram to the IPv6 default gateway of the ISP.

When the user host accesses the IPv4 Internet, the user host will use the private IPv4 address defined by RFC1918 [5] obtained from the CPE as the source address, and send the IPv4 datagram to the CPE. The CPE encapsulates the IPv4 datagram in an IPv4 over IPv6 softwire tunnel and forwards it to the AFTR. The other CPE typically converts private IPv4 addresses (as defined by RFC1918 [5]) into public addresses via NAT before forwarding them to the core device. However, in this case, the CPE directly forwards datagrams with the private IPv4 address as the source address to the core device (AFTR), bypassing NAT. When the AFTR receives the IPv6 datagram, it decapsulates the IPv6 datagram. The AFTR configures a public IPv4 address pool and converts the private IPv4 address defined by RFC1918 [5] into a public IPv4 address.

Because the IPv4 over IPv6 softwire tunnel is used, there is no need to plan the use of the RFC1918 [5] address space for each CPE. Overlapping address spaces can be uniquely identified by the IPv6 address of the IPv4 over IPv6 softwire tunnel endpoint, which comes from different CPE datagrams.

11.2.3 Stateful Tunneling Configuration

1. *Core Device AFTR*

The core device AFTR provides an IPv4 over IPv6 tunnel and IPv4 NAT functions. The IPv4 over IPv6 tunnels are from AFTR to multiple B4s.

The implementation details are as follows.

1) **Fragmentation and Reassembly**

If the MTU of the lower link cannot support the overhead of encapsulation for datagrams, AFTR must perform fragmentation and reassembly. Fragmentation must be performed after IPv6 datagram encapsulation, and reassembly must be performed before IPv6 datagram decapsulation, as detailed in RFC2473 [13].

Fragmentation at the tunnel entrance is a lightweight operation. In contrast, reassembly at the tunnel exit is a heavyweight operation. For example, if there are two fragments, when the first fragment is received at the tunnel exit, it must wait for the second fragment to arrive before assembling the IPv6 datagram and then decapsulating it. Therefore, the tunnel exit is required to cache and track fragments. Since AFTR is the convergence point of multiple tunnels, in the case of a large number of fragments, AFTR is required to consume a lot of resources to cache and track this traffic, which affects the performance of AFTR. When the hardware resources of the AFTR device are below the preset threshold, AFTR should notify the administrator.

2) **Extended Binding Table**

The NAT binding table of AFTR is extended from basic 5-tuple to also include the IPv6 source address of the IPv6 datagram and the (overlapping) RFC1918 [5] private IPv4 address used to support B4 devices. Through the extended binding table for reverse lookup, AFTR can correctly encapsulate the IPv4 datagram returned from the IPv4 Internet into an IPv6 datagram and return it to the corresponding B4 device, while maintaining a static configuration for each tunnel.

3) **Well-Known IPv4 Address (192.0.0.1)**

AFTR should use the well-known IPv4 address (192.0.0.1) defined by IANA to configure the IPv4 over IPv6 tunnel and use it for ICMP issues (such as traceroute output).

2. *Edge Device (B4)*

The B4 device creates a tunnel to AFTR. The specific implementation technical details are as follows.

1) **Fragmentation and Reassembly**

The use of encapsulation technology (IPv4 over IPv6 or any other method) to carry IPv4 over IPv6 traffic will reduce the available MTU. Unfortunately, path MTU discovery (RFC1191 [14]) is not a reliable method. The solution to this problem is for network operators to increase the MTU of all IPv6 links between B4 devices and AFTR devices by configuring (increasing at least 40 octets to accommodate the increased IPv6 header). However, not all network operators can increase the IPv6 link MTU, and B4 devices must perform fragmentation and reassembly. Fragmentation must be performed after the encapsulation of the IPv6 datagram, and reassembly must be performed before the decapsulation of the IPv6 datagram, as detailed in RFC2473 [13].

2) **AFTR Discovery**

In order to configure the IPv4 over IPv6 tunnel, the B4 device needs to know the IPv6 address of the AFTR device. This IPv6 address can be configured using various methods, including out-of-band mechanisms, manual configuration, or DHCPv6 options. To ensure interoperability, B4 devices should implement the DHCPv6 option defined in RFC6334 [15].

3) **DNS**

B4 devices are usually configured by network operators, and their upstream interface is IPv6-only. Therefore, their upstream DNS resolver needs to query via IPv6. The IPv6 address of the DNS resolver is obtained through DHCPv6 (or other similar IPv6 methods). The B4 device can pass this IPv6 address directly to the user's IPv6 host, but the B4 device must support the DNS proxy function (RFC5625 [9]) to support IPv4 hosts. The DNS security features that B4 devices need to support are detailed in RFC4033 [16].

4) **Interface Initialization**

Note: B4 devices can be hosts or CPEs. The host or CPE may also support the traditional dual-stack operation mode. Therefore, one must choose to start one mode during initialization: dual-stack or DS-Lite.

5) **Well-known IPv4 Address (192.0.0.1)**

Any locally unique IPv4 address can be configured on the endpoint of the IPv4 over IPv6 tunnel to represent the B4 device. To avoid conflicts with other addresses, IANA has defined a "well-known IPv4 prefix" (192.0.0.0/29) for DS-Lite.

(1) 192.0.0.0 is a reserved subnet identifier.
(2) 192.0.0.1 is reserved for AFTR.
(3) 192.0.0.2 is reserved for B4.

If an ISP prohibits B4 from using 192.0.0.2 for some reason, B4 can use other addresses within the range of 192.0.0.0/29.

11.2.4 Deployment Considerations

1. *Tunnel*

The tunnel must be configured according to RFC2473 [13] and RFC4213 [17], and the traffic class encoding of the IPv4 header (RFC2474 [18]) must be copied to the IPv6 header, and vice versa.

2. *NAT*

AFTR can configure multiple IPv4 address pools for NAT functions. Its range of IPv4 addresses can be disjoint but cannot overlap. Network operators can set IPv4 address pool policies in AFTR. For example, AFTR can have two link interfaces. Each link interface uses a different IPv4 address pool. Another example is that AFTR assigns the first group of B4s to use the first IPv4 address pool, while another group of B4s uses the second IPv4 address pool.

AFTR must provide NAT behavior of the operator that complies with RFC4787 [19], RFC5508 [20] and RFC5382 [21].

3. *Application Layer Gateway*

In order to share public IPv4 addresses, AFTR must perform NAT functions, which can lead to NAT-related issues. For instance, active FTP requires an ALG to function properly. Since AFTR is a core device that supports a large number of B4s, it is not feasible to support ALG on a large scale.

4. *Sharing Public IPv4 Addresses*

AFTR allows multiple users to share a single IPv4 address, thus addressing the issue of address scarcity. However, this also introduces some problems related to address traceability and address blocking (RFC6269 [22]).

5. *AFTR Horizontal Scaling and High Reliability*

DS-Lite is a tunnel-based solution. Therefore, tunnel endpoints can be set anywhere in the ISP's access network.

Using the DHCPv6 tunnel endpoint option (RFC6334 [15]), user groups sharing the same AFTR can be created. Therefore, a few centralized AFTRs can be used initially. When more capacity is needed, more AFTRs can be added, closer to the edge of the access network. Similarly, this method can also improve reliability.

11.2.5 Security Considerations

For security issues related to NAT, refer to RFC2663 [23] and RFC2993 [24].

However, moving NAT functions from CPE to the ISP's core device AFTR introduces new issues. To prevent malicious users from abusing port resources and implementing address tracing, AFTR should have the ability to record "tunnel ID, protocol, port/IP address," as well as the corresponding creation time and session length.

Since multiple users share an IPv4 address, the transport layer port becomes a crucial resource. Therefore, AFTR should have a limit on the maximum number of transport layer ports that each user can use concurrently (RFC6269 [22]).

AFTR should configure IPv6 ingress filters on the tunnel interface, only accepting IPv6 addresses from legitimate B4 devices.

11.2.6 Stateful Tunneling Example

The topology and data flow of the DS-Lite example are shown in Fig. 11.6. The left side shows the topology, and the right side shows the source and destination addresses of the datagrams on this link.

1. *Scenario*

An IPv4 network (client H1) initiates access to the IPv4 Internet (server H2) through an IPv6 network.

2. *DS-Lite Parameters*

   (1) B4 tunnel endpoint: 2001:db8:0:1::1.
   (2) AFTR tunnel endpoint: 2001:db8:0:2::1.
   (3) IPv4 address pool: [192.0.2.1–192.0.2.100].

3. *Host Addresses*

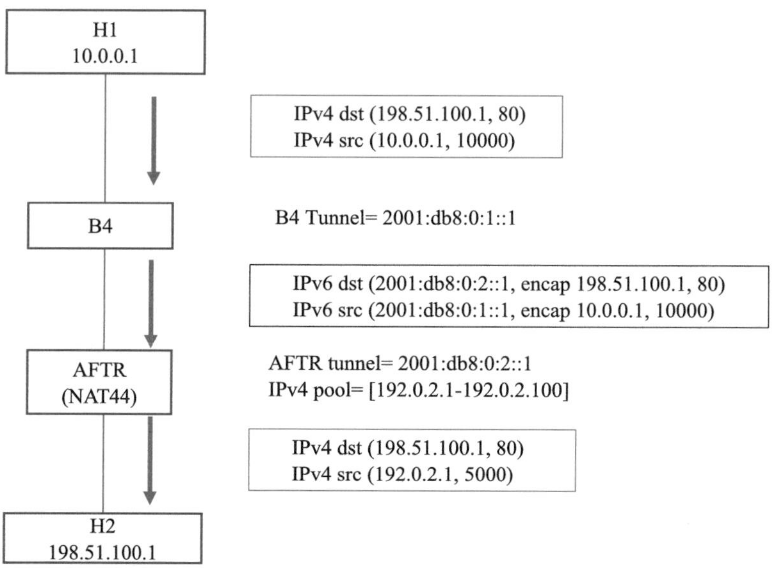

Fig. 11.6 DS-lite example

(1) H1: An IPv4 host (10.0.0.1) in the IPv4 network.
(2) H2: An IPv4 host (198.51.100.1) in the IPv4 Internet.

4. *Address and Port Mapping*
AFTR: Establish a session table to represent the mapping relationship of external and internal IPv4 addresses and ports determined by a specific IPv6 address (TCP or UDP or ICMP):
{2001:db8:0:1::1}:
(10.0.0.1, 10000) ← → (192.0.2.1, 5000).

11.3 Subscriber State Tunnel

In this book, subscriber state tunnel specifically refers to LW-4o6 technology, which is defined by RFC7596 [25]. LW-4o6 can be seen as an evolution of DS-Lite (RFC6333 [11]). LW-4o6 decentralizes some of the NAPT functions from DS-Lite and transfers them to the CPE. The central device only needs to maintain user-level status. The topology of LW-4o6 is shown in Fig. 11.7.

11.3.1 Background

For implementing DS-Lite, the AFTR dynamically performs centralized NAT44 function (assigning public IPv4 addresses and ports to requesting hosts, RFC3022 [26]); therefore, the AFTR's NAT44 function must maintain the session state of each flow. For network operators with a large number of B4 clients, there are scalability

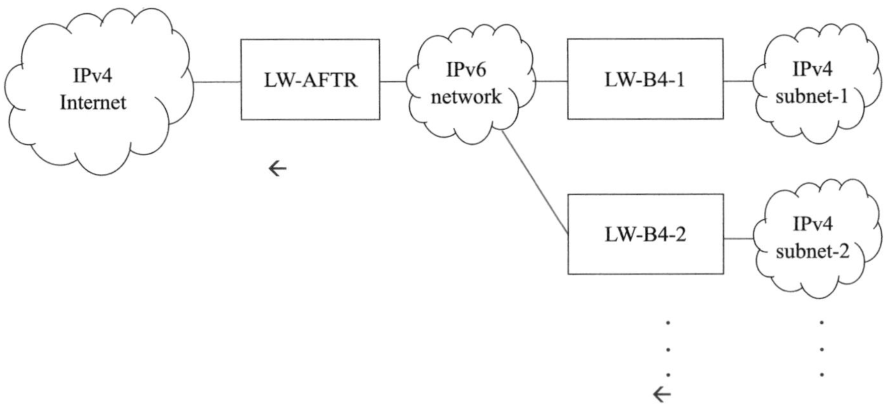

Fig. 11.7 Topology of LW-4o6

and maintainability issues. At the same time, according to the laws of the country where the operator is located, the requirement to keep the log of each NAPT session state also brings huge operational overhead.

LW-4o6 transfers the NAPT function from the centralized AFTR to the distributed B4, with the following advantages.

(1) Modern CPEs have widely supported and used NAT44 functions, so LW-4o6 uses CPE to provide the conversion from private IPv4 addresses to public IPv4 addresses, that is, network operators do not need to run centralized NAT44.
(2) The state centrally maintained by AFTR is reduced from per-flow to per-subscriber. This greatly reduces the resources (memory and processing capacity) that AFTR needs to maintain.
(3) The log overhead required by national laws to be logged is also greatly reduced.
(4) The allocation of IPv6 and IPv4 addresses by network operators can remain completely independent.

Note: The difference between MAP-E and LW-4o6 is that MAP-E establishes an algorithm-based relationship between IPv4 addresses and IPv6 addresses, so it is stateless. LW-4o6 does not establish an algorithm-based relationship between IPv4 addresses and IPv6 addresses, but introduces the concept of subscriber state, so it is a technology between stateless tunnel technology (MAP-E) and stateful tunnel technology (DS-Lite) called subscriber state.

11.3.2 Subscriber State Tunnel Basics

DS-Lite (RFC6333 [11]) defines a solution to provide IPv4 services through an IPv6-only network. The core technology it uses is: IPv4 over IPv6 (RFC2473 [13]) and NAT. LW-4o6 is functionally similar to DS-Lite. It runs an IPv6-only access network between lwB4 and lwAFTR. Both methods use IPv4 over IPv6 tunnels to provide IPv4 services. The main function of the LW-4o6 data plane is shown in Fig. 11.8.

LW-4o6 includes the following three components.

(1) lwB4: Performs NAPT and IPv4/IPv6 encapsulation/decapsulation.
(2) lwAFTR: Performs IPv4/IPv6 encapsulation/decapsulation.
(3) Configuration system: Notifies lwB4 of the available public IPv4 addresses and transport layer port sets.

The difference between lwB4 (LW-4o6) and B4 (DS-Lite) is that lwB4 performs the NAPT function. This means that a configuration system is needed to notify lwB4 of the available public IPv4 addresses and transport-layer port sets. This information can be obtained through DHCPv6 extension (RFC7598 [27]), or through the Port Control Protocol (PCP, RFC6887 [1]), or through the Broadband Forum's TR-69 specification.

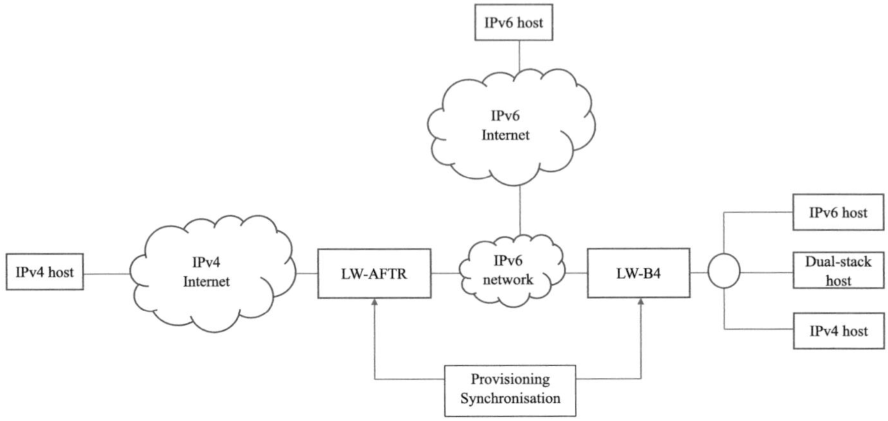

Fig. 11.8 Synchronization of LW-4o6 configuration

11.3.3 Subscriber State Tunnel Configuration

1. *Core Device (lwAFTR)*

Unlike the binding table (NAPT 5-tuple) of DS-Lite, the binding table of LW-4o6 is 3-tuple, including the following parts.

(1) The IPv6 address of lwB4.
(2) The public IPv4 address used by lwB4.
(3) The transport layer port set used by lwB4.

lwAFTR has two functions: encapsulating IPv4 over IPv6 for IPv4 packets received from the Internet, and verifying the legality and decapsulating IPv6 packets received from lwB4. lwAFTR does not need to perform NAPT, so it does not need to maintain session state.

lwAFTR must maintain a 3-tuple binding table for each lwB4 throughout the service process. If lwAFTR itself participates in the configuration process of public IPv4 addresses and transport layer ports, it must keep synchronized through an out-of-band mechanism. Therefore, the lifecycle of binding table entries must be synchronized with the lifecycle of address allocation.

Due to the similarity between LW-4o6's lwAFTR and DS-Lite's AFTR, lwAFTR must strictly follow the behavior of the AFTR data plane defined by RFC6333 [11], including the following aspects.

(1) Encapsulation and decapsulation (RFC6333 [11]).
(2) Fragmentation and reassembly (RFC6333 [11], RFC2473 [13]).
(3) Tunnel (RFC6333 [11], RFC2473 [13], RFC2983 [28]).

When lwAFTR receives an IPv6 datagram from lwB4, lwAFTR decapsulates the IPv6 header and verifies the source address and transport layer port in the binding table. If the IPv6 source address, the decapsulated IPv4 source address, and the transport layer source port match the entries in the binding table, lwAFTR forwards the datagram to the IPv4 destination node.

If no match is found (for example, there is no matching IPv4 address entry, or the transport layer port is out of the specified range), lwAFTR must discard the datagram or implement some policy (such as datagram redirection). lwAFTR can send an ICMPv6 Type 1, Code 5 (destination unreachable, source address failed ingress/egress policy) error message to the corresponding lwB4. Note: The ICMP policy should be configurable.

When lwAFTR receives an IPv4 datagram from the Internet, lwAFTR uses the IPv4 destination address and transport layer destination port to look up the corresponding IPv6 destination address (target lwB4) in the binding table. If a matching entry is found, lwAFTR encapsulates the IPv4 datagram. The source address of the encapsulated IPv6 datagram is the IPv6 address of lwAFTR, and the destination address is the matching IPv6 address in the binding table (the IPv6 address of the corresponding lwB4). Then, lwAFTR forwards the datagram to the corresponding lwB4 via an IPv6-only access network.

If no match is found, lwAFTR must discard the datagram. lwAFTR can send back an ICMPv4 Type 3, Code 1 (destination unreachable, host unreachable) error message. Note: The ICMP policy should be configurable.

lwAFTR must support hairpinning between two lwB4s, completing the decapsulation of datagrams sent from one lwB4 to another lwB4 in the same domain, and performing new encapsulation. Note: The hairpinning policy should be configurable.

2. *Edge Device (lwB4)*

The following parameters must be configured for lwB4.

(1) lwAFTR's IPv6 address.
(2) The public IPv4 address used by NAPT44.
(3) The transport layer port used by NAPT44.
(4) User-side IPv6 prefix.

lwB4 must use the DHCPv6 parameter extension OPTION_S46_CONT_LW (RFC7598 [27]). Note that the tunnel lifecycle and corresponding configuration information (such as shared IPv4 address, IPv4 address) should be consistent with the DHCPv6 lease lifecycle.

To correctly identify user-end devices, the user-side IPv6 prefix is used to construct the lwB4's IPv6 address (/128) as the source address of the lwB4 tunnel. Its construction method is consistent with MAP-E (RFC7597 [29]).

If for any reason (such as the expiration of the DHCPv6 lease), the IPv6 source address of lwB4 changes, the dynamic configuration process of lwB4 must be restarted. If for any reason, the public IPv4 address or transport layer port set of lwB4 changes, lwB4 must refresh the NAPT table.

lwB4 must support the dynamic configuration of the public IPv4 address and transport layer port set. Its transport layer port set is defined by RFC7597 [29]. Note that for LW-4o6, a-bits should be set to 0, so a continuous port set can be assigned to each lwB4.

DHCPv6 can only assign a single PSID to a single lwB4. If the client uses all the transport layer ports assigned to the lwB4 at the same time, it may not be able to initiate any more IPv4 connections. The current DHCPv6 does not provide a mechanism to provide more transport layer port numbers based on requests. If there is such a need, other mechanisms (such as PCP, RFC7753 [30]) should be used. RFC6269 [22] discusses the issue of IP address sharing in more detail.

When sharing a public IPv4 address, it is recommended that the transport layer port range assigned to lwB4 does not include system ports (0–1023). System ports are usually reserved for the servers. RFC6269 [22] analyzes the use of transport layer ports with IPv4 address sharing.

If lwB4 receives an ICMPv6 error message (Type 1, Code 5) originating from lwAFTR, lwB4 can understand that the binding table of lwAFTR did not find a matching entry, so lwAFTR cannot forward the IPv4 datagram. In this case, lwB4 should restart the DHCPv6 configuration process. Note: This "restart strategy" of lwB4 should be configurable.

After receiving such ICMP error messages, lwB4 must verify whether its source address is the same as the address of lwAFTR. If not, lwB4 must discard the ICMP error message.

To prevent the use of forged lwAFTR addresses as source addresses to send ICMP messages to lwB4, network operators should configure the network ingress filtering mechanism defined by RFC2827 [31].

In addition, LW-4o6 should also configure lwB4 according to the DNS considerations defined by RFC6333 [11].

Due to the similarity between LW-4o6's lwB4 and DS-Lite's B4, lwB4 must strictly follow the behavior of the B4 data plane defined by RFC6333 [11], including the following points.

(1) Encapsulation and decapsulation (RFC6333 [11]).
(2) Fragmentation and reassembly (RFC6333 [11], RFC2473 [13]).
(3) Tunneling (RFC6333 [11], RFC2473 [13], RFC2983 [28]).

lwB4 also needs to perform IPv4 address translation (NAPT44) during encapsulation and decapsulation. The address pool of this NAPT44 provides the public IPv4 address and transport layer port range of lwB4 (RFC3022 [26]).

The workflow of lwB4 is: The downstream interface of lwB4 connects the subnet to assign private IPv4 addresses (RFC1918 [5]). When lwB4 receives IPv4 datagrams sent by these hosts, lwB4 performs NAPT44 on the source address of the datagram, whose address is the public IPv4 address obtained by lwB4, and its transport layer port is the specified port range. Then it encapsulates the IPv4 datagram into an IPv6 datagram, whose IPv6 destination address is the IPv6 address of lwAFTR, and the IPv6 source address is the IPv6 tunnel endpoint address of lwB4. Finally, lwB4 forwards the encapsulated IPv6 datagram to lwAFTR through an IPv6-only access network.

When lwB4 receives an IPv6 datagram from lwAFTR, lwB4 decapsulates the IPv6 datagram, then through the NAPT44 state-mapping table converts the destination address of the IPv4 datagram into the original RFC1918 [5] address and transport-layer port.

If the source address of the IPv6 datagram received by lwB4 does not match the IPv6 address of lwAFTR, the datagram must be discarded. If the decapsulated IPv4 datagram does not match the configuration of lwB4 (i.e., the IPv4 destination address or port is not the public IPv4 address owned by lwB4 and the allowed transport layer port range), the datagram must be discarded. lwB4 can send an ICMP error message to lwAFTR (type 3, code 13—destination unreachable, communication administratively prohibited). Note: The ICMP policy should be configurable.

lwB4 should have application layer gateway functions (such as SIP, FTP) and other NAPT traversal mechanisms (such as Universal Plug and Play (UPnP) protocol, etc.).

lwB4 can also be implemented within the host. In this case, the host should have NAPT44 functionality and encapsulation/decapsulation functionality.

The NAPT44 in lwB4 for TCP and UDP must comply with the behavior defined in RFC4787 [19], RFC5508 [20] and RFC5382 [21]. If supporting DCCP, it must comply with the behavior defined in RFC5597 [32].

The NAPT44 in lwB4 for ICMP must comply with the behavior defined in RFC5508 [20].

If lwB4 receives an ICMP error message (error detected inside the IPv6 tunnel), the node needs to relay the ICMP error message to the original node source (lwAFTR), and must comply with the behavior defined in RFC2473 [13].

If two hosts sharing the same public IPv4 address, located inside lwB4, send fragmented datagrams to the same external IPv4 destination host, these hosts may use the same IPv4 fragment identifier, resulting in fragment reassembly errors at the IPv4 destination host. Given that the IPv4 fragment identifier is also a 16-bit field, it can be analogous to the transport layer port range. Therefore, compared to the rate of sending fragments, if the fragment identifier space is large enough, lwB4 can rewrite the IPv4 fragment identifier to the numerical range defined by PSID. However, this method will increase the probability of conflicts during fragment reassembly (RFC6864 [33]).

11.3.4 Deployment Considerations

1. Parameter Configuration

In LW-4o6, binding information must be synchronized among lwB4, lwAFTR, and the registration server.

In addition to the DHCPv6 mechanism, the following protocols can also be used to implement parameter configuration functions.

(1) DHCPv4 over DHCPv6 (RFC7341 [34]).
(2) PCP (RFC6887 [35]).

To prevent intercommunication complexity, it is recommended that network operators use a single parameter configuration mechanism. If multiple configuration mechanisms are required (for example, switching between different mechanisms is necessary), each configuration mechanism should have independent resources (such as public IPv4 address/PSID pool, lwAFTR tunnel address, and binding table, etc.).

2. ICMP Processing

For lwAFTR and lwB4, ICMPv6 must be processed according to RFC2473 [13].

In an address sharing environment, ICMPv4 must be specially processed according to RFC6269 [22]. The ICMP message processing of LW-4o6 is as follows.

1) **IwAFTR Processing ICMPv4**

For received ICMP messages, lwAFTR should implement the following functions.

(1) Check the ICMP "type" field.

① If the ICMP "Type" field is 0 (echo response) or 8 (echo request), lwAFTR must use the value of the ICMP "Identification" field as the source port to look up the binding table. If a corresponding value is found in the binding table, lwAFTR will encapsulate the ICMP datagram and forward it to the corresponding IPv6 address. Otherwise, the datagram must be discarded.

② If the ICMP "Type" field is any other value, lwAFTR must use the transport layer header included in the ICMP message defined by RFC5508 [20] to determine its source port. Then use the IPv4 destination address and the source port obtained from the ICMP datagram to look up the binding table. If a corresponding value is found in the binding table, lwAFTR will encapsulate the ICMP datagram and forward it to the corresponding IPv6 address. Otherwise, the datagram must be discarded.

(2) Note that these ICMP policies should be configurable in the device as needed.

2) **IwB4 Processing ICMPv4**

lwB4 must implement ICMP forwarding defined by RFC5508 [20]. For ICMP echo requests with IPv4 source addresses defined as private addresses by RFC1918 [5], lwB4 should implement the method defined by RFC6346 [36], using the transport layer port set defined by PSID as the ICMP identifier.

11.3.5 Security Considerations

LW-4o6's adoption of address sharing results in a reduction in the transport layer port space available to users, significantly reducing randomness. This means that attackers can more easily guess the port numbers in use, which could lead to denial-of-service attack incidents.

The transport layer port set for users can be a set of continuous or non-continuous ports. Using a continuous port set does not reduce the threat, but using a non-continuous port set (RFC6346 [36]), as long as the attacker does not know the transport layer port set generation algorithm, can increase randomness, thereby improving security.

LwAFTR must rate limit ICMPv6 error messages to prevent DoS attacks.

For the security risks of IP address sharing, refer to RFC6269 [22].

11.3.6 Subscriber State Tunnel Example

The topology and data flow of the LW-4o6 example are shown in Fig. 11.9. The left side is the topology, and the right side is the source and destination addresses of the datagrams on this link.

1. *Scenario*

The IPv4 network (client H1) initiates access to the IPv4 Internet (server H2) through the IPv6 network.

2. *DS-Lite Parameters*

   (1) lwB4 tunnel address: 2001:db8:abcd:ef00::c000:0212:0034.
   (2) lwAFTR tunnel address: 2001:db8:ffff::1.
   (3) IPv4 address in this case: 192.0.2.18, PSID = 52.

3. *Host Addresses*

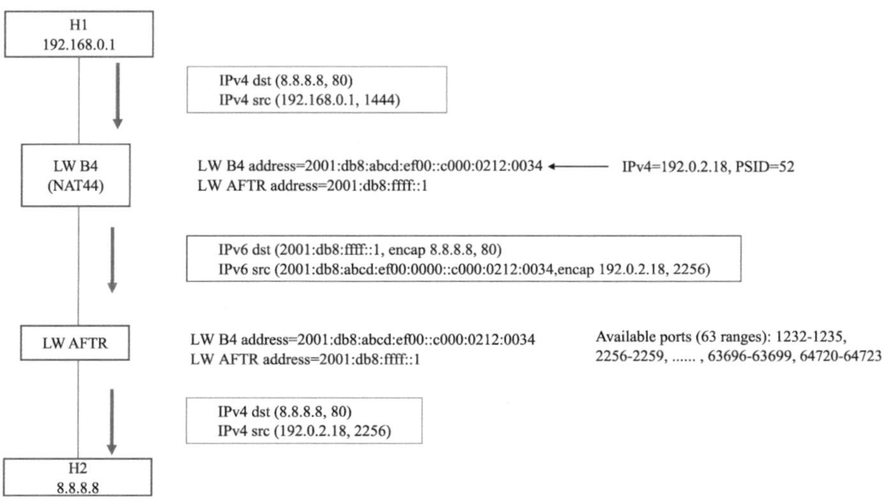

Fig. 11.9 LW-4o6 example

(1) H1: An IPv4 host in the IPv4 network (192.168.0.1).
(2) H2: An IPv4 host in the IPv4 Internet (8.8.8.8).

4. Notes on Address and Port Mapping
lwB4: Establish session table (TCP or UDP or ICMP):
{2001:db8:abcd:ef00:0000:c000:0212:0034}
(192.168.0.1, 1444) ← → (192.0.2.18, 2256)

11.4 Summary

This chapter introduces the stateful double translation (464XLAT), stateful encapsulation (DS-Lite), and subscriber state encapsulation (LW-4o6) technologies. The characteristic of the stateful double translation mechanism is to maintain the state on the core network equipment and keep the user-side equipment stateless. The advantage of this mechanism is that it requires less modification to the user-side equipment, making it easy to promote and apply. However, maintaining the state on the core equipment is not conducive to the scalability and security of the network. Therefore, it is recommended to choose the stateless mechanism first. When it is necessary to use the stateful mechanism, ensure that the scale of the core equipment deployment is not too large.

References

1. Mawatari M, Kawashima M, Byrne C. RFC6877: 464XLAT: Combination of stateful and stateless translation. IETF 2013-04.
2. Bagnulo M, Matthews P, Beijnum I. RFC6146: Stateful NAT64: Network address and protocol translation from IPv6 clients to IPv4 servers. IETF 2011-04.
3. Bao C, Li X, Baker F, et al. RFC7915: IP/ICMP translation algorithm. IETF 2016-06.
4. Bagnulo M, Sullivan A, Matthews P, et al. RFC6147: DNS64: DNS extensions for network address translation from IPv6 clients to IPv4 servers. IETF 2011-04.
5. Rekhter Y, Moskowitz B, Karrenberg D, et al. RFC1918: Address allocation for private internets. IETF 1996-02.
6. Bao C, Huitema C, Bagnulo M, et al. RFC6052: IPv6 addressing of IPv4/IPv6 translators. IETF 2010-10.
7. Troan O, Droms R. RFC3633: IPv6 prefix options for dynamic host configuration protocol (DHCP) version 6. IETF 2003-12.
8. Savolainen T, Korhonen J, Wing D. RFC7050: Discovery of the IPv6 prefix used for IPv6 address synthesis. IETF 2013-11.
9. Bellis R. RFC5625: DNS proxy implementation guidelines. IETF 2009-08.
10. Rosenberg J. RFC5245: Interactive connectivity establishment (ICE): A protocol for network address translator (NAT) traversal for offer/answer protocols. IETF 2010-04.
11. Durand A, Droms R, Woodyatt J, et al. RFC6333: Dual-stack lite broadband deployments following IPv4 exhaustion. IETF 2011-08.
12. Storer B, Pignataro C, Santos M, et al. RFC5571: Softwire hub and spoke deployment framework with layer two tunneling protocol version 2 (L2TPv2). IETF 2009-06.
13. Conta A, Deering S. RFC2473: Generic packet tunneling in IPv6 specification. IETF 1998-12.

14. Mogul J, Deering S. RFC1191: Path MTU discovery. IETF 1990-11.
15. Hankins D, Mrugalski T. RFC6334: Dynamic host configuration protocol for IPv6 (DHCPv6) option for dual-stack lite. IETF 2011-08.
16. Arends R, Austein R, Larson M, et al. RFC4033: DNS security introduction and requirements. IETF 2005-03.
17. Nordmark E, Gilligan R. RFC4213: Basic transition mechanisms for IPv6 hosts and routers. IETF 2005-10.
18. Nichols K, Blake S, Baker F, et al. RFC2474: Definition of the differentiated services field (DS Field) in the IPv4 and IPv6 headers. IETF 1998-12.
19. Audet F, Jennings C. RFC4787: Network address translation (NAT) behavioral requirements for unicast UDP. IETF 2007-01.
20. Srisuresh P, Ford B, Sivakumar S, et al. RFC5508: NAT behavioral requirements for ICMP. IETF 2009-04.
21. Guha S, Biswas K, Ford B S, et al. RFC5382:NAT behavioral requirements for TCP. IETF 2008-10.
22. Ford M, Boucadair M, Durand A, et al. RFC6269: Issues with IP address sharing. IETF 2011-06.
23. Srisuresh P, Holdrege M. RFC2663: IP network address translator (NAT) terminology and considerations. IETF 1999-08.
24. Hain T. RFC2993: Architectural implications of NAT. IETF 2000-11.
25. Cui Y, Sun Q, Boucadair M, et al. RFC7596: Lightweight 4over6: An extension to the dual-stack lite architecture. IETF 2015-07.
26. Srisuresh P, Egevang K. RFC3022: Traditional IP network address translator. IETF 2001-01.
27. Mrugalski T, Troan O, Farrer I, et al. RFC7598: DHCPv6 options for configuration of softwire address and port-mapped clients. IETF 2015-07.
28. Black D. RFC2983: Differentiated services and tunnels. IETF 2000-10.
29. Troan O, Dec W, Li X, et al. RFC7597: Mapping of address and port with encapsulation (MAP-E). IETF 2015-07.
30. Sun Q, Boucadair M, Sivakumar S, et al. RFC7753: Port control protocol (PCP) extension for port-set allocation. IETF 2016-02.
31. Ferguson P, Senie D. RFC2827: Network ingress filtering: Defeating denial of service attacks which employ IP source address spoofing. IETF 2000-05.
32. Denis-Courmont R. RFC5597: Network address translation (NAT) behavioral requirements for the datagram congestion control protocol. IETF 2009-09.
33. Touch J. RFC6864: Updated specification of the IPv4 ID field. IETF 2013-02.
34. Sun Q, Cui Y, Siodelski M, et al. RFC7341: DHCPv4-over-DHCPv6 (DHCP 4o6) transport. IETF 2014-08.
35. Wing D, Cheshire S, Boucadair M, et al. RFC6887: Port control protocol (PCP). IETF 2013-04.
36. Bush R. RFC6346: The address plus port (A+P) approach to the IPv4 address shortage. IETF 2011-08.

Chapter 12
Stateless IPv6 Prefix Translation

Stateless translation technology establishes an algorithm-based transformation relationship between IPv4 and IPv6. Naturally, this can also be done between IPv6 addresses without disrupting end-to-end address transparency. Similarly, IPv6/IPv6 double translation technology can also be introduced. This chapter introduces stateless IPv6 prefix translation (IPv6 Network Prefix Translation, NPTv6) technology and stateless IPv6 double prefix translation (double IPv6 network prefix translation, dNPTv6) technology.

12.1 IPv6 Prefix Translation

RFC6296 [1] defines a type of NPTv6 technology, which is a transport layer protocol-independent IPv6-to-IPv6 network prefix translation. NPTv6 can provide functionality similar to IPv4 NAT, i.e., decoupling internal and external network addresses, establishing a 1:1 mapping relationship between internal and external network addresses, and maintaining end-to-end reachability at the network layer. At the same time, because it is independent of the transport layer protocol, there is no need to distinguish and specially handle transport layer protocols without IP header checks (such as SCTP) and transport layer protocols that check and verify pseudo headers containing IP address information (such as TCP/UDP/DCCP, etc.). The reason NPTv6 is called "IPv6/IPv6 prefix translation" rather than "IPv6/IPv6 address translation" is that NPTv6 only maps the prefix part of the IPv6 address based on an algorithm, while keeping the rest of the IPv6 address unchanged. The topology of NPTv6 is shown in Fig. 12.1.

X. Li and C. Bao, *New IPv6 Transition Technology*,
https://doi.org/10.1007/978-981-95-8427-7_12

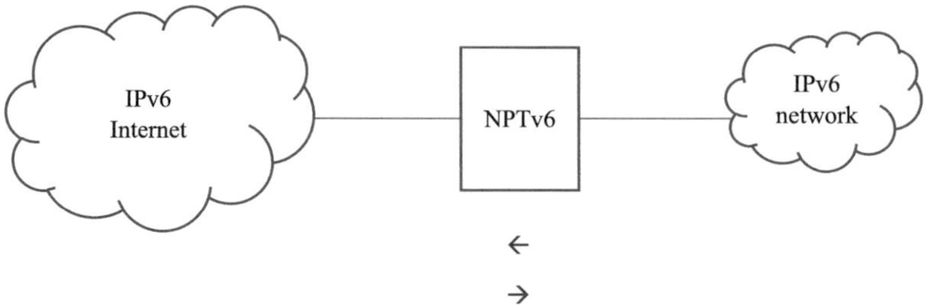

Fig. 12.1 Topology of NPTv6

12.1.1 Background

Based on the reasons stated in RFC2993 [2], the IETF generally does not recommend using IPv6 address translation technology. However, in some cases, it is necessary to convert IPv6 addresses, and the scenarios include: multi-homing and security management, etc. Because NPTv6 is a special type of IPv6 address translation technology, when implementing NPTv6, attention should be paid to the issues discussed in RFC4864 [3] and RFC5902 [4].

The NPTv6 technology defined by RFC6296 [1] has the following characteristics.

(1) NPTv6 supports bidirectional initiated communication, thus it does not provide any network security protection that NAPT44 might offer. If this type of network security protection is needed, an IPv6 stateful firewall (RFC6092 [5]) must be used.
(2) Although IPv6 prefix translation technology is used, the IPv6 address used by the internal network is different from the IPv6 address observed by the external network, but end-to-end reachability at the network layer can still be maintained. Note that this refers to the network layer. If application-layer programs directly call IPv6 addresses or provide address-based referrals, DNS or ALG processing mechanisms must be added to ensure that the application runs transparently and smoothly.
(3) If there are multiple NPTv6s with the same configuration between two IPv6 networks, these NPTv6s do not need to perform "state synchronization" because NPTv6 is stateless, and internal and external IPv6 prefix translation is entirely algorithm-based. Therefore, this mechanism supports asymmetric routing, load sharing, and failover.
(4) Because it is a 1:1 prefix translation, there is no need to modify the transport layer port number or other parameters.
(5) NPTv6 does not support any use of RFC3424 [6]. For example, NPTv6 does not support the TCP authentication option defined by RFC5925 [7] because the original IP address will be used to calculate the authentication code.
(6) When using applications of the Internet Key Exchange Version 2 (IKEv2) defined by RFC5996 [8], it must be able to make the end system's applications detect the presence of the translator (NPTv6), so that IKEv2 will switch

to using UDP to ensure communication. Interestingly, on the one hand, NPTv6 should make the end system's applications unable to perceive the existence of NPTv6, so as to transparently support all applications; on the other hand, NPTv6 must make certain end system's applications explicitly understand that there is an address translator in the communication path, in order to switch to UDP. These applications mainly involve security and the trust model of the end system, that is, whether the IP address must be trustworthy evidence for end system authentication. Further thinking: ① If IPsec is deployed throughout the entire network, then the IP address can be trustworthy evidence for end system authentication. ② Under controllable conditions, deploying dual NPTv6 can solve this problem.

1. *The Feature of IPv6 Address Independence*

    1) **From the Perspective of the Edge Network**
        (1) When using the provider-aggregatable address (PA address), when the upstream ISP changes, the IPv6 address used in the local network (for interface address, access list, and log) does not need to be changed.
        (2) When using the provider aggregatable address (PA address) and multi-homing, when reducing, adding, or changing upstream network operators, the IPv6 address used in the local network (for interface address, access list, and log) does not need to be changed.
        (3) The local network administrator does not need to coordinate with the upstream ISP to announce other IPv6 prefixes (including their own IPv6 prefixes or subsets of other ISPs' IPv6 prefixes in the case of multi-homing).
        (4) Unless the local network administrator wants to implement traffic engineering in the case of multi-homing through BGP, there is no need to establish BGP with the upstream network.
    2) **(2) From the Perspective of the Upstream Network**

Ensuring that the IPv6 address used by the edge network is the IPv6 prefix allocated by the upstream ISP eliminates the problems that may occur with configuring ingress filtering policies and announcing customer-specific IPv6 prefixes (RFC2827 [9]).

Adhering to "address independence" will have a significant impact on the edge network, upstream network, and the entire Internet. In fact, the demand for "address independence" is the main reason for medium and large enterprises to deploy NAT, including those with a large amount of "swamp space" of public IPv4 addresses. The demand for "address independence" is also the driving force for edge networks to become members of the Regional Internet Registry (RIR) community, seeking to obtain BGP autonomous system numbers and provider-independent addresses (PI addresses), which is also the cause of the explosion of the IPv4 routing table. Network operators have repeatedly stated that the lack of "address independence" leads to their customers' lack of control over routing, which has a negative impact on marketing.

RFC4864 [3] discusses local network protection issues and proposes the concept of address autonomy. Address autonomy is one of the important benefits brought by

NAPT44. For IPv6, RFC4864 [3] represents configuring multiple IPv6 addresses for all hosts of an edge network, which includes multiple IPv6 globally routable unicast addresses obtained from multiple upstream network operators, as well as RFC4193 [10]. Consider a scenario: a network is using Unique Local Address (ULA) to achieve internal connectivity; when a host needs to communicate with the Internet, an IPv6 globally routable unicast address can be assigned to that host.

The solution does not meet the requirement of "address independence." If the IPv6 prefix of the upstream ISP changes, all hosts, routers, DHCPv6 servers, access control lists, and firewalls of the edge network must modify their configured IPv6 addresses. Otherwise, communication with the Internet cannot be restored.

Using an IPv6 address independent of the ISP is another technology to meet the "address independence." However, this solution requires the edge network to be eligible to obtain a PI address, and its upstream ISP agrees to receive the PI address and to announce it to the global Internet. From the implementation perspective, for multi-homed networks with a wide geographical distribution and poor IP address aggregation, it is difficult to coordinate the announcement of a part of the PI address space to several different upstream network operators. This is one of the reasons why companies with a large amount of "swamp space" public IPv4 addresses choose to use IPv4 NAT instead of PI addresses.

2. *Applicability of NPTv6*

To meet the requirement of IPv6 address independence, NPTv6 provides a simple and practical solution. NPTv6's translation function for IPv6 prefixes has "address independence." The bidirectional, checksum-independent algorithm introduced by NPTv6 avoids the major problem introduced by NAPT44.

The characteristics of NPTv6's "keeping the transport layer port unchanged" and "checksum-independent address" mean that it can support any current and future transport layer protocols without upgrading NPTv6. At the same time, because NPTv6 does not rewrite the transport layer protocol header, NPTv6 will not affect the encryption processing of the IP payload.

The default NPTv6 address mapping mechanism is completely algorithm-based, so the NPTv6 translator does not need to maintain the state of nodes or connections, which has greater adaptability and scalability than using NAPT44. Since the default NPTv6 mapping can be initiated in either direction, it can directly support peer-to-peer applications, while if using NAPT44, a complex and costly application layer protocol must be used to achieve the same purpose.

It should be noted that although NPTv6 has advantages that NAPT44 does not have in many aspects, as described in RFC2993 [2], it does not eliminate all the architectural problems of IPv4 NAT.

(1) NPTv6 needs to modify the IP header, so it is not fully compatible with security mechanisms (such as IPsec authentication header).
(2) If applications that use embedded IP addresses or IP datagram headers are used, like NAPT44, a corresponding application-layer gateway needs to be specially developed.

(3) Using different internal IPv6 prefixes and external IPv6 prefixes will lead to the complexity of DNS deployment. For example, when an internal node communicates with other internal nodes, it uses an internal address, and when an external node communicates with this node, it needs to obtain the external address of this node. This leads to the phenomenon of split DNS, increasing the complexity of operation and management.

The selection of IPv6 addresses in the edge network is a complex issue. Using ULA has the advantage of address independence, but if the original intention of using ULA is to prevent any external device from accessing the internal network, then deploying NPTv6 can be considered as abusing ULA. In this case, a second ULA that does not provide NPTv6 service can be deployed on the internal network. The edge network can use an IPv6 PA address of a network operator and translate it into an IPv6 PA address of another network operator through NPTv6.

In any case, the introduction of any prefix translation mechanism including NPTv6 will bring many known and unknown problems. It is strongly recommended to consider RFC4864 [3] before deploying NPTv6 and the alternative solutions suggested by RFC5902 [4], some of which may cause fewer problems than NPTv6.

12.1.2 Basics of NPTv6

NPTv6 can be implemented in IPv6 routers, replacing the prefix of the IPv6 address with a specified algorithm when forwarding datagrams. The router function that implements NPTv6 prefix translation is called NPTv6 translation.

1. *Basic Form of NPTv6*

The NPTv6 translator connects two networks, one of which is an IPv6 "internal network" with a single exit, and the other is an "external network" connected to the IPv6 Internet. All hosts on the internal network are configured with IPv6 addresses in an IPv6 prefix with only local routing. When these addresses need to communicate with the IPv6 Internet, they are translated by NPTv6 into globally routable IPv6 addresses. In principle, the prefix lengths of the internal IPv6 prefix and the globally routable IPv6 prefix should be equal. If the lengths of these two prefixes are different, a 1:1 mapping cannot be achieved. The topology is shown in Fig. 12.2.

Figure 12.2 shows an NPTv6 translator connected to two networks. The internal network uses the local IPv6 address (ULA) defined by RFC4193 [10] to represent the internal IPv6 nodes, and the same node will use a globally routable IPv6 address when communicating with the IPv6 Internet.

When the NPTv6 translator forwards IPv6 datagrams from the internal network to the IPv6 Internet (outbound), NPTv6 replaces the source address of the datagram with the external prefix instead of the internal prefix. When the NPTv6 translator forwards IPv6 datagrams from the external IPv6 Internet to the internal network (inbound), NPTv6 replaces the destination address of the datagram with the internal

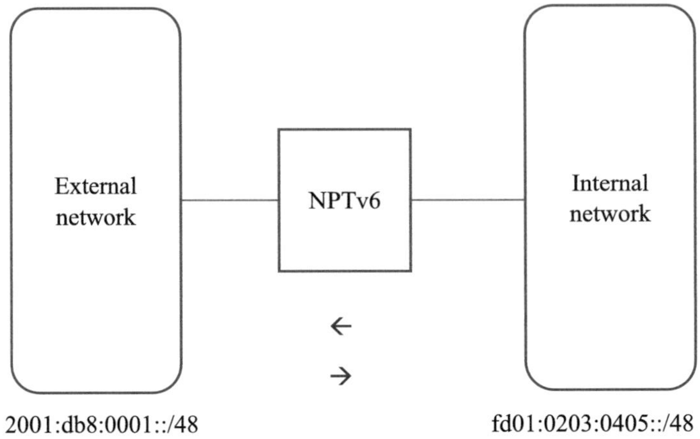

Fig. 12.2 Basic form of NPTv6

prefix instead of the external prefix. In Fig. 12.2, when the IPv6 datagram passes through the "outbound" of the NPTv6 translator, the source prefix (fd01:0203:0405::/48) is replaced by the external prefix (2001:0db8:0001::/48); when the IPv6 datagram passes through the "inbound" of the NPTv6 translator, the target prefix (2001:0db8:0001::/48) will be replaced by the internal prefix (fd01:0203:0405::/48). In both cases, only the local network's IPv6 prefix is replaced, and the external peer IPv6 prefix remains unchanged. It can be considered that the nodes on the internal network are hidden "behind the scenes" of the NPTv6 translator.

2. *NPTv6 Between Two Internal Networks*

NPTv6 can be used between two internal networks. In this case, both networks can use the ULA prefix, each subnet in one network maps to the corresponding subnet in the other network, and vice versa. Each internal network can also use the ULA prefix for internal addressing and use the global unicast address to communicate with other networks, as shown in Fig. 12.3.

3. *NPTv6 Redundancy and Load Sharing*

In some cases, an internal network can be connected to multiple NPTv6 translators, as shown in Fig. 12.4. In this case, the NPTv6 translators are configured with the same internal and external prefixes. Since NPTv6 is stateless, it naturally supports device redundancy and load balancing across multiple links.

4. *NPTv6 Multi-homing Function*

When the internal network has multiple affiliations, the internal network is connected to different external networks through two NPTv6 translators. In this case, the NPTv6 translators are configured with the same internal prefix and different external prefixes. Due to the existence of multiple different translation processes, in addition to using the NAT session traversal application (session traversal utilities for NAT, STUN)

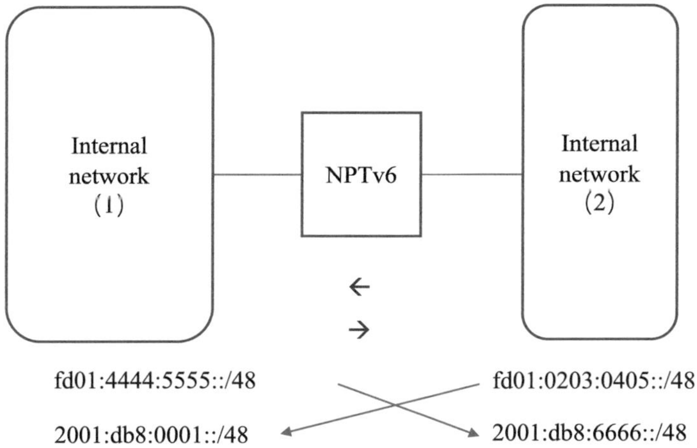

Fig. 12.3 NPTv6 between two internal networks

Fig. 12.4 Parallel translators

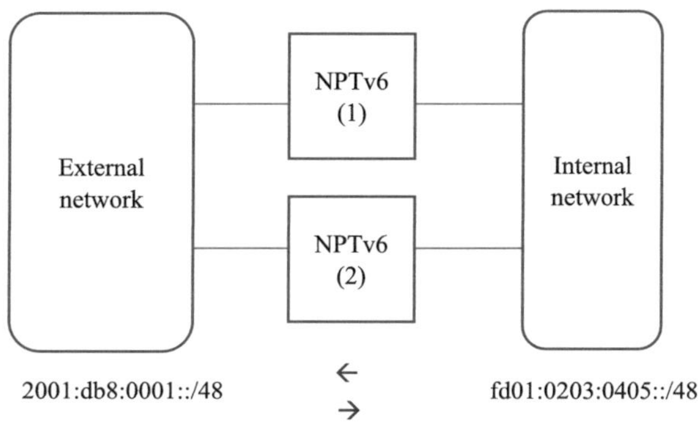

protocol defined by RFC8489 [11], the hosts of the internal network cannot determine which external prefix they are mapped to, as shown in Fig. 12.5.

Note: The multi-affiliation function of using translators is not exactly the same as the multi-affiliation function of using PI addresses. When a link failure causes the NPTv6 translator to switch, the IPv6 address prefix will change, resulting in session termination and address reference failure. Of course, this problem will not arise in a network with relatively stable routing.

5. *Bidirectional Session Initiation*

The default operating mode of NPTv6 is stateless, that is, it does not need to maintain the state of nodes or sessions, but only uses the information in the IPv6 header to perform translation through the algorithm. Therefore, NPTv6 supports bidirectionally initiated communication. This is a significant improvement over NAPT44 devices, but NPTv6 cannot be used as a firewall.

6. *Checksum-Neutral Mapping*

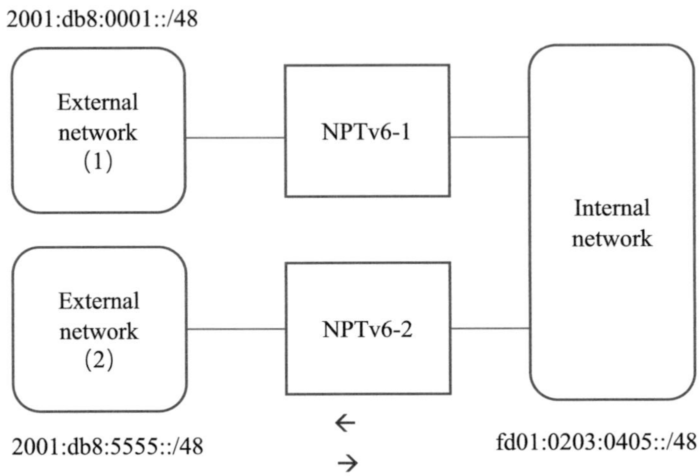

Fig. 12.5 Parallel converter with different upstream networks

When an IPv6 header field is changed, the IPv6 pseudo-header checksum will change, causing the transport-layer checksum verification to fail. Fortunately, according to the provisions of RFC1071 [12] on Internet checksums, these changes are clearly defined (RFC1624 [13]), so they can be compensated by modifying the part of the field covered by the checksum, resulting in the checksum unchanged.

Based on this principle, the default mapping mechanism of NPTv6 is irrelevant to the checksum. NPTv6 offsets by changing other parts of the IPv6 address, resulting in the IPv6 pseudo-header checksum remaining unchanged after mapping. That is, the IPv6 pseudo-header checksum of the internal network form and the external network form of the same IPv6 datagram does not change, so the NPTv6 translator does not need to update the checksum of the transport layer header (such as TCP or UDP).

When the IPv6 datagram of the internal network passes to the external network through NPTv6, its "outgoing direction" "checksum" is calculated by selecting the 16-bit field in the IPv6 source address. Similarly, when the IPv6 datagram of the external network passes to the internal network through NPTv6, its "incoming direction" "checksum" is calculated by the same algorithm.

Note that the use of a checksum-neutral algorithm will prevent edge networks from using subnets with 0xFFFF in the /48 external prefix.

12.1.3 NPTv6 Algorithm Specification

The IPv6 address structure defined by RFC4291 [14] is shown in Fig. 12.6.

1. *NPTv6 Configuration Calculation*

The parameters for configuring NPTv6 are as follows:

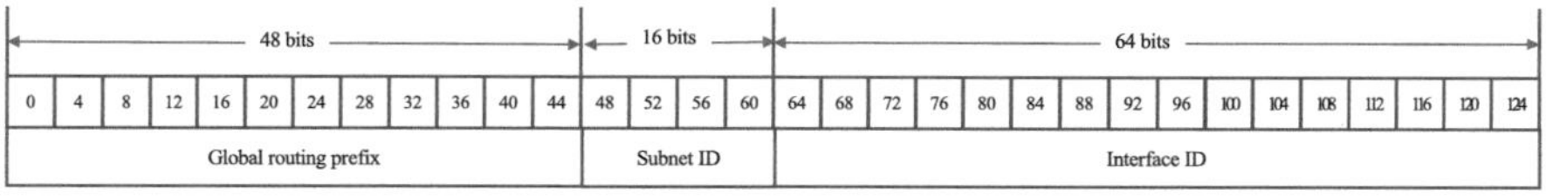

Fig. 12.6 IPv6 NPTv6 address structure

(1) One or more internal interfaces and their internal routing domain prefixes.
(2) One or more external interfaces and their external routing domains (if necessary, configure the corresponding domain name) prefix.

If a router provides NPTv6 translation services between multiple domains (such as multiple affiliations), it must logically be considered as several independent NPTv6 translators.

When configuring the NPTv6 translator, ensure that the internal prefix and the external prefix have the same prefix length (the shorter one of the two can be filled with 0), and then the prefix is filled with 0 to /64. Calculate the 16-bit complement sum of the external prefix /64 and the 16-bit complement sum of the internal prefix /64. Then calculate the difference between these two 16-bit complement sums: internal minus external. The obtained value is called the "adjustment value." This "adjustment value" is valid throughout the configuration lifecycle of the NPTv6 translator and is used for independent processing of each datagram.

2. *NPTv6 Translation from the Internal Network to the External Network*

When a datagram passes from the internal network through the NPTv6 translator to the external network, its IPv6 source address is either updated in the following way or the datagram is discarded.

(1) If its source address in NPTv6 does not belong to the internal network's IPv6 prefix or does not have a corresponding mapping table, or the subnet is 0xFFFF, then discard the datagram. At the same time, send an ICMPv6 destination node inaccessible error message.
(2) The internal prefix is replaced by the external prefix, but the "adjustment value" needs to be added. If the result is 0xFFFF, set it to 0×0000.

3. *NPTv6 Translation from the External Network to the Internal Network*

When a datagram passes from the external network through the NPTv6 translator to the internal network, its IPv6 destination address is updated in the following way: the external prefix is replaced by the internal prefix, but the "adjustment value" needs to be subtracted. If the result is 0xFFFF, set it to 0×0000.

4. *NPTv6 with /48 or Shorter Prefix*

When the internal prefix and external prefix configured by the NPTv6 translator have a prefix length of 48 bits (/48) or shorter, the "adjustment value" is adjusted in the range of 48–63 bits of the IPv6 address.

This type of mapping does not modify the interface identifier (IID), which is located at 64–127 bits of the IPv6 address, so it will not affect protocols using globally unique IIDs.

The NPTv6 translator must implement /48 prefix length mapping.

5. *NPTv6 with /49 or longer prefix*

When the internal prefix and external prefix configured by the NPTv6 translator exceed 48 bits (such as /52, /56, or /60), the adjustment must be made in the 48–63 bits, 64–79 bits, 80–95 bits, or 112–127 bits of the IPv6 address. Note that regardless of which segment is chosen, that segment must avoid 0xFFFF [15–17].

6. *NAT Behavior Requirements*

The NPTv6 translator should support hairpinning behavior (RFC4787 [18]). This means that when the NPTv6 translator receives a datagram at its internal interface with a destination address of the external prefix of its own network, the NPTv6 translator will map the address of the datagram and forward it back to the internal network. This allows internal nodes to communicate with other internal nodes, regardless of whether these nodes use the internal prefix or the external prefix.

Additionally, for security reasons, the NPTv6 translator can also be configured not to support hairpinning behavior, i.e., communication between internal devices must use the internal prefix.

NPTv6 does not perform port mapping and uses a one-to-one reversible mapping algorithm, so there is no need to consider other NAT behaviors.

7. *Impact on Applications*

NPTv6 will not cause the problems of other types of NAT discussed in RFC2993 [2]. The NPTv6 translator is stateless, so a "reset" or "momentary interruption" of the NPTv6 translator will not disrupt connection sessions through NPTv6. If there are multiple NPTv6 translators with the same configuration between two networks, load balancing will be automatically supported. In addition, the NPTv6 translator will not cluster the traffic of different internal hosts/interfaces through the mapping process from internal addresses to external addresses, so filtering a particular connection session will not affect other sessions. The NPTv6 translator can be used with a firewall, allowing network administrators to specify security policies more flexibly than using traditional NAT.

However, NPTv6 will indeed have an impact on some applications.

(1) The application program of the IPv6 internal network connected by the NPTv6 translator and its counterpart application program instance on the IPv6 Internet do not have the same 5-Tuple for the same connection session.
(2) The same node in the internal network will have at least two IPv6 addresses, i.e., the IPv6 address using the internal prefix and the IPv6 address using the external prefix. When NPTv6 supports hairpinning behavior, communication within the internal network can ignore this technical detail. But applications and domain systems may consider different addresses as different nodes.

8. *Considerations for Traditional NAT Traversal Techniques*

For IPv4, there are several traditional NAT traversal techniques, such as Session Traversal Utilities for NAT (STUN) (RFC8489 [11]), Traversal Using Relay NAT (TURN) (RFC8656 [19]), and ICE (RFC5245 [20]). When necessary, the NPTv6 translator can also use these techniques. All these techniques require the assistance of an external server (or NPTv6 function extension) to help the hosts of the internal network understand the external IPv6 address.

9. *Cooperation with IPv4/IPv6 Translators*

When deploying NPTv6, not only the relationship with NAT44 needs to be considered, but also the relationship and deployment with IPv4/IPv6 translators need to be considered consistently (RFC6144 [21], RFC6052 [22], RFC7915 [23] RFC6219 [24], RFC6146 [25], RFC7599 [26], RFC6147 [27]).

12.1.4 Security Considerations

NPTv6 supports bidirectionally initiated communication, allowing hosts on the IPv6 Internet to directly initiate communication with nodes in the internal network. This feature brings convenience for attacks from external networks. Although this does not pose a greater risk than using global IPv6 addresses, some companies may mistakenly believe that the NPTv6 translator can provide protection similar to NAT for the internal network.

The port mapping mechanism of NAT needs to establish a state in two directions. This has led to a misunderstanding in the industry that NAT functionality is the same as a stateful firewall. In fact, NAT functionality is different from a stateful firewall. NAT can initiate state establishment from the internal network, but NAT does not specify other policies. The NPTv6 translator should also have the function of an IPv6 firewall (RFC6092 [5]).

12.1.5 NPTv6 Example

The topology and data flow of the NPTv6 example are shown in Fig. 12.7. The left side is the topology, and the right side is the source and destination addresses of the datagram on this link.

1. Scenario
   (1) IPv6 network (client H1) initiates access to the IPv6 Internet (server H2).
   (2) IPv6 Internet (client H2) initiates access to the IPv6 network (server H1).
2. Translation Parameters

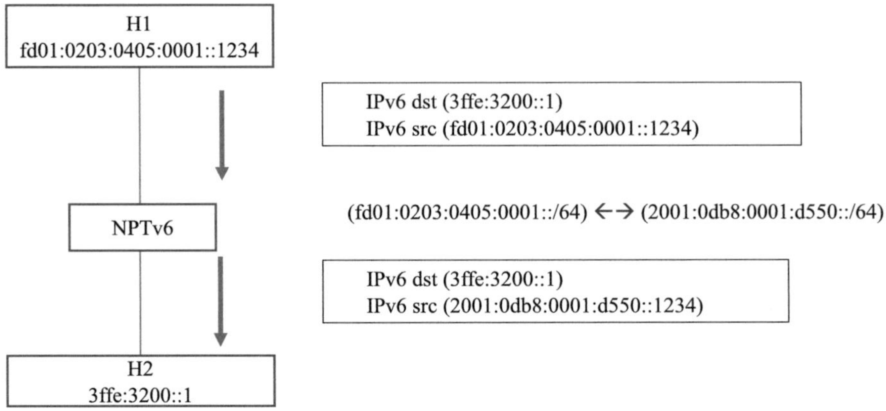

Fig. 12.7 NPTv6 example

(1) Internal IPv6 prefix: fd01:0203:0405:0001::/64.
(2) External IPv6 prefix: 2001:0db8:0001:d550::/64.

(3) Mapping unrelated to checksum.

(1) H1: An IPv6 host in the IPv6 network (fd01:0203:0405:0001::1234).
(2) H2: An IPv6 host on the IPv6 Internet (3ffe:3200::1).

3. Host Address:
4. Address Mapping Relationship Annotation

"Internal IPv6 Address":
(fd01:0203:0405:0001::1234) ←→ (2001:0db8:0001:d550::1234).

The selection of the "d550" field is based on the algorithm unrelated to the checksum.

12.2 Stateless Double IPv6 Prefix Translation

Based on the Stateless IPv6 Prefix Translation (NPTv6), the translator is cascaded to form the Stateless IPv6 Double Prefix Translation (dNPTv6), as shown in Fig. 12.8.

12.2.1 Background

Similar to stateless IPv4/IPv6 translation technology, NPTv6 devices can also be cascaded to form stateless IPv6 Double Prefix Translation (dNPTv6). In this case, for the hosts of the communicating parties, the basic characteristics of the IPv6 Internet end-to-end are maintained. Both hosts use ULA (RFC4193 [10]), and through the

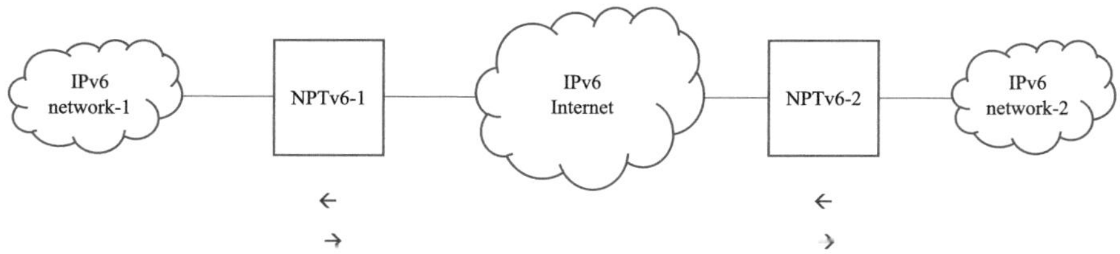

Fig. 12.8 dNPTv6

first NPTv6, the source and destination addresses of their datagrams are translated into globally unique IPv6 unicast addresses, allowing traversal of the IPv6 Internet. Through the second level NPTv6, the source and destination addresses of their datagrams are translated back to the original ULA. This is a process from IPv6 ULA to IPv6 global unicast address, and then to IPv6 ULA, that is, IPv6-IPv6-IPv6 (666).

Although the double translation technology makes the datagram with ULA addresses traverse the IPv6 Internet, it does not use encapsulation at the network layer when crossing the IPv6 Internet. The Internet ACL and rate-limiting techniques can be applied to individual ULA hosts without decapsulation.

12.2.2 Basics of dNPTv6

1. *Similarities and Differences with NPTv6*

Similar to NPTv6, dNPTv6 uses the prefix mapping mechanism of NPTv6 to translate the addresses in the datagram, but unlike NPTv6, dNPTv6 translates both the source and destination prefixes of the datagram.

(1) The 1st NPTv6 maps the source prefix for datagrams sent to the external network, and maps the destination prefix for datagrams received from the external network.
(2) Regardless of whether the datagram is sent to the external network or received from the external network, the 2nd dNPTv6 maps both the source and destination prefixes.

2. *Address Format*

dNPTv6 can be considered the cascading of two NPTv6 translators that translate both the source and destination addresses of the datagram, but due to the introduction of double translation technology, the use of addresses has more flexibility.

(1) The dNPTv6 is the address-mapping mechanism of NPTv6 that translates the source and destination addresses of the datagram through two translators.
(2) Because it is a double translation, as long as the address mapping rules are consistent between the two translators, different IPv6 prefix lengths can be chosen.

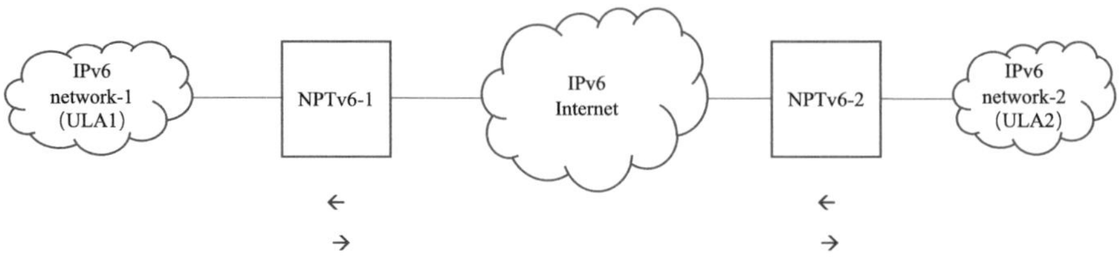

Fig. 12.9 dNPTv6 (666VPN)

(3) The source and destination addresses of the datagram usually need to use different IPv6 prefixes.

3. *Protocol Processing*

The protocol processing of dNPTv6 uses the processing method of NPTv6 defined by RFC6296 [1]. It should be pointed out that because it is a double-translation technology, "checksum neutral" requirement can be ignored.

4. *666 Virtual Private Network (666VPN)*

For double translation technology, an important application scenario is to build a virtual private network (666VPN) using IPv6 ULA addresses across the IPv6 Internet, as shown in Fig. 12.9.

The characteristics of implementing 666VPN with dNPTv6 are as follows:

(1) For the IPv6 Internet, what is transmitted are simple IPv6 datagrams (not any encapsulation, tunneling, or IPv6 segment routing (SRv6)), so standard network layer tools (ACL, rate-limiting, etc.) can be used without decapsulation.
(2) Compatible with higher layer security protocols.

12.2.3 dNPTv6 Configuration Discussion

1. *Routing and Forwarding*

The NPTv6 translator and the router connected to it are configured according to the standard IPv6 routing principles. Note that at the boundary of the NPTv6 translator, the internal and external IPv6 routes should not be leaked.

2. *DNS Configuration*

Configure the DNS of the internal network as needed on the internal network side of the NPTv6 system.

3. *Compatibility with NPTv6*

As mentioned above, dNPTv6 maps both the source and destination prefixes of the datagram at the same time. In contrast, NPTv6 only maps the source or destination prefix of the datagram based on the direction of data transmission. Therefore, devices that support dNPTv6 should be configurable, that is, decide whether to map the source and destination addresses at the same time based on the range of the source and/or destination addresses. In this way, access to the IPv6 Internet and 666VPN can be implemented on one device.

12.2.4 dNPTv6 Example

The topology and data flow of the dNPTv6 example are shown in Fig. 12.10. The left side is the topology, and the right side is the source and destination addresses of the datagrams on this link.

1. *Scenario*
   (1) IPv6 ULA network (client H1) initiates access to the IPv6 ULA network (server H2) through the IPv6 Internet.
   (2) IPv6 ULA Internet (client H2) initiates access to the IPv6 ULA network (server H1) through the IPv6 Internet.
2. *dNPTv6 Parameters*
   (1) Source IPv6 prefix of mapper dNPTv6-1: 2001:0db8:0001:d550::/64.
   (2) Destination IPv6 prefix of mapper dNPTv6-1: 3ffe:3200::/64.
   (3) Destination IPv6 prefix of mapper dNPTv6-2: 2001:0db8:0001:d550::/64.

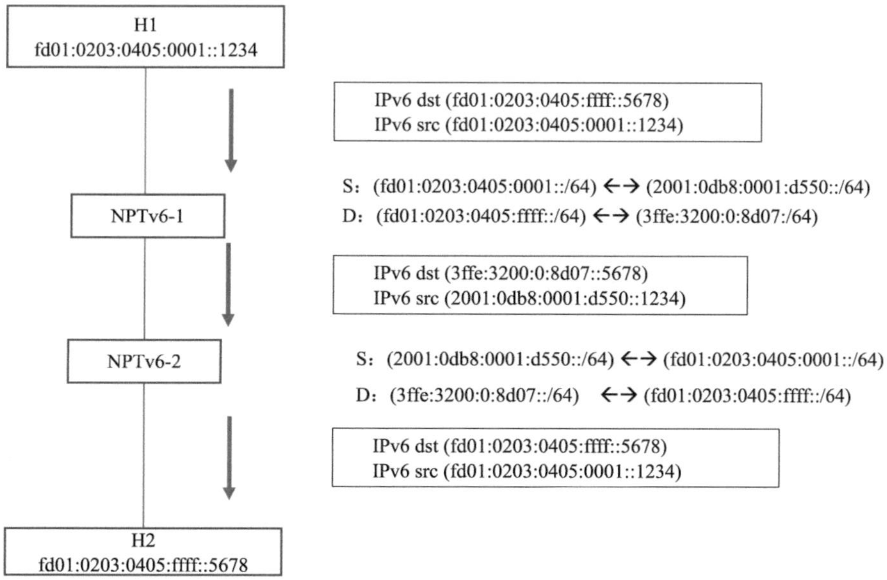

Fig. 12.10 dNPTv6 example

(4) Source IPv6 prefix of mapper dNPTv6-2: 3ffe:3200::/64.

3. *Host Address*

(1) H1: An IPv6 host in the IPv6 ULA network (fd01:0203:0405:0001::1234).
(2) H2: An IPv6 host in the IPv6 ULA network (fd01:0203:0405:ffff::5678).

4. *Address Mapping Relationship Notes*

(1) IPv6 source address:

(fd01:0203:0405:0001::/64)⟷ (2001:0db8:0001:d550::/64).

(2) IPv6 destination address:

(fd01:0203:0405:ffff::/64) ⟷ (3ffe:3200::/64).

12.3 Summary

This chapter introduces NPTv6 and dNPTv6. In the early design of IPv6, the IETF's idea was to remove the address translation mechanism introduced by IPv4 to restore the characteristic of end-to-end addresses on the Internet. However, with the development of the Internet, people gradually realized that it is impossible and unnecessary to completely ignore address translation in IPv6. This chapter introduces the mechanisms and design implementation schemes of stateless IPv6 prefix translation and double IPv6 prefix translation. Note that the IPv6 prefix translation is a new field, full of challenges, and opportunities in the future.

References

1. Wasserman M, Baker F. RFC6296: IPv6-to-IPv6 network prefix translation. IETF 2011-06.
2. Hain T. RFC2993: Architectural implications of NAT. IETF 2000-11.
3. Velde G T, Hain T, Droms R, et al. RFC4864: Local network protection for IPv6. IETF 2007-05.
4. Thaler D, Zhang L, Lebovitz G. RFC5902: IAB thoughts on IPv6 network address translation. IETF 2010-07.
5. Woodyatt J. RFC6092: Recommended simple security capabilities in customer premises equipment (CPE) for providing residential IPv6 internet service. IETF 2011-01.
6. Daigle L. RFC3424: IAB considerations for unilateral self-address fixing (UNSAF) across network address translation. IETF 2002-11.
7. Touch J, Mankin A, Bonica R. RFC5925: The TCP authentication option. IETF 2010-06.
8. Kaufman C, Hoffman P, Nir Y, et al. RFC5996: Internet key exchange protocol version 2 (IKEv2). IETF 2010-09.
9. Ferguson P, Senie D. RFC2827: Network ingress filtering: Defeating denial of service attacks which employ IP source address spoofing. IETF 2000-05.
10. Hinden R, Haberman B. RFC4193: Unique local IPv6 unicast addresses. IETF 2005-10.
11. Petit-Huguenin M, Salgueiro G, Rosenberg J, et al. RFC8489: Session traversal utilities for NAT (STUN). IETF 2020-02.

12. Braden R, Borman D, Partridge C. RFC1071: Computing the internet checksum. IETF 1988-09.
13. Rijsinghani A. RFC1624: Computation of the internet checksum via incremental update. IETF 1994-05.
14. Hinden R, Deering S. RFC4291: IP version 6 addressing architecture. IETF 2006-02.
15. Johnson D, Deering S. RFC2526: Reserved IPv6 subnet anycast addresses. IETF 1999-03.
16. Conta A, Deering S, Gupta M. RFC4443: Internet control message protocol (ICMPv6) for the internet protocol version 6 (IPv6) specification. IETF 2006-03.
17. Singh H, Beebee W, Donley C, et al. RFC6204: Basic requirements for IPv6 customer edge routers. IETF 2011-04.
18. Audet F, Jennings C. RFC4787: Network address translation (NAT) behavioral requirements for unicast UDP. IETF 2007-01.
19. Reddy T, Johnston A, Matthews P, et al. RFC8656: Traversal using relays around NAT (TURN): Relay extensions to session traversal utilities for NAT (STUN). IETF 2020-02.
20. Rosenberg J. RFC5245: Interactive connectivity establishment (ICE): A protocol for network address translator (NAT) traversal for offer/answer protocols. IETF 2010-04.
21. Baker F, Li X, Bao C, et al. RFC6144: Framework for IPv4/IPv6 translation. IETF 2011-04.
22. Bao C, Huitema C, Bagnulo M, et al. RFC6052: IPv6 addressing of IPv4/IPv6 translators. IETF 2010-10.
23. Bao C, Li X, Baker F, et al. RFC7915: IP/ICMP translation algorithm. IETF 2016-06.
24. Li X, Bao C, Chen M, et al. RFC6219: The China Education and Research Network (CERNET) IVI translation design and deployment for the IPv4/IPv6 coexistence and transition. IETF 2011-05.
25. Bagnulo M, Matthews P, Beijnum I. RFC6146: Stateful NAT64: Network address and protocol translation from IPv6 clients to IPv4 servers. IETF 2011-04.
26. Li X, Bao C, Dec W, et al. RFC7599: Mapping of address and port using translation (MAP-T). IETF 2015-07.
27. Bagnulo M, Sullivan A, Matthews P, et al. RFC6147: DNS64: DNS extensions for network address translation from IPv6 clients to IPv4 servers. IETF 2011-04.

Part III
Deployment and Outlook

Chapter 13
IPv6-Only Transition Roadmap

The core idea of the new-generation IPv6 transition technology is to promote the deployment of IPv6-only while maintaining interconnection with the IPv4 Internet, and ultimately complete the transition to IPv6.

13.1 Evolution and Future Directions

In 2016, the Internet Architecture Board (IAB) proposed [1]:

(1) The IETF will no longer require new protocols or extended protocols to support compatibility with IPv4. Future IETF protocol work will only optimize for IPv6.
(2) We encourage the industry to develop strategies that support IPv6-only operations.

In 2020, the Office of the President of the United States issued a memorandum [2], proposing the goal of migrating to IPv6-only.

In 2021, the Chinese Government issued a document titled "Accelerating the Large-scale Deployment and Application of the Sixth Version of the Internet Protocol (IPv6)" [3]. The document outlined a plan to complete the transition to IPv6-only by 2030.

Although the transition to IPv6 is still ongoing, the above decisions are timely. The evolution and future directions of the IPv6 transition can be divided into the following stages.

X. Li and C. Bao, *New IPv6 Transition Technology*,
https://doi.org/10.1007/978-981-95-8427-7_13

13.1.1 IPv4-Only

Since IPv4's inception in the 1980s, it has been the cornerstone of Internet development. Its 32-bit address space once supported global network expansion. However, with the rapid proliferation of the Internet of Things (IoT), mobile devices, cloud computing, and particularly artificial intelligence agents, address resources have rapidly depleted. Although the crisis has been delayed through NAT and IPv4 address allocation strategies, the limitations of IPv4 have become unable to meet modern demands. Currently, IPv4 still accounts for approximately 70% of global network traffic, but its lifecycle will eventually come to an end. Governments and enterprises worldwide are expediting the transition to IPv6 to anticipate and mitigate future challenges.

13.1.2 Dual Stack

Dual-stack technology was the first technical solution developed by the IETF to transition from IPv4 to IPv6. Since IPv6 is incompatible with IPv4, it is crucial to ensure that IPv6-upgraded devices can still communicate with IPv4 Internet. While dual-stack technology appears to be the most straightforward approach, its deployment has several drawbacks, including address space wastage (IPv4 addresses remain occupied), increased routing complexity, security vulnerabilities, and higher deployment and operational costs. Despite two decades of practical implementation, the transition to IPv6 has remained incomplete. In response, the IETF initiated a re-evaluation of this approach and developed a new-generation translation-based IPv6 transition technologies and standards.

13.1.3 IPv4-Reachable IPv6-Only and IPv6-Mostly

An IPv6-only network refers to a deployment model in which only IPv6 addresses are configured for devices within a specific scope, relying exclusively on the IPv6 protocol. This model effectively addresses the address shortage problem through its 128-bit address space, while also supporting more efficient routing, automated configuration, and enhanced security. However, IPv6-only networks that cannot communicate with the IPv4 Internet are not acceptable to users. To resolve this, the current term IPv6-only now refers to IPv6-only networks that employ IPv6 translation technologies, enabling IPv6-only devices to interoperate with the IPv4 Internet.

An IPv6-mostly network describes a deployment model where IPv4-reachable IPv6-only is the default configuration. In such networks, IPv4 addresses are optionally assigned to devices that do not support IPv6, ensuring their access to the IPv4 Internet.

In the following chapter of this book, the terms IPv6-only and IPv6-mostly are used to refer specifically to IPv4-reachable IPv6-only and IPv4-reachable IPv6-mostly networks, respectively.

13.1.4 IPv4/IPv6 Coexistent and IPv4 Sunset

The coexistence of IPv4 and IPv6, along with the gradual phasing out of IPv4 (IPv4 Sunset), can be achieved through the phased deployment of "IPv4-reachable IPv6-only and IPv6-mostly" networks. These new IPv6-only/IPv6-mostly networks ensure seamless interoperability with both IPv4 and IPv6 Internet. Key characteristics of these networks include the following:

(1) The IPv6-only hosts can communicate with the IPv4 Internet via translator.
(2) The IPv4 addresses are allocated exclusively to devices that lack IPv6 support, thereby significantly reducing the overall allocation of IPv4 addresses.
(3) The IPv6-to-IPv4 traffic is passing through translators only when the counterpart is IPv4-only.

This represents a new form of IPv4/IPv6 coexistence. As the number of IPv6-only and IPv6-mostly networks grows, end-to-end IPv6 traffic will gradually dominate, while IPv4 traffic will steadily decline. This transition occurs transparently, without the need for a "flag day" event. The timeline of this process is not critical; more importantly, the emergence of novel IPv6-only applications (applications that IPv4 cannot support) will surge during specific phases, ultimately driving the global Internet toward a fully IPv6-only infrastructure.

13.2 Which Transition Technology to Choose?

This book introduces the new generation of IPv6 transition technologies, but because IPv4 and IPv6 are not compatible, and the address space of IPv4 and IPv6 is vastly different. Especially after more than 50 years of development of the Internet, its scale is huge, and its application system has an undeniable diversity. Therefore, there is no single IPv6 transition technology that can adapt to all scenarios. The following discusses the issues that must be considered when specifically choosing IPv6 transition technology.

13.2.1 Interoperability with IPv4

Although to an IPv6-only Internet is currently the consensus for transition strategy. From a global perspective, IPv4 may continue to exist for a considerable period in the future. The value of the Internet lies in "interconnection and interoperability," so devices on the IPv6-only network need to support communication with devices on the IPv4 Internet.

IPv4/IPv6 translation technology is the only technology that can make IPv4 and IPv6 interconnect and interoperate at the network layer [4–6]. In other words, any IPv6-only deployment, to satisfy the following requirements, must deploy and use IPv4/IPv6 translation technology:

(1) Need to interconnect and interoperate with the IPv4 Internet.
(2) Need to interconnect and interoperate with other IPv4 networks.
(3) Need to continue to use applications that are not compatible with IPv6.
(4) Need to continue to use operating systems or dedicated hardware devices that are not compatible with IPv6.

After deploying IPv4/IPv6 translation technology, the IPv6-only hosts in IPv6-only network can interconnect and interoperate with IPv4.

Conclusion: The key building block of the new generation of IPv6 transition technology is IPv4/IPv6 translation.

13.2.2 Scalability, Security, and Traceability Issues

Routers on the Internet are stateless, that is, each data packet is forwarded independently according to the routing table, thereby ensuring the scalability of the Internet. In addition, stateless technology can ensure end-to-end address transparency, so it can precisely control security and traceability.

Stateful technology requires state synchronization between translators, and scalability is not as good as stateless devices. At the same time, stateful technology invalidates the uniqueness of the address, thereby destroying end-to-end address transparency and posing challenges to the security and traceability of the network.

Conclusion: To ensure scalability, security, and traceability, it is recommended preferring stateless translation technology.

13.2.3 IP Address-Embedded Applications

IETF standards suggest: Application layer protocols should not contain any IP address information, if IP addresses need to be referenced, they must be through the DNS. In this case, for example DNS64, which cooperates with the IPv4/IPv6 translator, can convert IPv4 addresses into IPv6 addresses (IPv4-converted IPv6 address) according to the pre-configured IPv6 prefix.

However, in reality, there are indeed a large number of non-regular situations. For example, not using (or unable to use) the DNS, the main form of which is embedding IP addresses in the application layer, including the following types:

(1) Active mode FTP, which embeds IP addresses in the application layer.
(2) Web pages that use IP addresses as hyperlinks.
(3) Other applications that embed IP addresses.

The above scenarios can be further divided into two situations.

(1) Controllable Situation. If the entity that deploys IPv6-only can fully control its application, such as running an IPv6-only server, the following processing can be done:

   ① Use standard application layer protocols, such as HTTP/HTTPS.
   ② All links in web pages (including javascripts, etc.) use DNS names instead of IP addresses.
   ③ Develop dedicated application layer proxies.

   Therefore, for controlled situations, deploying translation technology is a preferred solution.

(2) Uncontrollable Situation. IPv6-only clients often face the following completely uncontrollable situations:

   ① Users using this client may access any service on the Internet, including applications embedded with IPv4 addresses, especially web pages that still use IP addresses as hyperlinks.
   ② Providing corresponding ALG for any service on the IPv4 Internet is unrealistic. Because applications are constantly changing and it is theoretically impossible to develop a universal ALG. At the same time, it is impossible to develop ALG for encrypted protocols.
   ③ The client may run different operating systems and have different IPv6 access behaviors.

In this case, double translation technology or tunneling technology (encapsulation technology) is a practical solution. Chapters 8, 10 and 11 of this book provide solutions for application layer protocols embedding IP addresses, and the comprehensive discussion is as follows. A very good sign is that more and more modern operating systems are integrating stateless translation modules as part of the basic function (iOS, macOS, Android, etc.).

1. *The Operating System Supports Prefix Discovery Technology and Provides API*

The operating system supports prefix discovery technology (RFC7050 [7], etc.), and applications running on this operating system must call prefix discovery API. Apple's mobile operating system (iOS) and computer operating system (Mac OS) support this feature. It should be noted that only Apple's operating system can use this technology, because Apple is a closed system, and applications that do not call the API according to the specifications are not allowed to be listed on the Apple App Store.

2. *The Operating System Supports Pref64 Extension and Provides API*

A better method compared to prefix discovery is the operating system supports Pref64 extension (RFC8781 [8]), and applications running on this operating system must call this Pref64 extension technology's API. For the security reasons, new versions of the operating systems (e.g., MacOS, etc.) are supporting this option, rather than prefix discovery technology.

3. *The Operating System Supports Prefix Discovery Technology and Supports Double Translation*

The operating system supports prefix discovery (RFC7050 [7]) or configuration (RFC8781 [8]) technology and double translation technology (RFC6877 [9]), that is, the operating system itself provides IPv4/IPv6 translation function. The reason why Google's Android system supports double translation technology is that Android is an open system and cannot require its applications to call specific APIs. The double translation technology makes the Android system IPv6-only on the network side and dual stack on the application side. In other words, any IPv4-only application on the Android system can access and use the IPv6-only network that has deployed a translator on the network side, maintaining interconnection with the IPv4 Internet. In fact, Apple also supports the double translation mode because when the iPhone serves as a "hotspot" for the wireless local area network, its connected devices can be fully functional for IPv4-only and IPv4 address-embedding applications.

Since tunnel technology cannot make IPv4-only hosts and IPv6-only hosts communicate, making it difficult to transition to IPv6-only. In addition, the current mainstream operating systems do not support tunnel technology (encapsulation technology).

Conclusion: It is recommended to prefer translation technology or double translation technology.

4. *Supporting for Legacy IPv4-Only Operating Systems*

It is strongly recommended to set up DHCPv4 server with Option 108 support, so the subnet becomes IPv6-mostly [10].

13.2.4 IPv6 Transition Roadmap

This book discusses the new generation of IPv6 transition technology, including single translation, 464 double translation, 4over6 encapsulation (tunneling), and comparing them with the traditional "dual stack" and "IPv6-only," as shown in Fig. 13.1 (RFC6052 [4], RFC7915 [5], RFC2473 [11], RFC6219 [6], RFC7599 [12], RFC7597 [13], RFC6146 [14], RFC6877 [9], RFC6333 [15]).

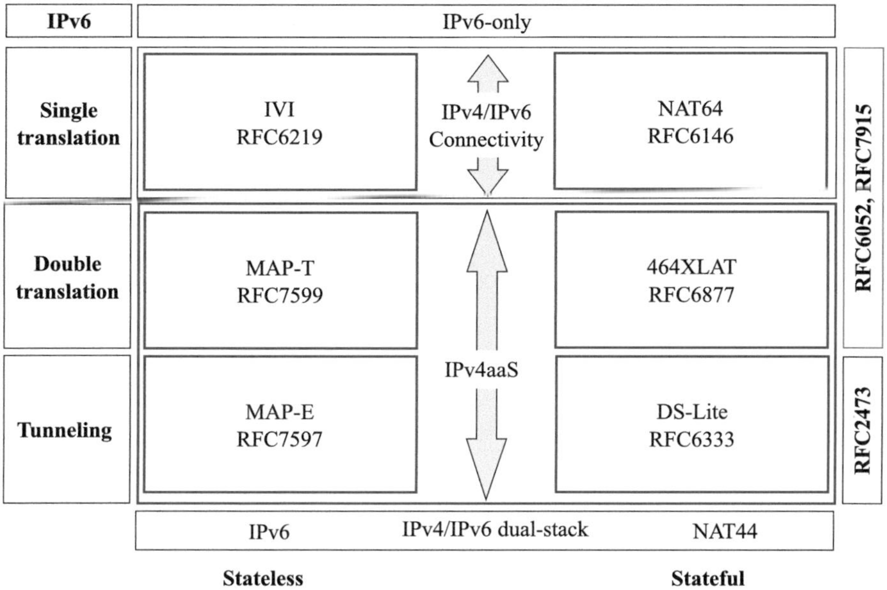

Fig. 13.1 New-generation IPv6 transition technology solutions

In Fig. 13.1, the left column is the stateless series technology (RFC6219 [6], RFC7599 [12], RFC7597 [13]), the main feature is that all address mapping relationships are algorithm-based, no need to maintain session states, support bidirectional initiated communication, and have better scalability and security. The right side is the stateful series technology (RFC6146 [14], RFC6877 [9], RFC6333 [15]), the characteristic is the need to maintain session states, only support client-to-server connection, but easier to deploy. For the protocol processing mechanism, the common component of all translation technologies is protocol translation (RFC7915 [5]), all encapsulation technologies' common component is encapsulation and decapsulation (RFC2473 [11]).

Since the basic design principle of the Internet is "connectionless, end-to-end, and best-effort," its implicit key idea is the statelessness of the network or, in other words, the state should be maintained on the end system. Therefore, we propose the following two suggestions [16]:

(1) Prefer the use of stateless IPv6 transition technology, and if necessary, stateful IPv6 transition technology can be used.
(2) Deploy stateless IPv6 transition technology in the backbone network, and if necessary, stateful IPv6 transition technology can be deployed in the edge network.

It needs to be emphasized that although the external characteristics of 464 double translation and 4over6 tunnel are the same, both provide IPv4 services through the IPv6 network (IPv4 as a Service, IPv4aaS). However, 464 double translation can degrade into single translation, achieving interconnection between IPv4 and IPv6. However, the tunnel technology and dual-stack technology cannot degrade to IPv6-only. Therefore, the recommended IPv6 transition strategy is “translation if you can, tunnel if you should, and dual-stack if you must.”

The strategy for building new networks or upgrading existing networks should prefer IPv6-only.

(1) When the communication peer is IPv6, use IPv6-only.
(2) When the communication peer is IPv4, prefer using single translation.
(3) When the application does not support IPv6 or the application embeds IPv4 address, use double translation.
(4) When it is necessary to preserve all the information of the IPv4 packet (such as the Option field in the IPv4 header), encapsulation technology could be used.

In the middle and late stages of the IPv6 transition, double translation will degrade into single translation, and finally the translator will have less and less traffic, entering the era of IPv6-only.

Adopting such an IPv6 transition roadmap can enable each network to transition to IPv6-only, efficiently use public IPv4, and keep the connection with the IPv4 Internet, thus maintaining smooth and transparent operation during the transition period from IPv4 to IPv6.

Lastly, but not least important, the IPv6-only transition compared with dual stack can significantly reduce costs while maintaining connectivity to the IPv4 Internet.

13.3 Summary

Based on the detailed discussion of IPv6 transition technology in the previous chapters, this chapter clearly proposes the roadmap from IPv4 to IPv6-only which addresses the scalability, security, and adaptation to various operating systems and applications.

References

1. IAB. IAB statement on IPv6. [2022-07-17]. https://www.iab.org/2016/11/07/iab-statement-on-ipv6.
2. Vought R T. Memorandum for heads of executive departments and agencies. [2022-07-17]. https://www.whitehouse.gov/wp-content/uploads/2020/11/M-21-07.pdf.
3. The People’s Republic of China Central People’s Government. Notice on accelerating the large-scale deployment and application of the Internet Protocol version 6 (IPv6). [2022-07-17]. http://www.gov.cn/zhengce/zhengceku/2021-07/23/content_5626963.htm.
4. Bao C, Huitema C, Bagnulo M, et al. RFC6052: IPv6 addressing of IPv4/IPv6 translators. IETF 2010-10.
5. Bao C, Li X, Baker F, et al. RFC7915: IP/ICMP translation algorithm. IETF 2016-06.

6. Li X, Bao C, Chen M, et al. RFC6219: The China Education and Research Network (CERNET) IVI translation design and deployment for the IPv4/IPv6 coexistence and transition. IETF 2011-05.
7. Savolainen T, Korhonen J, Wing D. RFC7050: Discovery of the IPv6 prefix used for IPv6 address synthesis. IETF 2013-11.
8. Colitti L, Linkova J. RFC8781: Discovering PREF64 in router advertisements. IETF 2020-04.
9. Mawatari M, Kawashima M, Byrne C. RFC6877: 464XLAT: Combination of stateful and stateless translation. IETF 2013-04.
10. Colitti L, Linkova J, Richardso M, et al. RFC8925: IPv6-Only Preferred Option for DHCPv4. IETF 2020-10.
11. Conta A, Deering S. RFC2473: Generic packet tunneling in IPv6 specification. IETF 1998-12.
12. Li X, Bao C, Dec W, et al. RFC7599: Mapping of address and port using translation (MAP-T). IETF 2015-07.
13. Troan O, Dec W, Li X, et al. RFC7597: Mapping of address and port with encapsulation (MAP-E). IETF 2015-07.
14. Bagnulo M, Matthews P, van Beijnum I. RFC6146: Stateful NAT64: Network address and protocol translation from IPv6 clients to IPv4 servers. IETF 2011-04.
15. Durand A, Droms R, Woodyatt J, et al. RFC6333: Dual-stack lite broadband deployments following IPv4 exhaustion. IETF 2011-08.
16. Bao Congxiao, Li Xing. Unified IPv4/IPv6 translation and encapsulation transition technology - IVI/MAP-T/MAP-E. ZTE Communications, 2013, 19(2): 7–11.

Chapter 14
IPv6-Only (and IPv6-Mostly) Network Design

This chapter discusses how to use the IPv4/IPv6 transition technologies in Chaps. 9, 10, 11 and 12, with the cooperation of Chaps. 7 and 8, to design IPv6-only (and IPv6-mostly) networks and achieve interconnection with the existing IPv4 Internet. Given the huge gap between IPv6 and IPv4 address spaces, the scarcity of public IPv4 addresses, and the limitations of network devices in supporting different technologies, there is no single solution that can fit to all scenarios. Actually, there may be multiple solutions for a single scenario. The following are recommended solutions for different scenarios. The solutions described here include topology, address, routing, DNS and firewall configurations, as well as server log analysis, etc. To help understand the essence of the solution, the communication process is given at the end of each section.

14.1 IPv6-Only Server

1. *Topology*

To complete the transition to IPv6-only, the servers should be IPv6-only, which can provide services to IPv4-only users through a translator.

This example uses stateless single translation (1:1 IVI), and the topology is shown in Fig. 14.1.

The building blocks are as follows:

(1) IPv4/IPv6 translator [1–3].
(2) Core routers (including IPv6-core router and IPv4-core router).
(3) Access router (IPv6-only).
(4) Server (IPv6-only).
(5) DNS server [4] (IPv4 and IPv6 dual stack).

2. *Address Configuration*

X. Li and C. Bao, *New IPv6 Transition Technology*,
https://doi.org/10.1007/978-981-95-8427-7_14

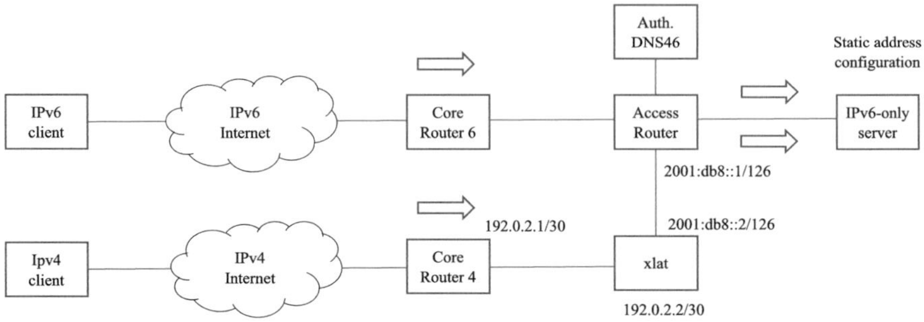

Fig. 14.1 Topology of IPv6-only server subnet

In this example, the IPv6-only server uses the IPv4-translatable IPv6 address defined by RFC6052 [1] (with u-oct) and uses Network Specific Prefix (NSP). The parameters are as follows:

(1) IPv6 prefix (NSP): 2001:db8:100::/40.
(2) The IVI4 address of the IPv4-translatable IPv6 address: 192.0.2.0/24.

Based on the above condition, the network design is as follows:

(1) The subnet of the IPv6-only server: 2001:db8:1c0:2::/64 (inside of 2001:db8:100::/40, with 192.0.2.0/24 embedded).
(2) Gateway address of the IPv6-only server: 2001:db8:1c0:2::1 (the 1st usable IPv6 address in subnet 2001:db8:1c0:2::/64. Note: This address does not need to use the IPv4-translatable IPv6 address, in order not to waste a public IPv4 address).
(3) IPv4 address corresponding to the IPv6-only server: 192.0.2.33. (Note: This is the IPv4 address embedded in the IPv4-translatable IPv6 address, see next item).
(4) IPv4-translatable IPv6 address used by the IPv6-only server: 2001:db8:1c0:2:21::.

3. *Routing Configuration*

The routing configuration is as follows:

(1) The IPv6 core router configures static or dynamic routes, pointing the IPv4-translatable IPv6 address (2001:db8:1c0:2::/64) to the access router.
(2) The access router configures the IPv6 default route (::0/0), pointing to the IPv6 core router.
(3) The IPv4 core router configures static or dynamic routes, pointing the IPv4 prefix (192.0.2.0/24) of the IPv4-translatable IPv6 address to the translator.
(4) The translator configures the IPv4 default route (0.0.0.0/0), pointing to the IPv4 core router.
(5) The translator configures the IPv6 route, pointing the IPv4-translatable IPv6 address (2001:db8:1c0:2::/64) to the access router.

(6) The access router configures the IPv6 route, pointing the Network Specific Prefix (NSP), which is used for translation (2001:db8:100::/40) to the translator.

4. *DNS Configuration*

The configuration of the authoritative DNS, which requires the DNS46 support, is as follows [4]:

(1) The AAAA record is the IPv4-translatable IPv6 address (2001:db8:1c0:2:21::).
(2) The A record is calculated through RFC6052 [1], and is the IPv4 address (192.0.2.33) corresponding to the IPv4-translatable IPv6 address.

5. *Security Policy and Firewall Configuration*

There are two methods to set up the security policies and firewalls.

(1) Deploy IPv6 security policies/firewalls between the IPv6 core router and the access router, as well as deploy IPv4 security policies/firewalls between the IPv4 core router and the translator, separately. In this case, maintaining the consistency of IPv4 and IPv6 security policies and firewalls is a challenge for the network and security management.
(2) Deploy IPv6 security policies and firewalls between access routers and IPv6-only servers. In this case, the IPv4 address is a subset of the IPv6 address, appearing in the form of IPv6, which can more easily maintain consistency.

6. *Log Analysis*

For IPv6-only servers, when providing services to clients on the IPv4 Internet, the IPv4 address is a subset of the IPv6 address, and its logs appear in the form of IPv6. That is, if the IPv6 address in the log appears within the subnet range of 2001:db8:100::/40, it is a record of a client's access from the IPv4 Internet. Therefore, only the logs in the form of IPv6 addresses need to be processed, reducing the development and operating costs of the log processing system.

7. *Communication Process*

The process of an IPv4 client (198.51.100.2) initiating access to the IPv6-only server (2001:db8:1c0:2:21::) is as follows:

(1) DNS query: A record = 192.0.2.33 (The AAAA record = 2001:db8:1c0:2:21::).
(2) Datagram in the IPv4 Internet: source address = 198.51.100.2; destination address = 192.0.2.33.
(3) After translation, the datagram in the IPv6-only subnet: source address = 2001:db8:1c6:3364:2::, destination address = 2001:db8:1c0:2:21::.
(4) Return datagram in the IPv6-only subnet:; source address = 2001:db8:1c0:2:21::; destination address = 2001:db8:1c6:3364:2::.
(5) After translation, the return datagram in the IPv4 Internet: source address = 192.0.2.33; destination address = 198.51.100.2.
(6) Loop until the communication process ends.

14.2 IPv6-Only Client

14.2.1 IPv6-Only DHCPv6 Client

1. *Topology*

To complete the transition to IPv6-only, IPv6-only clients should be able to access IPv4-only servers on the Internet through a translator.

There are two implementation scenarios for the IPv6-only subnet. This section discusses the first scenario, where the stateful DHCPv6 is used to assign addresses to IPv6-only clients, and the translator uses stateless single translation technology 1: *N* IVI, as shown in Fig. 14.2.

The building blocks are as follows:

(1) IPv4/IPv6 translator [1–3, 5].
(2) Core router (including IPv6 core router and IPv4 core router).
(3) Access router (IPv6-only), providing DHCPv6 proxy and RA services to this subnet.
(4) DHCPv6 Server.
(5) Client [6, 7] (IPv6-only), obtaining address through DHCPv6.
(6) DNS resolver [4] (IPv6 and IPv4 dual-stack access).

2. *Address Configuration*

The IPv6-only client in this example uses an RFC6052 [1]/RFC7915 [2] (no u-oct) defined "IPv4-translatable IPv6 address," which uses a Network Specific Prefix (NSP); in addition, the IPv4-converted IPv6 address and the IPv4-translatable IPv6 address use different IPv6 prefix lengths. The parameters are as follows:

(1) IPv4-translatable IPv6 address: 2001:db8:100::/40.
(2) IPv4: 1.2.4.0/24.
(3) The public IPv4 address sharing ratio: 2048.

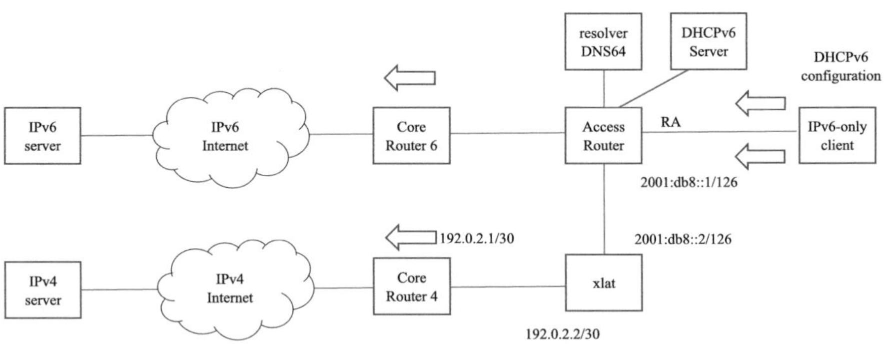

Fig. 14.2 Topology of the DHCPv6-based IPv6-only client subnet

(4) IPv4-converted IPv6 address prefix: 2001:db8:100::/96.

The client address is assigned through DHCPv6.

(1) IPv6-only client subnet: 2001:da8:ff01:0204::/64.

Note: In this mode, the IPv6 address pool of DHCPv6 is discontinuous, and the addresses in the pool must comply with the 1:*N* IVI address and port mapping rules.

(2) Default gateway address of the IPv6-only client subnet: 2001:da8:ff01:0204::1/64.

Note: This address is not the "IPv4-translatable IPv6 address" in order not to waste the public IPv4 address. The default gateway address is announced by RA, and the configuration parameters of RA are as follows:

AdvAutonomous off (A=0).

AdvManagedFlag on (M=1).

AdvOtherConfigFlag on (O=1).

(3) The IPv6 address obtained by the IPv6-only client in this example through DHCPv6: 2001:da8:ff01:0204:0300:0800:: (corresponding to PSID = 1).
(4) IPv4 address of the server on the IPv4 Internet: 198.51.100.2.
(5) IPv4-converted IPv6 address of the server on the IPv4 Internet: 2001:db8:1c6:3364:2::, which is obtained via DNS64.

3. *Routing Configuration*

The routing configuration is as follows:

(1) The IPv6 core router configures static or dynamic routing, pointing the IPv4-translatable IPv6 address (2001:da8:ff01:0204::/64) to the access router.
(2) The access router configures the IPv6 default route (::0/0), pointing to the IPv6 core router.
(3) The IPv4 core router configures static or dynamic route, pointing the IPv4 prefix (1.2.4.0/24), which is corresponding to the IPv4-translatable IPv6 address (2001:da8:ff01:0204::/64) to the translator.
(4) The translator configures the IPv4 default route (0.0.0.0/0), pointing to the IPv4 core router.
(5) The translator configures the IPv6 route pointing the IPv4-translatable IPv6 address (2001:da8:ff01:0204::/64) to the IPv6 access router.
(6) The IPv6-only access router configures the IPv6 route, pointing the Network Specific Prefix (NSP, 2001:db8:100::/96), to the translator.

4. *DNS Configuration*

Configuring the DNS64 resolver for the IPv6-only clients [4]. The DNS64 configuration parameter is: IPv6 prefix 2001:db8:100::/96.

For example, if the A record of the server on the IPv4 Internet is 198.51.100.2, then the AAAA record dynamically generated by DNS64 is 2001:db8:100::198.51.100.2.

5. *Security Policy and Firewall Configuration*

There are two methods for implementing the security policies and firewalls.

(1) Deploy IPv6 security policies/firewalls between the IPv6 core router and the access router, as well as deploy IPv4 security policies/firewalls between the IPv4 core router and the translator, separately. In this case, maintaining the consistency of IPv4 and IPv6 security policies and firewalls is a challenge for the network and security management.
(2) Deploy IPv6 security policies and firewalls between the access router and the IPv6-only client. In this case, the IPv4 address is a subset of the IPv6 address, appearing in the form of IPv6, which can more easily maintain consistency.

6. *Log Analysis*

For IPv6-only clients, their addresses are assigned by DHCPv6, and specific IPv6 addresses can be assigned based on the client's fingerprint (such as MAC address). User authentication can be done through browser portal authentication, 802.1x, and other methods. Since 1:N IVI is stateless, each IPv6-only client is assigned a specific public IPv4 address and a port range (in the form of PSID), which can greatly simplify the user's traceability process.

7. *Communication Process*

The process of an IPv6-only client (2001:da8:ff01:0204:0300:0800::) initiating access to any IPv6 server is the ordinary IPv6 communication process, which is not repeated here.

The process of an IPv6-only client (2001:da8:ff01:0204:0300:0800::) initiating access to the TCP 80 port of a server (198.51.100.2) on the IPv4 Internet is as follows:

(1) DNS query: DNS64 queries the IPv4 server's domain name, obtains the A record = 198.51.100.2 only; then DNS64 generates the AAAA = 2001:db8:1c6:3364:2:: from the A record.
(2) Datagram in the IPv6-only subnet: source address = 2001:da8:ff01:0204:0300:0800::; TCP source port = 9000; destination address = 2001:db8:1c6:3364:2::, TCP destination port = 80.
(3) After the translator, the datagram in the IPv4 Internet: source address = 1.2.4.3, TCP source port = 12,289 (mapped to the port range of PSID = 1, the translator maintains the port mapping state throughout the communication process); destination address = 198.51.100.2, TCP destination port = 80.
(4) The server's return datagram in the IPv4 Internet: source address = 198.51.100.2, TCP source port = 80; destination address = 1.2.4.3, TCP destination port = 12,289 (mapped to the port range of PSID = 1).

(5) After the translator, the return datagram in the IPv6-only subnet: source address = 2001:db8:1c6:3364:2::, TCP source port = 80, destination address = 2001:da8:ff01:0204:0300:0800::, and TCP destination port = 9000.
(6) Repeat until the communication process ends.

8. Operating System Support for DHCPv6 and IPv6-Only

It is important to consider the operating system support for the IPv6-only clients.

(1) Apple's mobile operating system (iOS) and MacOS [6, 7] support stateful DHCPv6. The iOS and MacOS also support the IPv6 Prefix discovery/configuration and IPv6-only API/double translation; therefore, they support access to any application on the IPv4 Internet, including applications with embedded IP addresses.
(2) Microsoft operating systems (Windows 7, 8, 10, and 11) support stateful DHCPv6. But they have not supported double translation yet; therefore, they can support access to most applications on the IPv4 Internet, but they cannot support the access to those with embedded IP addresses.
(3) Basic mode of Linux operating systems supports stateful DHCPv6. But most of the releases have not supported double translation in default mode; therefore, they can support access to most applications on the IPv4 Internet, but they cannot support the access to those with embedded IP addresses.
(4) Some customized Linux operating systems (RFC7050 [7], etc.) support stateful DHCPv6. They support the IPv6 Prefix discovery/configuration and double translation; therefore, they support access to any application on the IPv4 Internet, including applications with embedded IP addresses.
(5) Standard Android operating system does not support DHCPv6 and cannot be used in the DHCPv6 subnet. It seems Google will not support DHCPv6 even in the future.

9. 1:*N* IVI's Functional Decomposition and Cascading Deployment

1:*N* IVI function includes the protocol translation based on RFC7915 [2] and the address mapping function of RFC6052 [1], as well as the IPv6 suffix encoding and transport-layer port mapping functions. Therefore, it can be implemented in cascading two devices, as shown in Fig. 14.3.

1:*N* IVI cascading makes the deployment of IPv6-only networks simpler and more flexible, facilitating the transition to an IPv6-only Internet.

14.2.2 IPv6-Only SLAAC Client

1. *Topology*

In order to complete the transition to IPv6-only, the clients must be IPv6-only and can access IPv4-only servers on the Internet through a translator.

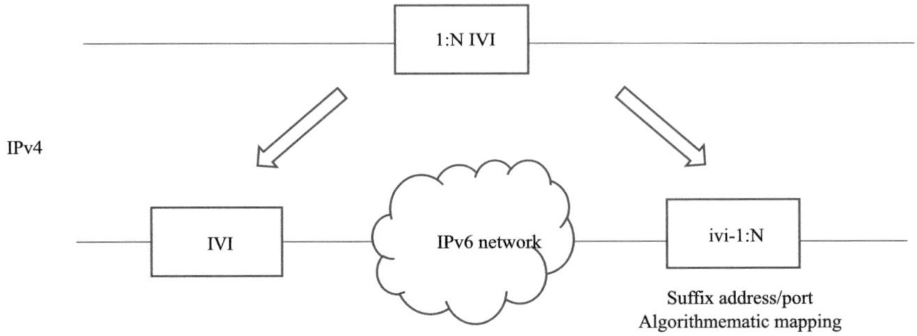

Fig. 14.3 Decomposition and cascading of 1:*N* IVI

This section is based on SLAAC to configure the address for IPv6-only clients, using stateful single translation. The topology is shown in Fig. 14.4.

The building blocks are as follows:

(1) IPv4/IPv6 translator [1, 2, 8].
(2) Core routers (including IPv6 core routers and IPv4 core routers).
(3) Access routers (IPv6-only), running RA (including DNS recursive server address extension (RFC8106 [9]), etc.).
(4) Client machines [6, 7, 9] (IPv6-only), address configured via SLAAC mode.
(5) DNS resolver [4] (IPv6 and IPv4 dual-stack access).

2. *Address Configuration*

In this example, the IPv6-only client uses SLAAC mode to configure the address. The IPv4-converted IPv6 address uses the "well-known prefix." The specific parameters are as follows:

(1) IPv6 address prefix: 2001:db8::/64.
(2) Translator's IPv4 address pool: 203.0.113.0/24.

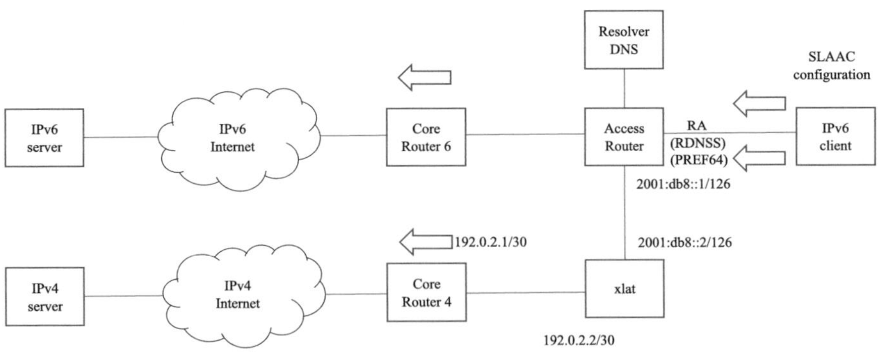

Fig. 14.4 Topology of SLAAC-based IPv6-only client subnet

(3) IPv4-converted IPv6 address prefix: 64:ff9b::/96 (RFC6052 [1] defined well-known prefix).

The address of the client accessing the IPv6-only subnet is configured via SLAAC.

(1) The default gateway address of the IPv6-only client subnet is 2001:db8::1, and the RA configuration parameters are as follows:

AdvAutonomous on (A=1).

AdvManagedFlag off (M=0).

AdvOtherConfigFlag off (O=0).

RDNSS 2001:db8::1 (gateway provides recursive DNS resolution service and DNS64).

(2) In this example, the IPv6-only client configures the IPv6 address via SLAAC: 2001:db8::111.

3. *Routing Configuration*

The routing configuration is as follows:

(1) The IPv6 core router configures static or dynamic routes, with the client machine's IPv6 prefix (2001:db8::/64) pointing to the access router.
(2) The access router configures the IPv6 default route (::0/0), pointing to the IPv6 core router.
(3) The IPv4 core router configures static or dynamic routes, pointing the translator's IPv4 address pool (203.0.113.0/24) to the translator.
(4) The translator configures the IPv4 default route (0.0.0.0/0), pointing to the IPv4 core router.
(5) The translator configures the IPv6 route, pointing the client machine's IPv6 prefix (2001:db8::/64) to the access router.
(6) The access router configures the IPv6 route, pointing the IPv4-converted IPv6 addresses (64:ff9b::/96) to the translator.

4. *DNS Configuration*

Configuring the DNS64 resolver for the IPv6-only clients [4]. The DNS64 configuration parameter is IPv6 prefix 64:ff9b::/96.

For example, if the A record of the server on the IPv4 Internet is 192.0.2.1, then the AAAA record dynamically generated by DNS64 is 64:ff9b::192.0.2.1.

5. *Security Policy and Firewall Configuration*

There are two methods for implementing the security policies and firewalls.

(1) Deploy IPv6 security policies/firewalls between the IPv6 core router and the access router, as well as deploy IPv4 security policies/firewalls between the IPv4 core router and the translator, separately. In this case, maintaining the

consistency of IPv4 and IPv6 security policies and firewalls is a challenge for the network and security management.

(2) Deploy IPv6 security policies and firewalls between the access router and the IPv6-only client. In this case, the IPv4 address is a subset of the IPv6 address, appearing in the form of IPv6, which can more easily maintain consistency.

6. *Log Analysis*

Under the SLAAC mode, two factors need to be considered for logs.

(1) The IPv6 address of the IPv6-only client is dynamic and random within the /64 range of the LAN (IPv6 privacy address: RFC3041 [10], RFC4941 [11], RFC8981 [12], RFC8064 [13]). Therefore, 802.1 × should be used for user authentication in L2, or user authentication should be done through a browser-based portal. Therefore, logs of the user and SLAAC address correspondence list must be kept according to management and security policies.
(2) When the IPv6-only client accesses the IPv4 Internet through NAT64, its IPv4 address and transport layer port are dynamic and random. Therefore, logs of the NAT64's IPv4 address and port, as well as the SLAAC address correspondence list, must be kept according to management and security policies.

Therefore, stateful systems are more complex and costly to manage user logs and traceability than stateless systems.

7. *Communication Process*

The process of an IPv6-only client (2001:db8::111) initiating access to any IPv6 server is the ordinary IPv6 communication process, which will not be elaborated here.

The IPv6-only client (2001:db8::111) initiates access to the TCP port 80 of the server (192.0.2.1) on the IPv4 Internet.

(1) DNS query: A record = 192.0.2.1; AAAA record generated by DNS64 = 64:ff9b::192.0.2.1.
(2) Datagram in the IPv6-only subnet: source address = 2001:db8::111::, TCP source port = 1500; destination address = 64:ff9b::192.0.2.1, TCP destination port = 80.
(3) After the translator: source address = 203.0.113.1, TCP source port = 2000 (dynamically generated port, the translator maintains the address and port state throughout the communication process); destination address = 192.0.2.1, TCP destination port = 80.
(4) Return datagram from the server in the IPv4 Internet: source address = 192.0.2.1, TCP source port = 80; destination address = 203.0.113.1, TCP destination port = 2000.
(5) After the translator, the return datagram in the IPv6-only subnet: source address = 64:ff9b::192.0.2.1, TCP source port = 80; destination address = 2001:db8::111::, TCP destination port = 1500.
(6) Repeat until the communication process ends.

8. *Operating System Support for SLAAC and IPv6-Only*

It is important to consider the operating system support for the IPv6-only clients.

(1) Apple's mobile operating system (iOS) and MacOS [6, 7] support SLAAC and get a DNS resolver address via RA (RDNSS). iOS and MacOS also support the IPv6 Prefix discovery/configuration and IPv6 only API/double translation; therefore, they support access to any application on the IPv4 Internet, including applications with embedded IP addresses.
(2) Microsoft operating systems (Windows 7, 8, 10, and 11) support SLAAC, but some versions do not support getting DNS resolver address via RA (RDNSS). In addition, they have not supported double translation yet; therefore, they can support access to most applications on the IPv4 Internet, but they cannot support the access to those with embedded IP addresses.
(3) Linux operating systems support SLAAC and get DNS resolver address via RA (RDNSS). But they have not supported double translation in the default mode; therefore, they can support access to most applications on the IPv4 Internet, but they cannot support the access to those with embedded IP addresses.
(4) Standard Android operating system [6, 7]: Android system supports SLAAC and getting DNS resolver address via RA (RDNSS). The Android also supports the IPv6 Prefix discovery/configuration and double translation, therefore they support access to any application on the IPv4 Internet, including applications with embedded IP addresses.

9. *Decomposition and Cascading of NAT64*

NAT64 function includes the protocol translation based on RFC7915 [2] and the address mapping function of RFC6052 [1], as well as dynamically mapping the transport layer ports between IPv4 and IPv6 for public IPv4 addressing. Therefore, it can be implemented in cascading two devices, as shown in Fig. 14.5.

NAT64 cascading makes the deployment of IPv6-only networks simpler and more flexible, facilitating the transition to an IPv6-only Internet.

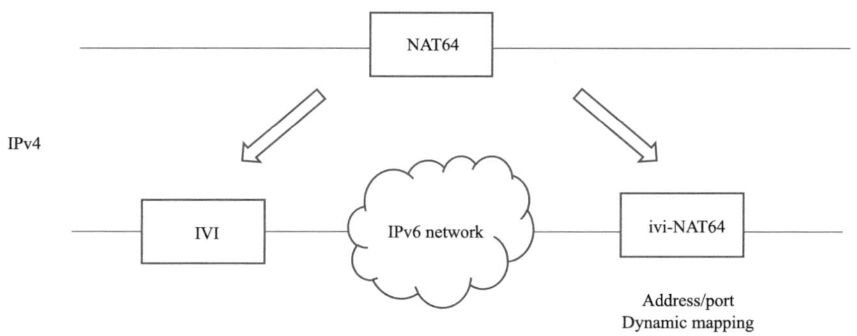

Fig. 14.5 Decomposition and cascading of NAT64

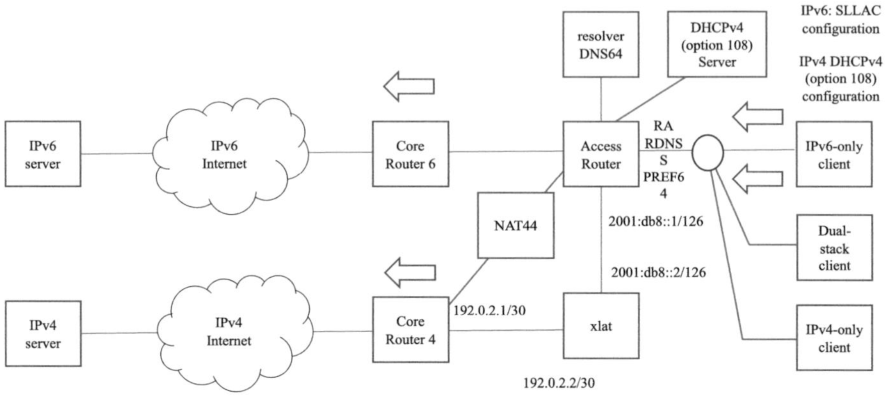

Fig. 14.6 Topology of SLAAC-based IPv6-mostly client subnet

14.2.3 IPv6-Mostly—Coexist with Dual Stack and IPv4-Only Hosts

To enable a gradual migration, network administrators need to identify which devices can function in IPv6-only mode and which cannot. Creating separate network segments for each type introduces complexity and scalability issues—a major hurdle to IPv6-only adoption.

A more desirable approach is to deploy a so-called "IPv6-mostly" network that provides IPv4 on demand [14]. This allows IPv6-capable devices to remain IPv6-only while seamlessly supplying IPv4 to those that require it.

1. *Topology*

The topology of the SLAAC-based IPv6-mostly client subnet is shown in Fig. 14.6

The building blocks are as follows:

(1) IPv4/IPv6 translator [1, 2, 8].
(2) Core routers (including IPv6 core routers and IPv4 core routers).
(3) Access routers (IPv6-only), running RA (including DNS recursive server address extension (RFC8106 [9]), etc.).
(4) NAT44.
(5) DHCPv4 server with Option 108 extension.
(6) Client machines [6, 7, 9] IPv6-only, the dual stack and IPv4-only. The IPv6 address is configured via SLAAC mode, while the IPv4 address is on demand based on the DHCPv4 Option 108 extension.
(7) DNS resolver [4] (IPv6 and IPv4 dual-stack access).

2. *Address Configuration*

The IPv6 address configuration is the same as the above SLAAC-based IPv6-only client subnet (see previous section).

The IPv4 address configuration is via DHCP. However, there are two methods to provide IPv4 service.

(1) Traditional dual-stack mode, i.e., there is an independent public IPv4 address pool maintained by a NAT44 device, shown in Fig. 14.6.
(2) Double translation mode, in this case the network itself could also be IPv6-only; the IPv4 address pool is obtained via double translation by a XLAT device, shown in Fig. 14.6.

3. *Routing Configuration*

The IPv6 routing configuration is the same as the above SLAAC-based IPv6-only client subnet (see previous section). The IPv4 address configuration is the ordinary routing.

4. *DNS Configuration*

The IPv6-only clients require the DNS64 support (see previous section). The dual-stack or IPv4-only is just use ordinary DNS service.

5. *Security Policy and Firewall Configuration*

Deploy IPv6 security policies/firewalls between the IPv6 core router and the access router, as well as deploy IPv4 security policies/firewalls between the IPv4 core router and the translator, separately. In this case, maintaining the consistency of IPv4 and IPv6 security policies and firewalls is a challenge for the network and security management.

6. *Log Analysis*

For IPv6 log analysis see previous Section. For IPv4 log analysis, it is the DHCPv4 log and NAT44 log combined records.

7. *Communication Process*

For IPv6, see the previous Section.

8. *Unique Features of IPv6-Mostly Network*

An IPv6-mostly network is very much similar to a dual-stack one with two additional key elements:

(1) The network provides NAT64 functionality (RFC6146 [8]), enabling IPv6-only clients to communicate with IPv4-only destinations.
(2) The DHCPv4 infrastructure processes DHCPv4 Option 108 as per RFC8925 [15].
(3) Upon connecting to an IPv6-mostly network subnet, an endpoint configures its IP stack based on its capabilities:

The client behaviors are as follows:

(1) IPv4-only Client: Acquires an IPv4 address through DHCPv4.

(2) Dual-Stack Client (Not IPv6-only Capable): Configures IPv6 addresses via Stateless Address Autoconfiguration (SLAAC) and, optionally, DHCPv6. Additionally, it obtains an IPv4 address via DHCPv4.
(3) An IPv6-only-capable client configures its IPv6 addresses and, while performing DHCPv4, includes option 108 (RFC8925 [15]) into the Parameter Request List. The DHCP server returns the option and, as per [RFC8925], the endpoint forgoes requesting an IPv4 address, remaining in IPv6-only mode.

Therefore, an IPv6-mostly subnet can support a mix of IPv4-only, dual-stack, and IPv6-only devices.

(1) IPv4-only Client: Can only access the IPv4 Internet, via NAT44.
(2) Dual-stack Client: Can access both the IPv4 as well as IPv6 Internet. The IPv4 access is via NAT44. The IPv6 access is native.
(3) IPv6-only Client: Can access both the IPv4 as well as IPv6 Internet. The IPv4 access is via IPv4/IPv6 translation. The IPv6 access is native.

9. *Benefits Compared to Dual-Stack Network*

IPv6-mostly networks offer significant advantages over traditional dual-stack models where clients have both IPv4 and IPv6 addresses:

(1) Drastically Reduced IPv4 Consumption: Dual-stack deployments don't solve the core problem of IPv4 address exhaustion. IPv6-mostly allows to significantly reduce IPv4 consumption, as well as to reclaim IPv4 space. This reduction depends on endpoint capabilities (DHCPv4 Option 108 and CLAT support). In real-world scenarios, like conference Wi-Fi, 60–70% of endpoints may support IPv6-only operation, potentially allowing 2–4 times smaller IPv4 subnets.
(2) Simplified Operations: Managing dual-stack networks means running two network planes simultaneously, increasing complexity, costs, and the potential for errors. IPv6-mostly allows to phase out IPv4 from many endpoints, streamlining operations and improving overall network reliability.
(3) Reduced Dependency on DHCPv4: As more devices operate seamlessly in IPv6-only mode, the criticality of DHCPv4 service diminishes significantly. This allows operators to scale down DHCPv4 infrastructure or operate it with less stringent Service Level Objectives (SLOs), optimizing costs and resource allocation.

Traditional IPv6-only adoption involved separate networks alongside dual-stack ones. IPv6-mostly offers significant improvements to integrate the IPv6-only, dual-stack and IPv4-only in a single network, without assigning an IPv4 address to IPv6-only capable clients, and therefore provides a smooth and transparent way to IPv6-only client subnets.

14.3 Home Broadband

1. *Topology*

In order to complete the transition to IPv6-only, the new constructed broadband access network should be IPv6-only, and the IPv4-only servers on the Internet can be accessed through the translators. It should be noted that the home network should provide both IPv6, as well as IPv4 services to all kinds of hosts.

The implementation scenario of IPv6-only home broadband is recommended to use stateless double translation technology (MAP-T, RFC7599 [5]), and its topology is shown in Fig. 14.7.

The building blocks are as follows:

(1) Core IPv4/IPv6 translator (BR) [5, 15].
(2) Core router (including IPv6 core router and IPv4 core router).
(3) Access router (IPv6-only).
(4) Home IPv4/IPv6 translator (CE, multiple) [5, 14].
(5) User hosts (IPv4, IPv6 or IPv4/IPv6 dual stack).
(6) Domain name server (IPv6 and IPv4 dual-stack access) [4].

2. *Address Configuration*

The MAP-T rules for BMR (DMR) are as follows:

(1) IPv6 prefix: BMR Rule IPv6 prefix = 2001:db8:0000::/40.
(2) IPv4 prefix: BMR Rule IPv4 prefix = 192.0.2.0/24.
(3) EA prefix length: BMR Rule EA-bit length = 16.
(4) Port-sharing length: PSID length = 8.
(5) Default prefix: DMR Rule IPv6 prefix = 2001:db8:ffff::/64.

The MAP-T rules for CEs are configured using RFC7598 [16]. That is, the access router is the DHCPv6 server, and the CE is the DHCPv6 client.

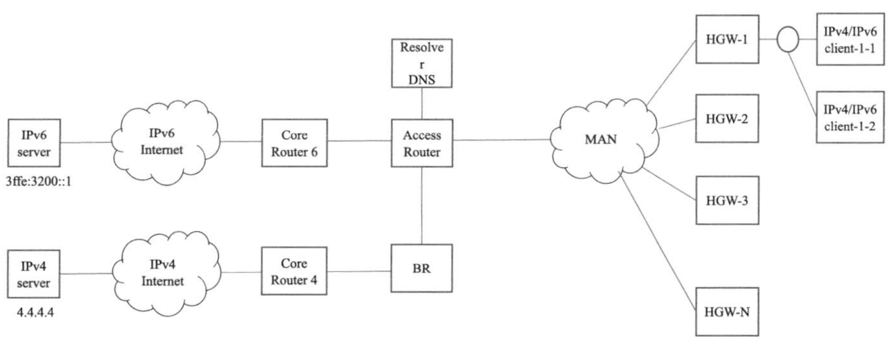

Fig. 14.7 Topology of IPv6-only home broadband

(1) IPv6 prefix: BMR Rule IPv6 prefix = 2001:db8:0000::/40.
(2) IPv4 prefix: BMR Rule IPv4 prefix = 192.0.2.0/24.
(3) EA prefix length: BMR Rule EA-bits length = 16.
(4) Port sharing length: PSID length = 8.
(5) Default prefix: DMR Rule IPv6 prefix = 2001:db8:ffff::/64.
(6) Port Set Identifier: PSID = 52.

3. *Routing Configuration*

The routing configuration is as follows:

(1) The IPv6 core router configures static or dynamic routes, directing the IPv6 prefix (2001:db8:0000::/40) to the access router.
(2) The access router configures the IPv6 default route (::0/0), pointing to the IPv6 core router.
(3) The IPv4 core router configures static or dynamic routes, directing the IPv4 prefix (192.168.0.0/24) to BR.
(4) The BR configures the IPv4 default route (0.0.0.0/0), pointing to the IPv4 core router.
(5) The BR configures the IPv6 route, directing the IPv6 prefix (2001:db8:0000::/40) to the access router.
(6) The access router, also acting as a DHCPv6 server, dynamically configures IPv6 routes for different CEs. For example, for a CE with PSID 52, its IPv6 route is 2001:db8:0012:3400::/64.

4. *DNS Configuration*

Because MAP-T is a double translation technology, it is an ordinary DNS resolver.

5. *Security Policy and Firewall Configuration*

There are two methods for implementing the security policies and firewalls.

(1) Deploy IPv6 security policies/firewalls between the IPv6 core router and the access router, as well as deploy IPv4 security policies/firewalls between the IPv4 core router and the translator, separately. In this case, maintaining the consistency of IPv4 and IPv6 security policies and firewalls is a challenge for the network and security management.
(2) Deploy IPv6 security policies and firewalls between the access router and the CEs. In this case, the IPv4 address is a subset of the IPv6 address, appearing in the form of IPv6, which can more easily maintain consistency.

6. *Log Analysis*

MAP-T uses stateless double-translation technology, so the logs for both IPv4 and IPv6 are bound to the user, which can conveniently carry out the security control and easy traceability.

(1) For IPv6, each CE uses a specific IPv6 prefix.

(2) For IPv4, each CE uses a specific port range in a specific public IP address.

7. *Communication Process*

The process of a client using IPv6 (for example, the client's address is 2001:db8:0012:3400:1:2:3:4) to initiate access to any IPv6 server is the ordinary IPv6 communication process, which is not repeated here.

IPv4 client (192.168.0.1) initiates access to IPv4 server (8.8.8.8).

(1) DNS query: A record = 8.8.8.8.
(2) Datagram in the user subnet: source address = 192.168.0.1, TCP source port = 1444; destination address = 8.8.8.8, TCP destination port = 80.
(3) After translation by CE, the datagram in the IPv6 network: source address = 2001:db8:0012:3400:0000:c000:0212:0034, TCP source port = 2256 (port range defined by PSID = 52); destination address = 2001:db8:ffff:0:0808:0808::, TCP destination port = 80.
(4) After translation by BR, the datagram in the IPv4 Internet: source address = 192.0.2.18, TCP source port = 2256 (port range defined by PSID = 52); destination address = 8.8.8.8, destination port = 80.
(5) Datagram returned from the server in the IPv4 Internet: source address = 8.8.8.8, source port = 80; destination address = 192.0.2.18, TCP destination port = 2256 (port range defined by PSID = 52).
(6) After translation by BR, the datagram in the IPv6 network: source address = 2001:db8:ffff:0:0808:0808::, TCP source port = 80; destination address = 2001:db8:0012:3400:0000:c000:0212:0034, TCP destination port = 2256 (port range defined by PSID = 52).
(7) After translation by CE, the datagram in the user subnet: source address = 8.8.8.8, TCP source port = 80; destination address = 192.168.0.1, TCP destination port = 1444 (mapped back to the original port number).
(8) Loop until the communication process ends.

8. *Operating System Support in Home Network*

Since the CE provides dual-stack services for users' hosts, it can support IPv4/IPv6 dual-stack clients, IPv4-only clients, or IPv6-only clients. Note: In the case of IPv4-only clients and IPv6-only clients, the client can only access the servers on the Internet that are in the same protocol family.

9. *MAP-T BR Function Decomposition and Cascading Deployment*

MAP-T BR can also be functionally decomposed into cascading of IVI and MAP-T (IVI-BR). IVI implements protocol translation based on RFC7915 [2] and RFC6052 [1]. The IVI-BR implements the address and transport-layer port mapping for IPv6 prefixes and suffixes for each CE. These two devices are connected through an IPv6 network, as shown in Fig. 14.8.

The decomposition of MAP-T BR function and the cascading of IVI make the deployment of an IPv6-only metropolitan area network simpler and more flexible, which is conducive to the transition to an IPv6-only Internet.

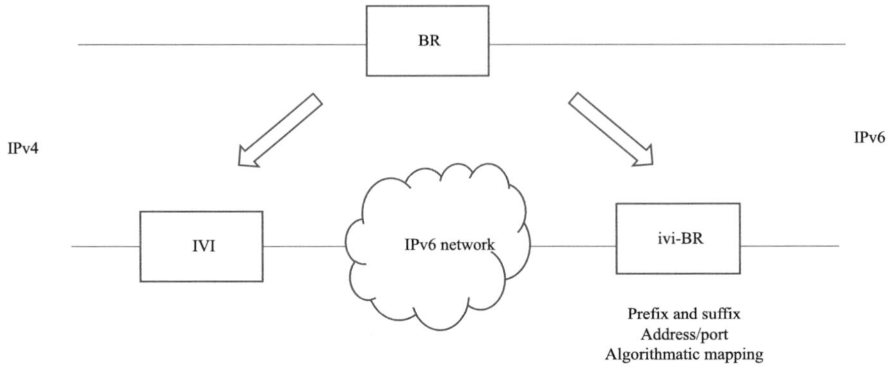

Fig. 14.8 Decomposition and cascading of MAP-T BR

14.4 IPv4 as a Service (IPv4aaS)

When ISP's backbone evolves to IPv6-only, the user's IPv4 virtual private network (IPv4 VPN) should be able to cross the IPv6 Internet. In fact, the massive addresses of IPv6 can make the 464 VPN have richer functions than IPv4 VPN using tunnel technology to cross the IPv4 Internet. In the long run, the user's IPv6 VPN can be upgraded to use the 666 VPN based on dNPTv6.

1. *Topology*

The IPv4 VPN crossing the IPv6 Internet is recommended to use stateless translation technology (IVI), and its topology is shown in Fig. 14.9.

The building blocks are as follows:

(1) IPv4/IPv6 translator-1 (xlat-1) [1–3].
(2) IPv4/IPv6 translator-2 (xlat-2) [1–3].
(3) Core router (R6).
(4) Access router (IPv6-only).
(5) IPv4 hosts (communication peers).

Note that the main differences between IPv4 public services via 464 double translation and IPv4 virtual private network (VPN) services via 464 double translation are as follows:

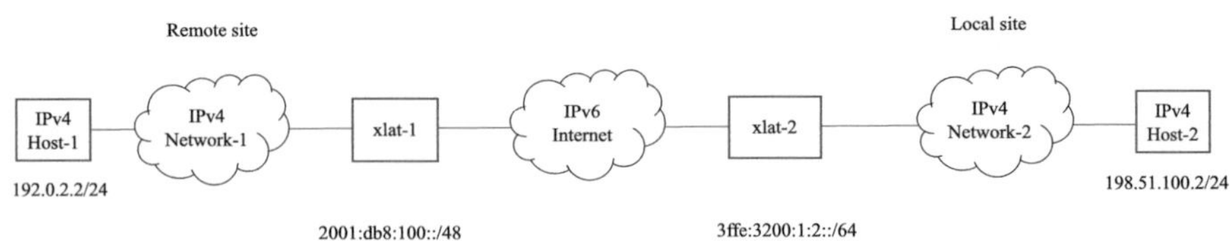

Fig. 14.9 Topology of IPv4 VPN crossing IPv6 Internet

(1) The IPv4 public services via 464 double translation use a public IPv4 address pool to access the global Internet. But it only supports communication initiated by user hosts.
(2) The IPv4 virtual private network (VPN) service via 464 double translation uses private IPv4 addresses. It can support bidirectional communication inside the VPN.

2. *Address Configuration*

The address used in the example is as follows:

(1) The xlat-1's IPv6 prefix1 = 2001:db8:100::/48.
(2) The xlat-2's IPv6 prefix2 = 3ffe:3200:1:2::/64.

Note that since the networks of the communication parties are usually in different administrative domains, different IPv6 prefixes should be used for each party's IPv4 address mapping, and the prefix length can be different.

(3) IPv4 prefix1 = 192.0.2.0/24.
(4) IPv4 prefix2 = 198.51.100.0/24.

Note that in this scenario, both parties' IPv6 addresses can be considered as IPv4-translatable IPv6 addresses. Specifically, for Network-1, its own IPv6 address is an IPv4-translatable IPv6 address, while Network-2's IPv6 address is an IPv4-converted IPv6 address. Conversely, for Network-2, the roles are reversed.

3. *Routing Configuration*

The routing configuration is as follows:

(1) Network-1 (192.0.2.0/24) is directly connected to xlat-1 and configures a default route (0.0.0.0/0) to xlat-1.
(2) Network-2 (198.51.100.0/24) is directly connected to xlat-2 and configures a default route (0.0.0.0/0) to xlat-2.
(3) The xlat-1 announces its IPv6 prefix-1 (2001:db8:100::/48) to the IPv6 Internet and makes a default route (::0/0) to the IPv6 Internet.
(4) The xlat-2 announces its IPv6 prefix-2 (3ffe:3200:1:2::/64) to the IPv6 Internet and makes a default route (::0/0) to the IPv6 Internet.

4. *DNS Server Configuration*

Because this is a double-translation technology, ordinary DNS servers and resolvers are used.

5. *Security Policy and Firewall Configuration*

There are two implementations of security policies and firewall configurations, which are equivalent and can be chosen according to the local considerations.

(1) Configure IPv4 security policies/firewalls on the IPv4 network.

(2) Configure IPv6 security policies/firewalls on the IPv6 network.

6. *Log Analysis*

There are two implementations for log analysis, which are equivalent and can be chosen according to local considerations.

(1) Record IPv4 logs on the IPv4 network.
(2) Record IPv4 logs in the form of IPv6 addresses on the IPv6 network.

7. *Communication Process*

The process of a host (198.51.100.2) on Network-2 initiating access to a server (192.0.2.33) on Network-1 is as follows:

(1) Datagram in Network-2: source address = 198.51.100.2; destination address = 192.0.2.33.
(2) After passing through xlat-2: source address = 3ffe:3200:1:2:c633:6402::; destination address = 2001:db8:100: c000:0221::.
(3) After passing through xlat-1: source address = 198.51.100.2; destination address = 192.0.2.33.
(4) The datagram returned in the IPv4 network: source address = 192.0.2.33; destination address = 198.51.100.2.
(5) The datagram returned after passing through the translator xlat-1: source address = 2001:db8:100:c000:0221::; destination address = 3ffe:3200:1:2:c633:6402::.
(6) Data datagram returned after passing through translator xlat-2: Source address = 192.0.2.33; Destination address = 198.51.100.2.
(7) Repeat until the communication process ends.

14.5 Summary

This chapter discussed the transition roadmap and specific solutions for typical scenarios of IPv6-only networks including:

(1) IPv6-only server.
(2) IPv6-only client.
(3) IPv6-mostly client.
(4) IPv6-only home broadband.
(5) IPv4 VPN cross IPv6 Internet (IPv4aaS).

The integrated solutions will be discussed in detail in the next chapter.

References

1. Bao C, Huitema C, Bagnulo M, et al. RFC6052: IPv6 addressing of IPv4/IPv6 translators. IETF 2010–10.

2. Bao C, Li X, Baker F, et al. RFC7915: IP/ICMP translation algorithm. IETF 2016–06.
3. Li X, Bao C, Chen M, et al. RFC6219: The China Education and Research Network (CERNET) IVI translation design and deployment for the IPv4/IPv6 coexistence and transition. IETF 2011–05.
4. Bagnulo M, Sullivan A, Matthews P, et al. RFC6147: DNS64: DNS extensions for network address translation from IPv6 clients to IPv4 servers. IETF 2011–04.
5. Li X, Bao C, Dec W, et al. RFC7599: Mapping of address and port using translation (MAP-T). IETF 2015–07.
6. Mawatari M, Kawashima M, Byrne C. RFC6877: 464XLAT: Combination of stateful and stateless translation. IETF 2013–04.
7. Savolainen T, Korhonen J, Wing D. RFC7050: Discovery of the IPv6 prefix used for IPv6 address synthesis. IETF 2013–11.
8. Bagnulo M, Matthews P, van Beijnum I. RFC6146: Stateful NAT64: Network address and protocol translation from IPv6 clients to IPv4 servers. IETF 2011–04.
9. Jeong J, Park S, Beloeil L, et al. RFC8106: IPv6 router advertisement options for DNS configuration. IETF 2017–03.
10. Narten T, Draves R. RFC3041: Privacy extensions for stateless address autoconfiguration in IPv6. IETF 2001–01.
11. Narten T, Draves R, Krishnan S. RFC4941: Privacy extensions for stateless address autoconfiguration in IPv6. IETF 2007–09.
12. Gont F, Krishnan S, Narten T, et al. RFC8981: Temporary address extensions for stateless address autoconfiguration in IPv6. IETF 2021–02.
13. Gont F, Cooper A, Thaler D, et al. RFC8064: Recommendation on stable IPv6 interface identifiers. IETF 2017–02.
14. Colitti, L., Linkova, J., Richardson, M., et al RFC8925: IPv6-Only Preferred Option for DHCPv4 IETF 2020–10.
15. Troan O, Dec W, Li X, et al. RFC7597: Mapping of address and port with encapsulation (MAP-E). IETF 2015–07.
16. Mrugalski T, Troan O, Farrer I, et al. RFC7598: DHCPv6 options for configuration of softwire address and port-mapped clients. IETF 2015–07.

Chapter 15
IPv6-Only Integration: Building Blocks and Strategies

Chapter 14 of this book discussed in detail the IPv6-only server, IPv6-only client, IPv6-only home broadband, and IPv4 VPN cross IPv6 Internet. This chapter will discuss the implementation plans using the above solutions as building blocks.

15.1 Campus Network

Whether it's IPv4, IPv4/IPv6 dual-stack, or IPv6-only campus network (including enterprise network), it is an ecosystem. Generally, a campus network includes the following components.

(1) Clients: Access servers locally or from the global Internet.
(2) External Servers: Can be accessed by the hosts outside campus.
(3) Internal Servers: Only open to the hosts in the campus.
(4) VPNs: Provide connectivity in closed communities.
(5) Supporting Systems: Network management system, security protection, user authentication, management and billing, etc.
(6) Others: Internet of Things, etc.

15.1.1 Dual-Stack Campus Network

The dual-stack campus network theoretically involves upgrading all network layer and above devices to support both IPv4 and IPv6 in dual-stack mode. This allows the campus network to logically function as two separate networks—one IPv4 and the other IPv6.

But from a practical perspective: since IPv4 can be used, users naturally lack the motivation to upgrade to use IPv6. Moreover, the construction and operation of a

X. Li and C. Bao, *New IPv6 Transition Technology*,
https://doi.org/10.1007/978-981-95-8427-7_15

dual-stack network obviously requires greater costs than a single-stack network. At the same time, according to the "barrel principle" of security, the security of the dual stack is the weaker one of IPv4 or IPv6.

Therefore, it is a good idea to construct an IPv6-only (IPv6-mostly) campus network.

15.1.2 IPv6-Only and IPv6-Mostly Campus Network

The IPv6-only campus network eliminates the complexity, high operating costs, and network security threats brought by running both IPv4 and IPv6 network protocols. Through translation technology, interconnectivity with the IPv4 Internet can be ensured.

The standards involved in the IPv6-only campus network mainly include RFC6052 [1], RFC7915 [2], RFC6219 [3], RFC6146 [4], RFC6147 [5], RFC7599 [6], RFC6877 [7], RFC7050 [8], and so on.

The advantages of constructing and operating an IPv6-only campus network are as follows:

(1) It conforms to the global trend of IPv6 transition.
(2) Through IPv4/IPv6 translation technology, the external characteristics of the IPv6-only campus network are dual stack, which can maintain interconnectivity with the IPv4 Internet.
(3) It eliminates the complexity, high operating costs, and network security threats brought by running both IPv4 and IPv6 network protocols.
(4) The massive address resources of IPv6 can naturally be "sliced," and different security policies and service-quality IPv6 prefixes can be configured for different services. At the same time, IPv6 segment routing and other functions provide new tools for the network.
(5) It better supports new applications such as the Internet of Things.

The topology of the IPv6-only campus network is shown in Fig. 15.1.

The design considerations are as follows:

(1) The data center (private cloud) of the campus network is IPv6-only. For servers (including VMs) that need to be accessed by IPv4 Internet users, configure IPv4-translatable IPv6 addresses. (See Chap. 13 of this book).
(2) The wired networks are dual stack provided by double translation technology in order to support legacy IPv4 hosts (see Chap. 13 of this book).
(3) The wireless LAN adopts the multi-SSID mode (see Chap. 13 of this book).

    ① One SSID serves non-Android systems, and it is recommended to use the DHCPv6 mode and the cascading mode.

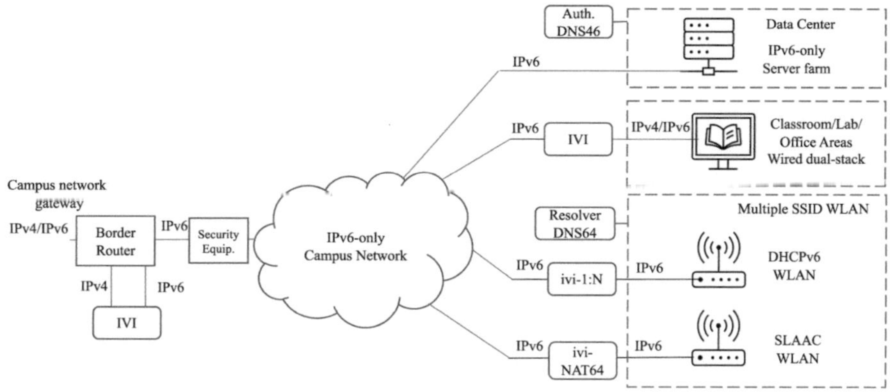

Fig. 15.1 IPv6-only campus network

② Another SSID can serve various modern operating systems (including Android systems) using the SLAAC mode; the cascading mode should be used.

Considering the recent IETF progress of the IPv6-mostly concept [9], the IPv6-mostly campus network can be constructed as shown in Fig. 15.2.

The design considerations are as follows:

(1) The data center (private cloud) of the campus network is the same as the IPv6-only case.
(2) The wired network and wireless networks can use the same IPv6-mostly technology.

① The IPv6 address is assigned via SLAAC, the connectivity to IPv6 is direct, and the connectivity to IPv4 is via translation.

② The IPv4 address is assigned via DHCPv4 option 108 on demand and the connectivity is provided by double translation.

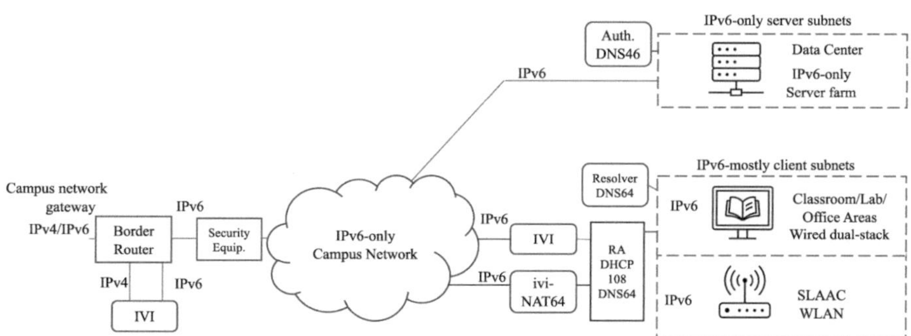

Fig. 15.2 IPv6-mostly campus network

The major technical plan involves the following:

1. *Address Plan*

The campus network's external exit is dual stack IPv4 and IPv6, deploying a stateless IPv4/IPv6 translator, and the internal campus network is IPv6-only. The IPv6 address of the campus network is generally /48, and the subnet is generally / 64, so a /48 contains 65,536 subnets.

In the above subnets, at least a few /64 s need to be reserved as Pref64 prefixes for IPv4/IPv6 translation technology. It is recommended that IPv6 servers and IPv6 clients use different Pref64s.

The campus network's public IPv4 addresses use the above Pref64 to map to the IPv6 address space, that is, the IPv4 address is mapped to the IPv4-translatable IPv6 address.

2. *Routing*

The campus network is IPv6-only; it is recommended that IGP (e.g., OSPFv3) only carries topology information. For scalability and routing control, it is recommended that the customer routes are carried by BGP (iBGP and eBGP).

3. *DNS*

The authoritative DNS server should provide DNS46 function and the DNS resolver should provide DNS64 function.

4. *Security*

The security device is IPv6-only. Because of stateless IPv4/IPv6 translation, the public IPv4 address (IPv4-translatable IPv6 address) appears in the form of IPv6, which is convenient for control. Therefore, the security control is simplified in an IPv6-only network, rather than in dual stack.

15.2 Metropolitan Area Network

In general, a metropolitan area network includes the following parts.

(1) Dedicated line users. Dedicated line users can be IPv4-only, IPv4/IPv6 dual stack, or IPv6-only. The hosts on the dedicated line users can be either clients or servers.

(2) Home broadband users. The devices used by home broadband users can be IPv4-only, IPv4/IPv6 dual stack, or IPv6-only. The host of home broadband users is usually client-only.

15.2.1 Dual-Stack Metropolitan Network

The dual-stack backbone means that all devices in the network layer and above have to support both IPv4 and IPv6. The biggest challenge facing the metropolitan network is the extreme shortage of public IPv4 addresses; the widespread use of NAT devices brings scalability problems, increased complexity, weakened security, and increased operational costs.

15.2.2 IPv6-Only Metropolitan Network

The IPv6-only metropolitan network eliminates the complexity, high operating costs, and network security threats brought by running both IPv4 and IPv6 protocols. Through translation technology, interconnection with the IPv4 Internet can be provided.

The IPv6-only metropolitan network involves the standards of RFC6052 [1], RFC7915 [2], RFC6219 [3], RFC6146 [4], RFC6147 [5], RFC7599 [6], RFC6877 [7], RFC7050 [8], RFC7598 [10], etc.

The features of an IPv6-only metropolitan area network are as follows:

(1) Through IPv4/IPv6 translation technology, the external characteristics of the IPv6-only metropolitan area network are dual stack, which can maintain interconnection with the IPv4 Internet.
(2) It eliminates the complexity, high operating costs, and network security threats brought by running both IPv4 and IPv6 network protocols.
(3) The massive address resources of IPv6 can be "sliced," and IPv6 prefixes with different security policies and service quality can be configured for different services. At the same time, functions like SRv6 provide new tools for the network.
(4) It supports new applications such as the Internet of Things.

The topology of the IPv6-only metropolitan area network is shown in Fig. 15.3.

The design considerations are as follows:

(1) The internal part of the metropolitan area network is IPv6-only. The core layer to the backbone is IPv4/IPv6 dual stack connecting multiple IPv4/IPv6 translators (IVIs).
(2) The Broadband Remote Access Server (BRAS) uses cascaded MAP-T technology (see Chap. 13 of this book). BRAS distributes IPv6 prefixes and shared public IPv4 addresses to users' home gateways in the form of IPv6 through DHCPv6-PD and DHCPv6's MAP-T extension.
(3) MAP-T CEs provide IPv4/IPv6 dual-stack service to the home users.
(4) The dedicated line users of the metropolitan area network can be IPv4-only, IPv4/IPv6 dual stack, or IPv6-only.

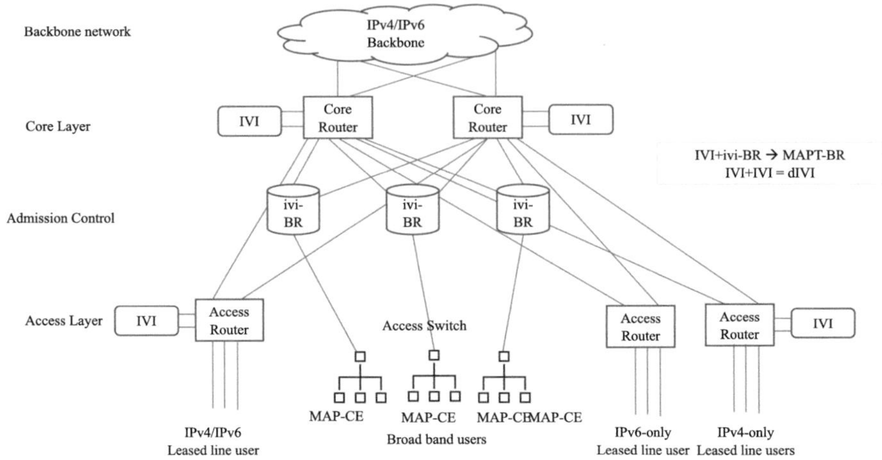

Fig. 15.3 Topology of the IPv6-only metropolitan area network

① IPv4-only or IPv4/IPv6 Dual Stack: The IPv4/IPv6 translators (IVIs) translate IPv4-translatable IPv6 addresses back to IPv4. The hosts on the dedicated line can either be a client or a server.

② IPv6-only: The user not only has a regular IPv6 prefix, but also has an IPv6 prefix of the IPv4-translatable IPv6 address. Hosts using the IPv4-translatable IPv6 address can achieve interconnection with the IPv4 Internet through the stateless translator of the core layer of the metropolitan area network. Note: In this case, DNS46 and DNS64 need to be used. The user can deploy a second IPv4/IPv6 translator (IVI) to make the internal network dual stack.

The major technical plan involves the following:

1. *Address Plan*

The metropolitan area network infrastructure is IPv6-only, and the internal infrastructure uses /48.

For home gateway users of the metropolitan area network, it is recommended that at least one/60 is allocated to each home gateway, so that the home gateway can allocate multiple/64 subnets to its subordinate networks. In addition, choose an appropriate public IPv4 address sharing ratio (recommended to be 1024). The total IPv6 and IPv4 address spaces required by the entire metropolitan area network are determined by the number of home gateways and the above IPv6 and IPv4 requirements for each home gateway.

For dedicated-line users of the metropolitan area network, depending on the business model and user needs, either the operator's IPv6 address (PA address) or the user's own IPv6 address (PI address) can be used. For each dedicated-line user, allocate /48, so each dedicated-line user can have 65,536 (/64) subnets. Among the above subnets, at least a few /64 s need to be reserved as Pref64 prefixes for IPv4/

IPv6 translation technology. It is recommended that IPv6 servers and IPv6 clients use different Pref64s. All public IPv4 addresses use the above Pref64 to map to the IPv6 address space, that is, map the IPv4 address to the "IPv4-translatable IPv6 address."

2. *Routing*

It is recommended that the Interior Gateway Protocol (IGP) only carries the topology information (OSPFv3 or IS-IS), and all customer addresses (including server addresses) are carried via Border Gateway Protocol (eBGP and iBGP).

For users with their own IPv6 address (PI address), their prefixes are announced via eBGP.

3. *DNS*

The metropolitan area network provides regular DNS service for native and double translation service. The DNS46 for IPv6-only servers and DNS64 for IPv6-only clients.

4. Security

The security device is IPv6-only. Because of stateless IPv4/IPv6 translation, the public IPv4 address (IPv4-translatable IPv6 address) appears in the form of IPv6, which is convenient for control. Therefore, the security control is simplified in an IPv6-only network, rather than in dual stack.

15.3 Backbone Network

The backbone network is a cross-regional IP network, usually with an independent Autonomous System Number (AS number), and is interconnected with other networks using border gateway protocol (BGP). The three types of BGP neighbors include the following.

(1) Connected to the "transit network" of the upper stream, in order to interconnect with the global Internet. In this case, the backbone network pays for the transit.
(2) Connected to peer networks. In this case, traffic is generally only exchanged between neighbors, without providing transit, and usually it is free peering.
(3) Connected to customer networks (metropolitan area networks, campus networks, corporate networks, etc.). In this case, transit services are provided for customer networks, and customers are charged.

15.3.1 Dual-Stack Backbone

The dual-stack backbone means that all devices in the network layer and above have to support both IPv4 and IPv6. The dual-stack backbone faces the challenges of increased complexity, increased costs of the deployment and operation, and weakened security.

15.3.2 IPv6-Only Backbone

The IPv6-only backbone reduces the complexity, high operating costs, and network security threats. Through stateless IPv4/IPv6 translation technology, interoperability with the IPv4 Internet can be ensured. In addition, with the maturity of SRv6 technology, some backbones have started to run SRv6, no longer using traditional MPLS technology.

The standards of transition technologies include RFC6052 [1], RFC7915 [2], RFC6219 [3], RFC6147 [5] and so on.

The features of the IPv6-only backbone are as follows:

(1) It conforms to the global development trend of IPv6 transition.
(2) Through IPv4/IPv6 translation technology, the external behavior of the IPv6-only backbone is dual stack, which can maintain connectivity with the IPv4 Internet.
(3) It reduces the complexity, operating costs, and network security threats compared to the dual-stack backbone.
(4) The massive address resources of IPv6 can naturally be "sliced," and IPv6 prefixes with different security policies and service quality can be configured for different services. At the same time, functions like SRv6 provide new tools for the backbone.

The topology of the IPv6-only backbone is shown in Fig. 15.4.

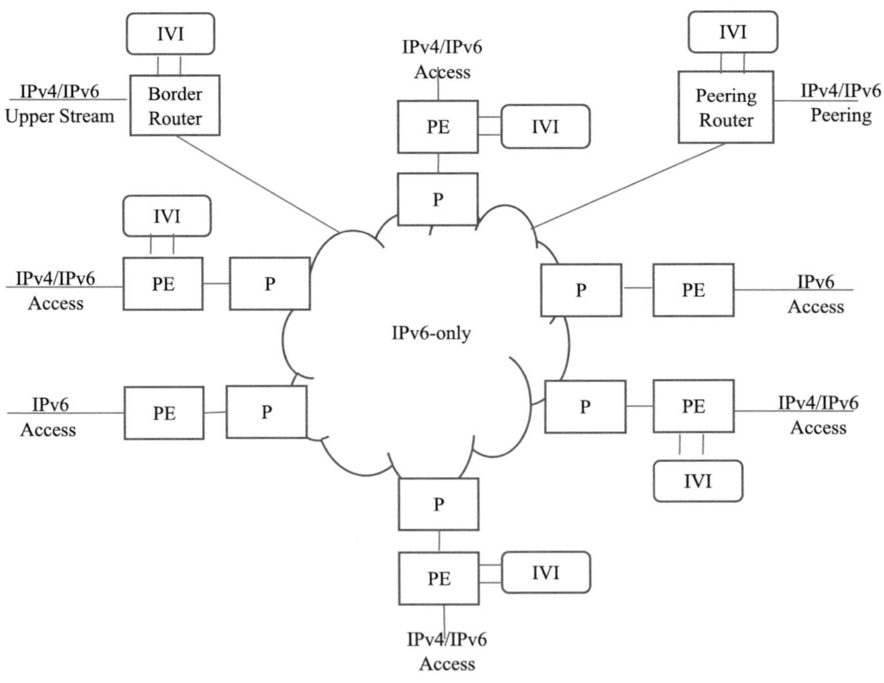

Fig. 15.4 IPv6-only backbone network

The design considerations are the following:

(1) The interface of the backbone to the upper streams and peers is IPv4/IPv6 dual stack. The stateless IPv4/IPv6 translators (IVI) are deployed in the border, and the internal network is IPv6-only, which includes core routers (provider router, P), backbone network edge routers (provider edge router, PE), and customer edge routers (customer edge router, CE, interconnected with PE, not shown in the figure).

(2) The customers (access networks) of the backbone network can be IPv4-only, IPv4/IPv6 dual stack, or IPv6-only.

① IPv4-only: This is achieved via double translation. For specific configuration details, refer to Chapter 13 of this book.

② IPv4/IPv6 Dual Stack: The IPv4 is achieved via double translation. For specific configuration details, refer to Chapter 13 of this book. The IPv6 is native.

③ IPv6-only: Besides native IPv6, it can also provide IPv4 access via single translation by configuring an IPv4-translatable IPv6 address. Note: In this case, DNS46 and DNS64 are needed. Furthermore, the IPv6-only customer network can also install its own translators to make its internal network support the dual-stack feature.

The major technical plan involves the following:

1. *Address Plan*

The backbone infrastructure is IPv6-only with a /48 and several /64 s as the Pref64 prefix should be reserved. The customer IPv6 prefixes are assigned with demonstrated needs. The public IPv4 addresses mapped into IPv4-translatable IPv6 addresses and assigned with demonstrated needs and the business model.

The backbone network needs to reserve several /64 s as the Pref64 for IPv4/IPv6 translation technology. It is recommended that IPv6 servers and IPv6 clients use different Pref64s.

2. *Routing*

It is recommended that the internal routing protocol only carry the topology information (OSPFv3 or IS-IS). All user addresses (including server addresses) are carried via BGP (eBGP and iBGP).

The users' own IPv6 and IPv4 prefixes (PI address) are announced via BGP.

3. *DNS*

The backbone can provide regular DNS service for native and double translation service. The DNS46 for IPv6-only servers and DNS64 for IPv6-only clients.

4. *Security*

The security device is IPv6-only. Because of stateless IPv4/IPv6 translation, the public IPv4 address (IPv4-translatable IPv6 address) appears in the form of IPv6, which is convenient for control. Therefore, the security control is simplified in an IPv6-only network, rather than in dual stack.

15.4 VPN

A virtual private network (VPN) is an IP network that spans the public Internet, usually using private IPv4 addresses and an internal domain name system, not interconnecting with the public Internet, or interconnecting with the public Internet with strictly configured firewalls and security systems.

When implementing IPv6 transition technology, whether the internal part of the VPN needs to be upgraded to IPv6 is still a controversial issue. The main considerations are as follows.

(1) Unless it is a very large-scale VPN, the private IPv4 address space is big enough, and there is no problem of address exhaustion.
(2) IPv4 has NAT, so when needed, the firewall system can be configured more securely to connect with the public Internet.
(3) The applications within the private network are usually custom developed and not very standardized (for example, embedding IPv4 addresses directly in the application, instead of using the domain name system), so upgrading to IPv6 requires redevelopment. However, future operating systems will have weaker and weaker support for IPv4. In the long run, it must be upgraded to IPv6. Sooner or later, it is expected that new communication mechanisms unique to IPv6 will appear. In this case, users of the VPN need to upgrade to IPv6 to use the new communication mechanism.
(4) The private address corresponding to IPv6 is ULA, but since IPv6 does not have NAT, when ULA needs to communicate with the public IPv6 Internet, it needs to use NPTv6 (RFC6296 [11]).

Therefore, this chapter mainly discusses the construction of a VPN that uses private IPv4 addresses internally. By analogy, a VPN that uses IPv6 ULA internally can be constructed, which is for the future IPv6-only inside VPN.

15.4.1 IPv4-Based VPN

Using IPv4 to build a VPN is based on encapsulation technology, such as GRE [12], IPsec [13, 14], L2TP [15] and VxLAN [16], etc. In this case, the source and destination addresses of the datagram are both the addresses of the IPv4 tunnel endpoints. The advantage is that if no decapsulation in the path is performed, the public Internet cannot understand the 5-tuple of user communication. However, the disadvantage is that thousands or even tens of thousands of communication processes may share the same pair of tunnel endpoints, which can easily hinder communication.

15.4.2 IPv6-Based VPN

When using IPv6 to build a VPN, the following two technologies can be chosen.

(1) Encapsulation Defined in RFC2473 [17]: Its advantages and disadvantages are similar to the above IPv4-based VPN.
(2) Double Translation Defined in RFC7915 [2] and RFC6052 [1]: In this case, there is a one-to-one correspondence between the private network address and the public IPv6 address, so it is not easy to hinder communication. Quality of service can be guaranteed for specific communication addresses. If encryption is needed, it can be done at the transport layer, or an additional layer of encapsulation can be added after translation.

The use of IPv6 to build a VPN involves the are including RFC6052 [1], RFC7915 [2], RFC6219 [3], RFC6296 [11], etc.

The behavior of building a VPN using double translation technology is as follows:

(1) It conforms to the global development trend of IPv6 transition.
(2) The VPN can continue to use private IPv4 addresses and continue to support existing application systems. In the future, ULA can be used to support the transition to IPv6 inside the VPN.
(3) By configuring different IPv6 prefixes in the Internet, different security policies and service quality can be guaranteed.
(4) There is a one-to-one correspondence between the private network address and the global IPv6 address, so it is not easy to hinder communication. Quality of service can be guaranteed for specific communication addresses based on the IPv6 prefix. If encryption is needed, it can be done at the transport layer, or an additional layer of encapsulation can be added after translation.

Using IPv6, multiple VPNs can be deployed and operated as shown in Fig. 15.5.

The design considerations are the following:

(1) The public Internet (AS1, AS2, AS3, and AS4) is IPv6. The internal protocol which VPN provides is IPv4.
(2) CE IVI: The configuration details are referred to in Chap. 13 of this book. If the IPv6 routing crosses different administration domains, the translator must use different IPv6 prefixes (Pref64).
(3) When the VPN uses ULA, it is recommended to use dNPTv6.
(4) In order to achieve better security and isolation, a 5-Tuple access-control table can be configured before and after the translation in CE IVI.
(5) When content encryption is needed, it can be done at the transport layer (RFC8446 [18]), or an additional layer of encapsulation can be added after translation.
(6) If needed, tunnels such as SRv6 can also be established on the public IPv6 Internet to further isolate.

The major technical plan involves the following:

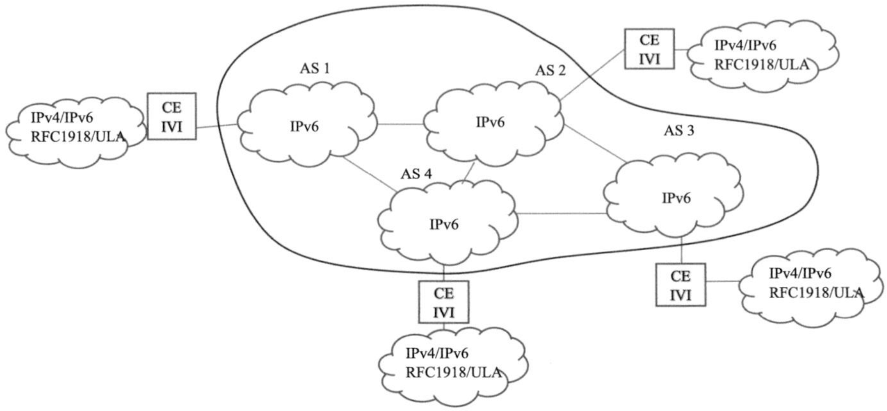

Fig. 15.5 IPv6-only virtual private network

1. *Address Plan*

Two address-planning issues need to be considered for the VPN.

(1) The external network address of the VPN is the public IPv6 address, and it is used as Pref64. If all access points of the VPN are in one administration domain, a single Pref64 can use (/48), which can automatically guarantee the optimal route. Otherwise, different Pref64 must be used (e.g., different /64 s).
(2) The internal network address of VPN uses private IPv4 addresses. When the internal network of the VPN is IPv6, use IPv6 ULA.

2. *Routing*

Through translation technology, the internal network addresses of the VPN are mapped to IPv4-translatable IPv6 addresses.

3. *DNS*

The virtual private network is a double translation, and the ordinary DNS system configuration can be used.

4. *Security*

The security device is IPv6-only. Because of stateless IPv4/IPv6 translation, the public IPv4 address (IPv4-translatable IPv6 address) appears in the form of IPv6, which is convenient for control. Therefore, the security control is simplified in an IPv6-only network, rather than in dual stack.

The internal security can use ordinary techniques, from the network layer to the application layer.

15.5 Data Center

Physical machines can be directly installed in the data center to provide services, but currently, data centers largely use virtualization technology to provide public cloud, private cloud, or hybrid cloud services. Generally, a data center includes the following components.

(1) External Servers: Users on the Internet can access the information services provided by the external servers.
(2) Internal Servers: Internal computing resources and storage resources.
(3) Supporting Systems: Including security protection systems, management billing systems, etc.

15.5.1 Dual-Stack Data Center

(1) **Physical Machine**

  (1) External Servers: Configure public IPv4 addresses, which can provide services to Internet users and also use the same public IPv4 address to access the IPv4 Internet. When transforming to dual stack, add the configuration of IPv6 addresses to provide services to IPv6 Internet users.
  (2) Internal Servers: Configure private IPv4 addresses for communication between internal servers in the data center. Private IPv4 addresses can access the IPv4 Internet via NAT. Generally, IPv6 addresses are not configured for internal servers.
  (3) Supporting Systems: Configure ACL according to the IPv4 and IPv6 "5-tuple" (protocol, source address, source port, destination address, destination port).

(2) **Virtual Machines in the Cloud**

  (1) All virtual machines are configured with private IPv4 addresses for communication between internal servers in the data center. Private IPv4 addresses can access the IPv4 Internet via NAT.
  (2) External Servers: When a virtual machine needs to provide external services, it binds to a randomly assigned public IPv4 address (floating IP) to provide services. When transitioning to a dual stack, add a configuration of IPv6 addresses to the virtual machine to provide services to IPv6 Internet users.
  (3) Supporting Systems: Configure ACL according to the IPv4 and IPv6 "5-tuple" (protocol, source address, source port, destination address, destination port).

Data centers face the challenges of increased complexity, weakened security, and increased operating costs for transit to dual stacks.

15.5.2 IPv6-Only Data Center

The IPv6-only data center reduces the complexity, high operating costs, and network security threats. Using translation technology, interconnection with the IPv4 Internet can be ensured.

The standards involved in the IPv6-only data center mainly include RFC6052 [1], RFC7915 [2], RFC6219 [3], RFC6146 [4], RFC6147 [5], RFC7050 [8], etc.

The behaviors of the IPv6-only data center are as follows:

(1) It conforms to the global development trend of IPv6 transition.
(2) Through IPv4/IPv6 translation technology, the external characteristics of the IPv6-only data center are dual stack, which can maintain interconnection with the IPv4 Internet.
(3) It reduces the complexity, high operating costs, and network security threats.
(4) By reusing public IPv4 addresses through IPv6, the public IPv4 address resources can be fully utilized.
(5) The massive address resources of IPv6 can naturally be "sliced," and IPv6 prefixes with different security policies and service quality can be configured for different services. At the same time, functions like SRv6 provide new tools for the network.

The topology of the IPv6-only data center is shown in Fig. 15.6.

The design considerations are the following:

(1) The external interface of the IPv6-only data center is dual stack.
(2) The server cluster of the data center is configured IPv6-only, and servers (virtual machines) that need to be accessed by IPv4 Internet users are configured with

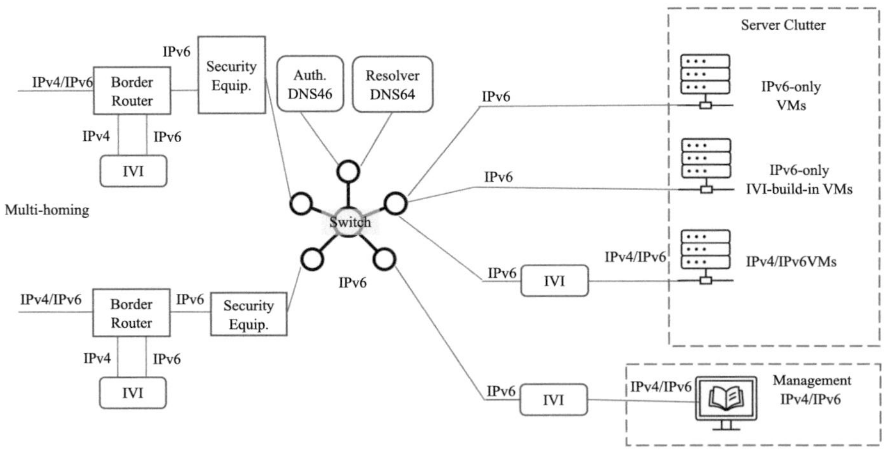

Fig. 15.6 IPv6-only data center

IPv4-translatable IPv6 addresses. For configuration details, refer to Chap. 13 of this book.

(3) The double translation technology can be used for the virtual machines. The translator itself can either be a physical one, or a function of a virtual machine.

The major technical plan involves the following:

1. *Address Plan*

   The data center is internally IPv6-only; the internal infrastructure uses /48.

   Data centers are generally multi-homed. For IPv4, data centers usually use provider-independent address (PI address) and interconnect using BGP. But for IPv6, there are two modes.

   (1) The data center uses a PI address and interconnects using BGP.
   (2) The data center uses PA addresses.

Regardless of which of the above modes is adopted, all public IPv4 addresses should use Pref64 to map to the IPv6 address space (IPv4-translatable IPv6 address).

2. *Routing*

   The data center is IPv6-only, and there are two modes for configuring its routing protocol.

   (1) The data center configures IGP and BGP. IGP only carries the topology information (OSPFv3 or IS-IS). All server addresses are carried through BGP (eBGP and iBGP).
   (2) The data center uses eBGP for routing.

3. *DNS*

Configure authoritative DNS servers adding DNS46 function and DNS resolvers adding DNS64 function.

4. *Security*

The security device is IPv6-only. Because of stateless IPv4/IPv6 translation, the public IPv4 address (IPv4-translatable IPv6 address) appears in the form of IPv6, which is convenient for control. Therefore, the security control is simplified in an IPv6-only network, rather than in dual stack.

15.6 Internet Exchange Center

Historically, there were no Internet Exchange (IX) points in the early days of the Internet, as there was only a single backbone, the NSFNET. Since 1995, with the gradual commercialization of the Internet, multiple backbones have emerged worldwide. Initially there was some form of interconnection between the backbones, but they often did not form the best path. To accelerate traffic exchange, Internet exchange centers emerged. Since then, due to continuous technological development, traffic exchange between different backbones has grown increasingly large. Over the past decade, many large networks have established direct connections with each other, no longer needing to send traffic to the exchange centers, and exchange centers have therefore tended to be neglected. However, market evolution often changes the demand for technology. With the further development of the Internet, as well as the demand for localization and reliability, more and more new types of Internet exchange centers are returning to the stage.

The new type of Internet exchange center generally has the following characteristics.

(1) Neutrality: Generally established and operated by a third party not controlled by telecom operators.
(2) Peer-to-Peer: When exchanging traffic between operators accessing the "exchange center" (Internet Exchange, IX) platform, a free peer-to-peer interconnection strategy is generally adopted.
(3) Microprofit or Nonprofit: The IX platform itself only provides access to the platform and does not participate in the traffic exchange between members. In terms of charging mode, only port occupancy fees are charged.

15.6.1 Dual-Stack Internet Exchange Center

Most Internet exchange centers are Layer 2 (L2). Operators can establish BGP neighbors with each other through L2 switches. In this case, whether it is IPv4-only, IPv4/IPv6 dual stack, or IPv6-only, the routing policy is executed on operators' own routers. At the same time, Internet exchange centers can provide route servers, which have independent autonomous systems. Therefore, operators accessing the Internet exchange center can establish BGP neighbor relationships with the route server, which can avoid the scalability problem of BGP neighbors (N^2).

As mentioned above, given the L2 characteristics of the Internet exchange center, the dual-stack transformation of the Internet exchange center seems relatively simple on the surface. However, data centers also face the challenges of increased complexity, weakened security, and increased operating costs brought by dual stacks.

15.6.2 IPv6-Only Internet Exchange Center

The IPv6-only exchange center reduces the complexity, operating costs, and network security threats. Through translation technology, interconnection with the IPv4 Internet can be ensured.

The IPv6-only exchange center involves RFC6052 [1], RFC7915 [2], RFC6219 [3], etc.

The characteristics of the IPv6-only exchange center are as follows:

(1) It conforms to the development trend of IPv6 transition worldwide.
(2) Through IPv4/IPv6 translation technology, the external characteristics of the IPv6-only Internet are dual stack, which can maintain interconnection with the IPv4 Internet.
(3) It reduces the complexity, high operating costs, and network security threats.
(4) The IPv6-only network can use the IPv4/IPv6 translation service for connecting to the IPv4 Internet.
(5) It can achieve dynamic scheduled interconnection. Using double translation technology, public IPv4 addresses can be traded on demand via IPv6.
(6) It can achieve extended interconnection. The current IPv4 address allocation only supports address allocation and assignment, but with the help of translation technology, it can be extended to allocate/assign factional public IPv4 address to users. An IPv4 address. After binding the port, it is allocated according to demand.
(7) Using SRv6 technology, the new type of exchange center can exchange different SRv6 slices according to different routing policies, and its profound impact will gradually emerge in future practice. In addition, fractional public IPv4 addresses can also associate with different slices for exchange.

The topology of the IPv6-only exchange center is shown in Fig. 15.7.

The design considerations are the following:

(1) The switch of the Internet exchange center is a layer-2 device, which is protocol-independent.
(2) Deploy routing servers.

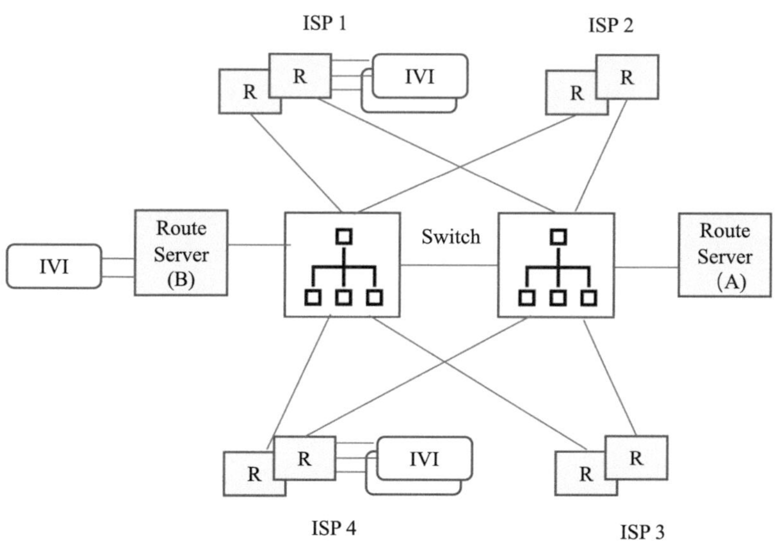

Fig. 15.7 Topology of the IPv6-only exchange center

(3) Deploy IPv4/IPv6 translators.

The major technical plan involves the following:

1. *Address Plan*

The route servers are IPv6-only (multiple /64 s from a /48). The translator requires several /64 s as the Pref64. All public IPv4 addresses use the above Pref64 to map to the IPv6 address space, that is, to map the IPv4 address to IPv4-translatable IPv6 address.

2. *Routing*

The route servers of the exchange center can generally be divided into two types.

(1) The first type is the IPv6-only route server (A), and each operator only establishes a BGP neighbor relationship with the IPv6-only routing server using IPv6. In this case, the operator runs its own translator. That is, the operator's network is dual stack, and in the IPv6-only Internet exchange center, it exchanges both regular IPv6 address traffic and IPv4-translatable IPv6 address traffic. In this case, BGP extension may be needed. Note that the routing server is a control plane device, and the actual traffic does not pass through the route server, but rather is directly exchanged through the L2 switch.
(2) The second type is the IPv4/IPv6 dual-stack route server (B) and translator (IVI). The operators establish IPv4 and IPv6 BGP neighbor relationships with the route server separately and the translator (IVI) provides translation services between IPv4 and IPv6 traffic. Note that the route server is a control plane device, the real traffic is directly exchanged through the L2 switch.

3. *DNS*

The Internet Exchange Center may provide the DNS service. For dual stack or double translation, it is just the regular DNS service. For single translation, configure authoritative DNS servers adding DNS46 function and DNS resolvers adding DNS64 function.

4. *Security*

The security device is IPv6-only. Because of stateless IPv4/IPv6 translation, the public IPv4 address (IPv4-translatable IPv6 address) appears in the form of IPv6, which is convenient for control. Therefore, the security control is simplified in an IPv6-only network, rather than in dual stack.

15.7 Internet

It can be expected that the global Internet will eventually complete the transition to IPv6-only, and the IPv4/IPv6 translation technology should be able to complete this mission. Although it is impossible to predict how long this IPv6 transition process will be at this moment, several conclusions can be drawn here.

(1) The core technology of the IPv6 transition is translation, which enables incompatible IPv4 and IPv6 to interconnect. Therefore, the IPv6-only network is still connecting to the global IPv4 Internet.
(2) The basis of translation technology is stateless, so it conforms to the essential characteristics of the Internet for maintaining the scalability and security of the Internet.
(3) Translation technology can be independently and incrementally deployed in individual networks, i.e., the internal network is IPv6-only and the external interface is dual stack.
(4) Through stateless translation technology, whether it is a public IPv4 address or a private IPv4 address, it can be regarded as a subset in a specific IPv6 address space. Therefore, in the future, IPv4 may still exist in the form of an IPv6 address and can continue to be used. The extremely difficult transition problem from IPv4 to IPv6 will be solved.

Based on the above discussion, the IPv6-only Internet is shown in Fig. 15.8.

The design considerations are the following:

(1) Each IPv6-only network exchanges reachable information through BGP to form a global IPv6 Internet.
(2) Some IPv6 addresses in each IPv6-only network contain IPv4 addresses (IPv4-translatable IPv6 addresses). The reachable information of IPv4-translatable IPv6 addresses is exchanged through BGP extension.
(3) When needed, these IPv4-translatable IPv6 addresses can be used in the form of IPv4 through the translator, or they can be used directly in the form of IPv6.

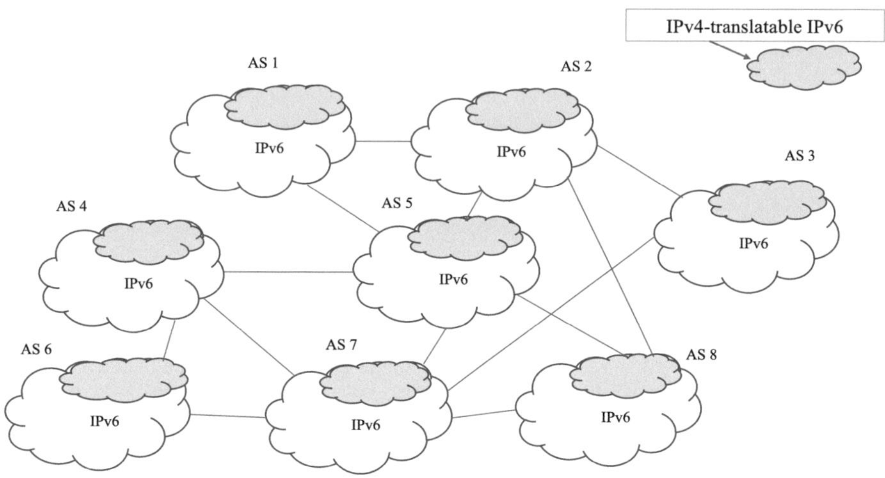

Fig. 15.8 IPv6-only Internet

15.8 Summary

This chapter introduces use cases of the IPv6-only networks, including the IPv6-only/IPv6-mostly campus network, IPv6-only metropolitan area network, IPv6-only backbone, as well as IPv6-only data center, IPv6-only Internet exchange center, and IPv6 VPN.

References

1. Bao C, Huitema C, Bagnulo M, et al. RFC6052: IPv6 addressing of IPv4/IPv6 translators. IETF 2010-10.
2. Bao C, Li X, Baker F, et al. RFC7915: IP/ICMP translation algorithm. IETF 2016-06.
3. Li X, Bao C, Chen M, et al. RFC6219: The China Education and Research Network (CERNET) IVI translation design and deployment for the IPv4/IPv6 coexistence and transition. IETF 2011-05.
4. Bagnulo M, Matthews P, Beijnum I. RFC6146: Stateful NAT64: Network address and protocol translation from IPv6 clients to IPv4 servers. IETF 2011-04.
5. Bagnulo M, Sullivan A, Matthews P, et al. RFC6147: DNS64: DNS extensions for network address translation from IPv6 clients to IPv4 servers. IETF 2011-04.
6. Li X, Bao C, Dec W, et al. RFC7599: Mapping of address and port using translation (MAP-T). IETF 2015-07.
7. Mawatari M, Kawashima M, Byrne C. RFC6877: 464XLAT: Combination of stateful and stateless translation. IETF 2013-04.
8. Savolainen T, Korhonen J, Wing D. RFC7050: Discovery of the IPv6 prefix used for IPv6 address synthesis. IETF 2013-11.
9. Mrugalski T, Troan O, Farrer I, et al. RFC7598: DHCPv6 options for configuration of softwire address and port-mapped clients. IETF 2015-07.
10. Colitti, L., Linkova, J., Richardson, M., et al RFC8925: IPv6-Only Preferred Option for DHCPv4 IETF 2020-10.
11. Wasserman M, Baker F. RFC6296: IPv6-to-IPv6 network prefix translation. IETF 2011-06.
12. Farinacci D, Li T, Hanks S, et al. RFC2784: Generic routing encapsulation (GRE). IETF 2000-03.
13. Kent S, Seo K. RFC4301: Security architecture for the internet protocol. IETF 2005-11.
14. Kent S. RFC4302: IP authentication header. IETF 2005-12.
15. Townsley W, Valencia A, Rubens A, et al. RFC2661: Layer two tunneling protocol "L2TP". IETF 1999-08.
16. Mahalingam M, Dutt D, Duda K, et al. RFC7348: Virtual extensible local area network (VXLAN): A framework for overlaying virtualized layer 2 networks over layer 3 networks. IETF 2014-08.
17. Conta A, Deering S. RFC2473: Generic packet tunneling in IPv6 specification. IETF 1998-12.
18. Rescorla E. RFC8446: The transport layer security (TLS) protocol version 1.3. IETF 2018-08.

Chapter 16
Transition to Future Network Protocols

16.1 Design Principles for Future Network Transition Technologies

One of the design principles of IPv6 is longevity, RFC1726 [1] points out: "It is very difficult to change a protocol as central to the workings of the Internet as IP. Even more problematic is changing such a protocol frequently. This simply cannot be done. We believe that it is impossible to expect the community to make significant, non-backward compatible changes to the IP layer more often than once every 10–15 years. In order to be conservative, we strongly urge protocol developers to consider what the Internet will look like in twenty years and design their protocols to fit that vision." However, people's demand for networks and the advancement of technology are inevitable. Sooner or later, there will be new network architectures and related protocols, which can currently be referred to as "future networks."

The architecture of future networks may continue to follow the Internet's design, with the first 4 bits of the header structure serving as a new version number (currently 10 to 15 available after excluding temporary test versions). Alternatively, it may adopt a completely different network architecture altogether.

In studying the history of the Internet [2, 3], understanding the design principles of ARPANET [4], IPv4 [5, 6] and IPv6 [1], as well as the research papers [7, 8] provides foundational insights into network evolution. Based on the experience of IPv6 transition technology, we suggest considering the following points for the transition technology of future networks.

X. Li and C. Bao, *New IPv6 Transition Technology*,
https://doi.org/10.1007/978-981-95-8427-7_16

16.1.1 General Principles

1. *New Features and Backward Compatibility*

In the foreseeable future, the address space of IPv6 is sufficient to meet the needs of mobile Internet, cloud computing, and the Internet of Things. Therefore, only revolutionary demands and breakthrough technological progress could possibly encourage suppliers, service providers, and users to switch to the future network. Hence, the future network protocol will not be fully compatible with the current Internet protocol (IPv4 or IPv6), nor can it be made fully compatible.

Therefore, the future network protocol itself must support new applications that the existing Internet protocol (IPv4 or IPv6) cannot support. Based on this consideration, the future network protocol does not need to consider backward compatibility.

It should be noted that compatibility refers to the direct intercommunication between the future network protocol and the existing network protocol. However, by deploying translators at the boundaries of different protocol networks, it is possible to achieve interconnection and intercommunication at the network layer. Therefore, not considering backward compatibility does not mean not considering translatability.

2. *Translatability*

The value of a network is the square of the number of users, and a future network that cannot interconnect and intercommunicate with IPv4 or IPv6 will be difficult to deploy on a large scale. Although theoretically, a dual-stack (or even "multi-stack") strategy can also be used between the existing Internet (IPv4 or IPv6) and the future network, the transition experience of IPv6 shows that "multi-stack" cannot achieve the complete transition to a new network protocol.

Based on the research and development insights from the IPv6 transition technologies explored in this book, the future network protocol should be designed to be translatable with IPv6 (since IPv6 is already translatable with IPv4). Furthermore, to align with the Internet's enduring fundamental nature, future protocols and IPv6 should prioritize translation capabilities at the network layer.

3. *End-to-End Address Transparency*

A very important concept of the Internet is "end-to-end address transparency" (RFC2775 [6]). According to the original definition of the Internet, end-to-end address transparency means globally unique addressing, and it also means that the source address and destination address of the datagram remain unchanged throughout the transmission process from source to destination.

Unfortunately, due to the exhaustion of public IPv4 addresses, security issues, etc., the current global Internet that has introduced stateful address translation (NAT), has largely lost end-to-end address transparency.

Because IPv6 has a massive addressing space, people hope to restore end-to-end address transparency through IPv6, that is, there is no NAT66, all networked devices on the IPv6 Internet have globally unique IPv6 addresses, and are reachable under permissible security policies.

The stateless IPv4/IPv6 Translation Transition Technology establishes a generalized end-to-end address transparency between IPv4 and IPv6. For example, the IPv4-translatable IPv6 Address on the IPv6 Internet has end-to-end address transparency with the IPv4 address on the IPv4 Internet.

The concept highlights that IPv6's addressing space has grown exponentially compared to IPv4. During the transition from IPv4 to IPv6, a subset of the IPv6 address space can be utilized first. This approach ensures end-to-end address transparency with the full set of IPv4 addresses.

When IPv6 becomes the mainstream network protocol, the IPv6 address space that does not have end-to-end address transparency with IPv4 can be enabled, as shown in Fig. 16.1.

Similarly, during the transition from IPv6 to future networks, a subset of the future network address space can be used first, which has end-to-end address transparency with the full set of IPv6 addresses. When the future network becomes the mainstream network protocol, the future network address space that does not have end-to-end address transparency with IPv6 can be then used, as shown in Fig. 16.2.

4. *Simplicity of the Architecture*

The perfection of the future network architecture is not reflected in the addition of all the necessary functions, but in the fact that no function can be removed. The future network continues to maintain the hourglass model of the Internet (IPv4 or IPv6), where any function implementable by a high-level protocol should be executed by

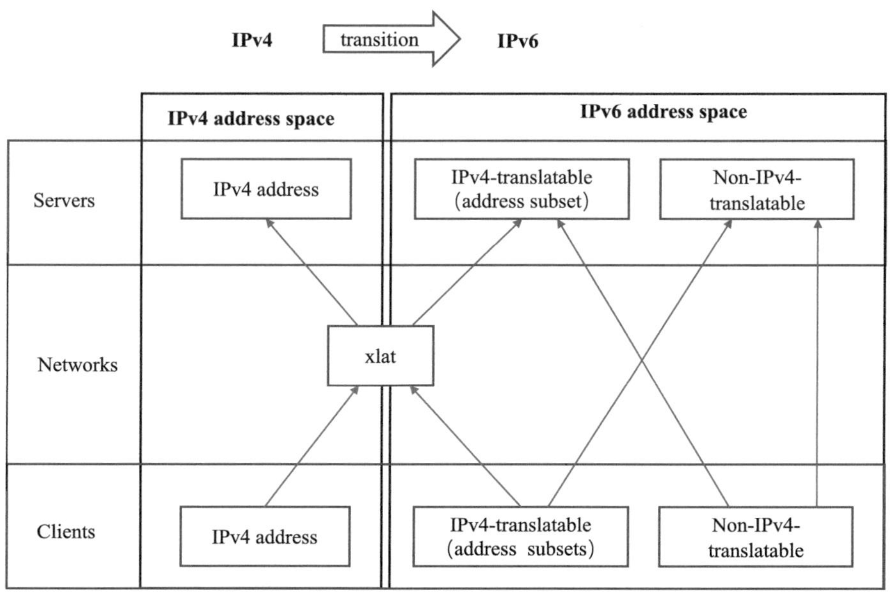

Fig. 16.1 IPv4 is a subset of IPv6 addresses

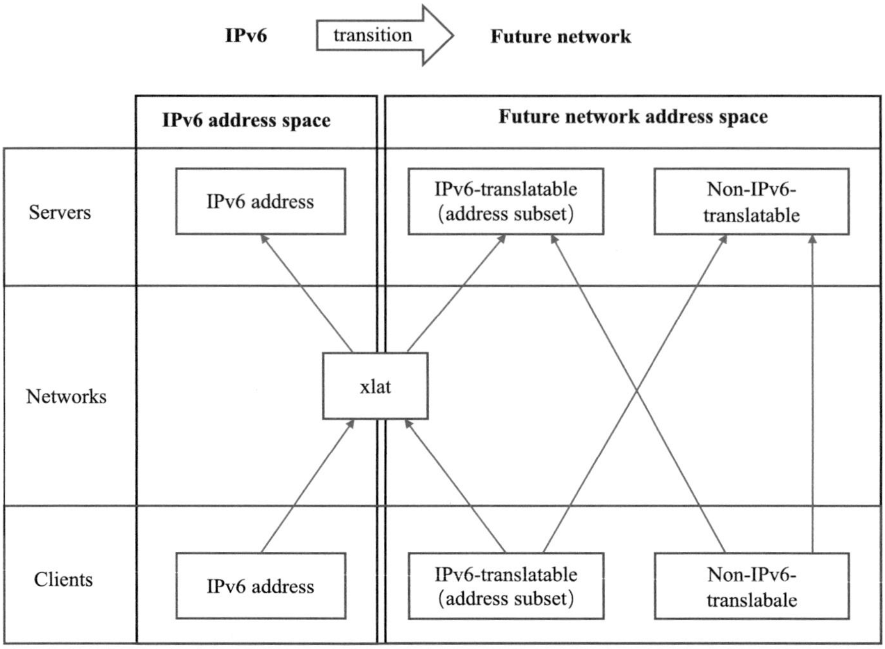

Fig. 16.2 IPv6 is a subset of future network addresses

that protocol. The future network must also be designed to operate seamlessly on any underlying communication protocol, including IPv4 and IPv6.

5. *Anarchy of Distribution and Cooperation*

One of the main reasons for the success of the Internet is that there is no single, centralized control point or policy issuer for the entire network. This decentralized and decoupled nature must be preserved in the future network. In other words, the entire future network community can only tolerate the minimum degree of centralization and forced cooperation. The benefits are:

① Easier to test new protocols and services;
② Eliminate single point of failure;
③ Allow distributed deployment and management.

16.1.2 *Tools and Technical Modules*

Future network devices are the entities that implement transition technologies and should have the following functions.

1. *Routing and Forwarding*

Routing is to determine the transmission path in order to send the datagrams to the destination node. Forwarding is to send the datagrams to the destination node efficiently according to the routing information.

The entity implementing the transition technology must implement the routing and forwarding of current Internet protocols (IPv6 and/or IPv4), as well as future network protocols.

2. *Address Mapping*

Address mapping is to establish a mapping relationship between network addresses of different protocols. Stateless address mapping refers to the bidirectional address mapping based on algorithms. Stateful address mapping is that the mapping in at least one direction between two protocols is dynamically generated.

The entity implementing the transition technology must implement the address mapping of Internet protocols (IPv6 and/or IPv4), as well as future network protocols. At the same time, it is recommended to prefer algorithm-based address mapping between two different protocols.

3. *Protocol Translation*

Protocol translation is the corresponding transformation between the headers of different protocols, that is, it must ensure that different protocols are "translatable" at the network layer. Translatability is the basis of interconnection, and protocol translation includes address mapping.

Entities implementing transition technologies must implement protocol translation for Internet protocols (IPv6 and/or IPv4), as well as protocols of future networks.

4. *Protocol Encapsulation*

Encapsulation is the technology of putting a network layer datagram (including payload) in the payload part of another datagram. Encapsulation cannot achieve interconnection between different protocols, but it can make datagrams cross the networks running different protocols. Tunneling is a special encapsulation mode. IPv6 extension headers can also be considered as encapsulation. It should be noted that SRv6 can also be understood as a special encapsulation mode.

Entities implementing transition technologies should implement encapsulation for Internet protocols (IPv6 and/or IPv4), as well as protocol of future networks.

Considering the above, future networks must be interconnected with IPv4 and IPv6, and their architecture and tools are shown in Fig. 16.3.

16.2 Review and Prospect of Transition Technology

From a historical perspective, the development history of human communication networks is a history of new technologies replacing old ones and constantly changing generations. At the same time, it is also a history of transitioning from the previous generation of technology to the new generation, as shown in Fig. 16.4.

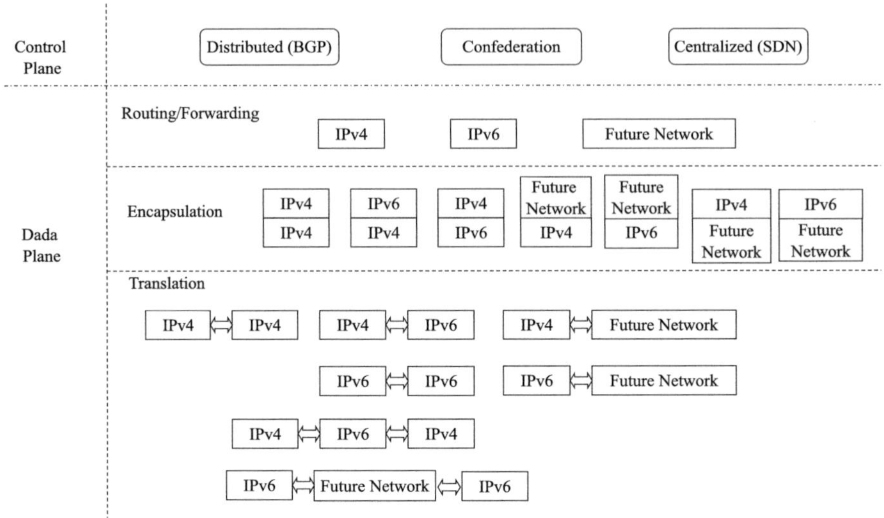

Fig. 16.3 Encapsulation and translation between different protocols

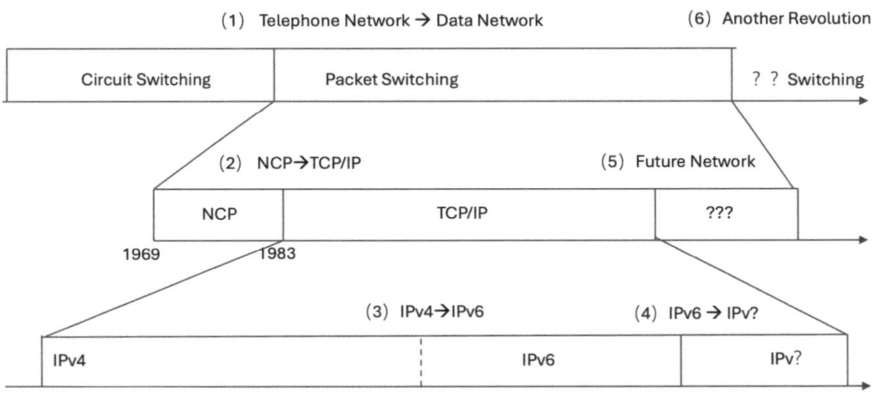

Fig. 16.4 The transition of communication networks: a historical perspective

16.2.1 From Telephone Network to Data Network

Traditional communication networks are based on circuit switching. Later, represented by ARPANET, the era of packet switching was initiated, leading to the birth of the Internet.

Interestingly, the principle of ARPANET designer Craig Partridge explicitly includes "don't worry about backward compatibility." David Clark's principle also does not mention compatibility issues with traditional communication networks (telephone networks, etc.). ARPANET is the world's first large-scale packet-switched network, which is revolutionarily different from the circuit-switched telephone network. It can be considered that if compatibility with the telephone network was considered when designing ARPANET, it would not be possible to produce revolutionary protocols.

From a technical point of view, the relationship between the first-generation packet network and the traditional circuit-switched network is a special kind of "encapsu lation," that is, the packet-switched network (network layer protocol) runs on top of the traditional telephone network (providing dedicated lines and switch lines at the edge).

More importantly, the packet network provides new applications (Telnet, FTP, E-mail, etc.), which traditional circuit switching cannot provide on a large scale.

16.2.2 From NCP to TCP/IP

The first transition of the Internet (from NCP to TCP/IP) was successful, and its key points are as follows:

(1) TCP/IP is incompatible with NCP, but TCP/IP has interconnection capabilities that NCP does not have, and there are no other alternative solutions.
(2) The transition from NCP to TCP/IP was implemented in a single management domain (ARPANET), which could be enforced. The scale of the network involved was not large, and the applications that needed to be supported (Telnet, FTP, SMTP, etc.) were not many.
(3) A clear transition period of one year was set. During the transition period, translation services were provided for all applications (i.e., NCP-only hosts and TCP-only hosts could communicate through "Relays"). At the same time, existing NCP-only hosts had to be upgraded to "dual-stack" hosts that support both NCP and TCP/IP, and new hosts had to be TCP/IP-only.
(4) A clear "flag day" was set, after which support for NCP was stopped.

16.2.3 From IPv4 to IPv6

IPv6 is not compatible with IPv4, so hosts using IPv6 cannot communicate with existing hosts using IPv4. The IETF initially recommended transitioning from IPv4 to IPv6 using dual-stack technology and tunneling technology, but neither dual-stack nor tunneling technologies can enable IPv6-only hosts to interconnect and communicate with IPv4-only hosts.

Today, the scale of the entire Internet makes it impossible to switch from IPv4 to IPv6 in a short period of time, so there is no "flag day." During the transition process, a large number of IPv4 applications will still exist for a long period of time and will gradually transition to IPv6 at a slow pace. During this transition period, the incompatibility between IPv4 and IPv6 makes it impossible for IPv6-only users to access resources on the IPv4 network, and at the same time, IPv4-only users cannot directly access resources on the IPv6 network. This poses a huge difficulty for the further deployment of the IPv6 network [9].

The new generation of IPv6 transition has introduced a series of transition technologies based on stateless translation.

(1) Clients on the IPv6-only network can access servers on the IPv4 Internet.
(2) Servers on the IPv6-only network can provide services for clients on the IPv4 Internet.
(3) Double translation can almost perfectly compatible with traditional IPv4 and applications, and can seamlessly evolve to single translation, and finally evolve to IPv6-only.
(4) IPv6-only further makes a smooth and transparent scheme to support the legacy hosts in an almost IPv6-only environment.

In this case, the value of the Internet is the square of the sum of IPv4 users and IPv6 users. In other words, users of the IPv6-only network will not lose the ability to communicate with the IPv4 Internet, and can enjoy new features of IPv6. There is no need to worry about when to turn off IPv4. Therefore, it can be expected that the transition to IPv6-only will truly start and eventually be completed.

16.2.4 From IPv6 to Future Networks

Whether the future network is a new version of the Internet protocol based on connectionless packet switching, or a completely different, revolutionary breakthrough, it is currently impossible to conclude. Therefore, there are two possibilities.

1. *The future network is a new version of the internet protocol based on connectionless packet switching*

If the future network is a new version of the Internet protocol based on connectionless packet switching, the protocol of the future network should be designed "translatable" with IPv6 to ensure interconnection and communication with IPv6.

2. *The future network uses a completely different mechanism from the current internet*

If the future network develops into a mechanism completely different from the current Internet, that is, the future network protocol cannot be "translatable" with the existing Internet protocol, then unfortunately the relationship between the future network and IPv6 is some form of "encapsulation" (i.e., adding multiple layers).

(1) The future network is encapsulated on top of IPv6, that is, the future network can run on top of IPv6, with IPv6 providing connections.
(2) IPv6 is encapsulated on top of the future network, that is, existing Internet applications can run on the future network through IPv6.

Note: A key point repeatedly emphasized in this book is that only translation technology can enable interconnection between incompatible network protocols, while encapsulation technology cannot achieve this. Therefore, any future network design considerations must take this into account to avoid the significant costs associated with non-translatable designs.

16.3 Summary

This chapter is the last chapter of the book. Through the description of the previous chapters, readers have understood the two Internet protocol transitions that have occurred, the first one (from NCP to TCP/IP) is finished, and the second one (from IPv4 to IPv6) is still in progress.

Through the author's decade-long research experience, including transitioning from IPv4 to IPv6, the authors have put forward their own observations and predictions for the evolution and development of future network protocols.

References

1. Partridge C, Kastenholz F. RFC1726: Technical criteria for choosing IP the next generation (IPng). IETF 1994–12.
2. Leiner B, Cerf V, Clark D, et al. A brief history of the internet. [2022–02–18]. https://www.internethalloffame.org/brief-history-internet
3. Li Xing, Bao Congxiao. The Evolution of Internet Technology - Commemorating the 50th Anniversary of the Birth of ARPANET. China Education Network, 2020, (1):5.
4. Clark D, The design philosophy of the DARPA internet protocols. ACM SIGCOMM Computer Communication Review, 1988, 18(4):106-114.
5. Carpenter B. RFC1958: Architectural principles of the internet. IETF 1996–06.
6. Carpenter B. RFC2775: Internet transparency. IETF 2000–02.
7. Clark D. Designing an Internet - Information Policy. Cambridge: The MIT Press, 2018.
8. Postel J. RFC801: NCP/TCP transition plan. IETF 1981–11.
9. Arkko J, Townsley M. RFC6127: IPv4 run-out and IPv4-IPv6 co-existence scenarios. IETF 2011–05.

Appendix A
Protocol Numbers

RFC791 defines an 8-bit field in the IPv4 header called "Protocol" to identify the next level protocol. In the IPv6 header defined by RFC8200, this field is called "Next Header", which is the value of the IPv6 extension header type. Refer to RFC5237, RFC7045. The protocol numbers currently registered with IANA are shown in Table A.1.

Table A.1 IP protocol numbers

Decimal	Keyword	Protocol	IPv6 extension header	References
0	HOPOPT	IPv6 Hop-by-Hop Option	Y	RFC8200
1	ICMP	Internet Control Message		RFC792
2	IGMP	Internet Group Management		RFC1112
3	GGP	Gateway-to-Gateway		RFC823
4	IPv4	IPv4 encapsulation		RFC2003
5	ST	Stream		RFC1190, RFC1819
6	TCP	Transmission Control		RFC793
7	CBT	CBT		
8	EGP	Exterior Gateway Protocol		RFC888
9	IGP	Used by Cisco for their IGRP		IANA
10	BBN-RCC-MON	BBN RCC Monitoring		
11	NVP-II	Network Voice Protocol		RFC741
12	PUP	PUP		

(continued)

X. Li and C. Bao, *New IPv6 Transition Technology*,
https://doi.org/10.1007/978-981-95-8427-7

Table A.1 (continued)

Decimal	Keyword	Protocol	IPv6 extension header	References
13	ARGUS (deprecated)	ARGUS		
14	EMCON	EMCON		
15	XNET	Cross Net Debugger		
16	CHAOS	Chaos		
17	UDP	User Datagram		RFC768
18	MUX	Multiplexing		
19	DCN-MEAS	DCN Measurement Subsystems		
20	HMP	Host Monitoring		RFC869
21	PRM	Packet Radio Measurement		
22	XNS-IDP	XEROX NS IDP		
23	TRUNK-1	Trunk-1		
24	TRUNK-2	Trunk-2		
25	LEAF-1	Leaf-1		
26	LEAF-2	Leaf-2		
27	RDP	Reliable Data Protocol		RFC908
28	IRTP	Internet Reliable Transaction		RFC938
29	ISO-TP4	ISO Transport Protocol Class 4		RFC905
30	NETBLT	Bulk Data Transfer Protocol		RFC969
31	MFE-NSP	MFE Network Services Protocol		
32	MERIT-INP	MERIT Internodal Protocol		
33	DCCP	Datagram Congestion Control Protocol		RFC4340
34	3PC	Third Party Connect Protocol		
35	IDPR	Inter-Domain Policy Routing Protocol		

(continued)

Table A.1 (continued)

Decimal	Keyword	Protocol	IPv6 extension header	References
36	XTP	XTP		
37	DDP	Datagram Delivery Protocol		
38	IDPR-CMTP	IDPR Control Message Transport Proto		
39	TP ++	TP ++ Transport Protocol		
40	IL	IL Transport Protocol		
41	IPv6	IPv6 encapsulation		RFC2473
42	SDRP	Source Demand Routing Protocol		
43	IPv6-Route	Routing Header for IPv6	Y	
44	IPv6-Frag	Fragment Header for IPv6	Y	
45	IDRP	Inter-Domain Routing Protocol		
46	RSVP	Reservation Protocol		RFC2205, RFC3209
47	GRE	Generic Routing Encapsulation		RFC2784
48	DSR	Dynamic Source Routing Protocol		RFC4728
49	BNA	BNA		
50	ESP	Encap Security Payload	Y	RFC4303
51	AH	Authentication Header	Y	RFC4302
52	I-NLSP	Integrated Net Layer Security TUBA		
53	SWIPE (deprecated)	IP with Encryption		
54	NARP	NBMA Address Resolution Protocol		RFC1735
55	Min-IPv4	Minimal IPv4 Encapsulation		RFC2004, Charlie_Perkins
56	TLSP	Transport Layer Security Protocol		
57	SKIP	SKIP		Tom_Markson

(continued)

Table A.1 (continued)

Decimal	Keyword	Protocol	IPv6 extension header	References
58	IPv6-ICMP	ICMP for IPv6		RFC8200
59	IPv6-NoNxt	No Next Header for IPv6		RFC8200
60	IPv6-Opts	Destination Options for IPv6	Y	RFC8200
61		any host internal protocol		IANA
62	CFTP	CFTP		
63		any local network		IANA
64	SAT-EXPAK	SATNET and Backroom EXPAK		
65	KRYPTOLAN	Kryptolan		
66	RVD	MIT Remote Virtual Disk Protocol		
67	IPPC	Internet Pluribus Packet Core		
68		any distributed file system		IANA
69	SAT-MON	SATNET Monitoring		
70	VISA	VISA Protocol		
71	IPCV	Internet Packet Core Utility		
72	CPNX	Computer Protocol Network Executive		
73	CPHB	Computer Protocol Heart Beat		
74	WSN	Wang Span Network		
75	PVP	Packet Video Protocol		
76	BR-SAT-MON	Backroom SATNET Monitoring		
77	SUN-ND	SUN ND PROTOCOL-Temporary		
78	WB-MON	WIDEBAND Monitoring		
79	WB-EXPAK	WIDEBAND EXPAK		
80	ISO-IP	ISO Internet Protocol		
81	VMTP	VMTP		
82	SECURE-VMTP	SECURE-VMTP		

(continued)

Table A.1 (continued)

Decimal	Keyword	Protocol	IPv6 extension header	References
83	VINES	VINES		
84	IPTM	Internet Protocol Traffic Manager		
85	NSFNET-IGP	NSFNET-IGP		
86	DGP	Dissimilar Gateway Protocol		
87	TCF	TCF		
88	EIGRP	EIGRP		RFC7868
89	OSPFIGP	OSPFIGP		RFC1583, RFC2328, RFC5340
90	Sprite-RPC	Sprite RPC Protocol		
91	LARP	Locus Address Resolution Protocol		
92	MTP	Multicast Transport Protocol		
93	AX.25	AX.25 Frames		
94	IPIP	IP-within-IP Encapsulation Protocol		
95	MICP (deprecated)	Mobile Internetworking Control Pro		
96	SCC-SP	Semaphore Communications Sec. Pro		
97	ETHERIP	Ethernet-within-IP Encapsulation		RFC3378
98	ENCAP	Encapsulation Header		RFC1241
99		any private encryption scheme		IANA
100	GMTP	GMTP		
101	IFMP	Ipsilon Flow Management Protocol		
102	PNNI	PNNI over IP		
103	PIM	Protocol Independent Multicast		RFC7761
104	ARIS	ARIS		
105	SCPS	SCPS		

(continued)

Table A.1 (continued)

Decimal	Keyword	Protocol	IPv6 extension header	References
106	QNX	QNX		
107	A/N	Active Networks		
108	IPComp	IP Payload Compression Protocol		RFC2393
109	SNP	Sitara Networks Protocol		
110	Compaq-Peer	Compaq Peer Protocol		
111	IPX-in-IP	IPX in IP		
112	VRRP	Virtual Router Redundancy Protocol		RFC5798
113	PGM	PGM Reliable Transport Protocol		
114		any 0-hop protocol		IANA
115	L2TP	Layer Two Tunneling Protocol		RFC3931
116	DDX	D-II Data Exchange (DDX)		
117	IATP	Interactive Agent Transfer Protocol		
118	STP	Schedule Transfer Protocol		
119	SRP	SpectraLink Radio Protocol		
120	UTI	UTI		
121	SMP	Simple Message Protocol		
122	SM (deprecated)	Simple Multicast Protocol		
123	PTP	Performance Transparency Protocol		
124	ISIS over IPv4			
125	FIRE			
126	CRTP	Combat Radio Transport Protocol		
127	CRUDP	Combat Radio User Datagram		

(continued)

Table A.1 (continued)

Decimal	Keyword	Protocol	IPv6 extension header	References
128	SSCOPMCE			
129	IPLT			
130	SPS	Secure Packet Shield		
131	PIPE	Private IP Encapsulation within IP		
132	SCTP	Stream Control Transmission Protocol		
133	FC	Fiber Channel		RFC6172
134	RSVP-E2E-IGNORE			RFC3175
135	Mobility Header		Y	RFC6275
136	UDPLite			RFC3828
137	MPLS-in-IP			RFC4023
138	manet	MANET Protocols		RFC5498
139	HIP	Host Identity Protocol	Y	RFC7401
140	Shim6	Shim6 Protocol	Y	RFC553
141	WESP	Wrapped Encapsulating Security Payload		RFC5840
142	ROHC	Robust Header Compression		RFC5858
143	Ethernet	Ethernet		RFC8986
144	AGGFRAG	AGGFRAG encapsulation payload for ESP		RFC9347
145	NSH	Network Service Header	N	RFC9491
146	Homa	Homa	N	HomaModule, John_Ousterhout
147	BIT-EMU	Bit-stream Emulation	Y	
148–252		Unassigned		IANA
253		Use for experimentation and testing	Y	RFC3692
254		Use for experimentation and testing	Y	RFC3692
255	Reserved			IANA

Appendix B
IPv4 Address Space Registry

The Regional Internet Registries (RIRs) allocate user IP address according to the "Global Policy", and other allocations require IETF review.

Table B.1 lists the allocation of the IPv4 address space. Initially, all IPv4 address spaces were directly managed by IANA. Subsequent parts of the address space have been allocated to other registries for specific purposes or for use by Internet service providers around the world. RFC1466 records most of these allocations, refer to RFC7249.

The following notes apply to Table B.1:

(1) Indicating the status of the address block, as follows.

  ① Reserved: Designated by the IETF for specific non-global unicast addresses.
  ② Legacy: Addresses allocated by the central Internet Registry (IR) before the establishment of the RIR. This address space is now managed by each RIR, including maintaining the address directory (who is, WHOIS) and reverse DNS records, and these addresses continue to be used globally.
  ③ Allocated: Fully delegated to the designated RIR.
  ④ Unallocated: Not yet allocated or reserved.

(2) For self-identification (RFC1122): 0.0.0.0/8 is reserved for the protocol, see iana-ipv4-special-registry.
(3) Reserved for private networks (RFC1918): Detailed registration information for 10.0.0.0/8, see iana-ipv4-special-registry.
(4) Reserved for public data networks (RFC1356): Restored in February 2008, allocated to APNIC in April 2010, see IANA Registry public data network number.
(5) Reserved for shared address space (RFC6598): Detailed registration information for 100.64.0.0/10, see iana-ipv4-special-registry.
(6) Used for loopback address (RFC1122): 127.0.0.0/8 is reserved for the protocol, see iana-ipv4-special-registry.

X. Li and C. Bao, *New IPv6 Transition Technology*,
https://doi.org/10.1007/978-981-95-8427-7

Table B.1 IPv4 address space registry

Prefix	Designation	Date	Status	Note
000/8	IANA–local identification	Sep-81	RESERVED	2
001/8	APNIC	Jan-10	ALLOCATED	
002/8	RIPE NCC	Sep-09	ALLOCATED	
003/8	Administered by ARIN	May-94	LEGACY	
004/8	Administered by ARIN	Dec-92	LEGACY	
005/8	RIPE NCC	Nov-10	ALLOCATED	
006/8	Army Information Systems Center	Feb-94	LEGACY	
007/8	Administered by ARIN	Apr-95	LEGACY	
008/8	Administered by ARIN	Dec-92	LEGACY	
009/8	Administered by ARIN	Aug-92	LEGACY	
010/8	IANA - Private Use	Jun-95	RESERVED	3
011/8	DoD Intel Information Systems	May-93	LEGACY	
012/8	AT&T Bell Laboratories	Jun-95	LEGACY	
013/8	Administered by ARIN	Sep-91	LEGACY	
014/8	APNIC	Apr-10	ALLOCATED	4
015/8	Administered by ARIN	Jul-94	LEGACY	
016/8	Administered by ARIN	Nov-94	LEGACY	
017/8	Apple Computer Inc	Jul-92	LEGACY	
018/8	Administered by ARIN	Jan-94	LEGACY	
019/8	Ford Motor Company	May-95	LEGACY	
020/8	Administered by ARIN	Oct-94	LEGACY	
021/8	DDN-RVN	Jul-91	LEGACY	
022/8	Defense Information Systems Agency	May-93	LEGACY	
023/8	ARIN	Nov-10	ALLOCATED	
024/8	ARIN	May-01	ALLOCATED	
025/8	Administered by RIPE NCC	Jan-95	LEGACY	
026/8	Defense Information Systems Agency	May-95	LEGACY	
027/8	APNIC	Jan-10	ALLOCATED	
028/8	DSI-North	Jul-92	LEGACY	
029/8	Defense Information Systems Agency	Jul-91	LEGACY	
030/8	Defense Information Systems Agency	Jul-91	LEGACY	
031/8	RIPE NCC	May-10	ALLOCATED	
032/8	Administered by ARIN	Jun-94	LEGACY	
033/8	DLA Systems Automation Center	Jan-91	LEGACY	
034/8	Administered by ARIN	Mar-93	LEGACY	
035/8	Administered by ARIN	Apr-94	LEGACY	
036/8	APNIC	Oct-10	ALLOCATED	

(continued)

Table B.1 (continued)

Prefix	Designation	Date	Status	Note
037/8	RIPE NCC	Nov-10	ALLOCATED	
038/8	PSINet, Inc	Sep-94	LEGACY	
039/8	APNIC	Jan-11	ALLOCATED	
040/8	Administered by ARIN	Jun-94	LEGACY	
041/8	AFRINIC	Apr-05	ALLOCATED	
042/8	APNIC	Oct-10	ALLOCATED	
043/8	Administered by APNIC	Jan-91	LEGACY	
044/8	Administered by ARIN	Jul-92	LEGACY	
045/8	Administered by ARIN	Jan-95	LEGACY	
046/8	RIPE NCC	Sep-09	ALLOCATED	
047/8	Administered by ARIN	Jan-91	LEGACY	
048/8	Administered by ARIN	May-95	LEGACY	
049/8	APNIC	Aug-10	ALLOCATED	
050/8	ARIN	Feb-10	ALLOCATED	
051/8	Administered by RIPE NCC	Aug-94	LEGACY	
052/8	Administered by ARIN	Dec-91	LEGACY	
053/8	Daimler AG	Oct-93	LEGACY	
054/8	Administered by ARIN	Mar-92	LEGACY	
055/8	DoD Network Information Center	Apr-95	LEGACY	
056/8	Administered by ARIN	Jun-94	LEGACY	
057/8	Administered by RIPE NCC	May-95	LEGACY	
058/8	APNIC	Apr-04	ALLOCATED	
059/8	APNIC	Apr-04	ALLOCATED	
060/8	APNIC	Apr-03	ALLOCATED	
061/8	APNIC	Apr-97	ALLOCATED	
062/8	RIPE NCC	Apr-97	ALLOCATED	
063/8	ARIN	Apr-97	ALLOCATED	
064/8	ARIN	Jul-99	ALLOCATED	
065/8	ARIN	Jul-00	ALLOCATED	
066/8	ARIN	Jul-00	ALLOCATED	
067/8	ARIN	May-01	ALLOCATED	
068/8	ARIN	Jun-01	ALLOCATED	
069/8	ARIN	Aug-02	ALLOCATED	
070/8	ARIN	Jan-04	ALLOCATED	
071/8	ARIN	Aug-04	ALLOCATED	
072/8	ARIN	Aug-04	ALLOCATED	
073/8	ARIN	Mar-05	ALLOCATED	

(continued)

Table B.1 (continued)

Prefix	Designation	Date	Status	Note
074/8	ARIN	Jun-05	ALLOCATED	
075/8	ARIN	Jun-05	ALLOCATED	
076/8	ARIN	Jun-05	ALLOCATED	
077/8	RIPE NCC	Aug-06	ALLOCATED	
078/8	RIPE NCC	Aug-06	ALLOCATED	
079/8	RIPE NCC	Aug-06	ALLOCATED	
080/8	RIPE NCC	Apr-01	ALLOCATED	
081/8	RIPE NCC	Apr-01	ALLOCATED	
082/8	RIPE NCC	Nov-02	ALLOCATED	
083/8	RIPE NCC	Nov-03	ALLOCATED	
084/8	RIPE NCC	Nov-03	ALLOCATED	
085/8	RIPE NCC	Apr-04	ALLOCATED	
086/8	RIPE NCC	Apr-04	ALLOCATED	
087/8	RIPE NCC	Apr-04	ALLOCATED	
088/8	RIPE NCC	Apr-04	ALLOCATED	
089/8	RIPE NCC	Jun-05	ALLOCATED	
090/8	RIPE NCC	Jun-05	ALLOCATED	
091/8	RIPE NCC	Jun-05	ALLOCATED	
092/8	RIPE NCC	Mar-07	ALLOCATED	
093/8	RIPE NCC	Mar-07	ALLOCATED	
094/8	RIPE NCC	Jul-07	ALLOCATED	
095/8	RIPE NCC	Jul-07	ALLOCATED	
096/8	ARIN	Oct-06	ALLOCATED	
097/8	ARIN	Oct-06	ALLOCATED	
098/8	ARIN	Oct-06	ALLOCATED	
099/8	ARIN	Oct-06	ALLOCATED	
100/8	ARIN	Nov-10	ALLOCATED	5
101/8	APNIC	Aug-10	ALLOCATED	
102/8	AFRINIC	Feb-11	ALLOCATED	
103/8	APNIC	Feb-11	ALLOCATED	
104/8	ARIN	Feb-11	ALLOCATED	
105/8	AFRINIC	Nov-10	ALLOCATED	
106/8	APNIC	Jan-11	ALLOCATED	
107/8	ARIN	Feb-10	ALLOCATED	
108/8	ARIN	Dec-08	ALLOCATED	
109/8	RIPE NCC	Jan-09	ALLOCATED	
110/8	APNIC	Nov-08	ALLOCATED	

(continued)

Table B.1 (continued)

Prefix	Designation	Date	Status	Note
111/8	APNIC	Nov-08	ALLOCATED	
112/8	APNIC	May-08	ALLOCATED	
113/8	APNIC	May-08	ALLOCATED	
114/8	APNIC	Oct-07	ALLOCATED	
115/8	APNIC	Oct-07	ALLOCATED	
116/8	APNIC	Jan-07	ALLOCATED	
117/8	APNIC	Jan-07	ALLOCATED	
118/8	APNIC	Jan-07	ALLOCATED	
119/8	APNIC	Jan-07	ALLOCATED	
120/8	APNIC	Jan-07	ALLOCATED	
121/8	APNIC	Jan-06	ALLOCATED	
122/8	APNIC	Jan-06	ALLOCATED	
123/8	APNIC	Jan-06	ALLOCATED	
124/8	APNIC	Jan-05	ALLOCATED	
125/8	APNIC	Jan-05	ALLOCATED	
126/8	APNIC	Jan-05	ALLOCATED	
127/8	IANA - Loopback	Sep-81	RESERVED	6
128/8	Administered by ARIN	May-93	LEGACY	
129/8	Administered by ARIN	May-93	LEGACY	
130/8	Administered by ARIN	May-93	LEGACY	
131/8	Administered by ARIN	May-93	LEGACY	
132/8	Administered by ARIN	May-93	LEGACY	
133/8	Administered by APNIC	Mar-97	LEGACY	
134/8	Administered by ARIN	May-93	LEGACY	
135/8	Administered by ARIN	May-93	LEGACY	
136/8	Administered by ARIN	May-93	LEGACY	
137/8	Administered by ARIN	May-93	LEGACY	
138/8	Administered by ARIN	May-93	LEGACY	
139/8	Administered by ARIN	May-93	LEGACY	
140/8	Administered by ARIN	May-93	LEGACY	
141/8	Administered by RIPE NCC	May-93	LEGACY	
142/8	Administered by ARIN	May-93	LEGACY	
143/8	Administered by ARIN	May-93	LEGACY	
144/8	Administered by ARIN	May-93	LEGACY	
145/8	Administered by RIPE NCC	May-93	LEGACY	
146/8	Administered by ARIN	May-93	LEGACY	
147/8	Administered by ARIN	May-93	LEGACY	

(continued)

Table B.1 (continued)

Prefix	Designation	Date	Status	Note
148/8	Administered by ARIN	May-93	LEGACY	
149/8	Administered by ARIN	May-93	LEGACY	
150/8	Administered by APNIC	May-93	LEGACY	
151/8	Administered by RIPE NCC	May-93	LEGACY	
152/8	Administered by ARIN	May-93	LEGACY	
153/8	Administered by APNIC	May-93	LEGACY	
154/8	Administered by AFRINIC	May-93	LEGACY	
155/8	Administered by ARIN	May-93	LEGACY	
156/8	Administered by ARIN	May-93	LEGACY	
157/8	Administered by ARIN	May-93	LEGACY	
158/8	Administered by ARIN	May-93	LEGACY	
159/8	Administered by ARIN	May-93	LEGACY	
160/8	Administered by ARIN	May-93	LEGACY	
161/8	Administered by ARIN	May-93	LEGACY	
162/8	Administered by ARIN	May-93	LEGACY	
163/8	Administered by APNIC	May-93	LEGACY	
164/8	Administered by ARIN	May-93	LEGACY	
165/8	Administered by ARIN	May-93	LEGACY	
166/8	Administered by ARIN	May-93	LEGACY	
167/8	Administered by ARIN	May-93	LEGACY	
168/8	Administered by ARIN	May-93	LEGACY	
169/8	Administered by ARIN	May-93	LEGACY	7
170/8	Administered by ARIN	May-93	LEGACY	
171/8	Administered by APNIC	May-93	LEGACY	8
172/8	Administered by ARIN	May-93	LEGACY	
173/8	ARIN	Feb-08	ALLOCATED	
174/8	ARIN	Feb-08	ALLOCATED	
175/8	APNIC	Aug-09	ALLOCATED	
176/8	RIPE NCC	May-10	ALLOCATED	
177/8	LACNIC	Jun-10	ALLOCATED	
178/8	RIPE NCC	Jan-09	ALLOCATED	
179/8	LACNIC	Feb-11	ALLOCATED	
180/8	APNIC	Apr-09	ALLOCATED	
181/8	LACNIC	Jun-10	ALLOCATED	
182/8	APNIC	Aug-09	ALLOCATED	
183/8	APNIC	Apr-09	ALLOCATED	
184/8	ARIN	Dec-08	ALLOCATED	

(continued)

Table B.1 (continued)

Prefix	Designation	Date	Status	Note
185/8	RIPE NCC	Feb-11	ALLOCATED	
186/8	LACNIC	Sep-07	ALLOCATED	
187/8	LACNIC	Sep-07	ALLOCATED	
188/8	Administered by RIPE NCC	May-93	LEGACY	
189/8	LACNIC	Jun-95	ALLOCATED	
190/8	LACNIC	Jun-95	ALLOCATED	
191/8	Administered by LACNIC	May-93	LEGACY	
192/8	Administered by ARIN	May-93	LEGACY	9, 10
193/8	RIPE NCC	May-93	ALLOCATED	
194/8	RIPE NCC	May-93	ALLOCATED	
195/8	RIPE NCC	May-93	ALLOCATED	
196/8	Administered by AFRINIC	May-93	LEGACY	
197/8	AFRINIC	Oct-08	ALLOCATED	
198/8	Administered by ARIN	May-93	LEGACY	11
199/8	ARIN	May-93	ALLOCATED	
200/8	LACNIC	Nov-02	ALLOCATED	
201/8	LACNIC	Apr-03	ALLOCATED	
202/8	APNIC	May-93	ALLOCATED	
203/8	APNIC	May-93	ALLOCATED	12
204/8	ARIN	Mar-94	ALLOCATED	
205/8	ARIN	Mar-94	ALLOCATED	
206/8	ARIN	Apr-95	ALLOCATED	
207/8	ARIN	Nov-95	ALLOCATED	
208/8	ARIN	Apr-96	ALLOCATED	
209/8	ARIN	Jun-96	ALLOCATED	
210/8	APNIC	Jun-96	ALLOCATED	
211/8	APNIC	Jun-96	ALLOCATED	
212/8	RIPE NCC	Oct-97	ALLOCATED	
213/8	RIPE NCC	Oct-93	ALLOCATED	
214/8	US-DOD	Mar-98	LEGACY	
215/8	US-DOD	Mar-98	LEGACY	
216/8	ARIN	Apr-98	ALLOCATED	
217/8	RIPE NCC	Jun-00	ALLOCATED	
218/8	APNIC	Dec-00	ALLOCATED	
219/8	APNIC	Sep-01	ALLOCATED	
220/8	APNIC	Dec-01	ALLOCATED	
221/8	APNIC	Jul-02	ALLOCATED	

(continued)

Table B.1 (continued)

Prefix	Designation	Date	Status	Note
222/8	APNIC	Feb-03	ALLOCATED	
223/8	APNIC	Apr-10	ALLOCATED	
224/8	Multicast	Sep-81	RESERVED	13
225/8	Multicast	Sep-81	RESERVED	13
226/8	Multicast	Sep-81	RESERVED	13
227/8	Multicast	Sep-81	RESERVED	13
228/8	Multicast	Sep-81	RESERVED	13
229/8	Multicast	Sep-81	RESERVED	13
230/8	Multicast	Sep-81	RESERVED	13
231/8	Multicast	Sep-81	RESERVED	13
232/8	Multicast	Sep-81	RESERVED	13
233/8	Multicast	Sep-81	RESERVED	13
234/8	Multicast	Sep-81	RESERVED	13, 14
235/8	Multicast	Sep-81	RESERVED	13
236/8	Multicast	Sep-81	RESERVED	13
237/8	Multicast	Sep-81	RESERVED	13
238/8	Multicast	Sep-81	RESERVED	13
239/8	Multicast	Sep-81	RESERVED	13
240/8	Future use	Sep-81	RESERVED	16
241/8	Future use	Sep-81	RESERVED	16
242/8	Future use	Sep-81	RESERVED	16
243/8	Future use	Sep-81	RESERVED	16
244/8	Future use	Sep-81	RESERVED	16
245/8	Future use	Sep-81	RESERVED	16
246/8	Future use	Sep-81	RESERVED	16
247/8	Future use	Sep-81	RESERVED	16
248/8	Future use	Sep-81	RESERVED	16
249/8	Future use	Sep-81	RESERVED	16
250/8	Future use	Sep-81	RESERVED	16
251/8	Future use	Sep-81	RESERVED	16
252/8	Future use	Sep-81	RESERVED	16
253/8	Future use	Sep-81	RESERVED	16
254/8	Future use	Sep-81	RESERVED	16
255/8	Future use	Sep-81	RESERVED	16,17

(7) Used for link-local address (RFC3927): 169.254.0.0/16 is reserved for the protocol, see iana-ipv4-special-registry.
(8) Reserved for private networks (RFC1918): Detailed registration information for 172.16.0.0/12, see iana-ipv4-special-registry.
(9) Reserved addresses.

① 192.0.2.0/24 is used for TEST-NET-1 (RFC5737). Detailed registration information for 192.0.2.0/24, see iana-ipv4-special-registry.
② 192.88.99.0/24 is used for 6to4 relay anycast (RFC7526). Detailed registration information for 192.88.99.0/24, see iana-ipv4-special-registry.
③ 192.88.99.2/32 is used for 6a44 relay anycast, which can work with 6to4 relay (RFC6751). See RFC7526.
④ 192.168.0.0/16 is reserved for private networks (RFC1918). Detailed registration information for 192.168.0.0/16, see iana-ipv4-special-registry.

(10) Reserved for IANA IPv4 special address registry (RFC5736): Detailed registration information for 192.0.0.0/24, see iana-ipv4-special-registry.
(11) Reserved for network interconnection device benchmark testing (RFC2544).

① Detailed registration information for 198.18.0.0/15, see iana-ipv4-special-registry.
② 198.51.100.0/24 is reserved for TEST-NET-2 (RFC5737). See iana-ipv4-special- registry.

(12) Reserved for TEST-NET-3 (RFC5737): Detailed registration information for 203.0.113.0/24, see iana-ipv4-special-registry.
(13) Multicast addresses registered with IANA (formerly "Class D" addresses) (RFC5771).
(14) IPv4 multicast addresses based on unicast prefixes (RFC6034).
(15) IP multicast within administrative scope (RFC2365).
(16) Reserved for future use (formerly "Class E" addresses) (RFC1112): Protocol reserved, see iana- ipv4-special-registry.
(17) Reserved for "limited broadcast" destination address (RFC919, RFC922): Detailed registration information for 255.255.255.255/32, see iana-ipv4-special-registry.

Appendix C
IPv4 Multicast Address Space Registry

The multicast address defined by the IP Multicast Host Extensions (*RFC1112*) is within the range of 224.0.0.0 to 239.255.255.255.

The address range between 224.0.0.0 and 224.0.0.255 is reserved for routing protocols and other infrastructure uses, such as gateway discovery and group member reporting. Regardless of the TTL value, routers should not forward any multicast datagrams with destination addresses in this range. The currently registered IPv4 multicast addresses with IANA are shown in Table C.1.

Table C.1 IPv4 multicast address space registry

Address	Name	CIDR	RFC
224.0.0.0–224.0.0.255	Local	224.0.0/24	RFC5771
224.0.1.0–224.0.1.255	Internet	224.0.1/24	RFC5771
224.0.2.0–224.0.255.255	AD-HOC I		RFC5771
224.1.0.0–224.1.255.255	reserved	224.1/16	RFC5771
224.2.0.0–224.2.255.255	SDP/SAP	224.2/16	RFC5771
224.3.0.0–224.4.255.255	AD-HOC II	224.3/16	RFC5771
	reserved	224.4/16	
224.5.0.0–224.251.255.255	DIS__	251/16 s	RFC5771
224.252.0.0–224.255.255.255	DIS__	224.252/14	RFC2365
225.0.0.0–231.255.255.255	reserved		RFC5771
232.0.0.0–232.255.255.255	SSM	232/8	RFC5771
233.0.0.0–233.251.255.255	GLOP		RFC3180
233.252.0.0–233.255.255.255	AD-HOC III	233.252/14	RFC5771
234.0.0.0–234.255.255.255	limited scope		RFC6034
235.0.0.0–238.255.255.255	limited scope		RFC5771
239.0.0.0–239.255.255.255	limited scope		RFC5771

X. Li and C. Bao, *New IPv6 Transition Technology*,
https://doi.org/10.1007/978-981-95-8427-7

Appendix D
Dedicated IPv4 Address Space Registry

The IANA IPv4 dedicated address registry is responsible for registering special IPv4 addresses, and its registration process refers to RFC5736, RFC6890, RFC8190. The IETF has reserved the 192.0.0.0/24 address block for special purposes related to protocol conversion. This registry includes the current allocation situation of the IETF. The address prefixes listed in the special purpose address registration table do not guarantee routability in any specific local or global network. The dedicated IPv4 addresses currently registered with IANA are shown in Table D.1.

Table D.1 Dedicated IPv4 address space registry

Address Block	Name	RFC	Allocation	Source	Destination	Globally
0.0.0.0/8	"This network"	RFC791	Sep-81	TRUE	FALSE	FALSE
0.0.0.0/32	"This host on this network"	RFC1122	Sep-81	TRUE	FALSE	FALSE
10.0.0.0/8	Private-Use	RFC1918	Feb-96	TRUE	TRUE	FALSE
100.64.0.0/10	Shared Address Space	RFC6598	Apr-12	TRUE	TRUE	FALSE
127.0.0.0/8	Loopback	RFC1122	Sep-81	False	False	FALSE
169.254.0.0/16	Link Local	RFC3927	May-05	TRUE	TRUE	FALSE
172.16.0.0/12	Private-Use	RFC1918	Feb-96	TRUE	TRUE	FALSE
192.0.0.0/24	IETF Protocol Assignments	RFC6890	Jan-10	FALSE	FALSE	FALSE

(continued)

X. Li and C. Bao, *New IPv6 Transition Technology*,
https://doi.org/10.1007/978-981-95-8427-7

Table D.1 (continued)

Address Block	Name	RFC	Allocation	Source	Destination	Globally
192.0.0.0/29	IPv4 Service Continuity Prefix	RFC7335	Jun-11	TRUE	TRUE	FALSE
192.0.0.8/32	IPv4 dummy address	RFC7600	Mar-15	TRUE	FALSE	FALSE
192.0.0.9/32	Port Control Protocol Anycast	RFC7723	Oct-15	TRUE	TRUE	TRUE
192.0.0.10/32	Traversal Using Relays around NAT Anycast	RFC8155	Feb-17	TRUE	TRUE	TRUE
192.0.0.170/32, 192.0.0.171/32	NAT64/DNS64 Discovery	RFC7050	Feb-13	FALSE	FALSE	FALSE
192.0.2.0/24	Documentation (TEST-NET-1)	RFC5737	Jan-10	FALSE	FALSE	FALSE
192.31.196.0/24	AS112-v4	RFC7535	Dec-14	TRUE	TRUE	TRUE
192.52.193.0/24	AMT	RFC7450	Dec-14	TRUE	TRUE	TRUE
192.88.99.0/24	Deprecated (6to4 Relay Anycast)	RFC7526	Jun-01			
192.168.0.0/16	Private-Use	RFC1918	Feb-96	TRUE	TRUE	FALSE
192.175.48.0/24	Direct Delegation AS112 Service	RFC7534	Jan-96	TRUE	TRUE	TRUE
198.18.0.0/15	Benchmarking	RFC2544	Mar-99	TRUE	TRUE	FALSE
198.51.100.0/24	Documentation (TEST-NET-2)	RFC5737	Jan-10	FALSE	FALSE	FALSE
203.0.113.0/24	Documentation (TEST-NET-3)	RFC5737	Jan-10	FALSE	FALSE	FALSE
240.0.0.0/4	Reserved	RFC1112	Aug-89	FALSE	FALSE	FALSE
255.255.255.255/32	Limited Broadcast	RFC8190, RFC919	Oct-84	FALSE	TRUE	FALSE

Appendix E
IPv6 Address Space Registry

Since December 1995, the management of IPv6 addresses has been formally delegated to IANA, see RFC1881. Starting from March 2010, its registration process has been confirmed by the IETF chairman. As described in RFC3513, IANA should limit the allocation of IPv6 unicast address space to the address range starting with the binary value 001. The rest of the global unicast address space (about 85% of the IPv6 address space) needs to be reserved for future definition and use, and is currently not allocated by IANA. The IPv6 addresses currently registered with IANA are shown in Table E.1.

Table E.1 IPv6 address space Registry

IPv6 prefix	Allocation	References	Notes
::/8	Reserved by IETF	RFC3513, RFC4291	This range has been partially allocated. See IANA registry iana-ipv6-special-registry for details.::/96, formerly defined as the “IPv4-compatible IPv6 address” prefix, was deprecated by RFC4291
100::/8	Reserved by IETF	RFC3513, RFC4291	This range has been partially allocated. See IANA registry iana-ipv6-special-registry for details
200::/7	Reserved by IETF	RFC4048	Deprecated as of December 2004 RFC4048. Formerly an OSI NSAP-mapped prefix set RFC4548
400::/6	Reserved by IETF	RFC3513, RFC4291	
800::/5	Reserved by IETF	RFC3513,RFC4291	

(continued)

X. Li and C. Bao, *New IPv6 Transition Technology*,
https://doi.org/10.1007/978-981-95-8427-7

Table E.1 (continued)

IPv6 prefix	Allocation	References	Notes
1000::/4	Reserved by IETF	RFC3513, RFC4291	
2000::/3	Global Unicast	RFC3513, RFC4291	The IPv6 Unicast space encompasses the entire IPv6 address range with the exception of ff00::/8, per RFC4291. IANA unicast address assignments are currently limited to the IPv6 unicast address range of 2000::/3. IANA assignments from this block are registered in IANA registry ipv6-unicast-address-assignments
4000::/3	Reserved by IETF	RFC3513, RFC4291	This range has been partially allocated. See IANA registry iana-ipv6-special-registry for details. 5f00::/8 (with 3ffe::/16, as noted at IANA registry ipv6-unicast-address-assignments) was used for the 6bone, but returned RFC5156
6000::/3	Reserved by IETF	RFC3513, RFC4291	
8000::/3	Reserved by IETF	RFC3513, RFC4291	
a000::/3	Reserved by IETF	RFC3513, RFC4291	
c000::/3	Reserved by IETF	RFC3513, RFC4291	
e000::/4	Reserved by IETF	RFC3513, RFC4291	
f000::/5	Reserved by IETF	RFC3513, RFC4291	
f800::/6	Reserved by IETF	RFC3513, RFC4291	
fc00::/7	Unique Local Unicast	RFC4193	See IANA registry iana-ipv6-special-registry for details
fe00::/9	Reserved by IETF	RFC3513, RFC4291	
fe80::/10	Link-Scoped Unicast	RFC3513, RFC4291	See IANA registry iana-ipv6-special-registry for details
fec0::/10	Reserved by IETF	RFC3879	Deprecated by RFC3879 in September 2004. Formerly a Site-Local scoped address prefix

(continued)

Table E.1 (continued)

IPv6 prefix	Allocation	References	Notes
ff00::/8	Multicast	RFC3513, RFC4291	See [IANA registry ipv6-multicast-addresses] for details

Note

(1)::1/128 is reserved for loopback address (RFC4291);
(2)::/128 is reserved for unspecified address (RFC4291);
(3)::ffff:0:0/96 is reserved for IPv4-mapped addresses (RFC4291);
(4) 0::/96 is deprecated (RFC4291) previously defined as "IPv4-compatible IPv6 address" prefix;
(5) 64:ff9b::/96 (RFC6052) IPv6 "well-known prefix" for IPv4/IPv6 address translation algorithm;
(6) 64:ff9b:1::/48 (RFC8215) reserved for local use of IPv4/IPv6 address translation algorithm's IPv6 "well-known prefix" extension;
(7) 2001:0::/23 reserved for IETF protocol assignments (RFC2928);
(8) 2001:0::/32 reserved for Teredo (RFC4380);
(9) 2001:2::/48 reserved for benchmarking (RFC5180);
(10) 2001:3::/32 reserved for AMT (RFC7450);
(11) 2001:4:112::/48 reserved for AS112-v6 (RFC7535);
(12) 2001:10::/28 deprecated (previously for ORCHID) (RFC4843);
(13) 2001:20::/28 reserved for ORCHIDv2 (RFC7343);
(14) 2001:db8::/32 reserved for documentation (RFC3849);
(15) 2002::/16 reserved for 6to4 (RFC3056).

Appendix F
Private IPv6 Address Space Registry

The address prefixes listed in the private address registry cannot guarantee routability in any specific local or global scope. The currently registered private IPv6 addresses with IANA are shown in Table F.1.

Table F.1 Private IPv6 address space registry

Address block	Name	RFC	Allocation	Source	Destination	Globally
::1/128	Loopback Address	RFC4291	Feb-06	FALSE	FALSE	FALSE
::/128	Unspecified Address	RFC4291	Feb-06	TRUE	FALSE	FALSE
::ffff:0:0/96	IPv4-mapped Address	RFC4291	Feb-06	FALSE	FALSE	FALSE
64:ff9b::/96	IPv4-IPv6 Translat	RFC6052	Oct-10	TRUE	TRUE	TRUE
64:ff9b:1::/48	IPv4-IPv6 Translat	RFC8215	Jun-17	TRUE	TRUE	FALSE
100::/64	Discard-Only Address Block	RFC6666	Jun-12	TRUE	TRUE	FALSE
2001::/23	IETF Protocol Assignments	RFC2928	Sep-00	FALSE	FALSE	FALSE
2001::/32	TEREDO	RFC4380, RFC8190	Jan-06	TRUE	TRUE	N/A
2001:1::1/128	Port Control Protocol Anycast	RFC7723	Oct-15	TRUE	TRUE	TRUE
2001:1::2/128	Traversal Using Relays around NAT Anycast	RFC8155	Feb-17	TRUE	TRUE	TRUE
2001:1::3/128	DNS-SD Service Registration Protocol Anycast		Apr-24	TRUE	TRUE	TRUE

(continued)

X. Li and C. Bao, *New IPv6 Transition Technology*,
https://doi.org/10.1007/978-981-95-8427-7

Table F.1 (continued)

Address block	Name	RFC	Allocation	Source	Destination	Globally
2001:2::/48	Benchmarking	RFC5180	Apr-08	TRUE	TRUE	FALSE
2001:3::/32	AMT	RFC7450	Dec-14	TRUE	TRUE	TRUE
2001:4:112::/48	AS112-v6	RFC7535	Dec-14	TRUE	TRUE	TRUE
2001:10::/28	Deprecated (previously ORCHID)	RFC4843	Mar-07			
2001:20::/28	ORCHIDv2	RFC7343	Jul-14	TRUE	TRUE	TRUE
2001:30::/28	Drone Remote ID Protocol Entity Tags (DETs) Prefix	RFC9374	Dec-22	TRUE	TRUE	TRUE
2001:db8::/32	Documentation	RFC3849	Jul-04	FALSE	FALSE	FALSE
2002::/16	6to4	RFC3056	Feb-01	TRUE	TRUE	N/A
2620:4f:8000::/48	Direct Delegation AS112 Service	RFC7534	May-11	TRUE	TRUE	TRUE
3fff::/20	Documentation	RFC9637	Jul-24	FALSE	FALSE	FALSE
5f00::/16	Segment Routing (SRv6) SIDs	RFC9602	Apr-24	TRUE	TRUE	FALSE
fc00::/7	Unique-Local	RFC4193, RFC8190	Oct-05	TRUE	TRUE	FALSE
fe80::/10	Link-Local Unicast	RFC4291	Feb-06	TRUE	TRUE	FALSE

Note

(1) related to the protocol, not allowed to assign;

(2) see RFC4380;

(3) see RFC3056;

(4) see RFC4193.

Appendix G
Common Transport Layer Ports

Service names and port numbers are used to distinguish between different services running on transport protocols such as TCP, UDP, DCCP, and SCTP. Service names are assigned on a "first come, first served" basis (RFC6335). The allocation of port numbers is as follows:

(1) System ports: 0~1023; allocated through the "IETF Review" or "IESG Approval" process as described by RFC8126.
(2) User ports: 1024~49,151; IANA uses the "IETF Review" process, "IESG Approval" process, or "Expert Review" process for allocation.
(3) Dynamic and/or private ports: 49,152~65,535. The registration process for service names and port numbers is described in RFC6335. System ports and user ports should not be used without IANA registration or prior to IANA registration. The commonly used transport layer ports that have been registered with IANA are shown in Table G.1.

Table G.1 Common transport layer port allocation table

Service Name	Port Number	Transport Protocol	Description
tcpmux	1	tcp	TCP Port Service Multiplexer
tcpmux	1	udp	TCP Port Service Multiplexer
rje	5	tcp	Remote Job Entry
rje	5	udp	Remote Job Entry
echo	7	tcp	Echo
echo	7	udp	Echo
discard	9	tcp	Discard
discard	9	udp	Discard
discard	9	sctp	Discard
discard	9	dccp	Discard

(continued)

X. Li and C. Bao, *New IPv6 Transition Technology*,
https://doi.org/10.1007/978-981-95-8427-7

Table G.1 (continued)

Service Name	Port Number	Transport Protocol	Description
systat	11	tcp	Active Users
systat	11	udp	Active Users
daytime	13	tcp	Daytime
daytime	13	udp	Daytime
qotd	17	tcp	Quote of the Day
qotd	17	udp	Quote of the Day
msp	18	tcp	Message Send Protocol (historic)
msp	18	udp	Message Send Protocol (historic)
chargen	19	tcp	Character Generator
chargen	19	udp	Character Generator
ftp-data	20	tcp	File Transfer [Default Data]
ftp-data	20	udp	File Transfer [Default Data]
ftp-data	20	sctp	FTP
ftp	21	tcp	File Transfer Protocol [Control]
ftp	21	udp	File Transfer Protocol [Control]
ftp	21	sctp	FTP
ssh	22	tcp	The Secure Shell (SSH) Protocol
ssh	22	udp	The Secure Shell (SSH) Protocol
ssh	22	sctp	SSH
telnet	23	tcp	Telnet
telnet	23	udp	Telnet
smtp	25	tcp	Simple Mail Transfer
smtp	25	udp	Simple Mail Transfer
time	37	tcp	Time
time	37	udp	Time
rlp	39	tcp	Resource Location Protocol
rlp	39	udp	Resource Location Protocol
name	42	tcp	Host Name Server
name	42	udp	Host Name Server
nameserver	42	tcp	Host Name Server
nameserver	42	udp	Host Name Server
nicname	43	tcp	Who Is
nicname	43	udp	Who Is
tacacs	49	tcp	Login Host Protocol (TACACS)
tacacs	49	udp	Login Host Protocol (TACACS)
re-mail-ck	50	tcp	Remote Mail Checking Protocol

(continued)

Table G.1 (continued)

Service Name	Port Number	Transport Protocol	Description
re-mail-ck	50	udp	Remote Mail Checking Protocol
domain	53	tcp	Domain Name Server
domain	53	udp	Domain Name Server
whoispp	63	tcp	whois ++
whois ++	63	tcp	whois+ +
whoispp	63	udp	whois ++
whois ++	63	udp	whois ++
bootps	67	tcp	Bootstrap Protocol Server
bootps	67	udp	Bootstrap Protocol Server
bootpc	68	tcp	Bootstrap Protocol Client
bootpc	68	udp	Bootstrap Protocol Client
tftp	69	tcp	Trivial File Transfer
tftp	69	udp	Trivial File Transfer
gopher	70	tcp	Gopher
gopher	70	udp	Gopher
netrjs-1	71	tcp	Remote Job Service
netrjs-1	71	udp	Remote Job Service
netrjs-2	72	tcp	Remote Job Service
netrjs-2	72	udp	Remote Job Service
netrjs-3	73	tcp	Remote Job Service
netrjs-3	73	udp	Remote Job Service
finger	79	tcp	Finger
finger	79	udp	Finger
http	80	tcp	World Wide Web HTTP
http	80	udp	World Wide Web HTTP
www	80	tcp	World Wide Web HTTP
www	80	udp	World Wide Web HTTP
www-http	80	tcp	World Wide Web HTTP
www-http	80	udp	World Wide Web HTTP
http	80	sctp	HTTP
kerberos	88	tcp	Kerberos
kerberos	88	udp	Kerberos
supdup	95	tcp	SUPDUP
supdup	95	udp	SUPDUP
hostname	101	tcp	NIC Host Name Server
hostname	101	udp	NIC Host Name Server

(continued)

Table G.1 (continued)

Service Name	Port Number	Transport Protocol	Description
iso-tsap	102	tcp	ISO-TSAP Class 0
iso-tsap	102	udp	ISO-TSAP Class 0
pop2	109	tcp	Post Office Protocol - Version 2
pop2	109	udp	Post Office Protocol - Version 2
pop3	110	tcp	Post Office Protocol - Version 3
pop3	110	udp	Post Office Protocol - Version 3
sunrpc	111	tcp	SUN Remote Procedure Call
sunrpc	111	udp	SUN Remote Procedure Call
auth	113	tcp	Authentication Service
auth	113	udp	Authentication Service
sftp	115	tcp	Simple File Transfer Protocol
sftp	115	udp	Simple File Transfer Protocol
uucp-path	117	tcp	UUCP Path Service
uucp-path	117	udp	UUCP Path Service
nntp	119	tcp	Network News Transfer Protocol
nntp	119	udp	Network News Transfer Protocol
ntp	123	tcp	Network Time Protocol
ntp	123	udp	Network Time Protocol
epmap	135	tcp	DCE endpoint resolution
epmap	135	udp	DCE endpoint resolution
netbios-ns	137	tcp	NETBIOS Name Service
netbios-ns	137	udp	NETBIOS Name Service
netbios-dgm	138	tcp	NETBIOS Datagram Service
netbios-dgm	138	udp	NETBIOS Datagram Service
netbios-ssn	139	tcp	NETBIOS Session Service
netbios-ssn	139	udp	NETBIOS Session Service
imap	143	tcp	Internet Message Access Protocol
	143	udp	Reserved
snmp	161	tcp	SNMP
snmp	161	udp	SNMP
snmptrap	162	tcp	SNMPTRAP
snmptrap	162	udp	SNMPTRAP
rsvd	168	tcp	RSVD
rsvd	168	udp	RSVD
bgp	179	tcp	Border Gateway Protocol
bgp	179	udp	Border Gateway Protocol

(continued)

Table G.1 (continued)

Service Name	Port Number	Transport Protocol	Description
bgp	179	sctp	BGP
irc	194	tcp	Internet Relay Chat Protocol
irc	194	udp	Internet Relay Chat Protocol
ipx	213	tcp	IPX
ipx	213	udp	IPX
imap3	220	tcp	Interactive Mail Access Protocol v3
imap3	220	udp	Interactive Mail Access Protocol v3
ldap	389	tcp	Lightweight Directory Access Protocol
ldap	389	udp	Lightweight Directory Access Protocol
https	443	tcp	http protocol over TLS/SSL
https	443	udp	http protocol over TLS/SSL
https	443	sctp	HTTPS
dhcpv6-client	546	tcp	DHCPv6 Client
dhcpv6-client	546	udp	DHCPv6 Client
dhcpv6-server	547	tcp	DHCPv6 Server
dhcpv6-server	547	udp	DHCPv6 Server
http-rpc-epmap	593	tcp	HTTP RPC Ep Map
http-rpc-epmap	593	udp	HTTP RPC Ep Map
nmap	689	tcp	NMAP
nmap	689	udp	NMAP
imaps	993	tcp	IMAP over TLS protocol
	993	udp	Reserved
pop3s	995	tcp	POP3 over TLS protocol
pop3s	995	udp	pop3 protocol over TLS/SSL (was spop3)

Appendix H
UDP, TCP, ICMP, ICMPv6, and Time-Related Protocol Constants

(1) UDP_MIN: 2 min (RFC4787).
(2) UDP_DEFAULT: 5 min (RFC4787).
(3) TCP_TRANS: 4 min (RFC5382).
(4) TCP_EST: 2 h 4 min (RFC5382).
(5) TCP_INCOMING_SYN: 6 s (RFC5382).
(6) FRAGMENT_MIN: 2 s.
(7) ICMP_DEFAULT: 60 s (RFC5382).

X. Li and C. Bao, *New IPv6 Transition Technology*,
https://doi.org/10.1007/978-981-95-8427-7

Appendix I
Terminology

(1) IPv4/IPv6 Translator (XLAT): A device that converts IPv6 datagrams and IPv4 datagrams to each other.
(2) IVI: Stateless IPv4/IPv6 translation technology.
(3) 1:*N* IVI: Stateless IPv4/IPv6 translation technology with public IPv4 address sharing.
(4) dIVI: Stateless IPv4/IPv6 double translation technology.

① IPv4-converted IPv6 address: An IPv6 address used by stateless and stateful translators to represent IPv4 hosts, which has a clear mapping relationship with the IPv4 address.
② IPv4-translatable IPv6 address: An IPv6 address assigned to an IPv6 host and has an algorithm-based mapping relationship with the IPv4 address, used for stateless translation technology.
③ Network Specific Prefix (NSP): A subset of the ISP's IPv6 prefix, which is globally reachable.
④ Well-Known Prefix (WKP): The IPv6 prefix (64:ff9b::/96) defined in RFC6052 for algorithmic mapping.
⑤ Well-Known Name (WKN): ipv4only.arpa (it only has an A record).
⑥ Well-Known Address (WKA): 192.0.0.170 and 192.0.0.171.
⑦ Pref64: The IPv6 prefix used to synthesize IPv4 addresses into IPv6 addresses, including NSP and WKP.

(5) DNS46: Converts AAAA records to A records.
(6) DNS64: Converts A records to AAAA records.
(7) MAP-T: Stateless IPv4/IPv6 translation technology with public IPv4 address sharing.
(8) MAP-E: Stateless IPv4/IPv6 encapsulation technology with public IPv4 address sharing.

① MAP Border Relay (MAP-BR, abbreviated as BR): A core router with specific functions (such as IPv4/IPv6 translation function or IPv4 over IPv6 encapsulation function).

X. Li and C. Bao, *New IPv6 Transition Technology*,
https://doi.org/10.1007/978-981-95-8427-7

② MAP Customer Edge (MAP-CE, abbreviated as CE): An edge router (home gateway) with specific functions (such as IPv4/IPv6 translation function or IPv4 over IPv6 encapsulation function).
③ Port Set Identifier (PSID): Identifies a range of transport layer ports assigned to a specific CE.
④ Embedded Address Bits (EA-bits): A field embedded in the IPv6 address, identifying several bits of the IPv4 subnet and PSID.

(9) NPTv6: Stateless IPv6/IPv6 prefix translation technology.
(10) NAT64: Stateful IPv4/IPv6 translation technology.
(11) NAT44: Stateful IPv4/IPv4 translation technology.

① 3-Tuple: (Source IP address, Destination IP address, ICMP identifier). The 3-Tuple uniquely identifies an ICMP session.
② 5-Tuple: (Source IP address, Source port, Destination IP address, Destination port, Transport protocol).
③ Binding Information Base (BIB): The binding table saved by NAT64.
④ Hairpin: The data packet "turns around" within the device and returns to the same side.

(12) 464XLAT: Stateful IPv4/IPv6 translation technology.

① PLAT: Provider XLAT.
② CLAT: Customer XLAT.

(13) DS-Lite: Stateful IPv4/IPv6 encapsulation technology.

① AFTR: Address Family Transition Router.
② B4: Basic Bridging BroadBand

(14) LW-4o6: User state IPv4/IPv6 encapsulation technology.

① lwAFTR: Lightweight Address Family Transition Router.
② lwB4: Lightweight Basic Broadband Bridge.

(15) RA: Router Advertisement.

① RDNSS: Recursive DNS server, used to provide DNS information of.
② DNSSL: DNS Search List (DNSSL).

(16) Tunneling and encapsulation.

① Tunneling: Establish two tunnel endpoints on the underlying network and use encapsulation technology to transmit data packets independent of the underlying network.
② Encapsulation: Use encapsulation/decapsulation to transmit data packets independent of the underlying network.

Afterword

It has been about thirty years since the authors of this book participated in the design and construction of CERNET in 1994. It has been over twenty years since the authors established China's first IPv6 test bed in 1998 and connected it to 6bone. It has been over ten years since the authors invented IVI technology in 2007. We deeply understand the profound meaning of the ancient Chinese saying "ten years to sharpen a sword", and hope to share with readers the experience of engaging in Internet research, technology development, and standardization work through this book.

In this process, the authors have always been encouraged by the spirit of the IETF. "We reject kings, presidents, and voting. We believe in rough consensus and running code."

Although the transition process of the next-generation Internet IPv6 is slower than expected, the authors firmly believe that the new generation of IPv6 transition technology is in the right direction. With the widespread deployment of IPv6, a new Internet ecosystem (connecting humans, devices, and robots) that is very different from IPv4 will be generated. The future is the era of new generation network researchers and engineers, and we hope that the spirit of the IETF and the Internet can be further promoted. "We do not predict the future, we create the future."

X. Li and C. Bao, *New IPv6 Transition Technology*,
https://doi.org/10.1007/978-981-95-8427-7